THE GREEKS AND

Ancient Greeks remembered their past before the rise of historiography, and after it poetry and oratory continued to serve commemorative functions. This book explores the field of literary memory in the fifth century BCE, juxtaposing the works of Herodotus and Thucydides with samples from epinician poetry, elegy, tragedy and oratory. Various socio-political contexts and narrative forms lent themselves to the expression of diverse attitudes towards the past. At the same time, a common gravitational centre can be observed, which is distinct from modern ideas of history. As well as presenting a broad overview on memory in various genres, Professor Grethlein sheds new light on the rise of Greek historiography. He views Herodotus and Thucydides against the background of memory in poetry and oratory and thereby elucidates the tension between tradition and continuity in which the shaping of historiography as a genre took place.

JONAS GRETHLEIN is Professor of Classics at the Ruprecht-Karls-Universität Heidelberg. He studied at Göttingen, Oxford and Freiburg before spending two years as a post-doctoral fellow at Harvard and teaching at the University of California, Santa Barbara. In 2006 he received the prestigious Heinz-Maier-Leibnitz award. In addition to numerous articles he has published *Asyl und Athen. Die Konstruktion kollektiver Identität in der griechischen Tragödie* (2003), *Das Geschichtsbild der Ilias. Eine Untersuchung des Geschichtsbildes der Ilias aus phänomenologischer und narratologischer Perspektive* (2006) and *Littells Orestie. Mythos, Macht und Moral in Les Bienveillantes* (2009), and edited (with A. Rengakos) *Narratology and Interpretation: The Content of Narrative Form in Ancient Literature* (2009).

THE GREEKS AND THEIR PAST

Poetry, Oratory and History in the Fifth Century BCE

JONAS GRETHLEIN

Professor of Classics, Ruprecht-Karls-Universität Heidelberg

CAMBRIDGE
UNIVERSITY PRESS

University Printing House, Cambridge CB2 8BS, United Kingdom

Published in the United States of America by Cambridge University Press, New York

Cambridge University Press is part of the University of Cambridge.

It furthers the University's mission by disseminating knowledge in the pursuit of education, learning and research at the highest international levels of excellence.

www.cambridge.org
Information on this title: www.cambridge.org/9781107656284

© Jonas Grethlein 2010

This publication is in copyright. Subject to statutory exception and to the provisions of relevant collective licensing agreements, no reproduction of any part may take place without the written permission of Cambridge University Press.

First published 2010
Reprinted 2010
First paperback edition 2013

A catalogue record for this publication is available from the British Library

ISBN 978-0-521-11077-8 Hardback
ISBN 978-1-107-65628-4 Paperback

Cambridge University Press has no responsibility for the persistence or accuracy of URLs for external or third-party internet websites referred to in this publication, and does not guarantee that any content on such websites is, or will remain, accurate or appropriate.

Contents

List of figures *page* vii
Preface ix
Abbreviations xi

1. Introduction 1
    1.1. Memory beyond historiography 1
    1.2. A phenomenological model of the idea of history 5
    1.3. Outline of the work 12

    PART I. *CLIO POLYTROPOS*: NON-HISTORIOGRAPHICAL
    MEDIA OF MEMORY 17

2. Epinician Poetry: Pindar, *Olympian* 2 19
    2.1. The structure 20
    2.2. Theron's victory and the history of his family 24
    2.3. Pindar's speech–act and the time of his ode 33
    2.4. The socio-political context 40
    2.5. Conclusion 43

3. Elegy: The 'New Simonides' and earlier elegies 47
    3.1. The content of Simonides fr. 11 W^2 48
    3.2. The idea of history in the 'New Simonides' and other elegies 54
    3.3. Elegy and epic 62
    3.4. The socio-political context 68
    3.5. Conclusion 72

4. Tragedy: Aeschylus, *Persae* 74
    4.1. The distanced past 75
    4.2. The idea of history 79
    4.3. Contingency of chance and reception 86
    4.4. The socio-political context 96
    4.5. Conclusion 97

v

5.	Epideictic oratory: Lysias, *epitaphios logos*	105
	5.1. The content and the idea of history	108
	5.2. The funeral speech – a speech-act	117
	5.3. The socio-political context	121
	5.4. Conclusion	122
6.	Deliberative oratory: Andocides, *de pace*	126
	6.1. The content and the idea of history	129
	6.2. Andocides, *de pace* vs. Lysias, *epitaphios logos*	133
	6.3. An oligarchic view of the past?	136
	6.4. Conclusion	139
	6.5. Summary of Part I	144

PART II.   THE RISE OF GREEK HISTORIOGRAPHY   147

7.	Herodotus	149
	7.1. Explicit criticism of other genres of memory: the Helen–*logos* (2.112–20)	151
	7.2. Implicit criticism of the use of the past in oratory (the Syracusan embassy scene (7.153–63); the speech duel at Plataea (9.26–7))	158
	7.3. Continuity in the idea of history: the Croesus–*logos* (1.26–94)	187
	7.4. Conclusion	203
8.	Thucydides	205
	8.1. Explicit criticism of other genres of memory (methodological reflections in 1.20–2; the digression on the tyrannicide (6.54–9))	206
	8.2. Implicit critisism of the use of the past in oratory (Pericles' funeral speech (2.35–46); the Plataean Debate (3.52–68))	220
	8.3. Continuity in the idea of history: The Sicilian Expedition	240
	8.4. Conclusion	279
9.	Epilogue: Historical fevers, ancient and modern	281

Appendix: Lengthy historical narratives in Tyrtaeus and Mimnermus?   291
Bibliography   297
Index locorum   332
Index of Greek words   340
General Index   341

List of figures

1. Cover of Stanley Lombardo's *Iliad* translation. © 1997 by Hackett Publishing Company, Inc. Reprinted by permission of Hackett Publishing Company, Inc. All rights reserved. *page* 282
2. Albrecht Altdorfer, *Battle of Issos*. Bayerische Staatsgemäldesammlungen – Alte Pinakothek. 284
3. Detail of Brygos Cup (AN1911.615). Ashmolean Museum, University of Oxford. 286

Preface

This book has taken shape in several places, each with its own distinctive environment. It was written in Widener Library in Cambridge MA, at the foot of the Black Forest in Freiburg, on the sunny shores of Santa Barbara and, finally, at Heidelberg in view of the *Philosophenweg*. Although *The Greeks and their Past* is less about space than time, more specifically about how Greeks in the fifth century BCE envisaged their past, it has benefitted from the experience of very different environments. The moves have, if nothing else, sensitized me to the different temporalities reigning in the Western world which, at least in this regard, is less unified than the discourse of globalization would lead one to believe. California's infatuation with youth and the present as well as the nostalgia of Heidelberg, the capital of Romanticism, may be clichés, but, as many clichés, they are not without significance. While the primary goal of this book is to chart the gravitational field of literary memory in fifth-century Greece, tracing back both the differences in the genres and the common ground they share, it is contemporary interest in memory that has triggered this study and continuously serves as a point of comparison, explicitly in the introduction and epilogue as well as implicitly throughout the book.

My argument requires close readings, but all texts are translated to make the book fully accessible to readers without knowledge of ancient Greek. Quotations from the *Iliad* are taken, with slight adaptations, from Lattimore (1951). For the translations of other texts, which do not aim at elegance, but stay close to the Greek, I have consulted the following editions: Aeschylus: Hall (1996); Andocides: Edwards (1995); Herodotus: Waterfield (1998); Isocrates: Norlin (1966); Lysias: Lamb (1976); Pindar: Nisetich (1980); Race (1997); Verity (2007). Simonides fr. 11 W^2: West in Boedeker and Sider (2001a), other elegiac poetry: Gerber (1999); Thucydides: Lattimore (1999). As to Greek names, I have taken latinized forms, except where familiarity dictates otherwise. The abbreviations of journals follow the *année philologique*, those of ancient authors the *Oxford Classical Dictionary*.

The following sections are revised versions of articles that have been published before: section 3.3: 'Diomedes Redivivus. A New Reading of Mimnermus fr 14 W²' *Mnemosyne* 60, 2007: 102–111; section 7.2.1: 'The Manifold Uses of the Epic Past. The Embassy Scene in Hdt. 7.153–163' *AJPh* 127, 2006: 485–509; section 8.2.1: 'Gefahren des λόγος. Thukydides' 'Historien' und die Grabrede des Perikles' *Klio* 87, 2005: 41–71; parts of section 8.3.2 (b): 'Eine herodoteische Deutung der Sizilischen Expedition (Thuc. 7.87.5f.)?' *Hermes* 136, 2008: 129–142. I am grateful for permission to use these articles for this book.

I was very lucky in finding on both sides of the Atlantic people with whom I could fruitfully discuss my work. It would be impossible to name all those to whom I am indebted, but I nonetheless wish to thank here Apostolos Athanassakis, Carolyn Dewald, Francis Dunn, Renaud Gagné, Ralph Galluci, Hans-Joachim Gehrke, Tonio Hölscher, Ted Lendon, David Konstan, Greg Nagy, Robin Osborne, Randy Pogorzelski, Kurt Raaflaub, Matthias Steinhart, Bernhard Zimmermann. I am particularly grateful to Stefania Tutino, Sara Lindheim and Robert Morstein-Marx for giving me such a warm welcome in California and making my time there a wonderful experience. The book has gained a great deal from the comments made by friends who have unflinchingly taken upon themselves the task of reading the entire manuscript: Deborah Boedeker, Bill Furley, Marianne Hopman, Christopher Krebs, Antonios Rengakos. In Heidelberg, Sabine Hug, Matthias Becker, Dominic Meckel and Hans-Josef Merz have been an immense help in preparing the manuscript for publication. I wish to thank finally Michael Sharp for his interest and his support of this project, and, last but not least, the two readers for Cambridge University Press whose comments have been very useful. One report in particular has enriched the book through a wealth of suggestions at different levels.

I dedicate this book to my teacher, friend and father, Christian.

JONAS GRETHLEIN
Heidelberg

Abbreviations

ANRW	Aufstieg und Niedergang der römischen Welt, ed. H. Temporini. (1970–97). Berlin
Bergk	T. Bergk (ed.). (1877–82) *Poetae Lyrici Graeci. I–III.* (4th edn). Leipzig.
Blass-Thalheim	F. Blass and T. Thalheim (eds.). (1914) *Antiphontis Orationes et Fragmenta.* Leipzig.
CEG	P. A. Hansen (ed.). (1983–89) *Carmina Epigraphica Graeca. I–II.* Berlin.
DK	H. Diels and W. Kranz (eds.). (1952) *Die Fragmente der Vorsokratiker. I–III.* (6th edn). Berlin.
FGrH	F. Jacoby (ed.). (1923–) *Die Fragmente der griechischen Historiker.* Berlin.
Gentili/Prato	B. Gentili and C. Prato (eds.). (1979/²2002) *Poetae Elegiaci. Testimonia et Fragmenta. I–II.* (Leipzig)
GG	Brunner, O. (ed.) (1972–1997) *Geschichtliche Grundbegriffe. Historisches Lexikon zur politisch-sozialen Sprache in Deutschland.* I–VIII. Stuttgart.
IG	*Inscriptiones graecae* (1873–) Berlin.
K. A.	R. Kassel and C. Austin (eds.). (1983–2001) *Poetae Comici Graeci.* Berlin.
LSJ	H. G. Liddell, R. Scott and H. S. Jones (eds.). (1996) *A Greek–English Lexicon.* With a revised supplement. (9th edn.) Oxford.
N²	A. Nauck (ed.). (1964) *Tragicorum Graecorum Fragmenta* (2nd edn). Hildesheim.
PMG	D. L. Page (ed.). (1962) *Poetae Melici Graeci.* Oxford.
PEG	A. Bernabé (ed.). (1988–2007) *Poetae Epici Graeci. I–II.* Leipzig/Berlin.
P. Oxy.	*The Oxyrhynchus Papyri.* (1898–) London.

RE	W. Pauly, G. Wissowa and W. Kroll (eds.). (1893–1980) *Realenzyklopädie der classischen Altertumswissenschaft.* Stuttgart/Munich.
SLG	D. L. Page (ed.). (1974) *Supplementum Lyricis Graecis.* Oxford.
TrGF	B. Snell, R. Kannicht and S. Radt (eds.). (1977–2005) *Tragicorum Graecorum Fragmenta. I–V.* Göttingen.
V	E.-M. Voigt (ed.). (1971) *Sappho et Alcaeus. Fragmenta.* Amsterdam.
W^2	M. L. West (ed.). (1992) *Iambi et Elegi Graeci. I–II* (2nd edn.). Oxford.

CHAPTER I

Introduction

1.1. MEMORY BEYOND HISTORIOGRAPHY

'We are all suffering from a consuming historical fever' wrote Friedrich Nietzsche in 1873 CE,[1] but his diagnosis now seems truer than ever before. Our culture, it is widely agreed, is obsessed with memory. David Lowenthal, for instance, speaks of a 'heritage crusade' and points out that we have enlarged the concept of heritage 'from the elite and grand to the vernacular and everyday; from the remote to the recent; and from the material to the intangible'.[2] Non-professional associations that are devoted to the preservation of local traditions or to the past of a community are thriving in the Western world, be it the *Freiburger Narrenzunft* ('Freiburg carnival guild') or the *Boston Historical Society*. Memorials are not a recent phenomenon, but, to give an example from Europe, the gigantic Shoa memorial in the centre of Berlin and the fierce public debate about it illustrate their current prominence.[3] In North America, the National Mall in Washington DC is a particularly striking example of a nation's attempt to monumentalize its past in the heart of its political power.[4] The boom of museums of all kinds has prompted some writers to dub the increasing efforts to preserve the past as 'musealization'.[5]

Our obsession with the past has also left its imprint in scholarship. Previous generations of scholars were convinced that historical awareness could only develop in literate cultures. Oral societies, both past and present, were believed to exist in a realm of timelessness without a sense of history.[6] Now, however, it is widely acknowledged that, while not all cultures may develop

---
[1] Nietzsche 1954: I 210 (my translation). [2] Lowenthal 1996: 14.
[3] On the debate about the '*Mahnmal Mitte*', see Jeismann 1999.
[4] Cf. Bodnar 1992 on public memory in the United States in the twentieth century CE.
[5] Cf. Preiß et al. 1990; Zacharias 1990; Huyssen 1995: 13–35.
[6] There are, however, remarkable exceptions. In anthropology, see Schott 1968; in prehistory, see Kirchner 1954. For a recent survey, see Holtorf 2005.

historiography, memory plays an important role in nearly all societies. The concepts of 'collective',[7] 'social'[8] and 'cultural'[9] memory suggest that groups of all sorts, ranging from the *Ventura Surf Chapter* to the *Académie française*, rely on the memory of specific events. The application of the term 'memory' to collectives has not remained without criticism,[10] but it is hard to deny that, on the one hand, individual memories are socially mediated and, on the other, individuals harbour memories related to groups to which they belong. While the concepts just mentioned vary in many regards, they all emphasize the significance of memory for the identities of individuals as well as of groups. Across cultures and ages, the past is an important tool for defining who we are and what we ought to do in the here and now.

Memories can be preserved in the various forms of 'texts, pictures, artifacts, buildings, songs, rites, customs'.[11] A large array of genres and media beyond historiography have therefore been examined as bearers of memory. Inspired by Pierre Nora, historians have become fond of '*lieux de mémoire*'.[12] The 'archaeology of the past' allows material relics to be interpreted as testimonies to the relation of humans to their past[13] and anthropologists such as Marshall Sahlins have transformed 'people without history' into 'islands of history'.[14] Not only material relics and oral traditions but also other media such as dance are being investigated as bearers of memory.[15]

An application of this broad interest in memory to ancient Greece promises to yield rich returns. As B. A. van Groningen noted, the Greeks were 'in the grip of the past'.[16] More recently, Nicole Loraux has examined the funeral speeches as semi-official history of Athens; the 'New Simonides' has forcefully confirmed Ewen Bowie's thesis that elegy could contain

---

[7] Halbwachs 1980. [8] Connerton 1989. [9] Assmann 1992.
[10] See, for example, Confino 1997, and, for further literature, Grethlein 2003a: 26–7.
[11] Assmann 2000: 524.
[12] Cf. Nora 1984–92. For an application of this approach to German history, see François/Schulze 2001; for an application in the field of Classics, see Jung 2006. For further broad approaches to memory in history, see n. 34 below.
[13] See, for example, Bradley and Williams 1998; Bradley 2002.
[14] Sahlins 1985; 2004. See already Rosaldo's study of the Ilongots (1980). For studies in attitudes towards the past in a wide range of cultures, see e.g. the papers in Layton 1994. Tonkin 1992 combines an investigation of oral history in Africa with many parallels from other cultures. On memory in modern Greece, see Herzfeld 1986; 1991; Sutton 1998.
[15] See e.g. Kuhnt-Saptodewo 2006, who examines dance on Java as a commemorative act.
[16] Van Groningen 1953. Dunn 2007, on the other hand, argues for a 'presentism' in the second half of the fifth century BCE. He argues that in various genres a new emphasis on the present comes to the fore. However, besides the fact that many of the phenomena described by him can be found earlier, I am not convinced that the past lost its relevance to the extent that Dunn argues for. Even some of his test cases such as Euripides rather attest to the continuing significance of the past. Moreover, the awareness of human fragility that he diagnoses in the sophists, particularly in Antiphon, can not only be traced back to Homer, but should be disentangled from the idea of 'presentism'.

historical narratives; Rosalind Thomas has discussed oral traditions; the concept of the 'archaeology of the past' has been applied to ancient Greece by Susan Alcock and Carolyn Higbie's study of the Lindian chronicle has elucidated the commemorative function of votives in temples.[17] While these studies have illuminated individual genres and specific aspects, historiography has remained the central focus of scholarship on ancient memory.[18] Even studies that are devoted to other genres tend to take Herodotus and Thucydides as their benchmark, viewing, for example, epic and elegy as predecessors to the rise of historiography.[19]

Given the prominence that historiography has for us, this focus is understandable. And yet, not only did Herodotus and Thucydides not supersede the pre-existing commemorative genres that continued to exist, but one may doubt whether historiography was the primary medium of memory in classical Greece.[20] On the contrary, it is likely that oratory and poetry reached a broader audience and were more influential in shaping perceptions of the past. Besides downplaying their relevance, the common teleological view prevents us from reading non-historiographic media in their own right. In particular, it leads to privileging the question of historical accuracy over others, an issue that is at the core of modern scholarship but the importance of which has been challenged for ancient historiography[21] and is even more questionable in the case of other genres.

At the same time, our tendency to take historiography as the prime genre of memory leads to a distorted view of its rise in the second half of the fifth century BCE. We are inclined to concentrate either on the influence of other genres in the historians' narratives or to focus on the dialectic of tradition and innovation within the genre of historiography.[22] These are

---

[17] Loraux 1986a; Bowie 1986; 2001; Thomas 1989; 1992; Alcock 2002; Higbie 2003. Further works may be mentioned: Hornblower 2004 juxtaposes Pindar with Thucydides. For an examination of the idea of history in the *Iliad*, see Grethlein 2006a. Another group of works focuses on the memory of particular events: Pallantza 2005 examines the reception of the Trojan War after Homer. Jung 2006 reconstructs the memory of Marathon and Plataea in classical antiquity. Luraghi 2008 investigates the construction of the Messenian past.

[18] See, for example, Deichgräber 1952; Gomme 1954; Chatelet 1962; Mazzarino 1966; Starr 1968; Lasserre 1976; Meier 1990; Fornara 1983; van Seters 1983; Sauge 1992; Shrimpton 1997; Marincola 2001; Clarke 2008.

[19] See e.g. Snell 1952; Strasburger 1972 on Homer; Steinmetz 1969 on elegy. Boedeker 1998 presents an important survey of memory in fifth-century Athens in art as well as in literature, but she privileges historiography too, as the outline of her argument reveals, 185–6: 'Then I will consider the paradox that historiography itself develops relatively late in a city so rich in memorials of its great past deeds ...'

[20] On this question, cf. Marincola 1997: 20–1.   [21] See, for example, Wiseman 1979; Woodman 1988.

[22] For Homer's influence on Herodotus and Thucydides, see, for example, Strasburger 1972; Rengakos 2006a; 2006b. For the influence of tragedy on historiography in general, see Walbank 1960; on Herodotus, see Stahl 1968; Saïd 2002; on Thucydides, Cornford 1907; Finley 1967; Macleod 1983a;

beyond doubt interesting questions, but it is equally important to see that, intruding into the crowded field of memory, the historians had to justify their new approach against the established genres. While recent studies such as *Herodotus in Context* by Rosalind Thomas (2000) have deepened our understanding of the first historians by contextualizing them in the intellectual milieu of their time, little has been done to view the rise of historiography against the background of contemporary media of memory.

In taking into account these considerations, this study aims at a non-evolutionist reconstruction of ancient attitudes towards the past. I juxtapose non-historiographic media of memory with historiography not so much to trace a development as to examine the different modes of remembering the past that coexisted. Needless to say, Herodotus and Thucydides open a new chapter in the history of memory, but since scholarship tends to foreground and focus on historiography, new facets of its rise, as well as of memory in general, can be elucidated by an approach that views Herodotus and Thucydides as part of a large field of commemorative genres. Besides identifying differences between these genres, I also aim to chart the common ground that distinguishes ancient Greek memory from concepts of history in other ages.[23]

My examination is limited in two regards: first, with a few exceptions, I concentrate on material from a single century to permit a synchronic reading. The rise of Greek historiography as well as, compared to other times, the richer textual transmission have made the fifth century BCE the most attractive choice. Second, I only rarely take into account archaeological material and discuss mainly literary texts. This restriction does not reflect the assumption that texts offer more interesting information – recent archaeological research gives ample evidence of how much art and material relics reveal about memory[24] – but, given the breadth of the question, it seems preferable to keep the focus as sharp as possible and to limit the analysis to literary genres.

As Mikhail Bakhtin and his circle emphasized, literary genres are not merely forms, but forms of knowledge.[25] It therefore makes sense to examine them as bearers of specific ways of representing the past. In

---

Shanske 2007. On tradition and innovation within the genre of historiography, see in particular Marincola 1997. See also Clarke 2008, whose examination of local historiography significantly broadens our understanding of the genre.

[23] For a stimulating collection of articles on the construction of time in Greek antiquity, see Darbo-Peschanski 2000.

[24] Besides the works on the 'archaeology of the past' mentioned in n. 13, see also Francis 1990; Castriota 1992; Csapo and Miller 1998; Hölscher 1998; Boardman 2002.

[25] Cf. Bakhtin 1981: 3–40; 259–422. See also Stierle 1979: 96, who draws on the concept of experience to define genres. Tonkin 1992: 50–65 applies the notion of genre to oral history. For a collection of important modern approaches to genre, see Duff 2000. The literature on genre in antiquity is vast, see e.g. Rossi 1971; Rosenmeyer 1985; Conte 1994; Depew and Obbink, 2000a.

particular, I will analyze to what extent the attitude towards the past and the scope, i.e. the historical agent and time covered in the narratives, are shaped by two generic features. In the oral world of the fifth century BCE, genres were still mostly defined by the occasion of their performance.[26] I will therefore assess prevailing modes of memory against the background of the socio-political and performative setting of their respective genres. At the same time, while being less defined by formal features than genres in the Hellenistic Age, fifth-century genres have specific narrative forms. This raises the question of the 'content of the form'. More specifically, I will try to elucidate whether narrative forms express attitudes towards the past, as I have claimed for the *Iliad*.[27] Narratives not only tell temporal sequences (narrated time), but they also unfold themselves in time (narrative time). It is worth asking whether the temporal organization of a narrative corresponds with its view of human life in time.[28] I will thus examine the presentation of the past in both historiography and other literary genres, depending on their socio-cultural setting and narrative forms.

I.2. A PHENOMENOLOGICAL MODEL OF THE IDEA OF HISTORY

If we not only look beyond historiography but also discard it as the yardstick, one question arises: how are we going to assess and compare the various commemorative genres? In this study, I replace an evolutionist perspective with an approach that draws on phenomenological and hermeneutical philosophy.[29] History is not the central topic of this tradition, but some of its adherents have reflected upon history and developed a characteristic view of it from which our current interest in memory, I believe, can greatly benefit. The phenomenological and hermeneutical approach is

---

[26] Cf. Depew and Obbink 2000b: 3–4.   [27] Grethlein 2006a: 180–310.
[28] For a theoretical discussion that starts from Ricoeur, see Grethlein 2006a: 180–204.
[29] I follow an 'etic' approach, i.e. I employ a theoretical framework with terms unknown in ancient Greece. An 'emic' approach, on the other hand, would rely on terms and concepts used by the object of the study (cf. Goodenough 1980: 104–19). One of the central aspects of my study, chance, has received, under the name of *tyche*, much attention from ancient Greek authors ranging from Hesiod (e.g. *Theog.* 360) to Lysias (e.g. 13.63). The concept of *tyche* becomes particularly prominent after the fifth century BCE in authors such as Menander (e.g. fr. 296) and, in historiography, Polybius, who frequently evokes *tyche* as an explanation for events which cannot be explained causally (cf. Walbank 1957: 16–26). I have nonetheless chosen to base my approach on the concept of contingency, as elaborated by Bubner 1984 and Marquard 1986. The notions of *tyche* in Greek texts are manifold and disparate – the polyphony of the term seems to mirror the phenomenon which it tries to denote. The concept of contingency, on the other hand, allows me to trace acts of memory back to their roots in temporality and, as we shall see, provides us with a typology that is useful for comparisons.

congenial for a study that tries to take into account a wide array of commemorative media while removing historiography from its centre.

Coined by Wilhelm Dilthey and Paul Yorck von Wartenburg, the concept of historicity ('*Geschichtlichkeit*') does not signify that something actually happened; in opposition to metaphysics and positivism, it rather points out that humans are always in history and somehow relate to it.[30] As Wilhelm Schapp noted, we are 'entangled in histories'.[31] In *Being and Time*, Martin Heidegger pushed this tradition further and argued that the 'vulgar time' of history is embedded in the level of historicity, which itself rests on the ground of temporality ('*Zeitlichkeit*').[32]

The link between memory and temporality is as plausible as it is fruitful. Not only is human temporality characterized by the ability to think about the future as well as to turn back to the past, but, whenever we remember the past, we confront our temporality. Viewing acts of memory as attempts to cope with temporality provides us with a framework broad enough to take into account various engagements with the past, ranging from monuments to historical scholarship, without privileging the latter. A phenomenological approach also goes beyond the functionalist approach that underlies some of the most influential current concepts.[33] The models of 'cultural memory', '*lieux de mémoire*', 'invented traditions' or 'intentional history' all have in common that they focus on the use of the past.[34] I believe, however, that the deeper starting point of temporality draws attention to crucial aspects neglected by these concepts and, in addition, lets us also better understand the manifold ways in which the past is used.

Temporality therefore provides the starting point from which I will develop a matrix of modes of memory. The temporality of human life is based on contingency, which tradition defines as '*quod nec est impossibile nec necesarium.*' Denoting what is, logically and ontologically, possible, but not necessary, contingency not only defines the realm in which human life unfolds, but also forms our ability to look ahead and back in time.[35]

---

[30] See in particular their correspondence as published by von der Schulenburg 1923 and Yorck von Wartenburg 1956. On the concept of historicity, see Bauer 1963; von Renthe-Fink 1964.
[31] Schapp ²1976.   [32] Heidegger ¹⁶1986: 372–404.
[33] I make this argument more fully in Grethlein (forthcoming b).
[34] On 'cultural memory', see Assmann 1992; on '*lieux de mémoire*', see Nora 1984–92; on 'invented traditions', see Hobsbawm and Ranger 1983; on 'intentional history', see Gehrke 1994; 2001; Foxhall and Gehrke (forthcoming). While most of these approaches are linked to historical research, Rüsen (1983; 1986; 1989) and Baumgartner ²1997 offer purely theoretical functionalist concepts.
[35] The term contingency stems from the translation of *endechómenon* from Aristotle's logic by Boethius, who seems to follow Marius Victorinus. On recent debates, see *Neue Hefte für Philosophie* 24/25 (1985); Makropoulos 1997: 7–32; v. Graevenitz and Marquard 1998a. Troeltsch 1913 is still a most valuable study.

Contingency is most often understood as being identical with chance. However, as Rüdiger Bubner has shown, it is the frame for actions as well as for chance. Where things are neither impossible nor necessary, human beings can act, but are at the same time constrained by chance.[36] There are thus two sides to contingency. I suggest they be called 'contingency of action' and 'contingency of chance'.[37]

Contingency, as the frame for both actions and chance, results in a tension between expectation and experience in our consciousness.[38] On the basis of previous experiences, expectations about the future are formed and guide our actions. If the outcome of our actions corresponds with our plans, our expectations are fulfilled. On the other hand, our expectations are disappointed if something crosses our plans. Such disappointments can be due to deficient planning or chance, implying also unforeseen actions of others. In all these cases, the new experience, as built on the old expectation, is the basis on which further expectations are formed.[39] Thus, contingency inscribes itself into human consciousness in the form of a dynamic interplay between expectations and experiences.

In his examination of the new temporality that emerged in the Modern Age, the historian Reinhard Koselleck points out, perhaps a bit schematically, that the acceleration of changes starting in the second half of the eighteenth century CE led to a new relation between experiences and expectations:[40] in earlier times, the 'horizon of expectations' ('*Erwartungshorizont*') was created by the 'space of experiences' ('*Erfahrungsraum*'); one expected things similar to one's own experiences. Around 1800 CE, however, the 'horizon of expectations' and the 'space of experiences' disintegrated. Due

---

[36] Bubner's reflections on contingency stand in the context of his investigation of the relation between history and practical philosophy (1984). For this, Aristotle proves helpful because he embeds chance in a theory of action.

[37] Marquard 1986 (cf. von Graevenitz and Marquard 1998b: XIV) makes a similar distinction in juxtaposing '*Beliebigkeitskontingenz/Beliebigkeitszufälligkeit*' with '*Schicksalskontingenz/ Schicksalszufälligkeit*'. On the one hand, Marquard argues, we can do and choose things; on the other, we are affected by events that are beyond our control. However, '*Schicksalskontingenz*' is not a very fortunate coinage, as it brings the ambiguous notion of '*Schicksal*' into play. A similar approach to contingency from a sociological perspective can be found in Makropoulos' analysis of the Modern Age as an epoch with a very strong awareness of contingency. Makropoulos points out the same two aspects (1997: 14–16; 1998: 60) and emphasizes that contingency is not a '*factum brutum*', but is constructed differently in different cultures (1997: 16–18).

[38] On the tension between expectations and experiences, see already Augustine's reflections in the eleventh book of his *Confessiones*, and Husserl's analysis of the temporal structure of intentional life (1928).

[39] However, experiences not only shape our current expectations, but as Liebsch 1996: 32–45 observes, experiences also affect our past expectations in our memory.

[40] Cf. Koselleck 1985: 3–69.

to radical changes, experiences transcended the horizon of expectations and consequently the future could not be extrapolated from the past anymore, but instead turned into an open space.[41] The past, on the other hand, was now perceived as a process with its own dynamic that led to the present, a view that found expression in the new terms 'new time' ('*Neuzeit*') and 'history' ('*Geschichte*') as singulars, signifying the process as well as its narrative account.[42]

While Koselleck's analysis affords an impressive illustration of the link between experience and expectation on the one hand and temporality on the other, it is important to notice that experiences can also disappoint expectations. This is at the core of Hans-Georg Gadamer's definition of experience. In looking to Aristotle, Gadamer emphasizes the negative character of experiences.[43] Real experiences, he argues, refute previous expectations. Though negative, experiences prove productive in so far as they lead to a new view of something. Following G. W. F. Hegel's view, Gadamer sees the productivity of experience as a dialectic process, a 'reversal of consciousness' ('*Umkehrung des Bewußtseins*').[44] He points out the historical character of this process. It takes place in time, and, what is more, human beings become aware of their historicity by experiencing their finiteness.[45]

Gadamer focuses on the tension between experiences and expectations and aligns them in a way different from Koselleck's approach. If we leave aside the discrepancy between philosophical reflection and historical analysis, we can note that, whereas in Gadamer's theory expectations are bound to be painfully disappointed, Koselleck deals with experiences that surpass expectations in a positive way. The structural negativity of experience, which the historian envisages as an experience of the freedom to shape the world, is defined as experience of finiteness in the philosopher's model.

Both modes of experience are relevant and can be traced back to the two aspects of contingency that I have mentioned. In the new alignment of experiences and expectations in the Modern Age, which is examined by Koselleck, the 'contingency of action' comes to the fore: the future opens as a space full of new possibilities that can be shaped by man. On the other hand, Gadamer's concept is based on the 'contingency of chance': contingency makes its force felt in the disappointment of expectations.

---

[41] On the new construction of the future, see Hölscher 1999.
[42] See Koselleck 1975: 647–91; 1985: 92–104.   [43] Gadamer ⁵1986: 346–84.
[44] See *ibid*.: 360.   [45] Cf. *ibid*.: 363.

Chance, broadly defined as that which is beyond the control of the acting subject, confounds human expectations and thereby undermines further plans and challenges identities. On what basis can the future be assessed if previous expectations have been thwarted by experiences? How can identities be stable if experiences reveal that we are merely toys in the hand of chance? Therefore, considerable efforts are made to bridge the gap between past expectations and experiences in order to be able to project new expectations onto the future. Three commemorative strategies serve this goal: to start with, past and present can be linked by traditions.[46] Traditions establish the **continuity** that rules out the perilous force of chance and makes the 'space of experiences' and the 'horizon of expectations' match. Furthermore, the wings of chance can be clipped by **regularity**. Here, it is not the assumption of a continuum but of recurrent patterns or even underlying laws that creates the stability necessary for identities and actions. The third strategy relies on the construction of **developments**. Developments are more dynamic than continuities and regularities and allow for change, but nonetheless the very direction of a development tells against the unpredictability of chance. If we add the **acceptance of chance** as a fourth option, we have four different modes of coping with contingency: the temporal unfolding of human life appears under the conditions of chance, continuity, regularity or development. Thus, acts of memory can be classified as accidental, traditional, exemplary or developmental (see Table 1).

Needless to say, these four modes rarely occur in pure form, but are often entangled with one another. For instance, traditional and exemplary views of the past often reinforce one another, and, in such cases, the distinction between continuity and regularity may seem casuistic. However, we shall also come across acts of memory that are traditional without being exemplary and vice versa. Other distinctions are more marked, as is the division into chance and attempts to overcome chance. Within the attempts to overcome chance, the idea of development squares neither with the notion

---

[46] The following typology is indebted to Rüsen's fourfold agenda of modes of historical narrative (1982; 1989: 39–61). By and large, the notions of continuity, regularity and development correspond with his traditional, exemplary and genetic modes. However, I cannot see that his fourth mode, the critical mode, establishes a form of historical narrative. It merely serves as a transition between the other modes. On the other hand, my fourth way of dealing with temporality, the acceptance of contingency, has no place in Rüsen's scheme. This is due to a fundamental difference: while Rüsen pursues a functionalist view and argues that memory must overcome chance in order to make action possible, in my phenomenological approach the experience of time precedes the use of history. Thus, in commemorative acts, we can note chance without necessarily overcoming it. For an extensive critique of Rüsen, see Grethlein 2006a: 32–41.

Table 1. *Phenomenological model of ideas of history*

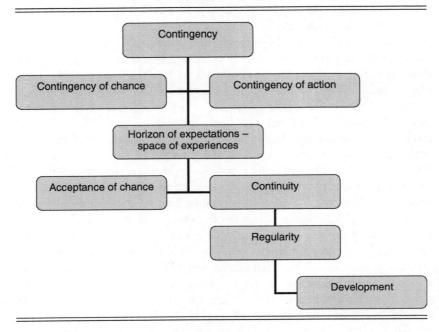

of regularity nor with the notion of continuity. As the particular arrangement of the four commemorative modes characterizes acts of memory, the approach outlined here not only traces memory back to its roots in human temporality, but also provides a classificatory scheme for comparisons. More precisely, it is the very mode of coping with temporality that serves as a criterion for the classification.

I suggest calling the particular arrangement of the four commemorative modes in an act of memory its 'idea of history'. Both parts of the term warrant some consideration. To start with the objective genitive, some scholars, most prominently Pierre Nora, juxtapose history with memory.[47] The gist of their argument is that the vanishing of traditions in the Modern Age has triggered our efforts to preserve the past. In other terms, the loss of memory, as incorporated in traditions, leads to the creation of 'history', an artificial reconstruction of the past. While I agree that Nora has identified

---

[47] Nora 1984–92. For a similar argument with a focus on Jewish memory, see Yerushalmi 1996. See also Lübbe 1977.

Introduction

an important development, I find the juxtaposition of memory with history misleading. It ignores theoretical approaches that have if not erased nonetheless blurred the boundaries between historiography and other forms of memory.[48] Seen from a phenomenological vantage point, the juxtaposition of memory and history disregards the common root of all commemorative acts in temporality. My use of 'idea of history' for poetry and oratory as well as for historiography acknowledges this common root and indicates a basic comparability that will allow us to explore the differences beyond a schematic dichotomy.

As to the '**idea** of history', despite its prominent use by R. G. Collingwood (1946) the term seems best suited to cover a wide range of attitudes to the past. 'Historical awareness' implies an evolutionist stance, as there are different degrees of awareness. 'Historical thinking' presupposes a theoretical reflection that does not apply to all forms of memories. 'Idea', on the other hand, is a broad denominator that implies neither an evolution nor a theoretical reflection.[49]

Besides tracing acts of memory back to human temporality, the emerging categories also shed new light on the function of acts of memory. The four modes of memory are congenial to different uses of the past. Traditions, which rest on continuity, are often constructed to create identities. No matter whether 'invented' or not, the continuity with the past as expressed, for example, by genealogies defines and legitimizes who we are in the present.[50] If, on the other hand, the notion of regularity is given a normative twist, then exempla, in juxtaposing the present with past precedents, provide parallels that give guidance in the here and now. Developments challenge continuities, but their dynamism lends itself to defining identities as the product of historical processes. At the same time, developments call into question an exemplary view of the past. The changes that come with the development impede a direct juxtaposition of different times and make it difficult to draw conclusions from the past about the present. While the notions of continuity, regularity and development cancel out chance and enable us to use the past in different ways, chance challenges both identities and the freedom of action. The destabilizing force of chance that we will encounter time and again in the course of this study alerts us to the fact that representations of the past are not necessarily serving a pragmatic purpose.

---

[48] White 1973 has proven as influential as controversial. For a more nuanced attempt at viewing historiography as a specific form of memory, see Ricoeur 2004.
[49] Cf. the reflections on various German terms by Goetz 1999: 18–25.
[50] On genealogies in general, see Legendre 1985; Heck and Jahn 2000. Lowenthal 1985: 61 points out that genealogies establish continuities. Zerubavel 2003: 62 emphasizes their legitimizing function.

1.3. OUTLINE OF THE WORK

This study pursues two major goals, one of which partakes of cultural history, while the other hopes to contribute to the study of Greek literature. Concerning cultural history, my aim is to reconstruct the literary field of memory in fifth-century BCE Greece, teasing out the diversity of attitudes towards the past as well as elucidating their common ground. The phenomenological model that I have just outlined allows us to take into account various genres without privileging historiography. On the literary side, the focus on memory, together with the comparative approach, helps us to shed new light on poetry and prose in fifth-century BCE Greece. Our understanding of the rise of Greek historiography, in particular, will be improved by viewing Herodotus and Thucydides against the background of memory in poetry and oratory. My study is divided into two parts. In the first, '*Clio polytropos*', I examine the content and idea of history in various non-historiographical genres of memory. The second, 'The rise of Greek historiography', presents a fresh assessment of Herodotus and Thucydides in the light of other genres, exploring the tension between tradition and innovation. While the book tries to advance a thesis about memory in the literature of fifth-century BCE Greece in general, I have tried to make the individual chapters also accessible to readers who are only interested in a single genre.

Needless to say, the genres discussed in Part I, that is epinician poetry, elegy, tragedy and epideictic and deliberative rhetoric, are rather different from one another in many regards, so it seems wise not to put them into the straitjacket of a single agenda. To give an example, the fragmentary transmission of elegy makes it necessary to deal first with the reconstruction of poems and nearly impossible to elaborate on their narrative forms. Nonetheless, the focus on the content, namely the time and the historical agent, and on the idea of history as outlined above together with the attempt to link the findings with the narrative forms and contexts of performance provide a template strong enough for a comparative reading. I have opted for close readings of select pieces from each genre, an approach that is not entirely unproblematic as the discussed texts may be more or less representative of their genres. And yet, given the awareness of this dilemma, the insights to be gained from close readings seem to me far preferable to the danger of commonplaces to which the broad focus of this study, both the question pursued and the ground covered, could lead. In order to avoid the danger of one-sided pictures, I broaden the view and take into account other texts from the same genre in the concluding sections of the individual chapters.

Praise of athletic victory in epinician poetry is framed by mythical narratives and *gnomai* in which human fragility figures prominently. In my reading of *Olympian* 2, I argue that Pindar presents Theron's athletic success as victory, albeit momentary, over the rule of time – through continuing a family tradition and modelling himself on exempla from the past, Theron manages to defy contingency of chance. Pindar's claim that the victor is dependent on his poetic praise in order to transcend time is mirrored by the temporal structure of his ode, which in its dense net of anachronies establishes a poetic continuum beyond the restraints of linear time. Despite the celebration of individual victory and the performance in the aristocratic setting of the symposium (after the victory festival, which will have been more public), the polis and its past have a prominent place in *Olympian* 2. The emphasis on human fragility facilitates the reintegration of the victor into his community.

The sparse evidence for elegy in the fifth century BCE has prompted me to support the examination of the 'New Simonides' with earlier fragments, particularly from Tyrtaeus and Mimnermus. Scanty though they are, the fragments reveal both the traditional and exemplary modes of memory and I suggest that the presentation of polis history as a continuum and the use of mythical foils are attempts to counterbalance contingency of chance, which looms large in other elegiac fragments. This allows a connection of two different strands of elegy that so far have been assigned to distinct subgenres of elegy, namely 'historical elegy' and 'sympotic elegy'. Given that, besides festivals, the symposium, an aristocratic institution, was the main occasion for elegiac performances, the focus on the polis is remarkable.

Tragedy, to which I turn next, stages contingency of chance in its full force, without the counterweight of continuity and regularity. At the same time, broadly speaking, the miseries and transgressions of tragedy take place in the 'other' and are distanced from the polis of Athens. The boundaries between Athens and the 'other' are, however, far from stable.[51] This is nicely illustrated by Aeschylus' *Persae*, which casts the very recent past, the Persian Wars, in a heroic mould and, unlike Phrynichus' *Halosis Miletou*, re-enacts a disaster that affected the enemies' camp, namely the battle at Salamis. Moreover, the perilous force of chance that rules on the stage contrasts with the continuity and regularity created by the ritual context of the Great Dionysia.[52] Nonetheless, a close reading of the *Persae* with the assistance of

---

[51] For a fine discussion of these ambiguities in tragedy, see Pelling 1997a: 16–19.
[52] This is not meant to detract from the polyphony of the Great Dionysia (see e.g. Goldhill 1990) and the tensions which emerge between the various performances, but, as I shall argue, the continuity and regularity of the ritual as a whole are in sharp contrast to the ruptures experienced by the characters on stage.

Aristotle's reflections on reception suggests that the Greek audience was invited to feel pity for their arch-enemies, the Persians.

While tragedy elaborates on experiences of contingency made by the 'other', the funeral speeches are an attempt to cope with contingency of chance that has affected Athenians. Lysias' *epitaphios logos* pits the individual death or experience of loss against the continuity of polis history that is reinforced by the chronological form of the narrative as well as by the ritualistic context of the funeral. Lysias presents his oration as a speech-act that not only, like the *Iliad*, compensates its heroes for their deaths through immortality, but also actively contributes to the continuity of Athens' history by providing the current generation with a model to emulate.

In all of the genres mentioned so far, the past is not presented for its own sake, but is always shaped by strong present interests. This grip of the present is strongest in the last non-historiographic genre that I will be discussing, deliberative oratory. Here, the past is not expounded in a continuous narrative, but selected events are chosen to buttress specific arguments. The exemplary mode of memory, which in the other genres appears mostly in the direct juxtaposition of mythic and more recent events, gains a normative twist and is used to give guidance in the present. As my example, Andocides' *de pace*, shows, the argumentative interests frequently lead to distortions. Another point makes *de pace* a particularly interesting object for this study: its view of the past, which has an aristocratic, if not oligarchic, leaning, strongly contrasts with the ideal image of Athens presented in the funeral speeches and therefore illustrates that the past figured as an important resource in socio-political conflicts.

Herodotus and Thucydides have not only been viewed as heirs of Homer and as the founding fathers of the historiographical tradition, but also as recipients of contemporaneous intellectual trends such as Ionian science or the sophists. In the second part of my study, I will complement these approaches by locating Herodotus and Thucydides in the field of memory as sketched in the preceding chapters. On the one hand, the first historians had to assert their new approach against the established accounts of the past in poetry and oratory; on the other, despite their polemics, they share much common ground with those genres.

After examining Herodotus' comments on Homer in the Helen–*logos*, I will argue that some embedded speeches can be read as an implicit critique of the rhetorical use of the past. The deficiencies of the historical arguments in the Syracusan embassy scene and the speech duel at Plataea throw into relief the *Histories*' superior take on the past. Nevertheless, Herodotus relies on an idea of history that resembles the commemorative modes to be found in poetry and oratory. Chance figures prominently in the *Histories*, and, what is more, is expressed by a narrative structure similar to that of the *Iliad*, particularly in that it includes a dense net of anachronies that forcefully pit expectations against experiences. Herodotus also uses the past in an exemplary way and not only draws on the Trojan War as a foil for the Persian Wars, but also uses the latter to shed light on later intra-Hellenic conflicts. Unlike the non-historiographic genres, the *Histories* does not follow the perspective of a single polis and, being a written text, is not determined by a specific performative context,[53] and yet the past is still in the grip of the present.

Thucydides' polemics against other commemorative media are more pronounced than Herodotus' and also address the orators. Here, a new reading of the methodological chapters 1.20–2 will be complemented by an examination of the tyrannicide digression in 6.56–9. Pericles' funeral speech and the Plataean Debate afford nice cases in which the questionable use of the past throws into relief the *History's* superiority over other commemorative genres. Like Herodotus, Thucydides emphasizes contingency of chance, and yet its destructive force is not distanced into the barbarian 'other' but unfolds in the very recent past of Greece. Moreover, neither *prolepseis* nor patterns offer a privileged stance to the readers who are fully exposed to the contingency of chance ruling at the level of action. Nonetheless, the exemplary use of the past that Thucydides envisages when he proclaims the usefulness of his account reveals that his narrative too is an attempt to overcome contingency of chance. Even more than Herodotus, Thucydides deviates in his use of the exemplary mode of memory from other genres by replacing the purposes of glorification and legitimization with a critical stance.

Despite the differences between the various genres, my investigation reveals a common tension around which their ideas of history gravitate, expressed in different narrative forms and embedded in various settings. The threat of chance looms large and is counterbalanced by the construction of continuities and regularities. On the other hand, there are only a few traces of the concept of development that has become so prominent since the Ages of Enlightenment and Historicism. In an epilogue, I will return to the beginning of this study and briefly point out crucial differences between this gravitational field and general tendencies of modern memory. Both times are 'in the grip of the past', but the ancient obsession with the past is different from our own historical fever.

---

[53] There is some evidence that Herodotus presented the results of his research in lectures (cf. Thomas 2000) and the language of his *Histories* bears the imprint of oral speech (Lang 1984), but the text, as we have it, was meant for publication. Clarke 2008: 363–9 elaborates on oral performances of local historians.

PART I
Clio polytropos: *Non-historiographical media of memory*

CHAPTER 2

Epinician Poetry: Pindar, Olympian *2*

As the title of a book by the Dutch classicist B. A. van Groningen has it, the Greeks were in the 'grip of the past'. One of the genres that illustrate this prominence of the past in ancient Greece is epinician poetry. Although its primary purpose is to praise an athletic victor, the past looms large in Pindar's and Bacchylides' odes.[1] With the exception of some brief poems, besides the praise of the victor and gnomic reflections, all victory odes contain myths as well. The coherence of these three basic parts and therefore the question of the unity of the odes have kept generations of scholars busy and continue to do so. In this chapter, I will explore a particularly complex poem, *Olympian* 2, which was written for Theron's victory in the chariot race in 476 BCE:[2] 'Nowhere is the question of unity so hard to answer as in the case of the second *Olympian*.'[3]

The focus on the idea of history, as outlined in the introductory chapter, permits a fresh look at *Olympian* 2. On the other hand, explicit reflections on time and a complex narrative structure make the poem an apt test case for my approach. After giving a brief outline of its structure (2.1), I shall examine the presentation of the past and a passage that deals with the future, the so-called eschatology. Is the traditional, exemplary, developmental or accidental mode of memory prevailing (2.2)? I will consider the 'content of the form' or what Glenn Most has called the 'compositional form'[4] and try to link the ode's idea of history to its narrative form (2.3). Then, the idea of history will be set against the background of the performative context (2.4). In conclusion, I will sum up the main points by illustrating them with examples from other victory odes (2.5).

---

[1] On the past in Pindar, see, for example, Huxley 1975; Mackie 2003: 39–76.
[2] On *Olympian* 2, see besides van Leeuwen's commentary (1964) also Hampe 1952; Bollack 1963; Woodbury 1966; Gianotti 1971; Demand 1975; Race 1979; Hurst 1981; Fitzgerald 1983; Lloyd-Jones 1985; Most 1986; Nisetich 1988; Verdenius 1989; Griffith 1991; Theunissen 2000: 698–786.
[3] Theunissen 2000: 698: 'Nirgends aber ist die Einheitsfrage so schwer zu beantworten wie im Falle des zweiten olympischen Lieds.'
[4] Cf. Most 1985: 42.

2.1. THE STRUCTURE

Let me first give a translation of *Olympian* 2:

Hymns, lords of the lyre,
what god, what hero, what man shall we celebrate?
Indeed, Pisa belongs to Zeus, while Heracles founded the Olympian Games,
firstfruits of war.
    But Theron, for his victorious four-horsed chariot,
      must be proclaimed, a man just in his regard for strangers, bulwark of
    Acragas,
the city's finest upholder from a line of famous ancestors, (1–7)

who suffered much in their hearts
and won a holy habitation at the river, and they were Sicily's
eye. Their allotted time sped on,
    adding wealth and popular favour
to their inborn virtues.
But o Cronian son of Rhea, ruling over the abode of Olympus
and the pinnacle of contests and the stream of Alpheus,
    warmed by songs
graciously preserve their ancestral land (8–14)

for their future offspring. Once deeds are done,
whether with justice or against it, not even
Cronus, the father of all,
    could make their outcome undone.
But oblivion may come with a fortunate destiny.
For under the force of noble joys pain dies,
with its malignancy being overcome, (15–20)

whenever a fate from a god sends
bliss towering high. This saying follows the fair-throned
daughters of Cadmus, who suffered greatly.
    But heavy sorrow falls
before greater blessings.
Long-haired Semele lives among the Olympians,
after dying in the roar of a thunderbolt;
    Pallas loves her for all times
and Zeus the father, and her ivy-bearing son loves her very much. (21–7)

They say, too, that in the sea
Ino has been granted imperishable life
among the sea-dwelling daughters of Nereus for all time.
    Truly, for mortals

death's end has not been fixed
nor when we shall complete a peaceful day, the child of the sun,
with unimpaired blessing.
   For various streams bearing
pleasures and toils come at various times upon men. (28–34)

And so it is that Moira, who holds the kindly destiny
that is their patrimony, adds to their heaven-sent bliss
also some suffering,
   to be reversed at another time,
from the time when his fated son met and slew Laius
and fulfilled the oracle
spoken of old at Pytho. (35–40)

When the sharp-eyed Erinys saw this,
she killed in mutual slaughter his warlike progeny.
Yet Thersander survived fallen
   Polyneices, gaining honour in new contests
and in battles of war,
a saving young shoot for the house of Adrastus' line.
From this seed the son of Aenesidamus has his root,
and it is fitting that he should enjoy victory songs and lyres. (41–7)

For at Olympia he himself
received the prize, while at Pytho and the Isthmus
the Charites shared by both awarded to his equally
   fortunate brother crowns for
the twelve-lap four-horse chariot. Winning
releases one who engages in competition from dark thoughts.
Truly, wealth adorned with virtues
   provides fit occasion for all manner of achievements
and supports a profound and questing ambition, (48–54)

a conspicuous star, the truest
light for man. If one has it and knows the future,
that the defenceless spirits
   of those who have died here immediately
pay the penalty – and that someone beneath the earth
judges the sins in this realm of Zeus,
declaring sentence with hateful necessity. (55–60)

But forever having the sun in equal nights
and in equal days, good men
receive a life with less toil, not troubling
   the earth with the strength of their hands

nor the water of the sea
for a paltry living, but, in company of the honoured
gods, those who delighted in oath-keeping
    spend a tearless
existence, whereas the others go through pain not to be looked at. (61–7)

But those, who had the courage to live three times
in either realm, keeping their souls entirely free from
unjust deeds, travel the road of Zeus to the
    tower of Cronus, where ocean
breezes blow
round the Island of the Blessed. Flowers of gold are ablaze,
some on land from radiant trees,
    while the water nurtures others.
With the wreaths of these they weave garlands for their hands and crowns, (68–74)

in accordance with the just counsels of Rhadamanthys,
whom the great father has ever beside himself,
the husband of Rhea
    who has the highest throne of all.
Peleus and Cadmus are numbered among them,
and Achilles, whom his mother brought, after she had persuaded
the heart of Zeus with her entreaties. (75–80)

He felled Hector, Troy's
indomitable mighty pillar, and brought Cycnus to death,
and Eos' Ethiopian son. I have many
    swift arrows under my arm
in the quiver,
that speak to those who understand, but in general they need
interpreters. Wise is he who knows things by nature,
    while those who have acquired their knowledge are boisterous
with garrulity like a pair of crows that cry in vain (81–7)

against the divine bird of Zeus.
Now aim the bow at the mark, come, my heart: Whom are we hitting,
when we launch this time from a kindly spirit
    the arrows of fame? Bending
the bow at Acragas,
I will proclaim a statement on oath with a truthful mind,
that no city in a hundred years has given birth
    to a man more beneficent to his friends
in spirit and more lavish of hand (88–94)

than Theron. But upon praise comes excess,
which does not keep to just limits, but, coming from greedy men,

babbling is eager
   to make obscure noble men's good
deeds. For grains of sand escape counting,
and how many joys this man has brought to others,
who could say? (95–100)

Even if scholarship is less and less inclined to follow E. L. Bundy in his claim that the praise of the victor is the only aim of all parts of epinician poems,[5] it will be hard to deny that it is a central aspect and, in the case of *Olympian* 2, the praise of Theron obviously constitutes the frame for the poem.[6] The ode starts with his praise (1–7), takes it up in its middle (46–9) and returns to it in the end (89–100).

In between the first and the second praise passages, there are two parallel sections, each of which embraces a twofold *gnome* (15–22; 30–4) and a myth (22–30; 38–45). The first *gnome* states that not even Chronus can reverse things done (15–17), but that with a happy fate past sorrow can be forgotten (18–22). The first myth tells the story of the two daughters of Cadmus, Ino and Semele, who suffered heavy blows, but then attained the gods' love and immortality (22–30). The uncertainty about when death comes (30–1) and man's general fragility (32–4) are emphasized in the second *gnome*. The following myth deals with Oedipus, his sons and Thersander. After the second praise this structure seems to be repeated, but the twofold *gnome* – it is athletic success that frees from worry, and wealth, and that embellished with virtue, is the truest light for man (51–6) – is followed instead by a long eschatological digression (57–81), which takes the place of the myth. After the eschatology, a meta-poetic reflection (83–9) leads to the final praise of Theron (89–100).

This analysis of the structure of *Olympian* 2 can be visualized as follows:

```
1–7 praise of Theron
    8–11 Theron's ancestors
    12–15a prayer for future generation
        15b–22a gnome
            15b–17 the past cannot be changed
            18–22a but sorrow can be forgotten
                22b–30a mythical foil
                    22b–27 Semele
                    28–30a Ino
        30b–34 gnome
            30b–31 time of death unknown
```

---

[5] See, for example, Carey 1995: 86.   [6] For another analysis of the structure, see Hurst 1981: 127–9.

>>> 32–4 fragility of life
>>>> 35–45 mythical foil
>>>>> 35–7 transition
>>>>> 38–42 Oedipus and sons
>>>>> 43–5 Thersander
>> 46–9a praise of Theron
>>> 49b–51a Theron's brother
>>>> 51b–56 *gnome*
>>>>> 51b–52 freedom from worry through athletic victory
>>>>> 53–6 praise of wealth
>>>>>> 57–83a afterlife
>>>>>>> 57–60 judgement
>>>>>>> 61–7a fate of good humans
>>>>>>> 67b fate of bad humans
>>>>>>> 68–83a fate of those who escape the circle
> 83b–89a meta-poetic reflection
> 89b–100 praise of Theron
>> 89–90a question about aim
>> 90b–95 praise of Theron: best *euergetes* in polis for last 100 years
>> 95b–98 limits of praise: other men
>> 99–100 limits of praise: deeds too numerous

2.2. THERON'S VICTORY AND THE HISTORY OF HIS FAMILY

It has not escaped the notice of interpreters that time is not only a thematic focus, but also structures *Olympian* 2.[7] André Hurst points out: 'The text makes different forms of time communicate with one another, on the one hand, the time of the mortals, on the other, the anti-time of the blessed.'[8] From a different angle, G. F. Gianotti observes that the ode progresses from the past to the future, first dealing with the past of Theron's family, then with the future of the individual in the afterlife. This movement is outlined in the first fifteen verses: the forefathers (8–11) stand for the past, which is taken up by the myth, Theron's success is the present, while the prayer for

---

[7] On time in epinician poetry in general, see Vivante 1972; Theunissen 2000; on narrative time in epinician poetry, see Segal 1974; Köhnken 1983; Hurst 1983; 1985; Calame 2000.
[8] Hurst 1985: 161–2: 'Il s'agit donc, dans le texte, de faire communiquer diverses phases du temps d'une part, le temps des mortels et le non-temps des bienheureux d'autre part.'

the coming generations anticipates the reflection on the future, which is given in the speculation about the afterlife.[9]

My focus on the idea of history allows for yet another approach to time in *Olympian* 2. In the introduction, I laid out an agenda that classifies acts of memory according to their way of coping with contingency. On the one hand, the detrimental force of chance may be acknowledged; on the other, the traditional, exemplary and developmental modes of memory seek to overcome contingency of chance through the construction of continuity, regularity and development. *Olympian* 2 can be fruitfully read as the confrontation of the dangerous force of chance and strategies to overcome it.[10] Pindar traces the history of Theron's family in the tension between chance on the one hand and continuity and regularity on the other (2.2.1) and further elucidates human temporality in his exposition of the afterlife (2.2.2).

2.2.1. *The past*

In the beginning, a strong line of continuity emerges.[11] The series of god, hero and man creates stability not only at the synchronic, but also at the diachronic level: Pisa belongs to Zeus – the god's claim precedes heroic and human times; Heracles has founded the Olympian games – this is the heroic past; and now, in the present time, Theron has won the chariot race.

Subtly connected syntactically through a relative clause, the continuity is then transferred from the cosmological level to human history (8), and Theron is embedded in the past of his family. The tradition in which Theron stands is implicit in his presentation as the 'bulwark of Acragas' ('ἔρεισμ' Ἀκράγαντος', 6), which corresponds with the foundation of the city by his forefathers (10). The family tradition is made explicit when Pindar calls Theron 'the city's finest upholder from a line of famous ancestors' ('εὐωνύμων τε πατέρων ἄωτον ὀρθόπολιν', 7). The continuity of the family is also projected further into the past, when the virtues ('ἀρεταί') with which Theron's forefathers acquired wealth are characterized as 'belonging to the race, inborn' ('γνήσιαι', 11). The prayer in 12–15, on the other hand, projects the noble tradition of the family into the future.

The following *gnome* hints that human life does not always proceed in a continuum of bliss: things done cannot be reversed and good luck can make

---

[9] Gianotti 1971: 33. See also Theunissen 2000: 740.
[10] Segal 1986: 126–7 notes the tension between man's achievements and his weakness in *Olympian* 2. See also Crotty 1982: 54.
[11] Cf. Theunissen 2000: 718–22.

man forget previous bad experiences (17–18). A third sentence introduces the vocabulary of death: 'For under the force of noble joys pain dies,// with its malignancy being overcome': ('ἐσλῶν γὰρ ὑπὸ χαρμάτων πῆμα θνᾴσκει// παλίγκοτον δαμασθέν', 19–20). However, the connotation of death is positive – it signifies the erasure of sorrow. Moreover, in the following mythical foil, the disruptive force of contingency of chance is displayed only at the individual level, in the lives of Semele and Ino, and, whilst their sorrow is only touched upon (23), their happy fate *post mortem* is dealt with at greater length (24–31).

Only the second myth reveals the dark side of Theron's family in the distant past:[12] Oedipus, an ancestor, who killed his own father (38–40), and the mutual murder of his sons Polyneices and Eteocles (41–2). The transition in 35–7 introduces the myth not only as an illustration of the preceding *gnome* that emphasizes human fragility, but also harks back to the first *gnome*: 'And so it is that Moira, who holds the kindly destiny// that is their patrimony, adds to their heaven-sent bliss// also some suffering, to be reversed at another time' ('οὕτω δὲ Μοῖρ', ἅ τε πατρώϊον// τῶνδ' ἔχει τὸν εὔφρονα πότμον, θεόρτῳ σὺν ὄλβῳ// ἐπί τι καὶ πῆμ' ἄγει, παλιντράπελον ἄλλῳ χρόνῳ.' 35–7). Underscored by the echo of παλίγκοτον δαμασθέν (20) in παλιντράπελον ἄλλῳ χρόνῳ (37)[13] and the repetition of πῆμα (19, 37), the quoted lines resume the message of the first *gnome* and alter its trajectory. Not only can good luck push bad experiences into the background, as is explicit in the first *gnome* and the following mythical foil, but the change can also take the opposite direction. The juxtaposition with the first *gnome* is maintained in the mythical narration where τέλεσσεν (40) evokes τέλος (17), stressing the unchangeability of bad deeds.[14]

The *gnome* in 35–7 modifies the first *gnome* in drawing attention to contingency of chance, to what is beyond human control, in general. In the same vein, the second myth, which deals with ancient ancestors of Theron, strongly contrasts with the presentation of his family at the

---

[12] While the genealogical link to the Labdacids is explicit (46), it is not mentioned for the daughters of Cadmus. However, see already the Scholion ad 39a: 'It is good to recall the story of Cadmus' daughters in order to use a related paradigm. For the family of Theron derives from here, as Pindar says in the ode which begins with ...' ('εὖ δὲ τὸ τῶν Κάδμου θυγατέρων μεμνῆσθαι, ἵνα οἰκείῳ παραδείγματι χρήσηται· τὸ γὰρ τοῦ Θήρωνος γένος ἐνθένδε κατάγεσθαί φησιν ὁ Πίνδαρος ἐν ἐγκωμίῳ οὗ ἀρχή ...'). See also Scholia ad 39b and c. Cf. Griffith 1991: 38–45.
[13] Cf. Gildersleeve 1885: ad loc.
[14] See also 32–3: 'nor when we shall complete a peaceful day, the child of the sun,// with unimpaired blessing.' ('οὐδ' ἡσύχιμον ἁμέραν ὁπότε παῖδ' ἀελίου// ἀτειρεῖ σὺν ἀγαθῷ τελευτάσομεν.').

beginning of the ode. The life of Oedipus is a frightening illustration of the limits of human knowledge and the power of contingency of chance to cross the plans of humans and to thwart their desire for continuity and regularity. More concretely, the mutual slaying of relatives, across as well as within generations, undermines the continuum in which the history of Theron's family is envisaged at the beginning. The tension is underscored by echoes of the prayer in 12–15 ('πατρώϊον// τῶνδ' ἔχει τὸν εὔφρονα πότμον', 35–6; 'εὔφρων ἄρουραν ἔτι πατρίαν', 14). Both passages are further juxtaposed by the repetition of the word μόρσιμος/μόριμος ('fated, allotted'): in 10, the life ('αἰών'), which brings wealth and popular favour, is called μόρσιμος; in 38, Oedipus, killing his father, is named μόριμος υἱός. The echoes draw attention to the contrast between the presentation of the family's past as a continuum of bliss and the havoc wreaked upon the family by Oedipus and his sons.

How does Pindar return from this dark chapter, which culminates in the mutual annihilation of relatives, to the praise of Theron, who, at the beginning of the ode, seemed safely embedded in an untarnished family tradition? Polyneices' son, Thersander, eases the transition. He is honoured for success in athletics and war (43–5) and, immediately after he is called 'a saving young shoot for the house of Adrastus' line' ('Ἀδραστιδᾶν θάλος ἀρωγὸν δόμοις', 45), the narrator turns to Theron: 'From this seed the son of Aenesidamus has his root,// and it is fitting that he should enjoy victory songs and lyres.' ('ὅθεν σπέρματος ἔχοντα ῥίζαν πρέπει τὸν Αἰνησιδάμου// ἐγκωμίων τε μελέων λυρᾶν τε τυγχανέμεν.' 46–7).

Despite the enormous temporal gap between this ancestor and Theron, continuity is created by various means.[15] Thersander is first called 'young shoot, scion' ('θάλος') and then the 'root of the seed' ('σπέρματος ... ῥίζαν') of Theron.[16] The plant imagery carries the idea of organic growth and is thus a metaphorical expression of continuity. Moreover, it is not insignificant that, where the continuity of the family tradition is stressed,

---

[15] Theunissen 2000: 731: 'In so far as the bliss, into which the sorrow is transformed with Thersandros, does not itself turn into sorrow again, the narrative and Chronus discover a new sort of continuum at a deeper level.' ('Sofern aber der Segen, in den das Leid sich mit Thersandros wandelt, nicht seinerseits wieder in Leid umschlägt, entdeckt die Erzählung an Chronus in einer tieferen Schicht eine neue Art von Dauer.') However, I disagree with Theunissen 2000: 715 when he argues that Theron breaks free from the constrictions of his family. On the contrary, as I try to show above, Theron is strongly embedded in his family background by continuity and regularity.

[16] See also the flower imagery in 50, though not pertaining to the family or one of its members, but to the present athletic victory: 'crowns for the twelve-lap four-horse chariot' ('ἄνθεα τεθρίππων δυωδεκαδρόμων'). On plant imagery in Pindar, see Carne-Ross 1976: 42–4; Steiner 1986: 28–39.

Theron is named with the patronymic.¹⁷ Finally, through another metaphor the 'new' continuity even harks back to the undisturbed continuum envisaged at the beginning of the ode. In the *gnome* that follows upon Theron's praise, wealth in combination with virtue is called 'a conspicuous star, the truest// light for man' ('ἀστὴρ ἀρίζηλος, ἐτυμώτατον// ἀνδρὶ φέγγος', 55–6). This echoes another visual metaphor for the glory of Theron's forefathers in 9–10: 'they were Sicily's// eye' ('Σικελίας τ' ἔσαν// ὀφθαλμός').

The force of contingency of chance, so threatening in the case of Oedipus and his sons, is not only restricted by the continuum that is created between Thersander and Theron, but also by Theron's imitation of Thersander's model. The repetition establishes regularity and thereby defies chance. The parallels between Theron and his ancestor are obvious: not only do the names resemble one another, but the epithet of Thersander, 'a saving young shoot for the house of Adrastus' line' ('Ἀδραστιδᾶν θάλος ἀρωγὸν δόμοις', 45), evokes Theron's description as 'the city's finest upholder from a line of famous ancestors' ('εὐωνύμων τε πατέρων ἄωτον ὀρθόπολιν', 7). W. C. Fitzgerald points out that Thersander's successes in games and war refer back to Heracles who founded the Olympic Games as ἀκρόθινα πολέμου (4).¹⁸ It also establishes a link to Theron.¹⁹ As Thersander was honoured ('τιμώμενος', 45) for his athletic victories, Pindar argues that Theron deserves honour now, linking both statements closely with the participle ἔχοντα (46).²⁰

Theron carries on a family tradition and repeats the model of Thersander. In establishing continuity and regularity, the athletic victory, a prime example of the realization of hopes, reasserts contingency of action against contingency of chance. However, the second *gnome* and the story of Oedipus and his sons bring in a more sinister tone, pointing out the fragility of human life and showing that, in the distant past, Theron's family was affected by contingency of chance. Looking at the structure, we can conclude that the threatening force of chance is embedded in the reassertion of continuity and regularity.²¹ This makes it less urgent, but does not ultimately take the sting out of it.

---

[17] One might add that the name Αἰνησίδαμος fits very well into the context of praise, evoking the stem αἰν-.
[18] Fitzgerald 1983: 56 n. 28. [19] Cf. Simpson 1969: 451.
[20] On the honour for Theron, see also 6: γεγωνητέον.
[21] Mackie 2003: 83–4 emphasizes the preponderance of the positive even in Thebes' dark history.

2.2.2. The eschatology

Contingency of chance seems finally to be overcome in the eschatology through which Pindar turns to the future (57–83).[22] However, the extent of the future upon which the eschatology reflects is limited. In *Olympian* 2, Pindar repeatedly shifts his focus between individual and collective fate. In the first stanza, he deals with the fate of Theron's family; the first *gnome* is exemplified by the individual lives of Semele and Ino; with Oedipus, Pindar returns to the frame of the family. In the eschatology, the focus is narrowed to the individual again.[23] Not the life of future generations, but the mere afterlife of the individual is at issue. The future of Theron's family remains a blank – it can be anticipated only in the form of a prayer (12–15).[24]

Nonetheless, for the future of the individual, the destructive force of chance is replaced with tranquillity in the eschatology. Pindar first describes the fate of good men (61–7), which he briefly contrasts with the toils that await the bad (67), and then elaborates on the Island of the Blessed, the destination of those who manage to escape the cycle of rebirths (68–83). The possible orphic background of this construction of the afterlife has attracted much attention;[25] for my reading its temporality is of interest. At the place to which the good are brought, there is a permanent equinox – a symbol of temporal stability[26] – and the Island of the Blessed knows, as Leonard Woodbury shows, neither day nor night.[27] The uninterrupted light sets the Island of the Blessed in the realm of timelessness.[28] The overcoming of contingency on the axis of time is underscored by spatial vagueness as the tower of Cronus and the Island of the Blessed are unlocated settings and in both places the boundary between water and earth is blurred.[29]

---

[22] Cf. the comment by Fitzgerald 1983: 49.
[23] On the possibility of knowing the future in Pindar, see Mackie 2003: 87–91. However, she does not comment on the restriction of the knowledge of the future in *Ol.* 2.56.
[24] On prayers and wishes as references to the future in Pindar, see Mackie 2003: 91–100. She sees a balance in the prayers between the acknowledgement of the future's uncertainty and 'confidence and optimism, thanks to the poet's evident ability to mediate successfully between the victor and the gods' (78).
[25] Cf. Hampe 1952; Demand 1975; Fitzgerald 1983; Lloyd-Jones 1985; Nisetich 1988; Griffith 1991; Currie 2005: 223; Hornblower and Morgan 2007: 29.
[26] Cf. Woodbury 1966; Gianotti 1971: 41–2.
[27] Woodbury 1966: 602–3. He goes further, linking the non-existence of day and night to the notions which come with the term 'ephemer'.
[28] Fitzgerald 1983: 58–61 tries to argue that the constraints of temporality are not broken on the Island of the Blessed. See, however, Theunissen 2000: 763, who rightly speaks of a 'lack of history' ('*Geschichtslosigkeit*') and elaborates on the eschatology's transcendence of time (741).
[29] 63–4: 'not troubling the earth with the strength of their hands// nor the water of the sea' ('οὐ χθόνα ταράσσοντες ἐν χερὸς ἀκμᾷ// οὐδὲ πόντιον ὕδωρ'). 72–3: 'Flowers of gold are ablaze,// some on land from radiant trees, while the water nurtures others ...' ('ἄνθεμα δὲ χρυσοῦ φλέγει,// τὰ μὲν

What is the function of the eschatology in our epinician ode? Some scholars claim that Pindar describes the Island of the Blessed in order to show Theron his future:[30] according to this interpretation, Theron will follow the heroes Peleus, Cadmus and Achilles and, like them, escape contingency on the Island of the Blessed. This view is as problematic as it is widespread. There is no explicit mention that Theron's future is prophesied, but the introduction to the eschatology is deliberately vague: 'If one has it [i.e. wealth] and knows the future,// that … ' ('εἰ δέ νιν ἔχων τις οἶδεν τὸ μέλλον,// ὅτι …', 56–7). Τις refers to Theron to whom the combination of wealth and virtues applies.[31] However the sentence is not about possession, but knowledge of the future, and even this knowledge of the future appears only in the *protasis* of a conditional clause that seems to be anacoluthic.[32]

Instead of representing Theron's future life, the description of the fate of the good and the Island of the Blessed rather serves as a foil to human life and its restricted possibilities of happiness.[33] The contrastive function of the eschatology is indicated by the great number of negations (62–7):

> … good men
> receive a life with less toil (ἀπονέστερον), not (οὐ) troubling
>   the earth with the strength of their hands
> nor (οὐδέ) the water of the sea
> for a paltry living, but, in company of the honoured
> gods, those who delighted in oath-keeping
>   spend a tearless (ἄδακρυν)
> existence.

While there is no safe day on earth, called 'sun's child' (32–3), the good have always equal days and nights enjoying the sun (61–2). Unlike Theron's forefathers ('καμόντες οἳ πολλὰ θυμῷ', 8), they do not have to toil (63–5). Moreover, the spatial vagueness of the eschatology contrasts with the precise locations that we find in the account of Theron and his family: Pindar mentions the foundation of Acragas at the river with the same name in Sicily

---

χροόθεν ἀπ' ἀγλαῶν δενδρέων, ὕδωρ δ' ἄλλα φέρβει …'). It is striking that in the first myth, in which Semele and Ino attain immortality, Mount Olympus (25) and the sea (28–30) provide the spatial frame of timelessness.

[30] Cf. Bollack 1963: 244 and Theunissen 2000: 744; Currie 2005: 3–4, who also refers to the hero–cult that Theron actually received (Diod. 11.53.2). See also Thummer 1957: 127 n. 1; Hurst 1985: 168–9. Against this interpretation, see Nisetich 1988: 15–16. Lloyd-Jones 1985: 259 is cautious, too.

[31] Cf. Hurst 1981: 128.

[32] For an attempt to avoid the anacoluthic construction, see Hurst 1981: 121–7, who takes the preceding sentence as *apodosis*.

[33] Cf. Gianotti 1971: 45–8, who emphasizes the discrepancy between heroes and human beings.

(8–10), Theron is called 'bulwark of Acragas' and even the prayer in 12–15 inscribes the temporal continuity into a stable spatial setting.[34]

It is therefore plausible to interpret the eschatology in *Olympian* 2 as a contrastive foil to human life as it is described in the preceding parts of the ode. And yet, there are a number of links between the eschatology and human life in general and Theron's in particular that blur the clear contrast and lend further significance to the eschatology. In 76, Cronus is introduced as 'the great father' ('πατὴρ ... μέγας'); in 77, he is called 'the husband of Rhea, who has the highest throne of all' ('πόσις ὁ πάντων 'Ρέας ὑπέρτατον ἐχοίσας θρόνον'). This evokes 12 where Zeus is introduced as 'o Cronian son of Rhea, ruling over the abode of Olympus' ('ἀλλ' ὦ Κρόνιε παῖ 'Ρέας, ἕδος Ὀλύμπου νέμων').[35] Some scholars even claim that Chronus and Cronus are identical and therefore see a reference to 'Chronus, the father of all' (17).[36] Regardless of whether we follow this argument, the repeated mention of Cronus and Rhea together is striking. It shows that the historical realm, in which the poet asks Zeus as son of Cronus and Rhea to grant further bliss to Theron's family, and the Island of the Blessed, where Cronus, the husband of Rhea, reigns over the greatest heroes, are not as separate as might first appear. The gap between the world full of contingencies and the timeless island is also bridged through Cadmus. Besides abiding on the Island of the Blessed, he is also named as the father of Semele and Ino (23).[37]

Two details establish a connection not only to the human world, but, more specifically, to Theron. Verses 48–9 'For at Olympia he himself// received (ἔδεκτο) the prize' are echoed by 62–3 'good men// receive (δέκονται) a life with less toil'. While the repetition of δέχεσθαι may seem random, a second parallel is more significant (72–4):

... Flowers of gold are ablaze,
some on land from radiant trees, while the water nurtures others.
With the wreaths of these they weave garlands for their hands and crowns ...
... ἄνθεμα δὲ χρυσοῦ φλέγει,
τὰ μὲν χερσόθεν ἀπ' ἀγλαῶν δενδρέων,
    ὕδωρ δ' ἄλλα φέρβει,
ὅρμοισι τῶν χέρας ἀναπλέκοντι καὶ στεφάνους ...

The garlands make the heroes resemble Theron. Garlands were awarded to athletic victors and their crowning is a recurrent theme in epinician

---

[34] 14–15: 'Graciously preserve their ancestral land/// for their future offspring.' ('εὔφρων ἄρουραν ἔτι πατρίαν σφίσιν κόμισον/// λοιπῷ γένει.').
[35] On Pindar's tendency to avoid the repetition of simple names, see Nisetich 1989: 85 n. 15.
[36] Griffith 1991: 48 with n. 18. Cf. Theunissen 2000: 707.   [37] Cf. Hurst 1981: 127.

poetry.[38] It figures prominently in *Olympian* 3, which Pindar composed for another celebration of the same victory (6–9): '... for the crowns woven in his hair (χαίταισι μὲν ζευχθέντες ἔπι στέφανοι)// exact from me this god-inspired debt,// to mix the many-toned lyre, the cry of pipes and the setting of words// for Aenesidamus in due measure.' Pindar goes on to tell how Heracles brought the olive tree, from which the garlands stem, to Olympia. In elaborating on the victory crown put on Theron's head, *Olympian* 3 makes explicit the parallel between Theron and the heroes on the Island of the Blessed and can therefore be read as a commentary on *Olympian* 2.[39]

These observations do not support the thesis that Pindar shows Theron his own future. As I have argued, such an interpretation would fail to do justice to the careful framing of the eschatology. However, the afterlife of the good and the Island of the Blessed cannot be reduced to a mere contrasting foil for human life either. The parallel between the heroes and Theron, both wreathed with garlands, suggests that the description of life on the Island of the Blessed illuminates the athletic victory – in particular its temporal dimension.[40] As the Island of the Blessed is elevated from time, Theron's victory at the Olympian games overcomes the supremacy of contingency of chance that otherwise rules human life: he perpetuates a family tradition, establishes regularity by following the paradigm of Thersander and even makes it possible to forget a past that was overshadowed by the arbitrariness of chance. In order to highlight Theron's transcendence of time, Pindar does not simply evoke a mythical foil, which would be rooted in time itself, but invokes the idea of a life beyond time.

However, as the parallels are only implicit, the case should not be pressed too hard, and we ought not to forget that Theron's transcendence of time is limited: according to the first *gnome*, things done cannot be undone, and, as the prayer in 12–15 reveals, the future remains open. The timelessness of the

---

[38] There is even a parallel instance in which crowns establish a connection between the mythic foil and the praise of the victor. In *Pyth.* 10.40, the Hyperboreans are said to be wearing ivy crowns. This underscores the similarity to the celebration of the victor who is praised for his crowns in 58. On the parallels between the Hyperboreans and the celebration of athletic victory, see Köhnken 1971: 162–3. He also notes the similarity between the land of the Hyperboreans in *Pyth.* 2 and the Island of the Blessed in *Ol.* 2 (170–2). On the other hand, I am not convinced by Fitzgerald's argument (1983: 60–1) that the wreathing on the Island of the Blessed evokes the binding of Cronus by Zeus.

[39] The parallel would be underscored if ἄνθεμα in 72 recalls the metaphor ἄνθεα τεθρίππων δωδεκαδρόμων in 50.

[40] This argument receives support from Nisetich's interpretation (1988: 6–8). He argues that 53–6 make the recipient expect the topos of immortalization through poetry that Pindar replaces by his scenario of the afterlife. Thus, the audience would be inclined to link the eschatology to the poetic immortalization of Theron. Mackie 2003: 96–7 gives parallels in which tranquillity is attained by athletic victory.

eschatology both illuminates and throws into relief the transcendence of time through athletic victory. Theron only achieves what, in another context, Simon Hornblower has called 'transient immortality'.[41]

To sum up, the history of Theron's family is presented in the tension between contingency of chance on the one hand and the traditional and exemplary modes of memory on the other. Theron, with his victory, reinforces the continuity of his family that was endangered by Oedipus and his sons, and, in paralleling Thersander, also establishes regularity. Therefore, the victory overcomes for a moment the perilous force of chance in the same way that the heroes on the Island of the Blessed have left time behind them. *Olympian* 2 nicely illustrates that the traditional and exemplary modes of memory serve as counterweights against contingency of chance that threatens human identities and actions. Against experiences in the sense of G. W. F. Hegel and Hans-Georg Gadamer, i.e. negative experiences that remind humans of their finiteness, continuity and regularity create the stability that is necessary for identities and actions.

2.3. PINDAR'S SPEECH–ACT AND THE TIME OF HIS ODE

In *Iliad* 9.411–16, Achilles reports a prediction by his mother Thetis:

I carry two sorts of destiny toward the day of my death. Either,
if I stay here and fight beside the city of the Trojans,
my return home is gone, but my glory shall be everlasting (κλέος ἄφθιτον ἔσται);
but if I return home to the beloved land of my fathers,
the excellence of my glory is gone, but there will be a long life
left for me, and my end in death will not come to me quickly.

Needless to say, Achilles goes for the first option and, through his *mors immatura*, he achieves 'imperishable glory' ('κλέος ἄφθιτον') in the medium of epic poetry. Here and in other passages, the Homeric epics present themselves as the *kleos* that bestows immortality on Achilles and his comrades. I would now like to show that Pindar claims a similar role for himself – he not only envisages Theron's athletic success as a victory over contingency of chance, but claims a role for himself in this transcendence of time (2.3.1). In a second step, I shall turn to the 'content of the form' and argue that the narrative structure of the ode enacts the transcendence of time that Pindar grants to the victor (2.3.2).

---
[41] Hornblower 2004: 92 on *Pyth.* 8.95–7.

2.3.1. Praise and transcendence of time

The end of *Olympian* 2 implies that, to transcend time, the victor is dependent on the praise of Pindar. After announcing that he is aiming at and shooting Theron, who has proven himself a great benefactor of his polis, Pindar continues (95–100):

> ... But upon praise comes excess,
> which does not keep to just limits, but, coming from greedy men,
> babbling is eager
> to make obscure noble men's good
> deeds. For grains of sand escape counting,
> and how many joys this man has brought for others,
> who could say?

> ... ἀλλ' αἶνον ἐπέβα κόρος
> οὐ δίκᾳ συναντόμενος, ἀλλὰ μάργων ὑπ' ἀνδρῶν,
> τὸ λαλαγῆσαι θέλον
> κρυφὸν τιθέμεν ἐσλῶν καλοῖς
> ἔργοις· ἐπεὶ ψάμμος ἀριθμὸν περιπέφευγεν,
> καὶ κεῖνος ὅσα χάρματ' ἄλλοις ἔθηκεν,
> τίς ἂν φράσαι δύναιτο;

Strong reverberations link the ode's ending to the first *gnome*: οὐ δίκᾳ (96) – ἐν δίκᾳ τε καὶ παρὰ δίκαν (16); κρυφὸν τιθέμεν (97) – ἀποίητον ... // ... θεῖεν (16–17); ἐσλῶν (97) – ἐσλῶν (19); ἔργοις (98) – ἔργων (17); χάρματ' (99) – χαρμάτων (19); δύναιτο (100) – δύναιτο (17).[42] Marked by these echoes, the end complements the reflection of the first *gnome*. While the second *gnome* harks back to its first part and spells out that bad experiences can overwhelm good, the poem's end refers back to the second part: not only bad deeds, but also good deeds, can be forgotten. It is Pindar's task to keep the good deeds visible. His claim to a 'truthful mind', literally a 'mind without oblivion' ('ἀλαθεῖ νόῳ', 92), can be read as the answer to 'oblivion' ('λάθα', 18), which threatens good and bad deeds alike. Hence, only the poet's engagement enables the athlete to transcend time. With his victory, the athlete causes sorrows to be forgotten (18–20 cf. 51–4), but he depends on the poet's praise not to sink into oblivion himself. Paradoxically, Pindar's praise also preserves the past sorrows that the victory itself makes vanish, Oedipus and his sons. However, he uses them to throw into relief the victor's success.[43]

---

[42] Cf. Theunissen 2000: 702.
[43] Memory and oblivion are also relevant within the Oedipus-story. Theunissen 2000: 733 points out that Oedipus kills his father since he is oblivious of his own origin. He juxtaposes this bad oblivion to the good oblivion that is described in 18–20.

Epinician Poetry: Pindar, Olympian 2

Pindar's assertion, namely that his praise enables the athletic victor to transcend time, resembles the claim of epic poetry to immortalize the objects of their praise.[44] I tentatively suggest that one passage not only points out that the poet helps the victor to transcend time, but also marks the similarity to epic (83–91):

> ... I have many
>   swift arrows under my arm
> in the quiver,
> that speak to those who understand, but in general they need
>   interpreters. Wise is he who knows things by nature,
> while those who have acquired their knowledge are boisterous
> with garrulity like a pair of crows that cry in vain
>
> against the divine bird of Zeus.
> Now aim the bow at the mark, come, my heart: Whom are we hitting,
> when we launch this time from a kindly spirit
>   the arrows of fame? Bending
> the bow at Acragas ...

> ... πολλά μοι ὑπ'
>   ἀγκῶνος ὠκέα βέλη
> ἔνδον ἐντὶ φαρέτρας
> φωνάεντα συνετοῖσιν· ἐς δὲ τὸ πᾶν ἑρμανέων
>   χατίζει. σοφὸς ὁ πολλὰ εἰδὼς φυᾷ·
> μαθόντες δὲ λάβροι
> παγγλωσσίᾳ κόρακες ὣς ἄκραντα γαρυέτων

> Διὸς πρὸς ὄρνιχα θεῖον·
> ἔπεχε νῦν σκοπῷ τόξον, ἄγε θυμέ· τίνα βάλλομεν
> ἐκ μαλθακᾶς αὖτε φρενὸς εὐκλέας ὀ-
>   ϊστοὺς ἱέντες; ἐπί τοι
> Ἀκράγαντι τανύσαις ...

These verses have puzzled scholars and prompted a variety of interpretations.[45] Whichever reading we follow, it is obvious that the many arrows that the poet has under his arms serve as an '*Abbruchformel*' ('break-off formula').[46] There are many stories which Pindar could tell, but, aiming at

---

[44] On epinician poetry referring to itself as *kleos*, see Nagy 1986: 89–90. He emphasizes that while in the epics *kleos* is restricted to the heroes, epinician poetry applies it to the athletes of the present as well as to the heroes of the past. On the similarity between the glory created by the epics and epinician poetry, see also Erbse 1999: 31. Currie 2005: 71–84, on the other hand, argues that while the epics only deal with immortality *via* renown, Pindar also takes into account literal immortality. On the various notions of *kleos* in Greek poetry, see Goldhill 1991: 69–166.
[45] Cf. Race 1979; Most 1986; Verdenius 1989.
[46] Cf. Ruck 1972: 162. For parallels, see Race 1979: 256 n. 16.

Theron, he turns to his praise again (83–5 and 89–91).[47] Perhaps the bow metaphor has further significance. It is not only the most elaborate of its kind in Pindar, but this is also the only time that Pindar says he is aiming at and shooting the victor. My suggestion is that the bow metaphor interacts with the preceding myth, namely that of Achilles, and thereby indicates a parallel between Pindar and Homer.

Achilles, the last of the heroes on the Island of the Blessed whom Pindar mentions (79–83), gains eternal fame only in exchange for his *mors immatura* (*Il.* 9.411–16). According to nearly all mythical traditions, Achilles dies from an arrow which is shot by Apollo and Paris. Pindar's announcement that he is going to shoot 'arrows of fame' at Theron, following immediately upon the reference to Achilles' afterlife, contrasts with the lethal arrows for Achilles. At the same time, the imagery implies the claim that Pindar's praise makes Theron transcend time, just as the shot of Apollo and Paris bestowed immortal glory on Achilles in the medium of epic poetry.[48]

Two points support this reading. In 79–80, the entreaties (λιταί) of Thetis are mentioned as the reason Achilles is on the Island of the Blessed. No matter whether these λιταί are only modelled after the λιταί in *Iliad* 1[49] or even, as I think is also possible, refer directly to them, Thetis' pleading that Zeus grant honour to her son is evoked. Thus, the λιταί call attention to the link between Achilles' death and glory. Moreover, Pindar calls his arrows εὐκλεεῖς. This can mean that his arrows, i.e. his poetry, are famous, but also, if we read it by hypallage, that his poems establish fame. Since *kleos* is what the epics claim to bestow, the analogy between Achilles and Theron at one level and between Homer and Pindar at another is forcefully underscored.

However, there is one significant difference between epic and epinician claims to negate contingency of chance. The epics grant immortality to dead heroes; Pindar, on the other hand, elevates a living man. Furthermore, he reaches out to the future of the living. It has been shown that Pindar

[47] On the bow metaphor, see Simpson 1969: 450–3, according to whom it serves the purpose of consoling Theron. Race 1979: 256–8 compares it to *Ol.* 13.93–7 and *Isthm.* 5.46–54 and points out that the poet refers to himself in the first person, that the arrows signify a quantity and that Pindar is ready to continue, but will return to the most essential thing.

[48] Another interpretation of Achilles in *Olympian* 2 is offered by Griffith 1991: 52–3. He argues that the myth of Achilles mediates between the myth of the daughters of Cadmus, in which love prevails, and the myth of the house of Laius, which shows utmost hatred. In the tension between love and hatred he sees the alternation of love and strife according to Empedocles. Interesting as this suggestion is, it seems a bit forced. For example, I am not convinced that the three victims of Achilles recall the three athletic victories in 46–51. The number three is too general to evoke such a reference by itself. On the function of Cadmus and Peleus in the myth, see Solmsen 1982a: 20.

[49] Cf. *ibid.*: 20–1. Nisetich 1988: 9–13 tries another tack and argues that there is a reference to the *Aithiopis*.

implicitly stylizes himself as a prophet in *Olympian* 2.[50] I would like to draw attention to a passage in which Pindar explicitly refers to the future, but in a non-prophetic way (12–15):

> But o Cronian son of Rhea, ruling over the abode of Olympus
> and the pinnacle of contests and the stream of Alpheus,
>   warmed by songs
> graciously preserve their ancestral land
> for their future offspring.
>
> ἀλλ' ὦ Κρόνιε παῖ 'Ρέας, ἕδος Ὀλύμπου νέμων
> ἀέθλων τε κορυφὰν πόρον τ' Ἀλφεοῦ,
>   ἰανθεὶς ἀοιδαῖς
> εὔφρων ἄρουραν ἔτι πατρίαν σφίσιν κόμισον
> λοιπῷ γένει.

If in a prayer within a song, songs are said to induce Zeus to grant further bliss, it is reasonable to read this as a statement about the function of the song itself.[51] In establishing contact with Zeus, Pindar's ode appears as the vehicle by which the continuity of the family can be preserved and be extended into the future. While a prayer does not come with the same authority as a prophecy, the attempt to influence the future through a speech–act nonetheless distinguishes Pindar from Homer. We will see that the funeral speeches give the epic claim to bestow immortality on the objects of their praise yet another twist.[52]

2.3.2. *The temporal organization of the ode*

I would now like to push my interpretation further and argue that Pindar not only claims to help Theron overcome contingency of chance, but that his very poem transcends time. Seen from this angle, the narrative form of the ode expresses its social function. The close relation between Pindar and time is implied in the very last question: '... for grains of sand escape counting,// and how many joys this man has brought to others,// who could say?' ('ἐπεὶ ψάμμος ἀριθμὸν περιπέφευγεν,// καὶ κεῖνος ὅσα χάρματ' ἄλλοις ἔθηκεν,// τίς ἂν φράσαι δύναιτο;' 98–100). The question harks back to the introductory question of the ode – 'what god, what hero, what

---

[50] Cf. Most 1986: 315–16 with more explicit parallels and further literature on p. 315 n. 64. See also Mackie 2003: 78–87, who, furthermore, argues that the quantifying style in 98–9 is reminiscent of prophecy.
[51] Cf. Willcock 1995: ad loc. Nisetich even translates ἀοιδαί as 'my song'. van Leeuwen 1964: ad loc. draws attention to the epic colouring of ἰανθεὶς ἀοιδαῖς.
[52] Cf. Chapter 5, section 5.2.

man shall we celebrate?' (2). The reverberation reinforces that, although a complete enumeration of Theron's deeds is impossible, Pindar is the one who is praising him most effectively. At the same time, the final question echoes: '... once deeds are done,// whether with justice or against it, not even// Chronus, the father of all, could make their outcome undone.' ('τῶν δὲ πεπραγμένων// ἐν δίκᾳ τε καὶ παρὰ δίκαν ἀποίητον οὐδ' ἄν// Χρόνος ὁ πάντων πατὴρ δύναιτο θέμεν ἔργων τέλος.' 15–17).

The parallel use of δύναιτο, in the first case in negation, in the second in a rhetorical question, juxtaposes Pindar with Chronus. The fact that Chronus cannot undo things done creates a further similarity to Pindar, who also reports the dark past of Theron's family. The link between Pindar and Chronus is perhaps reinforced by the word ἀποίητον. The use of ποιεῖν and its cognates to denote poetic composition is particularly common in prose texts from the second half of the fifth century BCE onward, but we also find it in earlier poetry.[53] This connotation would strengthen the juxtaposition of Pindar with Chronus. However, given that high poetry seems to avoid this use of ποιεῖν,[54] this must remain a tentative suggestion. Nonetheless, the reverberations raise the question: is Pindar, like Chronus, the father of all? In the following, I will take a brief look at the temporal organization of the ode and suggest that his poetry even allows him to master time.

Time is relevant at several levels in *Olympian* 2. The poem reflects on temporality, reports events which take place in time and itself unfolds in time. Therefore, I would like to raise the question of how the temporal organization of the narrative compares to the time in the narrative. What is the relation between narrated and narrative time? To start with narrative time, *Olympian* 2 is full of anachronies. While Pindar refers to different times, the temporal gaps and distances are glossed over.[55] When the poem turns from Theron to his ancestors, a relative clause makes it possible to step into the past without further ado (8). The following prayer jumps into the future by referring rather vaguely to 'their future offspring' ('λοιπῷ γένει', 15) The distance of the mythical past dissolves in the present of the narration when Pindar says: 'This saying follows the fair-throned// daughters of Cadmus ...' ("ἕπεται δὲ λόγος εὐθρόνοις// Κάδμοιο κούραις ...', 22–3). Furthermore, both Semele and Ino are elevated to a timeless sphere.[56]

---

[53] See for example, Solon fr. 20 W² 3. On the use of ποιεῖν and its cognates for poetic activity, see Ford 2002: 131–57.
[54] Ibid.: 137. [55] Cf. the analysis of Hurst 1985: 170–2.
[56] 26: αἰεί; 29: βίοτον ἄφθιτον; 30: τὸν ὅλον ἀμφὶ χρόνον. See also the present tense of the verbs: 25: ζάει; 26: φιλεῖ and the resultative perfect in 30: τετάχθαι.

The time of the story of Oedipus and his sons (38–9) is not marked, only the aorist indicates that it took place some time in the past.[57] The temporal gap between Thersander and Theron (46) is, as I have pointed out, concealed by the plant metaphor. Finally, the eschatology is set in timelessness.

How does this narrative treatment of time relate to narrated time? We have seen that in the account of Theron's history and that of his family continuity balances contingency of chance. In his extensive use of anachronies, Pindar does not unfold the past as a continuity. On the contrary, he dissolves it. Disregarding chronology, the form of the presentation undermines the idea of continuity that we find at the level of content. However, this does not mean that Pindar's narrative is ruled by contingency. On the contrary, the free jumps through the present, the historical past, the future and different phases of the mythical past blur the borderlines between times.[58] Pindar undermines the historical continuum, but only to create a new, poetic continuum. The medium of song in which the dense net of anachronies makes the boundaries between past, present and future collapse establishes an eternal present, comparable to the timelessness of the eschatology.

The narrative form negates contingency of chance not only through a poetic continuum, but also through regularity. The neglect of temporal distances and contexts provides a setting in which past and present can mirror one another, mediated by the timeless level of gnomic utterances. No direct link is indicated between the exemplum of the daughters of Cadmus and the present, but the fate of Semele and Ino exemplifies the first *gnome*: bad experiences can cede to good ones. At the same time their suffering leads to the second *gnome*, which points out the fragility of man. Then, the myth of Oedipus and his offspring not only exemplifies the second *gnome*, but also corresponds to the first. On the one hand, the history of the Labdacids reveals the weakness of human life, on the other, the shift from Oedipus and his sons to Thersander and Theron illustrates that fortune can erase the memory of a bad past. What the first myth has shown at the level of individual life, the second demonstrates for the family.

---

[57] Hurst 1985: 162 writes about ἄλλῳ χρόνῳ (37): ' ... in fact, in verse 37 Pindar avoids an adjective which would underline the passing of time.' (' ... en effet, au vers 37, Pindare évite un adjectif qui soulignerait l'écoulement du temps.').

[58] Hurst 1985: 172: 'Hidden jumps, levelled gaps, a timeless present, all these devices make the ode resonate with the tone of an "eminent present".' ('Sauts camouflés, écarts aplanis, présent intemporel, ces procédés font résonner l'ode dans une tonalité de "présent majeur".'). Crotty 1982: 98 notes that Pindar does not distinguish between the past and present, but focuses on 'the persistence through time of patterns in mortal life'. Huxley 1975: 41–3 points out that Pindar does not distinguish between myth and history.

Furthermore, the Labdacids serve as a negative and a positive foil to Theron. I have already elaborated on the parallels between Theron and Thersander. Unlike Thersander, Polyneices and Eteocles are negative foils and establish a strong contrast between the happy present and the dark past:[59] while Polyneices and Eteocles kill each other, expressed pointedly by ἀλλαλοφονίᾳ (42), Theron and Xenocrates are united in athletic victories: '.. at Pytho and the Isthmus// the Charites shared by both awarded to his equally fortunate brother crowns for// the twelve-lap four-horse chariot.' ('... Πυθῶνι δ' ὁμόκλαρον ἐς ἀδελφεόν// Ἰσθμοῖ τε κοιναὶ Χάριτες ἄνθεα τεθρίππων δυωδεκαδρόμων// ἄγαγον.' 49–51).[60]

Thus, Pindar not only creates a poetic continuum, but in his hands history also becomes a panopticon of events that mirror each other. This constitutes the exemplary use of the past, which directly juxtaposes events from whichever time. Through juxtapositions that disregard temporal distance, fixed patterns evolve and the ensuing regularity negates chance. The panopticon of events as well as the poetic continuum provides a narrative reply to the detrimental force of contingency of chance.

I started with the observation that only Pindar's praise allows Theron to overcome contingency of chance. Thus, the transcendence of time is the content as well as the function of the epinician poem. At the same time, the praise itself is processed in time. I have argued now that in the temporal organization of his ode's narrative Pindar transcends the constraints of time. More specifically, in establishing a poetic continuum and in setting up a panopticon of exempla, the function of the epinician poem – to help the victor transcend time – has inscribed itself into its narrative form. Form, function and content converge. Pindar's ode is a speech-act not only in helping the victor transcend time, but, more specifically, in transcending time through its own narrative form.

2.4. THE SOCIO-POLITICAL CONTEXT

It is the aim of this book to explore the ideas of history of various genres in light of their narrative forms and socio-political contexts. In the preceding

---

[59] Fitzgerald 1983: 56 offers a further observation: 'In the recitation of his victories (48–51) Theron is associated with his brother, just as the sisters Semele and Ino were associated through their eternal life in the corresponding position of the second triad.'
[60] Cf. Griffith 1991: 51. In both cases, only one of the brothers is named: Thersander and Polyneices. One could also argue that the patronymic (46: τὸν Αἰνησιδάμου) implies a contrast to Laius' murder at the hands of his son. The success at the Pythian games also contrasts with the Pythian oracle about Oedipus' crimes (39).

section, I have suggested an approach to the 'content of the narrative form' in *Olympian* 2; now it is time to take a look at the context in which its reception took place. Epinician poetry was composed for performance, but it was not restricted to a single occasion. Most *epinicia* seem to have been performed first at celebrations in the victor's hometown, either in his house or at more public places such as sanctuaries, but the odes could be re-performed at symposia.[61] When Pindar claims that 'faster than a magnificent horse// and a winged ship// I will send this message everywhere' (*Ol.* 9.23–5), he obviously alludes to the dissemination of his song in symposia all over Greece.[62] Perhaps, the double setting of celebration party and symposium also helps to answer the much-debated question of whether the odes were sung by a chorus or a soloist.[63] I am inclined to believe that at the celebration of the victory a chorus performed, but that later recitals in a sympotic setting were by individuals.[64]

In recent decades, numerous works have shown that culturally, socially and politically the symposium played a central role in archaic Greece.[65] It was the context for poetic performances,[66] was at the core of the development of pottery and vase painting[67] and was also crucial for the development of the polis, as is particularly clear in the Spartan *kosmos*.[68] Most importantly, the symposium helped aristocrats to establish, maintain and 'enact' their social identity.[69] Therefore, the symposium was an apt institution for the circulation of glory gained in the world of athletic games. Although the victors are far from forming a homogenous group – including tyrants as well as average citizens – the world of athletic competitions was by and large aristocratic.[70] Theron was tyrant of Acragas, and yet origin and ancestry, as praised in *Olympian* 2, were cornerstones of aristocratic identity in general.

---

[61] On the performance at public festivals, see Slater 1984: 244–5; Krummen 1990: 275–6. On re-performances, see Kurke 1991: 5; Currie 2004; Hubbard 2004. On the performance of some of the shorter odes right at the site of the games, see Gelzer 1985. Burnett 2005 examines how Pindar engages the specific audience in his odes for Aiginetean boys.

[62] Cf. Ford 2002: 121–2 with parallels.

[63] For the performance by a chorus: Burnett 1989; Carey 1989; 1991; Morgan 1993; for the performance by a soloist: Heath 1988; Heath and Lefkowitz 1991; Lefkowitz 1995; for a fuller bibliography see Clay 1999: 25 n. 1. See also Carey 2007a.

[64] Cf. *ibid.*: 208.   [65] I only give a few titles: Murray 1990a; Slater 1991; Schmitt Pantel 1992.

[66] See n. 61 above.   [67] Murray 1990b: 9. See the books by Dentzer 1982 and Schmitt Pantel 1992.

[68] The political aspect is emphasized by Murray 1982; 1983a: 265–8; Rossi 1983; Schmitt Pantel 1992: 33–4; 107–13.

[69] Murray 1983b; Bremmer 1990.

[70] See Carey 1995: 90 with n. 9 for the *communis opinio* that athletic competitions were an aristocratic domain. On the other hand, Young 1984 stresses that not only aristocrats competed at athletic games, and Hornblower 2004: 35 points out that symposia were not automatically antidemocratic. Rose 1982: 55 argues that 'the origin of the genre represented an aristocratic escalation of ideological warfare responding to the more threatening aspects of the relatively "democratic" tyrannies'. See, however, Thomas 2007 against the thesis that epinician poetry emerged as a reaction to the process of democratization.

Nonetheless, it is important to note that *Olympian* 2 ultimately embeds Theron and his family in the polis. When Pindar turns to Theron's ancestors, he mentions the foundation of the polis (8–9). Theron is not only called 'bulwark of Acragas' ('ἔρεισμ' Ἀκράγαντος', 6) at the beginning, but at the end Pindar directs his bow at Acragas and calls Theron the most generous son of the city born in the last hundred years (91–5). Pindar makes sure that the praise for the individual also elevates the polis. That poleis gained in reputation through athletic victories of their citizens comes to the fore in the speech with which Thucydides has the *Olympionikes* Alcibiades defend himself against accusations of his sumptuous lifestyle and political aspirations (6.16.2):

For the Greeks, who had previously expected that our city was exhausted by war, believed that it was greater than its actual power on account of the splendour of my representation at Olympia, since I entered seven chariots, more than any individual before, and I won and also came second and fourth and arranged everything in a manner worthy of the victory.[71]

In a similar vein, an epigram for the *Olympionikes* Ergoteles presents the claim that he 'gave to Himera an imperishable memorial of his excellence' (*CEG* 393.4).[72]

This observation ties in nicely with approaches emphasizing that victory odes served not only the function of praising the victor, but also of mediating between him and the polis and thereby easing the return of the outstanding individual into his community. Building on the work of Kevin Crotty, Leslie Kurke has argued that epinician poems worked towards reintegrating the victor on three levels, those of house, class and city.[73] The mediation between the aristocratic desire for distinction and the claims of the polis is not only owed to the public performances in which the odes were first performed, but also reflects on the institution of the symposium. Aristocratic as the setting of the symposium was, sympotic poetry nonetheless reveals that aristocrats were more and more obliged to pursue their ambitions within the frame of the polis. In the next chapter, we shall see that memory in another sympotic genre, elegy, is dominated even more by the polis.

---

[71] On the link between individual success and glory of the polis in Pindar, see e.g. Steiner 2001: 272–3.
[72] As we know from *Olympian* 12, Ergoteles had been exiled from Crete and had found his new home in Himera.
[73] See in particular Crotty 1982: 112–22, who argues that epinician poetry is an 'act of inclusion' and compares it to rituals (120); Kurke 1991: 6. Hornblower 2004: 28–30 draws attention to the limits of this approach. Furthermore, some scholars have emphasized the didactic aspect of epinician poetry, see e.g. Rose 1982; Carey 1995: 86.

The epinician reflection on time can be linked to the social reintegration of the victor and allows us to add yet another to Kurke's three levels at which the victor is reintegrated. The emphasis on human fragility in victory odes is striking and leads me to suggest not only that examples of human failure and misery throw the victory into relief,[74] but that the mixture of praise with a focus on the dark side of life also serves to integrate an outstanding success into a world in which chance looms large. The social return is embedded in a *nostos* to the temporality of human life that the victor has transcended for a moment. The reintegration at the cosmological level reinforces the social reintegration by calling attention to the human condition to which the victor is subjected in the same way as his fellow citizens.

2.5. CONCLUSION

We have seen that in *Olympian* 2 *gnomai* as well as myths draw attention to human fragility. Contingency of chance is prominent in nearly all odes of Pindar. While mythical exempla often illustrate the divine punishment awaiting men who do not accept the limits set on human life – e.g. Bellerophontes (*Isthm.* 7.43–8; cf. *Ol.* 13.91), Tantalus (*Ol.* 1.55–64) and Ixion (*Pyth.* 2.21–41) – *gnomai* forcefully alert the audience to the fact that men are exposed to forces beyond their control. For example, in a famous and much-discussed passage Pindar calls man 'ephemeral' and compares him to a shadow's dream (*Pyth.* 8.95–6). The brief ode *Olympian* 12 starts with a prayer to *tyche* under whose guidance 'swift ships pilot the seas' (3) and then continues the sea metaphor to elaborate on the insecurity of human life: 'Men's hopes,// are often tossed up and, at other times, down// as they voyage through vain falsehoods,/// no man has ever found a sure sign// regarding an impending action from the gods.' (5–8). In *Pythian* 12, a reflection on the fickleness of bliss even gives the poem's closure a sombre tone: 'If there is any bliss among men, it does not appear// without struggle. Still a god may bring it to pass today// – what is fated cannot be avoided – but there will come the time,// which, striking someone with surprise, will,// against expectation, give one thing, but defer another' (28–32). As Hugh Lloyd-Jones has claimed, 'no early Greek poet is more aware than Pindar of the mortality of man and of the impermanence of all human things.'[75]

However, in *Olympian* 2 the destructive force of chance is challenged by the regularity and continuity that Theron creates through his athletic victory.

---

[74] Cf. *ibid.*: 87.   [75] Lloyd-Jones 1985: 245.

The exemplary and traditional modes of memory serve as powerful counterweights against contingency of chance. The exemplary mode of memory figures prominently in other odes too. With the exception of some brief odes, all epinician poems evoke mythical heroes as foils for the athletic victors. To give a random example, in *Isthmian* 1 the mirror function of Castor and Iolaus is pointed out explicitly: 'But I render honour to Herodotus for his four-horse chariot,// whose reins he guided not with other hands, and I wish// to include him in a hymn to Castor or Iolaus,// for they were born as the mightiest charioteers of the heroes, one in Lacedaemon, the other in Thebes.' (14–17). In many other cases, the juxtaposition is not explicit, but is marked by similarities as when in *Isthmian* 4 Pindar first mentions the light stature of Melissus, victor in the pancration (67–9 (49–51)), and then turns to Heracles, whom he introduces as 'short of stature,// but adamant in spirit' (71–2 (53–4)). The implicit comparison of the victor with a mythical hero allows Pindar to praise his client effectively without the risk of making inappropriate claims for a living man.

If we turn to the only other classical poet besides Pindar from whom we have a number of victory odes, Bacchylides, we find a case in which a historical figure fulfils the function of the mythical foil. In an ode for the victory of Hieron in the Olympic chariot race in 468 BCE, Bacchylides narrates the rescue of Croesus from the pyre and presents it as Apollo's answer to his generous gifts. Croesus' generosity is invoked as a parallel for the rich presents that Hieron has given the gods (Bacchyl. 3.58–66). In the following chapters, we shall see that in other genres too, particularly in elegy, tragedy and funeral speeches, the recent past can be cast in a mythical register. The mythification of history is facilitated by the exemplary use of the past, which only focuses on direct juxtapositions of events and thereby neglects temporal distances.

In *Olympian* 2, contingency of chance is also challenged by continuity. Particularly at the beginning, the history of Theron and his family is presented as a continuum. We find the traditional mode of memory in other epinician odes as well. For example, the Thessalian Hippocleas who won the boys' long sprint race 'has walked in the footsteps of his father,// who was twice a winner at Olympia' (*Pyth*. 10.12–13) and Alcimidas of Aegina, winner in the boys' wrestling, set 'his feet in the tracks// of his own grandfather Praxidamas' (*Nem*. 6.15–16). In the case of the Argivian Theaeus, Pindar notes that 'many times has honour from victory in the games// come to the famous race of your mother's forbears' (*Nem*. 10.37–8) and after enumerating several victories, breaks off, 'as it is impossible to reckon the vast amount of bronze,// there is too little leisure to count it'

(*Nem.* 10.45–6). While in these examples the history of the family is envisaged as a continuum, in other poems the frame is larger, for example in *Pythian* 1, when Pindar remarks that Hieron founded Aetna 'with god-built freedom,// according to the ordinances of Hyllus' rule; for the descendants of Pamphylus,// and indeed of Heracles' sons,// who dwell under the heights of Taygetus,// desire always to keep to the statutes of Aegimius as Dorians.' (61–5). In these and other passages, the notion of continuity balances the force of chance.

I have argued that Pindar claims a role for himself in Theron's transcendence of time. Only his praise allows the victor to gain 'transient immortality'. The same claim also surfaces in other poems, for example when Pindar introduces his song as 'glorious recompense for the toil' of the victor (*Isthm.* 8.1) and states that 'virtue endures// in glorious songs for a long time' (*Pyth.* 3.114–15) whereas 'great deeds of strength,// are sunk in deep obscurity, if they lack songs' (*Nem.* 7.12–13).[76] In *Nem.* 6.28a–30, Pindar invokes the Muse: 'Come, Muse, direct// upon this house a glorious wind of verses –// for when men have passed away// songs and legends preserve for them their noble deeds.'

The complex temporal form of *Olympian* 2 establishes the transcendence of time that the victor gains through Pindar's praise. The numerous, more or less unmarked jumps through time create an eternal present in which the constraints of time disappear and past, present and future mirror one another. *Olympian* 2 is admittedly one of the more complex Pindaric odes, but there are other odes with the same density of anachronies and fascinating plays with narrative and narrated time. Hurst has examined the temporal complexity of *Pythian* 4, which, broadly speaking, repeats the same movement twice: a series of *analepseis* that lead further and further back in the past is followed by a return to the present.[77]

Olympian 7 is yet another interesting case. Pindar narrates three myths about Rhodes, the home of the victor Diagoras: Tlepolemus, who killed his great-uncle (20–33), the Heliadae, who failed to make proper sacrifices for Athena (34–53), and the rise of Rhodes out of the depths of the ocean (54–71). Narrated time inverses here the movement of narrative time; whereas the ode moves forward, Pindar goes, unhampered by the constraints of linear time, from myth to myth back in time. Even in poems without such intricate temporal structures, the mythical foils constitute free jumps through time.

---

[76] Cf. Mackie 2003: 97–8 with parallels.   [77] Hurst 1983.

However, the epinician transcendence of time is only temporary. The tension between continuity and regularity on the one hand and contingency of chance on the other remains ultimately unresolved. In *Nemean* 11, we find a reflection on virtue: 'Ancient qualities// put forth their strength in alternate generations of men.' While here the traditional and exemplary modes of memory converge, the following verses speak a different language: 'The black fields do not yield continual crops,// nor are trees wont to bear fragrant flowers// of equal richness with every turn of the years,// but they vary. In like fashion Moira leads// the mortal race. There comes from Zeus no certain sign// for men to read' (37–44).

We shall find similar ideas of history in other genres that also balance, albeit in their own, distinct ways, contingency of chance with the exemplary and traditional modes of memory. In the victory odes, the emphasis on human fragility also contributes to the social function of the genre. Performed at victory celebrations and circulating in symposia, epinician poetry is a product of aristocratic striving for distinction. Nonetheless, the fickleness of fate, which affects everybody alike, puts individual achievements into perspective and facilitates the reintegration of the victor into his community.

CHAPTER 3

Elegy: The 'New Simonides' and earlier elegies

Only a few articles had been devoted to the sparse evidence for historical narrative in elegy,[1] when in 1992 a new Oxyrhynchus papyrus was published that contained elegiac fragments on one or more sea battles and the battle at Plataea by Simonides.[2] The 'New Simonides' forcefully called to our attention that, besides martial exhortations and reflections on the human condition, elegy could also be used to narrate historical events.[3] The place of these narrative passages in elegies, however, is the object of dispute: while most scholars assume that a specific class of elegies was devoted to historical narratives, 'historical' or 'narrative elegy', which ought to be distinguished from 'sympotic elegy', Lawrence Kowerski and David Sider observe that the Greeks never attached such labels to elegies and therefore argue against such sub-genres.[4] Rather, as Sider puts it, elegies with historical narratives 'also incorporated myth (proto-history to the Greeks) and looked forward to (and gave advice on) the future, while including as well themes now thought of as sympotic.'[5]

The fragmentary transmission of elegy makes it not only difficult to figure out the links between historical subjects and other themes, but also to arrive at safe conclusions about the focus and temporal scope of the

[1] The most influential article was Bowie 1986, but see also Steinmetz 1969; Lasserre 1976. On the terms ἔλεγος, ἐλεγεῖον, ἐλεγεία see West 1974: 2–9; Lambin 1988; Gerber 1997: 94–6. The origin of elegy is the object of scholarly dispute (the fragments are collected in Gentili and Prato 1979/²2002; West ²1992). Lately, Page's theory of the threnodic roots of elegy (1936) has been taken up again, cf. Aloni 2001: 90; 105; Yatromanolakis 2001: 219–20 with n. 60; Kowerski 2005: 115–19. For earlier advocates of this theory, see Tsagarakis 1977: 15 n. 2. However, it is well known that there are only few dirges in elegiac couplets (Gentili 1968: 52 points out that the oldest funeral inscriptions are in hexameters) and only very few, if any, archaic elegies can be claimed to be lamentatory. See against the origin of elegy in lament Bowie 1986: 23–7; Fowler 1987: 86–7; Gentili 1988: 32–3; 63–4.
[2] The *editio princeps* is Parsons 1992; the new fragments are already included in West ²1992. On the life of Simonides, see Lefkowitz 1981: 49–56; Molyneux 1992. Most scholars follow the earlier date given in the Suda according to which he was born in the fifty-sixth Olympiad and died after eighty-nine years in the seventy-eighth Olympiad (468–464 BCE). The earlier Suda-date (birth in the sixty-second Olympiad) is favoured by Stella 1947.
[3] See the contributions in Boedeker and Sider 2001a; Kowerski 2005.
[4] Kowerski 2005: 63–73; Sider 2006.   [5] *Ibid.*: 328.

narratives. In addition, given the shortness of most fragments, it is virtually impossible to elaborate on narrative forms. Nonetheless, accounts of the past, whether as narratives for their own sake or embedded in a non-narrative context, are too prominent in elegy to be left aside in a study on ideas of history. It is possible to reconstruct, at least tentatively, elegy's idea of history, the genre's specific arrangement of the traditional, exemplary, developmental and accidental modes of memory.

Whereas in the preceding chapter I first focused on a single victory ode, *Olympian* 2, and then in the conclusion took into account other samples of the same genre, the fragmentary status of the 'New Simonides' requires me to back up the discussions right from the beginning with references to fragments of other poets, mostly Tyrtaeus[6] and Mimnermus,[7] both dating from the seventh century BCE, but also Archilochus, roughly their contemporary, and Xenophanes who lived at the same time as Simonides. In a first step, I will touch upon the problems of a reconstruction of the longest piece of the 'New Simonides', fr. 11 W^2, and examine its content (3.1). The following discussion of the underlying idea of history will suggest a link between seemingly disparate strands of elegy (3.2). I shall then attempt to deepen our understanding of historical narratives in elegy by discussing the genre's self-fashioning vis-à-vis epic (3.3). In the last section before the conclusion (3.4), I will relate elegy's idea of history to its socio-political context (3.4).

3.1. THE CONTENT OF SIMONIDES FR. 11 W^2

The Suda mentions Simonidean elegies on the Persian Wars, but only the publication of *P. Oxy.* 3965, which partly overlaps with scraps from *P. Oxy.* 2327, provided us with at least one lengthy passage dealing with the Persian Wars, fr. 11 W^2, which has been reconstructed and translated by M. L. West as follows:

> str[uck you ... and you fell, as when a larch]
>   or pine-tree in the [lonely mountain] glades
> is felled by woodcutters ...
>   and much ...

---

[6] According to some sources, Tyrtaeus was from Sparta where he is supposed to have served as a general in the Second Messenian War (defended by Rossi 1967–8). Others claim that he came from Athens or Miletus, cf. the testimonies and the discussion in Prato 1968: 1*–4*.

[7] The evidence for Mimnermus' lifetime is extremely scanty, but appears to confirm the Suda according to which his *akme* was in the thirty-seventh Olympiad (632–629 BCE). On Mimnermus' life, see West 1974: 72–6; Allen 1993: 9–19; Sanz Morales 2000. Jacoby 1918: 268–72 makes a strong case that he was from Smyrna and not from Colophon.

Elegy: The 'New Simonides' and earlier elegies

[A great grief seized] the war-host; [much they honoured you,]
   [and with Patr]oclus' [ashes mingled yours.]
[It was no ordinary mortal] laid you low,
   ['twas by Apoll]o's [hand that you were struck.]
[Athena] was at [hand, and smote the famous t]ow[n]
   [with Hera; they were wro]th with Priam's sons
[because of P]aris' wickedness. The car of God's
   Justice o'ertakes [the sinner in the end.]
[And so] the valiant Danaans, [best of warr]iors,
   sacked the much-sung-of city, and came [home;]
[and they] are bathed in fame that cannot die, by grace
   [of one who from the dark-]tressed Muses had
the tru[th entire,] and made the heroes' short-lived race
   a theme familiar to younger men.
[But] now farewell, [thou son] of goddess glorious,
   [daughter] of Nereus of the sea, while I
[now summon] thee, i[llustriou]s Muse, to support,
   [if thou hast any thought] for men who pray:
[fit ou]t, as is thy wont, this [grat]eful song-a[rray]
   [of mi]ne, so that rem[embrance is preserved]
of those who held the line for Spart[a and for Greece,]
   [that none should see] the da[y of slavery.]
They kept their co[urage, and their fame rose] heaven-high;
   [their glory in] the world [will] never die.
[From the Eu]rotas and from [Sparta's] town they [marched,]
   accompanied by Zeus' horsemaster sons,
[the Tyndarid] Heroes, and by Menelaus' strength,
   [those doughty] captains of [their fath]ers' folk,
led forth by [great Cleo]mbrotus' most noble [son,]
                     ... Pausanias.
[They quickly reached the Isthmus] and the famous land
   of Corinth, [furthest bounds] of Pelops' [isle,]
[and Megara, N]isus' [ancient] city, where the r[est]
   [then joined the army from] the country round.
[Again they marched, the ome]ns giving confidence,
   [and soon they reached Eleusis'] lovely plain,
driving [the Persians from Pan]dion's [land, by help]
   of that most godlike se[er, the Iamid.]
... overcame ...
      ...

   ...
παῖ[σέ] ο.[σὺ δ' ἤριπες, ὡς ὅτε πεύκην
   ἢ] πίτυν ἐν βήσ[σαι' οὔρεος οἰοπόλου
ὑλοτόμοι τάμ[νωσι
   πολλὸν δ' †ἥρῶσ[

ἦ μέγα πένθ]ος λαὸν [ἐπέλλαβε· πολλὰ δ' ἐτίμων,
  καὶ μετὰ Πατρ[όκλου σ' ἄ[γγεϊ κρύψαν ἐνί.
οὐ δή τίς σ' ἐδ]άμασσεν ἐφ[ημέριος βροτὸς αὐτός,
  ἀλλ' ὑπ' Ἀπόλλ]ωνος χειρὶ [τυπεὶς ἐδάμης.
Παλλὰς δ' ἐγγὺ]ς ἐοῦσα πε[ρικλεὲς ἄ]στ[υ καθεῖλεν
  σὺν δ' Ἥρῃ, Πρ]ιάμου παισὶ χ[αλεπτ]όμ[εναι
εἵνεκ' Ἀλεξά]νδροιο κακόφρ[ονο]ς, ὡς τὸν [ἀλιτρόν
  ἀλλὰ χρόνῳ]ι̣ θείης ἅρμα καθεῖλε δίκ[ης.
τοὶ δὲ πόλι]ν πέρσαντες ἀοίδιμον [οἴκαδ' ἵ]κοντο
  φέρτατοι ἡρ]ώων ἀγέμαχοι Δαναοί[,
οἷσιν ἐπ' ἀθά]νατον κέχυται κλέος ἀν[δρὸς] ἕκητι
  ὃς παρ' ἰοπ]λοκάμων δέξατο Πιερίδ[ων
πᾶσαν ἀλη]θείην, καὶ ἐπώνυμον ὁπ[λοτέρ]οισιν
  ποίησ' ἡμ]ιθέων ὠκύμορον γενεή[ν.
ἀλλὰ σὺ μὲ]ν νῦν χαῖρε, θεᾶς ἐρικυ[δέος υἱέ
  κούρης εἰν]αλίοιο Νηρέος· αὐτὰρ ἐγώ[
κικλήισκω] σ' ἐπίκουρον ἐμοί, π[ολυώνυμ]ε Μοῦσα,
  εἴ περ γ' ἀν]θρώπων εὐχομένω[ν μέλεαι·
ἔντυνο]ν καὶ τόνδ[ε μελ]ίφρονα κ[όσμον ἀο]ιδῆς
  ἡμετ]έρης, ἵνα τις [μνή]σ̣ε̣ται ὕ[στερον αὖ
ἀνδρῶ]ν, οἳ Σπάρτ[ῃ τε καὶ Ἑλλάδι δούλιον ἦμ]αρ
  ἔσχον] ἀμυνόμ[ενοι μή τιν' ἰδεῖν φανερ]ῶ̣[ς
οὐδ' ἀρε]τῆς ἐλάθ[οντο, φάτις δ' ἔχε]ν οὐρανομ[ήκ]ης
  καὶ κλέος ἀ]νθρώπων [ἔσσετ]αι ἀθάνατο<ν>.
οἳ μὲν ἄρ' Εὐ]ρώταν κα[ὶ Σπάρτη]ς ἄστυ λιπόντ[ες
  ὥρμησαν] Ζηνὸς παισὶ σὺν ἱπποδάμοις
Τυνδαρίδα]ις ἥρωσι καὶ εὐρυβίῃ Μενελάω[ι
  ἐσθλοὶ πατ]ρ̣ώιης ἡγεμόνες π[ό]λεος,
τοὺς δ' υἱὸς θείοιο Κλεο]μβ[ρ]ότου ἔξ[α]γ' ἄριστ[ος
                ]αγ. Παυσανίης.
αἶψα δ' ἵκοντ' Ἰσθμὸ]ν καὶ ἐπικλέα ἔργα Κορίν[θ]ου
  νήσου τ' ἐσχατιήν] Τανταλίδεω Πέλοπος
καὶ Μέγαρ' ἀρχαίην Ν]ίσου πόλιν, ἔνθά περ ὤ[λλοι
                          ] φῦλα περικτιόνων
θεῶν τεράε]σσι πεποιθότες, οἳ δὲ συν[
  ἷκον Ἐλευσῖνος γῆς ἐ]ρ̣α̣τὸν πεδίον
Μηδείους γαίης Παν]δίονος ἐξε[λάσα]ντες
  Ἰαμίδεω τέχναις μάν]τ̣ι̣ος ἀντιθέου[
            ].ς δαμάσαντ[
            ].ι εἰδομεν[
            -ώ]νυμον α.[

If we accept West's reconstruction, then fr. 11 W² starts with a tree simile that describes the death of Achilles and is followed by a reference to his burial. While West's suggestion that *P. Oxy.* 2327 fr. 5 (lines 1–4 of fr. 11 W²) precedes *P. Oxy.* 2327 fr. 6 is not beyond dispute and not all scholars believe that the verses deal with Achilles' burial and death,[8] we reach safer ground with the following lines, which describe the sack of Troy (10–14) and mention the fame the Greeks were given by the Muses (15–18). The reference to Troy is capped by an invocation of Achilles with which West's reconstruction of the beginning of the fragment ties in nicely (19–20). Then the narrator goes on to ask the Muses to help him bestow glory on those who fought at Plataea (20–8). In what seems to be the beginning of an account of the battle, the march of the Spartans and other Greeks to Plataea is narrated (28ff.) before the papyrus breaks off.[9]

A majority of scholars follow the Suda and assume that Simonides wrote a number of elegies each of which was devoted to a particular battle. According to this view, fr. 11 W² belongs to a poem on Plataea. However, the Suda not only mentions no Plataea–poem, but its testimony raises many problems in general. To touch upon only one, 'The reign of Cambyses and Xerxes and the sea-battle of Xerxes' ('ἡ Καμβύσου καὶ Δαρείου βασιλεία καὶ Ξέρξου ναυμαχία') are very unlikely to be titles of poems. Even if Theodor Bergk is right in his suggestion that the reference to the Persian kings rather defines Simonides' lifetime, we have to accept that the Suda's text is deeply corrupt. Moreover, the contradiction between the Suda's reference to an elegiac poem on the sea-battle at Artemisium and Priscian's quotation from a lyric poem with the same title has called into question the reliability of the titles and metres given by the Suda.[10]

On account of these and other problems, Kowerski postulates that the reconstruction of the Persian Wars elegies ought to rely only on the fragments.[11] Our fragments, he argues, do not support the assumption of several poems. Instead, Kowerski suggests that Simonides may have written one large poem that referred to different battles. While, as Kowerski admits, the tentative reconstruction of such a poem ultimately remains speculative, his critique successfully challenges the *communis opinio* that there was a Plataea–elegy. Neither in the Suda nor in any other source is such a poem

---

[8] West's reconstruction depends on the observation that *P. Oxy.* 2327 fr. 5 is the bottom of a column and fr. 6 (lines 5–14 W²) the top of another column. Yet, Lloyd-Jones 1994: 1 is doubtful and thinks it possible that the fragment came later. Parsons 1992: 28 suggests that the verses refer to Mardonius' or Masistius' death. Kowerski 2005: 44–5 is also sceptical about West's reconstruction. For a fuller discussion see Luppe 1993; Rutherford 2001: 43–4.
[9] However, Kowerski 2005: 74 casts doubt on the narrative character of the poem to which fr. 11 W² belonged.
[10] Cf. Rutherford 2001: 35–6 for a fuller survey of the testimonies and a discussion of the different possibilities.
[11] Kowerski 2005: 4–19.

mentioned, and we have to allow for the possibility that fr. 11 W² was part of a poem that dealt with more than Plataea alone. Moreover, Kowerski takes up the suggestion by Dirk Obbink and Sider that fr. 11 W² may have belonged to the same poem as some of the fragments from the papyrus that most scholars classify as sympotic. I will come back to this possibility in section 3.3; for now, it may suffice to note that the context of fr. 11 W² is less clear than scholars were inclined to believe in the immediate aftermath of its publication.

Even with Kowerski's caveats in mind, however, it is hard to disagree that the 'New Simonides' included an account of the battle at Plataea. Thus, the poem seems to have dealt with the recent past, a temporal scope that Ewen Bowie deems unique in elegy.[12] Indeed, most of the fragments of Tyrtaeus and Mimnermus tackle remote, albeit not mythical, events, but, on the other hand, there are a couple of earlier fragments that refer to the more recent past: Tyrtaeus fr. 5 W² mentions the capture of Messene two generations earlier[13] and Pausanias tells us that Mimnermus composed a poem about Gyges' attack on Smyrna (fr. 13a W²).[14] Nonetheless, Simonides fr. 11 W² seems to be distinct in devoting a rather long narrative to events that probably took place only a couple of years or even fewer before the poem was composed.[15]

What about the focus? Tyrtaeus' *Eunomia* deals with the Spartan constitution (fr. 4 W²) and in other fragments he mentions the Spartan capture of Messene (fr. 5 W²). Likewise, Mimnermus focuses on the history of Smyrna, and also other elegies of which we only have the names, Semonides' *archaiologia Samion* and, if in elegiac couplets, Xenophanes' *ktisis*–poem, seem to have narrated polis history.[16] An illustrious group of

---

[12] Bowie 2001: 55–6. On the date of the Plataea–elegy, see West 1993: 9; Boedeker 1995: 217–29; Aloni 2001.
[13] However, Schwartz 1899: 429 suggests that 'fathers of our fathers' (fr. 5 W² 6) refers to ancestors in general. See also Luraghi 2003: 110–11.
[14] See also fr. *adesp. eleg.* 62 W², which seems to be on the Lelantine War.
[15] Bowie 2001: 55–6 also argues that the Plataea–poem seems to have been shorter than other historical elegies, containing a couple of hundred lines. However, as I argue in the Appendix, the evidence for historical elegies that filled one or even more books is very scanty. In many further aspects, the 'New Simonides' resembles other narrative elegies, as Bowie acknowledges (2001: 56–8). Fr. 14 W² is very likely to contain a prophecy; thus, we have not only direct speech as in Mimnermus fr. 13a W², but something similar to the oracle in Tyrtaeus fr. 4 W². There is even a trace of divine agency, the Tyndaridae, who are said to march with the Spartans in fr. 11 W² 30–1. However, it is difficult to decide whether this is a real epiphany or whether Simonides is only referring to statues the Spartans had with them (cf. Hornblower 2001). For divine agency in Simonides' battle elegies, see also West's discussion of what he takes to be the Artemisium–poem (1993: 3–4).
[16] If we assume that the Ionian history by Panyassis was written in elegiacs, we would have a narrative elegy the focus of which transcends the past of a single polis. Cf. Bowie 1986: 32 with n. 102. See also Huxley 1969: 186.

scholars argue that the 'New Simonides' deviates from this focus on the polis in taking a pan-Hellenic stance.[17] And in fact, in fr. 11 W² 37–8, Peloponnesian troops are mentioned and Peter Parsons, in the *editio princeps*, suggests that in line 41 the Athenians join the army.[18] Furthermore, in fr. 15–16 W², which is likely to have belonged to the same poem as it comes from an account of Plataea, the Corinthians are praised.

Yet, if we first concentrate solely on fr. 11 W² and leave aside other fragments, the prominence of the Spartans is striking.[19] Their departure and march is described in detail (29–37) and their leader Pausanias is mentioned by name (34). In his appeal to the Muse, Simonides asks for glory to be bestowed on the Spartans (24–6). This suggests that they are the main subject of the poem, which is the medium of glory. The focus on Sparta would be further enhanced if lines 25–6, as in West's restoration, claim that the warriors defended Sparta (and Hellas) from the day of slavery.[20]

The mention of other cities does not necessarily conflict with a Spartan perspective, but seems natural given that the battle at Plataea actually involved other Greek cities too.[21] Thus, even the praise of the Corinthians in fr. 15–16 W² might suit a poem with a Spartan slant, particularly as the verses seem to be taken from the description of the battle order.[22] In his quotation, Plutarch points out that Simonides was not 'training a chorus in Corinth and did not compose an ode for the city, but nevertheless recorded these deeds in an elegy' (*de Herodoti malignitate* 872C–E). This comment shows that the poem was not composed for Corinth, but it does not exclude a focus on another polis.[23]

---

[17] Cf. Boedeker 1995: 225; 2001a: 127; 2001b: 154; Bearzot 1997: 78; Obbink 2001: 79–80; Kowerski 2005: 63–107. Schachter 1998 argues for a Peloponnesian stance.

[18] Cf. Rutherford 2001: 47.

[19] Here I side with Aloni 2001: 102–4, who emphasizes the Spartan slant of the 'New Simonides'. Going even further, Aloni presents the unprovable but interesting suggestion that 'while commissioning Simonides to write the inscription for the monument at Plataea and for the tripod at Delphi, the Spartans and/or Pausanias also commissioned an elegy that commemorated the dead and celebrated their victory *in situ* ...'. Pavese 1995 grounds a very different reconstruction of the poem on the Spartan bias. Arguing that Achilles served as a model for Leonidas, he proposes that first the battle at Thermopylae was reported, followed by the foil of Achilles and the battle at Plataea. For the Spartan focus, see also Burzacchini 1995: 23–6.

[20] Cf. Aloni 2001: 103. However, the mention of the 'sons of Dorus and Heracles' in opposition to 'Medes and Persians' in fr. 13 W² does not necessarily support the argument for a Spartan perspective as he claims. Boedeker 1995: 224 is right to point out that, as in fr. 15–16 W², 'the specific disposition of troops along the battle line' may be intended.

[21] On pan-Hellenism in the aftermath of Plataea, cf. Aloni 2001: 100–2.

[22] See Luppe 1994. For a different view, see Obbink 2001: 80.

[23] *Pace* Boedeker 1995: 225; Obbink 2001: 80.

To sum up, the fragmentary transmission makes it hard to arrive at safe conclusions about the temporal scope and focus of the 'New Simonides'. There are elegies that refer to the recent past, but, among the preserved material, Simonides' elegy seems to be unique in devoting a long narrative to contemporary history. While a majority of scholars believe that the poem of fr. 11 W² also deviates from other elegies in taking a pan-Hellenic stance, I have pointed out the possibility that the main focus is Sparta. I shall return to temporal scope and focus when I compare elegy with epic, but before that the modes of memory deserve closer examination.

3.2. THE IDEA OF HISTORY IN THE 'NEW SIMONIDES' AND OTHER ELEGIES

In the preceding chapter, I have argued that *Olympian* 2 foregrounds contingency of chance while at the same time balancing its detrimental force with the notions of continuity and regularity. Viewing the past as undisturbed by chance creates the stability necessary for identities and actions. Despite the scanty transmission of elegy, it is possible to trace in some fragments the exemplary and traditional uses of the past (3.2.1), whereas other elegiac fragments elaborate on human fragility. My theoretical approach and the parallel of Pindar allow us to suggest tentatively a link between seemingly distinct strands of elegy (3.2.2).

3.2.1. Regularity and continuity

It is debated whether or not in Simonides fr. 11 W² Achilles serves as a model for an individual – the names of Leonidas as well as of Pausanias have been thrown in the ring – but it is uncontroversial that, at a more general level, Simonides evokes the siege of Troy as a mirror for the Persian Wars.[24] He points out that the Greek heroes at Troy gained *kleos* from the Muses (15–18),[25] before he asks the Muse, this time in

---

[24] Pavese 1995: 22 argues that Achilles figured as a model for Leonidas and that thus the poem also dealt with the battle of Thermopylae; Shaw 2001: 180–1 claims that Achilles was used as a model for Pausanias; Rutherford 2001: 38 sees the link less in Achilles himself, but in the pan-Hellenic nature of both enterprises. See also Obbink 2001: 72. As long as we have no evidence about the occasion and the commissioner of the poem, it seems most reasonable to see in Achilles 'the archetypal mortal divinity/divinized mortal' (Obbink 2001: 72).

[25] Even the immortality of the glory seems to be expressed: ἀθά]νατον (15) is a likely complement and ὑπ[λοτέρ]οισιν (17) 'is guaranteed by the quotation at Theocr. 16.46.' (Parsons 2001: 61; cf. Lloyd-Jones 1994: 2). A meta-poetic significance can also be found in ἀοίδιμον in verse 13. Cf. Lloyd-Jones 1994: 1, who prefers West's πόλι]ν to Luppe's Τροίη]ν; Poltera 1997: 344.

the singular, to assist him in bestowing glory on the hoplites at Plataea (20–8).[26] Thereby, the achievement of the Greeks who fell against the Persians is compared with the bravery of the heroes who died at Troy. This comparison is an exemplary use of the past, which, without taking into account the time in between, directly juxtaposes two different events. Accordingly, Simonides ignores the different circumstances and modes of warfare so that contemporary hoplites and Homeric heroes mirror one another, and the present seems to re-enact the past. As I have argued in the introduction, such juxtapositions create regularity and thereby minimize the threat of chance. This use of the past parallels the myths with which Pindar illuminates the athletic successes of his clients.

In addition to the explicit comparison of the battles at Plataea and Troy, Simonides also casts the recent event in a heroic register. The strong epic colouring, for example in ἀοίδιμον (13) and ὠκύμορον (18),[27] gives contemporary history a heroic patina that prompted West to speak of a 'mini-epic in elegiacs'.[28] Not only epic words, but also features of epic narrative, such as the invocation of the Muse, distance the events from the here and now. We find this also in other elegies, for example in the brief Mimnermus fragment, which deals with Gyges' recent attack: 'So the men around the king charged, after he had given the word of command, making a fence with their hollow shields.' ('ὣς οἳ πὰρ βασιλῆος, ἐπε[ί ῥ'] ἐ[ν]εδέξατο μῦθον,/ ἤ[ϊξ]αν κοίληι[ς ἀ]σπίσι φραξάμενοι.' fr. 13a W²). The mention of μῦθος suggests that the elegy contained a speech. Besides, the introductory ὡς may indicate that our distich was the *comparandum* of a simile. To direct speech and simile, the proem that the poem had (fr. 13 W²) can be added as a further epic feature that endowed contemporary history with a heroic air. Here and elsewhere, the events described are not explicitly juxtaposed with other events, but, presented in an epic light, they appear as re-enactments of heroic grandeur and are therefore also evidence for an exemplary view of the past.

---

[26] Although the tenor seems clear, the gaps are large. None of the letters of 24 [μνή]σεται West or [μνήσετ' ἐν ...] Parsons can be safely deciphered. In 28, 'immortal' refers to fame, but it is difficult to decide whether κλέος (West), supported e.g. by Stehle 2001: 114–15, or φάτις (Parsons) was at the beginning of the line.

[27] Cf. Lloyd-Jones 1994: 1–3.

[28] West 1993: 5. Yet, a cautious note may be added: in many cases, the reconstruction draws on epic parallels, and thus arguments easily become circular.

56 *The Greeks and their past*

The heroization of contemporary history also facilitates the normative use of exempla. A case in point is Tyrtaeus fr. 5 W² 1–8, which deals with the conquest of Messene:[29]

.. to(?) our king Theopompus, dear to the gods,
through whom we captured spacious Messene,
Messene good to plough and good to plant.
For nineteen years the spearmen fathers of
our fathers fought ever unceasingly over it,
displaying steadfast courage in their hearts,
in the twentieth year those [i.e. the opponents] abandoned their rich farmlands
and fled from the high mountain range of Ithome.

ἡμετέρῳ βασιλῆϊ, θεοῖσι φίλῳ Θεοπόμπῳ,
ὃν διὰ Μεσσήνην εἵλομεν εὐρύχορον,
Μεσσήνην ἀγαθὸν μὲν ἀροῦν, ἀγαθὸν δὲ φυτεύειν·
ἀμφ' αὐτὴν δ' ἐμάχοντ' ἐννέα καὶ δέκ' ἔτη
νωλεμέως αἰεὶ ταλασίφρονα θυμὸν ἔχοντες
αἰχμηταὶ πατέρων ἡμετέρων πατέρες·
εἰκοστῷ δ' οἱ μὲν κατὰ πίονα ἔργα λιπόντες
φεῦγον Ἰθωμαίων ἐκ μεγάλων ὀρέων.

It may suffice to single out θεοῖσι φίλῳ Θεοπόμπῳ[30] and πίονα ἔργα[31] as examples of epic diction in this fragment. More specifically, together with νωλεμέως αἰεὶ ταλασίφρονα θυμὸν ἔχοντες,[32] the mention of twenty years is likely to evoke the image of much-toiling Odysseus who first besieged Troy for ten years and then wandered around for another ten years before he could return to his home on Ithaca. The conquest of Messene is thus presented as an enterprise worthy of an Odysseus. The heroization of the recent past gives it authority. While neither the fragment itself nor the quoting context permits a firm

---

[29] It should be noted that fr. 5 W² consists of three single fragments that West, following Bergk and other editors, has put together (fr. 5 W² 1–2; fr. 5 W² 3; fr. 5 W² 4–8). Indeed, all three fragments deal with Messene and its capture and seem to be linked to one another. However, it is not necessary that they directly followed upon one another (cf. von Blumenthal 1948: 1950; Page 1951: 12; Gentili and Prato 1979/²2002 in their edition); what is more, the change from the first (fr. 5 W² 2) to the third person (fr. 5 W² 4) has been deemed odd (cf. von Blumenthal 1948: 1950). I would therefore rather keep the three fragments separate, while assuming that they come from the same poem. Cf. Meier 1998: 258–60.
[30] Cf. Il. 20.347; Od. 10.2: φίλος ἀθανάτοισι θεοῖσι; Il. 22.41; 24.749: φίλος ... θεοῖσι.
[31] See Il. 12.283; Od. 4.318.
[32] See Prato 1968: 77, who suggests that the epitheton ταλασίφρων has been combined with the phrase ἐμὸν ἔχειν or that ταλασίφρων has been contaminated with τλήμονα θυμὸν ἔχειν. He also points out that the use first of a cardinal (ἐννέα καὶ δέκ' ἔτη, 4), then an ordinal number (εἰκοστῷ, 7) is Homeric.

conclusion, the argument for a paraenetic purpose is persuasive.³³ The perfunctory nature of the account makes it at least likely that the reference to the past served as an exhortation in the present.

In this case, an exemplary use of the past can be found not only in the heroization of the recent past, but also in its presentation as a model for the present. In the form of exempla, the juxtaposition of different times gains a normative twist – a parallel from the past is presented as the standard for which present men ought to aim. Concretely, Tyrtaeus appeals to his audience to be as brave as the Spartans who conquered Messene. The descriptive and normative aspects of the exemplary view of the past are intertwined, since the model of the recent past gains authority from its presentation as heroic. Here and in other cases, the heroization of the recent past underscores its paradigmatic function by allowing conclusions *a maiore ad minus*.

Tyrtaeus fr. 5 W² also reveals another mode of memory, the traditional mode, which presents history as a continuum. Not only does the phrase 'the fathers of our fathers' point out the sequence of generations, but the first person plural for a past action, εἵλομεν (2), envisages Sparta's past and present as one entity – the timeless collective in 'we captured spacious Messene' elides the distinction between past and present. This continuum of Spartan grandeur is also expressed by the personal pronoun in the first person plural that is applied to king Theopompus (1).³⁴

Mimnermus uses the same means to present the history of Smyrna as continuous (fr. 9 W²):

> ... leaving Pylus, the city of Neleus,
>   we came in our ships to desired Asia
> and with insolent violence we settled in lovely
>   Colophon, the instigators of painful hubris;
> and setting out from there, from the river ...,
>   by the will of the gods we captured Aeolian Smyrna.³⁵
>
> Αἰπὺ <   > τε Πύλον Νηλήϊον ἄστυ λιπόντες
>   ἱμερτὴν Ἀσίην νηυσὶν ἀφικόμεθα,
> ἐς δ' ἐρατὴν Κολοφῶνα βίην ὑπέροπλον ἔχοντες
>   ἑζόμεθ', ἀργαλέης ὕβριος ἡγεμόνες·
> κεῖθεν †διαστήεντος ἀπορνύμενοι ποταμοῖο
>   θεῶν βουλῇ Σμύρνην εἵλομεν Αἰολίδα.

---

[33] Cf. Meier 1998: 265. See also Jacoby 1918: 2 and 27; Bowra 1938a: 47–8; Prato 1968: 75.
[34] See also the use of the first person plural for the ancestors who arrived on the Peloponnese in the *Eunomia* (fr. 2 W² 15: ἀφικόμεθα). Similarly, in the same fragment the deictic 'this town' (13) links the act of the foundation to the present time of the performance.
[35] On the aspect of colonization in the fragment, see Dougherty 1993: 187–8.

In lines 2, 4 and 6, the first person plural is used for past actions. It creates a collective that embraces the founders of Smyrna as well as its present residents and thereby welds the ancient past and the present into a continuum. What renders this fragment extraordinary is that the phrases 'with insolent violence' and 'instigators of painful hubris' cast the past in critical terms. Some scholars argue that Mimnermus is criticizing the Greek settlement on Asian soil as the transgression of a natural boundary.[36] Others postulate that the heinous settlement of Colophon must have served as an explanation for present misfortune.[37] Instead of pressing the fragment into the Procrustean bed of a Herodotean reading or speculating about the lost context, the contrast between 'with insolent violence' and 'instigators of painful hubris' on the one hand and 'by the will of the gods' on the other leads me to suggest that the unjust settlement of Colophon throws into relief the righteous capture of Smyrna. Seen from this perspective, the poem expresses the colony's desire to distance itself from the founding polis and to foreground its own tradition. Nonetheless, it remains noteworthy that negative deeds are attributed to the time-transcending 'we'.

Perhaps, there is the same entwinement of the traditional with the exemplary mode that we have encountered in Tyrtaeus fr. 5 W². Strabo introduces his quotation with the words 'recalling that Smyrna was always the object of fights'. This, particularly the 'always', seems to imply that the foundation of Smyrna is introduced to shed light on later or even present fights. If part of the *Smyrneis*, the fights at the very beginning of Smyrna's history could serve as a mirror for the fight against Gyges, or, together and given a normative twist, both could be used as a foil for present conflicts. However far we are inclined to push this, Strabo's comment suggests that, in juxtaposing different events, Mimnermus also used the past in an exemplary way.

The fragments just discussed demonstrate that the exemplary and traditional modes of memory can reinforce one another. The idea of a continuum buttresses the notion of regularity – the equilibrium of a tradition facilitates the repetition of great deeds – and, conversely, the imitation and emulation of ancestors establishes a continuum. That being said, the two modes of memory should not be confused for they present different ways of coping with contingency. For example, Mimnermus fr. 14 W², which

---

[36] Jacoby 1918: 280–2; de Marco 1939–40: 339; Mazzarino 1966: 40–1; Szádeczky-Kardoss 1968: 945; Tsamo 1973: 372.
[37] von Wilamowitz-Moellendorff 1913: 283–4; Klinger 1930: 79–80; de Marco 1939–40: 339; Dihle 1962: 263; Mazzarino 1966: 40; Steinmetz 1969: 76–7.

Elegy: The 'New Simonides' and earlier elegies

I shall discuss in section 3.3, only illustrates the exemplary use of the past without the construction of a tradition. The difference between the traditional and exemplary modes of memory comes to the fore in the uses of the past to which they lend themselves, with traditions helping establish identities and exempla giving guidance for actions.

3.2.2. 'Narrative/ historical' and 'sympotic' elegy

Our remnants of elegy are scanty, but nonetheless the fragments of Simonides, Tyrtaeus and Mimnermus have allowed us to discover the exemplary as well as the traditional modes of memory. In the preceding chapter, we saw that in *Olympian* 2 regularity and continuity are means of restricting the destructive force of chance. Therefore, it is most interesting that contingency of chance plays a major role in elegy. For example in fr. 13 W^2, Archilochus mourns the death of some men at sea and adds on a more general note: '... but, my friend, for incurable woes/ the gods have set powerful endurance as an/ antidote. This woe comes to different people at different times. Now it has turned upon us/ and we bewail a bloody wound,/ but later it will pass to others.' (5–9).

The sea that, according to the poem, actually caused the death of the men serves in many other texts as a metaphor for the unpredictable as well as uncontrollable dangers to which human life is exposed.[38] Mimnermus fr. 2 W^2 takes up another image from nature, the epic simile of the leaves (1–2), not only to describe the sorrows of old age, but also to express that life is subjected to forces beyond man's control (11–16):[39]

> For many are the miseries that beset one's heart. Sometimes a man's estate
> wastes away and he has a painful life of poverty;
> another in turn lacks children and longing for them
> most of all he goes beneath the earth to Hades;
> another has soul-destroying illness. There is no human
> to whom Zeus does not give many ills.

My approach allows us to see a link between such general reflections on life and specific historical references, which most scholars have kept separate, ascribing the first to 'sympotic elegy' and the latter to 'narrative/ historical elegy'. I suggest that the construction of the past as continuity or regularity replies to elegy's emphasis on human fragility. What is

---

[38] See Lesky 1947; Péron 1974.
[39] For an interpretation of the leaves-simile against the Homeric background, see Griffith 1975. See further Garner 1990: 3–8 and Sider 2001: 280–3 with further literature on 281 n. 17.

presented in general reflections as dominating individual life, contingency of chance, is counteracted at the level of the polis, whose continuity extends from the past to the present and allows for the construction of regularities. We shall find a similar approach in the funeral speeches in which the eternal grandeur of Athens compensates for the individual experience of contingency (Chapter 5).

This link would gain in force if it were not only abstract, but if both narrative and reflection could be found in a single elegy. Unfortunately, however, other than the papyrus fragments, our knowledge of elegies depends on the selections of later authors who have taken passages out of their context for their quotes. Since the interest of authors such as Stobaeus is rather in the general and gnomic,[40] it ought not to surprise us that there is no fragment that combines a reflection on human fragility with a historical narrative.

The 'New Simonides' may offer some new evidence for this question. *P. Oxy.* 3965 contains not only fragments on battles against the Persians, but also 'sympotic' fragments. One of these, fr. 26 of *P. Oxy.* 3965, contains verses which, in part, overlap with an excerpt in Stobaeus.[41] In the first 5 lines in MS S of Stobaeus, which are inconsistent with the first four lines in the papyrus (fr. 20 W² 1–4), the 'man from Chios' is quoted with the comparison of men to leaves (fr. 19 W²);[42] the following part that is transmitted both in Stobaeus and the papyrus (fr. 20 W² 5–12) points out that man, as long as he is young and healthy, is not aware of his fragility. While the quote in Stobaeus breaks off at fr. 20 W² 12, in the papyrus eight badly damaged lines follow; their content is hard to reconstruct, but we can at least see that Simonides refers to Homer in line 14.[43] Sider offers the most likely reconstruction: fr. 19 and 20 W² both come from the same poem and fr. 19 W² preceded what we have in *P. Oxy.* 2327, fr. 6. They are run together in MS S of Stobaeus without indication that four lines are missing, since in the transmission something like ἐν τῷ αὐτῷ dropped out and two distinct quotations became one.[44] Sider's reconstruction yields the following text:

---

[40] Cf. Sider 2006: 329.
[41] Unless the poem was misattributed by Alexandrian scholars, then we have to assume that it was written by Simonides. However, see Hubbard 2001 who clings to his thesis that fr. 19–20 W² were written by Semonides of Amorgus. For literature on the authorship of the fragments that predates the 'New Simonides', see Sider 2001: 276 n. 6.
[42] The manuscripts MA which are generally supposed to be from the lesser family do not have the first five lines.
[43] For an interesting suggestion, see Sider 2001: 280–3.
[44] Sider 2001: 272–80. For a different reconstruction, see West 1993: 10–11, who suggests that both fragments come from the same poem, but that fr. 19 W² followed fr. 20 W².

The man from Chios said one best thing:
"As is the generation of leaves, so is the generation of men."
Few men hearing this take
it to heart. For in each man there is hope
which grows in the heart of the young.
...
   ...
... for a short time ...
   ... abide ...
As long as mortal has the desirable bloom of youth
with a light spirit he thinks many unaccomplished deeds.
For he has no expectation that he will grow old or die,
nor when healthy does he think about illness.
Fools are they whose thoughts are thus! Nor do they know
that the time of youth and life is short
for mortals. But you, learning this at the end of your life,
endure, delighting in good things in your soul
... Consider [the account of the man of] old.
Homer escaped [the forgetting of his words]
...
   ... false ...
   ... in feasts ...
   ... well-plaited ...
   ... here and [there] ...
   ...

ἓν δὲ τὸ κάλλιστον Χῖος ἔειπεν ἀνήρ·
«οἵη περ φύλλων γενεή, τοίη δὲ καὶ ἀνδρῶν»
παῦροί μιν θνητῶν οὔασι δεξάμενοι
στέρνοις ἐγκατέθεντο· πάρεστι γὰρ ἐλπὶς ἑκάστῳ
   ἀνδρῶν ἥ τε νέων στήθεσιν ἐμφύεται.
        .]ειθο[
         .]υτ[...].[
   .τυτ]θὸν ἐπὶ χρό[νον
......]ρλ[.....]ω παρμενο[
θνητῶν δ' ὄφρα τις ἄνθος ἔχει πολυήρατον ἥβης,
   κοῦφον ἔχων θυμὸν πόλλ' ἀτέλεστα νοεῖ·
οὔτε γὰρ ἐλπίδ' ἔχει γηρασέμεν οὔτε θανεῖσθαι,
   οὐδ' ὑγιὴς ὅταν ἦι, φροντίδ' ἔχει καμάτου.
νήπιοι, οἷς ταύτηι κεῖται νόος, οὐδὲ ἴσασιν
   ὡς χρόνος ἔσθ' ἥβης καὶ βιότοι' ὀλίγος
θνητοῖς. ἀλλὰ σὺ ταῦτα μαθὼν βιότου ποτὶ τέρμα
   ψυχῆι τῶν ἀγαθῶν τλῆθι χαριζόμενος.
      ]φράζεο δὲ παλα[
         ]γλώσσης ἔκφυγ' Ὀμηρ[
...... (.)]πα.δαμα[

```
..... (.)]ω ψυδρῆις ε[
..... (.)] ἐν θαλίηισι[
   ...]ι ἐϋστρέπτων [
 ....]ων, ἔνθα καὶ [
          ]. .[
```

A few scholars, Obbink, Ian Rutherford, Sider and most recently Kowerski, suggest that fragments 19 and 20 may have belonged to the same poem as fr. 11 W².[45] The reflection on the human condition in combination with a meta-poetic reflection makes for a broad common ground between the fragments. The Homeric quote and the comment on man's fragility in fr. 19–20 W² seem a fitting complement for the reference to epic poetry and the thoughts about the immortalizing power of poetry in fr. 1 W². In this reconstruction, the immortality that Simonides offers to the warriors at Plataea is highlighted by the contrast with the human condition. Intriguing as this reconstruction is, the fragmentary state of the text does not allow us to prove it; and yet, it illustrates what form the abstract link between historical narratives and reflections on human fragility that I have argued for could have taken. The poem negates contingency of chance for the warriors, whom it makes immortal, as well as for the audience, for whom it creates the continuity and regularity that are necessary to plan the future.

3.3. ELEGY AND EPIC

The fragmentary transmission has made it hard to explore elegy's idea of history, but, according to my tentative reconstruction, there is a tension between contingency of chance on the one hand, and the traditional and exemplary modes of memory on the other. This idea of history is not only reminiscent of Pindar's approach to the past, but also bears close resemblance to the genre to which elegy is most indebted, epic poetry. Elegy follows epic in its emphasis on human fragility, a debt which is particularly visible in the reception of the Homeric simile of the leaves in Mimnermus fr. 2 W² and Simonides fr. 19 W². Moreover, the construction of continuities and regularities in elegy parallels the traditional and exemplary uses of the past by the Homeric heroes as well as the reception of the epics, in which genealogies were traced back to epic heroes and their deeds were

---

[45] Rutherford 2001: 50, who considers fr. 19–20 W² as a *sphragis* in the Plataea–poem; Obbink 2001: 82–4; Sider 2001: 285–6; Kowerski 2005: 130–44, who emphasizes the connotation of lament in fr. 11 W² and sees this as a link to the other fragments from *P. Oxy.* 3965. Against the thesis that fr. 19–20 W² be attributed to the Plataea–elegy, see Bowie 2001: 54 n. 31.

used as exempla.⁴⁶ Nevertheless, there are crucial differences in temporal scope and focus: elegy primarily deals with the non-mythical past and its focus is not pan-Hellenic, but the polis. The distinction is not clear-cut though: there is evidence for elegy with mythic narratives⁴⁷ and Simonides fr. 11 W² may have been pan-Hellenic. On the other hand, there were epics including recent history.⁴⁸ However, it seems safe to claim that elegy drew on the language and style of epic to focus on the polis and its more recent past neither of which was at the core of epic poetry.

The debt to epic is acknowledged and reflected upon in elegy. In my reading of *Olympian* 2, I have suggested that Pindar hints that the transcendence of time, which he grants Theron, parallels the immortalization of heroes in epic poetry. The 'New Simonides' implies exactly the same parallel to Homer. Simonides not only compares the Greeks who died fighting against the Persians with Homeric heroes, but his prayer that the Muses bestow *kleos* on them also implies a juxtaposition of his song with epic poetry. Just as Homer immortalized Achilles,⁴⁹ Simonides makes the Greek soldiers immortal through his praise.⁵⁰ However, a significant difference indicates that Simonides may refer to the *Iliad* not only as a model to be imitated: Simonides invokes the Muse in the singular (21) whereas he names the Muses, or, to be exact, the Pierides, as the source of Homer's knowledge (16), and, what is more, he asks the Muse only to be an 'auxiliary' ('ἐπίκουρος') for his poem (21).⁵¹ By using a military epithet for his own poetic activity, Simonides blurs the borderline between *logos* and *ergon* and reinforces the contribution of his poem to the immortalization of the Greek soldiers. More significantly, he 'refuses to present himself as tapping a pre-existing, divine source of knowledge' and thereby sets himself off against Homer.⁵²

---

[46] Cf. Grethlein 2006a: 317–29.
[47] See Bowie 2001: 51–3 on Sacadas' *Sack of Troy* and on Archilochus fr. 286–9 W² that seem to stem from an elegy on Heracles. A new Archilochus fragment, *P. Oxy.* 4708, now gives us more than twenty consecutive lines on a mythical theme, the repulse of the Achaean army by Telephus. According to Obbink 2006: 8, 'the mythological narration seems not to have existed for its own sake, but as an *exemplum* or *ainos*.' West 2006: 15–16 agrees that the myth is introduced as an exemplum, but suspects that 'the re-telling of the myth was the main *raison d'être* of the poem'.
[48] Choerilus of Samos is said to have composed an epic poem on the Persian Wars. However, most archaic epics seem to have been restricted to the Mythic Age.
[49] Aloni 2001: 94 points out that for Simonides Homer figures as the origin of the whole tradition of the Trojan War: 'In fact, Simonides' text seems to dwell upon two events, the death of Achilles and the fall of Troy, that are certainly not at the center of the Homeric poems.'
[50] Boedeker 2001b believes that there is a further level to the comparison of epic heroes and the warriors of Plataea. She argues that Achilles' immortalization not only in poetry, but also in cult, is referred to and evoked as a model for the fallen who received at least hero-like cultic honours. See also Obbink 2001: 72.
[51] Cf. Stehle 2001: 108–9.   [52] Stehle 2001: 111. Cf. Aloni 2001: 95 Rutherford 2001: 45–6.

Subtle as this demarcation may be, it attests an agonistic tendency in the field of memory. Literary genres not only vary in their ideas of history and their scope, but can also draw attention to their differences from other genres. Such references may be merely part of an agonistic rhetoric or actual attempts to define their own approach to the past against other genres. In any case, they reveal a high degree of self-reflection and also indicate a degree of competitiveness in the literary field of memory.

In order to elucidate further the agonistic interaction between the various genres of memory, I shall now turn to Mimnermus fr. 14 W², which, in addition to affording a splendid example of the exemplary view of history, engages in a juxtaposition of contemporary soldiers with Homeric heroes and elegiac with epic poetry that is similar to, and more complex than, the comparison in Simonides fr. 11 W². According to my reading, which revives a conjecture of August Meineke,[53] Mimnermus fr. 14 W² praises a Smyrnean soldier, who is, presumably, dead but whose bravery Mimnermus has personally witnessed. To praise this contemporary, Mimnermus juxtaposes him with epic heroes, in particular Diomedes:

> I have not heard from my elders of such strength
>   and brave spirit, as are his, I who saw him,
> routing the dense ranks of the Lydian cavalry
>   on the plain of Hermus, a spear-bearing man.
> At no time whatsoever did Pallas Athena chide his heart's
>   fierce strength, when he sped among
> the fore-fighters in the combat of bloody war,
>   defying the enemies' bitter missiles.
> For none of his foes was better than he
>   in going about the task of strenuous war,
> when he rushed under (?) the rays of the swift sun.
> οὐ μὲν δὴ κείνου γε μένος καὶ ἀγήνορα θυμὸν
>   τοῖον ἐμέο προτέρων πεύθομαι, ὅς μιν ἴδον
> Λυδῶν ἱππομάχων πυκινὰς κλονέοντα φάλαγγας

---

[53] See Grethlein 2007a. Meineke conjectures ὅς for οἵ in v. 2. Therefore, the ἴδον is not a third person plural which refers to the 'elders', but a first person singular with the narrator as subject. For the traditional reading according to which present soldiers are unfavourably compared with their ancestor, see Jacoby 1918: 287–9, who argues for an encomium-like elegy; Klinger 1930: 80–2; Marsa Positano 1946: 361–2; Cook 1958–9: 28; Fränkel ²1962: 239; West 1974: 74; Vetta 1983: XXIII; Podlecki 1984: 60; Rösler 1990: 231; Allen 1993: 9–10; Gerber 1999: 97 n. 1. On the other hand, von Weber 1955: 68–71 and Steffen 1973: 66–7 reject Jacoby's thesis. Instead, von Weber 1955: 70 takes up von Wilamowitz-Moellendorff's claim that Mimnermus is defending a hero from rebuke (1913: 276). However, this thesis has been rightly rejected by Pasquali 1923: 298; Klinger 1930: 80; Steffen 1973: 66. A (too) ingenious interpretation along other lines is given by Pasquali 1923: 298. According to him, fr. 14 W² belongs to a poem in which Mimnermus justifies his poetic activity. By contrasting himself with a belligerent ancestor, he points out that he is only involved in love.

Elegy: The 'New Simonides' and earlier elegies

"Ερμιον ἂμ πεδίον, φῶτα φερεμμελίην·
τοῦ μὲν ἄρ' οὔ ποτε πάμπαν ἐμέμψατο Παλλὰς Ἀθήνη
δριμὺ μένος κραδίης, εὖθ' ὅ γ' ἀνὰ προμάχους
σεύαιθ' αἱματόεν<τος ἐν> ὑσμίνῃ πολέμοιο,
πικρὰ βιαζόμενος δυσμενέων βέλεα·
οὐ γάρ τις κείνου δῄων ἔτ' ἀμεινότερος φὼς
ἔσκεν ἐποίχεσθαι φυλόπιδος κρατερῆς
ἔργον, ὅτ' αὐγῇσιν φέρετ' ὠκέος ἠελίοιο.[54]

Pinpointing allusions in orally transmitted poetry is notoriously difficult and problematic for we do not know the exact form in which poems circulated in the Archaic Age.[55] But as Elizabeth Irwin has persuasively argued, in weighing the risk of such interpretations, 'perhaps more dangerous and certainly more prevalent recently, is that [i.e. the risk] of under-valuing verbal resonances and thereby implicitly circumscribing the potential for allusion between archaic poets and genres by our own difficulties in assessing it.'[56] If there are poems to which references can be legitimately pointed out, then it is the Homeric epics. Given the striking similarities in this case, it seems safe to argue for an allusion in Λυδῶν ἱππομάχων[57] πυκινὰς κλονέοντα φάλαγγας/ "Ερμιον ἂμ πεδίον, φῶτα φερεμμελίην to a particular passage in the *Iliad*.[58] In *Il.* 5. 85–94, the onslaught of Diomedes is compared to a river that runs so mightily that it breaks bridges and fences. This simile is closed by the following lines (*Il.* 5. 93–6):

> Like these the massed battalions of the Trojans were scattered
> by Tydeus' son, and many as they were could not stand against him.
> Now as the shining son of Lykaon, Pandarus, watched him
> storming up the plain scattering the battalions before him
> ...
> ὡς ὑπὸ Τυδείδῃ πυκιναὶ κλονέοντο φάλαγγες
> Τρώων, οὐδ' ἄρα μιν μίμνον πολέες περ ἐόντες.
> τὸν δ' ὡς οὖν ἐνόησε Λυκάονος ἀγλαὸς υἱός

---

[54] On this verse, see McKay 1975; Veneri 1976; Xydas 1982: 322–4. κεῖνος neither requires a corresponding οὕτως nor does it necessarily signify great temporal distance. It simply anticipates the following description of the hero. For this use of κεῖνος, see Kühner and Gerth ³1898 I: 650. On ἐκεῖνος in epic poetry, see Magnien 1922: 157–60.

[55] See e.g. Fowler 1987 and West 1995, who observes that there are very few clear allusions to Homer in archaic poetry.

[56] Irwin 2005: 100.

[57] There may even be one attestation of ἱππόμαχος in the *Iliad*. While the manuscripts have ἱππόδαμοι in 10.431, Aristarchus read ἱππόμαχοι.

[58] On the strong epic flavour of the fragment, see Fowler 1987: 46; Allen 1993: 140–1. Jacoby 1918: 287–9 provides a detailed list with epicisms. See also Klinger 1930: 80–1 and von Weber 1955: 66–72. Gentili 1965: 383–4 draws attention to the subtle transformations of epic diction in Mimnermus.

θύνοντ' ἀμ πεδίον, πρὸ ἕθεν κλονέοντα φάλαγγας
...

These are not the only uses of the phrase κλονεῖν φάλαγγας in the *Iliad*,[59] yet two details in Mimnermus 14 W² establish a link to this particular passage: the attribute πυκινός characterizing φάλαγγες as object of κλονεῖν recalls *Il.* 5.93 and, even more significantly, *Il.* 5.96 is the only active use of κλονεῖν with an object in the epics. Furthermore, κλονέοντα φάλαγγας in fr. 14 W² 3 repeats the phrase in the same grammatical form and has the same metrical position. This strong similarity brings another less striking parallel to the fore: ἀμ πεδίον, which is used in the same metrical position in *Il.* 5.96 and Mimnermus fr. 14 W² 4.[60] In envisaging the Smyrnean soldier as a Diomedes *redivivus*, Mimnermus elevates the Smyrnean to heroic heights, yet another illustration of the exemplary view of the past. This time, however, it is not combined with the traditional mode, as the Smyrnean is only compared to Diomedes without the notion of a continuum linking the two.

The epic intertext goes further for, as Felix Jacoby has already noted,[61] the comparison with earlier heroes is also modelled on a scene in *Iliad* 4 where Agamemnon tries to spur on Diomedes by unfavourably comparing him to his father Tydeus. He closes his speech with the following remark: 'This was Tydeus, the Aetolian; yet he was father/ to a son worse than himself at fighting, better in conclave' (*Il.* 4.399–400). However, Mimnermus inverts the comparison of generations that he borrows from the *Iliad*. The Smyrnean surpasses the old heroes, and therefore the glorious past does not tower above the mediocre present, but recent achievements 'leave behind' what is known from the past.[62]

Since the fragment appears to allude to the *Iliad*, it is tempting to see the deeds of the Homeric heroes in the standards that the Smyrnean surpasses. Two details support this interpretation. First, the reference to Athena in verse 5 has, I believe, special significance.[63] Diomedes is

---

[59] Cf. *Il.* 11.148; 15.448–9.
[60] See also *Il.* 5.87: θῦνε γὰρ ἀμ πεδίον ποταμῷ πλήθοντι ἐοικώς. For ἀμ πεδίον in the same metrical position, see *Il.* 6.71; 23.464.
[61] Jacoby 1918: 288–9.
[62] However, the inversion can draw on the original context. When Sthenelus defends Diomedes (*Il.* 4.404–10), he claims that their generation actually surpasses the generation of Tydeus, because they managed to capture Thebes with fewer men and abstained from their fathers' hubris. Cf. Grethlein 2006a: 53–5.
[63] For another take on Athena in the fragment, see Allen 1981, who connects her to the remnants of the Athena–temple in Smyrna and emphasizes the 'real-world' roots of verse 5. He rightly rejects Page's conjecture κεν for μέν. Athena is also mentioned in Tyrtaeus fr. 23a W² 18 and in Archilochus fr. 94; 95 W² 7.

generally linked to Athena in the *Iliad* and, more specifically, he is chided by her for withdrawing from the battle (5.800–24).[64] Mimnermus' claim that Athena did *not* chide his warrior, since he fought so bravely, contrasts with her rebuke of Diomedes for his lack of bravery in the *Iliad*.

This *auxesis* is reinforced by a second correspondence. Mimnermus points out that his hero was not hurt by any missiles. Though a minor detail, it gains in significance if we take into account that, after Athena admonishes Diomedes, he is hit by Lycaon's arrow.[65] Again, as in the case of Athena's favour, Diomedes serves as a contrast for our hero, the Smyrnean man: while the epic hero is hit, the contemporary warrior successfully evades arrows and spears. I concede that both Athena and the missiles in themselves are far from sufficient to establish parallels with the *Iliad*. However, seen together against the background of the allusion to Diomedes' commitment on the battlefield, they give the foil of Diomedes a new twist: the Smyrnean warrior is not only modelled on Diomedes, but he even outshines him.

As in Simonides fr. 11 W², the comparison of contemporary soldiers with epic heroes converges with a juxtaposition of the poetic media of praise. Besides using Diomedes as a foil for the Smyrnean, Mimnermus juxtaposes himself with Homer. In the same way that the explicit comparison in verses 1–2 is taken up by the implicit model of Diomedes, the 'elders' ('πρότεροι') of verse 2 can be identified with the epic tradition, in which Diomedes figures as a prominent character. We have seen that Simonides carefully demarcates his own poem from the Homeric model. Is the same the case in Mimnermus' fragment, which goes beyond a mere comparison and presents the Smyrnean as superior to Diomedes? Besides the tendency of ancient authors to link their literary assertions to the greatness of their subjects, Mimnermus' comment on the source of his knowledge suggests such an interpretation: he stresses that he has not only heard of but has also seen the hero. This can be read as a distancing of elegy from epic poetry for the *Iliad*'s narrator claims to have heard his account from the Muses (2.486) and the bards acquired their knowledge listening to each other. Given the widespread privileging of seeing over hearing,[66] Mimnermus seems to suggest

---

[64] On Diomedes in the *Iliad*, see Andersen 1978.
[65] Fr. 14 W² 8: πικρὰ ... βέλεα; *Il*. 5.99: πικρὸς ὀϊστός.
[66] See, for example, Heraclit. fr. 101a DK: 'for eyes are more exact witnesses than the ears' ('ὀφθαλμοὶ γὰρ τῶν ὤτων ἀκριβέστεροι μάρτυρες'). Hdt. 1.8.2: 'for ears are less reliable than eyes.' ('ὦτα γὰρ τυγχάνει ἀνθρώποισι ἐόντα ἀπιστότερα ὀφθαλμῶν'). Drawing on the juxtaposition of the senses, Mimnermus anticipates the historians' emphasis on autopsy, which, however, is grounded on methodological reflections.

that his elegy, though smaller and less significant, also excels epic poetry in some regards.

In summary, Mimnermus fr. 14 W² in a subtle way simultaneously acknowledges and challenges the epic heritage: by a paradoxical turn, the epics serve as an intertext to set off elegy from the epic tradition as another and surely not inferior medium of memory.[67] Such an agonistic interaction can also be found in other commemorative genres: '... we are not in need of Homer for praise nor of any other who will charm with his verses for the moment (τὸ αὐτίκα τέρψει), but whose claims the factual truth will destroy', Thucydides has Pericles assert in his funeral speech for the Athenians (2.41.4). Again, the authority of a speaker and the content of his presentation are intertwined, but, while in Mimnermus the superiority of his subject implies the poet's superiority over Homer, here the rejection of Homer is used to throw into relief the greatness of the deeds that the orator is lauding. Such agonistic tendencies in the field of memory are taken up and significantly intensified by the first historians. In the second part of this study, we will see for example that the claim of the Thucydidean Pericles just quoted also echoes the author's own rejection of the poets in his methodological reflections (1.21.1).[68] As the genres discussed in this part of my study show, the field of memory was already crowded before the rise of Greek historiography, and, intruding into this field, Herodotus and Thucydides had to work hard to legitimize their new approach.

3.4. THE SOCIO-POLITICAL CONTEXT

As outlined in the introduction, it is the aim of this book to explore the ideas of history in various literary genres, paying special attention to narrative forms and viewing the modes of memory against the backdrop of their performative contexts. While the scanty transmission of elegy makes it virtually impossible to elaborate on its narrative form, we are better off with regard to the context of performances. The main stage for poetry in archaic Greece was the symposium,[69] in addition to which West gives a list of seven further occasions for the performance of elegy. They range from battles to 'delivery of a quickly-improvised, entertaining piece in a place with a view of a public fountain'.[70] Bowie convincingly

---

[67] See also Schwinge 1997, who argues that in fr. 12 W² Tyrtaeus distances his poetry from the epics.
[68] See Chapter 8, section 8.1.1.
[69] Cf. Pellitzer 1990: 180. On elegy in the symposium, see Reitzenstein 1893: 45–85; Vetta 1983; 1992: 18–99; Gerber 1997: 92; Slings 2000: 5. See also, with a focus on memory, Rösler 1990.
[70] West 1974: 10–13, quotation from 12–13.

demonstrates that most of these occasions rest on rather naive readings of the poems as directly reflecting the contexts of their performance.[71] Nevertheless, he argues for a second occasion besides the symposium, also mentioned by West – public festivals.[72]

There are two major pieces of evidence for the performance of elegies at public festivals: First, Ps.-Plutarch, *de musica* 1134a claims that originally 'elegies set to music' ('ἐλεγεῖα μεμελοποιημένα') were sung by an *aulodos* and backs this up by a reference to an inscription on the musical *agon* at the Panathenaea. Second, Pausanias quotes the following inscription: 'Echembrotus from Arcas dedicated this gift for Hercules, winning it at the games of the Amphictyonies, singing lyrical songs and elegies for the Greeks' (10.7.6).

Although the evidence of these testimonies is not uncontested,[73] they make a strong case for elegiac *agones*. On the other hand, Bowie's further suggestion that narrative elegies were performed at public festivals is less compelling.[74] His major argument is that the historical narratives were too long to be performed at a symposium. However, not only is it hard to determine what length was appropriate for poems at symposia, but, more importantly, the evidence for lengthy historical elegies is scanty.[75] A brief review of Bowie's strongest candidates, Tyrtaeus' *Eunomia* and Mimnermus' *Smyrneis*, in the Appendix demonstrates how weak his case is. Since there are no other indicators of or reasons for public performances of 'historical elegies', it seems safe to assume that, as for elegies in general, symposia were the prime place for their circulation, without dismissing the possibility of performances at public festivals.

The strongest candidate for public performance may be Simonides fr. 11 W².[76] The hymn-like elements of this fragment would be particularly

---

[71] Bowie 1986: 15–21. Bowie 1990 demonstrates that even martial elegies were performed in symposia or symposium-like contexts.

[72] Bowie 1986: 27–34. His theory has met with approval: e.g. Dougherty 1994: 37; Gerber 1997: 92–3; Aloni 2001: 90–1, who adds that 'more or less sizable parts of these historical elegies might be used in symposia'.

[73] For a critical evaluation of both sources, see Rosenmeyer 1968: 222–5. Gentili 1968: 50 argues that the inscription about Echembrotus refers neither to hexameters nor to elegiacs, but to lyric poems. See also Fowler 1987: 88.

[74] See also Kowerski 2005: 67–73.

[75] Revisiting his argument, Bowie 2001: 46–7 concedes that he has become more sceptical that Tyrtaeus' *Eunomia* can be attributed to this class of elegies.

[76] Different settings have been suggested: Parsons 1992: 6; Boedeker 1995: 222–3; 2001a: 133 consider a performance at Plataea; similarly Aloni 2001: 95–104, who argues for a Spartan commission; Bearzot 1997 suggests a meeting at the Delphic Amphictyony; Schachter 1998 points to the Achilleium at Sigeum; Shaw 2001 thinks of the Isthmian games. Dissenting voices are West 1993: 4–5 and Sider 2001: 285, who consider a sympotic performance.

appropriate for a public setting, but they do not rule out the symposium. Thus, the performative contexts of epic and elegy appear to be complementary: while the primary occasion for the epics seems to have been public festivals, with episodes such as the *Aristeia* of Diomedes or the *Doloneia* being recited in a sympotic setting, elegies were also performed at public festivals, but primarily at symposia.

We have already encountered the symposium as the setting for recitals of victory odes.[77] It was clear that the aristocratic institution of the symposium provided an apt context for the praise of outstanding individuals, but at the same time I noted that Pindar is at pains to make the success of the victor fruitful for his polis. Elegy can help our understanding of the relation between memory, the aristocratic background of the symposium and claims of the polis. Xenophanes' symposium–elegy provides a good starting point. After describing the festive setting, mentioning the prayers and sacrifices and delicately determining how much to drink – one ought to be able to 'come/ home without an attendant unless you are very old' (17–18) – Xenophanes turns to the topics which are appropriate for sympotic poetry. While his positive assessment is rather brief, more time is given to the rejection of certain topics (fr. 1 W² 19–24):

> <it is meet > to praise that man who after drinking reveals noble thoughts,
>   so that there is a recollection of and striving for virtue;
> it is not meet to make an array of the battles of the Titans or Giants
>   or Centaurs, figments of our predecessors,
> or violent factions – there is nothing useful in them;
>   but it is meet always to have a good regard for the gods.[78]
> ἀνδρῶν δ' αἰνεῖν τοῦτον ὃς ἐσθλὰ πιὼν ἀναφαίνει,
>   ὡς ᾖ μνημοσύνη καὶ τόνος ἀμφ' ἀρετῆς,
> οὔ τι μάχας διέπειν Τιτήνων οὐδὲ Γιγάντων
>   οὐδὲ <   > Κενταύρων, πλάσμα<τα> τῶν προτέρων,
> ἢ στάσιας σφεδανάς· τοῖς οὐδὲν χρηστὸν ἔνεστιν·
>   θεῶν <δὲ> προμηθείην αἰὲν ἔχειν ἀγαθήν.[79]

Xenophanes does not reflect explicitly on elegiac poetry, but since he uses elegiac couplets to discuss poetry at the symposium,[80] it makes good

---

[77] Cf. Chapter 2, section 2.4.
[78] My translation is based on the assumption that αἰνεῖν, διέπειν and ἔχειν depend on 13: χρή. Other scholars take them to serve the function of imperatives.
[79] For parallels, see Reitzenstein 1893: 50; Vetta 1983: L.
[80] Deufert 2004: 36–41 argues that the poem itself was an '*Eröffnungslied*'. For this thesis, see already Reinhardt 1916: 126; Bowra 1938b: 354.

sense to refer his statement to elegies. The quoted lines discard myth and violent discord as topics, since they are of no use.[81] In the second part of this study, we shall see that usefulness is an important category for the first historians. And yet, while Thucydides' claim that his work is useful (1.22.4) is strongly reminiscent of Xenophanes' idea of poetic accounts of the past, the striving for usefulness does not prevent the historians from reporting on civil conflicts. Xenophanes' limitation of the content, on the other hand, ties in nicely with the elegies under scrutiny in this chapter, which focus on the non-mythical past and bolster the cohesion of the polis. Seen from this perspective, elegy contributes to the symposium as an institution that strengthened the polis community.

However, Xenophanes' objections to both topics must be read as a postulate rather than as a description.[82] Mythic subjects do surface in sympotic poetry – as already mentioned, there are traces of mythic narratives in elegy, e.g. in the Archilochus–fragment on Telephus (*P. Oxy.* 4708). More importantly, the scholia on Harmodius and Aristogeiton (*PMG* 893–6) illustrate that political strife was not alien to sympotic poetry.[83] The widespread view that elegy simply mirrors the rise of the polis has recently been challenged by Elizabeth Irwin. In *Solon and Early Greek Poetry*, she interprets exhortation elegy as heroic role-playing that 'may have served the purpose not solely, nor even primarily, of emphasising obligation to the polis and concern for the collective, but rather of justifying or asserting for its audience an economic/social position within their community, of flattering themselves, and reaffirming group identity.'[84] In comparing the poems by Tyrtaeus and Callinus with heroic boasting in the *Iliad* and in taking into account the performative context, Irwin makes a strong case for seeing exhortation elegy as 'an élite genre and its civic sentiments as asserting prerogative and division'.[85]

It is therefore important to see that the prominence of the polis, which is felt so strongly in some of the fragments of Tyrtaeus and Mimnermus, illustrates only one side of an institution that stood in the tension between claims of the polis and aristocratic assertions. The fragments that I have discussed reveal the relevance of the past for efforts to stress the cohesion of the polis in the aristocratic setting of the symposium. The

---

[81] Ford 2002: 53–8 persuasively challenges the thesis that the divisive songs criticized by Xenophanes are allusions to epic poetry. Bowra 1938b: 363–4 argues that the violence of the topics banned by Xenophanes 'introduce an element of discord into a harmonious occasion'.
[82] Reinhardt 1916: 133 and Vetta 1983: L argue that Xenophanes is recommending his own poetry, 'the foundation of Colophon and the colonization of Elea'.
[83] Cf. Rösler 1990: 231.   [84] Irwin 2005: 49.   [85] *Ibid.*: 50.

construction of a common past has a strong unifying force that allowed the symposiasts to envisage themselves as part of the larger community, just as Pindar made efforts to present his athletic victors as members of their poleis.

However, this should not lead us to the assumption that in the symposium the past was only used to establish social cohesion. It is true that in our elegiac fragments the past is mostly viewed from the perspective of the polis, but the texts that we have depend largely on the selection process of transmission, which is likely to have neglected partisan poems. We still have though some sympotic poetry in which the past is evoked in bitter polemics against political opponents within the polis, as, for example, in Alcaeus: 'They made the base-born Pittacus tyrant of the polis, lacking gall and pressed by a heavy fate, and the crowd supported this' (fr. 348 V). In the surviving part of a particularly interesting poem (fr. 298 V), Alcaeus seems to draw on a myth to slander Pittacus. A fragment from the Oxyrhynchus collection (*P. Oxy.* 2303 fr. 1a), which contains a description of the rape of Cassandra by the Locrian Ajax, was augmented by *Cologne Papyrus* nr. 2021,[86] which makes it very likely that Ajax's heinous deed is evoked as a model for the crimes of Pittacus.[87] In this case, the exemplary use of the past supports the case of a faction within the polis.

Important as it is to acknowledge elite interests and to take into account uses of the past for partisan purposes, the capacity of elegy to view the past from the perspective of the polis is remarkable and illustrates the impact that the rise of the polis had on the aristocratic institution of the symposium. The past could be brought into play to bolster the collective identity of the polis, to provide a model of action in battles against the enemies of the polis and to render the political order sacrosanct as in Tyrtaeus' *Eunomia*.[88]

3.5. CONCLUSION

It is difficult to find long self-sufficient historical narratives in elegy, but there are many references to the remote as well as the recent past in our fragments. In addition to this broad temporal scope, most elegies differ

---

[86] On the Cologne fragment, see Merkelbach 1967; Lloyd-Jones 1968. For the text of the song, besides fr. 298 in Voigt's edition, see also *SLG* 262.
[87] The present form ζώει in line 45 strongly suggests that the myth is used to shed light on the present and in line 47 Pittacus seems to be addressed in the patronymic. Against interpretations which assume that Alcaeus must have blamed Pittacus for some sacrilege, Rösler 1980: 204–21 argues convincingly that the foil of Ajax throws into relief Pittacus' crimes in general.
[88] On the *Eunomia*, see the Appendix.

from epic in focusing on the past of the polis, a focus worth noting given that, besides public festivals, the symposium with its aristocratic character seems to have been the primary setting for elegiac performances. My model of the idea of history allows us to link different strands that tend to be assigned to different forms of elegy and thereby supports Sider's critique of the notion of such sub-genres. The emphasis on human fragility, I have argued, is balanced by the presentation of polis-history in the traditional mode and by the exemplary use of the past. The time-transcending 'we' of the polis citizens creates a continuum and the heroization of the recent past as well as the presentation of past deeds as models for the present establishes regularity. Whereas the continuum helps corroborate identities, regularity gives guidance for actions. Both modes of memory converge in countering the force of chance. The past as presented in elegy is firmly in the grip of the present, more specifically in the tension between claims of the polis and the aristocratic desire for distinction. Whereas some fragments of sympotic poetry, notably by Alcaeus, illustrate that the past could be used for partisan interests, the elegiac fragments by Tyrtaeus and Mimnermus reflect the pressure on aristocrats to integrate themselves into the polis-community.

CHAPTER 4

Tragedy: Aeschylus, Persae

The prominence of tragedy, whose stories, in the eyes of the Greeks, constituted part of their past, makes it an important genre for this study, but doubts may arise as to whether my test case, *Persae*, actually offers an exemplary reading. *Persae* is the only preserved historical tragedy from the fifth century BCE and we know of only two further historical tragedies, Phrynichus' *Halosis Miletou* and *Phoenissae*. While in general the tragic subjects are taken from the mythic past, these tragedies deal with events of the Persian Wars.[1] And yet, this very peculiarity, together with a high degree of self-reflection,[2] makes *Persae* an intriguing illustration of the tragic mode of memory. As this chapter will show, *Persae* presents crucial aspects of tragedy as an act of memory in condensed form.

Performed in 472 BCE, *Persae* stages the Persian defeat at Salamis in 480 BCE.[3] In Susa, Atossa, Xerxes' mother, and the Chorus of Persian elders speculate about the fate of the king and his army, which have set out to conquer Greece. A messenger arrives to inform them about the defeat. After choral reflections on this news in the first *stasimon*, Atossa and the Chorus (in a second *stasimon*) invoke the dead Darius. In a necromancy, they tell him what has happened and ask for advice on what to do. The third *stasimon*, a song of praise for Darius, is followed by the return of the defeated Xerxes. His and the Chorus' mourning leads to the closure of the play.

---

[1] There are no fragments of the *Halosis Miletou*, about which we are informed solely through the famous account of its failed performance in Hdt. 6.21.2. For the *Phoenissae* see 3 TrGF F 8–12. As noted in the *Hypothesis*, the first lines of *Persae* allude to the first line of Phrynichus' play. On the comparison of both plays see Kitto ³1961: 33–5. On the *Halosis Miletou*, see Rosenbloom 1993; Mülke 2000 with further literature in 234 n. 1. On historical tragedies, see Castellani 1986; Hall 1996: 7–9. In addition to plays with mythical subjects, at least one play is attested, *Anthos* or *Antheus* by Agathon, in which the plot as well as the characters were freely invented, cf. Arist. *Poet.* 9.1451b 21.
[2] For this, see Grethlein 2007b.
[3] It was performed as the middle play with *Phineus* and *Glaucus*; the name of the satyr play was *Prometheus*. The few fragments of these plays do not allow for more than speculation about links to *Persae*; cf. Föllinger 2003: 237–41.

Tragedy: Aeschylus, Persae

In a first step, I will consider the content of memory and show that *Persae* casts contemporary history in a heroic register (4.1). I shall then examine the underlying idea of history and elaborate on the role of contingency within the play (4.2). The next section will be devoted to the *Persae*'s reception. I will discuss the stand from which the Athenian audience may have perceived the Persian disaster, ask to what extent the viewing of *Persae* would have involved an experience of contingency and discuss the relation of the tragic past to the present of the audience (4.3). I will then view the idea of history against the backdrop of the context of performance (4.4). Finally, in summing up the results, I shall show that, unconventional as *Persae* is, it draws attention to general features of tragedy as a commemorative genre (4.5).

4.1. THE DISTANCED PAST

When *Persae* was performed in 472 BCE, the traces of the Persian invasions were still visible, but, in the play, the battle of Salamis is forcefully distanced from the present of the audience. The remoteness that is characteristic of the mythical subjects of other tragedies is created in *Persae* at two levels. First, the action takes place in Persia, the Greek victory is focalized through the lens of the enemy and no Greek individuals are named.[4] Therefore, the lack of temporal distance is partially compensated for by spatial distance.[5]

Second, the battle of Salamis that had taken place only eight years earlier is presented in 'heroic vagueness'.[6] Not only do the strict formal conventions of tragedy remove the action from the world of the audience,[7] but the idiom drawing on lyric as well as epic language elevates the action and transfers it to the horizon of the heroic past.[8] As in other tragedies, there are

---

[4] Cf. e.g. Goldhill 1988: 192–1. Similarly, the funeral speeches and epigrams on the Persian Wars only rarely name individuals (cf. below p. 133). This seems to serve two functions: first, the polis comes to the fore as acting subject; second, the recent past is made more distant, since references to individuals who were still living would have tied the events to the present.

[5] Cf., e.g., Snell 1928: 66; 77; Kierdorf 1966: 50; Vidal-Naquet 1988a: 257; Vernant 1988: 244–5; Föllinger 2003: 246. The change of perspective from the victorious to the defeated party allows for a *peripeteia* from a good to a bad state. Cf. Kitto ³1961: 34; Gagarin 1976: 36–7; Meier 1988: 82; Nicolai 1998: 17. However, Snell 1928: 76–7 is right to note that tragedies can have positive endings. The 'renversement' in *Persae* is emphasized by Saïd 1988. See also Avery 1964: 174–9.

[6] Easterling 1997 has coined the term 'heroic vagueness' to signify the temporal setting of tragedy – not an indeterminate *illud tempus*, but a specific time that draws on and transforms the epic world and is therefore removed from the present.

[7] This, however, does not imply that tragedy excludes everyday life. I am grateful to one of the anonymous readers for drawing my attention to such passages as Eur. *Andr.* 166–7 and *Phaethon* TrGF 773, 11–14, in which housework is mentioned.

[8] On the epic influence on the tragic idiom, see Easterling 1997: 23–5.

many epic colourings in *Persae*.[9] To give just one example: in the *parodos*, the Chorus describes the departure of the Persian army (126–31):

> For all the cavalry
> and all the infantry,
> like a swarm of bees, have left with the leader of the army;
> crossing the forelands on both sides of the sea,
> yoked together.
>
> πᾶς γὰρ ἱππηλάτας
>   καὶ πεδοστιβὴς λεώς
> σμῆνος ὣς ἐκλέλοιπεν μελισ-
>   σᾶν ξὺν ὀρχάμῳ στρατοῦ,
> τὸν ἀμφίζευκτον ἐξαμείψας ἀμφοτέρας ἅλιον
> πρῶνα κοινὸν αἴας.

Not only is ὄρχαμος an epic word with just one other occurrence in the tragedies that have been transmitted,[10] but also the use of a bee–simile to highlight the size of an army stems from epic poetry.[11] The epic vocabulary and metaphor steep the army's departure in an epic light.

In many cases, Homeric phrases are transformed and adjusted to their new contexts.[12] For example: 'contrary to expectation I see the light of homecoming' ('καὐτὸς δ' ἀέλπτως νόστιμον βλέπω φάος', 261) is not a simple repetition of the Homeric 'to see the day of homecoming' ('νόστιμον ἦμαρ ἰδέσθαι'), but the similarity is strong enough to evoke the epic model. The word 'light' ('φάος'), which has replaced the epic 'day' ('ἦμαρ'), introduces an additional layer of meaning by drawing on the imagery of light that works throughout *Persae*.[13] Moreover, Sideras has argued that the phrase also reverberates *Il*. 18.61: 'as long as I know he is alive and seeing the light of day' ('ὄφρα δέ μοι ζώει καὶ ὁρᾷ φάος ἠελίοιο').[14]

The Homerisms in *Persae* are not restricted to verbal reminiscences and similarities. There are two larger structural units which evoke the background of the epics. Barrett points out similarities between the messenger who brings the news of the Persian defeat and the epic bard and suggests that the messenger draws on the authority that is ascribed to the Muses.[15] Even if we do not fully agree with Barrett's thesis that the messenger in

---

[9] Cf. Stanford 1942: 26; Sideras 1971: 98–200; 212–15; Saïd 1988: 326–7; Garner 1990: 22–4. Hall 1989: 79; 1996: 24 argues that epic language helps to present the Persians as aliens.
[10] TrGF III 451q.9. Cf. Belloni 1988: ad 125–32.
[11] Cf. Sideras 1971: 192; 247; Belloni 1988: ad 125–32. However, in the bee–simile in *Il*. 2.85–93 not ὄρχαμος ἀνδρῶν, but ποιμὴν λαῶν is used. On the bee–simile in epic poetry, see Fränkel ²1977: 71. On the different levels of significance in *Persae*, see also Broadhead 1960: ad 128.
[12] Cf. Hall 1996: 24.   [13] Cf. Kakridis 1975; Pelling 1997a: 2–6.   [14] Sideras 1971: 199.
[15] Barrett 1995; 2002: 40–55.

Greek tragedy should be viewed against the background of the epic bard, the particular echoes in *Persae* establish a link between the messenger's account of the battle at Salamis and the *Iliad's* narrative.

The other point may be even more significant in establishing an epic setting for *Persae*. Right at the beginning, the Chorus presents a list of Persian heroes who have joined the army. Containing some significant epicisms,[16] the '*catalogo "tragico"*'[17] names first the Persians (21–32) and then the allies (33–58). It not only draws on the epic form of a catalogue in general, but is reminiscent of the 'Catalogue of Ships' in particular. As in this list in *Iliad* 2, the catalogue of the Persians and Greeks comes at the beginning of the drama to bring in the departure of the army, which lies outside the temporal extension of the main action.

The numerous epicisms, the pointed similarities between messenger and epic bard and the imitation of the 'Catalogue of Ships' at the beginning evoke the *Iliad* as background for *Persae*. Even though some passages envisage the Persian defeat in terms of a siege,[18] the parallel to the conquest of Troy rests on an inversion.[19] While the attacking Greeks succeed against the Trojans, this time the invading party, the Persians, is defeated. Their return, which is called 'the light of homecoming' ('νόστιμον ... φάος', 261) and thereby appears in an epic light, turns into a disaster survived only by a small group. Besides distancing the recent event from the present, the foil of the Trojan War thus underscores the defeat of the Persians.

As we have already seen, the presentation of the recent past in a heroic register can be found in other genres too.[20] One could 'speak of recent events as if they were archaic', notes Isocrates (4.8). The Persian Wars, in

---

[16] εὐτλήμονι (epic τλήμων) (29); ἱπποχάρμης (*Il.* 24.257; *Od.* 11.259) (30); ἵππων ... ἐλατήρ (*Il.* 4.145; 11.702) (32); πολυθρέμμων Νεῖλος (*Il.* 3.89; 195; 265 etc.: πολυβότειρα χθών; cf. Belloni 1988: ad 33–40)(34); ἐφέπων (*Il.* 20.357: τοσσούσδ' ἀνθρώπους ἐφέπειν καὶ πᾶσι μάχεσθαι (38); cf. Belloni 1988: ad 33–40); βασιλῆς δίοποι (*Il.* 2.207: ὡς ὅ γε κοιρανέων δίεπε στρατόν) (44); στεῦνται (*Il.* 2.597; 3.83; 5.832 etc.) (49); τοξουλκῷ λήματι πιστούς (*Il.* 5.205: τόξοισιν πίσυνος) (55).

[17] Belloni 1988: ad 20ff. There are further catalogues in *Persae*, which hark back to the catalogue in the *parodos*: in 302–30, the messenger lists fallen Persians and in the *exodos*, the Chorus and Xerxes name dead warriors. Some of the names recur. The connections between the three catalogues are discussed by Saïd 1988: 332–3. On the epic background of the catalogues in *Persae*, see Albini 1967: 256; Holtsmark 1970: 20; Paduano 1978: 51–70; Michelini 1982: 15; 77. Saïd 1988: 329 compares the catalogue in the *parodos* to the 'Catalogue of Ships'. The differences from epic catalogues are stressed by Belloni 1982: 195–6. Hall 1989: 76 mentions as another background 'the cataloguing techniques of Ionian logography'. The Persian names are made up, cf. Lattimore 1943: 82–7; Bacon 1961: 23–4.

[18] Cf. Rosenbloom 1993: 191.

[19] My thesis that the Persian campaign is presented as an inverted Trojan War is supported by the similarities to the *Agamemnon* which have been noted by Michelini 1982: 72–4.

[20] I will return to this point in the Epilogue.

particular, seem to have invited heroization. While *Persae* directly epicizes the battle of Salamis, the 'New Simonides' compares the Trojan War with the Persian Wars. In a similar vein, the Eion epigrams play with the juxtaposition of the Athenians' current bravery with Menestheus' achievements.[21] This mode of presentation is not limited to literary sources and epigrams. For example, the Stoa Poikile showed the battle of Marathon and another recent fight, perhaps the battle at Oenoe, next to the Iliupersis and the Amazonomachy, casting the recent and the mythical past in the same register.[22] However, it was not only the Persian Wars that could be distanced from the present. We have seen that Tyrtaeus and Mimnermus epicize recent events in the history of Sparta and Smyrna. Another strong case is the third ode of Bacchylides in which a recent event takes the place that in epinician odes normally belongs to myths. Bacchylides evokes Croesus and his rescue by Apollo as a foil for Hieron, who, like the Lycian king, can count on the god's favour as reward for his rich gifts.

An interesting parallel to this tendency to present events of the recent past as distant is the 'inscriptional' 'once' ('ποτέ'). To give an example, an epigram that was placed next to the Council Hall in the Metroon recorded crowns for the men around Thrasybulus who defeated the oligarchs at Munychia in 404/3 BCE. As recorded by Aeschines, the epigram, which itself has been preserved only in mutilated form, reads: 'The ancient people of Athens have honoured these men on account of their bravery/ with crowns, for they, once upon a time (ποτε),/ were the first to stop those who ruled with unjust laws,/ putting their own lives at risk.' (*Aeschin.* 3.190). One would expect that the epigram and the list of the honoured were put up considerably later, but less than a year had elapsed since the victory over the oligarchs.[23] There are many other inscriptions in which a ποτέ takes the perspective of a future readership for whom the event remembered would already belong to ancient history.[24] The various acts of memory just mentioned share with the 'inscriptional' ποτέ the presentation of the past *sub specie aeternitatis*. This approach is typical of the exemplary mode of

---

[21] On one statue there were verses mentioning the victory at Eion and on another verses about Menestheus' participation in the Trojan War. The verses have been transmitted by Aeschin. *In Ctes.* 183–5 and Plut. *Cim.* 7.5. Erskine 2001: 69 n. 34 assumes that the statues were put up in the late seventies of the fifth century BCE and gives further literature.

[22] Cf. Francis 1990; Castriota 1992; Hölscher 1998: 163–9. On the comparison of the Trojan and the Persian Wars in general, see Boedeker 1998; Erskine 2001: 61–92. On the representation of the Persian Wars in literature, Kierdorf 1966 is still valuable.

[23] Cf. Raubitschek 1941b: 294–5.

[24] See the examples listed by Young 1983: 35–40 and Dillery 1995: 140. See also Ebert 1972: 93.

memory that neglects chronology and directly juxtaposes events from different times. In section 4.3.3, I will elaborate on the exemplary view of the past in *Persae*, and, in the conclusion, (4.5), I shall show that the play's distancing of contemporary history illustrates the importance of 'heroic vagueness' for tragedy in general.

4.2. THE IDEA OF HISTORY

We have seen that contingency of chance figures prominently in elegy as well as in epinician poetry and there is no need to argue that tragedy is another genre which foregrounds human fragility. Nonetheless, in order to elucidate the idea of history in tragedy, it is worth taking a closer look at *Persae*. In the introduction, I have pointed out that contingency, embracing freedom of action as well as chance, results in a tension between expectations and experiences in our consciousness. I shall therefore start with an examination of this tension at different levels (4.2.1), then investigate the use of counterstrategies such as continuity and regularity (4.2.2) and finally ask to what degree moral explanations minimize the force of contingency (4.2.3).

4.2.1. Expectations and experiences

It has been noted – often in combination with a negative judgement on the play's aesthetic value – that there is not much action in *Persae*. However, we ought to be careful not to judge Greek tragedy by the standards of modern drama. The static character that modern scholars are inclined to criticize as a deficiency is, I believe, rather a powerful device to draw attention to the dialectic of expectations and experiences and thereby to underscore contingency of chance.[25]

In the *parodos* and the first *epeisodion*, ample space is given to speculations about the welfare of Xerxes and his army. The Chorus is wavering: first they are worried (10); then, however, the listing of Persian nobles in the army soothes the old men (14–64) and instills confidence in them that nobody can withstand these powerful troops (87–92). This feeling is boosted by the

---

[25] Schadewaldt 1974b: 117 argues that *Persae* is dramatic insofar as it moves from ignorance to knowledge and suffering. Cf. Michelini 1982: 125–6. Paduano 1978: 59 calls the inquiry into the causes for the defeat 'la sostanza e la matrice del dramma'. The tension between expectation and experience can lead to fear, the prominence of which in Aeschylus has been pointed out by de Romilly 1985. She calls fear in Aeschylus 'une certaine condition humaine' (18–19). On fear in Aeschylus, see also Schnyder 1995 (on *Persae* see 34–65).

assertion that the military success of Persia has been ordained by Moira and gods (102–7). Yet, after that the Chorus takes into account god's power to deceive man (93–100), and this reflection turns them again to the possibility of defeat (114–25).

This lengthy alternation of fear and hope comes to an end when the Chorus decides to ascertain the army's fate from Atossa (140–3). The queen, however, does not know anything for sure either, but is filled with even more fear than the Chorus (161–7). Her anxiety has been raised by a dream and an ominous bird sign (181–210). In her dream, Atossa saw two women, one in Persian, the other in Dorian dress, who were yoked together by Xerxes. While the first stayed calm, the latter freed herself, Xerxes fell and, being mourned by his father, tore his clothes. When, terrified by this dream, Atossa wanted to sacrifice, she saw an eagle being chased to Apollo's altar by a falcon that attacked him there. After this account, the Chorus tries to soothe Atossa, advises her to sacrifice and judges ('κρίνομεν', 225) that everything will turn out well (215–25). However, once the Chorus has managed to restore Atossa's confidence, the messenger comes with the news of a total defeat. In the necromancy scene, Darius prophesies further disaster and finally the devastated Xerxes himself bears testimony to the catastrophe.[26]

I have summarized the *parodos* and first *epeisodion* to demonstrate that, despite a lack of action, the beginning of *Persae* subtly highlights the tension between expectation and experience by focusing on the Chorus' and Atossa's wavering between fear and confidence. The tension is heightened by the fact that, since the expectations concern distant events, the insecurity is about something that has already taken place. It is not a temporal but a spatial distance that opens the dynamic of expectation and experience.

The tension between expectation and experience comes to the fore not only at the main level of the action, but also in the embedded action, the defeat of the Persian army. Xerxes fails to realize his plans, his high-flying expectations are harshly disappointed.[27] In 744–6, the queen states: 'My son achieved this, uncomprehending in his youthful audacity,/ he who expected that he could constrain with fetters, like a slave,/ the sacred flowing Hellespont, the divine stream of Bosporus.'

---

[26] It is marked that the messenger's speech realizes the Chorus' fears, as 252: 'the Persian flower has fallen and is gone' ('τὸ Περσῶν δ' ἄνθος οἴχεται πεσόν') harks back to 60: 'such is the flower of men of Persian soil, which has gone' ('τοιόνδ' ἄνθος Περσίδος αἴας οἴχεται ἀνδρῶν'). On the other hand, the queen explicitly states that the Chorus' positive interpretation of her dream and the birds' fight were mistaken (518–20).

[27] See the list of passages that Avery 1964: 182 n. 17 gives.

Tragedy: Aeschylus, Persae

Besides the failure of the plan to conquer Greece, more specific expectations during the battle are disappointed. For example, the messenger reports that Xerxes, deceived by the Greeks' ruse ('οὐ ξυνεὶς δόλον/ Ἕλληνος ἀνδρός', 361–2),[28] stationed some troops around Psyttaleia with the following intention (369–73):

> If the Greeks escaped their horrid fate
> and found some way of fleeing secretly with their ships,
> it was decreed that all his men would lose their heads.
> So he said in full confidence of heart,
> for he did not comprehend what was to come from the gods.[29]

Turning to the future, Darius says about Xerxes' strategy in 803–4: 'he leaves the selected part of his army behind/ deluded by empty hopes'. Thus, the disappointment of the Chorus' hopes for good news repeats, with some delay, the failing of Xerxes' plans. The main action as well as the embedded report foreground negative experiences in the sense of G. W. F. Hegel and Hans-Georg Gadamer.[30]

4.2.2. The rupture of continuity and regularity

In elegy and epinician poetry, continuities and regularities counteract contingency of chance. For example, as we have seen, in *Olympian* 2 the havoc wreaked upon the family by Oedipus and his sons is balanced by the continuum and regularity created by the victory of Theron who takes up and re-enacts the successes of his ancestor Thersander. In *Persae*, on the other hand, continuities and regularities are forcefully challenged by the presentation of Xerxes' defeat as a rupture.[31] In the necromancy scene, Darius gives a list of the Persian rulers from Medus to Xerxes (759–86). The kings form a continuum in maintaining the Persian yoke over Asia and in augmenting the empire. The only interruption is Mardus (774–5), who, however, is but a usurper of the regal power and is quickly removed by Artaphrenes,[32] so that his does not compare to the rupture marked by

---

[28] See also 391–4: 'terror befell all barbarians/ mistaken in their expectation. For it was not as in flight/ that the Greeks then sang the paian,/ but rushing into the battle with courage and confidence.'
[29] Cf. 450–5: 'He [i.e. Xerxes] sent these men there, so that, when/ the enemies were shipwrecked and tried to save themselves on the island/ they could make an easy killing of the Greek army,/ and save their own comrades from the sea straits –/ so poorly did he understand what was to come.'
[30] Cf. p. 8.
[31] Saïd 1981 contrasts the rupture caused by Xerxes in *Persae* to Herodotus' emphasis on continuity between Darius and Xerxes.
[32] Cf. Saïd 1981: 36.

Xerxes' disaster, which is pointed out at the beginning and ending of the genealogy (759–62 ... 780–6):

> And so he has brought about a deed,
> as great and unforgettable as never before (οὐδέπω) –
> the fall and complete emptying out of the city of Susa –
> since Lord Zeus bestowed this honour on us
> ...
> And I went on many military campaigns with a large army,
> but I did not (οὐ) bring such a great catastrophe upon the city.
> My son Xerxes is a young man and thinks young thoughts
> and does not (κοὐ) remember my injunctions.
> For know this well, contemporaries of mine:
> None of us who have wielded this power
> could be shown to have wrought such suffering (οὐκ ἄν φανεῖμεν πήματ' ἔρξαντες τόσα).

The rupture is emphasized by repeated negations (760; 781; 786) and the *geminatio* of νέος in 782. The characteristics with which Darius credits his ancestors strongly contrast with Xerxes.[33]

Xerxes has not only interrupted a continuum, he has also failed to correspond to the exemplum of his father. Darius chides him for not 'remembering his injunctions' (782–3) and, asked by Darius how Xerxes came to commit such an act of hubris, the queen says (753–8):

> In the company of bad men, raging Xerxes learned
> this. They said that you had acquired great wealth for your children
> with your warlike spirit, but that he, due to a lack of manly courage,
> played the warrior at home, without increasing the inherited prosperity.
> He frequently heard such reproaches from wicked men
> and therefore planned this expedition of his army against Greece.

Atossa's claim that Xerxes was driven to the catastrophe by his desire to equal his father as well as Darius' reproach that Xerxes did 'not remember his injunctions' (782–3) point out his failure to re-enact the great deeds of his father. Xerxes has created something which is worthy of eternal memory (760), but only as a negative exemplum. We can thus note that, unlike in epinician and elegiac poetry, there are no exempla and traditions left to create stability.

---

[33] Cf. Föllinger 2003: 268–71. See also Holtsmark 1970: 17, who sees the traditions of praise and blame poetry (ἐγκώμιον and ψόγος) juxtaposed in the presentation of Xerxes and Darius (16). Griffith 1998: 59–60 emphasizes that Darius' genealogy establishes a strong link to Zeus, who, in *Persae*, is only named in connection with Darius.

4.2.3. Moral fault or contingency of chance?

Yet, to what extent is it contingency of chance that fails Xerxes' expectations? A majority of scholars assume that the disaster of the Persian army is presented as the result of Xerxes' hubris.[34] Seen from this angle, Xerxes is not the victim of forces beyond his power, but is responsible for his downfall, whereby contingency of chance would be transformed into moral guilt. Such an interpretation relies mainly on Darius' harsh judgement of his son's failure, which is taken to represent Aeschylus' view. Other scholars are inclined to give more weight to the power and malign intentions of the gods to which humans are subjected. As in Homer, it is argued, human and divine motivation cannot be disentangled. In Bruno Snell's words: 'Guilt and fate tie up the disaster.'[35]

Is the catastrophe due to Xerxes' failure or is the Persian king merely the victim of the gods? Is human fault (ἁμαρτία) at work or does the envy of gods (φθόνος θεῶν) rule? Is there liberty of human action or divine determination?[36] I think that most of the answers which argue for either side are flawed. Looking for the poet's opinion, they fail to account for tragedy's form. It should be a commonplace but is often overlooked that tragedy is pluriform and polyphonous.[37] There is no authority that announces the right interpretation, but competing voices open up various perspectives and angles. Even though this does not mean that every utterance comes with the same degree of plausibility, it is safe to claim that the generic form makes tragedy a genre better suited to raising questions and opening up tensions than providing clear cut answers.

In order to assess the role of contingency of chance, it is necessary to differentiate between speakers and to examine who says what in which context. To start with the Chorus: although the Persian elders are critical of

---

[34] Cf. e.g. Lloyd-Jones 1971: 87–9; Paduano 1978: 60–2; 78–82; Winnington-Ingram 1983: 14; Meier 1988: 87–8; 91; Nicolai 1998: 18, who even discovers 'Imperialismus-Kritik' and contrasts it to the other Aeschylean tragedies that show suffering without guilt (21).

[35] Snell 1928: 71 ('Schuld und Schicksal knüpfen das Verhängnis.'). See also Schadewaldt 1974a: 5; Gagarin 1976: 49–50; Saïd 1981: 20–1, who points out that, while in *Persae* divine and human motivation coincide, they are different in Herodotus' account of the Persian disaster. Podlecki 1993: 62 argues that Xerxes 'does not seem to have been acting quixotically or without forethought, nor did he, it appears, undertake the expedition against official advice from his councillors'. Hall 1996: 15 notes: 'The Persian catastrophe is multiply over-determined.' Föllinger 2003: 282–6 takes another tack in arguing that it is not only Xerxes' individual fault, but that he is determined as part of a family line.

[36] These questions have received much attention in scholarship on tragedy. For a recent discussion with an extended survey of earlier works, see Lurje 2004.

[37] Even if polyphony is seen, it can be condemned as weakness, see Kitto ³1961: 42 on *Persae*. On the polyphony and pluriformity of tragedy as features well-suited to the Athenian democracy, see Grethlein 2003a: 433–43; Grethlein 2003b: 64.

Xerxes and compare him unfavourably to Darius, they trace the disaster back to the will of gods. The Chorus emphasizes the unexpectedness of the calamity and refers to the daimon or the gods as its author(s).[38] In a similar vein, Atossa frequently mentions the gods' role.[39] However, in response to Darius' reproaches, she offers an explanation at the human level: Xerxes was driven to the Greek expedition by the pressure to emulate his father (753–8). In the messenger's account, the gods figure prominently as cause of the disaster.[40] At the same time, the messenger does not gloss over Xerxes' miscalculation. Both explanations are combined in 361–2: '... because he [i.e. Xerxes] did not understand the ruse/ of the Greek man nor the envy of the gods'. Darius elaborates on his son's fault.[41] Yet he also mentions the daimon: 'Alas, a mighty daimon came upon him, so that he lost his judgement.' (725). Nonetheless, from his point of view the main responsibility lies with Xerxes: 'But when someone hastens himself, god gives a hand, too.' (742). On the other hand, Xerxes himself invokes the gods to explain his defeat.[42] We can see that not only do the main characters differ in their assessment of the defeat, but that also one of them can give voice to Xerxes' responsibility as well as to the gods' envy. For example, the messenger and Darius mention both miscalculation and the gods' share. However, while in the messenger–speech Xerxes' hubris seems to be triggered by divine intervention (454–5), the gods merely come to add to one's folie according to Darius.

What about the authority of the utterances? Cannot Darius' judgement claim more authority than the views of the others? He stands at the centre of the play, he is the positive mirror to Xerxes and he is even able to predict the future. Is it not natural to take his words for the poet's view? Without questioning the weight of Darius' assessment, I am hesitant to follow this line for three reasons.[43] First, Darius is more ambiguous than most scholars allow.[44] Not only is it likely that the Athenian spectators would have been

---

[38] The Chorus mentions the deceit by a god for the first time in 93–100. Cf. Michelini 1982: 79. See then 158; 264–5; 282–3; 515–16; 532–4; 904–6; 920–1; 1005–7. There is, however, one badly corrupt passage which includes the word ἁμαρτία, 676–80: †περὶ τᾷ σᾷ δίδυμα διαὶ† γοέδν' ἁμάρτια;/ πᾶσαι <γὰρ> γᾷ τᾷ† ἐξέφθινται τρίσκαλμοι/ νᾶες ἄναες ἄναες. See the conjectures in Broadhead 1960: app. ad 674ff. and Belloni 1988: ad 672–80. On the Chorus' more conciliatory attitude towards Xerxes at the end, see Harrison 2000a: 84.
[39] 293–4; 472–3; 598–602; 724. [40] 345–7; 353–4; 373; 454–5; 495–9; 513–14.
[41] 744–6; 749–51. In 807–14, Darius explains the future defeat of the troops, which are still in Greece as punishment for their impious deeds. See also 818–31, where Darius further points out the hubris of the expedition.
[42] 909–11; 942–3; 1008.
[43] Belloni 1982: 185 is right to emphasize that the Darius scene is the only place in which Xerxes' hubris is blamed for the catastrophe.
[44] For straightforwardly positive readings of Xerxes, see e.g. Winnington-Ingram 1983: 8–15; Court 1994: 54; Georges 1994: 82.

reminded of Darius' own crossing of the Bosporus when he blames his son's crossing of the same strait,[45] but Darius' defeat at the hands of the Greeks is also mentioned explicitly in 244 and 473–5.[46] The audience's memory of Marathon and the hints at Darius' failures in the text cast a shadow over, if not subvert, his otherwise straightforwardly positive presentation. Second, it is striking that the gods figure prominently as explanation for the Persian disaster after the Darius scene as well. Not only is Xerxes allowed to give his version, which ignores any kind of moral fault, but also the Chorus, which is so critical of its king, continues to mention the gods as the source of the catastrophe. Third, the other character who might lay claim to some authority, the messenger, who is stylized as an epic bard, emphasizes the role of the gods.

All in all, there are voices that blame Xerxes for his mistakes, but man's dependence on the gods also looms large in *Persae*.[47] While the explanation of the defeat as Xerxes' fault negates contingency of chance, the reference to the gods' will merely transfers it to another level; life remains unpredictable when humans are at the mercy of the gods. How little the gods are a solution to contingency is revealed by the different names under which they figure in *Persae*: δαίμων, δαίμονες, θεός, θεοί, Ζεύς. The insecurity of human life comes to the fore in the difficulty of naming the force to which it is subjected. Linguistic denotation conveys control, its vagueness expresses helplessness.[48] *Persae* does not solve contingency of chance, it rather shows the audience human beings who have experienced a harsh disappointment of their expectations and desperately try to cope with it.

To sum up, contingency of chance is at the core of *Persae*. The static form, far from being an aesthetic deficiency, makes *Persae* into an intense study of the tension between expectation and experience, Xerxes' defeat is presented as the rupture of a tradition as well as the failure to follow an exemplum and the Persian disaster is not simply explained as the result of miscalculation, but is embedded in a view of the world in which the envy of the gods (φθόνος θεῶν) plays a major role.

---

[45] Cf. Sourvinou-Inwood 2003: 225–6.
[46] Cf. Podlecki 1993: 61–2. See also 236 with Hall 1996: ad loc.
[47] Cf. Sourvinou-Inwood 2003: 221, who sees both sides. See also Vernant 1988: 45–8 on the fundamental character of the tension between human responsibility and divine maliciousness. He also notes (38): 'In a tragic perspective man and human action are seen, not as things that can be defined or described, but as problems. They are presented as riddles whose double meanings can never be pinned down or exhausted.'
[48] On this point, see the illuminating reflections in Blumenberg 1979: 40–67.

4.3. CONTINGENCY OF CHANCE AND RECEPTION

While in elegy and epinician poetry chance is balanced by continuity and regularity, there is nothing to limit its threat in *Persae*.[49] The downfall of Persia is a total one. And yet, to what extent is the audience affected by contingency of chance reigning on the stage? I will first consider the stance from which the Athenian audience would have perceived the fate of the Persians (4.3.1), then elaborate on their experience of watching *Persae* (4.3.2) and finally point out the exemplary use of the past (4.3.3).

4.3.1. Pity for the Persians

Persae stages the downfall of enemies. Even more so, the Persian disaster marks an extraordinary success for the Athenians. The contrast is reinforced by the Chorus' role as an internal audience, particularly at the beginning of the play, when both spectators and Chorus first wait for the messenger to come and then figure as audiences for his account, one within the play and the other outside.[50] One passage even seems to hint at diverging attitudes towards the news: 'And he is bringing news of some event, whether it will make good or bad listening.' ('καὶ φέρει σαφές τι πρᾶγος ἐσθλὸν ἢ κακὸν κλυεῖν.' 248). Of course, the bipolar division of the news is owing to the Greek inclination to polarized expressions. At the same time, however, it can be read as a marker of the double audiences, describing their diverging receptions: the news which shocks the Persians on the stage must have delighted the Greeks in the audience.

The audience's distance from contingency of chance unfolding at the level of the play is crucial, as *Persae* itself, Aristotle's theory of reception and Phrynichus' *Halosis Miletou* show.[51] The reaction of the Chorus and Atossa to the bad news of Salamis reveals the difficulties of articulating one's own misfortune. In lines 285–9, the messenger and the Chorus lament:

---

[49] The comparison of tragedy with epinician poetry is particularly illuminating as the two genres are complementary in some regards. For example, whereas the victory odes hail the success of an outstanding individual in the present, tragedies focus on the downfall of outstanding individuals in the past. The fragility of human life that Pindar uses to frame the happiness of the moment is at the core of tragedy. For interesting comparisons of victory odes with tragedy, see Crotty 1982: 4–7 on the relation between *praxis* and *pathos*, and Kurke 1991: 6–7 on the relation between individual and community.

[50] Cf Grethlein 2007b: 373–4.   [51] For a more extended discussion of this, see Grethlein 2007b.

MESSENGER: Alas, how I groan as I remember Athens (ὡς στένω μεμνημένος).
CHORUS: Athens is indeed abhorrent to her enemies.
We have reason to remember (μεμνῆσθαι)
that she rendered the beds of many Persian wives
fruitless and manless.

To this the queen replies (290–5):

I have long been silent in my misery, stunned
at the terrible news; for this disaster is so overwhelming
that it is hard to speak or ask questions about what we have suffered.
Nevertheless it is necessary for men to endure the tribulations
the gods send. Unfold the whole disaster,
speak and compose yourself, even if you are groaning at our miseries.

As line 295 shows, the messenger is having trouble giving an account of the battle – of course, he recalls what has happened, but the articulation of this memory is impaired by groaning ('στένειν'). Before Atossa appeals to the messenger to start his report, she explains her own silence and points out that the events weigh too heavily to be remembered properly.[52] By the same token, the Chorus later shies away from informing the old king of his son's devastating defeat (694–702). They are filled with fear and are not capable of 'answering/ in words hard for friends to utter' ('ἀντία φάσθαι,/ λέξας δύσλεκτα φίλοισιν', 701–2). The memory of one's own sorrows is unsettling and easily leads to a loss of words.

This observation is conceptualized in Aristotle's theory of reception. According to Aristotle, tragedies allow the audience to attain a catharsis through the feeling of pity and fear. The much-debated meaning of catharsis can be left aside here;[53] what concerns my argument is merely one of the conditions on which pity and fear depend.[54] Aristotle points out that the relation between the audience and the tragic hero must be balanced between proximity and distance. On the one hand, there must be enough similarity and proximity to allow for identification; on the other, a certain degree of distance is necessary so that fear (for oneself) does not outweigh sympathy with the other.[55]

The heuristic value of this concept for Greek tragedy is proven by a comparison of Aeschylus' *Persae* with Phrynichus' *Halosis Miletou*. Whereas Aeschylus was awarded the first prize for *Persae* and the other plays of his

---

[52] On Atossa's marked silence, see Taplin 1972: 80, who draws attention to the contrast between her reactions to the news and that of the Chorus. See also Taplin 1977: 87 with n. 1 and, on silences in tragedy in general, Aélion 1983–4.
[53] See e.g. Halliwell 1998: 350–6.
[54] Arist. *Rh.* 1383a8–12; 1386a24–6. For an application of this theory and a meta-poetic reading of pity in tragedy, see Grethlein 2003b.
[55] Cf. Grethlein 2003b: 43–6.

trilogy, the presentation of 'own sorrows' ('οἰκεῖα κακά'), namely the capture of Miletus by the Persians in 494 BCE, upset the Athenians so much, according to Herodotus, that they decided to fine Phrynichus.[56] In *Halosis Miletou*, the audience is confronted with its own experience of contingency of chance, the failure of the Ionian revolt, in which Athens was involved. *Persae*, on the other hand, establishes enough distance between the audience and the tragic action by presenting the disaster in the camp of the Persians.

If we subject the examination of the Chorus as an internal audience to an Aristotelian reading, we can say that *Persae* is a successful tragedy that contains a failed tragedy. While the Chorus is too affected by the news to achieve a catharsis, the Athenian audience is protected from contingency of chance by distance and can relish the performance. Whereas the Athenians stage the battle of Salamis in their theatre, the Persians are left speechless.

However, this application of Aristotle raises one question: would the Athenian audience actually feel pity? Is empathy not outweighed by distance? Does the enmity with the Persians not prevent the Athenians from feeling the proximity to the tragic characters that is necessary for a catharsis to emerge? The damage from the last Persian attacks was still visible when *Persae* was performed, and Edith Hall has fruitfully applied the concept of 'orientalism' to the otherness of the Persians.[57] This being said, there are hints in the text that the Persian suffering has significance beyond the triumph over the defeated enemy.[58] In some ways, *Persae* is a hymn to the Athenian victory, but at the same time it is also a tragedy that invites the audience to empathize with the suffering characters.

First, Greeks and Persians are not simply pitted against each other. When Xerxes is said to stem from the 'goldborn race' (80), his line is implicitly traced back to Zeus who fathered Perseus through union with Danae as golden rain. Thus, the Persians are integrated into the Greek genealogical system. Moreover, in Atossa's dream, two sisters are yoked by Xerxes, one in Persian, the other in Doric dress. Obviously, the two women stand for the

---

[56] Cf. Rosenbloom 1993; Mülke 2000.   [57] Hall 1989; 1996.

[58] The tension between empathy and enmity is described e.g. by Meier 1988: 83 and Harrison 2000a: 103–15, who is one of the latest advocates for the view that the Greek audience would not have pitied the Persians. Hall 1989: 71–4; 99–100; 1996: 19 also concedes the possibility that the audience would 'work through the difficult emotions which they had themselves experienced', but lays more emphasis on the presentation of the Persians as the 'other'. However, Griffith 1998: 44–57 presents a most stimulating and subtle discussion of why spectators may have identified with Xerxes. A majority of recent scholars seem to argue for pity with more or less caution, e.g. McCall 1986; Goldhill 1988: 193 n. 35, who compares it with the pity that Achilles feels for Priam in *Iliad* 24; Sourvinou-Inwood 2003: 226–7. However, I cannot follow Föllinger 2003: 285–6 who also applies Aristotle's model, but argues that Xerxes' suffering is undeserved, since he is the victim of his family's fate. As I have pointed out, the guilt of Xerxes is far from being that clear-cut. Moreover, I do not see that Xerxes has inherited guilt.

Persian and Greek people. Although their reactions to the yoke are utterly different, it is remarkable that the enemies are envisaged as sisters; in the dual 'the two sisters from the same/ race' ('κασιγνήτα γένους/ ταὐτοῦ', 185–6) the family bond is forcefully marked.[59]

Second, we should not overlook the fact that the calamity of the Persians was shown in a setting in which the audience was used to reacting with pity to the suffering on stage. In addition, the epic background distances the recent event, but casts it in a register which otherwise served the Greeks well for purposes of identification.[60] Presented as a failed epic *nostos*, Xerxes' return appears in a pattern that may have encouraged the emergence of empathy in an audience used to feeling sympathy with suffering heroes such as Odysseus.

Third, the *gnomai* with which the Chorus and the characters comment on their calamity employ concepts on which the Athenians would draw to make sense of their own experiences. Both the envy of the gods and human fragility on the one hand and the temptation of wealth and man's liability to hubris on the other are Greek patterns. What is more, the *gnomai* are formulated as general utterances applicable to any man. For example, in 93–100 the Chorus says:

> But what mortal man will avoid
> the cunning deceit of a god?
> Who is the one who, with swift foot, masters the well-flying leap?
> Friendlily fawning upon a man at first
> Ate leads him into her nets.
> It is impossible for a mortal to escape from them and to flee.

Subsuming the particular disaster of the Persians under general patterns like this universalizes the experience of the Persians and must have made it easier for Athenians to develop some empathy with their sorrows.

Fourth, some *gnomai* seem to address the Greek audience specifically.[61] In 598–605, for instance, Atossa says:

> Friends, whoever has experience of disasters
> knows that when a wave of disasters
> rears against people they tend to fear everything,
> but that, when the daimon flows gently, they believe (πεποιθέναι)
> that always the same wind of good fortune will blow.
> I am already full of every kind of fear;

---

[59] Cf. Föllinger 2003: 277–9.
[60] Here, I disagree with Hall 1989: 79; 1996: 24, who argues that the epic background merely emphasizes the otherness of the Persians. Sourvinou-Inwood 2003: 15–16 rightly points out that the heroic age was distant as well as an integral part of the present.
[61] Sourvinou-Inwood 2003: 50–2 argues that the choruses of Greek tragedy were perceived not only as *dramatis personae*, but also as ritual performers.

> hostile images from the gods appear before my eyes,
> and a din – no *paian* – rings in my ears.

Commentators have been troubled by the question of why bad experiences enable man to understand the optimism of the prosperous.[62] I do not see what exactly the problem is – it makes sense that those shattered by fatal blows know that misfortune comes unexpectedly – but I agree that this part is noteworthy, for it is the fear of the ones with bad experiences which matters to Atossa, who uses the general *gnome* to buttress her own feelings. At first glance, the comment on the prosperous seems to be given to expand her point into a polar expression.

However, the comment is significant and has two possible references. The *gnome* alerts one to the danger that the prosperous tend to take their bliss for granted. Not only is an overdose of confidence generally bad in tragedy, but πεποιθέναι in particular has a sinister ring in *Persae*.[63] Atossa's words prepare the ground for the surprise that Darius shows about the sudden decline of his empire in the following scene (739–43). The Persians were used to success and, even though Darius knew oracles about a future decline, he assumed that his people would go on thriving. Thus, the prosperous can refer to the Persians who were too cocksure. Second, since the Persians were defeated by the Greeks and are constantly contrasted with them, one might well identify the prosperous with the Greeks. This does not constitute an open admonition, but raises the possibility that Athens, now prosperous, may be oblivious of its fate and therefore open to a blow similar to that received by the Persians.

The second passage which bears relevance for Athens is Darius' words in 818–28:

> Piles of corpses will mutely signify
> to the eyes of people even three generations hence
> that who is mortal must not think thoughts above his station;
> for hubris bloomed and produced a crop
> of calamity, from which it reaps a harvest of lamentation.
> Consider that the penalties for this are such,
> and remember Athens and Greece, so that no-one
> may scorn the current daimon,
> lust after what belongs to others and thereby pour out great prosperity
> (ὄλβον ἐκχέῃ μέγαν).

---

[62] Cf. Broadhead 1960: ad 598–602.
[63] Cf. the use of πείθεσθαι in 74–80 and 803–4, where it signifies vain expectations. On the ambiguity of πείθειν in the *Oresteia*, see Goldhill 1984: 44; Sommerstein 1989: ad *Eum.* 885.

Tragedy: Aeschylus, Persae

For Zeus is set above us as a punisher of minds
too arrogant, a stern assessor (εὔθυνος βαρύς).

In what follows, Darius appeals to the Chorus to pass these reflections on to Xerxes. However, I suggest that the moral message that the corpses have for the Persians rather addresses the Greeks in the audience.[64] First, the warning not to detest present fate and thereby to gamble away one's happiness applies much better to the Athenian audience than to the Persian protagonists. As presented in *Persae*, there is no 'great prosperity' ('ὄλβος μέγας') left that the Persians can put at risk, while it is the successful Greeks who are in danger of neglecting their present daimon. Moreover, it may be asked to what extent the piles of corpses, lying on Greek soil, will be a mute admonition to Persians. They would be visible not to Persians, but to Greeks; in fact, Herodotus reports that the Persian skeletons were the object of Greek inquiries (9.83). Finally, εὔθυνος not only echoes 213 where Xerxes is said not to be accountable to the polis, it also brings in the political reality of Athens where εὔθυνα is the technical term for the examination of the conduct of officials.[65]

Such an interpretation of the Chorus' warning, namely as being also levelled at the audience, is reinforced by the second person plural imperatives. In a theatre performance, second person plural imperatives can, if their message is general, easily slide from the internal communication system (stage) to the external communication system (stage–receiver).[66] The dramatic illusion is not automatically broken by this, but a general message can blur the borderline between stage and extra-dramatic reality and the audience can feel as if it is being directly addressed.

I am far from insinuating that Aeschylus was a Herodotus *avant la lettre* and warned against Athenian imperialism.[67] Such a claim does not do justice to the date of the performance. However, it is plausible to conclude that the audience's reaction was not limited to delight at the enemy's sorrow. The horizon of tragedy, the presentation of Persian suffering as a failed epic *nostos*, the general relevance of *gnomai* and the specific

---

[64] For conventional interpretations of this passage see Lenz 1986: 144, who sees a reference to Xerxes, and Fisher 1992: 258–63, who makes Darius' speech the cornerstone of his reading of *Persae* as an untragic play.

[65] Cf. Hall 1996: ad 213. [66] See for a parallel in the *Eumenides*, Grethlein 2003a: 223–4.

[67] This position is taken by Holtsmark 1970: 22–3; Melchinger 1979: 35–6; 39; Rosenbloom 1993: 190–1; 1995: 93; Nicolai 1998: 23. Gagarin 1976: 52–3 is more careful and argues that the connection between Persia's fate and Athens' imperialism is possible, but that there is no more than an implicit warning. I would like to suggest further that attempts to interpret *Persae* as a warning against Athenian imperialism bear testimony to the semantic richness of the text. Although the time of its performance makes it implausible that *Persae* was directed against Athens' imperialism, the play's texture allows such an interpretation to come to the fore as soon as later developments are taken into account.

significance of some *gnomai* for Athens all suggest that the Athenians would view the Persians not only as their defeated enemies, but also as fellow humans subject to the same condition. *Persae* not only distances the disaster from the audience, but also establishes enough common ground, which, according to Aristotle, is necessary for an audience to empathize with the tragic characters.[68] It goes without saying that the response will have varied from spectator to spectator, depending on the background of the individual, but if we allow for a complex response to the performance of *Persae*, pity cannot be left out.[69]

4.3.2. *The expectations of the audience*

In the chapter on epinician poetry, the fact that the odes not only present events that happen in time, but themselves unfold in time, led me to investigate the relationship between narrated and narrative time. The temporal panopticon and poetic continuum created by Pindar, I found, mirrors the transcendence of time by Theron. Let us transfer this angle to *Persae* and, instead of focusing on time itself, compare the audience's reception of the drama with the experiences on stage. The tension between expectation and experience comes to the fore not only in the embedded account of Xerxes' defeat and in the main action featuring the Chorus' and Atossa's forebodings about and (indirect) experience of the expedition's outcome, but the audience's reception of both main and embedded actions is an experience itself. Following the plot, the spectators have expectations about its further development that are either fulfilled or disappointed. One can thus discern three different levels of involvement, from most to least direct: Xerxes has expectations about what he is experiencing himself, the Chorus' expectations are directed to the experiences of others, who, however, are relatives, while the audience has an experience of something that is merely staged. With this difference in mind, I now turn to the question of how the experience of the audience compares to the experience of the characters.

It has been argued that Aeschylus is misleading his audience at two points in *Persae*.[70] In 529–31, the queen asks the Chorus to send Xerxes into the

---

[68] In Grethlein 2007c, I argue that Aristotle's concept, notably the balance between proximity and distance, also allows us to conceptualize modern performances of *Persae*, albeit in a diametrically opposite way. While in 472 BCE the battle of Salamis was so close that it needed to be distanced, in the Modern Age the battle of Salamis is so remote that many directors make it evoke more recent wars to make the play more significant for their audiences.
[69] See the careful assessment by Pelling 1997a: 17.
[70] Cf. Broadhead 1960: xxxvii–xl; Dawe 1963: 27–30; Avery 1964; Taplin 1977: 92–8; Thalmann 1980; Michelini 1982: 73; 136–8; Georges 1994: 92–4; Court 1994: 27–43.

house when he arrives. However, the next character to enter is not, as these lines suggest, Xerxes, but Darius. Furthermore, after Darius has left, the queen announces that she will go to meet her son and give him new clothes (849–51). Yet, when Xerxes enters, he has not met his mother and is still in rags.[71]

Atossa's first announcement creates suspense that is not resolved until Xerxes finally arrives. Moreover, when Darius instead of Xerxes enters the stage, his function as foil for his son is forcefully underscored. The second announcement serves to deepen the impression of the Persian calamity. As the pun on 'army' ('στόλος') and 'garment' ('στολή') in 1019 suggests, the clothes serve as cipher for the whole empire.[72] The disappointment of the expectation that Xerxes would appear in new clothes forcefully shows the extent of the catastrophe. In the end, there is only mourning, but no sign of a new rise of Persian power.[73]

Effective as the misdirections are, it must be noted that they do not weigh heavily: neither of them is an explicit and confirmed *prolepsis*, and, while the realization of the first is merely postponed, the second does not even refer to the question of whether Xerxes will enter, but only to the manner of his entry. Instead, it is safe to claim that the audience is well-informed about the plot.[74] Unlike the Chorus and the queen at the beginning, the spectators know about the Persian defeat and cannot be taken by surprise. Whereas the Persians on stage are exposed to a harsh experience of contingency, the reception experience is by and large free of disappointments. Thus, the theatre performance not only affords the pleasure of an aesthetic experience, but even within this indirect experience there is little place for contingency of chance.

4.3.3. 'Heroic vagueness' and the present of the audience

The contrast between the characters' and the audience's experiences of contingency also comes to the fore in other respects. We have seen that at the level of content Xerxes' defeat signifies a rupture that destroys continuity as well as regularity. I shall now argue that the audience, on the other hand, is given an exemplary view of the past that, through the assumption of regularity, minimizes the force of chance.

---

[71] I do not see any hint in the text that Xerxes is putting on new clothes at the end, as is argued by Avery 1964: 179–84; Gagarin 1976: 41–2.
[72] Cf. Avery 1964: 180–4; Thalmann 1980: 267–78.
[73] Cf. Harrison 2000a: 91.   [74] Cf. Mitsis 1988: 104–9.

In the chapter on elegy, I noted a tendency to epicize the recent past that is similar to the *Persae's* presentation of Salamis in 'heroic vagueness'. When Mimnermus and Tyrtaeus draw on Homeric vocabulary and narrative devices to glorify recent military achievements, they may not juxtapose two specific events with one another, but nonetheless the presentation of recent events as re-enactments of heroic grandeur establishes an exemplary view of the past. By the same token, in epicizing contemporary history *Persae* draws on the exemplary mode of memory. The presentation of a battle against the Persians as a heroic deed, comparable to the victory over the Trojans, creates regularity and thereby tells against contingency of chance.

The parallel between the elegiac fragments and *Persae* can be pursued further. The fragmentary status of elegy made it hard to arrive at safe conclusions, but there is enough material to warrant the conjecture that in some poems the heroization of the recent past reinforces its function as a model for the present, as it allows the drawing of conclusions *a maiore ad minus*. Thus, the descriptive use of the exemplary mode of memory – casting the recent past in an epic light – supports the normative application of exempla – presenting the recent past as a benchmark for the present and future. The same mechanism can be seen in *Persae*. I have shown that the *gnomai* are not restricted in their significance to the Persians and that some even seem to address the Greeks specifically. While I rejected the anachronistic thesis that *Persae* was a warning against the danger of Athenian imperialism, it is difficult to deny that the disaster of the Persians is presented as a lesson for all men including the Greeks. Thus, although the past is distanced from the present in *Persae*, it is nonetheless evoked to shed light on it. The twofold exemplary use of the past in *Persae* establishes for the audience the very regularity which Xerxes, in failing to imitate his glorious ancestors, destroys.

Let me suggest that the link between the past on stage and the present of the audience is mirrored within *Persae* in the Darius scene, which, as I have argued elsewhere, can be read as a *mise-en-abyme*.[75] Darius' necromancy is not only a play-within-a-play, but, more significantly, through Darius the past enters the present of the play in the same way that tragedies are the staging of past events. The embedding of a 'plu-past', a past prior to the time of the action, mirrors the relation of the present of the audience to the past of the tragic plot. In doubling its own relation to the present of the performance, *Persae* becomes self-reflexive and reveals the otherwise only implicit shape and function of its own presentation of the past.

---

[75] Cf. Grethlein 2007b.

Although Darius died not long ago, he is treated with great awe and reverence. The Chorus states that 'the soil of Persia/ has never covered his like before' (645–6) and Atossa addresses him as god-like: 'O you who in your happy fate outdid the prosperity of all men,/ as long as you looked upon the sun's rays, you were enviable/ and lived your fortunate life among the Persians, like a god.' (709–11). Embodied by the godlike apparition of Darius as a ghost, the recent past appears larger than the present, just as *Persae* presents the recent past in a heroic register. In both cases, the larger-than-life frame endows the past with significance and authority. Just as Darius is presented as a benchmark for Xerxes, the disaster of the Persians conveys an important message for the audience that gains in authority from its presentation in 'heroic vagueness'.

The *mise-en-abyme* of Darius illuminates yet another crucial aspect of the past in *Persae*. Darius is not only cast in a larger-than-life frame, but the past that he embodies strongly contrasts with the present.[76] In the third *stasimon*, the Chorus praises him and juxtaposes his glorious reign with the catastrophe that his son has brought about (852–906). The numerous negations in the praise illustrate how the Chorus evokes the past as a foil to the present.[77] The contrast between Darius and Xerxes also comes to the fore in the staging, which has Darius enter in full regal attire whereas Xerxes comes in rags. This contrast between past and present within the action mirrors the relation between the past as staged in *Persae* and the present of the audience. Here, however, it is not a glorious past that is juxtaposed with a desolate present, but, inversely, a miserable past that meets a prosperous present.

The exemplary mode of memory in *Persae* is only indirect, as there is no explicit juxtaposition of the past with the present. Nonetheless, the numerous *gnomai*, particularly those which seem to address the Greeks, indicate that Aeschylus is offering his audience a model, or, to be more exact, an exemplum to be avoided. Paradoxically, removing the action from the world of the audience increases its relevance for the present for the heroic vagueness lends it authority to shed light on the present *a maiore ad minus*. Although distanced from the present, the past is in the strong grip of the present.

---

[76] Cf. Alexanderson 1967: 2; 9; Michelini 1982: 73–4, who points out that Darius is 'Xerxes bettered' (74); Mitsis 1988: 112; Föllinger 2003: 254–67, with literature in 255 n. 107.
[77] ἀκάκας; ἄμαχος (855); ἀπόνους; ἀπαθεῖς (861); οὐ διαβὰς Ἅλυος ποταμοῖο/ οὐδ' ἀφ' ἑστίας συθείς (865–6); ἀκάματον (901). See also the phrase νῦν δέ (904) which is used already in the *Iliad* to mark a contrast between the past and the present. Cf. Grethlein 2006a: 122–3.

4.4. THE SOCIO-POLITICAL CONTEXT

It is widely acknowledged that Greek tragedies ought to be interpreted against the institutional background of their performances. Unlike modern drama, Greek plays were performed in a ritualistic context and were part of civic festivals. It is problematical to argue for a sharp division between public and private settings in ancient Greece, but, while the symposium as the major occasion for the dissemination of victory odes and elegies constitutes a more private setting, the civic festivals as well as the public funerals to which I will turn in the next chapter are events that were organized by the polis. Thus, we are now moving from a more private to a more public setting.

Persae was staged at the Great Dionysia, a most important festival with theatrical performances.[78] Established either under the tyrants or after the overthrow of the Peisistratid regime,[79] this festival included the performances of dithyrambs, four trilogies with satyr plays and, probably from 486 BCE onwards, comedies as well. In an influential article, Simon Goldhill has drawn attention to the frame around the dramatic performances, notably the libations by the ten generals, the honouring of individual citizens, the parade of the war-orphans and the display of the allies' tributes. He argues for a tension between this enactment and representation of the power of the polis and the questioning of values and conventions in the tragedies.[80]

Goldhill is surely right to point out the destabilizing force of many tragedies, which put central creeds of the polis to the test. However, it is worth noting that such challenges and transgressions tend to be projected into the 'other' – most importantly, the tragic action takes place outside of Athens, a point to which I shall return in the next section.[81] In my reading of *Persae*, I have focused on an instance of military disaster that is distanced from the present and affects an enemy of Athens. Moreover, not only does the theatre allow the audience to have experiences at the safe distance of the

---

[78] On the Great Dionysia see Deubner 1932: 138–42; Pickard-Cambridge ²1968: 57–125; Parke 1977: 125–36; Simon 1983: 101–4; Connor 1990. On the relation of the plays to this institutional setting, see Meier 1988: 62–74; Goldhill 1990 and 2000. Sourvinou-Inwood 2003: 67–200 makes an attempt at a new reconstruction of the ritual background and the genesis of tragedy.

[79] Against the common view that the Great Dionysia have a pre-democratic origin, see Connor 1990.

[80] Goldhill 1990; Goldhill 2000 is a comment on and reply to the discussion triggered by his earlier article.

[81] Goldhill 1990: 114–15 mentions the fact that the tragic action is distanced from the audience only as a *prolegomenon*, but does not really take it into account. In Grethlein 2003a: 439–42, I try to show that the dichotomy between questioning and affirming polis-values is misleading as tragedy also shaped the past as a foil which neither undermined nor backed up, but criticized the status quo.

'as-if', but the familiarity of myths sets its audience mostly free from tensions between expectation and experience. It is not so much the *what*, but the *how* that raises suspense.[82]

It is therefore possible, instead of seeing not so much a tension between the context and the content of tragedy, to argue that both reinforce one another in distancing contingency of chance from the polis. In addition to the projection of the tragic plot onto the 'other', the annual performance of tragedies and the ritual setting establish continuity and regularity that contrast with the fickleness of fate in the 'other' of the tragic setting. It is as tempting as it is dangerous to spell out this point for *Persae*, as we do not know exactly when the single rituals were introduced in the Great Dionysia. Yet, an obvious contrast would have arisen between the Persians' mourning that Asia was unmanned (117–19; 289; 579–80; 730) and the proud parade of the Athenian adolescents who, after losing their fathers in war, had been brought up by the polis.[83] The crowns for citizens and strangers who had benefited the polis would have corresponded negatively to the presentation of Xerxes as someone who had brought great harm to Persia.[84] The tributes of the allies can have been displayed only after the treasure of the Delian League had been transferred to Athens.[85] However, since already before that numerous strangers attended the festival, there would have been a strong contrast between the Athenian self-representation to the Hellenic world at the Great Dionysia and the mourning over the loss of the empire in *Persae*.[86] Thus, the ritual setting of tragedy reinforces the distancing of the tragic action into the 'other'; conversely, the suffering of the 'other' in *Persae* throws into relief the stability of the polis as presented at the Great Dionysia.

4.5. CONCLUSION

For many reasons, *Persae* is an extremely interesting act of memory. One of these reasons is its high reflectivity – the characters as well as the Chorus elaborate on memory and, in staging an embedded past, the apparition of

---

[82] Particularly Euripides presents well-known plots with new twists and turns. See, for example, Arnott 1973.
[83] On the parade, see Pickard-Cambridge ²1968: 59 with the ancient testimonies; Meier 1988: 68–70; Goldhill 1990: 105–14.
[84] Cf. Pickard-Cambridge ²1968: 59; 82 with n. 2 and Goldhill 1990: 104–5 on the honours for citizens and strangers.
[85] See Pickard-Cambridge ²1968: 58–9; Meier 1988: 68–70; Goldhill 1990: 101–4. Raubitschek 1941a: 356–62 argues that the display of tributes was introduced by a decree between the death of Pericles and the performance of the *Babylonians*.
[86] Cf. Pickard-Cambridge ²1968: 58–9.

Darius can be interpreted as a *mise-en-abyme*.[87] The high degree of reflection is perhaps due to the failure of *Halosis Miletou*, which obviously did not prevent Aeschylus from composing another historical play, but may have prompted him to explore the possibilities and limits of memory in tragedy. Fair enough, but is *Persae* representative of tragedy in general? Does not the fact that it is the only preserved historical tragedy make it the least apt case-study? On the contrary, I have chosen *Persae* because its special case condenses features which are crucial for tragic memory in general.

As we have seen, the battle of Salamis is spatially distanced and cast in an epic light. Thereby, *Persae* demonstrates not only the importance of 'heroic vagueness' for tragedy – even a historical subject must be presented in a mythical register – but it also indicates why 'heroic vagueness' is so crucial for tragic memory. In accordance with Aristotle's model of reception, I pointed out that the temporal distancing helps establish the balance between proximity and distance that is necessary to produce a catharsis in the audience. The reception of Phrynichus' *Halosis Miletou* illustrates what happens when the disaster is too close to the spectators. In *Persae*, on the other hand, the tragic plot is sufficiently removed from present day Athens, while at the same time *gnomai* allow the audience to see in the fate of the Persians an exemplum that is relevant to themselves.

The balance between proximity and distance is crucial for tragedy in general. To start with, the distancing of tragic actions from Athens has received much attention in scholarship. In her reading of Aeschylus' *Septem*, Sophocles' *Antigone*, *Oedipus Tyrannus* and *Oedipus Coloneus* as well as Euripides' *Supplices* and *Phoenissae*, Froma Zeitlin concludes that Thebes 'provides the negative model to Athens' manifest image of itself with regard to its notions of the proper management of city, society, and self.[88] While her analysis has not escaped criticism, especially for overstating the Athens–Thebes dichotomy and for glossing over the subtle differences between the various versions of Thebes,[89] her emphasis on the role of the 'other' in tragedy has been taken up and developed further. N. T. Croally, for example, challenges the tendency to privilege Thebes as the 'other' and notes a variety of alterities that, from an Athenian point of view, make tragic characters the 'other':

The characters who inhabit the fictional other-place are in cultural terms themselves consistently other to an Athenian democrat: kings, heroes, transgressors, barbarians, slaves, powerful and seductive women and so on. So, spatially,

---

[87] Cf. Grethlein 2007b: 379–88.   [88] Zeitlin 1990: 131. See also Vidal-Naquet 1988b.
[89] Cf. Easterling 1989; Saïd 1989; Rehm 2002: 236–8 is sceptical about the focus on the 'other' in general.

temporally, ethnically, socially and sexually the world of tragedy is other, represented for the benefit of Athens, the self.[90]

The importance of distance from the tragic plots comes also to the fore in the few plays with Athenian characters. Athens' most prominent role in tragedy is granting help and asylum to suppliants.[91] Euripides' *Supplices* deals with Athens' support for Adrastus and the Argivan mothers who were not allowed to bury their sons. Euripides has Theseus and the Athenians receive the suppliants and successfully defend their rights in a war with Thebes. In the *Heraclidae*, the Athenian kings Demophon and Acamas provide the sons of Heracles with shelter and defeat their persecutor, Eurystheus. While the myths of *Supplices* and *Heraclidae* are well-known from the surviving funeral speeches, tragedies dealing with other myths also envisage Athens as a haven for refugees, notably for Orestes (Aesch. *Eum.*) Medea (Eur. *Med.*), Heracles (Eur. *HF*) and Oedipus (Soph. *OC*). What is relevant for my argument here is that in all these plays Athens is not, or at least not seriously, affected by tragic turmoil – Athens in tragedy is untragic.[92] The plays are performed in Athens, but tragedy takes places elsewhere.

While in *Persae* the spatial distance and the heroization establish the distance that tragedies with mythic subjects automatically have, these plays need to create the nearness that the battle of Salamis had for the Athenian audience in 472 BCE. Not only did the tragedians play with the mythical tradition to make it interesting for present concerns, but they also made their stories resonate with their audience through what Christiane Sourvinou-Inwood has called 'zooming-devices'. Words and concepts from the world of the audience, but alien to the heroic cosmos 'had the effect of bringing the world of the play nearer, pushing the audience into relating their experiences and assumptions directly to the play'.[93]

For example in Aeschylus' *Supplices*, Argos, where the Danaids flee, is governed by the king Pelasgus. However, Pelasgus does not decide himself

---

[90] Croally 1994: 40–1.
[91] For an examination of the asylum tragedies, see Grethlein 2003a. There were also tragedies dealing with other Athenian myths such as Euripides' *Erechtheus* (TrGF 349–70), a play about the invasion of Eumolpus. Cf. Carrara 1977. That the portrayal of Athens was positive is strongly suggested by the quotation of a lengthy passage from Euripides (TrGF 360) by Lycurgus who praises him 'for he believed that the deeds of those men would become an excellent paradigm for the citizens' (Lycurg. 100).
[92] Cf. Parker 1997; Grethlein 2003a: 436. In some plays though, Athens is exposed to strong tensions. In the *Heraclidae*, Demophon is hard pressed to sacrifice a royal girl in order to save his suppliants. His rejection of this, however, does not weigh heavily as the Heracles daughter Macaria volunteers. The case of *Medea* is a bit trickier. According to some accounts Medea, once she has settled in Athens as wife of Aegeus, assassinates Theseus. However, this mythical tradition is not explicitly mentioned in the play. Cf. Grethlein 2003a: 348–9.
[93] Sourvinou-Inwood 1989: 136.

whether or not to accept the supplication of Danaus and his daughters, but refers the issue to an assembly, whose procedures, particularly the vote by show of hand (604, 607, 621), are strongly reminiscent of democratic Athens. 'The ruling hand of the people' ('δήμου κρατοῦσα χείρ', 604) even seems to allude to the word δημοκρατία. Moreover, the decision of the assembly is phrased in terms known from contemporary Athenian decrees, including the phrase 'The Argives have decided' ('ἔδοξεν Ἀργείοισιν', 605) as well as the word 'inviolability' ('ἀσυλία', 610). These 'zooming-devices' bring the world of the play closer to the time of its performance and render the dilemma whether or not to help the Danaids relevant to the audience.

To give another example, in *Orestes*, which was performed in 408 BCE, Euripides has the hero stay after the murder of his mother and be exposed to the attacks of the enraged mob in Argos. Menelaus' description of the unpredictable fury of the mass (696–703) and the messenger's account of the assembly featuring the worst sort of demagogues (884–949) parallel the unstable political situation in Athens, in particular the witch-hunt on potential enemies of the democracy after the failure of the short-lived oligarchic government in 411 BCE.[94] The similarities are reinforced by the word 'comradeship' ('ἑταιρεία') which is applied to the friendship between Orestes and Pylades (1072, 1079). The rarity of ἑταιρεία in tragedy – these are the only occurrences in the entire transmitted work of Euripides – makes its use in the context of a struggle between the *jeunesse dorée* and the people striking and would not have failed to evoke the contemporary clubs of young, often subversive aristocrats.[95] This and other zooming-devices permit an exemplary use of the past without explicitly juxtaposing it with the present. The 'zoom'-like allusions to the present suffice to establish the past as a foil, which sheds light on the world of the audience through contrast, similarity or refraction.

As these examples illustrate, the right degree of familiarity and distance between the world of the audience and the world of the play is crucial to tragedy as a genre. The distancing of the contemporary subject in *Persae* highlights the importance of this balance, which makes it possible to address and negotiate controversial issues without taking the stand of particular groups and dividing the polis. For example, in Euripides' *Supplices* various characters condemn the people's lack of reflection and particularly the belligerency of young men (160; 231–3; 728–30), the very points with which

---

[94] See e.g. Burkert 1974: 106–8.
[95] The only other use of ἑταιρεία in the extant corpus of tragedy is in Soph. *Aj.* 683.

aristocratic critics took issue in democratic Athens.[96] However, in *Supplices* the critique is put forward in the heroic world, it is levelled against Thebes and thereby 'displaced upon a city that is imagined as the mirror opposite of Athens'.[97] In N. T. Croally's words, 'tragedy performs its didactic function by examining ideology *otherwise*'.[98] That being said, the similarities to the situation current in Athens at the time of performance are striking and the boundaries between 'other' and self get easily blurred, or, as Chris Pelling puts it: 'The polarity is simultaneously challenged and asserted.'[99]

Persae shows that it is not only the distancing effect that makes the heroic world such an attractive playing ground for the tragedians. The *mise-en-abyme* of Darius reveals that its larger-than-life status endows the heroic world with authority. I have noted the same in my examination of elegiac fragments in which the heroization of recent history seems to reinforce its significance as a model for the present. At the same time, as I have already mentioned, myth is not fixed. Within undefined boundaries that the tragedians, particularly Euripides, never tired of exploring, myths could be altered and thereby rendered significant for the present.[100] The combination of flexibility and authority made myth eminently apt for the negotiation of present concerns. The temporal setting is remote, but nonetheless the heroic past is in the firm grip of the present.

Persae also nicely illustrates the contrast between the experience of the characters and the reception experience with which tragedy frequently plays. Whereas in the first part of the play Atossa and the Chorus waver between fear and hope, the audience knows that the messenger will bring news of a defeat. The historical subject augments the advantage in knowledge which in other tragedies the audience enjoys over the characters thanks to the familiarity of the myths. As a fragment from the comedy *Poiesis* by Antiphanes states: 'Tragedy is a blessed/ creation in all regards, if/ the spectators know the words,/ before somebody has said them. So the poet only/ has to remind them.' (fr. 189 KA 1–5). Tragic irony, 'the contradiction between "is" and "seems" in the working of destiny and circumstance',[101] is particularly prominent in the works of Sophocles. In *Oedipus Tyrannus* for example, when Oedipus commits himself to clarifying the murder of Laius with the words 'I fight in his defence as if for my father' (397), the gap between his and the audience's knowledge comes to the

---

[96] See the passages cited in Grossmann 1950: 146–53.   [97] Zeitlin 1990: 144.
[98] Croally 1994: 42.   [99] Pelling 1997a: 17.   [100] See, for example, Burian 1997.
[101] Sedgewick 1948: 21. For an exemplary treatment of tragic irony in Sophocles, see Kirkwood 1958: 247–87, who makes the important point that tragic irony is not limited to scenes in which 'the irony of the situation is verbally emphasized' (248).

fore.¹⁰² And when Oedipus points out the defeat of the Sphinx at his hands with the words 'I came,/ Oedipus, who knew nothing, and I stopped her' (397–8), the dramatic irony 'is here especially effective, since in, as he imagines, employing irony and sarcasm Oedipus is in fact voicing the essential truth'.¹⁰³

In *Persae*, the contrast between the merciless rule of contingency of chance on the stage and the audience's full knowledge of what will happen has particular force. The Persian invasion was a recent event that had shaken Greece and Athens in particular. Not only had the attack posed a serious threat to the political independence of the Greek poleis, but the war had inflicted much pain on individuals. Hence, *Persae* allows the audience to re-experience a recent event that involved an extreme experience of contingency;¹⁰⁴ however, the tragic re-enactment¹⁰⁵ comes without the tension between expectations and experiences and instead dramatizes the enemy camp under the sway of contingency of chance.

If we move from reception to the experience of the characters, the question arises as to how we should evaluate their shortcomings. I have argued that purely moral interpretations of *Persae* fall short of the complex and polyphonous assessment of the Persian defeat. Besides blaming Xerxes and his deficient leadership, the Chorus and characters also elaborate on human fragility and their dependence upon arbitrary gods. The issue of guilt and fate in tragedy has attracted much attention, most prominently in the discussion of Sophocles' *Oedipus Tyrannus*. Recently, German scholars have foregrounded the responsibility of Oedipus for his downfall. Arbogast Schmitt and Eckard Lefèvre apply Aristotle's concept of *hamartia* to Oedipus and argue that he is the victim of his own character.¹⁰⁶ In *Die Suche nach der Schuld*, M. Lurje deconstructs this position as effectively as polemically, tracing it back to the sixteenth century and unmasking its Christian presuppositions.¹⁰⁷

The very term '*Schuld*' is not only hard to translate into English, let alone into ancient Greek, but implies many aspects that are alien to classical Greece. Of course, responsibility is an issue in tragedy, but at the same time contingency of chance is so prominent that it would be pointless to start

---

[102] See e.g. Pucci 1992: 79–80.   [103] Dawe 1982: ad 397.
[104] On the broad reception in art and literature, see Kierdorf 1966; Francis 1990; Castriota 1992; Boedeker 1998.
[105] Meier 1988: 90 emphasizes that *Persae* is a 'repetition' of the war.
[106] See especially Lefèvre 1987 and Schmitt 1988. In 2001, Lefèvre applies his interpretation to all preserved Sophoclean tragedies.
[107] Lurje 2004, which is more or less a 500-page review of Lefèvre's and Schmitt's works on Greek tragedy, including an extended archaeology of their intellectual roots.

giving examples. It is worth noting that we shall encounter similar tensions and contradictions between different models of explaining disasters in the first historians. Particularly in Herodotus, concepts such as a cycle of good and bad fate, divine retribution and the envy of the gods surface and compete with one another in the narrative (Chapter 7, section 7.3.1). The absence of an all-embracing concept and the pluralism of explanations forcefully express the power of contingency, which is hard to master even in retrospect.

In elegy and epinician poetry, the destructive force of chance is balanced by constructions of continuity and regularity. The disaster of the Persians, on the other hand, is unmitigated. As presented by Aeschylus, the continuum and chain of great deeds by Persian kings has been irreversibly broken by Xerxes' total defeat. Many tragedies offer a similar picture and even those that have a more or less happy ending shatter the belief in the contingency of action, man's ability to steer his own course. For instance, in *Eumenides* Orestes is finally acquitted, but the closure is only brought about with the help of a goddess and there are still repercussions of the corruption of language, the inversion of gender and dubious attempts to appropriate justice at the end.[108]

That being said, one may wonder whether the unrestricted emphasis on contingency of chance in tragedy is not itself a strategy to tame its power. Displacing the exploration of contingency into a fixed context has the effect of banning its danger. What is more, the performative context creates regularity and continuity. The annual performance of tragedies at the Great Dionysia reinforces the discharging of contingency of chance into the 'other' at the level of the action.

Before turning to the funeral speeches in the next chapter, which will lead us to prose literature and in this regard bring us closer to historiography, it may be worthwhile to give a brief review of memory in the poetic genres that I have examined so far. Epinician, elegiac and tragic poetry differ in what past they refer to and what function these references have. While victory odes evoke mythical foils for the athletic victory of an individual, elegies focus on the remote and recent history of the polis. Tragedy, however, deals with myths or, in the case of *Persae*, with mythicized history, mostly outside of Athens. The differences extend to the performative contexts: besides festivals and victory celebrations, symposia were the

---

[108] See, in particular, Goldhill 1984; 1986: 33–56. On the process at Athens, see also Vellacott 1977, and for an attempt to understand the tensions as an expression of Greek legal thought, Grethlein 2003a: 232–47.

primary occasion for the presentation of elegies and victory odes, whereas tragedy belongs in the public setting of the Great Dionysia.

These differences notwithstanding, in all three genres the past tends to be in the grip of the polis and the present. The prominence of the polis is most obvious in elegy, but the Pindaric odes also attempt to reintegrate the victor into his polis community and, while the majority of tragedies are set outside of Athens, this distance is used to negotiate issues of political life in Athens. In all three genres, the past serves as a model for the here and now, be it positive or negative, even when the present is not invoked explicitly. Besides the exemplary mode of memory, we have also encountered the traditional mode of memory, notably in the victory odes and elegies. Both regularity and continuity can be seen as counterstrategies to the most striking parallel between the genres, the prominence of contingency of chance. Epinician, elegy and tragedy all constitute attempts to cope with human fragility, albeit in distinct ways.

CHAPTER 5

Epideictic oratory: Lysias, epitaphios logos

In his *Panegyricus*, Isocrates draws on the *logos–ergon* dichotomy to state that no account has done justice to the deeds of the Greeks in the Persian Wars (4.82):

So they produced in the persons of those who fought against the men from Asia men of such great valour that no one, either of the poets or of the sophists (μηδένα ... μήτε τῶν ποιητῶν μήτε τῶν σοφιστῶν), has ever been able to speak in a manner worthy of their achievements.

In this version of the topos '*verbis facta exaequare*' ('to equal deeds in words'), Isocrates distinguishes two forms of accounts, those composed by poets and those by sophists. The first probably refer to epic, tragedy, elegy and lyric poetry, the second to speeches. After discussing various genres of poetry in the preceding chapters, I will now turn to the second group mentioned by Isocrates – oratory.[1] In our journey through various genres of memory, the prose of oratory brings us a step closer to historiography and is therefore the last station of the first half on non-historiographical modes of memory.

The prominence of the art of persuasion in ancient Greece is obvious. To start with Homer, in the *Iliad*'s embassy-scene, Phoenix mentions that Peleus sent him out to make Achilles 'a speaker of words and a doer of deeds' (9.443).[2] Besides physical strength, oratorical skills are crucial to the Homeric heroes. Phoenix' attempt to persuade the sulking Achilles to return to the ranks of the Greeks also illustrates the prominence of the past in the heroes' speeches. At the core of Phoenix' appeal, we find the story of Meleager (9.524–99): when, a long time ago ('πάλαι', 9.527),[3] the

---

[1] On the use of the past in oratory, see Jost 1936; Schmitz-Kahlmann 1939; Pearson 1941; Perlman 1961; Nouhaud 1982; Loraux 1986a; Worthington 1994; Gotteland 2001; Clarke 2008: 245–303.
[2] On the heroes' art of persuasion, see, for example, the study by Martin 1989, which draws on speech–act theory, and, more recently, Roisman 2007.
[3] However, Meleager belongs only one generation before the heroes of the Trojan War, cf. Grethlein 2006a: 56. Thus, the distancing of the recent past that I have noticed in elegy and tragedy can be traced back to Homer. On the instructive example of Nestor in the Homeric epics, see Grethlein 2006d.

Curetes were besieging Calydon, Meleager was caught by anger, withdrew from the battle and could not be lured back, not even by rich presents. Only when the city was on the verge of capture did Meleager return to combat and help to defend Calydon. However, owing to his late return, he did not receive presents. Thus, Phoenix argues, Achilles should give up his anger while he can still expect presents for his return.

There are many other cases in which Homeric heroes draw on exempla from the past to buttress their arguments.[4] And yet, no matter what reconstruction we follow, it is not until the Classical Age that we can find the first theoretical reflections on the art of speaking.[5] A well-known product of this development is Aristotle's treatise *ars rhetorica* from the fourth century BCE. In the third chapter of this work, Aristotle distinguishes three types of oratory, judicial, deliberative and epideictic,[6] which are defined by the function of the audience. In judicial and deliberative speeches, the audience is a judge, i.e. a decision is to be made, in the first concerning past events, in the second the future. Epideictic speeches, on the other hand, do not ask the audience to make a practical judgement, but bestow either praise or blame on somebody or something. While judicial and deliberative speeches are given respectively in a law court and in a political assembly, epideictic speeches are situated in the frame of ceremonies. This distinction between three species of rhetoric is not without problems and we can think of other ways of categorizing oratory; yet, the history of reception has made it Aristotle's 'most distinctive contribution'[7] to the theory of rhetoric.

The past comes into play in all three types of oratory, but since in judicial speeches the focus is mostly on the case under discussion and references to the past are limited, I will discuss only deliberative and epideictic oratory. Owing to the differences in function and setting, they draw on the past in different ways. The use of the past in the same narrative form, albeit in different settings, is particularly interesting for a study that examines the ways in which ideas of history are shaped by narrative form and communicative context. I will first examine Lysias' *epitaphios logos* as an example of an

---

[4] For a survey, with references to scholarly literature, see Grethlein 2006a: 43–62.
[5] The development of rhetoric as the theory of the art of speaking is debated. While older scholarship tended to follow the ancient tradition that Tisias and Corax wrote the first rhetorical treatise in the fifth century BCE in Sicily (e.g. Kennedy 1963: 58–61), scholars have recently argued that only the fourth century BCE saw the rise of rhetoric as a discipline, cf. Cole 1991; Schiappa 1999.
[6] Arist. *Rh.* 58a36–59a5. Cf. e.g. Hellwig 1973: 111–77.
[7] Kennedy 1994: 58. Carey 2007b: 236 points out that Aristotle only codified pre-existing distinctions, but did not create them.

Epideictic oratory: Lysias, epitaphios logos

epideictic speech and then, in the next chapter, look at a deliberative speech, Andocides' *de pace*.

We have to start with a difficulty: our evidence for the funeral speeches from the fifth century BCE is very scanty. Most scholars would agree that Thucydides' *History* does not contain a reliable account of an *epitaphios logos* delivered by Pericles; in Chapter 8, section 8.2.1, I shall argue that the Periclean speech serves a meta-poetic or meta-historical function. There are only very few fragments from Pericles' Samian funeral speech[8] and from an *epitaphios* by Gorgias (DK 82 B 5–6). All other examples, the speeches by Lysias, Demosthenes (60), Hypereides (6) and Plato's *Menexenus*, are from the fourth century BCE.[9]

However, Loraux convincingly argues that, owing to the strong generic conventions, fourth-century funeral speeches were not too different from fifth-century ones.[10] The preserved speeches follow more or less a common structure: they start with an introductory reflection on the orator's task and the relation between words and deeds, then present a canon of highlights from Athenian history up to the present and close with a consolation. Thus, it seems justifiable to elaborate on one of the fully transmitted funeral speeches from the fourth century BCE. I have chosen the funeral speech by Lysias,[11] which, probably dating from 392/391 BCE, is still close to the fifth century,[12] and which is also particularly interesting for its lengthy account of the Athenian past.[13]

---

[8] For the fragments of the Samian funeral speech, see Blass ²1887: 37. For a speculative reconstruction, see Weber 1922.

[9] For historical and archaeological studies of the public funerals, see Stupperich 1977; Clairmont 1983; for philological approaches to the funeral speeches, see e.g. Schneider 1912; Schroeder 1914; Pohlenz 1948; Ziolkowski 1981. For cultural historical approaches, see after Loraux 1986a also Carter 1991; Wilke 1996; Prinz 1997. Herrman 2004 offers a collection of the funeral speeches in English translation.

[10] Loraux 1986a. On the consistency of the genre, see also Stupperich 1977: 39–40; Wilke 1996: 237.

[11] The authenticity of the speech has been subjected to doubts, as, being a metic, Lysias could not be chosen to deliver a funeral speech, cf. Carey 2007b: 242. The discussion of whether the speech was written, but not delivered by Lysias or stems from another author is not relevant to my argument on the underlying idea of history. For a recent survey of earlier scholarship, see Kartes 2000: 126–44, who regards Lysias as the author.

[12] Lysias hints at the battle of Cnidus (59) and the reconstruction of the destroyed walls (63), which was not finished until 391 BCE. According to Walz 1936: 51–3, Iphicrates' victory over a Spartan corps, which goes unmentioned in Lysias' speech, is the *terminus ante quem*. He dates this victory to 390 BCE. Yet, this date is not undebated (cf. the literature in Kartes 2000: 117 n. 11). Kartes 2000: 118–25 argues that the *epitaphios logos* fits best into the time of negotiations between Athens and Sparta in autumn/winter 392/391 BCE. Cf. Loraux 1986a: 123 n. 200; Prinz 1997: 234 with n. 17.

[13] Loraux 1973: 14 notes that Lysias' *epitaphios logos* gives a lot of space to the past, but deems this typical of funeral speeches.

I shall first discuss the idea of history and argue that the experience of contingency of chance, the loss of relatives and friends, is compensated for by the presentation of polis-history as a continuum (5.1). Then, I will try to show that the speech claims an important role for itself in the establishment of this continuum. Similarly to, but also differently from Homer, Pindar and Simonides, Lysias presents his *logos* as a speech–act (5.2). I will deepen the examination of the funeral speech by taking into account its performative setting (5.3). Finally, I will summarize the results of the close reading and buttress them by looking at other funeral speeches (5.4).

5.1. THE CONTENT AND THE IDEA OF HISTORY

In the preceding chapter, I argued that tragedy foregrounds contingency of chance, but at the same time distances it from Athens at various levels – non-Athenian heroes set in 'heroic vagueness' are the victims of misfortune. The *epitaphios logos*, on the other hand, responds to painful experiences in the lives of present-day Athenians. Death is the strongest manifestation of contingency of chance: with the exception of suicide, death is beyond our control and not only contradicts the basic assumption that everything will go on as before, but annihilates the very possibility of expectations and experiences. However, contingency of chance is virtually absent from the funeral speeches. If chance is mentioned, then only as an explanation for minor defeats that do not seriously affect the stability of Athens.[14] In the chapters on memory in poetic genres, we have encountered the traditional and exemplary modes of memory as powerful counterstrategies against human fragility. I would now like to explore how the funeral speeches employ continuity and regularity to discharge the experiences of contingency of chance made in one's own ranks.

To start with, Lysias suggests that the polis will compensate for individual loss. In the final part of his speech, a rather atypical mourning,[15] he appeals to the Athenian community to fill the void that the deaths of the soldiers have left in the lives of their relatives (75):

It seems to me that we have this one way of expressing our gratitude to those who lie here: if we hold their parents in the same high regard as they did, if we are as affectionate to their children as though we were ourselves their fathers, and if we offer ourselves as assistants to their wives as they did while they lived.

---

[14] Cf. Parker 1997: 155, who argues that chance or the gods are referred to as explanation for defeat in the funeral speeches, since it would be unthinkable to blame the fallen.
[15] Cf. Wilke 1996: 248–9.

Epideictic oratory: Lysias, epitaphios logos

This is not a mere *façon de parler* for the Athenian polis did take over part of the responsibilities of the dead and raised the war orphans, who, at the threshold of manhood, were given the hoplites' armour in a spectacular act at the Great Dionysia.[16]

In the following, I will argue that the polis not only helps the bereaved to cope with their loss, but that the history of the polis, as outlined in the speech, overcomes the individual experience of contingency of chance. While the lives of individuals are prematurely stopped by the force of chance, the *epitaphios logos* presents the history of the polis as a long continuum which is maintained by a chain of re-enactments of heroic bravery. The fragility and mortality of the individual is counterbalanced by the eternal strength of Athens. The individual may die, but as part of Athenian history, he gains a rank in eternity. This relation has a further twist: only the heroic acts of individuals give Athens an existence that defies temporality. Thus, through their very deaths Athenian soldiers establish the tradition of the polis that helps them gain immortality.

This argument requires a closer look at the account of Athens' past, by far the longest part of the speech, and its temporal organization. In a first step, I shall show not only that the history of Athens is told in chronological order, but that the sequentiality of events is frequently marked (5.1.1). In a second step, I will argue that the sequentiality is blurred by the continuity of virtue, which makes it hard to distinguish between different stages of the past and transforms Athens into a transhistorical entity (5.1.2).

5.1.1. Athens' history: a sequence of great deeds

Lysias presents Athenian history from the beginning to the present in chronological order. Needless to say, the narrative has a strong patriotic bent and, of course, only few selected events are mentioned.[17] Whole periods are skipped; for example, the Archaic Age is left out completely and the Peloponnesian War is only touched upon most perfunctorily. Yet, despite this patriotic cherry-picking, Lysias' account somehow looks like an uninterrupted sequence, since temporal markers link the single events to each other and transform the 'best-of' collection into a coherent succession.

Starting with the 'adventures long ago' ('παλαιοὶ κίνδυνοι'), Lysias tells in temporal order what we would call mythical stories, the fight against the Amazons (4–6), the support for Adrastus (7–10) and the intervention against

---

[16] See Isoc. *de pace* 82; Aeschin. *in Ctes.* 154; cf. Goldhill 1990: 105–6.
[17] Cf. Kartes 2000: 82. On the distortions of history in the *epitaphios logos*, see Loraux 1973: 18–24.

Eurystheus in favour of the Heraclidae (11–16). The sequentiality is not made explicit for the transition from the Amazons to Adrastus and the Argives, but the battle with the Amazons is given a very archaic ring by the explanation for the Amazons' military successes against their neighbours before they encountered the Athenians. Being the first to use iron and ride horses, they were superior to their opponents (4). This obviously dates the story back to the beginning of civilization. Following the supplication of Adrastus, the help for the Heraclidae is introduced by the temporal marker 'later' ('ὑστέρῳ δὲ χρόνῳ', 11). Moreover, the time is determined by the date of Heracles' death ('ἐπειδὴ Ἡρακλῆς μὲν ἐξ ἀνθρώπων ἠφανίσθη …', 11).

From the Amazonomachy and the wars against Thebans and Argives, Lysias moves on to the Persian Wars without even touching upon the Archaic Age. It is debated whether or not the Greeks drew a clear borderline between myth and history.[18] While it is wise to avoid generalizations and to allow for various concepts, it seems safe to say that the Greeks distinguished between myth and history, but not as categorically as we do – they rather regarded them as ancient and recent past. Lysias' transition from the rescue of the Heraclidae to the defence against the Persians deserves a closer look as it at the same time links and sets off history from myth, for which Lysias gives a closing summary in 17: 'Now in many ways it was natural to our ancestors, moved by a single resolve, to fight for justice.'

This remark is followed by references to Athenian autochthony and democracy.[19] German scholars have argued that the passage adheres to the chronological frame of Lysias' account:[20] the Athenians could not be called autochthonous before the beginning of Greek colonization and only then could democratic structures have emerged. However, this reading neglects the temporal markers in the text and imposes an alien historical construction on it. Lysias explicitly turns back to the beginning of history ('ἀρχή', 17), when he refers to autochthony.[21] Moreover, democracy, as Lysias describes it in 18–19, creates exactly the attitude that underlies the great deeds presented in 3–16, namely the love of freedom, justice and unity. Thus, in 17–19 Lysias does not follow chronology, but presents an

---

[18] See, for example, the discussion by Gotteland 2001: 89–102 and, on ancient historiography, Feeney 2007: 68–86.

[19] On the Athenian myth of autochthony, see Ermatinger 1897; Loraux 1986a: 148–50; Rosivach 1987; Wilke 1996.

[20] Cf. Schneider 1912: 43–4 on autochthony; Walz 1936: 14 n. 36 on democracy; Kartes 2000: 51, who agrees with this explanation and adds observations about the brevity with which Lysias touches upon autochthony.

[21] Loraux 1973: 30 stresses the difference between autochthony and the establishment of democracy. The first is given by nature, the latter is a development.

analepsis. His look back to the very beginning closes the account of the early stories and sets them off against the Persian Wars, the account of which starts with 20.[22]

At the same time, the *analepsis* establishes a link between the archaic and the more recent events at the level of content. The attitudes that Lysias describes in 17–19 are the basis not only for the ancient deeds, but also for later achievements. The same desire for justice and freedom that prompted the Athenians to fight off the Amazons and to intervene on behalf of the Heraclidae and Argives motivates the resistance against the Persians and the opposition to Greek aggressors. In pointing out common features, the passage on autochthony and democracy bridges the gap between ancient and recent history and presents Athens' past as an uninterrupted continuum.

The introduction to the Persian invasion also links the historical and mythical events to one another and, what is more, ties them to the present (20):

For indeed, being of noble stock and having the same minds, the ancestors of those who lie here (οἱ πρόγονοι τῶν ἐνθάδε κειμένων) did many noble and admirable deeds; but ever memorable and mighty are the trophies left behind by their descendants (οἱ ἐξ ἐκείνων γεγονότες) everywhere, owing to their virtue.

The soldiers of the Persian Wars, introduced as οἱ ἐξ ἐκείνων γεγονότες, continue the tradition of virtue and even surpass their ancestors,[23] who are called οἱ πρόγονοι τῶν ἐνθάδε κειμένων. The genitive 'of those who lie here' embraces not only the men who fought against the Persians, but also the subsequent generations up to the ones who have just been buried. Thus, while acknowledging some kind of boundary between mythical and historical stories, Lysias glosses over the enormous gap of the whole Archaic Age and bridges it by embedding both the mythical and recent past in a sequence that extends to the present. This temporal construction accords with the observation of anthropologists that in oral societies the memory of the last few generations is directly linked to the mythical past.[24] While the memory of the origin is more or less stable, the

---

[22] Gotteland 2001: 100–1 emphasizes the rupture which suggests a hierarchy between different parts of the past. Loraux 1986a: 137 is more balanced.
[23] Kartes 2000: 55 n. 93.
[24] Cf. Vansina 1985: 23–4. See also Henige 1974: 27, who describes the devices of telescoping (27–38) and artificial lengthening (38–64) of time in oral traditions. As Nouhaud 1982: 20–3 notes, there are only very few references to archaic history in Athenian speeches.

memory of the recent past moves with every generation, thereby creating a 'floating gap'.

The Persian Wars are told in chronological order: starting with Marathon (21–6), Lysias proceeds to Thermopylae, Artemisium and Salamis (27–43) and then comes to Plataea (44–7). The transition from Darius to Xerxes is marked by 'after that' ('μετὰ ταῦτα', 27) and Xerxes' invasion is dated as happening 'in the tenth year' ('δεκάτῳ ἔτει', 27).[25] Compared to the mythical stories, the account of the Persian Wars becomes increasingly detailed and, accordingly, the temporal markers become more precise. The advancing of the Persian army after the battles at Thermopylae and Artemisium and before the battle at Salamis is dated as 'not many days later' ('οὐ πολλαῖς δ' ὕστερον ἡμέραις', 34), and when Lysias comes to the battle of Salamis, even shorter time spans come into view: 'For a long time (πολὺν χρόνον) the sea-battle was evenly balanced and at one moment (τοτὲ μέν) they seemed to have won and been saved, at another (τοτὲ δ') to have been defeated and destroyed' (38).

After the Persian Wars, Lysias briefly touches upon the internal wars in Greece ('ὑστέρῳ δὲ χρόνῳ Ἑλληνικοῦ πολέμου καταστάντος', 48). He mentions a battle with Aegina (48) and then elaborates on the Corinthians' attack, which had to be repulsed by the young and old as the Athenian army was out of town (49–53). Paragraphs 54–7 close the account of the wars against Persians and Greeks: a reflection on the limits of narrative representation that harks back to the introductory remarks[26] leads to the praise of Athens, which ruled over the sea for seventy years (55), protected its allies and saved Greece from the Persian threat (56–7). Thus, Lysias concludes, Athens rightly gained the Greek hegemony.

From this point on, the account still follows chronological order, but the temporal sequence is not marked anymore. Instead, the reported events are structured by thematic aspects. First, Lysias turns to Athens' greatness even in disasters, which he downplays as 'misfortunes' ('δυστυχίαι') and which do not affect the continuum of Athenian grandeur (58). He touches upon the loss of ships in the Hellespont and the defeat at Aegospotamoi, quite shattering events which he nonetheless manages to integrate into his praise by pointing out that the defeats reveal how much the other Greek states are indebted to Athens.[27] Only after the mentioned events did the Persians dare

---

[25] See the interesting comparison of Salamis with Marathon by Loraux 1973: 39–40: while Salamis is carefully described, Marathon is only a *logos*.
[26] Cf. Kartes 2000: 79–80.
[27] Lévy 1976: 39–40 on δυστυχία as excuse for defeat. Kartes 2000: 83 notes the correspondence between the description of δυστυχία in 59 and the emphasis on Athens' strength in 57.

to interfere in Greek politics again. Seen from this angle, even defeat is an expression of Athens' greatness. From here, Lysias turns to internal affairs, including in his praise those who helped to re-establish democracy after the tyranny of the Thirty (61–5). Among them, he explicitly mentions the foreigners (67).[28] Finally, Lysias comes to the men who are being buried now. The failure of their attempt to help the Corinthians who were at loggerheads with the Spartans (67–70) leaves the Peloponnesians in slavery to Sparta (69).

How can we explain the decline of temporal markers for the very recent events? I think it is not only due to the fact that here Lysias could take for granted that his audience was familiar with the sequentiality of the events, but the thematic ordering – first Athens' brillance even in military disaster and then its internal affairs – serves, I suggest, to throw into relief the achievement of those who are being buried. The reference to Athens' greatness even in defeat prepares for the portrayal of the failed expedition in support of the Corinthians as a manifestation of Athens' power. In the same way as Athens' loss of hegemony is taken as an indicator of its greatness, since only then did the Persian threat come back into existence, it is due to the failed expedition that the Peloponnesians remain under the Spartan yoke. Similarly, the account of internal conflicts helps to pay tribute to the recent expedition. Already those who fought at the Piraeus deserved the highest praise; the ones being mourned now are even worthier of honour for sacrificing themselves on foreign soil (70).

To sum up: although Lysias skips long phases of Athenian history and mentions only select events, the temporal markers make the account look like a gapless sequence. Athens' history is portrayed as a long chain of great deeds, and even the less than successful enterprises of the very recent past are integrated into the list of achievements as expressions of Athenian virtue.

5.1.2. Beyond sequence

I would now like to go one step further and argue that the sequence of virtuous enterprises establishes a continuum that ultimately transcends the sequentiality of Lysias' account. Beneath the sequentiality, there is the continuity of virtue (ἀρετή),[29] which blurs the temporal distinctions on

---

[28] This is evidence for Patterson's argument against Morris that formal burials were not limited to citizens in Greek poleis (2006: 52).

[29] Lévy 1976: 163 with n. 3 lists all occurrences of ἀρετή in Lysias' *epitaphios logos* and points out its central role.

which a sequence is based. The transhistorical stance of Athens also comes to the fore in the stability of space.[30]

A number of terms that mark temporal relations are used for a wide range of times and thus lose their specificity.[31] For example, both the heroes of the ancient past (3; 6; 17) and the soldiers in the Persian Wars (20; 23; 32) are called 'forebears' ('πρόγονοι'). In the same vein, not only are the account of the battle against the Amazons, the supplication of Adrastus and the help for the Heraclidae introduced as 'adventures long ago' ('παλαιοὶ κίνδυνοι', 3), but the Persian Wars are also mentioned as 'deeds performed long ago' ('πάλαι τῶν ἔργων γεγενημένων', 26). The use of the same temporal terms for different ages blurs the distinction between them and makes us envisage Athenian history as a long continuum so that, for example when in 60, 61 and 69 the intelligence ('διάνοια'), virtue ('ἀρετή') and good deeds ('ἀγαθά') of the forefathers are invoked, it is impossible to pin the reference down to a particular generation – it is the heritage of the past as a whole that is hailed. Thus, Lysias' presentation of Athens' history illustrates the traditional mode of memory. We have already encountered an application of this mode to polis history in elegy. While in some fragments from Tyrtaeus and Mimnermus the traditional view of the past comes to the fore in the time-transcending 'we',[32] Lysias' funeral speech expresses it through the equalizing attribution of the same positive predicates to all phases of Athenian history.

The temporal continuum of Athenian history has a spatial expression in deictic pronouns. Time and again, Lysias refers to ἥδε ἡ πόλις or ἥδε ἡ χώρα. Throughout the different time periods, it is 'this city' and 'this land'. It is striking that all occurrences of this phrase refer to mythical Athens or to the Athens of the Persian Wars, while none can be found in the account of the recent past. This suggests that the deictic pronouns are used specifically to forge a link between past and present Athens. The spatial deixis creates stability on the temporal axis.

---

[30] Loraux 1986a: 121–9 gives a most stimulating analysis of the temporal concepts of the funeral speeches and emphasizes the aspect of timelessness. However, when it comes to Lysias, I part company from her. According to Loraux 1986a: 123, 'the epitaphioi of the early fourth century display no such certainties and make no attempt to reconcile all temporalities in a present that is open to action'. On the contrary, as I try to show above, the sequentiality of the account leads to the establishment of a continuum reaching from the past into the present. Moreover, Loraux 1986a: 134 argues against the creation of continuities in the *epitaphioi logoi*. However, the element of repetition which she emphasizes does not exclude continuity.

[31] Gotteland 2001: 85 notes that παλαιός, ἀρχαῖος, πρόγονοι most often refer to the mythical time.

[32] See pp. 57–8.

The temporal continuum is even embodied by a spatial mark within 'this city'. The burial ground assembles generations of dead and thus creates a present that has absorbed Athens' past. The dissolving of time in place shows in the undifferentiated use of 'those, who lie here' ('οἱ ἐνθάδε κείμενοι') for the deceased of different eras. In 60, this phrase denotes those who have died in the battles that deprived Athens of its hegemony. In 54, neglecting that the public burial for the war dead was a historical institution of rather recent origin (see section 5.3), 'the men who are lying here' ('οἱ ἐνθάδε κείμενοι ἄνδρες') refers to the Athenians of the Persian Wars. In 64, when the rebellion against the tyranny of the Thirty is compared to the deeds of 'those, who lie here' ('οἱ ἐνθάδε κείμενοι'), the reference is ambivalent. οἱ ἐνθάδε κείμενοι could signify the dead from the Corinthian expedition, but is more likely to include also the soldiers from earlier wars. And when Lysias starts with a reflection on the possibility of describing 'the virtue of the men, who lie here' ('τὴν τῶν ἐνθάδε κειμένων ἀνδρῶν ἀρετήν', 1), he refers neither to the recently dead nor to another particular generation, but praises the whole range of past Athenians who have sacrificed themselves for their polis.[33] The undetermined reference expresses a view of history in which individual events and times merge into an eternity.

That the continuum of virtue erases the borderlines between different stages of the past comes to the fore in the following claim: 'It is therefore no wonder that, although these deeds have been performed long ago (πάλαι τῶν ἔργων γεγενημένων), nowadays the virtue of these men is still envied by all, as if their deeds were recent.' (26). Linear time is doubly blurred. First, the battle of Marathon is attributed to the level of πάλαι, thus, as already mentioned, being assigned to the same stage as the mythical deeds. Simultaneously, the virtue shown at Marathon is still remembered as if it were recent, so that a certain quality of deeds seems to transcend the boundaries of linear time.

We have seen that traditional views of the past are often entangled with exemplary uses of the past. While they constitute distinct modes of memory – traditions lend themselves to the construction of identities, exempla guide specific actions – they can reinforce one another. Continuities are produced by repetitions and, conversely, regularities rely on some kind of

---

[33] Cf. Kartes 2000: 32, who stresses that the present dead are called 'those, who are being buried now' ('οἱ νῦν θαπτόμενοι'). However he does not do justice to the differences between the single occurrences, when he claims that 'those, who lie here' ('οἱ ἐνθάδε κείμενοι') always refers to the entire war dead from the past.

continuity. We find yet another interaction of these two commemorative modes in Lysias' *epitaphios logos*, in which the continuity of great deeds is generated by the emulation of ancestors by each generation. When Lysias explains the courage of those who unseated the regime of the Thirty, he says: 'Imitating in fresh adventures the ancient valour of their ancestors …'(61). The liberation of Athens from tyranny not only continues earlier manifestations of Athenian virtue, but, what is more, it is an act of imitation. Similarly, Lysias says about those who have just been buried: 'For they were first trained in the excellences of their ancestors, and then in manhood they preserved that ancient fame intact and displayed their own prowess.' (69). Again it is claimed that the great deeds of the ancestors have taught the soldiers how to be brave.

The pedagogical function of the past is also illustrated by the interaction of two generations in the fight against the Corinthians, who captured Geraneia when the Athenian army was out of town. Instead of waiting for the army to return, the young and old who had been left in Athens endeavoured to fight the Corinthians. In 51, Lysias says: 'These had often proved their own worth, and those would imitate them, and while the seniors knew how to command, the juniors were able to carry out their orders.' Although half of the Athenian troops were too frail to fight properly and the other half lacked experience, the Athenians succeeded, since the young obeyed the commands of the old and imitated their earlier deeds.[34] The cooperation of the two generations demonstrates that the continuum of Athenian history is based on the imitation of the ancestors by each new generation.

It can be concluded not only that Lysias' funeral speech presents the past as a sequence, but that Athens' history forms a continuum that is based on the imitation of the ancestors' model. The continuity of the Athenians' performances and achievements is so strong that the differences between the eras of the past become blurred. Athenian virtue becomes a timeless constant. This transcendence of time parallels the timelessness created in *Olympian* 2, which, as I have argued, Pindar implicitly compares with the eternity on the Island of the Blessed, and it is therefore not surprising to find that funeral speeches instil in the Platonic Socrates for several days the feeling that he is living on the Isles of the Blessed (*Menex.* 235c4–5).

In the context of the funeral speech, this temporal construction has a particular function, namely that the eternal continuum of the polis

---

[34] Lysias concludes the episode with: 'Returning with fairest renown to their own land, these [i.e. the young] resumed their education and those [i.e. the old] considered the next steps.' (53).

overcomes the personal experience of contingency of chance. While the individual has fallen prey to forces beyond his control, by being part of the polis, he gains an eternal life. This effective use of the traditional and exemplary modes of memory enables the funeral speeches to make contingency of chance virtually disappear at an occasion that ritually reflects on the strongest experience of contingency, death. There may be single 'misfortunes' ('δυστυχίαι') but they are far from seriously disturbing Athens' equilibrium.

5.2. THE FUNERAL SPEECH – A SPEECH–ACT

As we have seen in Chapter 3, Simonides takes up the epic claim to compensate the heroes for their deaths with eternal memory in the medium of poetry. The same assertion can be found in Lysias' funeral speech which, like the 'New Simonides', applies the 'imperishable glory' ('κλέος ἄφθιτον') with which the epics endow individual heroes to the collective of dead. I shall argue that Lysias gives the immortalization of the dead yet another twist, but let me start with the traditional topos of immortality through praise. In 6, Lysias calls memory immortal: 'Thus, they made our city's memory imperishable (ἀθάνατον <τὴν> μνήμην) through virtue.' About the Athenians' fighting in the Persian Wars, Lysias says: 'but ever memorable (ἀείμνηστα) and mighty are the trophies left behind by their descendants everywhere, owing to their virtue' (20). At the end of his speech, Lysias makes the general claim: 'For their memory can never grow old (ἀγήρατοι) ...'(79). And, referring to the recently dead, he states: 'They have left behind an immortal (ἀθάνατον) memory through their virtue' (81).

'Memory' ('μνήμη') grants great deeds eternity. It is obvious that the funeral speech itself is a memorial and thus a medium that makes the dead immortal. In 3, Lysias explicitly calls his speech an act of memory: 'First, I shall go through the ancient adventures of our ancestors, drawing remembrance (μνήμην) thereof from their renown. For those are worthy to be remembered (μεμνῆσθαι) by all men ...'[35]

The immortalization through *logos* is spelled out in 23:[36]

But our ancestors, without calculating the risks in war, but holding that a glorious death leaves behind it a deathless account of deeds well done (τὸν εὐκλεᾶ

---

[35] See also 61: 'These men are worthy of being remembered (μεμνῆσθαι) in private as well as in public.'
[36] Cf. Loraux 1973: 32–3 and Kartes 2000: 59–60 on this passage.

θάνατον ἀθάνατον περὶ τῶν ἀγαθῶν καταλείπειν λόγον), did not fear the multitude of their adversaries, but rather trusted their own valour.

In a chiasm, the 'glorious death' produces a 'deathless account'. What is more, Lysias has the heroes themselves voice a reference to speeches like his own: not only do they gain immortality through the *logos*, but it is the knowledge of this that drives and motivates their courage.

Even the phrasing, including words such as 'famous' ('εὐκλεής'), 'immortal' ('ἀθάνατος') and 'ageless' ('ἀγήρατος'), makes Lysias' assertion that he immortalizes the dead through his praise reminiscent of the poetic topos. However, Lysias' claim goes further. Poetry grants the dead its own eternity, which means that, since the poem is a *monumentum aere perennius*, the object of its praise becomes immortal too. In the funeral oration, the immortalization relies on the eternity of the praise as well, but it also has a further aspect that gives the speech an additional function. The dead Athenians gain immortality through being part of the eternal history of Athens. I have already pointed out that, in dying for their community, the soldiers contribute to the continuum of Athens' glory, and I shall now argue that Lysias not only presents Athenian history as a timeless entity, but that he implicitly claims that his speech, due to its pedagogical function, helps to sustain the reproduction of virtue, thereby blurring the borderline between *logos* and *ergon*.

At the beginning of the praise of Athens' past, Lysias states that one ought to remember the deeds of the ancestors (3),

glorifying them in their songs (ὑμνοῦντας μὲν ἐν ταῖς ᾠδαῖς), describing them in the records of good deeds (λέγοντας δ' ἐν ταῖς τῶν ἀγαθῶν μνήμαις),[37] honouring them on such occasions as this (τιμῶντας δ' ἐν τοῖς καιροῖς τοῖς τοιούτοις), and educating the living through the achievements of the dead (παιδεύοντας δ' ἐν τοῖς τῶν τεθνεώτων ἔργοις τοὺς ζῶντας).

Syntactically, the four participles are parallel, but at the level of content they make two pairs.[38] The first two signify different modes of memory, praise in the form of songs and speech. Songs probably refer to elegies or lyrical

---

[37] The manuscripts have different readings for the second word. The *Heidelberg. Pal. Gr. 88* has γνώμαις, the *Laurent. LIX. 15* and the *Paris. Coisl. 249* read μνήμαις. γνώμαις is evidently wrong, as something parallel to ᾠδαῖς is needed, i.e. a medium of praise. Hude 1912 and Avezzù 1985 therefore follow the *Laurentianus* and *Parisinus*. Thalheim, on the other hand, proposes the conjecture τοῖς ... ἐγκωμίοις, which is taken up by Albini. At first glance, μνήμαις looks a bit strange, as μνήμη in the meaning 'memory' and μεμνῆσθαι have just been used. Yet, this could also be taken as a reflection on the process leading from memory to memorials such as funeral speeches.

[38] On the structure, see also Kartes 2000: 35–6.

poems, the λέγειν obviously implies Lysias' own speech. The second pair of participles defines the act of memory by its relation to its object and its receivers: it honours the dead and educates the living. Both functions are closely intertwined with one another, as the missing object to τιμᾶν has to be supplied from the genitive τῶν τεθνεώτων, which stands in the second half, qualifying the deeds by which the recipients are educated.

It is reasonable to take the second pair of participles as an elaboration on the acts of memory mentioned by the first pair. Thus, Lysias claims an educational function for his own speech.[39] Presenting the great deeds of the past, Lysias sets out the exempla to guide the present generation. Seen from this angle, there is a dialectical relationship between words and deeds: as pointed out in the proem, the words, albeit ever-failing, aim at giving a proper presentation of deeds. At the same time, the words have an impact on deeds by presenting the benchmark for future deeds and inviting the current generation to emulate their forefathers.

In accordance with this dialectic, a few passages blur the borderline between word and deed. In the proem, Lysias emphasizes the deficiencies of his narrative representation and thereby reinforces the gap between words and deeds:[40] 'For their valour has provided (παρεσκεύασεν) matter in such abundance, alike for those who are able to compose in verse and for those who have chosen to make a speech ...' (2). However, the verb describing the action of Athenian virtue is exactly the same as the one applied to the *logos* in 1: 'But as for all mankind all time would be insufficient to produce (παρασκευάσαι) a speech to match their deeds ...' The implicit parallel introduces an equivalence of speaking and doing into the discourse on the deficient representation of deeds in words and thereby subtly subverts it.

Immediately following upon the proem, the passage on memory that I have already discussed (3) establishes a smooth transition from words to deeds. The four parallel participles are all complemented by adverbial expressions, in each case ἐν with a noun: 'in their songs' ('ἐν ταῖς ᾠδαῖς'); 'in the records of good deeds' ('ἐν ταῖς τῶν ἀγαθῶν μνήμαις'); 'on such occasions as this' ('ἐν τοῖς καιροῖς τοῖς τοιούτοις'); and 'through the achievements of the dead' ('ἐν τοῖς τῶν τεθνεώτων ἔργοις'). The series leads from songs through speeches and the funeral ceremony to deeds.

---

[39] See also in the account of Athenian history in 19: ὑπὸ λόγου ... διδασκομένους. On the educational function of the funeral speeches, see Carter 1991: 227–30.
[40] See also 54: 'To recount in detail the perils undergone by many men is not easy for a single person, nor to show forth in a single day what has been done in all past times. For what speech or time or orator would suffice to declare the virtue of the men who lie here?'

Thus, the speech is embedded in a sequence that links words and deeds. The decisive step is the καιροὶ οἱ τοιοῦτοι. The ceremony itself stands somewhere between words and deeds. It comprises both speech and ritual, and it signifies the point where words turn into acts. The funeral ceremony is both the wording of acts – great deeds are praised – and the enactment of words – by being part of a ceremony, the exempla of the past lead to great actions in the future.

In another revealing passage, Lysias refers to his own activity as an *ergon*: '... so that to enumerate even the nations that followed in his train would be a lengthy task (ἔργον)' (27). Lysias takes up the traditional topos that words fall short of the events they describe, but at the same time blurs the clear dichotomy between words and deeds. Owing to a dialectical relationship, in which words not only represent events but also generate deeds, Lysias' words become a speech–act directed at the dead as well as the living.[41] The funeral speech not only helps the dead to overcome contingency of chance, like Homer's and Simonides' poetry, but it also provides the present and future generations with exempla as guidance and thereby contributes to the continuity of Athens' history that, in turn, lends immortality to the fallen.

The pedagogical function of memory in Athens is underscored by the negative examples of the Amazons and the Persians. While the exemplary use of the past is the basis for the continuity of Athens' success, it does not work for the opponents of Athens. About the Amazons Lysias states: 'They alone could not learn from their mistakes and take better counsel in future actions; they would not return home and report their own misfortune and our ancestors' valour' (6). The Athenians gain immortal memory – the Amazons, however, cannot learn their lesson from the past, as none of their fighters returns from the battlefield. The case of the Persians is slightly different (22):

Besides, from former actions they had conceived a particular opinion concerning our city, notably that if they march against another city first, they would be at war with these men and Athens as well, for the Athenians would be zealous in coming to defend their injured neighbours. But if they will come here first, none of the other Greeks will dare to save others and for their sake incur an open enmity with them.

The Persians do take into account the past, but they draw the wrong conclusion, underestimate Athens and, instead of refraining from an

---

[41] This reading of Lysias ties in with Beale's claim that epideictic is a 'significant social action in itself' (1978: 225). See also the interpretation of Pl. *Menex.* as a ritual by Carter 1991.

invasion, decide to attack Athens.[42] Both the Amazons and the Persians therefore throw into relief the successfully applied lessons of the past that underlie the Athenian success. The failures to learn from the past highlight the special case of Athens, where memory in the form of the funeral speech provides each new generation with a model and thereby helps to transform history into a continuous display of virtue.

5.3. THE SOCIO-POLITICAL CONTEXT

Lysias' funeral speech pits the continuity and regularity of Athens' history against the individual experience of contingency of chance. The dead gain immortality by being part of the polis. As with the poetic genres that I have discussed in the preceding chapters, it is important to contextualize this view of history in its performative setting. Thucydides introduces the *epitaphios logos* of Pericles by a detailed description of the ceremony in which the speeches were held (2.34.1–7):

In the same winter, the Athenians, in accordance with their ancestral custom, buried at public expense the first to die in this war, in the following manner. They lay out the bones of the deceased for three successive days, after setting up a tent, and each person brings to his own relative something if he wants to. When the procession takes place, wagons carry cypress coffins, one for each tribe. Inside are the bones of each man, according to tribe. One empty bier, fully decorated, is carried for the missing, all who were not found and recovered. Any man who wishes, citizen or foreigner, joins the procession, and female relatives are present at the grave as mourners. They bury them in the public tomb, which is in the most beautiful suburb in the city and in which they always bury those killed in wars, except of course for the men who fought at Marathon; on account of their outstanding virtue, they gave them burial right there. After they cover them with earth, a man chosen by the state, who seems to be of sound judgement and enjoys high reputation, makes for them an appropriate speech of praise. After this they depart.

As Thucydides notes, the burial ceremony was public and was even paid for by the polis. This setting gave the image of Athens projected in the *epitaphioi logoi* significance and authority. In her book *The Invention of Athens*, Nicole Loraux points out the relevance of the funeral speeches for the political identity of Athenians. While the values praised by the orators defined what it meant to be an Athenian, the standardized account of the past presented the semi-official version of Athens' history.

---

[42] But see also 56: The Athenians 'did not weaken their allies, but made them strong too and presented their own power as such that the Great King no more longed for the goods of others, but yielded some of his own and feared for what remained'.

The public setting distinguishes the funeral speech from epinician and elegiac poetry, which circulated, after and besides public performances, primarily in symposia, but renders it comparable to tragedy and its performance at the Great Dionysia. I suggest that the parallel with tragedy goes further and also extends to the interaction between context of performance and idea of history. In my discussion of tragedy, I argued that the public context reinforced the distancing of contingency of chance at the level of content and a similar argument can be made for the funeral speech. There were only few years in which Athens would have no casualties to mourn. Therefore, the public funerals and speeches tended to be an annual ritual. Year after year, the same events, for example the help for the Heraclidae and Marathon, and the same rhetorical topoi such as '*verbis facta exaequare*' ('to equal deeds in words') would be presented to a large gathering of citizens. The regularity and tradition established thereby tied in well with the presentation of Athens' history as a continuum and helped to counterbalance the individual experience of loss.

The pervasiveness of the notion of continuity is highlighted by Thucydides' assumption that public burials for the war dead were of ancient origin, although the ceremony at the Kerameikos was probably not institutionalized until after the Persian Wars.[43] While in tragedy the ritual setting further distances contingency of chance presented on the stage, the ritualistic character of the funeral speeches supports the explicit portrayal of the polis as the instance which overcomes contingency of chance. In other words, the ritual of the funeral enacts the continuity and regularity in which the speeches cast Athens' history.[44]

5.4. CONCLUSION

The chain of orators who were entrusted with the task of lauding the war dead in Athens made the funeral speeches a genre with a more or less fixed form that repeated the same topoi over and over. The core of the *epitaphioi logoi* is a survey of Athens' history from its beginnings to the battles that had just taken place. The *praeteritio* with which the Thucydidean Pericles,

---

[43] On the origin of the public burial with the *epitaphioi logoi*, see Jacoby 1944; Loraux 1986a: 28–42. On the Kerameikos as burial place, see Clairmont 1983. Recently, Patterson 2006 has argued that the Kerameikos was not so much a cemetery as 'a multi-use area, notable especially for the prevalence of tombs (Athenian and non-Athenian) and pottery workshops (as well as prostitutes and public gatherings)' (56).

[44] An interesting suggestion is made by Carter 1991: 223, who argues that the funeral oration itself is removed from ordinary time as a ritual.

Aspasia in the report of the Platonic Socrates and Hyperides gloss over the mythical deeds does not challenge the notion of standard topoi, but forcefully illustrates it in presupposing the familiarity of the catalogue of deeds from the long tradition of funeral speeches.[45]

In addition to the ritualization of the ceremony, the standardization of the account of the past makes the form correspond to the content for, as we have seen, Lysias envisages Athenian history as a long continuum that relies on the re-enactment of great deeds by each generation. The same view can be found in other funeral speeches, for example when the fictive Aspasia asserts that 'virtuous they were because they were sprung from men of virtue' (*Menex.* 237a7). When she praises, at the end of the historical account, the deeds 'of the men, who lie here' ('τῶν ἀνδρῶν τῶν ἐνθάδε κειμένων', 246a5), the indiscriminate reference to all the generations which fought and died for the polis merges the single stages of Athenian history in a continuum, just as in Lysias. Demosthenes explicitly points out that his praise aims at reflecting the continuum of great deeds (60.12):

But I choose, after recalling their noble birth and the magnificent deeds done by their ancestors, to link as closely as possible my speech with the deeds of these [i.e. the men just buried], to the end that, just as they were akin by nature, so I may make the words of praise spoken over them apply to both alike. I assume that this would be gratifying to those and, best of all, to both, if they should come to share one another's virtue not only by nature but also through our words of praise.

We can therefore say that the continuity of the genre of the *epitaphioi logoi* corresponds to the ritualized setting and mirrors the continuum which the orators envisage Athenian history to be. In abstract terms, the form of the speeches establishes the tradition that they set out on the level of the content. The continuum of the genre and ritual as well as of Athenian history helps to discharge the experience of contingency of chance that funeral speeches have to address.

Besides reflections on their own generic tradition, for instance in Demosthenes' announcement that he shall 'treat the theme in the same vein as those who have previously spoken here' (60.1), we also find references to other media of praise. Demosthenes caps his discourse on the mythical past by stating that he is now turning to 'deeds, which, though in point of merit no whit inferior to the former, still, through being closer in point of time, have not yet been mythicised (μεμυθολόγηται) or even

---

[45] Nilsson 1951: 86 on the *praeteritio* in Demosthenes: 'The recounting of these topics is monotonous and so it seemed probably to the ancients themselves who heard them repeatedly. Therefore they are passed over with a brief mention, they could not be absent.' See also Wilke 1996: 241–2.

been lifted to heroic rank (εἰς τὴν ἡρωϊκὴν ἐπανῆκται τάξιν)' (60.9). Demosthenes goes on to suggest that the achievements of the men just buried even surpass the campaign against Troy (60.10–11).

This comparison, which we also find in Hyperides (6.35) and which may have also figured in Pericles' speech on the fallen in the Samian War,[46] may remind the reader of Mimnermus' presentation of a contemporary Smyrnean hero as a stronger Diomedes (fr. 14 W²).[47] Demosthenes only demarcates his speech from poetry as a medium that also lauds recent deeds, but perhaps the superiority of his subject also reflects on himself. Even in this case though, the claim would be far from the polemical assertion which Thucydides has Pericles make in his funeral speech: 'We are not in need of Homer for praise nor of any other who will charm with his verses for the moment, but whose claims the factual truth will destroy.' (2.41.4). Nonetheless, we may note not only that poetic genres competed with one another, but that oratory formed also part of the agonistic field of memory.

A striking parallel between Lysias' *epitaphios logos* and various poetic genres is the claim to immortalize the war dead through glory. Hyperides' statement that 'if they did not share in mortal old age (γήρως θνητοῦ), but attained un-aging glory (εὐδοξίαν ἀγήρατον), they have been entirely fortunate' (6.42) strongly evokes the epic notion of glory, particularly Achilles' choice between a long unglorious life and a *mors immatura* with unfading fame (*Il.* 9.411–16).[48] Pericles, in the Samian funeral speech, seems to have pushed this even further in claiming that 'the men who died in Samos have become immortal just like the gods. For we do not see those themselves, but only from the honours they have and the good things they grant do we conclude that the immortals exist. The same applies to the men who have died for their fatherland.' (Stesimbrotus FGrH 107 F 9 *apud* Plut. *Per.* 8).

I have argued that the immortalization in Lysias' speech goes beyond the poetic topos, as it relies not so much on the eternity of the praise as on the eternal excellence of Athens to which the speech makes a contribution in

---

[46] In Plutarch's *Life of Pericles*, we find the following quote from Ion, 'that Pericles, after he had defeated the Samians, had strange and presumptuous thoughts, for while Agamemnon captured a barbarian city in ten years, he captured in nine months the first and mightiest of the Ionians'. (Plut. *Per.* 28). For the view that this is a quotation from Pericles' Samian funeral speech, see e.g. Weber 1922: 382–3 and Jacoby 1944: 14–15. For further parallels, see Nouhaud 1982: 15–16.

[47] See Chapter 3, section 3.3.

[48] For another strongly antithetical play with death and immortality, see the end of Gorgias fr. 6 DK: 'While they have died, the desire for them has not died with them, but is immortal and lives in the not immortal bodies of those who do not live.' ('τοιγαροῦν αὐτῶν ἀποθανόντων ὁ πόθος οὐ συναπέθανεν, ἀλλ' ἀθάνατος οὐκ ἐν ἀθανάτοις σώμασι ζῇ οὐ ζώντων').

offering the audience a model to be imitated. In Hyperides, the model character of the dead is put forward in the form of an indirect question that considers the reaction of the young and children to the sacrifice of the war dead: 'Will they not admire their death and themselves hurry to imitate as a model their life, in the place of which they have left behind virtue?' (6.32). The *Menexenus* directly addresses its own exhortatory function: 'We need a speech which will adequately praise the dead and give kindly exhortation to the living, appealing to their children and their brothers to imitate the virtues of these heroes.' (236e3–7). This makes the *epitaphioi logoi* a speech-act; in preparing the ground for the re-enactment of the great deeds of the past in times to come, the speeches actively contribute to the continuum as which they present Athenian history.

All in all, we may note that the funeral speeches share with the commemorative genres of poetry the basic tension between contingency of chance on the one hand and the traditional and exemplary modes of memory on the other, but at the same time balance it in their own distinctive way. The comparison with tragedy is particularly instructive for both genres are embedded in public settings. Whereas tragedy consequently locates the destructive force of chance at the safe remove of the 'other', the *epitaphioi logoi* set out to cope with contingency of chance affecting Athens. However, the individual experience of death and loss is balanced by an account of polis history that emphasizes continuity and regularity. The compensation of individual experiences at the level of the polis is clearly expressed in the *Menexenus*: 'She [i.e. the polis] stands towards the fallen in the position of heir and son, towards the sons in that of father, and towards the parents in that of guardian, thus exercising towards all all manner of care throughout all time.' (249b8–c4).

In presenting Athens' past as an untainted positive model, the funeral speeches are far more one-dimensional and affirmative than tragedy whose 'heroic vagueness' and polyphonous form allow the creation of ambiguities as well as the tackling of controversial issues.[49] However, the ritualistic context of both genres buttresses the construction of continuity and regularity and celebrates Athens as the place where contingency of chance is kept at bay. In the next chapter, Andocides' *de pace* will illustrate a very different view of Athens' history.

[49] Cf. Grethlein 2003a: 433–40.

CHAPTER 6

Deliberative oratory: Andocides, de pace

In the preceding chapters, it has proved fruitful first to examine the content and idea of history and then to relate the findings to the context of the performance. For elegy and epinician poetry, we found an interesting tension between the focus on the polis and the rather aristocratic institution of the symposium. In the case of tragedy and the *epitaphios logos*, the ritualist context of the performances further distances contingency of chance from Athens. However, it would be very difficult to adhere to this order of investigation – first explore the content and idea of history, then take into account the performative context – in an examination of deliberative oratory. This difficulty reveals one of the genre's crucial aspects: in deliberative speeches, the past is invoked to buttress a specific argument in a particular situation and therefore it would be impossible to discuss their idea of history without taking into account the context. Of course, we have seen that the past in elegy, epinician poetry, tragedy and the funeral speeches is not dealt with for its own sake, but that present concerns shape its presentation and that in many cases it is the major goal of the historical narrative to shed light on the present. However, in deliberative speeches the grip of the present is even stronger – here, the past is not the main focus and is not unfolded in a continuous narrative, but references to select events help the orator to argue specific points in the present.

We find the first instances of deliberative speeches in Homer when the heroes are discussing what to do. For example, in *Iliad* 2 the Greeks gather for a consultation and Thersites, who argues for a return to Greece, is overpowered both verbally and physically by Odysseus, who, in Helen's words, knows 'every manner of shiftiness and crafty counsels' (3.202). The institutionalization of assemblies in the Archaic Age led to the cultivation of deliberative oratory and the central place of public speeches in the Athenian democracy made oratorical skills an essential asset for every politician. The assembly as the main place for deliberative speeches adds yet another public setting for memory to this investigation, albeit a setting that, unlike festivals and the state funerals in the Kerameikos, was part of the everyday life of the polis.

Despite their central place in Athens's politics, we have far fewer deliberative than judicial speeches[1] – in the assembly orators had to speak freely and could not rely on the manuscript written by a *logographos*. With the exception of the fragmentary Lysias 34, the only samples of deliberative oratory that we have from the fifth century BCE are speeches in Herodotus and Thucydides.[2] However, classical scholars now agree more or less unanimously that the speeches in the historians are not faithful reproductions of speeches actually delivered.[3] It is more appropriate to read the speeches as artful compositions of the historians and to explore their functions within the historical narratives. In my chapters on Herodotus and Thucydides, I shall even argue that some speeches serve a metahistorical function.

Nonetheless, for the sake of credibility, the content of embedded speeches in historical works cannot have essentially deviated from the rhetorical practice of their day. Like fourth-century speeches, they feature frequent references to the past. For example at the beginning of *Histories* Book 7, Xerxes invokes a council to discuss whether or not to attack Greece. While Mardonius enthusiastically supports plans for an invasion, Artabanus voices his qualms and recommends caution (7.9–10).[4] Both spend much time buttressing their positions with historical arguments. Or, to give a Greek example to which I will return in Chapter 8, section 8.2.2, Thucydides adds to his account of the fall of Plataea a speech duel between the Plataeans, who plead for mercy, and the Thebans, who insist on their annihilation (3.52–68). As we will see, the past is crucial for the arguments of the Thebans as well as for those of the Plataeans. This prominence of the past in deliberative oratory is not surprising given the authority of the past that we have seen in different genres so far. A past that is greater than the present lends itself to conclusions *a maiore ad minus* and offers a rich archive of exempla.

In deliberative speeches, we encounter a specific form of the exemplary mode of memory. As defined in the introduction, the exemplary mode of memory presupposes regularity and directly juxtaposes different events with one another. Mimnermus, for example, pits a Smyrnean warrior

---

[1] For a recent survey of our corpus of deliberative speeches, see Usher 2007.
[2] On speeches in Old Comedy as evidence for the relevance of the past in fifth-century oratory, cf. Burckhardt 1924; Nouhaud 1982: 37–40.
[3] See e.g. Marincola 2007: 120–7. For a recent examination of speeches in Herodotus and Thucydides, see Scardino 2007.
[4] For a fresh reading of this passage, see Grethlein 2009b.

against the foil of Diomedes and Simonides compares the Greek soldiers at Plataea with the Greek heroes besieging Troy (Chapter 3). While in these cases the exemplary use of the past is descriptive – the foil of one event helps to illuminate another – in others exempla are normative. In the preceding chapter, we have seen that Lysias' *epitaphios logos* presents the deeds of their ancestors as a paradigm to be followed by the young in his audience (Chapter 5). Here, a parallel from the past, instead of shedding light on another past event, offers a model for how to act in the present and the future. The construction of regularity not only prepares the ground for contingency of action in general, but suggests a particular action. This normative use of exempla is particularly prominent in deliberative oratory, which is involved in the making of decisions.

For my analysis, I have chosen the earliest fully preserved deliberative speech, Andocides' *de pace*, a plea before the assembly to accept the terms for peace that Andocides and his fellow ambassadors have negotiated at a peace conference at Sparta. Other sources inform us that, contrary to this, the assembly penalized the embassy – without awaiting judgement, they went into exile.[5] The internal chronology of *de pace* seems to support 392/391 BCE as the date for these events, but 393/392 BCE and 387/386 BCE have also been suggested.[6]

Besides the date, there is another uncertainty: most scholars simply assume that we have the speech that Andocides delivered in the assembly. Yet, the relation of our text to the speech actually delivered by Andocides is far from clear.[7] Was it published by Andocides himself and if so, how could he do so, since he went into exile? Or was the speech never delivered like this, but published by the exiled Andocides as an *apologia*? Or, to entertain yet another possibility, was it published by somebody else on the basis of notes taken during the delivery? These questions are interesting and ought not to be ignored,[8] and yet, the focus on the idea of history allows us to leave them aside. Unless we assume that *de pace* is a later forgery,[9] the exact date

---

[5] Cf. Philochorus FGrH 328 F 149a; Demosthenes 19.276–80; Ps.–Plut. *Moralia* 835a; Photius 261b. It seems safe that Andocides *de pace* and the Philochorus fragment deal with the same embassy, cf. Pownall 1995: 142.

[6] For 392/391 BCE, which goes back to Didymus (FGrH 328 F 149a), see Accame 1951: 112; Strauss 1987: 138 with n. 67; Pownall 1995: 140–4; Edwards 1995: 106–7; for 394/393 BCE, see Momigliano 1936; Albini 1964: 49; and for 387/386 BCE, see Bruce 1966.

[7] Dover 1968: 188 raises the same question for Lys. 1. On the publication of speeches, see Hansen 1984; Worthington 1991; 1994. See also, for Roman oratory, Morstein-Marx 2004: 25–30.

[8] For further questions along these lines, see Todd 1993: 21.

[9] Recently, Harris 2000 has argued that *de pace* is not authentic. His major point besides the historical blunders is the comparison with Aeschines' *de falsa legatione*. While most scholars have argued that the very similar account of fifth-century history is due to Aeschines' copying Andocides, Harris points out

and the circumstances of its publication can be neglected in an examination of how the past is used in it.

After reading *de pace* as an illustration of the mode of memory in deliberative oratory (6.1), I will allow myself to discuss features that are not characteristic of the genre as such, but enable us to see a point that is as hard to grasp as it is crucial to an investigation of memory in classical Greece. *De pace* gives us the rare opportunity to catch a glimpse of a view of the Athenian past that is very different from the semi-official version of the *epitaphioi logoi*. Reading *de pace* against the background of Lysias' funeral speech alerts us to the fact that Athenian memory was far more polyphonic than many studies including Loraux's *Invention of Athens* make it seem. I will therefore point out crucial differences from Lysias' funeral speech (6.2) and discuss to what extent Andocides' speech represents an oligarchic view of history (6.3). In a concluding section, I will broaden the scope of this chapter by taking into account the evidence of other deliberative orations as well as judicial speeches (6.4).

6.1. THE CONTENT AND THE IDEA OF HISTORY

Andocides not only draws heavily on exempla to reinforce his plea that the Athenians accept the peace offered by Sparta, but he also reflects on exempla in abstract terms. Right at the beginning, he states:[10] 'For it is necessary, Athenians, to use past events (τοῖς πρότερον γενομένοις) as indications of the future (τῶν μελλόντων).' (2). Similar remarks can be found later in the speech: 'For it is necessary to recall the past (τὰ γεγενημένα) to find good counsel.' (29) and: 'For the examples from the past (τὰ ... παραδείγματα τὰ γεγενημένα) of our mistakes are sufficient to deter sensible men from making any more mistakes.' (32). Besides highlighting the prominence of the exemplary mode of memory in deliberative rhetoric, Andocides' reflections alert us to a crucial difference from the funeral speeches that feature similar reflections. While there the past is envisaged only as an archive of positive paradigms, Andocides considers the logic of exempla in more general terms: that it is possible and reasonable to make all kinds of inferences from the past about the future. Accordingly, Andocides also picks negative paradigms from the past and employs exempla for critical purposes.

that there are more historical errors in *de pace*. Thus, *de pace* must be a copy of *de falsa legatione*. However, the number of historical errors seems a weak argument for an intertextual dependency as a copy can both increase and reduce the number of errors, cf. Nouhaud 1982: 231 n. 344.
[10] For parallels in other orators, see Albini 1964: ad 2.

De pace uses two larger sets of exempla, each consisting of three cases, and one rather perfunctory reference to the past at the end. In the first part of his speech, Andocides argues that peace with Sparta would pose no danger for the Athenian democracy (1–12). For this, he adduces three exempla: the peace after the war in Euboea (446 BCE), the peace after the war because of the Aeginetans (457/456 BCE), and the Nicias peace (421 BCE). In none of these cases, Andocides argues, was the Athenian democracy challenged, but, on the contrary, the times of peace made possible the accumulation of riches and the building of new ships and walls. Thus, peace has proved most conducive to the Athenian Empire. The installation of the regime of the Thirty in 404 BCE, Andocides carries on to argue, does not disprove his point, since it was the result not of a peace treaty but of a truce that victorious Sparta could impose on Athens (10–12).

After Andocides has drawn on the past to make the general point that peace is beneficial for Athens, he turns to the present situation (13–27): there is not only no necessity to continue the war (13–16), but peace would be good for all major Greek states, Sparta, Boeotia and particularly Athens (17–23), which should make use of the extremely favourable conditions offered by the Spartans despite their military superiority. A continued alliance with Corinth and Argos, on the other hand, would prove detrimental to Athens (24–7).

A second set of historical exempla (28–32) illustrates Andocides' anxiety that Athens will choose weak allies over strong ones and fight the strong on behalf of its friends. He gives three examples for this mistake: the peace of Epilycus with the Persian king which was abandoned due to intrigues set up by Amorges; the choice of the Syracusans instead of the Egestans as allies;[11] and the decision to dissolve the peace with the Spartans in favour of an alliance with the Argives in 414 BCE. In all three instances, the rejection of the strong partners led to disasters.

In the third part of his speech, Andocides justifies the ambassadors' referral of the decision to the assembly and renews his appeal to accept the peace (33–41). He first objects to those who argue that, instead of turning to the assembly, the embassy should have acted right on the spot (33–4). This argument is balanced by the rejection of the opposite view that walls and ships are not sufficient and that therefore a continuation of the war is necessary (35–6). Andocides then mentions the emergence of the Athenian Empire in a rather general way to underscore his plea to vote for

---

[11] On the difficulties of dating these events, see Edwards 1995: 198–9.

Deliberative oratory: Andocides, de pace

the peace offer: since it was walls and ships on which Athens' rise to power was founded, the treaty offered by Sparta provides them with all they need.

As this reading shows, historical arguments from the past form the backbone of Andocides' argument. While the funeral speeches linger solely on positive exempla, Andocides gives both positive and negative exempla, all from the recent past of Athens. In his first set, Andocides presents the positive exempla that underscore his suggestions, the second set provides negative exempla that show the scenario to come should his advice not be heeded, and, at the end, we find a general positive exemplum that uses Athens' success in the past as a model for Athens in the present.

In two cases, the exempla carry special significance and lend additional authority to Andocides. The second exemplum in the first set is the peace that was made with Sparta after the war because of the Aeginetans (6). Andocides mentions that his grandfather of the same name was among the ten *presbeis autokratores*. In the second set of exempla, Andocides refers to the peace with the Great King that was abandoned owing to the intrigues of Amorges (29). Again, Andocides makes the point that this peace had been negotiated by a relative of his, this time his uncle.[12]

Such references to ancestors by aristocrats in public speeches were not unproblematic. As Josiah Ober notes, 'several passages in Athenian speeches suggest that the demos distrusted and even actively disliked aristocratic pretension'.[13] I doubt though that Andocides' references to his grandfather and uncle would have aroused negative emotions in his audience, since he mentions his ancestors for their services to the polis.[14] The point that interests me more is that Andocides inserts himself into a family tradition of political conduct and thereby combines the traditional and exemplary modes of memory. Since both grandfather and uncle served as ambassadors, they are models for Andocides. In his attempt to persuade the assembly to make peace, he follows the exemplum of his ancestors who had successfully negotiated peace treaties. While the peace negotiated by his grandfather illustrates the advantages that can be expected from the peace that he is advocating, the rejection of his uncle's peace treaty exemplifies the dangers of deciding against his proposal. The exempla gain relevance as part of his family tradition and, conversely, the tradition of his family becomes significant through the exempla.

---

[12] There is epigraphic evidence for this embassy: Meiggs and Lewis 1969: 201–3 (nr. 70); cf. Meiggs 1972: 134–5.
[13] Ober 1989: 255.   [14] On this strategy, cf. Ober 1989: 265–6.

Seen from this perspective, there is a double use of exempla: on the one hand, previous peace treaties and the choice of wrong allies serve as positive or negative models for the present situation. On the other, Andocides' ancestors stand as exempla for his own plea for peace. Andocides not only uses exempla to drive home his point about the positive impact of peace and the importance of joining the right allies, but he also employs models from his own family tradition to enhance his authority as speaker.

Scholars have not failed to note the many historical blunders in *de pace*.[15] For example in 3, Andocides mentions that Miltiades was recalled to Athens from exile in 452 BCE so that he could negotiate a truce with Sparta. However, it was Cimon who had been ostracized after the Athenian expedition to Mt. Ithome in 461 BCE. The fifty-year peace which he gains from the Spartans must be the five years' truce mentioned by Thucydides (Thuc. 1.112.1). The elements of the war in Euboea and the war because of Aegina are so mixed up that it is difficult to relate them to what we find in Thucydides.[16] There are also mistakes in the account of the more recent events: for example, according to *de pace* 29 the Athenians' support for Amorges prompted the Great King to provide the Spartans with 5,000 talents, which helped the Spartans to defeat the Athenians. However, if we follow Thucydides, Athens supported Amorges only *after* the Persian aid for Sparta.[17]

Some of the mistakes may be due to a lack of reliable sources. The mixing up of Miltiades and Cimon, which we also find in Demosthenes, seems to be such an error.[18] On the other hand, some references appear to have been distorted for the sake of the argument. In the second case that I have just mentioned, the support for Amorges, the temporal order seems to be inverted to establish a causal link between the choice of the wrong allies and defeat. In exempla, the past not only is invoked to buttress assertions, but the orators were willing to bend the historical truth for their argumentative needs.[19] Of course, the distortions could not conflict with the audience's knowledge, as this would have seriously undermined the argument.[20] And yet, as *de pace* indicates, the orator had some freedom to change the chronology, to establish causal relationships and even to make

---

[15] See, for example, Nouhaud 1982: 230–4. For further literature, see the list in Missiou 1992: 59 n. 6.
[16] Cf. Thomas 1989: 121.   [17] Cf. Westlake 1977.
[18] Cf. Dem. 23.205. On the disappearance of Cimon in oral tradition, see Thomas 1989: 203.
[19] See, for example, Perlman 1961; Missiou 1992: 59–60 with further literature in n. 6.
[20] Pearson 1941 elaborates on the knowledge that the orators presupposed in their audience. Worthington 1994: 117–18 suggests that some historical blunders were introduced only in the revised versions of the speeches for publication.

up events.[21] This freedom, combined with the general authority of the past, made the exemplary use of the past a powerful tool in political oratory just as the flexibility of myth allowed tragedians to render their subjects significant for their audiences.

6.2. ANDOCIDES, *DE PACE* VS. LYSIAS, *EPITAPHIOS LOGOS*

It is not unproblematic to compare the account of the past in Andocides' *de pace* with Lysias' *epitaphios logos*. While the former uses select exempla from the past to buttress specific points in the present, the latter presents a chronological account of Athens' history. And yet, despite the different forms, striking discrepancies concerning the view of Athens' past can be noted: Andocides mentions individuals, he does not gloss over defeat, he argues that Athens owes its prosperity to peace and he even casts its history in a tragic frame.

To start with, the funeral speeches generally avoid naming individuals. In Lysias' funeral speech, only Themistocles and Myronides are mentioned. The same tendency can be found in Aeschylus' *Persae*, which deals with Salamis, but does not even mention Themistocles.[22] Cimon was allowed to put up herms for his victory at Eion, and yet he could not put his name in the inscriptions. Democratic forms of memory foregrounded the achievements of the polis and, by and large, ignored individual merits. Andocides, on the other hand, does not shy away from referring to individuals; he even mentions, as we have seen, his ancestors, risking estranging his audience.[23]

The funeral speeches focus on military victories and give little consideration to defeat. If failures are referred to at all, they are twisted so that they prove Athenian superiority. Andocides, on the other hand, names quite a few debacles of Athens, not sparing its humiliation in the Peloponnesian War. Moreover, contrary to the image of a flourishing Athens in the funeral orations, he concedes that Athens would not have the power to face Sparta at the moment (15–16).

Andocides' view of the past deviates from the funeral speeches' portrayal not only with regard to defeat, but also Athens' great achievements. In a passage representative of the tenor of funeral speeches in general, Lysias states: 'By means of countless toils, conspicuous struggles and glorious perils

---

[21] For example, the Syracusan embassy in 30 seems to be made up, cf. Albini 1964 and Edwards 1995: ad loc.
[22] Cf. above p. 75.
[23] Missiou 1992: 78–82 goes even further, pointing out that 'Andokides ... in this speech refers to practically everybody by name *except* Perikles and ... Themistokles'.

they made Greece free, while displaying the outstanding greatness of their fatherland ...' (55). Andocides, on the other hand, argues that Athens owed its prosperity to times of peace. In contrast to the semi-official version of the funeral speeches, not war, but peace figures as the cause of Athens' success in the fifth century BCE.

Andocides even casts Athens in a tragic frame. This contradicts the ideal image of Athens in the funeral speeches and also goes against the conventions of tragedy in which Athens tends to be untragic. *De pace* applies to Athens the very frame that, as I have argued in Chapter 4, section 4.5, tragedy distances from it at the levels of content and context: 'For this peace raised the Athenian people so high (ὑψηλὸν ἦρε) and rendered them so strong ...' (7). The phrase ὑψηλὸν αἴρειν is used several times in tragedy[24] and also implies a concept that is at the core of many tragedies: whoever rises too high, is bound to fall. This is spelt out in Eur. TrGF 1113a (= 1040N²), where we find the synonymous πρὸς ὕψος αἴρειν:

> If you see somebody raised high
> through splendid wealth, priding himself on noble descent
> and lifting his eyebrows above fortune,
> expect straightaway fast retribution in his case.
> ὅταν ἴδῃς πρὸς ὕψος ἠρμένον τινά
> λαμπρῷ τε πλούτῳ καὶ γένει γαυρούμενον
> ὀφρύν τε μείζω τῆς τύχης ἐπηρκότα,
> τούτου ταχεῖαν νέμεσιν εὐθὺς προσδόκα.

Cast in this mould, Athens' rise already implies its fall. And indeed, the rise and prosperity in peace is followed by defeat in the Peloponnesian War. As Andocides writes, 'the land was wasted and they were deprived of many goods' (8).

In another passage, Andocides uses an epic intertext to give his presentation of Athens' history a sinister ring. When he adduces the last of three exempla for Athens' tendency to reject strong allies in favour of the weak, he writes: 'Afterwards, we were persuaded by the same Argives, who are here today to persuade us to make war, to sail against Laconia, while we were at peace with the Spartans, and excite their anger, the beginning of many evils (ἀρχὴν πολλῶν κακῶν).' (31). ἀρχὴ πολλῶν κακῶν has an epic ring, as similar phrases occur in two crucial passages in the *Iliad*. In 5.62–3, the narrator says about Phereclus: 'He it was who had built for Alexander the balanced ships,/ the beginning of the evil, fatal to all Trojans.' ('ὃς καὶ Ἀλεξάνδρῳ τεκτήνατο νῆας ἐΐσας/ ἀρχεκάκους, αἳ πᾶσι κακὸν

---

[24] See e.g. Eur. *Supp.* 554–5; *Heracl.* 321–2; *Phoen.* 404.

Τρώεσσι γένοντο'). When Achilles sends Patroclus to Nestor in *Iliad* 11, the narrator foreshadows the disaster to come: '... and he heard it from inside the shelter,/ and came out like the war god, and this was the beginning of his evil'. ('... ὃ δὲ κλισίηθεν ἀκούσας/ ἔκμολεν ἶσος Ἄρηϊ· κακοῦ δ' ἄρα οἱ πέλεν ἀρχή', 11.603–4).

Whereas in my samples from epinician and elegiac poetry epic intertexts serve to glorify recent events, the epic reverberation in *de pace* evokes the great suffering in the *Iliad* and thus underscores the bitter consequences of the wrong choice of allies. As we have seen in Chapter 4, section 4.5, tragedy can also evoke the heroic past to throw into relief pitfalls of the present, which, however, are illustrated at a safe distance from Athens. In the second part of this study, I shall argue that the use of the heroic past for critical purposes figures prominently in the first historians. The similarity between their practice and what we find in Andocides is underscored by the fact that both Herodotus and Thucydides employ the same epic echo as the orator to mark crucial points, more precisely, steps to be regretted, in their narratives.[25]

As we see, Andocides uses the registers of tragic and epic poetry to call attention to the consequences of mistakes in Athenian politics. The poetic echoes highlight his critical view of Athens' history, which significantly diverges from the account in the funeral speeches. The image of an uninterrupted series of great successes is replaced by a history full of changes, a ride with ups and downs. The contrast nicely illustrates that the past was not only used in different ways, but that accounts could openly contradict one another. Memory in classical Greece was more polyphonous and at times even more cacophonous than accounts that focus on the *epitaphioi logoi* and rely on concepts such as ideology argue for.

That being said, it is also important to notice that, while the views of Athens' past are divergent, Andocides uses the same modes of memory that we find in other genres, notably the exemplary and traditional modes. He thus shares the same idea of history, and yet applies it in a very different way. There are not only positive, but also negative exempla that, instead of glorifying the present, rather alert the assembly to possible mistakes. The frame of the tragic hero is not distanced from Athens, but applied to its own history.

---

[25] When the Athenians decide to send a fleet in support of the Ionians, Herodotus anticipates the impending disaster: 'These ships became the beginning of evils (ἀρχὴ κακῶν) for both Greeks and barbarians.' (5.97.3). In Thucydides, the Spartan Melesippus, who has been sent as herald to Athens to explore the possibility of a peaceful reconciliation, but returns without being admitted to the city, says (2.12.3): 'This day will be the beginning of great evils (μεγάλων κακῶν ἄρξει) for the Greeks.'

6.3. AN OLIGARCHIC VIEW OF THE PAST?

Elegy, tragedy and the funeral orations present a past that is firmly in the grip of the polis. Epinician poetry stems from the aristocratic world of athletic competitions, and yet the praise of the individual is carefully aligned with the claims of the polis. Now, in Andocides' *de pace*, we have seen a view of the past that goes against creeds crucial to the semi-official memory of the funeral speeches. Can we attribute the view of *de pace* to a subversive political stance? In a stimulating monograph, Anna Missiou links Andocides' plea for peace to his aristocratic background,[26] explains his opposition to war as an oligarchic stance and argues that his speech was not so much an attempt to persuade the audience as to subvert democracy.

Thought-provoking as Missiou's book is, some of its premises are open to challenges. The economic determinism – Andocides was an oligarch and thus against the war – and the assumption of clearly defined political parties – oligarchs versus democrats – do not do full justice to the complexities of Athenian politics.[27] Moreover, it is hard to believe that Andocides did not aim at persuading the assembly with his speech.[28] That being said, Missiou is right that Andocides' position does not tie in with the democratic mainstream, but has rather oligarchic leanings.[29] Andocides' very starting point that peace does not foster the abandonment of democracy reveals that advocates of peace were at least denounced as oligarchs. As the condemnation of the ambassadors shows, the political climate was in favour of war.[30] At the same time, the fact that Epicrates was a member of Andocides' embassy indicates that there were also democrats favouring peace.[31]

There were, however, specific reasons for oligarchs to oppose the war. The war particularly affected rich Athenians, who had to shoulder liturgies.[32] Of course, not all rich Athenians were oligarchs nor were all oligarchs so rich that they had to pay liturgies, yet it would be difficult to deny a certain connection between wealth and oligarchic leanings. Moreover, their philolaconism inclined oligarchs to favour peace with Sparta. The pro-Spartan slant of *de pace* strongly supports its interpretation as oligarchic:[33]

---

[26] Missiou 1992. On Andocides' *persona*, see Furley 1996: 49–69.
[27] Cf. Ober 1989: 279. [28] Cf. Furley 1996: 61 n. 47.
[29] Cf. Albini 1964: 21–2. Furley 1996: 59–61 is convinced that Andocides was an oligarch in 415 BCE and 411 BCE, but doubts if this holds true for 391 BCE. Thomas 1989: 119 n. 77 and Harris 1998 also question the oligarchic leanings in *de pace*.
[30] Cf. Seager 1967: 104–8.
[31] Strauss 1987: 140 argues for a coalition of 'oligarchs, stingy liturgists and the war weary' and sees Epicrates' support for peace as a 'pragmatic' position.
[32] See Strauss 1987: 140. [33] Cf. Jacoby, FGrH III B Suppl. II, p. 413; Strauss 1987: 139.

according to Andocides, it was Sparta that saved Athens from total destruction in 404 BCE (21–2),[34] and now, despite three victories, the Spartan terms for peace are extremely generous. When Andocides raises the rhetorical question of what kind of peace the Athenians would have offered the Spartans after only a single victory, the Spartans appear to be not only militarily but also morally superior to the Athenians (18–19).

However, two things are important to note. First, Andocides distances himself from the oligarchs. In 33, he mentions that some advocates of peace recommend not referring the question back to the assembly, because the *demos* needs to be deceived for its own sake. The contempt for the *demos* and the conviction that the assembly is not capable of making the right decisions are oligarchic convictions. Andocides, however, argues against this that in times of peace politics should be transparent. By objecting both to oligarchs in favour of secret agreements and to radical democratic warmongers, Andocides tries to stylize his own position as the 'golden mean'. Of course, this may be not much more than a rhetorical strategy by Andocides, an attempt to endear himself to the assembly, but, nonetheless, it challenges Missiou's thesis that Andocides did not really try to persuade his audience.

Second, Andocides does not, as Missiou claims, argue against the Athenian Empire.[35] On the contrary, his argument implies a positive view of the empire: ships, walls and riches, which Andocides adduces as precious fruits of peace in his account of the Pentecontaetia, are closely linked with the idea of an empire. In the end, when Andocides evokes Athens' rise in the fifth century as a model for the present, he explicitly mentions and plays with the very word ἀρχή. The intertwining of the meanings 'foundation (for successes)' and 'empire' reveals a positive notion of empire: 'There was once a time, Athenians, when we did not possess walls and ships; but when we had these, we laid the foundation for our successes (γενομένων δὲ τούτων τὴν ἀρχὴν ἐποιησάμεθα τῶν ἀγαθῶν)' (37). The governing verb ποιεῖσθαι and the objective genitive τῶν ἀγαθῶν leave no doubt that ἀρχή means 'foundation' and signifies the walls and ships as a starting point.[36] However, both come after ἀρχή and, when the listener first hears ἀρχή, he may be inclined to expect that it denotes 'empire', for the content

---

[34] Missiou 1992: 92–108 tries to show that this is a slanted version of what actually happened in 404 BCE.
[35] See in particular *ibid*.: 73–82. Strauss 1987: 141 rightly notices that for Andocides the empire has value.
[36] Cf. Thuc. 1.128.4: 'He first conferred the benefit from this on the king and started the whole affair (τοῦ παντὸς πράγματος ἀρχὴν ἐποιήσατο).' Isoc. 12.120: 'Therefore I have preferred to start very far back in the past (πορρωτέρωθεν ποιήσασθαι τὴν ἀρχήν).'

of the previous sentence, the acquisition of walls and ships, describes the foundation of the empire. In particular the verb κτᾶσθαι may induce the listener to expect the meaning 'empire'.

Only a few sentences later, the signifier ἀρχή has changed its signified and means 'empire': 'By using force against our enemies, we acquired sovereignty over the Greeks (τὴν ἀρχὴν τῶν Ἑλλήνων). These successes (ταῦτα τὰ ἀγαθά) were achieved (ἐγένετο) in eighty-five years.' (38). This new use of ἀρχή is strongly linked to the previous one by the following sentence, in which γίγνεσθαι and ἀγαθά are employed again in a new syntagmatic order. The repetitions establish a close link between the 'empire' and the 'foundation for successes' that, thanks to peace, walls and ships made possible.

In 40, ἀρχή recurs: 'Now, although we possess the same foundation for successes (τὴν αὐτὴν ... ἀρχὴν ἀγαθῶν) as our ancestors, some say that this peace must not be made.' Here, ἀρχή signifies 'foundation (for successes)' again. Yet, the previous use of it in the meaning 'empire' and the context, the acquisition of walls and ships, make it likely that the signified 'empire' at least rings in the background. The floating of the signifier ἀρχή along the signifieds 'foundation (for successes)' and 'empire' shows that Andocides presents the empire as something positive that would benefit from peace.

Andocides establishes further subtle links between empire and peace, for instance when he uses ποιεῖσθαι with ἀρχή and εἰρήνη as objects (41). In one passage, εἰρήνη is even the object of both verbs that rule ἀρχή as object in the meaning 'foundation' and 'empire': '... we once more made peace (τὴν εἰρήνην ἐποιησάμεθα), the one which Nicias, son of Niceratus, achieved (κατηργάσατο) for us' (8). It is only a small and very subtle point, but the use of ἀρχή and εἰρήνη with the same verbs deepens at the linguistic level the link that Andocides tries to establish between peace and empire. The phrase εἰρήνην ἄγειν ('to make peace', twice in 40) may have a similar effect. Commentators have suggested different ways of understanding the phrase.[37] What strikes me is that εἰρήνη is made the object of a verb signifying activity and action. Perhaps this helps to bridge the gap between peace, a rather passive state, and empire which is associated with bustling activity. As this subtle play with ἀρχή and εἰρήνη shows, Andocides is at pains to create a connection between peace and empire.

Nonetheless, with the two qualifications that Andocides presents himself as an advocate of the 'golden mean' and that he does not challenge the value

---

[37] See the survey in Albini 1964: ad 40, who argues for the meaning 'godere la pace, vivere in pace'.

of the empire, his argument bears if not an oligarchic, then at least an aristocratic imprint. The contrast between his arguments and the semi-official history in the funeral speeches is not so much a result of his argumentative needs in this special case as the clash of two divergent views of Athens' past. The comparison illustrates that the past is a semantically highly charged terrain for socio-political struggles.

Besides giving us a glimpse of an aristocratic view of the past, *de pace* may also illustrate aristocratic traditions of memory. While some scholars argue that Andocides relies on historical works and pamphlets, Rosalind Thomas points out that he refers to events in which members of his family were involved and makes the interesting suggestion that his version of the Pentecontaetia derived from the tradition of his family.[38] If this is the case, *de pace* would be one of the few testimonies to the oral traditions of aristocratic families in democratic Athens.

6.4. CONCLUSION

The prominence of exempla in *de pace* illustrates the important role that the exemplary mode of memory had in deliberative speeches. Similarly, though to a lesser degree, references to past deeds are found in judicial speeches, which, in the following, I will also take into account in order to give my examination a broader basis. As Isocrates, unaffected by false modesty, puts it: 'The deeds of the past are, indeed, an inheritance common to us all; but the ability to make proper use of them at the appropriate time, to conceive the right sentiments about them in each instance, and to set them forth in finished phrase, is the peculiar gift of the wise.' (4.9). Parallels from the past allowed the orators to buttress their points and to make their arguments more appealing. Thus, in deliberative and judicial oratory the past is even more in the grip of the present than in elegy or tragedy.

At the same time, formulaic phrases, including the rhetorical questions 'who has not heard' (e.g. Lycurg. 62) and 'who does not know' (e.g. Lycurg. 106) reveal that the orators were at pains to avoid the impression of erudition, which would have smacked of elitism and estranged large parts of the audience.[39] The pressure on orators to stylize themselves as common citizens led to a peculiar tension between a rhetoric of the average and a

---

[38] Cf. Thomas 1989: 119–23. Thompson 1967 argues for Hellanicus as Andocides' source. Nouhaud 1982: 124–5 thinks it probable that Andocides used oligarchic pamphlets and notes similarities to Thucydides, yet leaves it open whether the historian's account served as a source.

[39] Cf. Jost 1936: 163–7; Pearson 1941: 214–19; Ober/Strauss 1990: 253.

most sophisticated eloquence, with a well-equipped quiver, exempla being one of the arrows.[40]

While the *epitaphioi logoi* presented solely positive exempla, Andocides, in his plea for peace with Sparta, also refers to past experiences that ought not to be repeated. Negative exempla are employed in other speeches too, for example in the defence against a *dokimasia* charge written by Lysias, who backs up the importance of unity among the people by two historical references, first to the discord among the Thirty which strengthened the case of the democrats (25.21–3) and second to the detrimental consequences of the factional strife pursued by some democrats after the Four Hundred lost power (25.25–7).

This pair of negative exempla also illustrates a further distinction. While the first exemplum takes an event from the history of the opponents, the second refers to an experience which the audience has had themselves. Exempla from one's own tradition were said to have greater persuasive potential: 'For not from foreign, but from your own exempla can you learn, what you ought to do.' (Dem. 13.21).[41] In parallels from one's own history, the exemplary mode is reinforced by the traditional mode of memory. This ties in nicely with my observation about various poetic passages as well as the *epitaphioi logoi* that the notion of continuity increases the significance of exempla.

A traditional view of Athenian history can be found in many speeches. To give a random example, in defending himself against the accusation of impiety, the speaker in Lysias 30 plays his own ritual practice as embodying the tradition of the polis off against the idiosyncratic claims of his opponent (30.18):

But of course, gentlemen of the jury, we are not to be instructed in piety by Nicomachus, but are rather to be guided by the ways of the past. Now, our ancestors, by sacrificing in accordance with the tablets, have handed down to us a city superior in greatness and prosperity to any other in Greece; so that it behoves us to perform the same sacrifices as they did ...

The traditional view of the past is particularly prominent in the Isocratean speeches, albeit in a special form, as the *patrios politeia* is evoked as a contrast to the corrupted present that has lost the standards of the glorious past, but ought to revive them.[42] *De pace*, on the other hand, effectually deconstructs the traditional view of Athenian history, which is

---

[40] Cf. Ober 1989: 177–82.
[41] The problematical status of exempla from others is illustrated by the blame which Dem. 20.105–6 levels at Leptines for holding up Sparta and Thebes as examples for Athens. Cf. Perlman 1961: 157–8.
[42] See e.g. Jost 1936: 126–59; Schmitz-Kahlmann 1938.

even cast in a tragic frame. The interactions between tragedy and oratory are manifold,[43] but the application of a tragic frame to Athens is noteworthy. Robert Parker has amply demonstrated the different views of the gods in tragedy and oratory.[44] The cruelty which is ascribed to gods in a number of tragedies is, with some qualifications, absent from speeches which foreground divine benevolence towards the polis.[45] While Andocides does not blame the gods for Athens' fate, he does apply to its history a template which looms large in tragedy.

A parallel to this can be found in Demosthenes' assessment of Athens' fight with Philip in *de corona* (18.194):

If the hurricane that burst upon us has been too strong, not for us alone, but for every Hellenic state, – what then? As if a ship-owner, who had done everything in his power for a prosperous voyage, who had equipped his craft with every appliance he could think of to ensure her safety, should encounter a great storm, and then, because his tackle was overstrained or even shattered, should be accused of the crime of shipwreck! 'But,' he might say, 'I was not at the helm – nor was I in command of the army – and I could not control fortune, but fortune controls all'.

G. O. Rowe notes that Athens 'is conceived as the tragic protagonist who can regret her fate but not her actions' and adds that 'though Athens was destined to lose the war and her liberty, it remained within her power to preserve her dignity and to assert her moral choice – it is in the expression of this view that the language of Demosthenes reaches the heights of tragic poetry'.[46] While neither the emphasis on forces beyond human control nor the ship metaphor is specific to tragedy,[47] it is striking that, just as in *de pace*, Athens' history is cast in a template that is well-known from tragedy, although, in tragedy, it is located at a remote 'other'. If we stay within the genre of oratory, we can note the enormous discrepancy between this view of Athens and the image projected in the funeral speeches. On the one hand, defeat and rupture are admitted and given a poetic emplotment, on the other, great efforts are made to present the past as an undisturbed

---

[43] See Wilson 1996, who examines the use of tragedy in fourth-century oratory, in particular references to tragedy as a symbol of the great past and its use for slander. See also Ober/Strauss 1990 for a more general exploration of drama and political rhetoric in classical Athens.
[44] Parker 1997.
[45] See also Mikalson 1983: 58–60, particularly his observation that 'in this passage "the daimon", "the god", and "fortune" seem to merge into one force, and as elsewhere in Demosthenes responsibility for failure is deflected from the gods to a daimon or fortune'. (59–60).
[46] Rowe 1966: 404–5.
[47] Rutherford 1982 makes the important observation that often what is labelled as 'tragic' in Greek literature can also be found in the Homeric epics. In a similar vein, Macleod 1983a argues that tragic influences that scholars have seen in Thucydides are more likely to be debts to Homer.

continuum. Memory in classical Greece was not only far more polyphonous than is often assumed, but the comparison just made demonstrates that contradictory views of the past could be voiced even in the same genre.

De pace also reveals the socio-political relevance of memory.[48] We have already seen in the elegy chapter that sympotic poetry draws on the past to underscore partisan polemics as well as to strengthen the coherence of the polis. As Alcaeus' poems illustrate, Xenophanes' reflections on the absence of strife from sympotic poetry were more a wish than an observation (Chapter 3, section 3.4). After tragedy and funeral speeches have illustrated the major commemorative efforts of the democratic polis, *de pace* has now offered us a precious glimpse of an aristocratic view of the past. Andocides uses the same idea of history, but applies the commemorative modes in a different way and with different purposes. Democrats and aristocrats fought fiercely over the capital of the past, and yet in doing so they relied on the same idea of history.

If we turn from the idea of history to the content, it is noteworthy that all exempla discussed by Andocides are historical; there are no references to myths in his speech. This is typical of deliberative and judicial rhetoric, which, while not completely ignoring myths, prefer historical examples, nearly all of them from the fifth and fourth centuries BCE.[49] This preference is addressed in some speeches. To give an example from a speech in a historical account, Thucydides has the Athenians start their speech at a meeting in Sparta with a reflection on how to present their claims most effectively (1.73.2):

Now as for the remote past (τὰ ... πάνυ παλαιά), what need is there to speak of events for which the audience would have the evidence of hearsay accounts rather than their personal experience? As for the Persian War, however, and all events of which you have knowledge of your own, even if it is rather tiresome for us to bring them up constantly, we are forced to speak.

While the reason for the rejection of myths is reminiscent of Thucydides' own methodological reflections,[50] the explicit privileging of history over myth is amply paralleled in our corpus of fourth-century oratory. Isocrates, for example, considers possible exempla for successfully mastering difficult situations (6.42):

---

[48] For anthropological investigations of the past as a political resource, see the papers in Gathercole and Lowenthal 1990.
[49] Cf. Nouhaud 1982: 12–23. See also Clarke 2008: 252–74 for a comparison of the references to the past in Demosthenes, Aeschines and Isocrates. The frequency of references to myths in Isocrates seems to be due to the greater number of epideictic speeches in his corpus.
[50] Cf. Hornblower 1991–6: ad 1.73.2. See also Rood 1999: 145 for interesting thoughts on the passage.

Now if I were to recount the wars of old which they fought against the Amazons or the Thracians or the Peloponnesians who under the leadership of Eurystheus invaded Attica, no doubt, I should be thought to speak on matters ancient and remote from the present situation; but in their war against the Persians, who does not know from what hardships they arose to great good-fortune?

When Demosthenes searches for evidence that Athens' freedom and power depends on its navy, he gives two pairs of exempla. He first caps a reference to the Persian Wars with the comment 'Well, but that is ancient history. Take something that you have all seen' (22.14) and mentions as a more recent example the help for the Deceleans in 357 BCE. In the same vein, he then turns from the Decelean War to the last war with the Spartans in the 370s: 'And why should one discuss ancient history?' (22.15). While in the passage from Isocrates mythical events are dismissed in favour of the Persian Wars, Demosthenes rejects not only the Persian Wars, but also the Peloponnesian War and instead refers to wars from the fourth century. This indicates that the neglect of myths in oratory is due not so much to a rigid divide between myth and history as to a gradual distinction between recent and remote events.

It is worth noting though that Isocrates and Demosthenes, while dismissing ancient history, still bother to mention it. In what has been called 'kinship diplomacy', myths seem to have constituted important argumentative capital.[51] For example, Xenophon reports that the Athenian Callias invoked mythic history to support his argument for peace at a conference in Sparta in 371 BCE (*Hell.* 6.3.6):

The right course, indeed, would have been for us not to take up arms against one another in the beginning, since the tradition is that the first strangers to whom Triptolemus, our ancestor, revealed the mystic rites of Demeter and Core were Heracles, your state's founder, and the Dioscuri, your citizens; and, further, that it was upon Peloponnesus that he first bestowed the seed of Demeter's fruit.

Callias' argument has particular force for he came from the family of the Ceryces which traditionally held one of the chief offices of the Eleusinian Mysteries. Of course, we cannot say if Callias actually said what we find in *Hellenica*, but Xenophon's narrative proves at least the currency and plausibility of such arguments.

The case of 'kinship diplomacy' notwithstanding, the predominance of historical arguments in speeches makes the conclusion inevitable that, in the world of politics, exempla from recent history were felt to be more

---

[51] See Jones 1999: 27–35 on 'kinship diplomacy' in classical Greece and Clarke 2008: 347–63 for an illuminating discussion of more cases of 'kinship diplomacy', mostly from the Hellenistic Age.

persuasive than ancient parallels – they were closer and better known.[52] In poetic texts, on the other hand, the authority of myth is so strong that even more recent events are envisaged in 'heroic vagueness'. Other than the obvious case of Aeschylus' *Persae*, I have argued that in some elegies recent events were cast in an epic register to increase their authority as models for the present.[53] The same applies to the funeral speeches, which erase the distinctions between recent and mythical achievements.[54] The comparison of the various genres alerts us to the relevance of the context for memory. The remoteness of the heroic world made it well-suited to negotiate issues of identity and moral conduct in the elevated settings of the symposium and public ceremonies, but, with exceptions such as 'kinship diplomacy', it was disadvantageous for the pragmatic interactions in the everyday world of the assembly, the law-courts and diplomatic conferences.

6.5. SUMMARY OF PART I

Before I try to assess anew the rise of historiography against the background of poetry and oratory, let me review briefly my examination of the non-historiographical media of memory. I have investigated the content and idea of history of five genres, epinician poetry, elegy, tragedy, funeral speeches and deliberative oratory, relating the results to their narrative forms and socio-political contexts. Some of them, namely epinician poetry and tragedy, favour mythical topics; elegy and the *epitaphioi logoi* also take into account the recent past, which is even privileged in deliberative speeches. More interestingly, the boundaries between mythical and more recent history are far from fixed. As particularly *Persae*, but also elegies and Lysias' funeral speech show, the very recent past could be cast in a heroic register. It is not so much the temporal distance as the character of an event and its function in a specific commemorative context that shape its presentation.

The focus of memory in most genres is on the polis, which figures as the hero in elegies and *epitaphioi logoi*. Even Pindar who praises an individual, often of aristocratic standing, embeds the victor in his community, past and present, and tragedy, while mostly dealing with myths set outside of Athens, presents them from an angle that sheds light on current concerns of the

---

[52] Since we strongly rely on evidence from Athens, another reason for the preference of exempla from the fifth century may have been that this was the time of Athens' great political and military successes and therefore provided the orators with the best exempla. Cf. Worthington 1994: 113.
[53] Cf. Chapter 3, section 3.2.1; 3.   [54] Cf. Chapter 5, section 5.1.

polis. It is striking that the polis is at the centre not only of genres more or less commissioned by the community, i.e. tragedy and the funeral speeches, but also of those genres that were performed in the arguably aristocratic setting of the symposium, notably elegies and also re-performances of victory odes. On the other hand, the subversive stance of Andocides' *de pace* alerts us to the fact that the past was a powerful tool in socio-political struggles.

The idea of history that underlies all genres pits contingency of chance against continuity and regularity. This common idea of history, however, is articulated in different ways. In my examination of elegy, I have suggested viewing the presentation of polis history as a continuum and the use of mythical foils as an attempt to balance the perilous force of chance. While this link remains hypothetical due to the fragmentary status of the textual transmission, the same tension is at the core of the victory odes. I argued furthermore that the narrative form of *Olympian* 2 mirrors the transcendence of time that the victor achieves through his success and with the help of Pindar. In tragedy, human fragility takes the whole stage, but is projected onto the 'other' and contrasts with the continuity and regularity established by the ritual performance in Athens. The ritualized recital of funeral speeches offered a similarly stable frame, underscored by the standardization of the content, but had to grapple with losses in the Athenian camp. However, the individual experiences of contingency of chance are compensated for by the eternal greatness of the city of Athens. The *epitaphioi logoi* not only promise, just as Homer and Simonides, immortal glory as reward for heroic deeds, but give the poetic topos a new twist: in providing the present generation with models, they actively contribute to the maintenance of Athens' grandeur. Deliberative oratory is set apart in that it refers only selectively to the past in order to buttress arguments about the present and the future, but the exemplary mode of memory aligns it with other genres. It is now time to turn to the rise of Greek historiography and to explore the place of the first historians in the field of memory in fifth-century Greece.

PART II

The rise of Greek historiography

CHAPTER 7

Herodotus

This book not only aims at examining the idea of history in a variety of genres, it also tries to shed new light on the rise of historiography by exploring Herodotus' and Thucydides' relation to memory in poetry and oratory.[1] My approach brings a shift of emphasis that may seem minor at first sight, but is, I believe, quite important for our understanding of the first historians. It is, of course, well-known that Herodotus and Thucydides criticize Homer and are, at the same time, heavily indebted to epic narrative. And yet, this view not only tends to neglect other poetic genres besides epic and, perhaps even more detrimentally, ignores oratory, but it also takes for granted that historiography is the primary medium of memory. However, Herodotus and Thucydides could not rely on an established genre. Instead, they had to assert themselves in the vast field of memory, part of which I have sketched in the first half of my study. Thus, the criticism of other genres is more essential and also goes further than is generally assumed. I shall argue that Herodotus and Thucydides define their new approach not only explicitly, but also implicitly against other commemorative genres. More specifically, I will suggest that some embedded speeches in the historical narratives have meta-historical significance. Questionable uses of the past by characters in the narrative throw into relief the superiority of historiography and can therefore be read as implicit meta-history. This implicit critique of oratory is more marked in Thucydides, but we also find in Herodotus a subtle deconstruction of the rhetorical use of the past.

At the same time, my phenomenological model of the idea of history makes it possible to elucidate a common ground between the first historians and commemorative poetry and oratory that deserves more attention than it

---

[1] More recent scholarship, e.g. Fowler 1996; 2006; Porciani 2001, has effectively challenged Jacoby's influential thesis that Herodotus was the first historian, but a study like this that needs sizable amounts of narrative for interpretation is still dependent on Herodotus and Thucydides for the fifth century BCE. On local historiography, see also Clarke 2008.

has received so far. I shall argue that Herodotus and Thucydides share a basic idea of history with the poets and orators whose authority they challenge. On the one hand, contingency of chance figures prominently in their accounts, which employ similar narrative means for expressing it as the epics or tragedy. On the other, both Herodotus and Thucydides use the exemplary mode of memory, albeit in an unprecedented way. It is the aim of this and the next chapter to assess anew the rise of Greek historiography by exploring the tension between tradition and innovation with respect to poetic and rhetorical memory.

My examination of both authors will follow the same structure: I will first discuss their explicit criticism of other genres of memory (7.1 and 8.1) and then elaborate on the implicit criticism of oratory (7.2 and 8.2). In a third step, I shall point out that despite this demarcation from poetry and oratory, the works of both historians share common ground in their ideas of history with their competitors in the field of memory (7.3 and 8.3).

Before I start my examination of Herodotus' explicit and implicit critique of other forms of memory, let me point out three fundamental differences concerning the scope of the narrative and the context of its reception, which, though very obvious, nonetheless deserve mention. First, the non-historiographical media of memory that I have discussed deal with both the archaic and recent past. However, a certain preference for the mythical past, including a tendency to epicize recent events, is discernible. Herodotus, on the other hand, expressly dismisses accounts of conflicts between Greeks and barbarians that predate Croesus, 'who, to my knowledge, first began criminal acts against the Greeks' (1.5.3). Despite his dismissal, Herodotus devotes a number of elaborate paragraphs to Io, Europa, Medea and Helen at the very beginning of his narrative (1.1–5), and yet it is worth noting that the central event of his narrative, the Persian Wars, belongs to the more recent past. This shift of attention was continued by Thucydides who, for similar methodological reasons, focuses on even more recent events. The only genre in which we could note a comparable preference for the recent past was deliberative oratory.

Second, all my examples for works of memory besides historiography were more or less in the grip of the polis, albeit in different ways. Elegies and funeral speeches focus on the past of the polis, the victory odes aim at reintegrating an outstanding individual into the polis, in deliberative speeches it is frequently the past of the polis that is invoked and even tragedies, which deal with non-Athenian myths, shed light on issues of concern for the polis. While poleis are a crucial factor in Herodotus' account, he does not limit his focus to one polis, but takes a pan-Hellenic stance and even devotes large parts of his work to non-Greeks.[2] One could say that he transfers the pan-Hellenic perspective of the Homeric epics from heroic subjects to the recent past.

Lastly, another, perhaps even more significant innovation concerns what I have called the 'socio-political context of performance' in the first part of this book. All poetic and rhetorical genres that I analyzed were composed for performance in a specific setting; in some cases, notably the victory odes and elegies, there were re-performances, but even these were oral presentations in a fixed setting, the symposium. Herodotus may have orally presented parts of the *Histories* and his narrative reveals features of oral speech, but the work as we have it was nonetheless written and intended for publication.[3] Of course, written texts are not free of contexts, and yet their context is far less defined than in the case of oral performances.[4] We will see that, despite the focus on the recent past, the pan-Hellenic perspective and the independence from a specific performative context, the past in the *Histories* is still strongly linked to the present.[5]

7.1. EXPLICIT CRITICISM OF OTHER GENRES OF MEMORY: THE HELEN–*LOGOS* (2.112–20)

In the first part of this study, I detected an agonistic spirit in the field of memory, for example when Simonides and Mimnermus compare their elegies with epic accounts of the past. In the hands of the first historians, who had to legitimize and establish their new genre, such comparisons are intensified and become attempts to define their own approach against others. In a much discussed chapter, Thucydides reflects on his method and distinguishes his own work from the accounts of poets and *logographoi*

---

[2] For a new reading of Herodotus' pan-Hellenism as dislocation, see Friedman 2006.
[3] On the ancient tradition of oral presentations by Herodotus, see Flory 1980: 14–15; on the *Histories* between orality and literacy, see Lang 1984; Rösler 1991; 2002; Thomas 2000.
[4] Cf. Kurke 2000: 140. Rösler 1991 demonstrates that Herodotus addresses an indeterminate future audience, and Boedeker 2000: 113 adds that the implied audience is not spatially defined either.
[5] In all three aspects, temporal focus, local perspective and performative context, Herodotus, and also Thucydides, seems to be distinct from the group of historians whose scanty fragments have been assembled by Jacoby in the third volume of FGrH under the name 'Geschichte von Völkern und Städten (Ethnographie und Horographie)'. Clarke 2008 argues that local historians, while also dealing with more recent events, privileged mythical subjects (see also Chaniotis 1988: 142–3 on historiographies written on stone), tried to embed local history in a wider perspective and disseminated their works in oral performances. It therefore seems that in many regards the local historians bridge the gap between Herodotean and Thucydidean historiography on the one side and poetic and rhetorical accounts of the past on the other. Interesting as the potential conclusions for the rise of Greek historiography may be, they are hard to draw, as nearly all the material on which Clarke's analysis rests is later than the fifth century BCE.

(1.20–2). Herodotus does not provide his readers with a similar general statement. Yet, when he uses poetry as a source, a rather critical attitude to its reliability comes to the fore, which resembles Thucydides' reflections.[6] As an example, I will turn to Herodotus' discussion of the story of Helen and the Trojan War (2.112–20). Herodotus not only critically reviews the *Iliad's* testimony, but uses the discussion of it to juxtapose his work with epic poetry as an alternative approach to the past.[7]

In his survey of Egyptian kings, Herodotus mentions a temple of 'Aphrodite, the stranger' besides that of Memphitis or – in Greek – Proteus (2.112). His conjecture that 'Aphrodite, the stranger' is actually Helen, who is said to have stayed with Proteus, is corroborated by the Egyptian priests:[8] when Alexander left Sparta with Helen and his booty, strong winds carried them to the Egyptian coast. Upon arrival, some of his slaves fled to a temple asylum and told the local priest about Alexander's crime. The king, informed by the priest, strongly disapproved of the Trojan's breach of the law of hospitality. However, respecting Alexander's status as guest, he did not kill him, but merely expelled him, confiscating Helen and the stolen goods (2.113–15).

According to Herodotus, Homer, who presents a different version of the rapture of Helen, knew this story. Herodotus reads *Il.* 6.289–91, where *peploi* that Alexander brought from Sidonia are mentioned, as an obvious reference to the Egyptian tradition (2.116).[9] Moreover, he argues, this passage also reveals that Homer cannot be the author of the *Cypria*, according to which Alexander sailed directly from Sparta to Troy (2.117).[10]

Upon further enquiry, Herodotus continues, the Egyptian priests told him that they knew the whole story from Menelaus himself. Only after the fall of Troy did Menelaus believe the Trojans' assertion that Helen was not

---

[6] Cf. Lateiner 1989: 99–100. On Herodotus' critique of poets in general, see Verdin 1977; Marincola 2006. See also Boedeker 2000: 103–8 for a stimulating examination of how comments on other genres help Herodotus define his own (master-)genre.

[7] On Herodotus' discussion of the Egyptian Helen-*logos* and the *Iliad's* evidence, see Dalfen 1974: 284–5; Hunter 1982: 52–61; Fehling 1989: 59–65; Austin 1994; Boedeker 2000: 104–5; Gumpert 2001: 21–2; 56–7; Munson 2001: 143–4; Pallantza 2005: 106–7. On the development of the figure of Helen in epic poetry, see Clader 1976; for later transformations, see Kannicht 1969: 21–77; Backès 1984.

[8] In this context, the question of whether Herodotus really draws on reports from Egyptians or has only made up this source can be neglected. For two extreme positions, see von Fritz 1967: 166, who strictly believes Herodotus' claim, and Fehling 1989: 59–65, who takes a most sceptical stance. See also Moyer 2002 and Rebuffat 1966, who argues for a Phoenician source.

[9] The transmitted text gives two further quotations from the *Odyssey*. Neither of them, however, refers to Alexander and Herodotus' following comment is only on *Il.* 6.289–91. Thus, I am inclined to follow Stein [8]1969; How and Wells 1912; Hude [3]1927; Lloyd 1988 in the *athetesis* of the *Odyssey* quotation. Rosén 1987–97, however, keeps the transmitted text.

[10] Herodotus presents similar arguments about the *Epigonoi* and the *Melampodia* in 4.32 and 2.49.

in Troy and sailed to Egypt where he went to Proteus to pick her and his goods up. However, when he sacrificed two local kids in order to calm the sea, he angered his hosts and had to flee to Libya (2.118–19). Herodotus adds that he approves of this account for the following reasons: it is hard to believe that Priam bore the deaths of many sons and let the whole city suffer only to make sure that Alexander could be with Helen. Even if Priam was too old to reign, not Alexander, but Hector would have been in charge of Trojan affairs. In a concluding remark, Herodotus suggests that the *daimonion* induced the Greeks not to believe the Trojans so that men would learn that serious crimes are severely punished (2.120).

Very artfully, Herodotus' narrative combines the evaluation of the Egyptian tradition with a chronological account of the Trojan War. Herodotus first presents the Egyptian *logos* about Alexander's stay in Egypt, including the traces of this version in Homer, and then has the Egyptian priests defend the reliability of their version. What the Egyptians say to prove their account, namely the Trojan War and its aftermath, complements the story line that begins with Alexander's arrival in Egypt. Thus, in Herodotus' evaluation of the Egyptian tradition the story of Helen unfolds in chronological order.

Let us take a closer look at Herodotus' reference to the *Iliad*. First of all, it is worth noting that Herodotus does not cast any doubt on the historicity of the Trojan War,[11] which he takes for granted, when, in a rather subversive reading, he uses the *Iliad* to corroborate an alternative tradition to the epic account. With his critical attitude towards the epic tradition, Herodotus aligns himself with a series of authors, ranging from Pindar to Xenophanes and Hecataeus, who question the reliability of Homer, but do not challenge the historicity of his tales.[12] More specifically, in reviewing the Homeric account of Helen, Herodotus follows Stesichorus. The Egyptian *logos* to which Herodotus subscribes resembles what we know about Stesichorus' *Palinode* (fr. 192–3 *PMG*). Both argue that Helen was not in Troy, yet Herodotus is more rationalistic in dispensing with the *eidolon*.[13] It is striking that Herodotus does not mention Stesichorus' *Palinode*, which would be much closer to his version, but instead adduces a rather weak allusion in Homer as support for it. This underlines the fact that, despite his critical attitude, Herodotus considers Homer a testimony worth engaging with.[14]

---

[11] Cf. Vandiver 1991: 127.
[12] For the critical reception of Homeric epic, see e.g. Buffière 1956; Lamberton and Keaney 1992; Richardson 1993: 25–35.
[13] Cf. Fehling 1989: 59; Austin 1994: 118–36. It is debated if already Stesichorus places Helen in Egypt, cf. Pallantza 2005: 106–7 with the relevant sources and literature.
[14] Cf. Pallantza 2005: 154–5, who questions the widespread opinion that Herodotus only criticizes Homer.

What is most interesting is that Herodotus' discussion of the Homeric evidence creates a juxtaposition of the *Histories* with epic poetry as different media of memory.[15] Herodotus applies to Homer an *interpretatio Herodotea*, which throws into relief the crucial differences that define the *Histories* against poetic accounts of the past. To start with, Herodotus' view of Homer makes the epic account look very similar to his own. According to Herodotus, Homer not only knew the version of the Trojan War to which he himself was introduced by the Egyptian priests, but also inserted it in his own poem.[16] The transmitted text is corrupt (2.116.2):

This is obvious for in the *Iliad* he alludes to Alexander's travel (and he corrected himself in no other passage) – how he was carried off course with Helen and how in the course of his wanderings he came, among other places, to Sidon in Phoenicia.

δῆλον δέ, κατὰ γὰρ ἐποίησε ἐν Ἰλιάδι (καὶ οὐδαμῇ ἄλλῃ ἀνεπόδισε ἑωυτόν) πλάνην τὴν Ἀλεξάνδρου, ὡς ἀπηνείχθη ἄγων Ἑλένην τῇ τε δὴ ἄλλῃ πλαζόμενος καὶ ὡς ἐς Σιδῶνα τῆς Φοινίκης ἀπίκετο.

κατὰ γὰρ ἐποίησε can be conjectured either to κατάπερ ἐποίησε or to κατὰ παρεποίησε.[17] Both conjectures are palaeographically and philologically sound. The latter assumes a meaning of παραποιεῖν for which we have no other evidence, but which is etymologically plausible: in general, παραποιεῖν signifies the process of altering or even counterfeiting; here, however, the meaning must be something along the lines of 'to introduce as an episode into a poem' (*LSJ*).[18] Despite the *petitio principii*, this reading is clearly preferable to κατάπερ ἐποίησε. It would be very awkward if Herodotus first points out that Homer ignores Alexander's visit to Egypt and then adds that he composed a πλάνη Ἀλεξάνδρου. παραποιεῖν, on the other hand, would signify that Homer only alludes to Alexander's visit

[15] Hunter 1982: 50–92 reads Book 2 as an attempt to establish Egyptian longevity, 'which, together with the reliability of Egyptian tradition, formed the basis of his challenge to the poets and his own revision of early Greek history and tradition' (91). See also Moyer 2002: 84, who argues that Herodotus draws on the memorial culture of Late Period Egypt.
[16] Cf. Hunter 1982: 54; Ford 2002: 149.
[17] κατάπερ ἐποίησε was suggested by Reiz. κατὰ παρεποίησε was proposed by Bekker and is preferred by Hude, Asheri, Rosén. A further conjecture is presented by Stein who athetizes γάρ.
[18] How and Wells 1912: ad loc. remark that 'in this sense the verb is a ἅπαξ λεγόμενον'. There is, however, at least one further possible use of παραποιεῖν with the meaning 'to introduce as an episode'. In the fragment of a work on literary criticism, παραποιεῖν is plausibly restored in two places (*P. Oxy.* 1611.165, 175, dating from the early third century CE). Unfortunately, the fragmentary state of the papyrus does not allow any safe conclusions about the exact meaning of παραποιεῖν. Yet, most occurrences of παραποιεῖν in the meaning 'make falsely, alter' are later: Diod. 1.78; Just. *Nov.* 73 praef. In Thuc. 1.132.5, the manuscripts have παραποιησάμενος σφραγῖδα. This, however, barely makes sense and thus editors have preferred παρασημηνάμενος, relying on Poll. 8.27, who quotes the phrase παρασημηνάμενος σφραγῖδα from Thucydides. In Arist. *Rh.* 1412a28–9 τὰ παραπεποιημένα signifiy what runs contrary to expectation in jokes.

in which case the text gains an intriguing paradoxical twist: the verb which generally denotes the process of counterfeiting is used to signify the embedding of the right version in the wrong account. More importantly, Herodotus' assumption that Homer embeds in his narrative an allusion to an alternative account establishes an *interpretatio Herodotea*. Implausible as Herodotus' reading may be,[19] it projects onto the *Iliad* the structure of the *Histories*, which frequently hints at and juxtaposes various accounts.

At the same time, Herodotus strongly marks the difference: he points out that, in his choice of the wrong tradition, Homer is led by other criteria than he himself is.[20] The Egyptian version was not 'as suitable for an epic poem as the other one that he used' ('ὁμοίως ἐς τὴν ἐποποιίην εὐπρεπὴς ... τῷ ἑτέρῳ τῷ περ ἐχρήσατο', 2.116.1). As this implies, different criteria underlie the presentation of the past in different genres. Herodotus does not spell out what criteria determine epic poetry,[21] but his statement καὶ οὐδαμῇ ἄλλῃ ἀνεπόδισε ἑωυτόν (2.116.2) reveals what epic poetry does not do. The meaning of ἀναποδίζειν, another 'spatial' verb like παραποιεῖν, is illustrated by another passage:[22] '... as he walked through the grain, he kept questioning the messenger and made him go back on himself concerning why he had come from Corinth ...' ('... διεξήιε τὸ λήιον ἐπειρωτῶν τε καὶ ἀναποδίζων τὸν κήρυκα κατὰ τὴν ἀπὸ Κορίνθου ἄπιξιν ...' 5.92ζ2). As the use in conjunction with ἐπειρωτᾶν shows, the basic meaning of 'making step back' can evolve into 'make go back on oneself', implying an act of critical scrutiny (*LSJ*). Thus, unlike Herodotus, Homer does not 'question' or 'examine' the alternative tradition that he mentions. This interpretation is backed up by another passage in which Herodotus mentions Homer: 'The one who has spoken about Oceanus has referred to something obscure and does not admit of refutation (οὐκ ἔχει ἔλεγχον). For I do not know of the existence of any

---

[19] See, for example, Lloyd 1988: ad loc. with serious doubts about the reference. On the other hand, Herodotus' reading is congenial to the poststructuralist interpretation of Helen by Gumpert 2001, who argues that already in the *Iliad* 'Helen herself unsettles our faith in origins and realities' (10; on Herodotus' reference to different Helen–versions in Homer, cf. 56–7). Gumpert uses the term 'graft' for Helen's enigmatic and elusive nature in the literary tradition, which illustrates the instability of meaning in general. For example in considering Herodotus' emphasis on Helen's foreign status in Egypt, Gumpert suggests that 'once again geographic displacement ... seems to be an acting out of metaphorical displacement: forced transfers of meaning, illegitimate acts of grafting'. (22).

[20] Cf. Lanata 1963: 230–1; Koster 1970: 13; Verdin 1977: 60–1; Boedeker 2000: 105; Ford 2002: 150.

[21] Dalfen 1974: 285 speaks of 'poetische Qualität'; Ford 2002: 150 suggests that in Herodotus' eyes the epics follow the requirements of praise poetry. Pallantza 2005: 154 focuses on the 'ästhetisierende Tendenz der Dichtung (εὐπρέπεια)'. This, however, is misleading, as Herodotus does not state that Homer strives for εὐπρέπεια; he merely follows what is ἐς τὴν ἐποποιίην εὐπρεπής.

[22] Most scholars assume something like to 'correct': How and Wells 1912: ad loc.; van Groningen 1945: ad loc.; *LSJ* s.v. However, the verb's etymology and the context of its use suggest a weaker meaning, cf. Stein [8]1969: ad loc.: 'darauf zurückkommen'. Powell 1938 states: 'The meaning is not clear'.

River Oceanus, but I think that Homer or one of the earlier poets invented the name and introduced it into poetry.' (2.23).

The epics do not apply the critical scrutiny to which Herodotus claims to subject his own account. Herodotus does not explicitly reflect on what his own scrutiny consists of, but his discussion of the Egyptian Helen–*logos* nicely illustrates it. He starts from autopsy, adducing the temple of 'Aphrodite, the stranger' as evidence of Helen's stay in Egypt, then takes into account both written and oral traditions, the *Iliad* and the reports of the Egyptian priests, and assesses their value as sources. While Homer follows the principles of epic poetry, the Egyptians' approach is similar to his own: they draw on an eye-witness, Menelaus, apply *historie* and acknowledge the limits of their knowledge in a manner that reminds the reader of Herodotus himself.[23] In addition to autopsy and the collection and evaluation of different traditions, Herodotus subjects the results of his enquiry to a rationalistic examination, asking how plausible the epic tradition is according to rational standards.

As we see, in the discussion of the Egyptian account the *Iliad* is not only used as a source, but also figures as a backdrop for Herodotus' way of reconstructing the past. Herodotus makes Homer resemble himself insofar as he knows and mentions different traditions, but marks that, unlike the *Iliad*, his account is the product of a critical approach that employs autopsy, the evaluation of sources and the assessment of plausibility according to rationality. While the epics claim to stem from the Muses, Herodotus' work is the product of *historie*.[24] Though not being named 'historiography', Herodotus' *Histories* reveals an awareness of presenting an approach to the past that is distinct from poetic accounts.[25] The implicit comparisons that I have noticed in poetic genres have evolved into open polemics against other commemorative genres.

Yet, even in the Helen–*logos* where Herodotus marks off his own approach to the past, an interesting similarity between the *Iliad* and the *Histories* emerges. In a closing comment, Herodotus offers an explanation for why the Greeks did not believe the Trojans' claim that Helen was in Egypt until they had conquered Troy[26] (2.120.5):

---

[23] μοι ... ἱστορέοντι (2.113.1) (Hdt.) ~ ἱστορίῃσι φάμενοι (2.118.1); ἱστορίῃσι ... ἐπίστασθαι (2.119.3) (Egyptian priests). In 2.119.3, Herodotus has the Egyptians acknowledge the limits of their knowledge.
[24] Cf. Marincola 2006: 15–16.
[25] One point is worth adding: Herodotus argues that Homer cannot be the author of the *Cypria*, according to which Alexander returned from Sparta to Troy without incident. Although Herodotus criticizes Homer's presentation as being unfettered by critical concerns, he assumes that Homer is consistent in his account of the past even in different works.
[26] On the prominence of this comment, see Hellmann 1934: 56 n. 1.

But they did not have Helen to give back and the Greeks did not believe that they spoke the truth. To declare my own opinion, this was because the *daimonion* arranged things so that, in their complete annihilation, they should make this clear to mankind that for severe crimes the punishment at the gods' hands is severe.

ἀλλ' οὐ γὰρ εἶχον Ἑλένην ἀποδοῦναι οὐδὲ λέγουσι αὐτοῖσι τὴν ἀληθείην ἐπίστευον οἱ Ἕλληνες, ὡς μὲν ἐγὼ γνώμην ἀποφαίνομαι, τοῦ δαιμονίου παρασκευάζοντος ὅκως πανωλεθρίῃ ἀπολόμενοι καταφανὲς τοῦτο τοῖσι ἀνθρώποισι ποιήσωσι, ὡς τῶν μεγάλων ἀδικημάτων μεγάλαι εἰσὶ καὶ αἱ τιμωρίαι παρὰ τῶν θεῶν.

It is plausible to read the reference to the deterrent function of the Troy story as a self-reflexive comment, as Herodotus' Helen–*logos* forcefully demonstrates that crimes are followed by punishment. It presents two corresponding violations of hospitality, by Alexander and Menelaus, both of whom are punished. Their crime is highlighted by the contrast of the Egyptian king Proteus who not only sticks to the rules of hospitality himself, but also explicitly condemns Alexander's crime and thus gives the moral judgement a voice at the level of the action. Moreover, the message 'great crime will be severely punished' recurs in the *Histories*.[27] In this context, it may be significant that the verb ἀποφαίνομαι, which Herodotus uses for his own activity, is a cognate of καταφανές, which signifies the dissemination of the divine message. The correspondence underscores that the *Histories* serves as a medium in which the consequences of great crimes are revealed.[28]

Yet, the most prominent account of the Trojan War and thus the medium that makes the heroic deeds 'clear' to men is epic poetry. Though not mentioned explicitly, the *Iliad* immediately springs to mind.[29] The reference to it is reinforced by πανωλεθρίῃ ἀπολόμενοι: while πανωλεθρίῃ has a rather general poetic ring, the idea of the total destruction of the generation of the heroes is an epic concept. We find it not only in the *Cypria's* proem,[30] but also in the *Iliad*, for example when Odysseus says to Agamemnon: 'Ruinous! I wish you directed some other unworthy/ army, and were not lord over us, over us to whom Zeus/ has appointed the accomplishing of wars, from our youth/ even into our old age until we are dead, each of us (ὄφρα φθιόμεσθα ἕκαστος).' (14.84–7). One might even argue that the phrase καταφανὲς

---

[27] Cf. below section 7.3.1. [28] Cf. Munson 2001: 186.
[29] Waters 1985: 101 and Vandiver 1991: 130 note that Herodotus takes up the traditional epic view of the Trojan War, but do not specify the reference.
[30] If one shares the conviction that the Διὸς βουλή in *Il.* 1.5 alludes to Zeus' plan to destroy the heroes in the *Cypria's* proem, one could even argue that Herodotus refers to this. However, this thesis, argued e.g. by Kullmann 1956, is rather problematic, cf. Grethlein 2006a: 261 n. 130 with further literature.

ποιεῖν evokes the Homeric account, because Herodotus uses ποιεῖν to signify the process of poetic composition.[31]

We may be reluctant to attribute to the *Iliad* the strongly moral outlook that Herodotus invokes – man's general fragility and the gods' unpredictability seem to figure more prominently in it than a concept of divine justice[32] – but there are passages that anticipate moralist interpretations.[33] In 16.31–2 for example, Patroclus addresses Achilles: '… What other man born hereafter shall be advantaged/ unless you beat aside from the Argives this shameful destruction?' When Patroclus mentions the utility of the exemplum of Achilles, the *Iliad*'s hero, to later generations, the *Iliad*'s self-reflection on its own relevance is obvious. While here the *Iliad*'s paradigmatic meaning is rather general, in a prayer by Menelaus the message to later generations concerns exactly the point that comes to the fore in Herodotus, the punishment for breaking the law of hospitality:[34] 'Zeus, lord, grant me to punish the man who first did me injury,/ brilliant Alexander, and beat him down under my hands' strength/ that any one of the men to come may shudder to think of/ doing evil to a kindly host, who has given him friendship.' (3.351–4).

Thus, in combining a reference to the *Iliad* with an essential pattern of the *Histories*, Herodotus' final assessment of the Trojan War reveals that, besides the differences to which he alerts his readers, the *Histories* also shares a common horizon with the epic account of the past. Before I elaborate on the similarities between the ideas of history underlying the *Histories* and other media of memory, Herodotus' critique of his competitors in the field of memory deserves further attention. In the next section, I will argue that some embedded speeches reveal the pitfalls of the rhetorical use of the past.

7.2. IMPLICIT CRITICISM OF THE USE OF THE PAST IN ORATORY (THE SYRACUSAN EMBASSY SCENE (7.153–63); THE SPEECH DUEL AT PLATAEA (9.26–7))

As I pointed out in the introduction to this chapter, Herodotus, though not the only one writing prose accounts of the past in his time, could not rely on generic conventions, but had to assert a place for his new approach against the established commemorative genres. I shall now argue that, besides the polemics against Homer, which I have just discussed, there is also an implicit criticism of the use of the past in speeches. The *Histories* contains

---

[31] For this meaning of ποιεῖν see Boedeker 2000: 103; Ford 2002: 134–5.
[32] See the interpretation in Grethlein 2006a.
[33] Cf. Grethlein 2006a: 322–3.   [34] Cf. Munson 2001: 143–4.

quite a few speeches with historical arguments. So far, scholarship has concentrated on the (non-)authenticity of the speeches and on their interaction with the narrative.[35] I would like to open up a new perspective by reading some speeches as 'meta-historical', i.e. as an implicit self-reflection. 'Meta-history' usually signifies theoretical reflections on memory and history.[36] In the case of the speeches however, this reflection is implied in the narrative. The speeches mirror or throw into relief the historian's work and thereby serve as an implicit self-reflection, comparable to meta-poetics. Thus, my reading enriches the concept of meta-history with the form of 'meta-poetics'.[37]

Needless to say, writing history is different from using the past in arguments. Nonetheless, the historical narrative of the past and the characters' invocation of the past in it are similar in that both are acts of memory. Recent works in the theory of history have challenged the claim to scientific objectivity of positivist historians and have, if not eradicated, at least made less distinct the borderline between historiography and other commemorative media.[38] More specifically, the character of ancient historiography makes the differences from rhetorical uses of the past smaller than they may appear to us at first glance. Tony Woodman may go too far in his claim that history was considered as part of rhetoric, but it is hard to deny the close links between the two genres throughout antiquity.[39] While modern historians strive to make their investigations as independent from present interests as possible, not only Polybius, but many other ancient historians stress the pragmatic dimension of their work.[40]

Therefore references to the past by characters invite a meta-historical interpretation. In many cases the use of the past in the speeches is rather questionable and throws into relief the superiority of the historian's work.

---

[35] On speeches in the *Histories*, see Jacoby 1913: 492–6; Deffner 1933; Hellmann 1934; Solmsen 1943; 1944; Steinger 1957; Waters 1966; Hohti 1976a; Heni 1977; Lang 1984; Pelling 2006a; Scardino 2007.

[36] White 2005: 302 defines meta-history as 'the presuppositions – conceptual, figurative, and metaphysical – regarding the nature of historical reality required for belief in the possibility of a distinctively historical kind of knowledge'.

[37] Chiasson 2003 makes a similar case for the Lydian *logos* in which the appropriation of tragic forms can be seen as a self-conscious engagement with another genre.

[38] See in particular White 1973, whose tropology goes very far in blurring the borderline between historical and fictional narratives. Although few historians will completely subscribe to his approach, White has forcefully called to our attention the rhetorical character of historiography. For another approach to the narrative side of historiography from the angle of hermeneutics and phenomenology, see Ricoeur 1990.

[39] Woodman 1988 with studies of Greek as well as Roman historians. For a critique of Woodman's far-reaching conclusions, see e.g. Rhodes 1994; Lendon (forthcoming).

[40] See Fornara 1983: 104–20; Luce 1991, who focuses on Tacitus' *'praecipuum munus annalium'*, but also illuminates the various notions of the *utile* in other ancient historians; Raaflaub (forthcoming).

Seen from this perspective, the level of the action contains a commentary on the narrative itself. In addition to explicit polemics, the implicit critique of memory in embedded speeches allowed Herodotus to define his approach to the past by demarcating it from other genres. I would like to discuss two cases in which the deficiencies of rhetorical uses of the past come to the fore: the Syracusan embassy scene (7.153–63) and the speech duel between the Tegeans and Athenians at Plataea (9.26–7) can be read as an implicit criticism of the use of the past in oratory. At the same time, the speeches indicate that, despite the differences, Herodotus shares common ground with oratory. The examination of speeches as foil to the *Histories* will allow us to figure out important aspects of Herodotus' work in the tension between continuity and innovation.

7.2.1. The Syracusan embassy scene[41]

In 7.153–63, Herodotus tells of an embassy the Greek alliance sends to Gelon of Syracuse, who, they hope, will be talked into joining their fight against Xerxes.[42] In his first reply to the embassy's appeal, Gelon points out that he received no help when he was threatened by the Carthaginians, but signals that he is nonetheless willing to support the alliance. He indicates the exact number of ships and manpower that will be provided by Syracuse and even promises to take care of the food supply for the whole army. Everything on one condition: that he be the leader of the Greek army (7.158). Syagrus, the Spartan envoy, harshly rejects this request (7.159). In a second speech, Gelon states that he would content himself with commanding either the navy or the army (7.160), but against this the Athenian envoy protests (7.161) and Gelon decides not to join the Greek alliance (7.162).

Both Syagrus and the Athenian envoy turn to the heroic past to buttress their claims. After Gelon has requested that he be the leader of the Greek army, Syagrus exclaims that Agamemnon would groan aloud if he knew that Gelon had taken the hegemony from the Spartans (7.159). The Athenian envoy quotes Homer in order to draw attention to Athens' role in the Trojan War, when he objects to Gelon's offer to command only the navy

---

[41] For an extended version of this section, see Grethlein 2006c.
[42] The authenticity of the Syracuse embassy is disputed. While Meyer 1899: 219 and Treves 1941 point out that the story in Herodotus is merely fictional, Brunt 1953: 158–62 lists accounts of it by other historians and argues that there actually was an embassy to Sicily. This question touches upon the more fundamental discussion about the reliability of Herodotus which has centered on the scepticism of Fehling 1989. On the historical background in Sicily, see Luraghi 1994: 273–88.

(7.161.3). Being the tyrant of Sicily, Gelon cannot invoke the heroic past to underscore his claim. Instead he calls his army the 'spring of Greece' (7.162). Against the references to the ancient past Gelon pits the youthful vigour of his rather recent superpower.

In the following, I will suggest that there is not only a general epic background in the embassy scene, but that Syagrus' words echo a specific passage from the *Iliad* and create a dense net of meanings.[43] It will be argued that the epic reverberation serves a dual purpose: on the one hand, Syagrus draws on the epic past to legitimize his claims; on the other, the epic parallels undermine his intentions and shed new light on the action for the recipients of the *Histories* (a). I shall then take a brief look at the Homeric quote in the Athenian's speech (b). In the next step, I will examine the rhetorical strategy that Gelon pursues with the spring metaphor and argue that it gains additional meaning at the level of reception through a fifth-century intertext (c). The tension between the meaning of the speeches at the level of the action and the meaning they gain through the intertextual foils for the readers of the *Histories* sheds a critical light on the use of the past in oratory, while at the same time revealing some common ground between Herodotus and orators (d).[44]

(a) Syagrus' use of the epic past
'Surely, he would groan aloud, Agamemnon, the son of Pelops, if he heard that Spartiates had been robbed of their leadership by Gelon and the Syracusans.' ('ἦ κε μέγ' οἰμώξειε ὁ Πελοπίδης Ἀγαμέμνων πυθόμενος Σπαρτιήτας τὴν ἡγεμονίην ἀπαραιρῆσθαι ὑπὸ Γέλωνός τε καὶ Συρηκοσίων.' Hdt. 7.159). Commentators have noted the similarity of Syagrus' exclamation to *Il.* 7.125:[45] 'Surely, he would groan aloud, Peleus, the aged horseman.' ('ἦ κε μέγ' οἰμώξειε γέρων ἱππηλάτα Πηλεύς ...'). However, the meaning of this instance of intertextuality has not received due scholarly attention[46] and recently, Deborah Boedeker went so far as to argue that there might be neither an allusion to a particular passage nor even an epic reminiscence. According to her, it is likely that Syagrus' exclamation is merely a rhetorical commonplace.[47] In a first step, I will present the linguistic similarities which make the lines a

---

[43] On Herodotus' use of the epics, see Steinger 1957; Huber 1965; Huxley 1989; Boedeker 2002; Pelling 2006b. The importance of the epic tradition for Greek historiography is stressed by Strasburger 1972 and ³1975: 62–9.
[44] For a cautious note on intertextuality in the *Histories*, see Grethlein 2006c: 487–8.
[45] See, for example, Stein ⁸1969: ad 7.159; Butler 1905: ad 7.159; Smith and Laird 1908: ad 7.159; How and Wells 1912: ad 7.159.
[46] Huber 1965: 32 compares only their embarrassment and complaints about Greece's misfortune.
[47] Boedeker 2002: 101.

clear and distinctive quotation (i). Second, I will draw attention to the similarities of the old and new contexts of the quotation that underline the reference (ii). Third, I will point out the meaning of the quotation as a rhetorical device in Syagrus' speech (iii). Finally, I will argue that the quotation turns against Syagrus and undermines his claim (iv).

(i) The epic character of Syagrus' words is obvious: κε is an Aeolic form, which is not attested in the *Histories* outside of oracles;[48] this is the only time Herodotus uses οἰμώζειν and the first part of the sentence nearly scans as a hexameter.[49] The rather un-Herodotean words, which stem from epic poetry, and the rhythm make it hard to see it as just a rhetorical commonplace. It must be added that this is not, as Boedeker claims, the only epic echo in the passage. In the parallel speech by the Athenian envoy, the *Iliad* is quoted explicitly (cf. 2.1b).

But we can go further: Syagrus' exclamation has not only a general epic ring, it also unmistakably refers to *Il.* 7.125. The phrase ἦ κε μέγ' οἰμώξειε is used only there in epic poetry; the formula γέρων ἱππηλάτα Πηλεύς is replaced by ὁ Πελοπίδης Ἀγαμέμνων.[50] At a linguistic level the reference of Syagrus' words to *Il.* 1.125 is unmistakable – it is a quotation which has been adjusted to its new context. The modification is not only formally reflected by the 'limping' of the hexameter, it even marks the exclamation as a quotation, as the mention of Agamemnon draws the recipients' attention to the origin of the quote in the *Iliad*.[51]

(ii) The verbal echo in combination with the marker 'Agamemnon' makes for a high degree of intertextuality. The intertextual link is underscored at the level of content by similarities between the new and old contexts. In the seventh book of the *Iliad*, the fighting comes to a halt and Hector challenges the best of the Greeks to a duel (7.67–91). When no one rises to the challenge, Menelaus offers to face Hector (7.96–102), but Agamemnon convinces him

---

[48] Hdt. 1.174.5; 4.159.3; 6.86γ2.
[49] Hornblower 1994: 66 argues that Herodotus intentionally avoids a hexameter, as he could have written *Tantalidēs* instead of *Pelopidēs*. He explains his choice of *Pelopidēs* by the negative associations which would have come with Tantalus, the meaning of Pelops for Spartan hegemony and an intentional or unintentional allusion to *Peleus* in *Il.* 7.125. Griffiths 1976 takes a different position: he is convinced that Herodotus wrote a hexameter and conjectures *Pleisthenidēs* for *Pelopidēs*. Although Herodotus, as Hornblower notes, avoids hexameters in general, there are a couple of hexameters and hexameters *manqués* in the *Histories*. See for example 7.178.2: ἐξαγγείλαντες χάριν ἀθάνατον κατέθεντο. Boedeker 2001a: 124 suggests that not all the hexameters are accidental, but that some are supposed 'to create an epic effect' or are 'adapted from epic or elegiac accounts of recent events'. On hexameters in the *Histories*, see also Norden ⁹1983: I: 45; Aly ²1969: 273 n. 3.
[50] Hornblower 1994: 66 deems it possible that the patronymic *Pelopidēs* evokes *Pēleus*, particularly as it is the closed syllable *Pel* that interrupts the rhythm of the hexameter.
[51] For further passages in which Herodotus alludes to specific verses in the *Iliad*, see Grethlein 2006c: 490.

that he would not be afforded a fair chance (7.109–19). In this embarrassing situation Nestor intervenes with an elaborate speech. He describes how Peleus would react, if he knew about the Greeks' cowardice (7.124–8):

> Oh, for shame! Great sorrow settles on the land of Achaea.
> Surely, he would groan aloud, Peleus, the aged horseman,
> the great man of counsel among the Myrmidons, and their speaker.
> Once, as he questioned me in his house, he was filled with great joy
> as he heard the generation and blood of all of the Argives.

Then Nestor embeds a story from his own youth into the wish that he himself be rejuvenated (7.132–3; 157): as a young chap, he fought a duel with mighty Ereuthalion, who owned Areithoos' club (7.133–56) – and now nobody is willing to accept Hector's challenge (7.157–8). The persuasiveness of this exemplum is revealed when seven heroes volunteer to face Hector.

Three obvious similarities between Nestor's and Syagrus' speeches are to be noted. First, the situations resemble each other. In the context of a pan-Hellenic war against barbarians there is a similar controversy: while in *Iliad* 7 the best of the Achaeans is challenged to a duel,[52] Herodotus describes the Greeks' struggle for the supreme command. That the argument over leadership corresponds to the search for the best hero becomes evident when the Athenians back up their claim to command the navy by referring to the fact that Menestheus was the 'best man' ('ἀνὴρ ἄριστος') of the Greeks.

Second, Nestor and Syagrus pursue the same rhetorical strategy. Both not only refer to a tradition, but more specifically imagine the reaction of a great hero of the past in order to criticize somebody in the present who does not live up to a tradition. In Nestor's speech, the authority of tradition appears at different levels: Nestor himself is the embodiment of a glorious past. Again and again, he reports his own deeds as exempla to be followed by the other heroes.[53] Moreover, Peleus is a hero of a former generation.[54] The obligation to tradition is even made explicit: Peleus' groaning contrasts with his delight when he hears about the origins of the heroes.

Third, the situation to which Nestor refers resembles the embassy scene. As Nestor reports more extensively in another passage (11.765–90), he and Odysseus went to Phthie in order to pick up Achilles for the Trojan War.[55]

---

[52] Cf. *Il.* 7.50–1; 73–4.   [53] On Nestor, see Dickson 1995 and Primavesi 2000.
[54] Although Achilles assumes that Peleus is still living, he belongs to a sphere that is distanced from the present. See Grethlein 2006a: 55–8 on the distance that separates the heroes of the Trojan War from their fathers and Grethlein 2006d on the case of Nestor.
[55] Cf. Kirk 1990: ad *Il.* 7.127–8: 'Nestor will describe the occasion more fully in another reminiscence at 11.769ff.: he and Odysseus were visiting Peleus in Phthie to recruit his son (and Menoitios') for the war against Troy.' Cf. Ameis and Hentze ³1896/⁵1894: ad *Il.* 7.127.

Peleus' enquiry about the heroes' origin is motivated by his desire that Achilles will follow their example.[56] As Nestor and Odysseus came to fetch Achilles for a war, the Greek embassy comes to Syracuse to persuade Gelon to join the fight against the Persians.

Possibly the epic intertext in general and the mention of Agamemnon in particular evoke a further similarity, not with Book 7, but with another passage. In the first book of the *Iliad*, Achilles challenges Agamemnon's leadership and withdraws from the battle. While he is absent, the Greeks come under pressure, and they eventually send an embassy to persuade him to return to the ranks of the army (Book 9). The present passage of Herodotus concerns another embassy dispatched to persuade somebody to join a Greek alliance. When finally Syagrus not only quotes the *Iliad*, but backs up his claim to leadership by referencing Agamemnon, the one who started the fight with Achilles in the *Iliad*, it seems possible that Gelon's rejection appears against the background of Achilles' dismissal of the embassy in *Iliad* 9.

(iii) Surely, I would be overstating my case if I were to claim that every ancient recipient of the *Histories* recognized the intertextual link to Nestor's speech. But the marked quotation, the salient similarities between the contexts and the status of the *Iliad* as a canonical text make it likely that ancient readers would grasp the reference. It is important to stress that the individual recipients will have pursued the comparison between old and new contexts to varying degrees and in different ways. However, this should not prevent us from examining intertextual relations and I will therefore trace back all discernible similarities and differences, albeit without claiming that every ancient recipient will have followed up all details of the intertext. I shall first look at the level of the action, analyzing the rhetorical function of the quotation, and then show that at the level of the reception the epic foil undermines Syagrus' claim. The dubiousness of the rhetorical use of the past throws into relief Herodotus' superior approach and helps him claim a place in the field of memory.

Syagrus acquires an epic gravity with his quotation and draws on Nestor's reputation in particular. Who would be better suited to lend emphasis to a speech than Nestor? When in Plato's *Symposium* Alcibiades is searching for somebody with whom he can compare Socrates, he gives as an example the juxtaposition of Pericles and Nestor (221c). By quoting and imitating Nestor, Syagrus follows the example of *the* hero of eloquence and wisdom.

---

[56] Cf. Phoenix in *Il.* 9.438–43 and Nestor in *Il.* 11.783–4 on the pedagogic aspect of the Trojan War.

Additionally, the content of the quotation underlines Syagrus' point. He puts Gelon under pressure when he evokes as foil a situation in which nobody dares to face the enemy. Thus, Gelon stands to look like a coward should he not join the alliance.

At the same time, Syagrus does not name a random epic hero, but Agamemnon, who was regarded as a Lacedaemonian by Spartans in the fifth century BCE.[57] Moreover, Agamemnon's putative disappointment if the Sicilians were to lead the Greek army gains authority from his function as the leader of a Greek alliance in the past.[58] As a former leader of a pan-Hellenic army, Agamemnon is a figure of authority for the Greeks; and as a Lacedaemonian, he belongs to the Spartan tradition. With both aspects Syagrus underlines the Spartan claim to command the Greeks – Agamemnon is an example of Spartan leadership.

Finally, the story that Nestor mentions in the original context can serve as a precedent for the present situation. Nestor went to Phthie to fetch Achilles and bring him to the Greek army that was to conquer Troy. When the attempt to recruit Gelon against Xerxes is seen against this foil, Syagrus' appeal to Gelon gains weight from the epic model.

(iv) As we have seen, the epic background lends authority to Syagrus' statement as a speech-act which draws on Nestor's eloquence, while also buttressing its content, since the heroic parallel backs up the Spartan claim to hegemony and reinforces the appeal to Gelon. By the same token, however, the epic background turns against Syagrus. As can be shown for each aspect, the comparison with the epic model emphasizes the shortcomings of his argument.

Syagrus tries to follow Nestor's eloquence, imitates his rhetorical strategy, and even quotes him. However, he falls short of his model.[59] While Nestor refers to the tradition to encourage the Greeks, Syagrus employs it to pressure Gelon. The differences can be pursued further: Nestor adds in a very elaborate composition an exemplum to his projection of Peleus' reaction. He carefully avoids posing an explicit request. In contrast, Syagrus continues with a negative imperative, tells Gelon to forget about the command of the army and brusquely confronts him with the choice either to serve under Sparta or to stay away. Nestor's strategy works – there

---

[57] Cf. How and Wells 1912: ad 7.159 and Boedeker 1993: 167, who presents evidence that Sparta claimed the Pelopidae as its ancestors in the fifth century BCE. For archaeological evidence of a cult of Agamemnon in Sparta, see Salapata 2002 with further literature.
[58] On this aspect of Agamemnon, cf. Plut. *Ages.* 6.6–11.
[59] There is already a fundamental difference in their positions. While Nestor's wish to be rejuvenated shows that he is not directly involved and can only give advice, Syagrus is a party in the dispute.

are seven volunteers after his speech – while Syagrus' embassy does not succeed. Syagrus tries to invoke Nestor's authority, but the persuasiveness of Nestor's subtle argument underlines the failure of his own aggressive and implicitly insulting request.

Furthermore, we have to ask how far Agamemnon is suited to establish a claim to leadership. In the *Iliad* he confesses himself that he has wronged Achilles and by this caused the Greeks a lot of trouble.[60] Insofar as Agamemnon is a bad model for leadership in the *Iliad*, it can be argued that Syagrus, in trying to found his claim on him, undermines his own point.[61]

Also the implicit precedent of the recruitment of Achilles not only strengthens Syagrus' appeal, but generates a contrast highlighting its failure. While Achilles actually joins the Greek army and goes to Troy, Gelon stays away from the alliance against Xerxes. Possibly, another parallel comes to the fore: as I have already pointed out, there are similarities to the embassy in *Iliad* 9. The failure of the Greek embassy in Syracuse may remind the recipient more of this equally unsuccessful embassy than the successful pick-up of Achilles.

Let us conclude: Syagrus' quote from the *Iliad* creates a dynamic between the present situation and the epic precedent. On the one hand, the similarities help Syagrus to back up his argument; on the other, the contrasts shed a rather critical light on his speech: his imitation of Nestor places him in a most honourable tradition; at the same time, the discrepancies highlight his shortcomings. Agamemnon is an exemplum of Spartan leadership, though a questionable one. The recruitment of Achilles is a precedent for his appeal to Gelon; its success, however, contrasts with Syagrus' failure.

If we compare the ways in which Nestor and Syagrus employ the past, we can note a significant discrepancy: Nestor uses the past as an *obligation* in order to motivate the Greeks to stand up to Hector's challenge whilst Syagrus draws on the past to legitimize a *claim*. But when his claim itself reveals that he does not live up to the heroic past, it proves to be hollow. I will discuss the meta-historical function of his speech under (d), but already now we can see that Syagrus' use of the past is highly questionable and contrasts with Herodotus' approach to the past.

---

[60] *Il.* 9.115–20 and 19.78–144. There he tries to trace back his mistake to Ate's intervention. On Agamemnon's character in the *Iliad*, see Taplin 1990.

[61] An objection to this argument would be that Agamemnon is mentioned as a positive model for leadership time and again in the classical period. See, however, Grethlein 2006c: 495–6 for a parallel use of Agamemnon as an ambiguous foil in Thucydides.

(b) The Athenian's Homeric quote

When Gelon says that he would be content with leading either the army or the navy, the Athenian envoy states that the Athenian command of the navy would be endangered by Gelon's leadership. In his rejection of Gelon's proposal, he points out that Athens has the strongest fleet and mentions Athenian autochthony (7.161.2–3).[62] Moreover, he draws attention to Athens' role in the Trojan War: 'Even Homer, the epic poet, declared that from them [i.e. the Athenians] there came to Ilium the best man in deploying and marshalling the army.' ('τῶν καὶ Ὅμηρος ὁ ἐποποιὸς ἄνδρα ἄριστον ἔφησε ἐς Ἴλιον ἀπικέσθαι τάξαι τε καὶ διακοσμῆσαι στρατόν.' 7.161.3). It is difficult to say whether this is a reference to epic verses that have not been transmitted or a slightly modified reference to the mention of Menestheus in the 'Catalogue of Ships': 'Never on earth before had there been a man born like him/ for the arrangement in order of horses and shielded fighters.' ('τῷ δ' οὔ πώ τις ὁμοῖος ἐπιχθόνιος γένετ' ἀνήρ/ κοσμῆσαι ἵππους τε καὶ ἀνέρας ἀσπιδιώτας.' Il. 2.553-4).[63]

However, unlike Syagrus the Athenian envoy quotes the epic tradition explicitly and explicitly derives a claim for his city from its role in the Trojan War. Moreover, the legitimizing function of the past is far less ambiguous than in Syagrus' argument. This can be linked to the observation that, unlike the Spartan envoy, the Athenian envoy remains anonymous. Perhaps this is due to Herodotus' sources, but maybe both points taken together direct the focus more on Spartan than on Athenian claims to leadership. This would go very well with Herodotus' statement that the Athenians restrained themselves during the Persian Wars and sought hegemony only afterwards (8.3.1–2).[64]

There is one aspect which may make the Athenian's epic quotation a bit more complex than it appears at first glance: it is not evident how far Menestheus' ability to lead the *army* has an impact on the Athenians' claim to command the *navy*. However, we should not press the case too hard, as the contrast between navy and army is not marked. The ambivalence is thus much weaker than the tensions that come with Gelon's claims.

---

[62] The Athenian's speech is subtly linked with Gelon's reply to Syagrus, which starts with the following words, 7.160.1: 'Spartan stranger, the confrontation with blame (ὀνείδεα κατιόντα) tends to excite anger in a man.' The Athenian refers to this reproach when he closes his statement, 7.161.3: 'So there is no blame (ὄνειδος) attached to us for saying this.'

[63] Weber 1922: 377 notes the similarities and differences in the wording and draws attention to the parallels in the third Eion epigram (Aeschin. 3.185; Plut. *Cim.* 7.6). However, there is no reason to follow his thesis that Herodotus took the quotation from the Samian funeral speech by Pericles.

[64] See p. 184.

(c) Gelon's rejoinder

Being the tyrant of a recent superpower, Gelon cannot compete for the semantic ground of the epic past and has to draw on another source to buttress his claims. When Gelon announces that he will not join the Greek alliance, he calls his troops the 'spring of Greece': 'Since you do not give in at all and want to possess it all, you had better leave as fast as possible and tell Greece that spring has been taken from her year.' ('ἐπεὶ τοίνυν οὐδὲν ὑπιέντες ἔχειν τὸ πᾶν ἐθέλετε, οὐκ ἂν φθάνοιτε τὴν ταχίστην ὀπίσω ἀπαλλασσόμενοι καὶ ἀγγέλλοντες τῇ Ἑλλάδι ὅτι ἐκ τοῦ ἐνιαυτοῦ τὸ ἔαρ αὐτῇ ἐξαραίρηται.' 7.162.1). As the following explanation has it, Gelon presents his troops as the 'most excellent part' ('δοκιμώτατον', 7.162.2) of Greece.[65] What is more, his words establish a reply to the rhetorical strategy of Syagrus and the Athenian at different levels: regarding the form, Gelon changes the register of speech. While the ambassadors have drawn on the semantics of epic poetry, the Syracusan tyrant employs nature imagery. At the level of content, Gelon uses the spring metaphor to counter the references to ancient glory with his present vigour:[66] whereas the Spartan and the Athenian turn to the past, his empire has a future.

In the analysis of Syagrus' speech, I have distinguished the level of action from the level of reception arguing that the Spartan uses the cultural capital of the heroic past, but that for recipients who grasp the intertextual link the epic foil undermines the claims. Although Gelon pursues a different rhetorical strategy, his words, too, at the level of reception gain additional meaning from an intertext that undermines his claim and, furthermore, establishes a link to a later time. Adolf Kirchhoff has already pointed out that Herodotus has Gelon quote the spring metaphor from Pericles' funeral speech on those who died in the Samian War.[67] It has been transmitted in two passages in Aristotle's *rhetoric* (1365a31–3; 1411a2–4):

... for example, Pericles said in the funeral oration that the youth had been taken from the city as if spring had been taken from the year.

... οἷον Περικλῆς τὸν ἐπιτάφιον λέγων, τὴν νεότητα ἐκ τῆς πόλεως ἀνηρῆσθαι ὥσπερ τὸ ἔαρ ἐκ τοῦ ἐνιαυτοῦ εἰ ἐξαιρεθείη.

---

[65] Some scholars have argued that the explanation is an interpolation. On the other hand, Loraux 1975: 10 with n. 35 thinks it is authentic. See also Treves 1941: 327. Whether an interpolation or not, the explanation grasps the meaning of the metaphor at a first level; it would not make sense to connect the spring to the Greek soldiers who are going to die, since ἐξαιρεῖσθαι is used in the perfect tense: spring has already been taken out of the year.

[66] The echo of ἀπαραιρῆσθαι (7.159) in ἐξαραίρηται (7.162.1) invites the reader to juxtapose Gelon's use of nature imagery with Syagrus' invocation of Sparta's epic heritage.

[67] Kirchhoff ²1878: 19 n. 1; von Wilamowitz-Moellendorff 1877: 365 n. 51; Meyer 1899: 221; Treves 1941: 322–6 and Loraux 1975: 9 n. 34 with further literature.

... as when Pericles said that the youth killed in the war vanished from the city as though someone took the spring from the year.

... ὥσπερ Περικλῆς ἔφη τὴν νεότητα τὴν ἀπολομένην ἐν τῷ πολέμῳ οὕτως ἠφανίσθαι ἐκ τῆς πόλεως ὥσπερ εἴ τις τὸ ἔαρ ἐκ τοῦ ἐνιαυτοῦ ἐξέλοι.

It is difficult to imagine that the recipients of the *Histories* would have missed the allusion: the similarities are not only striking, but these are the only transmitted instances of the image in the classical period.[68] If Aristotle in the fourth century BCE still knew the passage from the funeral speech and considered it worthy of being quoted twice, it is a fair guess that educated fifth-century recipients would have noticed the intertextuality.

The obvious quote from a later speech has puzzled scholars. From the point of view I am taking here, it gains new significance. The specific use of the metaphor by Pericles works as a contrast. The comparison of young soldiers who have died to spring is a metonymy of the epic plant metaphor for the *mors immatura*:[69] in Pericles' words, dying soldiers are not compared to flowers or plants in spring, but to spring itself. Gelon, however, employs the spring metaphor for an army that is not even fighting. The foil of Pericles underlines the inappropriate use of the spring metaphor by Gelon. As when Nestor's reference to the past as an obligation for the present reveals its reduction to a legitimizing function in Syagrus' speech, here the foil of a well-deserved honour uncovers mere pretensions.[70] Therefore, I would like to argue against Hans van Wees that in the embassy scene not only Sparta's, but also Syracuse's aspirations to the chief command appear in a rather critical light.[71]

---

[68] Gossmann 1908: 45 n. 2 and 66 n. 4 gives the following passages as parallels: Dem. 60.23: '... it seems to me that if somebody said that the valour of these men was the soul of Greece he would say the truth'. ('... δοκεῖ δέ μοί τις ἂν εἰπὼν ὡς ἡ τῶνδε τῶν ἀνδρῶν ἀρετή τῆς Ἑλλάδος ἦν ψυχή τἀληθὲς εἰπεῖν'.), Eur. *Supp.* 447–9: 'For how could a city be strong/ when somebody cuts and plucks off the young/ like the ears in a spring field?' ('πῶς οὖν ἔτ' ἂν γένοιτ' ἂν ἰσχυρὰ πόλις/ ὅταν τις ὡς λειμῶνος ἠρινοῦ στάχυν/ τομαῖς ἀφαιρῇ κἀπολωτίζῃ νέους;'). However, these are not real parallels, but rather similar images.

[69] E.g. Euphorbus in *Il.* 17.53–60; Achilles in *Il.* 18.56–60 = 437–41; Hector in *Il.* 22.86–7. Since Loraux 1975 has pointed out that, unlike epic heroes, democratic hoplites are represented as adults, it is tempting to see an epic claim in Gelon's use of the metaphor.

[70] Gelon's pretentious attitude may be enhanced by the solemn ring of his words, which sound nearly gnomic. In Simonides' epigram on the dead at Thermopylae, 'Stranger, tell the people of Lacedaemon/ that we who lie here obeyed their commands' ('ὦ ξεῖν', ἀγγέλλειν Λακεδαιμονίοις ὅτι τῇδε/ κείμεθα τοῖς κείνων ῥήμασι πειθόμενοι', Hdt.7.228), ἀγγέλλειν is followed by an indirect object and a ὅτι-clause. Although Herodotus quotes this epigram, the similarities do not warrant reading an allusion to it in Gelon's words. Nevertheless, the parallels in the syntax reveal the high tone of Gelon's words.

[71] van Wees 2002: 341–2.

Furthermore, the spring metaphor jolts the recipient from the Persian Wars into a later time. More specifically, for the contemporaries of Herodotus it must have recalled the recent and current struggles of Athens against other Greeks for hegemony. In 6.98.2, Herodotus mentions explicitly the in-fighting among the Greeks: 'After all, during the reigns of Darius the son of Hystaspes, Xerxes the son of Darius and Artaxerxes the son of Xerxes, for these three successive generations, Greece suffered more evils than it had for twenty generations before Darius, partly those inflicted by the Persians here, partly those inflicted by the leading states in their wars for power.'[72] As the quote from the Pericles speech evokes the later and grimmer time when Greeks stood against Greeks, the controversy about the supreme command, *hegemonia*, foreshadows the fight for hegemony, that is to say political leadership.[73] Herodotus' readers knew only too well that fierce discussions like the one in the Syracusan embassy scene had given way to military confrontations.

The subtle *prolepsis* of the spring metaphor increases the temporal complexity of the embassy scene. Not only does the ancient past of the Homeric heroes mirror the recent past of the Persian Wars, but at the same time the later internal struggle for hegemony is evoked as a horizon for the embassy scene. The Athenian restraint in the Persian Wars and their subsequently aggressive politics highlight each other. This interpretation can be backed up by the observation that Herodotus explicitly mentions the Syracusan embassy when he comments on the change of Athens' attitude in foreign affairs.[74]

Thus, the Syracusan embassy scene is one of many passages in the *Histories* in which Herodotus plays with the 'future past', events that for the historical characters are still in the future, but for him and his readers already belong to the past. Particularly in the last book of the *Histories*, we find a dense net of *prolepseis* that evoke the intra-Hellenic conflicts after the Persian Wars. I have just quoted 6.98.2, an explicit comment, and in my examination of Herodotus' account of Plataea we will encounter numerous subtle references.

(d) The embassy scene as foil to the Histories

The Syracusan embassy scene deconstructs the use of the past in speeches. Paradoxically, it is the epic past itself, invoked by Syagrus to back up his

---

[72] Fornara 1971a: 32 notes that 6.98.2 refers to the Peloponnesian War. Cf. Nenci 1998: ad 6.98.9–10.
[73] This is also argued by Munson 2001: 218–19.
[74] Cf. 8.2.2–3.2. On the references back to the Syracusan embassy, see Masaracchia 1977: ad 8.2.7–9, who adds the observation that Λάκων is used only here and in 7.161.2. On Herodotus' criticism of the struggle for hegemony, see van Wees 2002: 341–2.

claims, that undermines his argument and shows how questionable such historical arguments in speeches can be. This deconstruction is particularly striking since the juxtaposition of the Trojan and the Persian Wars was prominent; it can be found not only in elegy and tragedy (see Chapter 3, Sections 3.2.1 and 3.3 and Chapter 4, section 4.1), but also in inscriptions, e.g. the Eion epigrams, and in numerous archaeological sources such as the Stoa Poikile.[75]

Herodotus, on the other hand, is very cautious with the comparison of the two wars – their explicit juxtaposition in the *Histories* is mostly focalized by Persians.[76] In Book 1, it is a Persian *logos* according to which the Trojan War was the first military encounter that led to the Persian Wars. Herodotus sets his own account off against this version and starts with Croesus (1.5–6). In 7.43, a link between the two wars is established by Xerxes, who sacrifices in Ilium on his way to Europe. Another Persian draws an analogy at the end of the *Histories*, when Artayctes asks Xerxes to give him the plot of land where Protesilaus is buried, so that he can show what consequences invaders of the Persian Empire have to face. Once he gets it, he uses the holy ground for agricultural purposes and desecrates the sanctuary by sexual debauchery (9.116).[77]

The juxtaposition of the Trojan and Persian Wars is a case of the exemplary use of the past. We have found this mode of memory in all genres under consideration in the first part of this study. Pindar evokes mythical foils to highlight athletic victories; the elegiac poets cast recent events in a heroic register and present them as models for the present; in tragedy, 'heroic vagueness' helps to negotiate present issues; the funeral speeches envisage the history of Athens as an unbroken chain of great deeds that are repeated by each new generation; and, in deliberative oratory, exempla buttress the orators' claims and arguments. Do Herodotus' deconstruction of the speeches in the Syracusan embassy scene and his reticence about the juxtaposition of Trojan with Persian Wars signal that he objects to this wide-spread mode of memory?

On the contrary, Herodotus himself envisages the past in an exemplary way. He not only has his characters juxtapose the Trojan and Persian Wars,

---

[75] See pp. 77–8.
[76] See Nesselrath 1996: 281–8, who argues that it is not Herodotus who attributes the comparisons to Persians, but that Herodotus draws on pre-existing traditions, and Erskine 2001: 83–7. When Herodotus points out the unique dimension of Xerxes' campaign in 7.20, he compares it to the Trojan War, but only as part of a large number of wars.
[77] For an analysis of the meaning of this reference to the Trojan War at the end of the *Histories*, see Boedeker 1988.

but also himself uses the heroic mirror to create meaning beyond the intention of the speakers – the dispute between Agamemnon and Achilles highlights the struggle of the Greek poleis for leadership during the Persian Wars. Throughout the *Histories*, different events and times are implicitly juxtaposed to each other. At the macro-level, the *Histories* is structured by the pattern of the rise and fall of an empire, which gets repeated over and over again. Works in the tradition of H. R. Immerwahr's *Form and Thought in Herodotus* have extensively examined foils and patterns in the *Histories* as devices for creating historical meaning, a point to which I will return in section 7.3.3 of this chapter.[78]

What is more, as we have just seen, these quarrels are made to foreshadow the later disastrous fight for hegemony. Many scholars have made a strong case for the position that Herodotus uses the *prolepseis* to later internal conflicts to indicate that Athens will follow Persia in the cyclic rise and fall of empires.[79] While it would be exaggerated to claim that Herodotus narrates the Persian Wars solely in order to warn Athens, it is hard to ignore the fact that his account also offers a lesson to the present. Herodotus thus uses the exemplary mode of memory not only descriptively, but also normatively. In his hands, history unfolds as a complex panopticon of different times mirroring each other. The heroic 'plu-past', the past of the Persian Wars and the 'future past' extending to the present shed mutual light on each other.

However, it is worth noting that Herodotus gives the exemplary use of the past a new twist. His juxtaposition of Trojan and Persian Wars deviates from the common analogy. In the 'New Simonides', in the Eion epigrams and on the Stoa Poikile, the comparison of the Trojan and Persian Wars is invoked to glorify the recent achievements of the Greeks. Herodotus too may play with the model of the Trojan War to highlight the 'epic' dimensions of the Persian Wars, but, as I have argued, he also uses the juxtaposition to draw attention to problematical aspects such as internal conflicts of the Greeks.[80] While this critical use of the past may be reminiscent of Andocides' *de pace*, it distinguishes Herodotus from most deliberative

---

[78] Immerwahr 1966. Hunter 1982: 176–225 for example has pointed out the structural similarity between Cambyses' expedition to Ethiopia, Darius' campaign against the Scythians and Xerxes' invasion into Greece. Recently, Raaflaub 2002a has argued that the Persian invasion under Xerxes is modelled on the Athenian expedition to Sicily in 427–424 BCE. See also Cobet 1971: 114–16; Fornara 1971b; Stadter 1992; Moles 2002: 48–52. On the importance of analogy in the *Histories*, see Corcella 1984. For a critical attitude to the emphasis on patterns, albeit only in a restricted field, see Waters 1971, who argues that there is not a constant (and moralizing) attitude towards tyrants in the *Histories*.

[79] Cf. Fornara 1971b; Raaflaub 1987; 2002a; Moles 1996; 2002. Rengakos 2004: 78 points out that the foreshadowing of Athens' later history resembles the *prolepseis* beyond the main action in the *Iliad*.

[80] Marincola 2006: 17–19 compares Herodotus' concept of glory with the poetic idea of glory.

speeches, in which, as the Spartans' and Athenians' arguments in the Syracusan embassy scene illustrate, the references to the epic past serve to buttress claims in the present.

Not only the purpose, to legitimize or to criticize, but also the explicitness of the link between past and present is rather different. In deliberative speeches, the comparison of the past with the present is spelled out and a precedent from the past is invoked for a specific argument in a particular situation. In Herodotus, on the other hand, the reference to the present is much vaguer and the juxtaposition much more complex. This is linked to a fundamental difference between the non-historiographic media of memory and Herodotus' work that I mentioned in the introduction to this chapter. The *Histories* is far more independent from a specific context. Unlike the poems and speeches discussed in the first part of this book, the *Histories* was not composed for a specific performance, but, being a written text, it could be read in very different settings. Nonetheless, the adumbration of later intra-Hellenic wars establishes links to the present which may be far less specific than the invocation of the past in speeches, but show that the past is nonetheless in the grip of the present. While Herodotus replaces straightforward glorification and legitimization with an indirect form of criticism, he still draws on the exemplary mode of memory.

7.2.2. *The speech duel at Plataea*

In the previous section, I have argued that the Syracusan embassy illustrates the problematical use of the past in oratory. The integration of speeches that reveal the deficiencies of their approach to the past helps to throw into relief the superiority of the *Histories*, which uses the past not so much to glorify and to legitimize but to shed critical light on the present. I would now like to offer a similar reading of the speech duel at Plataea.[81] While in the Syracusan embassy scene the criticism of oratory is implied in the epic foil that has different meanings at the levels of action and reception, the legitimizing use of the past is explicitly questioned in the discussion between the Tegeans and the Athenians at Plataea and the meta-historical significance of the speech is reinforced through an echo of an authorial reflection (a). Moreover, the criticism is not only directed towards deliberative

---

[81] The similarity of the Athenians' argument to funeral speeches has attracted the most attention, cf. n. 91 below. Otherwise, Solmsen 1944: 249 sees a 'proof of the persistence of Athenian bravery to the present time'; similarly, von Fritz 1967: 269 argues that the speech duel serves to explain and compensate for the minor relevance of the Athenians in the battle.

speeches, but also applies to epideictic oratory (b). The subsequent narrative of the battle at Plataea reinforces the implied criticism (c). As in the Syracusan embassy scene, the critique of historical arguments in speeches is linked to the adumbration of later intra-Hellenic conflicts. Since in these conflicts Plataea was an important point of reference, the *prolepsis* gives the critique of historical arguments a further twist (d).

(a) Explicit criticism of the use of the past in speeches
When the Greeks manage to defeat the Persian navy at Salamis, there remains the Persian army under Mardonius' command in Thessaly. After failing to win the Athenians as allies, Mardonius leads his troops to Athens, burns it for a second time and then goes back to Boeotia where he encounters the Greek army. A first skirmish takes place at Erythrae, after which the Greeks move to the area of Plataea, which has a spring and appears to be better suited for a battle (9.25.2–3). Here, the Tegeans and Athenians get into an argument over the battle formation.[82] The Spartans, it is agreed, can pick a wing, but both the Athenians and the Tegeans lay claim to the other wing. Instead of simply reporting who asserted themselves, Herodotus gives speeches to both parties.[83]

The Tegeans argue that they have always enjoyed a privileged position (9.26.2–7). When the Heraclidae tried to invade the Peloponnese, Hyllus suggested a duel between himself and the best of the Peloponnesians who had gathered at the Isthmus to defend their land. If he won, the Heraclidae would be allowed to settle, in the case of a victory for his opponent, the Heraclidae would be barred from the Peloponnese for a hundred years. In the duel, the Tegeans' king Echemus killed Hyllus and thus the Spartans could not settle in the Peloponnese for a hundred years. Since that time, the Tegeans claim, they have received special honours. Echemus not only exemplifies the Tegeans' excellence, he also offers a parallel to the present situation. In their attempt to conquer Greece, the Persians resemble the Heraclidae who tried to push into the Peloponnese. Similar to the ancient Peloponnesians facing the sons of Heracles, the present residents of the peninsula gathered at the Isthmus and only hesitantly joined the Athenian forces outside their own land.

---

[82] This conflict contrasts with the role of Chileus, a Tegean, who not much earlier convinced the Spartans to follow the Athenians' request for help (9.9).
[83] My interpretation is not linked to the question of whether the debate was historical; against its historicity, see already Maass 1887: 589 n. 1. What is important is that the manner of argument, in particular to use the past, is typical.

Herodotus 175

In their reply (9.27), the Athenians first question the whole discussion by contrasting mere words to deeds, then nevertheless come up with a whole catalogue of achievements themselves: they defended the rights of the Heraclidae, helped the Argives to bury their dead, fought off the Amazons and were not outshone by anybody at Troy. However, the Athenians continue, these ancient events should not count for too much – who was strong in the past can now be weak and vice versa. They therefore refer to their victory at Marathon, a recent display of virtue. Despite this evidence of their excellence, they would fight in any position and pass the decision on to the Spartans.

The Spartans unanimously decide that the Athenians should command the second wing,[84] a fair response to the debate where the Athenians clearly make a stronger case than the Tegeans. Already by questioning the discussion and agreeing to take any position, the Athenians show themselves to be superior.[85] Moreover, they take up the Tegeans' distinction between ancient and recent deeds (9.26.2; 7) and, by challenging the relevance of ancient deeds, undermine the Tegeans' exemplum. The battle of Marathon, which the Athenians juxtapose as *monomachia* to Echemus' duel (9.27.5), is not only more recent, but also establishes a closer parallel to the present situation, in which the Greeks are facing the Persians.[86] Even in the field of myth the Athenians outdo their opponents, adducing more than one event. In particular their first reference cleverly turns the tables on the Tegeans: while the Tegeans try to derive authority from a victory over the Spartans, the Athenians recall their support for the Heraclidae and thereby evoke an obligation that the Spartans, the arbiters of the controversy, have towards them.

At first glance, the Athenians' rejection of ancient deeds is a rhetorical strategy that throws into relief their strongest point, Marathon.[87] Such a reading is supported by the fact that, despite their criticism, the Athenians

---

[84] Herodotus' report on the Spartans' decision ironically harks back to the Tegeans' claim to superiority, 9.28.1: 'The entire army of the Lacedaemonians shouted that the Athenians were worthier (ἀξιονικοτέρους) than the Arcadians to hold the wing.' Cf. 9.26.6: 'Even independently of this achievement which we have mentioned, we are worthier (ἀξιονικότεροι) to have this position.'

[85] Thus, in accordance with the argument of the Athenian ambassador in 7.161.2 and Herodotus' authorial comment in 8.3, the Athenians' speech emphasizes the willingness to subordinate their own business to the common fight against the Persians, cf. Kierdorf 1966: 100; von Fritz 1967: 269.

[86] This is obvious when Pausanias mentions Marathon in his argument for swapping sides with Athenians (9.46.2). It is noteworthy that the number of nations the Athenians claim to have defeated exactly corresponds to the number in Herodotus' account in 7.60–80, cf. Meyer 1899: 219 n. 1.

[87] Cf. Pallantza 2005: 167–8, who criticizes Cartledge 1993: 28–9 for seeing a distinction between *spatium mythicum* and *spatium historicum*, and herself emphasizes the 'okkasionelle Element dieser Aufwertung der Gegenwart'. On the central role of Marathon in the Athenians' speech, see also Solmsen 1944: 249.

actually do mention a series of ancient achievements.[88] At the same time, the Athenians' argument, even if only used as a rhetorical device, parallels the scepticism toward ancient exempla and the preference for recent events which we have found in deliberative and judicial oratory.[89] It also calls to mind Herodotus' own reservations. Even though the Athenians do not invoke Herodotus' epistemological scepticism towards the reconstruction of events in the distant past,[90] their position echoes the *Histories'* proem, which closes with the remark that great cities can become small and, inversely, small cities great: 'For most of those which were great in the past have become small, and those which were great in my own time were small in times past. Since I know that human happiness never remains in the same place, I will mention both equally.' (1.5.4).

The echo of this central narratorial statement gives the point weight beyond its rhetorical function within the Athenians' speech and invites the readers to read the Athenians' statement as a reflection about memory in general. More specifically, it draws the reader's attention to a general flaw of exemplary uses of the past: any exemplum presupposes that the present resembles the past. Only on this condition can the past serve as a legitimization for the present. In the Syracusan embassy scene, the use of exempla for legitimizing purposes is implicitly questioned by their ambivalence; the epic parallels quoted do not so much buttress the characters' claims as undermine them. The Athenians' comments in the speech duel at Plataea, on the other hand, explicitly call attention to the highly questionable assumption on which exempla rest – the assumption of regularity which squares badly with the mutability of life that, as we will see (section 7.3), is at the core of the *Histories*. Herodotus thereby challenges an essential aspect of memory in the orators who frequently use exempla, as we have seen in the Andocides chapter. Despite this criticism, the debate at Plataea and the following narrative reveal that Herodotus himself draws on the exemplary mode of memory, replacing however the purpose of legitimizing with a critical view. Before I elaborate on this, I would like to take my

---

[88] Pallantza 2005: 167–8 sees here even 'logische Widersprüche'.   [89] See pp. 142–4.
[90] The Athenians in Thuc. 1.73.2, on the other hand, in their rejection of old deeds adduce epistemological reasons reminiscent of Thucydides' own reflections: 'Now as for the remote past (τὰ ... πάνυ παλαιά), what need is there to speak of events for which the audience would have the evidence of hearsay accounts rather than their personal experience?' For yet another reason why one should reject references to ancient deeds, see the Thebans in Thuc. 3.67.2: 'Do not be moved to pity by hearing old achievements, if they actually happened, achievements which should assist those who are being wronged, but for those acting shamefully mean double punishment, because they sin not in accordance with their heritage.' See also p. 235 n. 108.

interpretation of Herodotus' criticism of oratory and its uses of the past a step further.

(b) The Athenians' criticism and funeral speeches
The Athenians' speech not only questions the use of the past in deliberative rhetoric, it also casts a critical light on epideictic oratory. Scholars have noted that the Athenians' speech contains central topoi of the *epitaphioi logoi*.[91] The help for the Heraclidae, the support of the Argives, the fight against the Amazons and the battle of Marathon are the core of the funeral speeches' historical sections. The change of the usual order of the argument gives prominence to the help for the Heraclidae, which forms a direct reply to Echemus' victory over the Heracles-son Hyllus.[92] While it is true that 'praises of Athens must surely have been made before the formal introduction of a "funeral speech", and the sorts of praises used here by the Athenians are familiar from some parts of tragedy',[93] it is striking that the list of deeds follows so closely the catalogue of the *epitaphioi logoi*.

Moreover, the question arises how relevant the individual exempla are for the Athenians' case. The help for the Heraclidae is directed against the Tegeans' exemplum and the attack of the Amazons may prefigure the Persian invasion,[94] but there is no particular reason why the support for the Argives should be mentioned. Like the Athenian support for the Heraclidae, this myth not only propagated another polis' obligation towards Athens, but helped to sell an aggressive foreign policy as selfless help.[95] Thus, it does not really fit into an argument at a time when Athens had yet no claim to hegemony. Of course, the story of the Argives may be used merely to reflect Athenian grandeur and I would not go so far as to call it blatantly anachronistic in the Athenians' argument, but the impression of a slight displacement reinforces the reference to the tradition of funeral

---

[91] Cf. Meyer 1899: 219–21; Jacoby 1913: 491; Schmitz-Kahlmann 1939: 63–5; Solmsen 1944: 249; West 1970: 275; Loraux 1986a: 65. Kierdorf 1966: 107 makes the interesting argument that the canon of mythical deeds was not formed in the funeral speeches, but derives from speeches about foreign affairs. On this link, see also the literature cited by West 1970: 274 n. 16. On *epitaphioi logoi*, see Chapter 5.

[92] Cf. Schulz 1933: 40; Kierdorf 1966: 98. Moreover, the reference to the Trojan War distinguishes the Athenian speech from the preserved *epitaphioi logoi*, only two of which mention the Trojan War (Dem. 60.10–11 and Hyp. 6.35–6), yet never as a part of the catalogue of deeds. Cf. Gotteland 2001: 218. Kierdorf 1966: 98–9 argues that the reference to the Trojan War is a relic from the propaganda before the Persian Wars.

[93] Flower and Marincola 2002: ad 9.27.1–6.

[94] The parallel between the Amazons' invasion and the Persian attack is even marked: according to the Athenians' speech, the Amazons came from the river Thermodon (9.27.4). Later, the Persians are said to come from the same river (9.43.2).

[95] Cf. Neumann 1995: 149–67. On the asylum motive in tragedy, see Grethlein 2003a.

speeches.[96] Even though the public funeral speeches were probably introduced after the Persian Wars, there can be little doubt that the Athenians' speech would have reminded Herodotus' readers of this institution.

It can therefore be argued not only that the Athenians challenge the exemplary use of the past in deliberative speeches, but that their criticism also applies to epideictic oratory. Seen from this angle, the subversive potential of what at the level of the action may be no more than a rhetorical device reaches quite far, affecting the genre in which Athens was 'invented'. While the *epitaphioi logoi*, as we have seen, envisage Athens' history as an untainted continuum, Herodotus has the Athenians question the validity for the present of virtues exhibited in the past. In doubting the relevance of topoi central to the funeral speeches, the Athenians' own words question an institution that was crucial in defining their political identity.

This interpretation ties in well with the observation that time and again Herodotus' *Histories* deviates from the 'official' version of Athenian history in the funeral speeches. The Amazons, for example, figure in the *epitaphioi logoi* as the 'other', warrior women, whose transgressive nature threatens Greek identity. As in the Athenians' speech at Plataea the Amazons were portrayed as invaders who were fought off like the Persians. Herodotus does not directly question this version, but, as R. V. Munson shows, he 'radically revises its ethical slant'.[97] In the Sauromatian *logos* (4.110–17), some of the Amazons who survive the defeat at the Thermodon River escape and, after roaming about, come to Scythia. The Scythians send out young soldiers to shadow them; these, however, get entangled with the Amazons and finally live together with them. One might object that, from the Greek perspective, the Scythians themselves are the 'other', but it is nonetheless remarkable that the story dissolves the radical alterity that defines the Amazons in oratory. The Amazons refuse to assimilate with the people of their young lovers and stick to their military activity, but they do settle down, each becoming the wife of a young Scythian. Particularly the fact that the Amazons get married reduces their otherness.

The representation of the Amazons reveals interesting differences between the 'official' history of Athens and Herodotus' account of the past; in other

---

[96] Cf. Kierdorf 1966: 109: 'Die Athenerrede bei Herodot ist insofern ein wenig anachronistisch, als sie die mythischen Parallelen (Hikesie-Geschichten) zu einem Ereignis bietet, das sich zu der angenommenen Zeit noch gar nicht ereignet hat.' See also Munson 2001: 220, who notes that the speech 'conforms to the manner of fifth-century hegemonic rhetoric'.

[97] Munson 2001: 123–32, quotation on 125. See also Gotteland 2001: 144 (131–61 on Amazons in speeches in general). However, Herodotus' account runs against the version in Lysias' funeral speech, according to which no Amazon survived the battle.

cases, there are even outright contradictions. While in the funeral speeches Athens has always been united and powerful, Herodotus notes that, under the rule of the Peisistratids, Athens was torn by civil strife and therefore rather feeble (1.59).[98] There is only one mention of Theseus in the transmitted funeral speeches (Dem. 60.28),[99] but in other sources he is made to prefigure many of the virtues of democratic Athens in the mythic age.[100] Herodotus, on the other hand, portrays him as a highly ambiguous figure and accuses him of hubris when he mentions his abduction of Helen.[101]

To sum up: the Athenians may reject the relevance of ancient exempla only to highlight their own achievements in the recent past, and yet the echoes of the proem invite readers to ponder generally on the use or abuse of the past in speeches and to compare it with the approach of the *Histories*. The critique is not limited to deliberative oratory, but also challenges the portrayal of Athens in the funeral speeches, central topoi of which the Athenians repeat in their speech. In the next section, I will demonstrate that the following account of the battle at Plataea illustrates the Athenians' emphasis on the discrepancy between reputation and reality and thereby reinforces the critique of historical arguments in speeches.

(c) The speech duel and the battle

As we have seen, the Tegeans adduce the *monomachia* of Echemus, and the Athenians counter their claim by calling Marathon a *monomachia*. The idea of a duel is taken up in the following narrative (9.46–49.1): after the Macedonian king Alexander has secretly visited the camp of the Greeks at night to alert them to the imminent attack, the Spartans, who face the Persians in the battle line, are gripped by fear and suggest that they swap positions with the Athenians, who have experience in fighting the Persians. The Persians, however, notice the change and themselves change their battle formation so that the Spartans come to face the Persians again. Mardonius sends a messenger who mocks the Spartans and challenges them, suggesting that an equal contingent of Persians and Spartans fight, either to decide the battle or as a prelude to the clash of the whole armies. The Spartans' reply to this challenge is silence.

The Persians' challenge not only takes up the theme of the *monomachia*, but it also illustrates the gap between reputation and reality that the

---

[98] Cf. Moles 2002: 37.   [99] Cf. Loraux 1986a: 65–6.
[100] Cf. Mills 1997: 1–42. Walker 1995: 55 emphasizes the relevance of Theseus as a mythical figure in the time of the Persian Wars.
[101] See below pp. 182–3, for the critical presentation of Theseus in Thucydides, see Walker 1995: 195–9. Isoc. 10.18–9 offers an apologetic presentation of the abduction of Helen.

Athenians have mentioned. The messenger sharply contrasts the Spartans' reputation for never fleeing or leaving the battle line with what they have just done (9.48.1–2).[102] This tension between the glory and actual performance of the Spartans is also pointed out when the Greeks decide to retreat (9.53.2):

> There the other *taxiarchs* were prepared to obey Pausanias, but Amompharetus the son of Poliadas, who was the *lochagos* of the company from Pitana, declared that he would not flee from the strangers nor, of his own free will, bring shame to Sparta. He was puzzled by what he saw going on, since he had not attended the earlier discussion.

Amompharetus' refusal to follow orders highlights the fact that the retreat contradicts the Spartan code of honour. Even critics who emphasize the problematic aspect of his disobedience[103] will have to concede that the fierce quarrel of the Spartans whether to stay or to go does not reflect positively on them. A critical view of the Spartan retreat is also supported by Mardonius' comment in which he compares the Spartans' cowardice to their alleged bravery (9.58.2–4). Thus, the Spartans' behaviour is compared critically to their reputation by one of themselves as well as by their opponents.

Finally, however, when the Persians attack, the Spartans prove to be brave and live up to their standards. Since most other Greeks have left for the Heraeum and the Athenians are engaged in a battle with the Greek allies of the Persians, a *monomachia* of some sort does take place – the Spartans fight alone with the Tegeans against the Persians.[104] And here, they show their valour:[105] 'Here the Spartans gained justice from Mardonius for the murder of Leonidas, just as the oracle had predicted, and Pausanias the son of Cleombrotus and grandson of Anaxandridas won the most glorious victory of any known to us (νίκην ... καλλίστην ἁπασέων τῶν ἡμεῖς ἴδμεν).' (9.64.1).[106]

Nevertheless, the Spartans' earlier attempts at evading a confrontation with the Persians tie in badly with their reputation. The swapping of positions with the Athenians and the retreat are less than heroic. This does not necessarily mean that, possibly induced by an Athenian source,

---

[102] See, for example, the Spartans at Thermopylae, Hdt. 7.207–28.

[103] For such an interpretation, see von Fritz 1967: 271–2, who emphasizes the stubbornness of Amompharetus and somehow argues that the Spartans have no fear. On the military aspect, see Tritle 2006: 219.

[104] 9.59.1: '... he [i.e. Mardonius] went for the Lacedaemonians and Tegeans alone (μούνους) ...'; 9.61.2: 'So, left alone (μουνωθέντες), the Lacedaemonians and Tegeans ...'

[105] This behaviour of the Spartans corresponds exactly to the words of the Spartan Demaratus, who discusses the Spartans' bravery with Xerxes (7.104.3).

[106] See also 9.71.1: 'Among the Greeks, although the Tegeans and the Athenians proved their worth, the Lacedaemonians excelled in valour (ὑπερεβάλοντο ἀρετῇ).'

Herodotus aims at denigrating the Spartans – in the passage just quoted, he goes out of his way to praise their victory. The narrative rather conveys that, even with soldiers as brave as Spartans and even in a victory as celebrated as that of Plataea, there may be a gap between reputation and actual performance. Thus, the narrative of the Plataean battle illustrates the Athenians' scepticism about the significance of past deeds for the present and thereby further challenges the legitimizing use of past exempla in speeches.

(d) Criticism of oratory's use of the past and the future of Greece
In the Syracusan embassy scene, the questionable use of the past is linked to *prolepseis* so that the claim to leadership that is backed up by the invocation of the heroic past simultaneously foreshadows the later intra-Hellenic fights for hegemony. Similar references to the future can be found in the debate between Tegeans and Athenians and the following account of the battle at Plataea. I would like to show not only that, as in the Syracusan embassy scene, Herodotus unveils the deficiencies of rhetorical exempla, but that the foreshadowings also establish the exemplary mode of memory, which, however, is distinct from the orators' use of this commemorative mode. We have seen that the catalogue of deeds from the *epitaphioi logoi* bears the imprint of Athenian imperialism and thereby jolts the readers into a later time when Athens had to defend its empire. Essential terms for the ensuing conflicts such as 'supremacy' ('ἡγεμονία') and 'faction, sedition' ('στάσις')[107] are already present in the discussion between Athenians and Tegeans. As in the Syracusan embassy scene, the foreshadowings establish an exemplary use of the past which differs from the exempla used by the orators.

The foreshadowing in the Athenians' speech is reinforced by a dense net of *prolepseis* in the account of the battle at Plataea. Most strikingly, Herodotus uses the introduction of the two seers of the Greek and Persian armies to look back to the past and at the same time to allude to the later fights between Greek poleis. In adding *prolepseis* to *analepseis*, Herodotus transfers the function of seers, i.e. to prognosticate the future, from the level of the action to the level of the plot, using it for his own narrative.

The Greeks' seer, Teisamenes, had received an oracle, according to which he would 'win five crucial contests' ('ἀγῶνας τοὺς μεγίστους ἀναιρήσεσθαι πέντε', 9.33.2). At first he thinks that he is destined to win the Olympic pentathlon, but it turns out that ἀναιρήσεσθαι signifies 'foreseeing' instead of 'winning'. Due to this gift, Teisamenes manages to

---

[107] τὸν Πελοποννησίων ἡγεμόνα (9.26.4); ἡγεμονεύειν (26.5); ἡγεμονεύειν (26.6); στασιάζειν (27.6).

gain Spartan citizenship for himself and his brother, an exceptional honour which prompts Herodotus to include an *analepsis* into the very distant past, namely to Melampus, who was the only other man whom the Spartans granted their citizenship.[108] This retrospective is immediately followed by the *prolepsis* of the five battles that Teisamenes was to predict, after Plataea, the battles at Tegea (c. 473–470 BCE), Dipaea (c. 470–465 BCE), probably Mt. Ithome and Tanagra (458–457 BCE).[109]

Teisamenes' opponent in the Persian camp is the Elean seer Hegesistratus (9.37). He had been condemned to death by the Spartans, but had managed to escape by cutting off his own foot by which he was fettered and fled to the Tegeans, who were at loggerheads with the Spartans at that time.[110] Herodotus adds that he would later be caught in Zacynthus and killed by the Spartans.[111]

In his presentation of the two seers, Herodotus mentions intra-Hellenic fights before and particularly after the Persian Wars. The story of Hegesistratus evokes a previous conflict between Sparta and Tegea[112] and the four wars to be predicted by Teisamenes are all domestic fights. This view of the future forcefully reminds the readers that the quarrel over positions in the battle formation at Plataea would turn into real fights for hegemony. The term ὠθισμός ('thrusting', 'struggling') is used as a metaphor for the word *agon*, but its literal meaning anticipates martial encounters.

The introduction of Teisamenes and Hegesistratus is not the only passage in the account of Plataea that refers to later conflicts between Greeks. To give another example, Mardonius was killed by the Spartan Arimnestus, who, Herodotus adds, himself died after the Persian Wars in a clash with the Messenians (9.64.2). A further passage deserves a closer look, since it combines an *analepsis* with a *prolepsis* that extends to the Peloponnesian War (9.73). The Decelean origin of the single Athenian who excelled at Plataea, Sophanes, brings Herodotus to the mythic past. After Theseus had raped Helen and hidden her somewhere, her brothers, the Tyndaridae, invaded Attica and threatened to destroy everything in their search. Either Decelus himself or other Deceleans, angry about Theseus' hubris and concerned about Attica's fate, revealed to them the

---

[108] Teisamenes is said to have 'imitated' Melampus. For a similar case, Cleisthenes, see 5.67.1. The phrasing raises the question of whether the imitation is a conscious act by the character or inferred by Herodotus.
[109] For the single battles, see Flower and Marincola 2002: ad 9.35.2.
[110] He is not the only one whom Herodotus reports to have fled from Sparta to Tegea, see also Leotychidas in 6.72.2.
[111] On possible dates, see Macan 1908: ad 9.37.4.
[112] For earlier wars between Sparta and Tegea, see also 1.66–8 with the interpretation by Boedeker 1993.

place, Aphidnae, where Theseus had hidden Helen. For this, the Deceleans were awarded privileges from Sparta (9.73.3):

> On account of this achievement, the Deceleans have enjoyed in Sparta exemption from tax and the privilege of front seats, all the way down to today, so that even during the war which was fought many years later between the Athenians and the Peloponnesians, although the Lacedaemonians devastated the rest of Attica, they kept away from Decelea.[113]

In a zigzag course, the affiliation of Sophanes, who excelled at Plataea, prompts Herodotus to turn to the mythic past, whence he jumps straight to the recent past. Put in technical terms, a far reaching *analepsis* leads to a *prolepsis* that comes close to the narrator's present. Irrelevant as the Decelean origin of Sophanes is, it could be argued that it is merely introduced to establish a link to the Peloponnesian War *via* myth. In their commentary, Flower and Marincola suggest that the Theseus–story serves not only as an *aition* for the saving of Decelea, but also as a mirror for the Peloponnesian War:

> The hubris of Theseus here in provoking a Spartan invasion may allude to Athens' (or Pericles'?) role in the outbreak of the Peloponnesian War. Decelus, we are next told, revealed Helen's whereabouts because 'he feared for the whole land of Attica'. In Alcman's version of this myth (Paus. 1.41.4 = PMG 21) the Dioscuri actually captured Athens; by not accepting that version H[erodotus] is perhaps providing contemporary Athenians with a mythic paradigm for preserving their city in the current war: by following the example of Decelus and coming to terms with Sparta, they could still save themselves from destruction.[114]

I am not so sure that the example of Decelus is intended to suggest a solution for current problems, but it is difficult to deny that the Theseus–story serves as a mirror to the recent past or present. In both cases, Attica is invaded by Spartans and the recent saving of Decelea is causally linked to the Tyndaridae's attack. Seen from this perspective, Theseus' hubris not only squares badly with his public image in Athens, but also sheds a rather critical light on Athens in the Peloponnesian War.

Thus, Herodotus' account of the battle of Plataea not only exemplifies the tension between reputation and reality that the Athenians pointed out, but also reinforces the *prolepseis*, which are encapsulated in the speech duel itself, and thereby makes the diplomatic disputes anticipate the later conflicts that would lead to outright hostilities. As in the Syracusan embassy

---

[113] For later ancient testimonies, see Macan 1908: ad 9.73.2. See also Mills 1997: 7–10.
[114] Flower and Marincola 2002: ad 9.73.2. If Theseus figures as a mirror for Pericles, this would have a parallel in Thucydides, cf. Walker 1995: 195.

scene, the juxtaposition of different times relies on the exemplary mode of memory. While Herodotus demonstrates in the Plataean debate how questionable the exemplary use of the past for legitimizing purposes is, he employs the same mode of memory for critical purposes, namely to highlight issues of his own time.

In the Plataea Debate, the foreshadowing enhances the significance of the Athenians' speech further in two regards. First, the *prolepseis* give an additional level of meaning to a particular point in the Athenians' speech for the *Histories'* readers. The statement that everything is changeable applies only too well to Athens itself. At Plataea, the Athenians subordinate their own claims to the necessity of unity in the fight against the Persians. Yet, as Herodotus explicitly remarks, this would change (8.3.1–2):

> But when the allies protested, the Athenians gave way, because they deemed it important that Greece survived and knew that if they made leadership a point of dispute, Greece was lost. And they were right, for internal dissension is worse than a united war to the same degree that war is worse than peace. So it was from appreciation of this fact that they did not resist, but gave way, as long as they badly needed them [i.e. the other Greeks], as they later demonstrated. For once they had repulsed the Persian and fought already for his territory, they used Pausanias' arrogant behaviour as a pretext and deprived the Lacedaemonians of the leadership. But all this happened later.

The further development of Athens' foreign politics gives an ironic slant to the emphasis that the Athenians put on changeability. The irony gets even sharper against the backdrop of the Peloponnesian War, which made Athens into an excellent example for a state that loses its power.

Second, as in the Syracusan embassy scene, the *prolepseis* indicate that the controversy about the battle formation would turn into actual fighting. More specifically, the *prolepseis* jolt the readers forward in time to when the battle of Plataea had itself gained the status of symbolic capital that was fiercely fought over.[115] Seen from this perspective, the speech duel at Plataea gets a new twist: the use of the past for legitimizing purposes is questioned in the context of an event that itself served to found claims in Herodotus' time.

A glimpse of this relevance of Plataea can be caught even in the *Histories*: Herodotus reports that the dead were buried separately at Plataea (9.85). The Spartans, Tegeans and Athenians gave their dead graves of their own. What is more, even poleis that were not involved in the fighting erected

---

[115] For a discussion of the reception of Plataea in antiquity, see now Jung 2006: 225–383 with further literature.

mounds. As an example, Herodotus mentions Aegina, for which ten years after the battle Cleades, the Aeginetan *proxenos* in Plataea, built a mound.[116] The poleis' efforts to mark or even 'create' their share in the victory against the Persians demonstrate Plataea's value as symbolic capital.[117] The *anathema* that the Greek alliance put up at the Delphic temple of Apollo is a further testimony to rival claims over the memory of Plataea.[118] At first, an inscription was added that declared the Spartan Pausanias as its dedicator.[119] Yet, owing to the protest of other poleis, his inscription was removed. Neither the appropriation by an individual nor by a single polis was accepted.

Moreover, the famous Plataean Debate in Thucydides (3.53–67), which may not be historical but employs fairly typical arguments and thus represents diplomatic conventions, attests the prominence of Plataea's heritage.[120] While the Plataeans invoke the battle as reason for their autonomy, the Spartans employ it as a mirror for their war against Athens.[121] In Athens, on the other hand, the victory, which was primarily due to the Spartans, had to step back behind the Athenian successes at Marathon and Salamis or was newly interpreted as an Athenian victory.[122]

As these examples show, Plataea, like Marathon in the Athenians' speech, was soon to be invoked to justify claims in the present.[123] Thus, the historical arguments in the speech duel make the account of Plataea entail *in nuce* its own history of reception. Herodotus not only criticizes historical arguments, but in combining his deconstruction of historical arguments with foreshadowings of later intra-Hellenic wars, he challenges the attempts of Greeks in his own time to instrumentalize the heritage of Plataea for their claims. As in the Syracusan embassy scene, Herodotus employs the exemplary mode of memory and uses the presentation of the Persian Wars to

---

[116] Cf. Huxley 1963. [117] Cf. Jung 2006: 259–60. [118] Cf. Jung 2006: 243–55.
[119] 'As leader of the Hellenes Pausanias destroyed the army of the Medes/ and dedicated this memorial to Phoibos' (Ἑλλήνων ἀρχηγὸς ἐπεὶ στρατὸν ὤλεσε Μήδων,/ Παυσανίας Φοίβῳ μνῆμ' ἀνέθηκε τόδε). The text of the inscription is to be found in Thuc. 1.132.2, and later in Demosthenes 59.97 and Plut. *Malign. Herod.* 42.
[120] Cf. Chapter 8, section 8.2.2.
[121] The Spartans' attempt to cast the Athenians as the new Persians is most obvious in the neologisms ἀττικίζειν and ἀττικισμός (3.62.2; 64.5).
[122] For example, in Pl. *Menex.* Marathon and Salamis are praised at great length. Plataea, however, comes third and gets only a single sentence (241c4–6). In the *Panegyricus*, Isocrates even closes his account of the war against Xerxes (4.89–97) with Salamis. Lys. 2. 44–7, on the other hand, emphasizes Athenian merits: when the Spartans and Tegeans were already starting to flee, the Athenians turned the battle around with their bravery. Cf. Jung 2006: 289–93.
[123] Another act of memory that could be a polis' attempt at appropriating Plataea for itself is the 'New Simonides'. What we have of it shows a focus on Sparta, but there are also aspects implying a pan-Hellenic perspective and the orientation of the whole poem is debated. See pp. 51–4.

shed light on his own time. Once more, his juxtaposition is far more subtle and complex than exempla in speeches, it is not instrumentalized for a particular purpose in a specific situation and it replaces glorification and legitimization with a critical perspective.

7.2.3. Conclusion

Herodotus not only explicitly criticizes epic poetry as an alternative commemorative genre, but some speeches can be read as an implicit critique of the use of the past in oratory. I have argued that the speeches in the Syracusan embassy scene and at Plataea unveil the deficiencies of the exemplary use of the past in deliberative speeches, and that the latter also challenges the portrayal of Athens in the *epitaphioi logoi*. Strikingly, this criticism is linked to later domestic fighting – in both passages, the discussion about leadership foreshadows the struggle for hegemony. Thus, we may note that much as Herodotus criticizes the exemplary mode of memory, he employs it himself in his *Histories*, descriptively and also normatively when he juxtaposes the Persian Wars with current intra-Hellenic conflicts. As the rape of Helen shows, Herodotus does not shy away from evoking even the mythic past as a mirror for the recent past or the present.[124] Despite his critical eye on exempla in oratory, Herodotus himself sets up a whole panopticon, in which the mythic past, the time of the Persian Wars and more recent events mirror each other.

That being said, there are crucial differences between Herodotus' exemplary use of the past and exempla in speeches. Instead of glorifying the present or legitimizing claims, Herodotus uses the foil of the past rather to highlight problematical aspects. While this critical stance may seem reminiscent of some of the exempla found in Andocides' *de pace*, the legitimizing use of the past that Herodotus challenges is widespread in oratory. Moreover, the subtlety and complexity of the juxtaposition of past and present distinguishes the historian from the orator. For example, in the Syracusan embassy scene Herodotus plays with different intertexts and pits

---

[124] The similarity between the Tegeans' argument and the link that Herodotus notes between past and present shows in the parallel phrasing: 'As a result of this achievement (ἐκ τούτου τοῦ ἔργου), we gained among the Peloponnesians of the time also other great privileges which we continue to hold (τὰ διατελέομεν ἔχοντες)' (9.26.5). 'On account of this achievement (ἀπὸ τούτου τοῦ ἔργου), the Deceleans have enjoyed in Sparta exemption from tax and the privilege of front seats, until today (διατελέει ἐς τόδε αἰεὶ ἔτι ἐοῦσα)' (9.73.3). Nonetheless, the difference is obvious: while the Tegeans use the past to legitimize a claim, Herodotus observes a link between the past and the present.

the level of reception against the level of action, and, in the account of Plataea, the speeches closely interact with the narrative. These differences from the orators are linked to a fundamental distinction between Herodotus and all commemorative genres that I have discussed in the first half of this study. While elegies, victory odes, tragedies, funeral and deliberative speeches are intended for performance in a particular setting, the *Histories* are a written text and therefore independent of a specific context. Accordingly, the *Histories* are not written from the perspective of a single polis as most of the texts discussed in the first half are, but return to the pan-Hellenic perspective of the Homeric epics. While Herodotus' account of the past is firmly embedded in the present, it does not buttress specific claims of a particular community.

7.3. CONTINUITY IN THE IDEA OF HISTORY: THE CROESUS–*LOGOS* (1.26–94)

My examination of Herodotus' critique of Homer as well as my meta-historical reading of the speeches have revealed that, even where Herodotus tries to set his own approach off against other commemorative genres, important similarities can be noted. Herodotus concludes his Helen–*logos* with an explanatory pattern that seems to align his *Histories* with the *Iliad*, and in the Syracusan embassy scene as well as in the speech duel at Plataea, the rhetorical use of the past is deconstructed, but nonetheless both passages show Herodotus using the past in an exemplary way. In this section, I would like to elaborate further on this observation and prove that the idea of history underlying Herodotus' work resembles what we know from non-historiographic genres of memory. Much as Herodotus calls attention to the innovation of his approach, the understanding of human life in the *Histories* belongs to the tradition formed by poetic and rhetorical accounts of the past.

The first part of this book has presented ample evidence that different genres have different ideas of history. Depending on the topic – e.g. distant or recent past, history of the polis or of Greece – and depending on the socio-political context – festival, symposium etc. – different views of human life in time emerge in accordance with the narrative forms of the genres. However, I have argued that there is a shared tension that underlies the genres' individual ideas of history, different as they may be from each other. On the one hand, contingency of chance figures prominently: life is subject to forces which are beyond man's control and human plans constantly fail. On the other hand, in viewing the past, continuities and regularities are established that limit the danger of contingency of chance; traditions help to form identities and exempla are given to guide actions.

In the following, I try to insert the *Histories* into this scenario, taking the Croesus–*logos* as an example, but also referring to other passages. The story of the Lydian king stands programmatically at the beginning of the *Histories* and presents patterns which will recur again and again.[125] Herodotus' account of Croesus has been much discussed; particularly works that try to figure out Herodotus' philosophy of history tend to start with the Croesus–*logos*. Instead of adding to Herodotean scholarship another lengthy retelling of it, I will restrict myself to briefly pointing out the underlying idea of history (7.3.1). I shall then argue that this idea of history is expressed by the *Histories*' narrative form (7.3.2) and finally consider the relation between historical characters and readers with regard to time, showing that Herodotus does not dissolve contingency of chance in a philosophy of history, but masters it through narrating the past (7.3.3).

7.3.1. The idea of history

Croesus extended the Lydian Empire and subjected some peoples in Asia, among them the Greeks at the west coast of Anatolia. His empire was then conquered by the Persians, who became the new rulers of Asia. These are the basic political events covered by Herodotus' Croesus–*logos*. His narrative, however, is not restricted to a bare account of events and goes beyond the replacement of one Eastern monarchy by another, yielding a more general view of man in history. A distinct idea of history emerges in the interplay between plot, protagonists' speeches and narratorial comments.

The central scene that provides the account of Croesus with an interpretative frame is his encounter with Solon.[126] Asked by Croesus whom he deems the most blessed man, Solon bluntly defies Croesus' expectations – that, of course, he himself will be the one – and names first an Athenian citizen, Tellus (1.30), and then two Argive brothers, Cleobis and Biton (1.31).[127] When Croesus is irritated and asks how these rather simple folks can compare to

---

[125] Cf. Regenbogen 1930: 228; Erbse 1979: 198–200; Raaflaub 2002b: 167–8; Pelling 2006a: 105. Harrison 2000b: 43–63 offers a detailed comparison of Croesus with Cyrus, Polycrates, Xerxes and other characters.
[126] On this scene, see Miller 1963; Schneeweiß 1975; Stahl 1975; Chiasson 1986; Harrison 2000b: 31–63.
[127] On these stories, see still Regenbogen 1961; on the ritualist background of the Cleobis and Biton story, see Chiasson 2005. On Tellus as *nom parlant* that alludes to τέλος, a central term in Solon's reflections, see Immerwahr 1966: 156 with n. 21; Nagy 1990: 245 n. 129. Long 1987: 65–6 lists all the repetitions of the stem τελ-.

his bliss, Solon points out the unpredictability of the future and emphasizes that only from the end can a life's quality be assessed (1.32.1–9):

> Croesus, when you ask me about human affairs, you put your question to someone who is well aware of how utterly jealous and given to troubling the divine is. In a long time span it is possible to see many things which one would rather not, and also to suffer much ... Of all these days in seventy years, 26,250, one day does not bring exactly the same thing as another. Hence, Croesus, man is entirely a matter of chance ... It is necessary to consider the end of anything, how it will turn out. For the god often offers prosperity to many, but then destroys them completely.[128]

Herodotus not only has Solon lecture about the jealousy of the gods, the changeability of life and the need to wait for the end, but he gives his reflection significance at the level of the plot, when Croesus, who sneers at Solon, has experiences that conform only too well to Solon's words. After the encounter with Solon, Croesus' bliss is ruined in two steps.[129] First, Croesus dreams that his beloved son will die (1.34.2) and not only despite, but precisely because of his efforts to avert this, his son is killed.[130] A guest–friend whom Croesus has instructed to keep an eye on his son while he is hunting misses the boar and kills Atys with his spear (1.34–45). Second, Croesus starts a war with the Persian king, Cyrus, is defeated and loses his empire (1.71–85). Thus, the further development makes Solon's general words retrospectively look like a specific prediction or warning to Croesus.[131]

The interpretative frame set out by Solon is also given authority by its correspondence to a point made by Herodotus himself at the end of his proem: 'For most of those [i.e. cities] which were great in the past have become small, and those which were great in my own time were small in times past. Since I know that human happiness never remains in the same place, I will mention both equally.' (1.5.4). Just as with the Athenians' emphasis on general changeability in the debate at Plataea, the echo of Herodotus' authorial reflection lends weight to Solon's comments on human fragility.

---

[128] See Harrison 2000b: 38–9 with references to parallels and scholarship. Mikalson 2003: 147–53 emphasizes the poetic origin, which he strictly distinguishes from popular religion.

[129] One could argue that Croesus' twofold disaster, first the personal loss of his son, then the political loss of his country, follows the structure outlined by Solon, who points out that men resemble countries insofar as they can never quite achieve *autarkeia*. Solon's paradigmatic juxtaposition unfolds syntagmatically in Croesus' life.

[130] Erbse 1992: 16 notes that Atys embodies the future of the dynasty, because his brother is mute. Thus, one could argue, already Atys' death fulfils the oracle according to which the Mermniads' rule will only extend over five generations.

[131] In 1.86.3, Croesus calls Solon's reflection 'being said with god' ('σὺν θεῷ εἰρημένον'). Cf. Stahl 1975: 13.

In the interplay between plot, characters' comments and narratorial reflection, the fickleness of fate comes to the fore at the beginning of the *Histories*. Not even, or precisely not, Croesus, the most powerful and richest man of his age, is protected from harsh experiences. Croesus sets a pattern that is repeated several times in the *Histories*, which, besides the encounter of East and West, is structured by the rise and fall of Eastern despots.[132] Manifesting itself in the fates of the powerful, the changeability of life is the tenor of the *Histories*. This aligns Herodotus with the non-historiographic media of memory that I have examined in the first part of this study.[133] Contingency of chance is at the core of tragedy, frames the praise of the victor in epinician poetry and is the backdrop against which the construction of regularities and continuities in speeches and elegies is to be viewed. The strong awareness of human fragility can be traced back to the Homeric poems.[134] To give an example, in one of the *Iliad's* most famous passages, Glaucus compares men to leaves (6.145-9).[135] On the one hand, the organic development of leaves mirrors the human passage from birth to death, on the other, the wind that moves the leaves signifies man's general fragility and hence prepares the ground for the account of the fate of Bellerophontes, who, first a darling of the gods, was later ruined all of a sudden and for no reason.

Yet, there are models in the *Histories* that aim at reducing the force of contingency of chance, notably the idea of a cycle and the notion of divine retribution. Some utterances seem to presuppose regularity in human lives and thus to restrict the utter unpredictability of the future. After Croesus' miraculous rescue on the pyre,[136] Cyrus keeps his former enemy as a counsellor in his entourage. In his function as adviser, Croesus says to Cyrus:[137] 'If you are aware that you are a human being and command such an army, then you should first learn that there is a cycle of human affairs, and that as the wheel turns around it does not permit the same people always to prosper.' (1.207.2). Scholars have not tired of identifying the 'cycle' or 'wheel of human affairs' as the essence of Herodotus' philosophy of history.[138] Such an interpretation, however, is

---

[132] Cf. Immerwahr 1966; Cobet 1971.
[133] See Chiasson 2003, who argues that Herodotus in the Lydian *logos* 'intentionally appropriates and modifies the techniques of tragic narrative' (7) and that this appropriation can be seen as drawing on and transforming elements from Greek tragedy. He also suggests that this use of tragedy can be seen as Herodotus' attempt to define his own genre.
[134] Cf. Grethlein 2006a.
[135] Cf. Grethlein 2006b with further literature on 3 n. 2.   [136] See below p. 199.
[137] For Herodotus' account of Croesus' career as counsellor after his defeat against Cyrus, see Burkert 1985 with further literature on 13 n. 41.
[138] See, for example, Hellmann 1934: 56–7; Nicolai 1986: 20–1; Erbse 1992: 26; van der Veen 1996: 4.

Herodotus 191

a bit rash.[139] The image of a cycle or wheel signifies that man is subject to changes, but suggests at the same time that these changes follow a regular pattern.[140] When Herodotus, however, comments on changes in his narratorial voice, as for example in 1.5.4, he does not indicate any such regularity.

It is worth lingering a moment on the context of Croesus' comment on 'the cycle of human affairs', as it illustrates the power of contingency of chance and challenges the notion of regularity that is suggested by the image of the wheel:[141] Cyrus has just started his expedition against the Massagetae and their queen has offered to battle either on her or on his own territory. While all others recommend the second option, Croesus advises fighting in the Massagetae's land and in addition proposes a wicked strategy: to leave the weakest part of the army with alcohol and abandon them to the Massagetae, who will try the alcohol and hence become an easy prey (1.207). Croesus' argument is sound – battling on Persian soil would raise the risk in the event of a defeat and reduce the gain deriving from a victory. And indeed, his stratagem works out and it does not take the Persians much to overcome the enemies in their drunken stupour.

Yet, the final result of the expedition, a devastating defeat of the Persians in an open battle including the death of Cyrus, raises the question of how wise Croesus' advice actually is. Of course, the issue debated is not whether or not, but *where* to fight;[142] at the same time, Croesus explicitly points out his role as wise adviser: 'King, I told you before, when Zeus gave me to you, that I would avert, as far as it is in my power, any catastrophe which I see threatening your house. My own sufferings have taught me unpleasant lessons.' (1.207.1). Croesus' own words underscore that, although he gives strategically sound advice, he fails to live up to his promise to protect Cyrus from disaster.[143] Such a perspective is reinforced by a later comment of

---

[139] Cf. Munson 2001: 183.   [140] Cf. Gould 1989: 79.
[141] The interpretation of this passage is debated. According to Stahl's detailed argument (1975), Croesus fails as 'wise adviser'. Shapiro 1994, on the other hand, argues that Croesus gives sound advice and cannot be held responsible for Cyrus' disaster (see already Aly ²1969: 58; Flory 1987: 95–6). I do not follow Stahl's reading in every point, but, by and large, it is more convincing than Shapiro's (see above). A further interpretation which strikes me as a bit too ingenious is offered by Erbse 1992: 27–8. He follows Stahl in seeing a failure of Croesus, but argues that, comparable to Agamemnon in *Iliad* 2, Croesus only pretends to support the expedition, but actually tries to dissuade Cyrus from it by giving outlandish advice.
[142] Cf. Shapiro 1994: 351.
[143] The passage gains further emphasis from Croesus' concluding words, 1.207.7: 'If I am not mistaken, when those [i.e. the Massagetae] see all these good things, they will turn towards them, and then we have the chance for a display of great deeds (ἡμῖν τὸ ἐνθεῦτεν λείπεται ἀπόδεξις ἔργων μεγάλων).' The phrase ἀπόδεξις ἔργων μεγάλων reminds us of Herodotus' claim to present

Cambyses. Rejecting Croesus' recommendation not to kill his brother (beyond doubt wise advice!), he reminds him of his failures as ruler of Lydia and as counsellor of Cyrus (3.36.3). Cambyses' accusation that Croesus is to be blamed for Cyrus' death may put things too strongly,[144] but it draws attention to Croesus' failure to save his master from disaster. It is tempting to argue that Croesus loses 'that deep sense of humanity',[145] and yet, particularly since Croesus himself introduces his plea with a reference to his own experiences, it seems more balanced to see Croesus' failure as marking the limits of human wisdom. Neither does sound advice protect against a downfall[146] nor does insight into the human condition grant the right decisions in every situation.[147]

The end of Cyrus not only highlights the force of contingency of chance, but more specifically undermines Croesus' notion of a cycle to which regularity is attached. As the disaster comes despite Croesus' advice, it shows that there is no regularity that would allow man to overcome contingency of chance. Even Croesus who has learned from his own suffering cannot prevent the downfall of Cyrus. To put it bluntly, the only consistency is life's inconsistency.

Let us turn to another thought–pattern that seems to restrict contingency of chance, divine retribution.[148] Some passages suggest that the gods take care that crimes are punished.[149] If conversely misfortune is assumed to be

---

ἔργα μεγάλα and to give an ἱστορίης ἀπόδεξις and thus reinforces the gap between Croesus' expectation and Herodotus' assessment: indeed, Cyrus' expedition figures in the *Histories*, but it is not so much a great achievement as an example of human failure.

[144] Cf. Immerwahr 1966: 75 n. 81.   [145] Stahl 1975: 24.

[146] A similar view is presented by Artabanus when he first tries to dissuade Xerxes from invading Greece (7.10β2); Themistocles, on the other hand, is confident about the success of good plans (8.60γ).

[147] Lloyd-Jones 1971: 62 points out that in Herodotus human deliberation is always fallible. In Grethlein 2009b, I examine the Council scene at the beginning of Book 7 as another test case for the question whether or not Herodotus' characters are able to learn from history.

[148] Cf. de Romilly 1971, who downplays the role of divine retribution by seeing it as theoretical background of human revenge; Erbse 1979: 192–5, who argues that Herodotus transfers Anaximander's law of the world to the past. Yet, he is aware that not all connections can be figured out by man; Harrison 2000b: 102–21 with emphasis on the inscrutability of the divine; Munson 2001: 183–94 on the interaction of the characters' and the narrator's reflections; Mikalson 2003: 142–6, who argues that in Herodotus the gods 'are concerned with actions that affect them and their property and specific human institutions under their protection. They do not, in broader terms, attend to all matters of justice among human beings' (143). In a similar vein, Scullion 2006: 194 argues that the gods only persecute religious offences. For parallels for the idea of divine retribution not only from ancient literature, see Friedrich 1973: 97–112.

[149] Here, the problem arises how individual action and divine plan and intervention can be reconciled. There is no system that does justice to all cases. The fact that Homeric scholars grapple with similar problems concerning divine and human agency indicates that this issue derives at least partly from a modern perspective based on concepts like freedom of action. For a treatment of the problem in Herodotus, cf. Gould 1989: 63–85; Harrison 2000b: 223–42; for a comparison of Herodotus with the different registers of *Iliad* and *Odyssey*, cf. Nagy 1990: 240–3.

the consequence of misdeeds,[150] contingency of chance is replaced with a just world order and history becomes an ethical affair. For example in 4.205, Herodotus refers to divine retribution, when he mentions the death of Pheretime: 'For, while still alive, she became infested with worms, as excessive cases of vengeance make the gods hostile towards men (ὡς ἄρα ἀνθρώποισι αἱ λίην ἰσχυραὶ τιμωρίαι πρὸς θεῶν ἐπίφθονοι γίνονται).' The gruesome death is explained as the consequence of a ghastly deed: Pheretime had the leaders of Barca impaled and the breasts of their women cut off.[151]

Yet, other passages where Herodotus explicitly refers to divine retribution yield a rather complex image. I have already quoted the end of the Helen–*logos*:[152] owing to the arrangement of the *daimonion*, the Greeks besieged Troy for ten years, although Helen was in Egypt all the time, to illustrate that great crimes are severely punished by the gods. Herodotus explicitly marks this as his own interpretation, but his explanation raises questions: who is punished – the Trojans and/or the Greeks – and, if the Greeks, what for?[153] And what is the *daimonion* and what is its relation to the gods?[154] It is rather striking that when speaking of divine retribution Herodotus shies away from naming individual gods.[155]

Another story in which Herodotus applies the idea of divine punishment is the killing of Persian messengers by the Athenians and Spartans (7.133–7).[156] While Herodotus is unable to adduce a specific punishment for the Athenians – the burning of their city and land in the recent past seems to be due to another cause (7.133.2)[157] – he can make out the retribution of Talthybius in the case of the Spartans. When, after the

---

[150] Cf. Harrison 2000b: 105–7 with examples for this view in the *Histories*.
[151] Upon closer inspection, Herodotus' comment on Pheretime's death is more complex than it may at first seem. The word ἐπίφθονοι brings in the notion of divine jealousy which, in other passages, is rather free of moral considerations. Cf. Munson 2001: 187.
[152] See pp. 156–8.
[153] The majority of scholars assumes that the Trojans are meant, cf. the translation by Marg 1991; Hohti 1976b: 42; Boedeker 1988: 47. Waters 1985: 87 and Pallantza 2005: 157–8, however, argue that the punishment is directed at the Greeks.
[154] On the different terms for the divine, ranging from personal names to the abstract *daimonion*, see Linforth 1928; Nicolai 1986: 26; Harrison 2000b: 158–81.
[155] This is noted by Mikalson 2003: 151, who also points out that the use of general names such as ὁ θεός or τὸ θεῖον is no indicator for disbelief on Herodotos' side. Cf. Harrison 2000b: 180, and on 'the limits of knowledge and inquiry', 182–207; Scullion 2006: 194–8.
[156] Cf. Scullion 2006: 198.
[157] Immerwahr 1966: 214 and Shimron 1989: 69 stress the irony in the passage. Munson 2001: 191–4 argues that Herodotus draws attention to the future of Athens as an 'anticipated, not yet consummated paradigm' (194).

murder of the Persians, they failed to gain good signs from sacrifices, they sent two Spartans to Xerxes to atone for the crime. Xerxes let them return and the 'wrath of Talthybius' was appeased. Later, however, Herodotus adds, it flared up again and the sons of the two that had been sent to Xerxes were killed as messengers by the Athenians. As this account reveals, the time and extent of the retribution is unpredictable.[158] The Spartans failed in their attempt to atone for it and received their due punishment later, and the Athenians seem not to have paid for their crime yet – when will they, or will they at all, and if so, how?

Even where Herodotus explicitly invokes divine retribution, the time, the exact agency and the link between crime and punishment are rather obscure. In some cases, Herodotus even concedes uncertainty as to whether a misfortune is the consequence of an earlier action.[159] On Cambyses' late confusion and frenzy against his relatives, he writes: 'Cambyses committed these mad acts against his closest relatives, either because of Apis or for another reason, as generally many evils afflict humans.'[160] (3.33). It is astonishing, Herodotus notes, that no Persians fled into the temple of Demeter at the battle of Salamis, and one might well see the goddess' revenge at work; yet, it is rather questionable whether it is seemly to speculate about the gods' affairs: 'I believe, if it is necessary to speculate (δοκέειν) about divine matters, that the goddess herself did not let them in, because they had burnt her temple in Eleusis.' (9.65.2). Thus, the concept of divine retribution does little to overcome contingency of chance, but rather reinforces it at a higher level. Man is subjected to forces that are not only beyond his control, but that are difficult to identify even in retrospect.[161]

Moreover, another, rather sinister, image of the gods figures in the *Histories* parallel to the model of divine retribution.[162] The assumption of a just regime of the gods is discarded in the notion of divine envy, which, unbound by moral consideration, brings to fall whoever rises too high. The tension between the two concepts can already be grasped in the Croesus–*logos*. While Herodotus refers to divine nemesis and Croesus acknowledges his guilt in the end, Solon characterizes the divine as jealous and given to causing

---

[158] Cf. Parker 1983: 201–2.
[159] Harrison 2000b: 115 argues that it is such an ambiguity 'that allows for the belief in the possibility of divine intervention to be maintained'.
[160] The maltreatment of the Apis–bull is told in 3.29. Cf. Friedrich 1973: 116–20.
[161] On the ambiguity of communication between gods and men in general, see Gould 1985: 22–4.
[162] However, Lloyd-Jones 1971: 67–8 rightly points out that in the *Histories* the gods are not so much hostile as inscrutable. See also Lang 1984: 61, who notes that 'nowhere in his narrative does Herodotus himself attribute to divine jealousy the defeat or fall of any great leader who might have been thought to be exceeding human limits'.

trouble (1.32.1).¹⁶³ In his discussion with Xerxes at the Hellespont, Artabanus voices a position that strongly reminds us of this view and includes the *gnome*: 'So death, since life is wretched, becomes the most attractive refuge for man. God gives a sweet taste of life, but in its course he turns out to be grudging (φθονερός).' (7.46.4).¹⁶⁴ Polycrates' Egyptian friend, Amasis, casts the gods in a similar vein, presenting himself as one who knows 'that the gods are jealous of success' when he argues that Polycrates ought to abandon his dearest possession (3.40.2).¹⁶⁵ In this episode, the idea of divine jealousy is underscored by the plot and seems to receive even narratorial confirmation.¹⁶⁶ As is well known, Polycrates tries to reduce his fortune by sacrificing a ring, which, however, returns to him. It would have been easy to present his death as punishment, particularly since greed makes him reject his daughter's warnings and go to Oroites. Yet, in accordance with Amasis' view of the gods, Herodotus states in his narratorial voice that Polycrates died in a manner 'worthy neither of himself nor of his ambitions' (3.125.2).¹⁶⁷

Where does this leave contingency of chance in the *Histories*? There are different models such as a cycle of good and bad fate, divine retribution or the envy of the gods to explain human suffering in the *Histories*. None, however, can claim to overcome contingency of chance. This resembles the ambiguity which I have detected in *Persae*, where various explanations for the Persian defeat are voiced, ranging from Xerxes' fault to the unpredictability of the gods.¹⁶⁸ In the *Histories* as well as *Persae*, the pluralism of concepts testifies to the difficulty of mastering contingency of chance in a

---

¹⁶³ Accordingly, scholars have disagreed on the interpretation. Most scholars assume that Croesus is punished for his hubris, see e.g. Heuß 1973: 395. Gould 1989: 80, however, argues that there is no punishment of hubris in Croesus' case, and in his comparison of the *Histories'* Solon with the historical person, Chiasson 1986: 259 argues that 'Herodotus ... has de-moralized or a-moralized Solon's views on the transience of wealth'. Munson 2001: 184–5 notes the tension between Solon's emphasis on the gods' envy and Herodotus' moralist invocation of divine nemesis.

¹⁶⁴ See also Artabanus' reflections in 7.10ε.

¹⁶⁵ The similarity to Solon's reflections is obvious in 3.40.3: 'For I do not know anybody, not even from hearsay, who did not end up completely ruined (οὐ κακῶς ἐτελεύτησε πρόρριζος), but did well in everything.' 1.32.9: 'For the god often offers prosperity to many, but then destroys them completely (προρρίζους ἀνέτρεψε).' There is only one further occurrence of πρόρριζος in the *Histories*, in 6.86δ. Cf. Regenbogen 1961: 114.

¹⁶⁶ Some scholars argue that Polycrates' downfall is a punishment for his crimes, according to others it is due to divine envy, cf. the survey by van der Veen 1996: 6 n. 13 and 14, who himself thinks that Polycrates is punished for his 'incapacity of curtailment' (6–22). I agree that there are points which indicate guilt on Polycrates' side, but Amasis' reflection and Herodotus' final comment (see above) give emphasis to divine envy.

¹⁶⁷ Cf. Friedrich 1973: 120–5. On the 'worthy', see Kurke 1999: 120, who stresses that the word is used three times in the closing passage, linking this to her interpretation of the Polycrates-story against the backdrop of gift-exchange (101–29).

¹⁶⁸ Cf. Chapter 4, section 4.2.3.

coherent system even in retrospect. Herodotus leaves his readers with a string of different explanations which indicates that contingency's force cannot be overcome in an abstract explanation. It is therefore questionable to attribute to Herodotus an elaborate philosophy of history or to see his aim in detecting '*Gesetzmäßigkeiten*'.[169] Still, as the next two sections will reveal, we do not do justice to Herodotus if we argue that he is merely voicing traditional wisdom when he emphasizes human fragility.[170] His narrative is both an artful in-depth presentation of contingency of chance and an ambitious attempt at mastering it.

7.3.2. *Narrative form as expression of idea of history*

Narratives not only tell events that take place in time, but also unfold themselves in time. The comparison of narrative time with narrated time has proved fruitful in the first part of this study, in which I suggested that the chronological account of Lysias' funeral speech reinforces the continuum on which Athens' history is envisaged and that Pindar's temporal zigzag course in *Olympian* 2 enacts formally the transcendence of time that Pindar promises Hieron. I would now like to read the narrative form of the *Histories* as an expression of its idea of history. To be more precise, I will argue first that the negative character of Croesus' experiences is underscored by the shaping of the *fabula* and then, in the next section, that the narrative form frees readers from experiences of contingency of chance.[171] As in tragedy, the characters' exposure to contingency contrasts with the reception experience, which is, by and large, free of disappointed expectations.[172]

Time and again, the temporal structure and the change of perspective juxtapose Croesus' vain expectations with his experiences.[173] On the one

---

[169] Nicolai 1986 is an extreme example of seeing the *Histories* as the exposition of a philosophy of history ('Erfassung und Darstellung der Gesetzmäßigkeiten des Geschichtsprozesses', 47). Yet, there are many other scholars who see Herodotus too much on the theoretical side: see, for example, Fornara 1971b: 76–80; 1990. Such approaches are duly criticized by Harrison 2000b: 240–1. See already the balanced view by Hellmann 1934: 13: 'Nicht darum handelt es sich nun aber bei Herodot, Gesetze für das göttliche Walten aufzustellen und zu erweisen, sondern darum, im frommen Schauen auf die verwirrende Fülle des Geschehens Wiederkehrendes zu erkennen und das ordnende Walten des θεῖον zu erahnen.'

[170] *Pace* Harrison 2000b.

[171] The narrative form of the *Histories* has been examined from many different angles. For a recent analysis with narratological terminology, see de Jong 1999; 2001. Rengakos 2004; 2006a shows Herodotus' manifold narratological debts to Homer, in particular retardation, dramatic irony and the misleading of expectations.

[172] Stahl 1975: 6 notes the similarity to tragedy, which has a comparable 'poet–audience relationship'.

[173] On Croesus' '*Selbstsicherheit*', see Marg ²1965: 290–5.

hand, the narrator focalizes Croesus' expectations and anticipates the corresponding experiences; in some cases, the narrator changes perspective for the *prolepseis*, in others, the foreshadowing is given at the level of the action, but there it is either not obvious or ignored. On the other hand, in *analepseis*, the narrator or Croesus himself looks back to his initial expectations from the vantage point of the experience.

Let us first turn to some cases of *prolepsis*. Upon killing Candaules and seizing the Lydian throne, Gyges faces resistance and agrees to consult Delphi. The oracle confirms Gyges' power, but adds that in the fifth generation Gyges' crime will be punished (1.13). Gyges is followed by Ardys, Sadyattes, Alyattes and Croesus. Although Herodotus does not call attention to the fact that Croesus is the fifth descendant, the oracle is an early hint at Croesus' downfall at the level of the action, where, however, no attention is paid to it (1.13.2).[174]

Solon's reflections on man's fragility are rather general; yet, in the transition from the Solon scene to the further narrative, Herodotus marks that they will have significance for Croesus:[175] 'After Solon's departure, the mighty retribution of god took hold of (ἔλαβε ἐκ θεοῦ νέμεσις) Croesus, in all likelihood because he believed that he was the happiest of all men.' (1.34.1). With his narratorial comment, Herodotus not only foreshadows Croesus' fall, but also establishes an even stronger link to Solon's words by suggesting that the coming disaster is due to Croesus' hubristic self-praise. The adumbration of Croesus' downfall strongly contrasts with his unquestioning assurance and self-confidence.

While the death of Croesus' son is not foreshadowed in more precise terms, there are *prolepseis* announcing the defeat against the Persians. Asking the Pythia whether he should attack Persia, Croesus is told that he would destroy a great power and receives the recommendation that he ally himself with the most powerful of the Greeks (1.53.3). Croesus takes this oracle as an affirmation that he would defeat Persia, and Herodotus does not explicitly contradict him (1.54.1). Yet, knowing that the reign of the Mermniads will end with Croesus and expecting that his end will be rather unpleasant, readers are very likely to grasp the oracle's ambiguity and read it as a *prolepsis* of a military disaster.[176]

---

[174] Herodotus even points out that the Lydians did not pay proper attention to the oracle: 'To this prediction, neither the Lydians nor their kings paid attention, until it was fulfilled.' (1.13.2).
[175] Cf. Regenbogen 1930: 227–8; Harrison 2000b: 36.
[176] Perhaps such a reading is fostered by Croesus' ὑπερήδεσθαι ('to be pleased exceedingly'). The prefix ὑπερ- may indicate an inappropriate reaction. Yet, as Chiasson 1983: 115 n. 2 points out, unlike περιχαρής ('exceedingly glad'), ὑπερήδεσθαι is not generally ambivalent in the *Histories*. On the semantics of ἥδεσθαι in Herodotus, cf. Bischoff 1932: 36 with n. 1.

Moreover, the following digression contains an episode that offers a parallel for such a misunderstanding of an oracle. In making his narrative follow the perspective of Croesus, who enquires which Greek state he should choose for an ally, Herodotus gives an account of Athenian and Spartan history (1.56.2–68). When the Spartans, who were very eager to expand their territory, consulted the Pythia about whether or not they should conquer Arcadia, she replied that they would not acquire Arcadia, but: 'I will give you Tegea, struck with the foot, to dance/ and to measure out her beautiful plain with a rope.' ('δώσω τοι Τεγέην ποσσίκροτον ὀρχήσασθαι/ καὶ καλὸν πεδίον σχοίνῳ διαμετρήσασθαι.' 1.66.2). Assuming that this means they would own Tegea, the Spartans attacked Tegea. They were, however, defeated and fulfilled the oracle by working the Tegeans' fields as slaves. This oracle strongly resembles the one that Croesus receives: asked if a neighbour ought to be attacked, the Pythia gives an oracle which is taken as confirmation of a victory, but which turns out to have predicted a defeat.[177] The similarity is highlighted by the adjective κίβδηλος, which is applied to both oracles, the only two occurrences of this word in the meaning 'ambiguous/deceptive' in the *Histories*.[178] The mirror of the Spartans' oracle calls attention to Croesus' misinterpretation of the Pythia's advice and invites the readers to compare Croesus' aspirations with his disastrous end.

The first explicit *prolepsis* is focalized by the Lacedaemonians and follows the digression on Athenian and Spartan history. Herodotus continues by saying that Croesus opts for the Spartans, who accept his offer (1.69–70), and then pursues the Spartan thread further beyond the main storyline. Presenting different accounts of what happened to a *krater* that the Spartans send to Croesus to confirm their alliance, Herodotus has the Spartans mention that Sardis and Croesus were captured (1.70.3). In the transition to the main narrative, Herodotus contrasts in his authorial voice the *prolepsis* explicitly with Croesus' expectation and links it to the oracle: 'Due to the misunderstanding of the oracle, Croesus invaded Cappadocia, assuming that he would bring down Cyrus and the Persian Empire.' (1.71.1).

For the readers, the vanity of Croesus' plans is further underscored when the Lydian Sandanis puts forward his doubts about the expedition (1.71.2–4). As the case of Croesus illustrates, a dense net of *prolepseis*, partly at the level of

---

[177] It can be argued that the Spartans' oracle is far less equivocal than the one given to Croesus, cf. Shimron 1989: 43. This, however, does not impinge on its function as mirror.
[178] 1.66.3 and 1.75.2. The only other occurrence, 5.91.2, has the meaning 'spurious'. Cf. Flower 1991: 71 n. 96 and, with different emphasis, Harrison 2000b: 152 n. 109.

the action, partly only presented to the readers by the narrator, anticipates experiences that clash with the current expectations of the characters and thereby emphasize the force of contingency of chance.

Herodotus also uses *analepseis* to highlight the disappointment of expectations. He often looks back to, and has his characters hark back to, the expectations or, even more dramatically, signs that offered them some insight into the future, but were not heeded or misunderstood. For example, in 1.43.3, Herodotus reports the death of Atys: 'Since it was a spear that hit him, he fulfilled the prophecy of the dream ...' ('ὁ μὲν δὴ βληθεὶς τῇ αἰχμῇ ἐξέπλησε τοῦ ὀνείρου τὴν φήμην ...'). The actual event appears in a participle, while the main verb marks it as a fulfilment of the dream. Not only does Atys' death violate the expectations of Croesus, who assumes that his son is safe, particularly since he has him go with a guardian, but the reference back to the dream recalls the anticipation of the death that Croesus failed to prevent despite his knowledge. Croesus himself establishes the same link when he tries to work out the responsibility for the death of his son and says to Adrastus: 'You are not alone to blame for the terrible thing that has happened to me, in so far as you did it involuntarily, but also somehow one of the gods, who even warned me a long time ago what was going to happen.' (1.45.2).

In 1.85, Herodotus tells how Croesus survived the capture of Sardis. He starts his account with an *analepsis*, quoting an oracle that Croesus' mute son would start speaking on a most unfortunate day. Accordingly, the son speaks his first words when a Persian is about to kill his father, alerting him to the identity of his opponent and thereby saving his father's life. Again, an event is seen through the lens of its anticipation, this time an oracle, a perspective that underscores the tension between expectation and experience. Although it had been predicted – a day most unfortunate to Croesus on which his mute son would gain speech – the actual experience comes rather unexpectedly.

At the end of the Croesus–*logos*, Herodotus has Croesus himself look back in two separate reflections and thereby shed light on the relation between experiences and expectations. First, when already on the pyre, Croesus calls out 'Solon' (1.86). Asked by the Persians what this means, he reports his encounter with Solon and adds the wish that every tyrant be granted a meeting with Solon stating that 'for him everything had gone the way that he [i.e. Solon] had said' (1.86.5). Thus, Croesus not only contrasts his experience with his expectations, but notes that he had had an opportunity to get his expectations straight, but missed it.

Second, after Croesus has been saved, he views his disaster from a different angle and blames Apollo for having led him astray with his oracles

(1.90.3–4). However, the Pythia rejects this accusation and argues that his downfall had been fated and was even postponed by Apollo, who could not completely prevent it. Moreover, she points out that Croesus has misinterpreted the oracles. Croesus did destroy an empire, yet not Cyrus' but his own, and the mule that would bring to an end his power signified Cyrus who is the offspring of a socially superior mother and an inferior father (1.91.1–5). Upon this reply, Croesus accepts that he is to be blamed himself for his downfall (1.91.6). Thus, the look back at the oracles carries a stronger moral notion than his reflection on the encounter with Solon. In both cases the *analepsis* from a character's perspective emphasizes the discrepancy between expectations and experiences, but the different assessments show that human plans can fail for various reasons including miscalculations as well as unpredictable obstacles.

To sum up: *prolepseis* and *analepseis* juxtapose expectations with experiences and thereby stress that the characters are liable to miscalculations and subject to forces beyond their reach. Particularly *prolepseis* that are given at the level of the plot and *analepseis* focalized by the characters draw attention to the failure of expectations, the first reinforcing the possibility of right expectations, the latter introducing a reflection on contingency at the level of the plot.

7.3.3. Narrative as solution for contingency of chance

We have seen that contingency of chance figures prominently in the *Histories* and is emphasized by its narrative form. At the same time, Herodotus presents his account in a way that protects his readers from the disappointments of expectations ruling at the level of the action. Without affecting the dynamics of the reading process, *prolepseis* and patterns safely guide the readers through what is open and insecure at the level of the plot. *Prolepseis* not only highlight the tension between expectation and experience at the level of the action, they also provide the readers with insights into the future and thus privilege them over the characters. The readers are led to expect what comes as a surprise for the characters. This gap is particularly obvious in oracles and signs that foreshadow the future at the level of the action: being frequently misunderstood by the characters,[179] they prepare the readers for the further development of the plot. The double function of oracles and signs, being part of the action and directing the attention of the readers as narrative devices, ties characters and

---

[179] Cf. *ibid.*: 230.

readers together and simultaneously deepens the gap between them. Thus, the *Histories* not only resembles non-historiographic media of memory in their emphasis on contingency of chance, but also expresses it in a narrative form reminiscent of epic and tragedy which creates a similar discrepancy between audience and characters.[180]

As in Homer and tragedy, the *prolepseis* tend to be vague. For example, as we have seen, the reference to an oracle that the Mermniads will rule for only five generations and Solon's reflections in combination with a narratorial comment foreshadow Croesus' downfall. Yet, what and in which way exactly he will suffer is not revealed. Thus, while the *prolepseis* privilege the readers over the characters, they are vague enough not to interfere with the forms of epic suspense that Irene de Jong and Antonios Rengakos have found in the Herodotean narrative.[181] The vagueness of the foreshadowing combined with, for example, retardation even contributes to suspense as it makes the readers desire to learn how the known end will come about.

In addition to *prolepseis*, Herodotus develops patterns in his narrative that prepare readers for the further development of the plot. I have already mentioned the pattern of the rise and fall of rulers that structures the *Histories*.[182] This 'corset' contains a set of smaller patterns. For example, time and again the Eastern monarchs are warned by 'wise advisers' before they set out on their fateful expeditions:[183] Croesus is warned by Sandanis and, indirectly, by Solon, and then, after his downfall, serves himself as adviser to Cyrus and Cambyses. Darius neglects warnings by Artabanus, Coes, Gobryas and Megabazus and Xerxes fails to heed the advice given by Artabanus and Demaratus. Other examples of significant action include laughing, which expresses unjustified self-assurance,[184] and the crossing of rivers, which often converges with moral transgressions.[185]

Such patterns work like *prolepseis* at the level of reception, preparing readers for the further development of the plot. The rejected warning, the despot's laughing or his crossing of a great river signal not only a hubristic attitude, but also alert the reader to the impending downfall. Yet the information given is even vaguer than in explicit *prolepseis* and thus makes

---

[180] Cf. Grethlein 2006a: 257–83 on Homer and above pp. 101–2 on tragedy.
[181] De Jong 1999: 242–51, who adduces 'prolepses, connaissance, identification, conflit/contraste' as suspense-creating devices; Rengakos 2006a, who examines suspense that is established through retardation, misdirection, dramatic irony.
[182] Cf. p. 172.   [183] Cf. Bischoff 1932; Lattimore 1939.   [184] Cf. Lateiner 1977; Flory 1978.
[185] Cf. Immerwahr 1954: 28 with n. 22; Konstan 1983; Lateiner 1989: 129–30 and, on physical and moral boundaries in general, 126–44; Munson 2001: 9–11.

the process of reading highly dynamic: how and when the transgression will lead to disaster remains in the dark.[186]

Patterns introduce regularity into the plot and thus restrict the force of chance. As in the various poetic and rhetorical genres discussed in the first part of this study, the exemplary mode is a powerful counterstrategy against contingency of chance, which looms large in the *Histories*. The repetitions suggest that human life is not as unpredictable as it seems. This regularity, however, only unfolds at the level of reception – and even here the effect is limited owing to the vagueness of the foreshadowing.

Nonetheless, the patterns that emerge in the *Histories* not only make different events in the narrative shed light on one another and thereby reinforce the *prolepseis* in sparing the readers the disappointment of expectations, but also enable the readers to understand their own time better. As I pointed out in section 7.2.1, Herodotus frequently refers in the last books to more recent and current intra-Hellenic conflicts and thereby hints that Athens will be next in the cycle of empires. The fate of the Eastern monarchs not only illustrates dangers that affect all men alike, but implies more specifically a lesson for Athens. Therefore, besides establishing regularity in the account of the past, the exemplary mode of memory in the *Histories* also has normative force. Unlike Thucydides, Herodotus does not proclaim the usefulness of his work, but he implicitly suggests that the patterns emerging in the *Histories* will help his readers to understand the present better and, as far as possible, to assess the future.

The *Histories'* anachronic structure and the dense net of patterns, we can sum up, create a gap between the characters and the readers. *Prolepseis* and the repetition of significant structures protect the reader from the insecurity that rules at the level of the action. Through foreshadowing and the establishment of patterns, the *Histories'* narrative masters contingency of chance. Herodotus does not offer a philosophy of history that solves the problem of contingency; yet, he overcomes it in the act of narrating. If we link this to the results of the last section, we can claim that the *Histories* simultaneously highlights contingency of chance – at the level of the action – and masters its force – at the level of the narration and reception.[187]

---

[186] Cf. Immerwahr 1966: 152.
[187] The difference is obviously due to the complementary perspective: the readers view in retrospective what is prospective for the characters. In Grethlein 2009b, I argue that Herodotus emphasizes that he can only write about historical developments that have come to an end. This constitutes a major difference from Thucydides who prides himself on 'having begun his work right when the war broke out, expecting that it would be a major one and notable beyond all previous wars' (1.1).

7.4. CONCLUSION

Recent studies have made an effort to contextualize Herodotus in the fifth century by pointing out his debts to natural scientists, medical writers and sophists.[188] While these studies take their cue mainly from Herodotus' ethnographic and geographic investigations, I have tried to assess anew Herodotus' account of the past in the context of commemorative genres. Two major differences between Herodotus on the one hand and poetry and oratory on the other are scope and context. A single polis is at the core of most non-historiographical genres of memory; Herodotus, on the other hand, follows a pan-Hellenic perspective that is reminiscent of the Homeric poems. Moreover, his *Histories* is a written work and therefore far more independent of a particular context than poems and speeches, which are composed for performance.

While Herodotus does not call his account a 'possession for all time' and does not emphasize its literariness as strongly as Thucydides, he explicitly sets his approach off against poetic memory, particularly against Homer. The *Histories* is written in prose and based on *historie*, thus establishing a genre different from the epics. I have also argued for a meta-historical significance of some embedded speeches which illustrate the rather questionable use of the past in oratory, notably the use of exempla for glorifying and legitimizing purposes, and thereby throw into relief the *Histories'* superiority.

Despite Herodotus' efforts to delimit his new approach to the past, the idea of history that comes to the fore in his work shares much ground with the non-historiographic genres of memory. Contingency of chance figures prominently in the *Histories* and is forcefully expressed by its narrative structure, which, like the *Iliad*, contains a dense net of anachronies and thereby juxtaposes expectations with experiences. The *Histories* does not propose a philosophy of history and dissolve contingency of chance in a formula, but *prolepseis* and patterns keep the readers safely posted about the further development of the plot without taking away the suspense concerning the *how*. In addition, patterns, particularly the arch-pattern, the rise and fall of empires, establish regularity. Thus, Herodotus simultaneously highlights and masters contingency of chance, the former at the level of the action, the latter at the level of the narrative.

As the prominence of patterns shows, Herodotus not only criticizes exempla in speeches, but also uses the exemplary mode of memory himself. His *Histories* establishes a panopticon in which the heroic past, the Persian

---

[188] Cf. Thomas 2000; 2006; Raaflaub 2002b.

Wars and the more recent intra-Hellenic fights shed light on one another. Unlike Thucydides, Herodotus does not explicitly proclaim the usefulness of his work, but the subtle hints that Athens will follow upon Persia in the cycle of empires give the patterns of the *Histories* significance for the present. That being said, Herodotus differs in his use of exempla from other commemorative genres in replacing glorification and legitimization with critical analysis.[189] In their critical use of the past, the *Histories* resemble Andocides' *de pace*, but Herodotus' comments on the present are only indirect and in this regard closer to the indirect negotiation of current issues in tragedy.

The critical foreshadowing of Athens' role as hegemonic power illuminates a further aspect of Herodotus' place in the tension of continuity and innovation with respect to other commemorative genres. While the epics, tragedy and epinician poetry highlight contingency of chance in the heroic past and thus at a safe distance from the present, Herodotus applies this idea of history to the recent past. At the same time, Herodotus' major cases for the fickleness of fate are Eastern despots[190] and the *Histories* only hints that Athens could suffer the same fate as Persia. Thus, not only the narratorial guidance, but also the focus on the 'other' somehow distances contingency of chance from the readers.

However, as every reader of Herodotus knows, the borderline between Greeks and barbarians is far from stable in the *Histories*.[191] It is a Persian whom Herodotus has predict the utter defeat of the Persian army at a banquet with Thebans. Asked by his Greek fellow symposiast if he should not share this prediction with the other Persians, the Persian replies: 'Guest–friend, what has been decreed by the god cannot be averted by man, for no one is willing to believe even those who tell the truth.' (9.16.4). Not only is the Persian's prediction right, but his words have a strong Herodotean ring and it is tempting to read them as a pessimistic self-reflection by Herodotus. Yet, even in this case it is worth pointing out that Herodotus has made an effort to offer his readers a narrative panopticon in which heroic and recent past and present mirror and refract one another.

---

[189] I thus agree with Boedeker 1998: 197–9 that Herodotus and Thucydides deviate from other commemorative genres through their critical spirit. However, I part company with her when she argues that the historians do not show 'a timeless world full of paradigms and analogies, but rather a time-bound picture of development, inconsistency, and change' (202). Instead, I argue that Herodotus and, in the next chapter, Thucydides use the exemplary mode that is well known from the non-historiographic media of memory for their critique. Thus, the relation between continuity and innovation is even more complex than Boedeker suggests.

[190] Cf. Mikalson 2003: 152, who argues that divine retribution is ultimately good in the *Histories*, as it saves Greece from the Persians.

[191] See e.g. Pelling 1997b.

CHAPTER 8

Thucydides

After dealing with Herodotus, I now turn to the second major historian of the fifth century BCE whose work, though obviously unfinished, has been fully transmitted, Thucydides. I propose to view his *History* as being at the intersection of tradition and innovation with respect to non-historiographic media of memory. To read the Thucydidean account of the Peloponnesian War from this angle may seem even more provocative, since, whereas Herodotus was dubbed 'father of history', Thucydides is hailed as the 'father of critical historiography' and many scholars are more inclined to align him with other historians, ancient as well as modern, than to envisage him against the backdrop of, say, elegy and tragedy.[1] At the same time, the *History* itself strongly suggests being seen against the background of non-historiographic memory, as Thucydides' efforts to set himself off against poets and orators, directly as well as indirectly, are more pronounced than Herodotus'. Though being a bit later than Herodotus and several other writers, Thucydides still did not write in an established genre, but was very much concerned to define his approach against other commemorative genres.

The examination of Thucydides' idea of history will not only help us contextualize the *History* in the wider field of memory, but it will also open a new angle on the old comparison of Thucydides with Herodotus. I will follow the same steps as in my Herodotus chapter: first, I will discuss the explicit critique of non-historiographical genres of memory in chapters 1.20–2, which have been widely discussed but have also often been

---

[1] See, however, Cornford 1907 and Macleod 1983a for comparisons of Thucydides with tragedy, and Hornblower 2004, who juxtaposes Thucydides with Pindar. Shanske 2007 argues that Thucydides relies on a tragic temporality in his invention of historiography. I agree that there are many similarities between Thucydides' and the tragedians' notion of time. However, many of her points are not specific to tragedy, but can be found in a wide array of other genres. Moreover, while Shanske sees a strong contrast between Thucydides' and Herodotus' temporalities, I believe that, by and large, Thucydides' idea of history resembles Herodotus' idea of history, albeit expressed in a different narrative form.

misunderstood. A new reading of this *locus classicus* will be supplemented by an analysis of the digression on the tyrannicide in 6.54–9 (8.1). I shall then make a case that Thucydides deconstructs the use of the past in speeches and thereby throws into relief the superiority of his own work. Strong echoes of Thucydides' methodological reflections reinforce the meta-historical significance of my two test cases, Pericles' funeral speech and the Plataean Debate (8.2). After elucidating Thucydides' explicit and implicit critique of other commemorative genres, I will examine his idea of history, which shares much common ground with these genres as well as with Herodotus but is expressed in a novel narrative form (8.3).

8.1. EXPLICIT CRITICISM OF OTHER GENRES OF MEMORY (METHODOLOGICAL REFLECTIONS IN 1.20–2; THE DIGRESSION ON THE TYRANNICIDE (6.54–9))

We have seen that Herodotus engages in critical discussions of the evidence given by Homer. To be more specific, I have argued that the Helen–*logos* in Book 2 implies a juxtaposition of the *Histories* with epic poetry as different media of memory. Thucydides is more explicit than Herodotus in his attempt to define his new approach to the past in contrast to other commemorative genres and provides his readers with a reflection on his method at the beginning of the *History*.[2] I will first offer a new reading of this famous passage (8.1.1) and then turn to Thucydides' discussion of the tyrannicide in 6.54–9 (8.1.2).

8.1.1. *Thucydides' methodological reflections in 1.20–2*

The chapters 20–2 in Book 1 of the *History* are often discussed as Thucydides' exposition of his method.[3] This is not wrong because Thucydides explicitly reflects on his method, but it is important to take into account the narrative context of these reflections. Thucydides starts the *History* with the thesis that the Peloponnesian War is the greatest upheaval so far. In the so-called 'archaeology', Thucydides goes through Greek history, showing that previous wars do not compare to 'his' war (1.1–19). This survey is capped by a methodological reflection on the difficulties that he was facing in his reconstruction of archaic history (1.20–21.1). Then, the rephrasing of the starting point – 'nonetheless it will be obvious to those

---

[2] Cf. Hornblower 1991–6: 59.
[3] Cf. the critique by Woodman 1988: 47–8 and the examples listed in n. 47.

who consider this war from the facts themselves that it has been greater than the others' (1.21.2) – leads Thucydides to a methodological reflection on his reconstruction of this rather recent war, divided into the famous sentence on speeches and a parallel sentence on events, and to the claim that his account will be useful to his readers (1.22). While chapter 1.20–21.1 serves as a cap to the 'archaeology', chapter 1.22 introduces an elaboration on the statement that the Peloponnesian War is greater than previous wars (1.23.1–3).[4] Thus, the name '*Methodenkapitel*', by which chapters 1.20–2 are known in German scholarship, is misleading in so far as the methodological reflections are divided into two sections serving different functions in an *auxesis*. Still, numerous parallels between the two parts, such as the emphasis on the toils of proper investigation, justify treating them together as methodological reflections.[5] I will first clarify who the object of Thucydides' criticism is (a), then ask what distinguishes the *History* from their works (b) and finally show that even Thucydides' critique is indebted to the very genres that he challenges (c).

(a) Poets and logographoi

In 1.21.1, Thucydides dissociates his work from the accounts of poets and *logographoi*:

> In the light of the evidence I have cited, however, one would not go wrong in supposing that the events which I have related actually happened like this, and in not believing that they happened as the poets have sung in their praise, adorning them with their exaggerations, nor like the reports which the *logographoi* have composed, more attractive for listening than with regard to truthfulness, reports which are beyond proof and for the most part have forfeited credibility over time by winning victories as patriotic fiction (μυθῶδες),[6] but in regarding what has been found from the clearest possible evidence as adequate for what concerns antiquity.

For a long time, it seemed clear that this criticism of poets was directed at Homer and given the prominence of the epics and the polemics against Homer in the 'archaeology', the Homeric poems are surely an object of Thucydides' critique. However, the 'New Simonides' has alerted us to the

---

[4] On this rupture between 1.21.1 and 1.21.2, see Hammond 1952: 134.
[5] See also 1.20.3, where Thucydides envisages both the archaic past and the present: 'And there are many other things, present as well as not yet forgotten with time …'
[6] Flory 1990 argues convincingly that the basic meaning of μυθῶδες in Thucydides is 'flattering'. Such tainting of stories is also implied in 1.22.3: 'Finding out these facts involved great effort, because eye-witnesses did not report the same specific events in the same way, but according to individual partisanship or ability to remember.'

fact that there were other poetic accounts of the past besides the epics. Deborah Boedeker has made a strong case that Thucydides' criticism is not restricted to Homer, but also applies to elegies.[7] If we assume that 'reports which are beyond proof and for the most part have forfeited credibility over time by winning victories as patriotic fictions (μυθῶδες)' (1.21.1) refers to the works not only of *logographoi*, but also of poets, it is rather plausible to see a reference to non-epic poems dealing with the past such as elegies, most of which have a patriotic slant. It is also worth considering that tragedies are implied in Thucydides' criticism. The representation of the past in tragedy is in the grip of the polis and some tragedies, most prominently the Athenian asylum tragedies, have a patriotic colouring. Moreover, the 'competition-piece' ('ἀγώνισμα') with which Thucydides contrasts his *History* in 1.22.4 applies well to tragedies, which were performed in competitions.[8]

What about *logographoi*? For some time, scholars tended to follow G. F. Creuzer's thesis that *logographos* is a *terminus technicus* for the pre-Herodotean historians mentioned by Dionysius.[9] Yet, the existence of such historians has been forcefully questioned by Felix Jacoby and there is no evidence for such a meaning of *logographos*.[10] Therefore, the present *communis opinio* assumes that *logographos* means 'prose author' and that Thucydides is taking a stand against Herodotus and other contemporary historians.

This view, however, also has serious flaws. A look at all the uses of *logographos* in fifth- and fourth-century literature reveals that there is not a single passage where *logographos* can be safely assumed to mean 'prose author'.[11] Its conventional meaning is 'speech writer' or 'orator'. Given that the funeral speeches are an important commemorative genre and that the past figures prominently in deliberative oratory, this meaning makes perfect sense for our passage in Thucydides, and there is no reason whatsoever to insist on a lexical *petitio principii*.

Moreover, the meaning 'orator' is supported by the context. As I have already mentioned, Thucydides reproaches the *logographoi* and poets for telling patriotic stories.[12] Obviously, this criticism cannot be directed at Herodotus, who follows a pan-Hellenic perspective,[13] but it makes good sense if it addresses oratory, as the past is tainted by a patriotic slant in both epideictic and deliberative speeches. Thucydides' rejection of a

---

[7] Boedeker 1995: 226–9. [8] The theme of competitions is already implicit in 1.21.1: ἐκνενικηκότα.
[9] Creuzer ²1845. See also Lipsius 1886.
[10] Cf. Curtius 1886; Jacoby 1949; Bux 1960; von Fritz 1967: 337–47.
[11] Cf. Grethlein 2004. [12] Cf. Flory 1990. [13] *Pace* Flory 1990: 201.

'competition piece to be heard for the moment' ('ἀγώνισμα ἐς τὸ παραχρῆμα ἀκούειν') could be aimed at the recitations of historical works as transmitted for Herodotus. Yet, the criticism of an ἀγώνισμα applies even better to oratory. Speeches are often called ἀγῶνες in classical literature and we find this use even in the *History*.[14] Furthermore, Thucydides blames the *logographoi* for being 'attractive to listen to' ('προσαγωγός'). Words related to προσαγωγός, such as προσάγεσθαι (3.42.6; 43.2), ἐπάγεσθαι (5.45.1) and ἐπαγωγός (5.85; 6.8.2), describe the effect of speeches in several passages in Thucydides.

Another point that may support the thesis that speeches are the object of Thucydides' criticism is the transition between the reflections on the representation of archaic history and the Peloponnesian War: 'And even though men always consider the war which they are currently fighting the most significant, but, once they have ended it, admire more the ancient ones, nonetheless it will be obvious to those who consider this war from the facts themselves that it has been greater than the others.' (1.21.2). Thucydides speaks of the evaluation of wars in general, but it is striking that both the magnification of the actual war and the high esteem for ancient wars can be found in the historical section of the funeral speeches.

The lexical evidence as well as the semantics of the context clearly favour the meaning 'orator' for *logographos* in the *History* and we can conclude that Thucydides' criticism addresses not solely Homer and prose authors such as Herodotus, but poets (including Homer) and orators. I do not want to rule out the possibility that Herodotus is implied in Thucydides' criticism – after all, he probably recited parts of his work in oral presentations – but it is important to note that the main targets besides poets are orators. Given that poetry and oratory were the most important media of memory, it makes good sense that Thucydides defined his own approach to the past in contrast to these genres. It is difficult to assess how many prose accounts of the past were being written at the end of the fifth century BCE,[15] but it is obvious that, compared to poetry and oratory, their relevance was rather minor and that no fixed genre of historiography had been established yet.

(b) Thucydides' new approach
What then distinguishes the *History* from the accounts of the past produced by poets and orators? Four aspects, namely production, product, its effect

---

[14] Cf. *LSJ* s.v. III 4. In the *History*, see Cleon's critique of political oratory as agonistic in 3.38.3–4. On ἀγώνισμα, see also Greenwood 2006: 21.
[15] See Fowler 1996; 2006; Porciani 2001.

on recipients and its medium, form the core of the new hermeneutics of memory that Thucydides outlines. While he emphasizes the pains he has taken in writing the *History*, the others 'turn toward what is ready available' (1.20.3). Consequently, the products are rather different. Thucydides claims that his thorough investigation leads to an accurate account (we will return to this in due course).[16] The poets, on the other hand, embellish the past and also the orators stray from the truth in their attempts to please their audiences.[17] Thucydides' concern about accuracy is linked to the choice of his topic. While poets and orators do not shy away from myths, he opts to deal with the very recent past that can be constructed more accurately than the archaic events of myth.

Owing to their embellishments and the tendency to flatter audiences, poetry and speeches are rather 'enjoyable' for their recipients (1.21.1; 22.4). The *History*, on the other hand, may be less enjoyable,[18] but Thucydides hopes that his work will be 'judged useful' by those 'who will wish to look at the plain truth about both past events and those that at some future time, in accordance with human nature, will recur again in similar or comparable ways' (1.22.4).[19] The exact character of the *History*'s usefulness is the subject of fierce debate. Some scholars argue that Thucydides claims to provide his readers with insights that help them better assess the present and the future.[20] Others are sceptical about the political relevance of the *History* and restrict its usefulness to the cognitive level, assuming that it only improves the readers' understanding of the past.[21] However, 1.22.4 unmistakably states that Thucydides' work not only elucidates the past, but also enables the readers to better assess things to come through the knowledge of

---

[16] Cf. 1.21.1; 22.4. The crucial word is σαφές ('clear') which according to Woodman 1988: 24–8 only refers to the level of presentation. See, however, Moles 1993: 107 for a defence of the *communis opinio* that sees a reference to truth.

[17] Cf. 1.21.4. On Homer, see also 1.10.3.

[18] However, Thucydides' phrasing does not exclude the possibility that his work can bring some pleasure, cf. Moles 1993: 102. On the negative connotations of words denoting pleasure in Thucydides, cf. de Romilly 1966. See also Flory 1990: 198–200. On the topos that poetry brings pleasure and enchantment, see Walsh 1984.

[19] I follow the common construction of the sentence which puts a comma after ἔσεσθαι. On the other hand, Goodwin 1866, followed e.g. by Flory 1990: 193, puts the comma after κρίνειν. However, I do not see how the genitive γενομένων can depend on ὠφέλιμα. Even in Goodwin's reading though, the *History* lays claim to usefulness for a better understanding of the future.

[20] Cf. Classen and Steup 1862–1922: ad 1.22.4; von Fritz 1967: I: 530–3; II: 247–50 (n. 15); de Ste. Croix 1972: 29–33; Connor 1984: 242–8 with good remarks on the transformation of Thucydides' methodological claims in his narrative; Erbse 1987: 340–6; Farrar 1988: 131–7; Lendle 1990: 234–5; Nicolai 1995 (who shows the prominence of the political dimension in ancient interpretations).

[21] Kapp 1930: 92–4; Gomme, Andrewes and Dover 1945–81: I 149–50; de Romilly 1956a; Edmunds 1975: 149–55; Stahl 2003: 15–17; Schwinge 2008: 32 n. 49.

'human nature' ('τὸ ἀνθρώπινον'). I will come back to the *History's* usefulness at the end of this chapter.

Finally, the oral performance of poems and speeches is contrasted with the written form of the *History*: 'it is composed rather as a possession for all time than a competition piece to be heard for the moment' (1.24).[22] This juxtaposition gains an additional level of significance if we follow John Moles' argument that Thucydides draws on the concept of an inscription in the presentation of his work.[23] I have already argued for Herodotus that the medium of writing sets off his work against poetic and rhetorical accounts, which are composed for a particular setting. As we see now, Thucydides explicitly points out the independence from a particular context that the medium of writing establishes.

(c) Thucydides' debt to poetry and oratory
As we have seen, in a passage placed prominently in the introductory assessment of his topic Thucydides defines his own work against the media that dominate Greek views on the past: poetry and oratory. There are two scholarly approaches to this self-definition, which elaborate on important aspects of the methodological reflections, one from a historical, the other from a more literary angle. Both make important observations, but, taken by themselves, they lead to rather unsatisfactory interpretations. To start with the more established view, modern historians emphasize Thucydides' methodological rigour, which reminds them of their own work. Indeed, Thucydides' claim to veracity and his critical treatment of sources sound very much like the creeds of modern historians.

However, Nicole Loraux has rightly asserted: 'Thucydides is not a colleague'.[24] Thucydides' methodological rigour ought not to be mistaken for scientific objectivity. The accuracy that Thucydides propagates is not a goal in itself, but aims at establishing insights that are useful.[25] This pragmatic intention not only adds a dimension that scientifically minded historians are eager to avoid, it is also linked to a notion of veracity that is rather different from the ideal of objectivity pursued by many modern historians. I will return to this point at the end of this chapter when I discuss the usefulness of the *History* in more detail. Here, it may be worth adding that the notion of usefulness also plays a role in poetic memory,

---

[22] On the oral nature of oratory, see also 1.21.1. Cf. Havelock 1964: 53–4; Hunter 1982: 287–9; Gentili and Cerri 1983: 8–11. On the role of writing for Thucydides, see Loraux 1986b; Edmunds 1993; Morrison 2004.
[23] Moles 1999: sections 2 and 6.   [24] The title of Loraux 1980: 'Thucydide n'est pas un collègue'.
[25] Cf. Nicolai 1995: 7, who contextualizes Thucydides.

for example when Xenophanes rejects in his symposium-elegy tales of strife for 'there is nothing useful (χρηστόν) in them' (fr. 1 W² 23).²⁶

The second approach that I would like to mention contextualizes Thucydides' methodological reflections in his time. Our evidence of fifth-century speeches is scanty, yet what we have and later speeches indicate that not only Thucydides' presentation but also his method strongly tap into contemporary rhetoric.²⁷ For example, the claim that other accounts may have greater aesthetic value, but are less useful than one's own is a widespread rhetorical topos²⁸ and key terms of Thucydides' methodological reflections, such as 'truth' ('ἀλήθεια'), 'proof' ('σημεῖον'), 'that which is needful' ('τὰ δέοντα') and 'precision, clarity' ('τὸ σαφές'), figure prominently in speeches. Another, at least partial, parallel is the preference for the recent past, which we have also found in deliberative oratory (Chapter 6, section 6.4).

Tony Woodman uses a close reading of the rhetorical structure of the beginning of the *History* to argue against the interpretation of Thucydides as a scientific historian and to demonstrate that even Thucydides' methodological claims merely reproduce rhetorical commonplaces.²⁹ Woodman's reading of the proem is impressive and his emphasis on the rhetorical side of Thucydides effectively challenges the portrayal of Thucydides as a scientific historian.³⁰ However, Woodman has not only been accused of pushing his conclusions too far,³¹ but he also disregards a crucial aspect that makes Thucydides' relationship with rhetoric more complex, namely his attempt to set the *History* off against accounts of the past in oratory.

Is this not a contradiction – how can Thucydides aggressively reject oratory as a commemorative medium and at the same time build his method on rhetorical practice?³² I think it is not so much a contradiction as a fruitful tension. Most importantly, Thucydides does not simply employ rhetorical devices, but rather he transforms them. Stewart Flory comments on 1.22.4: 'Other writers and speakers before and since Thucydides have

---

²⁶ See pp. 70–1.
²⁷ Cf. Moraux 1954; Kennedy 1963: 47–9; Gommel 1966; Parry 1972: 51; Macleod 1983b; Connor 1984: 6; 27–9; Siewert 1985; Woodman 1988: 1–69; Tsakmakis 1998; Plant 1999.
²⁸ See e.g. Gorgias, *Helen* 13. Cf. Crane 1998: 52; Plant 1999: 72–3. See also Greenwood 2006: 9–10, who draws attention to Thucydides' complex and innovative use of the topos.
²⁹ Woodman 1988: 1–69. See also Fox and Livingstone 2007: 543–4, who point out that historiography and rhetoric were far less distinguished from one another in antiquity than they are now.
³⁰ It is also worth noting that modern theorists such as White 1973 or Ricoeur 1990 have emphasized the rhetorical or narrative character of scientific historiography.
³¹ Cf. Moles 1993: 116–18. See also p. 159 n. 39 for scholars, who offer a more radical critique of Woodman's approach.
³² Cf. Fox and Livingstone 2007: 549.

sought an audience's sympathy by graceful apologies at the beginning of their works for the unworthiness of their efforts. But Thucydides' diction adds complexity and dignity to a standard opening ...'[33]

Something similar can be said about the overall structure of the proem. As Woodman shows, the proem has the form of an *auxesis*.[34] Thucydides points out the size of the Peloponnesian War that surpasses all earlier wars. Implicitly, the dimension of his topic elevates Thucydides himself above Homer and Herodotus.[35] At the same time, Thucydides claims that his work is not 'a competition piece' and criticizes the poets for their embellishments. Obviously, there is something of a 'performative tension' – the very argument that no war compares to Thucydides' war contains the rejection of such comparisons, or, inversely, the criticism of *epideixis* is itself embedded in an *epideixis*.[36] And yet, the form of the *auxesis* may be rhetorical, but the critical reflections on which Thucydides builds his argument, for example the evaluation of archaeological relics as evidence (1.10), are carried by genuine criticism and clearly go beyond rhetoric.

There is a similar tension with poetry. For instance, Thucydides' criticism of the poets may remind us of Pindar's comment on Homer's representation of Odysseus' exploits.[37] While Pindar's critique of epic magnification parallels Thucydides' rejection of poetic embellishments, Thucydides' discussion of the size of the Trojan War also taps into the methods of Ionian science.[38] Thucydides may draw on poetic forms, but he transforms them into something new. Another example of such a transformation is Thucydides' claim to have produced a 'possession for all time' ('κτῆμα ἐς αἰεί'). Gregory Crane notes that the idea of a 'possession for all time' draws on the topos of 'imperishable glory' ('κλέος ἄφθιτον') and concludes that 'Thucydides replaces Homer as the true giver of undying fame'.[39] The reference is unmistakable, but it is also important to see the

---

[33] Flory 1990: 207. Tsakmakis 1995: 51 emphasizes that the rhetorical presentation does not impede the scientific character of the *History*. See also Parry 1972: 51.

[34] Woodman 1988: 6–7.

[35] See in Chapter 3, section 3.3 my interpretation of Mimnermus fr. 14 W² according to which the superiority of a recent Smyrnean hero over epic heroes parallels an implicit juxtaposition of Mimnermus with Homer.

[36] Cf. Ober 1998: 55–6. Connor 1984: 29 calls the 'archaeology' an *epideixis*.

[37] See, for example, Pind. *Nem.* 7.20–4. Cf. Richardson 1986; Hornblower 1987: 19; 2004: 287–93. On early ancient literary criticism, see Ford 2002 with further literature on 2 n. 4.

[38] Pindar, on the other hand, may also reject an account of the past for theological reasons. In *Ol.* 1.28–55, he argues that the gods cannot have eaten Pelops' shoulder as this is incompatible with their nature, an argument that would be alien to Thucydides.

[39] Crane 1996: 211–15 (quotation from 215). See also Greenwood 2006: 6, who notes the similarity to Herodotus' proem. For another, less convincing interpretation, see Lendle 1990, who argues that 'for all time' is restricted to the lifetime of Thucydides' contemporary readers.

transformation. Whereas poetic works define their own eternity *via* their objects, Thucydides claims eternity in relation to his readers. Fame has been replaced with usefulness.

To sum up: Thucydides explicitly juxtaposes the *History* with poetry and oratory in order to define his new approach to the past. Careful investigation, the orientation toward truth (implying both the particular and the general), usefulness and the medium of writing are all adduced to distinguish the *History* from other accounts of the past. At the same time, the very criticism of poetic and rhetorical accounts of the past draws on poetic and rhetorical forms and elements. Thus, Thucydides' attempt to define his *History* in contrast to other acts of memory reveals the tension between continuity and innovation that characterizes the rise of historiography.

8.1.2. The digression on the tyrannicide (6.54–9)

In his methodological reflections, Thucydides touches upon the Athenians' belief about the tyrannicide. While it is widely assumed that the victim of the assassination by Harmodius and Aristogeiton, Hipparchus, was tyrant, Thucydides points out that actually his brother, Hippias, ruled (1.20.2). In Book 6, Thucydides revisits and elaborates on the tyrannicide when he describes the turmoil that the Mysteries scandal and the mutilation of the Herms triggered in 415 BCE (6.54–9).[40] I will now turn to this discussion, in which Thucydides forcefully pits against the current accounts his own reconstruction that illustrates some of the principles outlined in 1.20–2.

Thucydides introduces his discussion with the following words: 'For the exploit of Aristogeiton and Harmodius was undertaken because of a love affair, which I shall describe in full to show that neither the others nor the Athenians themselves say anything accurate about their own tyrants and about what happened.' (6.54.1). Scholars have argued that this criticism addresses Hellanicus and Athenian writers,[41] but this unjustifiedly narrows the focus. Authors such as Hellanicus may be implied, but Thucydides does not specify the object of his criticism as writers. Instead, he speaks of 'the Athenians' and starts with the impact that the belief about the tyrannicide

---

[40] On Thucydides' discussion of the tyrannicide, see Pearson 1949; Lang 1954–5; Schneider 1974: 62–6; Forde 1989: 32–7; Rood 1998a: 180–1. Meyer 2008 was published too late for me to take into account. Older scholarship considers the passage a later addition, cf. Schwartz ²1929: 180–6 and the literature given by Pearson 1949: 187 n. 1. Momigliano 1971: 33–4 emphasizes the tension between the embedding of the episode and its significance. See also Schadewaldt 1929: 93; Schneider 1974: 65. On the historical background, see Furley 1996: 13–48.

[41] Cf. Hornblower 1987: 83–4; Thomas 1989: 244 and the further literature given by Tsakmakis 1995: 223 n. 111, who himself argues that Thucydides criticizes Herodotus.

had on the general political climate at Athens. Hence, his criticism is directed against a popular view that was not bound to a specific author or genre, but found expression in a variety of media ranging from statues to scholia.[42]

I will first briefly sketch Thucydides' own account of the tyrannicide and discuss his criticism of the popular view, with particular attention to the subversive stance on democracy (a), and then show that Thucydides uses this deconstruction to throw into relief his striving for accuracy (b).

(a) The critique of the Athenians' beliefs about the tyrannicide
At the beginning of the digression, Thucydides outlines the conflict (6.54.1–4). Hipparchus fails to seduce the handsome young man Harmodius. Nonetheless, Harmodius' 'lover' ('ἐραστής'), Aristogeiton, is outraged and 'fearing that Hipparchus' power might bring him round with force (βίᾳ), he immediately plots in accordance with his social position the overthrow of the tyranny' (6.54.3). Hipparchus, on the other hand, 'did not want to apply force (βίαιον ... δρᾶν), but arranged to insult him [i.e. Harmodius] in a surreptitious way, as though quite unconnected' (6.54.4).[43] This leads Thucydides to two reflections. He first elaborates on the character of the Peisistratids' tyranny, which handled Athenian affairs rather well and did not interfere with the constitution (6.54.5–7), and then goes on to present evidence that Hippias, not Hipparchus, was tyrant, adducing inscriptions and giving reasons from probability (6.55).

After these clarifications Thucydides returns to the narrative. Harmodius' sister is first enlisted to serve as a basket-carrier in a procession, but is then dismissed as being unworthy (6.56.1). This subtle revenge of Hipparchus is countered by Aristogeiton's plan to overthrow the tyranny at the Panathenaea (6.56.2–3). However, when one of the conspirators is seen talking to Hippias, Harmodius and Aristogeiton fear betrayal and hastily kill Hipparchus (6.57). Hippias reacts calmly to the conspiracy and punishes those involved in it (6.58). Thucydides does not stop his account here, but reports that the assassination attempt instilled fear into Hippias and prompted him to make his rule brutal and to strengthen his links with other tyrants (6.59.1–3). Finally, three years after the assassination attempt, he was expelled by the exiled Alcmaeonids with the support of the Spartans and, after a brief stay in Sigeum and Lampsacus, joined the Persian king Darius for whose troops he fought at Marathon (6.59.4).

---

[42] Cf. Brunnsaker ²1971; Taylor ²1991.
[43] On this contrast, see Stahl 2003: 3. See also Tsakmakis 1995: 197.

Thucydides corrects the popular view in three important respects:[44] first, Hipparchus was not the tyrant of Athens. Moreover, the assassination was not so much a political act, but rather the result of a love affair. Finally, only after the assassination did the Peisistratids' reign become violent. In Thucydides' view, Hans-Peter Stahl rightly observes, the popular version of the tyrannicide has mixed up cause and effect: the assassination did not aim at overcoming a cruel tyranny, but rather made the tyranny cruel.[45]

In her examination of the oral traditions about the Alcmaeonids, Rosalind Thomas demonstrates that Felix Jacoby's juxtaposition of an 'official' tradition with the Alcmaeonids' version of the expulsion of the tyrants cannot be maintained. It does not do justice to the accounts in Herodotus and Thucydides and disregards the nature of oral traditions. As Thomas shows, various versions of the tyrannicide circulated in the fifth century BCE, all of them open to transformations.[46] Yet, even in this new more complex reconstruction of the traditions about the tyrannicide, Thucydides' account forcefully questions general tenets of Athenian collective memory. The Athenians may have been aware that the murder of Hipparchus did not end the tyranny – Thucydides himself notes that[47] – but the assertions that Hippias was tyrant and that the conspirators were driven by rather base personal motives effectively chip away at the story of two young aristocrats who sacrifice their lives to fight a hateful regime.[48] As the numerous statues and the mention of Harmodius and Aristogeiton in scholia show, the tyrannicide figured prominently in the Athenians' memory and Thucydides deconstructs a deeply ingrained creed about the beginnings of democracy.[49]

Three minor points underscore the deconstruction. Thucydides mentions in both Books 1 and 6 that Hipparchus was murdered at the Leocoreion (1.20.2; 6.57.3). I suggest that the semantics of this place reinforce the dismantling of democratic memory. According to the legend, Leos, the eponymous hero of one of the phylai, had not hesitated to sacrifice his three daughters when this was needed to save Athens from famine or a plague.[50] The death of the daughters forms a powerful contrast to the murder of Hipparchus and thereby reinforces Thucydides' deconstruction: while Leos

---

[44] Cf. Taylor ²1991: 81–2; Tsakmakis 1995: 187–8.   [45] Stahl 2003: 8.
[46] Thomas 1989: 238–82.   [47] Cf. *ibid.*: 244.
[48] It is also noteworthy that Harmodius and Aristogeiton wrongly expect that their assassination would find support from citizens who are not part of the conspiracy (6.56.3). Cf. Tsakmakis 1995: 198.
[49] However, the traditional story of the tyrannicide also seems to have attracted scorn, see Kinzl 1978, who argues that a vase painting presents a drunken couple in the pose of the tyrant-slayers, and Boedeker 1998: 202, who draws our attention to decrees against the slander of Harmodius and Aristogeiton.
[50] For the famine, see the scholion ad Dem. 54 7 and the scholion ad Thuc. 1.20 Suid.; for the plague, see Aristid. *Panath.* 119; Hieron. *Adv. Iovinian.* 1.41. For further evidence, see Kock 1925: 2000–1.

sacrificed his daughters in the interest of the polis and thereby helped the Athenians, Harmodius and Aristogeiton pursued personal motives and seriously worsened the situation of Athens.

Furthermore, Thucydides not only gives a positive assessment of the early phase of the Peisistratids' regime, but the tyranny that worked within the Athenian constitution reminds one of the 'golden age' under Pericles when 'what was in name a democracy became in actuality rule by the first man' (2.65.9).[51] Thucydides' description of the Peisistratids' reign evokes particularly the Athens of Pericles' funeral speech. Successful wars (6.54.5), proper sacrifices (6.54.5-2.38), the rule of the laws (6.54.6-2.37.3) and *arete* (6.54.5-2.37.1; 40.4) correspond to Pericles' ideal image of democratic Athens. Even an aspect that at first sight seems to underline the inequality under tyranny echoes the funeral speech: Aristogeiton plotted against Hipparchus 'in accordance with his social status' ('ὡς ἀπὸ τῆς ὑπαρχούσης ἀξιώσεως', 6.54.3).[52] In the funeral speech, Pericles points out that in Athens citizens are 'singled out for public service in accordance with social status ('κατὰ ... τὴν ἀξίωσιν'), the reputation one enjoys, not by rotation but by merit' (2.37.1). The description of the Peisistratids' regime in the very terms that characterize the ideal democratic Athens of the funeral speech effectively undermines the belief that Athens had to be liberated from the tyrants.

On the other hand, the blurring of the borderlines between the public and the private spheres that Thucydides foregrounds in his account of 415 BCE contrasts with the description of Athens in the funeral speech. Particularly the regime of general suspicion ('ὑποψία') that comes to the fore in the reactions to Alcibiades' licentious lifestyle contradicts Pericles' claim that 'in public life we conduct ourselves with freedom and also, regarding that suspicion (ὑποψία) of others because of their everyday habits, without anger at a neighbour if he does something with pleasure' (2.37.2). I further tentatively suggest that the dismantling of the founding moment of democracy as the culmination of an erotic affair can be linked to Pericles' appeal in the funeral speech that the Athenians become lovers of their polis.[53] This is the only occurrence of the word 'lover' ('ἐραστής')

---

[51] Stahl 2003: 4 with n. 2 points out that Thucydides' positive evaluation of the Peisistratids ought not to be taken as a positive verdict on tyranny in general.
[52] On Aristogeiton's social status in Thucydides' account, see Wohl 2002: 7–8; on the word ἀξίωσις and its economic connotation, see Allison 2001.
[53] The motif of *eros* also links the discussion of the tyrannicide to the Sicilian Expedition and Alcibiades, cf. Connor 1984: 178–9; Forde 1989: 32–4; Vickers 1995: 196; Allison 1997a: 183. For a psychoanalytical approach to *eros* and Athenian democracy, see Wohl 2002, in particular 30–72 on the Periclean funeral speech, and 171–214 on the Sicilian Expedition.

outside the Harmodius–Aristogeiton story,[54] and, if this suffices to establish a link, one could read the erotic nature of the 'tyrannicide' as an ironic comment on the image of the democratic citizens as lovers of Athens. In that case, the non-metaphoric involvement of *eros* in the beginnings of democracy subverts the *eros*–metaphor for the citizens' adherence to democracy.

(b) Thucydides' method

Many scholars assume that Thucydides contrasts his account with the popular view that rests on hearsay.[55] The general thrust of this argument is right, but it disregards crucial aspects of Thucydides' discussion and thereby deprives it of its complexity. The *differentia specifica* between Thucydides and the *communis opinio* is not the 'hearsay', on which Thucydides himself relies, as he explicitly points out (6.55.1, see also 1.4). Nevertheless he stresses that his sources are more accurate (6.55.1). This does not necessarily indicate, as scholars are prone to assume, that Thucydides had connections with later members of the Peisistratid clan.[56] This is possible, but it seems more plausible to interpret Thucydides' claim against the background of his reflections in Book 1. While the Athenians pay attention to the questionable testimonies of 'scoundrels', Thucydides considered 'it his responsibility to write not as he learned from the chance informant' (1.22.2).

Moreover, Thucydides adduces epigraphic evidence for his reconstruction. As scholars have noted, Thucydides only rarely refers to or even quotes inscriptions.[57] I suggest that there is a simple explanation for the striking accumulation of inscriptions in the discussion of the tyrannicide. Thucydides wants to drive home the point that the truth about the tyrannicide is not that difficult to establish: 'One might also understand it simply from the following' (6.55.1). Seen from this angle, the references to the inscriptions are neither owed to a scientific attitude nor are they supposed to give the readers insight into the historian's workshop, but they demonstrate the Athenians' sloppiness – they do not bother to take into account even what is open to everybody (to say nothing about serious research).

---

[54] Cf. Allison 1997a: 184–5.
[55] See, for example, Connor 1984: 178; Rawlings 1981: 102–3, who establishes a link between 6.53 and 1.20 without noticing the obvious positive correspondences.
[56] Cf. Hornblower 1987: 77. Taylor ²1991: 78 n. 5, on the other hand, emphasizes Thucydides' research as the reason for his superior knowledge.
[57] On Thucydides and epigraphy, see Gomme, Andrewes and Dover 1945–81: I: 30–9; Smarczyk 2006.

Thucydides contrasts his approach not only with the Athenians' assumptions about the past, but also with their attitude towards the present. His description of the Athenian 'investigation' of the scandals ('ζήτησις', 6.53.2) echoes the reflections on his own project that he calls an 'investigation of the truth' ('ζήτησις τῆς ἀληθείας', 1.20.3): both the Athenians and Thucydides use 'proof' ('πίστις', 6.53.2–1.20.1; 21.1) and are involved in the process of 'approving' ('(ἀπο)δέχεσθαι', 6.53.2–1.20.1). These similarities are reinforced by a striking allusion: the Athenians wanted rather to 'examine the affair closely and find out than to let anyone accused, however worthy he seemed, escape without trial on account of the informer's vileness' ('βασανίσαι[58] τὸ πρᾶγμα καὶ εὑρεῖν ἢ διὰ μηνυτοῦ πονηρίαν τινὰ καὶ χρηστὸν δοκοῦντα εἶναι αἰτιαθέντα ἀνέλεγκτον διαφυγεῖν', 6.53.2). This clearly echoes 1.20.1:[59] 'Such, then, I found (ηὗρον) to be ancient history, although it was difficult to trust every piece of evidence. For men accept one another's accounts of past events, even if they are about their own countries, with a uniform lack of examination (ἀβασανίστως).' A little further on, Thucydides sets off his own account against the poets' and the *logographoi*'s versions which are 'without proof' ('ἀνεξέλεγκτα', 1.21.1). The correspondences between the Athenians' investigation in 415 BCE and Thucydides' own methodological reflections are reinforced by the explicit mention of the tyrannicide as one of the examples of erroneous memory in 1.20.2.

The striking similarities throw into relief the underlying discrepancy. Thucydides critically remarks that the Athenians arrested 'some very honest citizens because of their own trust in worthless men' (6.53.2). As with the tyrannicide, the Athenians fail to rely on the right sources. At another level, however, their assessment of the recent past contrasts with the assessment of the more distant past. In 415 BCE one of the accused citizens makes a confession about the mutilation of the Herms. Thucydides comments that nobody knew if this confession was right, but although 'it was unclear whether in this the victims had been punished unjustly, it was nonetheless unmistakable that for the time the rest of the city benefitted from this' (6.60.5). At the same time, Alcibiades was still suspected of having been involved in the affair of the Mysteries and when a small Spartan army came to the Isthmus, the Athenians were only too willing to see this as part of Alcibiades' conspiracy against democracy, although the Spartans had been sent out to deal with the Boeotians (6.61.1–2).[60]

---

[58] On the legal connotation of βασανίζειν, see Hornblower 1987: 107; Tsakmakis 1998: 252 n. 47.
[59] Cf. Morrison 2004: 106–7. [60] Cf. Rawlings 1981: 110–11.

This over-sensitivity toward conspiracies constitutes a marked contrast with the treatment of the past. The efforts to investigate the present situation are clearly disproportionate; on the other hand, the reconstruction of the past is more than sloppy. Hence, the Athenians' investigative efforts are unbalanced, and since they abuse the arsenal of critical inquiry in their evaluation of the present, their reconstruction of the past suffers from carelessness. The opposite tendencies in assessing the past and the present highlight the shortcomings of both.

To sum up: Thucydides challenges the Athenian tradition about the tyrannicide. The Athenians' sloppiness in looking at the past paired with their paranoia regarding the present throws into relief the accuracy of the *History*.[61] In his thorough investigation, Thucydides takes into account and carefully weighs various sources. Popular belief, on the other hand, illustrates the kind of 'patriotic fiction' against which Thucydides polemicizes in 1.21.1. The deconstruction of the tyrannicide as the culmination of a love affair is politically highly charged and reveals a subversive stance that will be further illustrated in the next chapter's discussion of the Periclean funeral speech.

8.2. IMPLICIT CRITICISM OF THE USE OF THE PAST IN ORATORY (PERICLES' FUNERAL SPEECH (2.35–46); THE PLATAEAN DEBATE (3.52–68))

Much work has been devoted to embedded speeches in the Greek historians, and the elaborate speeches in Thucydides have received particular attention. Scholars have concentrated on two major questions, the authenticity of the speeches and their interaction with the narrative.[62] In my Herodotus chapter (Chapter 7, section 7.2), I suggested a meta-historical reading of speeches with historical arguments. The references to the past in the speeches parallel the historian's account of the past as another act of memory and therefore form a *mise-en-abyme*. I argued that the use of the past in the Syracusan embassy scene and the speech duel at Plataea is questionable and throws into relief the *Histories'* superiority. This approach to speeches is a particularly powerful tool for reading Thucydides who, as we have just seen, explicitly polemicizes against oratory. Thus, the

---

[61] The meta-historical interpretation of the digression on the tyrannicide is developed further on p. 271–3.
[62] On the authenticity of the speeches in Thucydides, see e.g. Hornblower 1987: 45–72; Garrity 1998. On the links between speeches and narrative, see de Romilly 1956b; Hunter 1973; Stahl 2003; Morrison 2006. See also the articles in Stadter 1973.

meta-historical significance of speeches can be read as continuing the critique of 1.21.1. Moreover, we will see that Thucydides reinforces the function of speeches as foil through echoes of his own methodological reflections. I will first discuss the Periclean funeral speech and, in the next section, the Plataean Debate as illustrations of this implicit, yet forceful meta-historical critique of oratory in Thucydides.

8.2.1. Pericles' funeral speech (2.35–46)

The *epitaphios logos* that Thucydides has Pericles deliver after the first year of the Peloponnesian War is one of the most prominent passages of the *History*. While some still grapple with the issues of authenticity and historical context, most scholars focus on the function of the speech in the *History*.[63] Commonly, Pericles' funeral speech is read as a representation of the Athenian ideal before Athens was brought low by the Peloponnesian War. In a more challenging reading, Hellmut Flashar points out numerous tensions and contradictions and suggests that these serve to unveil the imperialist ideology of Athens.[64]

The approach that I am taking in this book paves the way to a new interpretation of the Periclean *epitaphios logos*. Thucydides could not rely on a firmly established genre, but had to justify his new approach against the claims of other commemorative genres, among others the public funeral speeches. As we have seen in Chapter 5, the funeral speeches presented a semi-official polis–history in which Athens' past appears as an uninterrupted chain of great deeds.[65] Seen from this perspective, Pericles' funeral speech figures as an alternative medium of memory in Thucydides' account of the past. I will therefore pursue the thesis that the *epitaphios logos* is embedded as a foil that throws into relief the advantages of the *History*. The general description of public funerals in the Kerameikos (2.34) makes it easy to read the speech as an implicit commentary on the *epitaphioi logoi* in general. My interpretation starts out from the observation that Thucydides has Pericles echo the methodological reflections in 1.20–2 (a). I will then argue that these similarities draw

---

[63] On authenticity and context of Pericles' funeral speech in Thucydides, see, more recently, Sicking 1995; Bosworth 2000. On Pericles' funeral speech in Thucydides in general, see Flashar 1969; Landmann 1974; Gaiser 1975; Ziolkowski 1981; Loraux 1986a; Yunis 1996: 79–82; Crane 1998: 312–22; Ober 1998: 83–9; Wohl 2002: 30–72; Dunn 2007: 181–92. For a more detailed version of the interpretation given above, see Grethlein 2005.
[64] Flashar 1969.   [65] See Loraux 1986a; Thomas 1989: 196–237.

attention to more fundamental differences between *History* and the *epitaphios logos* (b). Pericles addresses the core problem of funeral speeches at the beginning of his speech (c). At the same time his speech itself illustrates the shortcomings of funeral speeches (d).

(a) Echoes of Thucydides' methodological reflections
The methodological reflections, goals and content of Pericles' funeral speech are reminiscent of the *History*. In 2.41.4, Pericles criticizes Homer and other poets: '... we are not in need of Homer for praise nor of any other who will charm with his verses for the moment (τὸ αὐτίκα τέρψει), but whose claims the factual truth will destroy'. This recalls Thucydides' rejection of poets in 1.21.1:

> In light of the evidence I have cited, however, one would not go wrong in supposing that the events which I have related actually happened like this, and in not believing that they happened as the poets have sung in their praise, adorning them with their exaggerations, or like the reports which the *logographoi* have composed, more attractive for listening than with regard to truthfulness, reports which are beyond proof and for the most part have forfeited credibility over time by winning victories as patriotic fiction, but in regarding what has been found from the clearest possible evidence as adequate for what concerns antiquity.

More specifically, the critique of verses that 'will charm for the moment' (τὸ αὐτίκα τέρψει) echoes Thucydides' assertion: 'And the results, by avoiding patriotic storytelling, will perhaps seem the less charming (ἀτερπέστερον) for listening ... It is composed rather as a possession for all time than a competition piece to be heard for the moment (ἐς τὸ παραχρῆμα).' (1.22.4).

These marked echoes are reinforced by more general similarities. Pericles reproaches the poets for deviating from the truth (2.41.4) while claiming that he gives a truthful account: 'And that these are not boastful words for the occasion but factual truth the very power of this city, which we acquired because of these characteristics, indicates.' (2.41.2). In a similar vein, Thucydides distances himself from others who fall short of the truth in 1.20.3 and 1.21.1. Moreover, Thucydides has Pericles strive for trustworthiness ('πίστις'), present evidence ('τεκμήριον', 'σημεῖον', 'μαρτύριον') and aim at exactness ('τὸ σαφές'), core elements of Thucydides' methodological claims.[66]

---

[66] πιστεύειν: 2.35.1; 2 (cf. e.g. 1.20.1); τεκμήριον: 2.39.2 (cf. e.g. 1.20.1); σημεῖον: 2.41.4; 42.1; ἀμάρτυρος: 2.41.4 (cf. e.g. 1.8.1); σαφέστατον: 2.40.3 (cf. e.g. 1.22.4). On Thucydides' use of τεκμήρια, see, for example, Schwinge 2008: 15–18.

Not only the methodological reflections, but also the goals put forward by Pericles resemble those of Thucydides. Both emphasize that their object is worthy of their attention (1.1.1; 2.36.2) and Thucydides' assertion that he creates a 'possession for all time' (1.22.4) corresponds with Pericles' claim that his praise is eternal: 'For in giving their lives in common cause, they individually gained ageless praise and the most distinctive tomb, not the one where they are lying but the one where on every occasion for word and deed their glory is left eternally.'[67] (2.43.2).

Like Thucydides (1.22.4), Pericles expects his account to be useful for the recipients, as, besides 2.46.1 'I have said, in accordance with the custom, in words as many useful (πρόσφορα) things as I could say ...', 2.36.4 shows:

After setting forth the devotion by which we came into this position and the form of government and the characteristics from which its greatness resulted, I will move on to the praise of these men, since I believe that, at the present occasion, these are not inappropriate to mention and advantageous (ξύμφορον) for the whole gathering, both citizens and foreigners, to hear about.

In addition to method and goals, the scope and content of Pericles' funeral speech and the *History* are similar. Thucydides by and large leaves the ancient past aside and hails the most recent war as the greatest. Similarly, Pericles touches upon the archaic past only in a *praeteritio*, while calling the most recent achievements the greatest (2.36.3).[68] Furthermore, as H. R. Immerwahr notes, both Thucydides and Pericles focus more on attitudes and mentalities than on deeds.[69] Thus, striking echoes of Thucydides' methodological reflections and more general similarities with the *History* pit Thucydides' new approach to the past against the well-established genre of the *epitaphios logos* and invite the readers to compare them.

(b) Differences between the epitaphios logos *and* History
Upon closer inspection, the similarities turn out to be rather superficial and fundamental differences emerge: 'As to the qualities for which I have praised (ὕμνησα) the city, the virtues of these men and men like them have given honour (ἐκόσμησαν) to them ...' (2.42.2). Pericles criticizes the poets, but at the same time he refers to his own speech as 'praise' ('ὑμνεῖν'), the very activity for which Thucydides blames the poets: 'In the light of the evidence I have cited, however, one would not go wrong in supposing that the events

---

[67] For a close reading of this passage, see Grethlein 2005: 52–5.   [68] Cf. Landmann 1974: 77.
[69] Immerwahr 1960: 285. While he concludes that 'the effect of the Oration, then, lies in the fact that it completes the picture of Athens drawn by Thucydides himself', I will argue that the similarities serve to tacitly compare the *epitaphios logos* with the *History*.

which I have related actually happened like this, and in not believing that they happened as the poets have sung in their praise (ὑμνήκασι), adorning them with their exaggerations (ἐπὶ τὸ μεῖζον κοσμοῦντες) ...' (1.21.1). The echo is underscored by the use of κοσμεῖν in both sentences, by Pericles, however, ascribed to the praised themselves.[70]

Thus, Pericles may reject poetic accounts for their excessive praise, but his speech itself implicitly admits to having the very features that Thucydides criticizes in poetry. The same tension can be found in other assertions. As we have seen, Pericles' polemic against Homer and 'any other who will charm (τέρψει) with his verses for the moment' (2.41.4) is reminiscent of Thucydides' concession that his account 'will perhaps seem the less charming (ἀτερπέστερον) for listening' (1.22.4). At the same time, however, Pericles says in 2.44.4: 'For love of honour alone has no old age, and in the uselessness of age it is not profit, as some claim, but being honoured that charms more (τέρπει).' Since the honour that Pericles mentions consists in the praise given by him, it is implied that the *epitaphios logos* offers the very charm that Thucydides rejects.

Thucydides also refuses to deliver a 'competition piece' ('ἀγώνισμα', 1.22.4).[71] In Pericles' speech, on the other hand, the idea of an *agon* figures prominently. In 2.42.1, Pericles says: 'For this reason I have spoken at length about the affairs of the city, teaching (διδασκαλίαν ... ποιούμενος) why the *agon* is not about the same for us and those who do not share these values ...' Taken together, διδασκαλία and *agon* perhaps evoke the image of a dramatic competition and thereby invoke the sinister connotations of a *theatrokratia* (cf. 3.38.4). The sentence also implies what Lysias (2.2) makes explicit, namely that the funeral oration is part of an *agon*.[72] Later on, Pericles points out that his speech constitutes not only an *agon* with foreigners, but also an internal *agon* between the generations: 'For the children of these men who are present, or the brothers, however, I see that the *agon* will be a great one, for everyone tends to praise the one who is no longer, and not easily will you be judged only slightly inferior, let alone equal, on account of their surpassing merit.'[73] (2.45.1).

Thus, a closer look reveals that the striking echoes and similarities draw attention to crucial differences between *History* and *epitaphios logos*. Pericles' speech illustrates the very shortcomings for which Thucydides blames poets and orators, in particular the embellishments that stray from the truth.

---

[70] For κοσμεῖν, see also 1.10.3; 2.46.1.
[71] Nonetheless, the beginning of his work has epideictic character, see above p. 213.
[72] There is even evidence for an *epitaphios agon*, cf. Loraux 1986a: 37–8.   [73] See also *agon* in 2.46.1.

Hence, the *epitaphios logos* allows Thucydides to implicitly reinforce the critique that is explicit in 1.20–2.

(c) Pericles' critique of the funeral orations
I would now like to push my analysis further by arguing that the major reason for the deficiencies of the funeral speech is voiced by Pericles himself at the beginning of the speech, to which scholars have paid little attention. His objections to the *epitaphios logos* are not merely a topical attempt to highlight the challenge that he as the orator is facing, but constitute a serious critique.[74] To start with, Pericles sets up a strict dichotomy between words and deeds (2.35.1):

> To me it would seem sufficient that, as the men have proved good in deed (ἔργῳ), the honours be bestowed also by deed (ἔργῳ), just as you now see carried out at public expense (δημοσίᾳ) for this burial, rather than that the virtues of many men are put at risk by a single man and whether he speaks well or badly (ἐν ἑνὶ ἀνδρὶ ... εὖ τε καὶ χεῖρον εἰπόντι).

The *logos* of the funeral speech is markedly juxtaposed with both the *ergon* of what the dead have done and the *ergon* of the funeral rite. The use of *ergon* for both heroic deeds and funeral rite suggests that the rite is a more appropriate way of honouring the dead than the mere words of the speech. The *antithesis* is reinforced at two levels, first through the juxtaposition of individual and community: the *ergon* of the ritual that is carried out on behalf of the public contrasts with the *logos* delivered by an individual. Second, the listening to the *logos* ('ἀκροατής', 'ἀκούοι', 'ἤκουσεν', 2.35.2) contrasts with the seeing of deeds ('ὁρᾶτε', 2.35.1).[75] Thus, words such as the funeral speech are ontologically, ethically and epistemologically inferior to deeds.[76]

In the following paragraph, Pericles touches upon the reason why the funeral speech falls short of giving an appropriate representation of reality: 'To speak in due proportion is difficult where grasp of the truth itself is hardly assured.' ('χαλεπὸν γὰρ τὸ μετρίως εἰπεῖν ἐν ᾧ μόλις καὶ ἡ δόκησις τῆς ἀληθείας βεβαιοῦται.' 2.35.2). There are two possible ways of construing ἐν ᾧ. Either it either refers to τὸ μετρίως εἰπεῖν or the

---

[74] For a topical reading, see Gaiser 1975: 26; Krischer 1977: 123–5; Loraux 1986a: 247; Prinz 1997: 100–2. For a more interesting reading, see Ober 1998: 84.
[75] Cf. the similar juxtapositions of seeing and hearing in 1.73.2; 7.48.3. On the ancient preference for seeing over hearing, see Marincola 1997: 63–86.
[76] A similar yet even more complex juxtaposition of words and deeds can be found in 2.43.2, cf. Grethlein 2005: 52–5.

antecedent has dropped out.⁷⁷ I would prefer the second construction, but in either case Pericles pits the topos '*verbis facta exaequare*' ('to equal deeds in words') which has been toned down to 'to speak in due proportion' against an '*verbis expectationes exaequare*' ('to equal expectations in words' – 'where grasp of the truth is hardly assured'). He then continues to elaborate on why it is difficult to establish δόκησις τῆς ἀληθείας.⁷⁸ Either the listener is familiar with the topic ('ξυνειδώς') and of good will ('εὔνους') or he is ignorant ('ἄπειρος') and envious ('φθονῶν'). Thus, the listeners' knowledge and attitude, but not the veracity of the account, decide whether the speech will be accepted. At the same time, Pericles' closing sentence reveals that the expectations of the audience are what guides the orator: 'But since it was so judged by those of long ago that this speech is a fine thing, I too must follow the custom and try to conform with the wishes and opinions (βουλήσεώς τε καὶ δόξης) of each one of you as far as possible.' (2.35.3).

This sentence is closely linked with the preceding discussion of receptive modes. Βούλησις harks back to εὔνους and φθονῶν, δόξα takes up δόκησις as well as ξυνειδώς and ἄπειρος. In the *Menexenus*, Plato has Socrates mock the speaker's tendency to butter up the audience by describing his reaction to the funeral speeches: 'I myself, Menexenus, when praised by them, feel mightily ennobled, and every time I stand listening with fascination, believing that I have become all at once taller and nobler and more handsome.' (235a6–10).

It is this desire to flatter the audience that gets in the way of a truthful account and therefore marks the crucial distinction between *epitaphios logos* and *History*. While the funeral speeches take the expectations of the audience as their gauge, Thucydides aims at the facts themselves.⁷⁹ A further parallel reinforces the contrast: the two aspects that underlie the expectations of the audience and thereby lead to corrupted accounts in funeral speeches, knowledge and attitude, are mentioned as major impediments to Thucydides' research in 1.22.3: 'It took much effort to find out the facts, because eye-witnesses did not report the same about the same events, but according to individual favour or ability to remember (ὡς ἑκατέρων τις εὐνοίας ἢ μνήμης ἔχοι).'

Pericles' introductory objections to the funeral oration are all the more revealing, as Thucydides emphasizes in a very prominent passage that,

---

⁷⁷ Cf. Grethlein 2005: 49 n. 36.
⁷⁸ I assume that δόκησις τῆς ἀληθείας signifies the subjective conviction that something is right.
⁷⁹ The orientation of epideictic speeches toward the recipients is pointed out by Arist. *Rh.* 3.1415b28–32 and 1.1367b7–9 citing Pl. *Menex.* 235d.

unlike his successors, Pericles did not aim at merely pleasing the *demos* in his speeches (2.65.8). Thus, Pericles' critique not only highlights a feature that makes him the exceptional politician in the *History*, but also touches upon an aspect that proves detrimental in Athens' history. As Thucydides points out, the orators' willingness to pander to the audience's expectations and preferences plays a prominent role in the disaster of post-Periclean Athens.[80] The juxtaposition of his own orientation towards the facts with the orators' desire to please their audiences indicates the political relevance of the *History*, a point to which I will return in due course.

(d) Pericles' speech as illustration of the flaws of epideictic oratory
Despite Pericles' critique, his funeral oration illustrates the very faults that result from an orientation toward the expectations of the audience. The radiant image of Athens that Pericles sketches stands in pointed contrast to the misery of the plague that follows nearly immediately in the narrative.[81] While this tension can be explained as a temporal development, there are other points in which the Athens of Pericles' oration not only contrasts with the Athens that was subsequently wrecked by the war, but also with Periclean Athens.[82] Most glaringly, the assertions about Athens' selfless benefactions in 2.40.5 are a far cry from the cold and calculating power politics that the Athenians pursue in Thucydides' narrative.[83] Strikingly, the contradiction is marked in the assertion itself: 'We are unique in helping someone without fear not out of calculation of advantage but with the reliability of our freedom.' (2.40.5). Of course, antithetical or dual expressions are common in Greek literature and here Pericles negates one explanation in order to emphasize his positive assertion through the contrast. However, I suggest that the twofold expression has further significance, as the negated part points toward the truthful assessment that emerges in the narrative. What is merely a rhetorical ploy at the level of the action alerts the readers to the discrepancy between claim and reality.

Similarly to the treatment of foreign affairs, the praise of the stable constitution and the harmonious polis–life contrasts not only with later politics, but also with Pericles' own experiences when he first was fined and

---

[80] Cf. Yunis 1996: 59–86; Ober 1998: 152–221.
[81] Cf. Gaiser 1975: 58–60; Ziolkowski 1981: 6; 195; Allison 1983; Macleod 1983a: 151; Schwinge 1996: 311.
[82] For a detailed discussion of the tensions and contradictions within the funeral oration, see Flashar 1969. For a further interesting tension, see Ober 1998: 85, who points out that the emphasis on 'great demonstrations' (2.41.4) contrasts with Thucydides' scepticism towards the evidence of monuments (1.10.1–2).
[83] Cf. Gomme, Andrewes and Dover 1945–81: ad loc.; Flashar 1969: 24–5, who points out that the assertion of 2.40.5 is already undermined by 2.40.4.

then re-elected as general (2.65.3–4).⁸⁴ At a meta-level, these contradictions are marked by the *logos–ergon* dichotomy itself. While in his critical reflection Pericles considers the tension between *logos* and *ergon*, in his speech he unashamedly claims that Athens' achievements do not fall short of the praise (2.41.2; 3; 4; 42.2).⁸⁵ Thus, the Periclean funeral oration illustrates that the need to please the audience leads to *logoi* that are out of touch with *erga*.

In his methodological reflections, Thucydides denounces rhetorical accounts of the past that indulge in 'patriotic fiction' and aim to sway audiences in performances. This critique is indirectly continued in Pericles' funeral speech, which illustrates the very shortcomings pointed out by Thucydides. What is more, echoes of Thucydides' methodological reflection prompt the readers to compare the funeral speech with the *History*. The orator's desire to please his audience throws into relief Thucydides' orientation towards the facts.

In the chapter on Herodotus, I noted that whereas the non-historiographic genres of memory are more or less in the grip of the polis, the *pater historiae* does not take the perspective of a single polis and sheds critical light on the present. Thucydides deviates from memory in poetry and oratory even more. The deconstruction of the *epitaphioi logoi*, the semi-official version of Athens' past, and the demystification of the tyrannicide, a charter myth for democratic Athens, reveal the critical stand that Thucydides takes on Athens and democracy. Given our scanty knowledge about Thucydides' life, a biographical approach to his work is rather problematic, but it is not difficult to see that the *History* was written by somebody who had been condemned to exile for twenty years by his own polis.

8.2.2. The Plataean Debate (3.52–68)

Thucydides' implicit criticism is not limited to epideictic oratory, he also casts a critical eye on other kinds of speeches.⁸⁶ For my argument, those diplomatic speeches are of particular interest that engage in discussions of the past and therefore invite a meta-historical reading. A particularly interesting example is the *agon* between Plataeans and Thebans in 3.52–68 which

---

⁸⁴ *Ibid.*: 18–19.
⁸⁵ Cf. Grethlein 2005: 64. Furthermore, Ober 1998: 88 points out that the praise for the central role of speech in Athenian politics (2.40.3) sits uneasily with Thucydides' tendency to privilege *erga* over *logoi*.
⁸⁶ For a general analysis of the precarious role of oratory in the *History*, see Yunis 1996: 59–86; Ober 1998: 52–121.

allows us to revisit Plataea, the place where in Herodotus' *Histories* the Tegeans and Athenians argue about the battle formation before the famous victory over the Persians (479 BCE).[87] In my reading of this passage, I argued that the deconstruction of historical arguments gains special significance from its setting, the battle of Plataea, which would figure prominently as historical capital in Herodotus' own time.[88] The Plataean Debate in Thucydides, held some fifty years later, is an excellent example of this use of Plataea as historical argument. Its examination will show us that, like Herodotus, Thucydides implicitly criticizes the use of the past in diplomatic speeches, albeit from a different angle.

I will first argue that the juxtaposition of the two speeches reveals how easily the truth is bent in diplomatic affairs (a). I shall then briefly discuss echoes of Thucydides' methodological reflection that are not as strong as the ones in Pericles' funeral speech, but nonetheless reinforce the contrast between the use of the past in oratory and his *History* (b). Finally, I will show that the Plataean Debate helps Thucydides to throw into relief another crucial point besides his accuracy (c).

(a) The rhetorical use of the past
The destruction of Plataea by the Spartans in 427 BCE did not have any major military or political significance.[89] Yet, Thucydides gives it a prominent place in his work and starts his account of the Peloponnesian War with the capture of Plataea by Thebes in 431 BCE.[90] Supported by Plataean oligarchs, a small group of armed Thebans enters Plataea at night. Taken by surprise, the Plataeans at first agree to abandon the alliance with Athens and to join the Boeotians. However, when they discover how small the Theban force actually is, they revolt. Many Thebans are killed, others are captured. With the captives in their hands, the Plataeans persuade a Theban army to return to Thebes. Nonetheless, they kill the 180 Thebans in their power (2.2–6).

Two years later, in 429 BCE, Archidamus comes to Plataea with a Spartan army. He fails to persuade the Plataeans to join the Spartans or even to remain neutral and therefore lays siege to the town.[91] Although the

---

[87] Cf. Chapter 7, section 7.2.2. On the Plataean Debate in Thucydides, see Hogan 1972; Macleod 1983b; Cagnetta 1984; Erbse 1987; Debnar 1996; 2001: 125–46; Price 2001: 103–26; Jung 2006: 282–9.
[88] See above pp. 185–6.   [89] Cf. Gomme, Andrewes and Dover 1945–81: II: 354.
[90] Cf. Cagnetta 1984: 203; Debnar 2001: 96 draws attention to the detailed determination of the time, which underscores the significance of the event.
[91] The exact legal status of Plataea is debated, as the category of an autonomous polis seems to have emerged only in the course of the fifth century BCE. Cf. Jung 2006: 283–5 with further literature.

expected help from Athens does not materialize, the Plataeans resist the Spartans for two years. In the summer of 427 BCE, however, the scarcity of food forces them to hand over the town to the Spartans who promise 'to punish only the unjust, and no one without justice' (3.52.2). The judges from Sparta make no particular charges, but instead ask the Plataeans what good things they have done for Sparta during the present war. The Plataeans present a rather lengthy speech (3.53–9), in which they express their anxiety, invoke their merits in the Persian Wars and reflect on what would be most expedient for the Spartans. The Thebans' rejoinder (3.61–7) is roughly the same length, by and large has the same structure[92] and picks up many details of the Plataeans' speech.[93] After the speeches, the Spartan judges repeat their question and have the Plataeans killed.

In an important article, C. W. Macleod examined the rhetorical techniques used by the Plataeans and Thebans and showed that, in a way similar to the Mytilinean Debate, the speeches at Plataea reveal the corruption of morality and the abuse of rhetoric in war.[94] Neither the Plataeans' nor the Thebans' self-justification is convincing.[95] There are flagrant discrepancies in their speeches bordering on outright contradictions. For example, the Plataeans claim that they have defended themselves 'in accordance with a law valid for all' ('κατὰ τὸν πᾶσι νόμον καθεστῶτα', 3.56.2) and even call their defence 'holy' ('ὅσιον', 3.56.2). At the same time, the Plataeans appeal to the Spartans to spare them because 'it is law for the Greeks not to kill these [i.e. captives]' ('ὁ δὲ νόμος τοῖς Ἕλλησι μὴ κτείνειν τούτους',

---

[92] Price 2001: 113–14 notes that the Thebans add the problem of Boeotian loyalty and leave aside the issue of expediency. Hornblower 1991–6: 1: 444–5 points out that the Thebans' speech is 'clearer and more logical' than the Plataeans' (cf. Price 2001: 105). While the Plataeans 'jump nervously around', the Thebans follow a chronological order. I agree that the Thebans' speech is better organized and more lucid. Yet, I would like to add that, although the Plataeans come back to their resistance to the Persians time and again, the basic structure of the main part of their speech is chronological too.

[93] In their rebuttal, the Thebans frequently pick up phrasings and often give them a new twist. See, for example, 'For they thrust away (ἀπεώσαντο) the better allies by their own choice.' (3.67.5) ~ 'And we have been pushed aside (περιεώσμεθα) from all, we the Plataeans, devoted to the Greeks beyond our power, lonely and undefended.' (3.57.4) '... as to those who stretched out their hands (χεῖρας προϊσχομένους) and were taken prisoners, you promised us later not to kill them, but lawlessly destroyed them ...' (3.66.2) ~ '... considering that you caught us by our own will and with hands outstretched (χεῖρας προϊσχομένους) (the Greeks have the law not to kill in this case) ...' (3.58.3). 'For those who lead commit a worse crime than those who follow.' (3.65.2) ~ '... those who follow are not to blame if something was not done properly, but those who lead with respect to what does not work out' (3.55.4).

[94] Cf. Macleod 1983b. On the close links to the Mytilinean Debate, see besides *ibid.*: 118–22 also Crane 1998: 194–5; Rood 1998a: 120–1.

[95] I am not convinced by Debnar's argument that the Plataeans cut a good figure, whereas the Thebans' speech is rather poor (1996). Price 2001: 103–26 gives a more balanced assessment of the deficiencies of both speeches.

3.58.3). *Nomos* proves to be highly ambiguous; it is invoked to justify the killing of the Theban captives as well as to argue that the Plataeans, who are themselves captives, should be spared.

On the other hand, the Thebans' denial that their invasion of Plataea constituted a wrong (3.65.2) does not square with their admission that their men were killed 'in accordance with a kind of law' ('κατὰ νόμον ... τινα') and that their infiltration was 'not entirely fair' ('ἀνεπιεικέστερον', 3.66.2).[96] The Plataean Debate, a 'travesty of legal forms', not only complements the Mytilinean Debate, but also corresponds to the following Corcyrean Pathology. In an interesting discussion, Jonathan Price reads the speeches against the backdrop of the 'transvaluation of words' that is characteristic of *stasis*.[97] There is, however, another important feature of this debate that has been neglected so far and that I wish to discuss – the use of the past by both Plataeans and Thebans.

The Plataeans' central argument is that they made a stand against the Persians.[98] It recurs in nearly every part of their speech. At the beginning, the Plataeans emphasize that they were the only Boeotians to stand up to the Persians. They participated in all of the battles, even the sea-battle at Artemisium (3.54.3–4). When the Plataeans try to assess what would be most expedient to the Spartans in the present situation, they resort to their own expediency and dwell on the past, thereby squeezing in their merits from the Persian Wars (3.56.4–5). Even in the part of their speech addressing the Spartan reputation, the Plataeans refer to their resistance against the Persians and contrast it with their potential annihilation (3.57.2–3). Finally, in the *peroratio*, the Plataeans underscore their earlier reference to the Persian Wars by invoking the graves to buttress their supplication (3.58.5; 3.59.2).

Since the Plataeans adduce the glory of their earlier deeds to strengthen their position in the here and now, they emphasize the links between past and present, for example by referring to the Greek *anathema* at Delphi: 'And it will seem monstrous that the Lacedaemonians have destroyed Plataea and that your fathers have recorded the city on the tripod at Delphi for its bravery, while you have erased (ἐξαλεῖψαι) it *in toto* from the Hellenic world for the sake of the Thebans.' (3.57.2). Being a memorial, the tripod at Delphi preserves and 're-presents' the past. The link between past and present is underscored further by the metaphoric use of ἐξαλείφειν, which is a technical term 'for erasing a name or a sentence from a public record.'[99] In drawing on the imagery of memorials to

---

[96] Cf. Price 2001: 116–17.   [97] Cf. *ibid.*: 103–26.   [98] Cf. Hornblower 1991–6: 445.
[99] Gomme, Andrewes and Dover 1945–81: ad 3.57.2. For further discussion of this passage, see below.

express their physical annihilation, the Plataeans intertwine the present threat with their past merits and make the point that destroying their town implies undoing the memory of the Persian Wars as it is preserved in the tripod.

Even more than the tripod at Delphi, the graves embody the continuity from the Persian Wars to the present on which the Plataeans' argument hinges. The tombs directly mark the place of those who fell in the battle and are the place where the Plataeans enact the memory of the dead in annual sacrifices. The Plataeans' imperative of 'look at them' ('ἀποβλέψατε', 3.58.4) implies that they are visible to the Spartans. The invocation of the tripod at Delphi and the graves underscores the relevance of past deeds and virtues in the present and thereby implies the traditional mode of memory that envisages history as a continuum.

Perhaps the Plataeans' interest in establishing a strong link between the Persian Wars and the present allows us to understand better a passage that has caused scholars many headaches so far (3.57.3):

We have arrived at this pitch of misfortune, we who, when the Medes were victorious, were at the brink of destruction, and who now face defeat by the Thebans in your hands – you who were our closest friends – and have been subjected to two dire ordeals, then destruction by famine if we did not surrender our city and now condemnation to death.

ἐς τοῦτο γὰρ δὴ ξυμφορᾶς προκεχωρήκαμεν, οἵτινες Μήδων τε κρατησάντων ἀπωλλύμεθα καὶ νῦν ἐν ὑμῖν τοῖς πρὶν φιλτάτοις Θηβαίων ἡσσώμεθα καὶ δύο ἀγῶνας τοὺς μεγίστους ὑπέστημεν, τότε μέν, τὴν πόλιν εἰ μὴ παρέδομεν, λιμῷ διαφθαρῆναι, νῦν δὲ θανάτου δίκῃ κρίνεσθαι.

Most commentators understand 'then' ('τότε') as referring to the Plataeans' very recent surrender, particularly since starvation played a major role in their decision. A. W. Gomme, on the other hand, rightly points out that 'then' ('τότε') can only refer to the years 480/479 BCE. As he notes, only three lines later, the Plataeans call the allies against the Persians 'former allies' ('οἱ τότε ξύμμαχοι'). It can be added that 'now' ('νῦν') refers back to the first 'now' ('νῦν') and that the dichotomy 'then ... now' ('τότε μέν ... νῦν δέ') obviously harks back to 'were at the brink of destruction, and who now ('νῦν') face defeat ...' Gomme concedes that 'there may well have been a story, even a true story, of a siege and much suffering', but the reference to starvation prompts him to suspect that the text is corrupt. If, however, we take into account the Plataeans' effort to link the present to the past, the parallel between the sieges by the Persians and the Spartans makes good sense. In this case, the Plataeans not only strive to link the past and present through continuity, but they also try to make them resemble one another. The similarity between the two situations supports the Plataeans' plea for mercy based on their merits. The traditional mode of memory – constructing a continuity between the past and present – is supported by the exemplary mode of memory, a specific parallel between the then and now.

And what about the Thebans? What do they say to outdo the Plataeans' history lesson? One would expect the Thebans to counter the historical arguments with reflections on expediency.[100] And yet, they rebut the Plataeans' claim by providing an alternative account of the past. First, they present a very different evaluation of the same events. For example, the Plataeans make their stand against the Persians their major point while they also blame the Thebans for their medism. The Thebans, however, attribute their medism only to a minority of oligarchs and denigrate the Plataeans' participation in the Persian Wars as being nothing but a favour to the Athenians.[101] The Plataeans' claim that they are the 'only Boeotians' who supported the Greek alliance (3.54.3) is transformed into a reproach for being the 'only Boeotians' to have entered an alliance with Athens (3.61.2–62.2)

Second, the Thebans use the same events as the Plataeans for opposite purposes. The Plataeans invoke the Persian Wars to gain authority. The Thebans, on the other hand, use the Persian Wars to accuse the Plataeans of *attikismos*.[102] The term *attikismos* is modeled on *medismos* and therefore creates a parallel between supporting the Persians and the Athenians. The Thebans thereby imply that Athens is the successor of the Persian Empire in threatening the freedom of Greece. Like the Plataeans, the Thebans establish a link between the Persian Wars and the present, but while the Plataeans argue the continuity and regularity of their conduct, the Thebans use the exemplary mode of memory differently when they evoke the Persian Wars as a foil for a present in which Athens has taken over the role of Persia.[103] By accusing the Plataeans of *attikismos*, the Thebans manage to turn the tables and redirect all the blame they have themselves received for their *medismos* onto the Plataeans.

---

[100] Cf. Price 2001: 114.
[101] Similarly, Herodotus suspects that the Phocaeans did not medize only due to their hatred of the Thessalians (Hdt. 8.30).
[102] This is the first evidence for the noun *attikismos*, which is also used in 4.133.1; 8.38.3; 87.1. In Xen. *Hell.* 1.6.13; 6.3.14, we find the verb *attikizein*. For epigraphic evidence, see the Athenian inscription IG 2²33 dating from 385 BCE. Erbse 1987: 336 argues that *attikismos* was coined by Thucydides and according to Orwin 1994: 72 n. 10 it is an 'ad hoc rhetorical expedient'. See also Cogan 1981: 69–73; Macleod 1983b: 116; Jung 2006: 288. For later parallels of similar coinages, see Gehrke 1985: 269–70.
[103] Cf. Jung 2006: 287.

Finally, the differences between the accounts of the Thebans and Plataeans even include factual evidence. The Plataeans make it seem as if they joined the Athenians after the beginning of the Persian Wars (3.55.1). The Thebans, however, place the Plataeans' alliance with the Athenians at the beginning of Plataean history. This is a significant difference because it allows the Thebans to belittle the Plataeans' participation in the Persian Wars as only a favour to Athens.[104]

In Herodotus' Plataean speech duel, the controversy between the Tegeans and the Athenians over the left wing, it is the notion of changeability that challenges exempla and traditions – since the power and strength of poleis is likely to change in the course of history, the past is ill-suited to legitimize present claims. Thucydides too deconstructs the rhetorical use of the past as tradition and exemplum in an *agon* located at Plataea, roughly fifty years later. However, his critique rather focuses on the distortions to which the past is subject in such arguments. The discrepancies between the speeches by the Plataeans and Thebans unveil that the past can be easily bent in the rhetoric of foreign affairs. The evaluation of events borders on the arbitrary, the same events are utilized for very different arguments and facts are deliberately misrepresented.

Thucydides' criticism is far-reaching. The fact that in the Melian Dialogue the Athenians deem it necessary to state explicitly that they will not engage in accounts of the past indicates that it was common practice to draw on the past to buttress one's arguments in diplomatic affairs.[105] In what has been called 'kinship diplomacy', ancient traditions and exempla constituted precious argumentative capital.[106] There are many instances of arguments relying on the past in Herodotus and even in Thucydides who seems to have transferred his own scepticism regarding historical arguments to his characters.[107] To give two examples from the *History*, exiles from Epidamnus invoke a common ancestry and refer to certain graves in order to appeal for support in Corcyra (1.26.3), and, in Sparta, the Athenians elaborate on their merits in the Persian Wars (1.73.4–74).[108]

---

[104] According to Thucydides, the Thebans are at least right in so far as the Athenian alliance antedates the Persian Wars (3.68.5). There are further points where the facts are wrong: for example, the Plataeans were not, as they claim (3.54.3), the only Boeotians to join the Greek alliance against the Persians. Cf. Gomme, Andrewes and Dover 1945–81: ad loc., who call it 'a notable falsehood'. On the other hand, the Thebans' claim that their medism was due only to a few oligarchs squares badly with the evidence from Herodotus, cf. Flower and Marincola 2002: ad 9.87.2. Price 2001: 119 stresses that the Thebans misrepresent Boeotian history.
[105] Cf. Gomme, Andrewes and Dover 1945–81: ad 5.89. See also above p. 143.
[106] Cf. Jones 1999. For a case-study, see Luraghi 2008 on the Messenians and their past.
[107] Cf. Hornblower 1991–6: 118 and, for a more differentiated view, Rood 1999: 145.
[108] While dealing with the Persian Wars, the Athenians point out that they will not speak of 'ancient deeds' ('παλαιά') for a rather Thucydidean reason, the lack of reliable evidence (1.73.2). It is for a different reason that Pericles decides not to elaborate on the ancestors' deeds, their familiarity to his audience (2.36.4).

The sharpness of Thucydides' critique is reinforced by Plataea's prominence. As I have already pointed out, the battle of Plataea was an important *lieu de mémoire* in Greece, a semantic terrain over which the Greek poleis fought with much verve, trying to secure their share of the glory or even to appropriate all the glory for themselves.[109] It is remarkable that Thucydides chooses an event that is so deeply ingrained in the cultural memory as Plataea to deconstruct the traditional and exemplary uses of the past in oratory.

(b) Oratory and history

As embedded acts of memory, historical references to the past form a *mise-en-abyme* and invite the readers to compare them with the historian's account. I would now like to argue that in the case of the Plataean Debate the meta-historical significance is reinforced by two points: first, Thucydides and the speakers in the Plataean Debate refer to the same events; second, some claims made by the Plataeans and Thebans evoke Thucydides' methodological reflections.

In his narrative, Thucydides leaves aside the Persian Wars, which form an important part of the Plataean Debate. Yet, the Plataeans and Thebans refer to other events that are part of the preceding narrative. For example, the Plataeans mention their support for Sparta at Ithome (3.54.5) during the revolt of the Helots, which Thucydides reports in his account of the Pentecontaetia (1.101–3; 2.27.2).[110] Another example, this time from the Thebans' speech, is the subjection of Aegina (3.62.5), which is also mentioned by Thucydides in his account of the growth of the Athenian Empire (1.105.2–3; 108.4–5; 2.27).[111] Seen from this angle, the Plataeans' introductory remark that they will present their speech to 'knowing ones' (3.53.4) applies not only to the internal audience of the Spartans, but also to the external audience: Thucydides' readers. In narratological terms, the speeches contain internal *analepseis* focalized by characters. The parallel narratives of characters and narrator invite the readers to compare the different accounts in particular, but also the different ways of dealing with the past in general.

---

[109] See pp. 184–5.
[110] There are some other cases in which the speeches offer details not covered by Thucydides' narrative. For example, both Plataeans and Thebans mention that the Thebans attacked in a holy month (3.56.2; 3.65.1), on which there is nothing in Thucydides.
[111] Further examples include Thebes' participation in the fight against Athens (3.62.5; 2.12.5; 22.2) and Athens' attempt at subjecting Boeotia (3.62.5; cf. 1.108.3; on Coroneia, which is mentioned in 3.62.3, see 1.113.2; 4.92.6).

What is more, some claims and arguments made by the speakers resemble Thucydides' reflections on his own method. Most of the resemblances are rhetorical commonplaces that show a general similarity between the *History* and oratory. Some, however, are more significant. Let us start with rather general similarities. The Thebans emphasize that truth should be the basis for the Spartans' judgement: '... and you will hear the truth about both and decide'.[112] (3.61.1). This is 'a standard opening in ancient speeches,'[113] but it also corresponds to Thucydides' claim to veracity, and, in addition, the appeal to have both sides heard recalls Thucydides' assertion that he collected his data from both sides of the war (5.26.5). Like Thucydides, the Plataeans invoke 'testimonies' ('μαρτύρια', 3.53.4) and the Thebans present a 'proof' ('τεκμήριον', 3.66.1).[114] Again, the use of μαρτύρια and τεκμήρια is common in rhetoric and constitutes a general parallel between oratory and the *History*.

A pointed echo occurs in 3.67.6, where the Thebans appeal to the Spartans to present a paradigm for the future:

... but establish an exemplum for the Greeks and set out contests not of words, but of actions, of which a brief recital suffices when they are good ones, while artfully adorned speeches serve as screens for wrongs committed.
... ποιήσατε δὲ τοῖς Ἕλλησι παράδειγμα οὐ λόγων τοὺς ἀγῶνας προθήσοντες ἀλλ' ἔργων, ὧν ἀγαθῶν μὲν ὄντων βραχεῖα ἡ ἀπαγγελία ἀρκεῖ, ἁμαρτανομένων δὲ λόγοι ἔπεσι κοσμηθέντες προκαλύμματα γίγνονται.

Not only does the παράδειγμα parallel Thucydides' didactic intentions, but the rejection of 'contests of words' ('λόγων τοὺς ἀγῶνας') echoes Thucydides' claim that he has produced 'rather a possession for all time than a competition piece to be heard for the moment' ('κτῆμά τε ἐς αἰεὶ μᾶλλον ἢ ἀγώνισμα ἐς τὸ παραχρῆμα ἀκούειν', 1.22.4). Moreover, the criticism of 'artfully adorned speeches' ('λόγοι ἔπεσι κοσμηθέντες') recalls: '... what the poets have sung in their praise, adorning it with their exaggerations (ἐπὶ τὸ μεῖζον κοσμοῦντες) ...'[115] (1.21.1). The echoes of Thucydides' methodological reflections reinforce the juxtaposition of the rhetorical use of the past with the *History* and make the corrupt accounts of the past given by the Plataeans and Thebans throw into relief Thucydides' accuracy.

---

[112] See also 3.64.4: 'You have now demonstrated that the nobility which once was yours is not ingrained, but what your nature always wanted has been exposed as the truth (ἐξηλέγχθη ἐς τὸ ἀληθές).'
[113] Price 2001: 113.   [114] On τεκμήριον in Thuc., see Hornblower 1987: 101–7.
[115] Price 2001: 113 points out that the Thebans are themselves liable to the reproach they direct against the Plataeans.

(c) The usefulness of the past

Thucydides not only unmasks the willingness of orators to distort the past, he also draws attention to another point besides accuracy in which the *History* is superior to speeches. His account of Plataea's destruction also suggests that historical arguments ultimately do not count for much in power politics. Some scholars argue that the Plataeans' speech is so convincing that the Thebans feel forced to counter the argument and finally convince the Spartans.[116] Yet, this argument rests on speculation and Thucydides explicitly mentions another reason why the Spartans decide to annihilate Plataea: 'In virtually every respect, the Lacedaemonians turned, concerning the Plataeans, a deaf ear on account of the Thebans, since they thought they were useful to them in the war which had recently broken out.' (3.68.4). This brief narratorial statement effectively contrasts with the rhetorical 'fuss' of the speeches.[117] Nothing the opponents, neither the Plataeans nor the Thebans, have to say about the past influences the Spartans; their decision is driven only by what is most conducive to their present interests. The past is outweighed by expediency. The irrelevance of historical arguments in power politics that is implicit at Plataea is explicitly pointed out by the Athenians in the Melian Dialogue (5.89):[118]

We will neither ourselves present a lengthy and unconvincing speech with nice words, either that we destroyed the Mede and therefore have the right to rule or that we are now attacking on account of wrongs we have suffered, nor will we deem it worthy that you think you can convince us by saying either that you are colonists of the Lacedaemonians and therefore did not march with us, or that you have done us no injury, but to obtain what is possible according to what both of us really think, since we as well as you understand that in human considerations justice is decided when pressure is equal, while those who are superior do what is possible and the weak acquiesce to it.

While in the Plataean and Melian Debates expediency trumps historical arguments, Thucydides asserts that the *History* is useful (1.22.4). What is the reason for this discrepancy in the value of the past? Why is it useful in Thucydides', but not in the orators', hands? As the internal contradictions and the discrepancies in the Plataeans' and Thebans' accounts forcefully show, truth does not really count in speeches, whose views on the past are

---

[116] Cf. Hogan 1972: 243. Cogan 1981: 14–15; 67. For the view I am advocating here, see also Connor 1984: 93–4; Cagnetta 1984: 205; Hornblower 1991–6: 1: 462.
[117] Cf. Schwinge 2008: 61.
[118] Cf. Morrison 2000: 128–9 on 'the "disconnect" between the rhetoric of justice found in debates and the decisions themselves, which were based on expediency'.

determined by their present interests. In contrast, Thucydides' account does not hinge on any particular interest.

Let us turn to his account of the events that are also referred to in the Plataean Debate. In the introduction to his *Pentecontaetia*, Thucydides writes (1.23.5–6):

As to why they broke the peace, I have first recorded the causes and disputes so that no one may ever search for the reasons why so great a war broke out among the Hellenes. For I consider the truest cause, which, however, was the one least openly expressed, that the Athenians became mighty, caused the Lacedaemonians fear and thereby forced them to go to war. The following are the openly stated charges made by both sides on account of which they broke the treaties and began the war.

What follows are the Corcyrean and the Potidaea Episodes.[119] Similarly to the Plataeans and Thebans, the Athenians and Spartans draw on the past to legitimize present assertions; Thucydides, on the other hand, engages with it to explain causes. This difference is linked to the different communicative contexts and media of oratory and the *History*.[120] As I have mentioned before, while speeches are delivered for a particular audience in a particular situation, the *History* is a written text and therefore its reception is not bound to any particular circumstances.[121]

Thucydides also outperforms the orators through the depth of his own engagement. While he claims to dig for hidden reasons – in his methodological reflections, he stresses his exertions (1.22.3) – the Plataeans concede that they will not be offering anything new: 'If we were unknown to one another, we might have benefitted by bringing in evidence of which you were unaware; as it is, everything said will be what you know …' (3.53.4).

Furthermore, the diverging interests in the past have different foci. Both the Plataeans and the Thebans see the past from a moralistic point of view. What was done in the past is evaluated in moral terms in order to buttress present assertions. Thucydides, however, rarely makes moral assessments. Ethics matter in the *History*, but they are discussed mostly at the level of the action, while the narrative rather emphasizes the underlying mechanisms of power.

---

[119] On Thucydides' famous distinction between the 'truest cause' and the 'openly stated charges', see the literature in Hornblower 1991–6: 1: ad 1.23.6.
[120] The *History*'s independence from a specific context is stressed by Moles 2001; Greenwood 2006: 3–4. For a recent attempt to tie the *History* more strongly to a specific historical situation, see Munn 2000.
[121] On the *History* as a written text, see e.g. Loraux 1986b; Edmunds 1993; Crane 1996.

Inevitably, the rhetorical use of the past for present purposes chips away at the relevance of arguments from the past and renders them ultimately useless. A past that is deliberately bent to bolster present assertions loses its authority. In Thucydides, on the other hand, the past is subjected not to a legitimizing purpose, but to close scrutiny. Paradoxically, making less use of history makes history more useful. In tracing and exposing the mechanisms of power and expediency, Thucydides establishes a type of knowledge that he believes is of great use. The Plataean Debate throws into relief not only the accuracy, but also the usefulness of the *History*.

I postpone a more detailed discussion of Thucydides' claim to usefulness to the end of this chapter and instead close with a brief summary: in the Plataean Debate, both parties draw on the past to make their cases. Yet, their contradictory accounts reveal how dubious using the past in oratory can be. Diplomatic speeches bend the truth to buttress specific assertions. Nonetheless, the historical arguments have no impact on the Spartans' final decision, which is based on expediency. By making references to the same events, drawing general similarities and placing one or two marked echoes, Thucydides juxtaposes the use of the past in speeches with the *History*. This embedded foil highlights the advantages of Thucydides' account, which, despite, or because of, being more detached from a particular situation and not being guided by a particular interest, yields useful knowledge while the speeches prove futile.[122]

8.2.3. Conclusion

Embedded in historical accounts, we often find a past previous to the past of the main narrative. Particularly in speeches, characters invoke their own past, which for the readers is a 'plu-past'. Since the characters' references to the past mirror the historians' narrative in being another act of memory, I have suggested a meta-historical interpretation of such speeches, reading them as an implicit commentary on how (not) to use the past. This approach has proved fruitful for Herodotus, but the 'plu-past' is an even more powerful tool in the hands of Thucydides. In his *History*, the implicit critique of historical arguments in speeches not only continues the explicit polemic against orators, but their function as foil for Thucydides' new approach is also underscored through echoes of his methodological reflections.

---

[122] I will return to the Plataean debate and elaborate further on its meta-historical significance, see p. 273.

Like Herodotus, Thucydides uses a speech duel at Plataea to unveil the shortcomings of historical arguments in diplomatic encounters. While in the Herodotean speech duel between the Athenians and Tegeans the exemplary use of the past is challenged by the general changeability, the numerous tensions and contradictions between the Plataeans' and Thebans' references to the past in Thucydides reveal that the truth is sacrificed for argumentative needs. By the same token, in my other test case, the Periclean funeral oration, historical accuracy is a victim of the desire to please the audience. While Thucydides reveals a strong awareness of changes, most prominently in his discussion of ancient history in the 'archaeology', he takes issue not so much with the notions of continuity and regularity themselves, but with applications of the traditional and exemplary modes of memory that bend the truth.

The Plataean Debate furthermore reveals that the stark distortions ultimately make historical arguments futile. The tendency to satisfy the audience's expectation that comes to the fore in the funeral speech is even more detrimental as Thucydides' reflections about Pericles and his successors show. Both throw into relief the usefulness that Thucydides explicitly claims for his work. We also find the meta-historical use of embedded speeches in later historians, but it has particular relevance for Thucydides, who is not only concerned to set his new approach to the past off against other commemorative genres, but also emphasizes the pragmatic dimension of his narrative.

8.3. CONTINUITY IN THE IDEA OF HISTORY: THE SICILIAN EXPEDITION

In Chapter 7, section 7.3, we have seen not only that Herodotus sets his own work off against poetic accounts of the past, but that at the same time his *Histories* relies on an idea of history that is very similar to what we find in oratory and poetry. A similar tension between innovation and continuity can be found in Thucydides. While the preceding section dealt with Thucydides' explicit and implicit criticism of other commemorative genres, I will now discuss Thucydides' interest in the relation between expectations and experiences and the prominence of chance in his narrative. This is not a new point in Thucydidean scholarship, but, read against the backdrop of the first part of this book, it draws our attention to the common horizon that Thucydides shares with poets and orators. Moreover, I hope that the examination of the *History*'s narrative form as an expression of its idea of history will deepen our understanding of its artful composition. As we will see, the shaping of narrative time and perspective emphasizes contingency of chance, albeit in a way very different from Herodotus (8.3.1). In a second step, I shall discuss whether Thucydides explains contingency of chance in abstract terms or whether, as in Herodotus, the narrative can be said to master it (8.3.2). This will lead us to a reconsideration of Thucydides' claim to usefulness (8.3.3). The passage I have chosen to illustrate the continuity in Thucydides' view of history is the Sicilian Expedition in Books 6 and 7, a pivotal point in the narrative which has been described as an *en miniature* war within the Peloponnesian War.[123]

8.3.1. Narrative and chance

The phantom of a positivist Thucydides who aims at presenting objective data still haunts many scholarly accounts, but a number of scholars, following a variety of different approaches, have elaborated on Thucydides' interest in human psychology.[124] Thucydides devotes ample space to his characters' motivation, their intentions and plans. This is well illustrated by the Sicilian Expedition. Time and again, Thucydides refers to the Athenians' expectations in his narratorial voice: the Athenians undertook the Sicilian Expedition not so much to help the Egestans, but they rather hoped to incorporate the whole island into their empire (6.6.1; 30.2–31.1).[125] More specifically (6.24.3):

And desire for sailing away afflicted everyone alike: the older men, since they believed they would subject the places to which they sailed or that a great force could meet with no harm; the young men, who longed for the sight and experience of what is far away and expected to be saved; the broad mass and the soldiers, since they believed that they would earn money for now and acquire dominion from which everlasting pay would derive.[126]

We have seen that in Herodotus authorial *prolepseis*, more or less explicit, and narrative patterns give the readers insights into the outcomes of plans and thereby throw the expectations of characters into relief. Thucydides, on the other hand, by and large avoids such foreshadowing. Of course, the

---

[123] Cf. Finley 1967: 122–62; Schwinge 2008: 135 ('paradigmatisches Abbild dieses Krieges'). On the Sicilian Expedition in general, see de Romilly 1963: 200–27; Green 1970; Connor 1984: 158–209; Rood 1998a; 133–201; Kallet 2001; Stahl 2003: 173–222; Schwinge 2008: 119–61.
[124] See e.g. de Romilly 1956b; Hunter 1973; Schneider 1974; Edmunds 1975; Rood 1998a: 61–130; Stahl 2003; Morrison 2006. Cornford 1907: 65 regards the ancient historians' interest in human psychology as the major difference from modern historians.
[125] Rengakos 1984: 102 counts thirteen references to the Athenians' goal to conquer Sicily.
[126] On the special ambitions of Alcibiades, see 6.15.2.

readers have the advantage of hindsight, but the narrative restricts their temporal focus to the perspective of the characters and only rarely evaluates expectations by leaps into the future.[127] In the following, I will first elucidate Thucydides' presentation of his characters' expectations (a), then link the results to studies of Thucydidean *enargeia* and the concept of 'sideshadowing' (b) and finally elaborate on the notion of chance in the *History* (c).

(a) Expectations and experiences
Instead of a *prolepsis*, Thucydides uses a retrospective to shed light on the Athenians' initial expectations. In the introduction of the 'Sicilian archaeology', the sketch of Sicily's history, geography and ethnology, he points out the Athenians' ignorance.[128] Thus, without anticipating the disaster, Thucydides alerts his readers that the Sicilian Expedition was ill conceived.

More importantly, Thucydides illuminates expectations by pointedly juxtaposing various perspectives.[129] In the case of the Sicilian Expedition, contrasting expectations are put forward in a triple-pair of speeches held at Athens, which, like other speech–pairs, shed light on one another and correspond closely with the narrative.[130] The expectations linked to the Sicilian Expedition are further illuminated by a parallel set of three speeches held in Syracuse. Before I turn to the experiences that follow the expectations, I will briefly elaborate on the expectations put forward in the speeches and elucidate how they shed light on one another.[131]

---

[127] See, however, 6.15.4 on Alcibiades: 'The masses, frightened by the magnitude of his license in conducting his personal life and of his aims in absolutely everything he did, whatever it was, developed hostility toward him as an aspiring tyrant, and while he as a public person managed the war with the utmost skill, they as private individuals detested him for his behaviour, and by entrusting the city to others they ruined it in short order.' However, this *prolepsis* does not juxtapose an expectation with an experience and is so vague that it triggered a scholarly debate as to what event Thucydides refers to. On the rarity of *prolepseis* in Thucydides, see Finley 1967: 127; Erbse 1989: 45–6. Dunn 2007: 116 emphasizes that Thucydides 'anticipates the future in order to motivate judgement of the episode at hand, rather than to demonstrate a connection between earlier and later events'. On *prolepseis* in Thucydides, see also, with different emphasis, Rengakos 2006b: 298–9.

[128] Cf. Ober 1998: 105–6; Kallet 2001: 31. Kagan 1981: 165–6 and Buck 1988 argue that the Athenians cannot have been ignorant of the size and history of Sicily after their earlier expedition. This would make Thucydides' comment even more striking. On the 'Sicilian archaeology' see also Rawlings 1981: 65–70, who draws attention to the similarities to the 'archaeology' in Book 1, and Tsakmakis 1995: 167–75. See p. 270 for a meta-historical interpretation of the 'Sicilian archaeology'.

[129] Cf. Gribble 1998: 59. Crane 1996: 38–50 points out that Thucydides gives more space to motivation than Herodotus does.

[130] On correspondences between speech and narrative in Thucydides, see particularly de Romilly 1956b; Hunter 1973; Stahl 2003; Morrison 2006.

[131] On the speeches by Nicias and Alcibiades, see Tompkins 1972; Connor 1984: 158–68; Bloedow 1990; 1996; Yunis 1996: 102–9; Ober 1998: 107–20; Kallet 2001: 31–48; Stahl 2003: 177–84. On the speeches by Hermocrates, Athenagoras and the anonymous general, see Connor 1984: 168–76; Kallet 2001: 66–9.

Five days after the Athenians have voted to invade Sicily, Nicias, with Alcibiades and Lamachus, one of the elected commanders, tries to convince the assembly to reconsider their decision (6.9–14). His main concern is the risk that Athens would run attacking Sicily while being threatened by her Greek enemies at the same time. On the other hand, Nicias argues, there is no real obligation to help the Egestans in their fight with Leontinoi and Syracuse.

Nicias' fierce invective against Alcibiades, who is accused of jeopardizing the public welfare for his private ambitions, provokes Alcibiades to deliver a counter-speech (6.16–18). Besides defending his own sumptuous lifestyle and elaborating on the relevance of alliances, Alcibiades argues that Sicily will prove easy prey – the Sicilians are torn by civil strife and therefore they will not be able to oppose the Athenians with united forces.

Noting that the Athenians are swayed by Alcibiades' argument, Nicias changes his strategy and, in a second speech, tries to deter his compatriots from an invasion by elaborating on the supplies that will be required (6.20–3). His view of Sicily is utterly different from Alcibiades': Sicily is not weakened by *stasis*, but on the contrary its poleis are strong and have large armies at their command. In case of an attack, they would be able to rely on their cavalry and safe supplies. An Athenian army, on the other hand, would be on its own, as the promises of the Egestans are mere words. However, Nicias' rhetorical strategy backfires, his postulations fail to discourage the Athenians and rather instill in them the feeling that an invasion would be a safe enterprise. It is not Nicias' scepticism but Alcibiades' confidence that carries the day.

The outcome of the Sicilian Expedition not only proves Nicias' scepticism right in general, but verifies specific warnings. The supply problems that Nicias mentions (6.20.4) will indeed affect the Athenian army (6.42.1; 48; 71.2) and the superiority of the Syracusan cavalry will pose a major problem: 'Cavalry harms the Athenians by cutting off free access to the land: it hinders plundering (52.2), pursuit in victory (70.3), gathering stones for the wall of circumvallation (98.3), and the collection of water and firewood (vii.4.6); and it influences Athenian decision-making (64.1, 66.1), above all the decision to withdraw from Syracuse in the winter of 415/14 BCE (71.2).'[132] As Nicias predicts, other Greek poleis will be prompted to rise against Athens.[133] Nicias also anticipates another point that is given a prominent place in the explanation of Athens' defeat, the similarity between

---

[132] Rood 1998a: 165–6. [133] Cf. 6.88.8 for Corinth and 6.93.2 for Sparta.

Athenians and Sicilians.[134] 'The greatest of all adventures' ('μέγιστον ... τῶν πρὶν κίνδυνον', 6.13.1) that he warns against becomes 'the greatest reversal' ('μέγιστον τὸ ... διάφορον', 7.75.7).[135]

In a Herodotean narrative, Nicias' warnings would be endorsed by the pattern of the 'tragic warner' and authorial foreshadowing.[136] In Thucydides, however, there is no pattern of the 'tragic warner' nor are Nicias' warnings confirmed by authorial *prolepseis*. Yet, at a more subtle level, the speeches closely interact with the narrative and thereby receive some evaluation.[137] For example, Nicias' words about the current situation of Athens closely correspond with Thucydides' own assessment. In 6.12.1, Nicias appeals to the Athenians: 'We must also remember that we have only recently had a little respite from a great plague and from war, so as to gain some strength in material wealth and manpower.' In 6.26.2, Thucydides notes: 'The city, because of the armistice, had just recovered from the plague and continuous warfare in respect to both the number of young men who had grown up and the accumulation of material wealth so that everything was easier to procure.'

The parallel assessment of the present state of Athens does not verify Nicias' predictions, but it gives him authority in general. Another correspondence is more significant: Nicias' warning that the money promised by the Egestans merely exists in their words (6.22; cf. also 6.12.1), is backed up by a preceding narratorial comment (6.8.2). Here, one of Nicias' warnings is endorsed by the narrative.

On the other hand, Alcibiades' over-confidence is likely to disconcert the alert reader,[138] brilliant as his rhetoric may be. And yet, Alcibiades' reflections on the Athenian Empire are reminiscent of points made earlier by Pericles,[139] as when he remarks that 'there is no possibility for us to regulate the amount of empire we want but a need, now that we have reached this stage, to make aggressive plans while allowing no defections, because of the danger of being ruled by someone else if we do not rule others'. (6.18.3). This reflection echoes Pericles' words in 2.63.2: 'You cannot abdicate from it

---

[134] 6.20.3. Cf. the authorial voice in 7.55.2 and 8.96.5. [135] Cf. Hunter 1973: 126.
[136] Nicias has been called a 'wise adviser' (e.g. by Marinatos 1980). Yet, there are crucial differences from most Herodotean 'wise advisers' (cf. Pelling 1991; Rood 1998a: 166–7).
[137] Von Fritz 1967: 727–8; Kagan 1981: 174–91; Connor 1984: 162–4; Ober 1998: 108–9; Kallet 2001: 42–8 present rather critical assessments of Nicias' speech, whereas de Romilly 1963: 206; Hunter 1973: 123–7; Bloedow 1990 and Yunis 1996 find it fairly reasonable.
[138] Cf. Hunter 1973: 136–40; Ober 1998: 110–12. For a more positive reading of Alcibiades' speech, see Kagan 1981: 181–6. On Alcibiades in Thucydides in general, see Gribble 1999: 159–213.
[139] Cf. Kagan 1981: 184–5 and Rengakos 1984: 106–12, who argues that the echoes underline the differences. See also de Romilly 1963: 204; 210–13, who, however, denies that there is no intentional juxtaposition.

[i.e. the empire], even if someone, full of fear in the current situation and in love of a quiet life, propagates this as the right course; for you now hold it like a tyranny that seems unjust to acquire but dangerous to let go.'[140] However, a closer inspection yields crucial differences, most strikingly that Alcibiades and Pericles use the same argument for different purposes. Whereas Pericles considers the preservation of the current empire, Alcibiades aims at further conquests.[141] Thus, the echoes of Pericles' speech do not so much lend authority to Alcibiades' argument as highlight the difference from Pericles.

Another echo illuminates Alcibiades' assessment of the situation in Sicily. Harvey Yunis states that 'Alcibiades recycles a paltry myth of Sicily (which only a distant, uninformed Greek could accept) as consisting of poorly armed, disorganized, primitive poleis and full of useless barbarians.'[142] While there can be no doubt that Alcibiades is wrong about the development of Sicily and that he errs about the Sicilians' ability to unite against a foreign intruder, his emphasis on the instability of Sicily is to some extent confirmed by the 'Sicilian archaeology' in which changes and wars loom large.[143]

Furthermore, the context makes the evaluation of Alcibiades' expectations more complex than it may look at first glance. In the brief introduction of Alcibiades that precedes his speech, Thucydides points out the Athenians' anxiety about Alcibiades' aspirations 'was very soon to harm the polis' (6.15.4).[144] The exact temporal reference of this has been much debated[145] and Thucydides does not say that Athens would not have suffered defeat had Alcibiades remained as one of the commanders, but the statement gives Alcibiades a rather positive entry into the narrative.[146] All in all, the juxtaposition of Nicias' and Alcibiades' speeches and correspondences with the narrative convey a very complex picture that highlights many aspects, but is far from clear-cut.

---

[140] Cf. 1.75.4.
[141] Rengakos 1984: 109–10. Connor 1984: 166, however, praises Alicibiades' speech for 'its understanding and illumination of Athenian character'.
[142] Yunis 1996: 106.
[143] Cf. Kagan 1981: 182; Rood 1998a: 164–5. Taking another angle, Connor 1984: 160 (cf. 165–6) notes that Sicily defies the assumption underlying the 'archaeology' in Book 1 that changeability impedes the development of strong forces.
[144] See p. 242 n. 127.
[145] While some scholars see a reference to the banishment of Alcibiades in 415 BCE, others argue for the banishment in 406 BCE. Cf. the survey in Gribble 1999: 183 n. 71, who is inclined to prefer 406 BCE, but points out that 'Thucydides must *also* have intended that the reader think of the similar deposition of 415 BCE ...' See also Connor 1984: 164 n. 17.
[146] Cf. Kagan 1981: 180–1; Connor 1984: 165.

The Athenians' expectations concerning an invasion of Sicily are further illuminated by the parallel set of three speeches held in Syracuse.[147] In the first speech, Hermocrates warns the Syracusans that the Athenians are on their way to Sicily (6.33–4). This, he argues, is not worrisome – the threat will make the Sicilians stand together and the Athenians will run into problems with their food supply – but nevertheless he suggests affirming old alliances and adding new ones. Moreover, the Syracusans ought to send out quickly a fleet to Tarentum and thereby terrify the Athenians.[148]

However, only a few Syracusans believe Hermocrates, and Athenagoras, who is introduced as 'the leader of the people and, at the time, the one who had most influence over the masses' (6.35.2), argues that, reasonable as they are, the Athenians would never plan such an expedition while they are still entangled in another war (6.36–40). And if the Athenians did actually come, they would be hopelessly inferior. Athenagoras goes on to insinuate that oligarchs have spread the rumors about an Athenian invasion in order to harm democracy. The debate is then cut short by a general who decides to prepare for an attack, but not to send out troops as Hermocrates had suggested (6.41.2–4).

The three speeches at Sicily parallel the three speeches in Athens and thereby invite comparison of the two poleis,[149] indicating the similarity that has been touched upon by Nicias and that will prove detrimental to Athens.[150] Moreover, the Syracusans' views on a potential invasion shed light on the Athenians' expectations. On the one hand, concerns raised by Nicias receive confirmation. Both Hermocrates and Athenagoras are confident that the Athenians will be defeated. More specifically, Hermocrates mentions the scarcity of food that the Athenians would be likely to suffer from (6.33.5), and Nicias' warnings are likewise echoed by Athenagoras, who mentions the war in which Athens is already involved (6.36.4) and points out that the lack of horses and equipment would disadvantage an Athenian army in Sicily (6.37.1–2). Athenagoras' argument that the Athenians could not come up with such a foolish plan,[151] as well as

---

[147] Cf. de Romilly 1963: 206–7.
[148] Kallet 2001: 66–9 finds Hermocrates' confidence suspicious and Gomme, Andrewes and Dover 1945–81: ad 6.34.4; Westlake 1969: 181–2 and Kagan 1981: 221 find fault with his plan. Hunter 1973: 157–60; Bloedow 1993 and Stahl 2003: 195–8, on the other hand, defend it.
[149] Cf. Connor 1984: 170–1; Kallet 2001: 66.
[150] Cf. Finley 1967: 154–6. It is, however, worth taking into account the differences as well. While in Syracuse the debate is closed by a general who makes a decision himself, Nicias, the Athenian general, defers to the assembly. It is tempting to see in the Syracusan general a foil who throws into relief Nicias' weakness as leader.
[151] 6.36.3 echoes Thucydides in 6.1.1 (ἔμπειρος-ἄπειρος).

Hermocrates' acknowledgment that his warning will seem untrustworthy ('ἄπιστα', 6.33.1) underscore how questionable the expectations are that prompt the Athenians to start another war.[152]

On the other hand, Athenagoras' speech may add some credibility to a point made by Alcibiades. W. R. Connor claims that the debate in Syracuse fails to 'provide an especially helpful analysis of what is so crucial for the outcome of the expedition: the political situation within Syracuse'.[153] I think the opposite is the case: the debate presents a democratic assembly that is very similar to the Athenian *ekklesia*, and no matter what we make of Athenagoras' argument, it testifies to fierce factionalism and partisanship within Syracuse. This confirms Alcibiades' view of the political situation in Sicily; if even individual poleis are torn by party-strife, the reader is invited to share his doubts that Sicily as a whole can unite (against Hermocrates' assumption in 6.33.4).

As we see, Thucydides gives ample space to the expectations that lead the Athenians to attack Sicily. While this focus aligns him with epic, tragedy and Herodotus, he differs from them in that he does not evaluate the expectations by *prolepseis* – the readers do not receive much information about the future at the level of the action. At the same time, the various expectations as outlined in the sets of speeches shed light on one another, and the speeches further interact with the narrative. However, far from giving the readers clear guidance about what is going to happen, Thucydides rather conveys a very complex picture of the situation and forces his readers to carefully weigh and assess different options.

While being cautious with *prolepseis*, Thucydides uses *analepseis* to underscore the fact that experiences disappoint expectations. These *analepseis* range from the implicit evocation of expectations through parallels to explicit references. For instance, Borimir Jordan gives a list of motifs that link the final battle in the harbour of Syracuse to the departure of the Athenian navy from Piraeus:[154] Thucydides elaborates on the visual effects and partly focalizes both scenes through internal spectators, those who have come to say farewell to the departing troops and the soldiers on land. In the Piraeus as well as in the harbour of Syracuse, the troops compete with one another: in 6.31.3–4 the competition centres on equipment and beauty, in 7.70.3 the soldiers try to excel in combat. While the exact degree of the correspondences may be disputed, it is hard to deny that the Sicilian

---

[152] Cf. Hunter 1973: 155 n. 4; Bloedow 1996: 157. Kallet 2001: 68–9 points out that not only the irrational nature, but also the 'incredible' nature of the Athenians' deeds is underlined.
[153] Connor 1984: 169–70.   [154] Cf. Jordan 2000: 76–7.

Expedition starts with a great spectacle in a harbour and culminates in another spectacular harbour scene. This 'ring composition'[155] juxtaposes the initial high hopes with the devastating defeat.

The Athenian departure after the defeat has even stronger links to the pompous farewell scene.[156] At the outset, Thucydides in passing refers back to the high hopes that had inspired the departure (7.75.3; cf. 6.31.6). While in the harbour of Piraeus people gathered, 'escorting ... comrades, relatives, or sons' (6.30.2), in the harbour of Syracuse 'whenever anyone saw one of his comrades or relatives, they clung to the messmates who were about to leave and followed as far as they could ... so that the entire army was filled with tears ...' (7.75.4). The picture of the defeated army, in which everybody carries their own belongings (7.75.5), strongly contrasts with the abundance and the boastful presentation of equipment in the Piraeus. Finally, in 7.75.6–7 Thucydides describes the feelings of the defeated Athenians and markedly juxtaposes their experiences with their initial expectations:[157]

The general suffering and equal apportionment of misery, although alleviated somewhat by being shared, nonetheless were not regarded as easy to bear in the present situation, particularly in view of what miserable end they had arrived at after what original splendour and pride. For this was certainly the greatest reversal for any Hellenic army; instead of coming to enslave others, they rather left, as it happened, fearing that they would suffer this, instead of prayers and *paians*, with which they had sailed off, they were setting out again with contrasting words of ill omen, proceeding as infantry instead of sailors, relying on the hoplite army rather than the navy.

(b) Enargeia *and 'sideshadowing'*

As we see, Thucydides gives emphasis to the disappointment of expectations not so much through *prolepseis* as through *analepseis*. This shaping of narrative time contributes to the strong mimetic dimension of Thucydides' account which has been remarked upon by the *History*'s readers since antiquity: following Plutarch's lead, scholars have elaborated on Thucydides' *enargeia*. In vignettes such as the final battle in the Syracusan harbour, the focalization of the action through an internal

---

[155] Hornblower 2004: 346–7.
[156] Cf. Stahl 2003: 192–3, who, however, argues that only this scene, but not the battle itself corresponds with the departure of the fleet from Piraeus (193 n. 5). I do not see why the echoes of both scenes should be mutually exclusive, and although the references in the battle scene are less explicit, there are striking similarities.
[157] Already 'the greatest reversal' ('μέγιστον ... τὸ διάφορον', 7.75.7) contrasts with 'the greatest passage' ('μέγιστος ... διάπλους') in 6.31.6.

audience gives the readers the feeling of directly witnessing the event.[158] Others have examined the temporal structure of the *History*, which sticks rather rigidly to chronology.[159] In addition to this, Thucydides' reluctance to intrude on his narrative beyond a few explicit reflections and a set of fixed phrases raises the impression that the narrative unfolds itself in step with the events themselves.[160]

My position tallies with these approaches. The effects that the focus on the characters' expectations and the avoidance of *prolepseis* have can be further elucidated by G. S. Morson's concept of 'sideshadowing'. Taking his cue from Mikhail Bakhtin's interest in chronotopes, Morson starts from the tension between the openness of time in our experience and narrative's tendency to closed time. While in our experience the future is undetermined, 'in a well-constructed story, everything points (or will turn out to point) to the ending and to the pattern that will eventually be revealed'.[161] This is most obvious in the case of foreshadowing since it 'involves backward causation, which means that, in one way or another, the future must already be there'.[162] However, 'by restoring the presentness of the past and cultivating a sense that something else might have happened'[163] devices of 'sideshadowing' recreate the openness of our experiences.

Morson uses the works of Dostoevsky and Tolstoy to illustrate the concept of 'sideshadowing',[164] but his definition applies well to Thucydides, whose narrative also recreates the openness of time to some extent: 'Whenever I re-read Book VII of Thucydides I keep hoping it'll go the other way this time,' remarks Peter Green.[165] In concentrating on the perceptions of the characters and unfolding all their different plans and options without making use of hindsight, Thucydides brings his readers as close as possible to the past

---

[158] Cf. Plut. *de glor. Ath.* 347a-c. In modern scholarship, see Connor 1985: 10–11; Davidson 1991: 24; Walker 1993: 355–6; Jordan 2000: 68–9; Hornblower 2004: 342–6; Greenwood 2006: 19–41. Bakker 1997: 37 suggests that 'this use of the imperfect is not so much a reference to an event as the displacement of its observation into the past' and thereby brings the reader close to the action.

[159] Kitto 1966: 298–9; Dunn 2007: 111–50. On the temporal organization of the *History*, see also Dewald 2005.

[160] Cf. Gribble 1998 for an analysis of narratorial interventions in Thucydides. See also Rood 2006: 243–4, who gives the narratorial interventions a more prominent role. Morrison 1999 elaborates on the consequences of Thucydides' narrative style on the process of reading. The multiplicity of perspectives, the authorial reticence and the episodic structure require an 'engaged reader'.

[161] Morson 1994: 7.   [162] *Ibid.*   [163] *Ibid.*: 6–7.

[164] Morson's application of 'sideshadowing' is extremely broad, including cases of pseudo-foreshadowing (134–7) and even paraquels and parodies (151–2). I wonder if a narrower focus would not enhance the utility of the concept. Furthermore, I am hesitant to follow Morson when he advocates 'sideshadowing' as a preferable temporal mode of narrating and gives it political relevance.

[165] Green 1970: xii.

perspective of the characters. Time and again, he even points out explicitly the possibility of another course of events. In a famous passage that figures as a decisive turning-point in the Sicilian Expedition, Thucydides remarks that Gylippus and the Spartan support arrived at the last minute (7.2.4):[166]

He happened to come (ἔτυχε ... ἐλθών) in the nick of time when the double wall to the Great Harbour, to a length of seven or eight stades, had already been completed by the Athenians, except for a short part at the sea (they were still busy building this), and along the rest of the circuit toward Trogilus on the other shore, stones had already been set down for the major portion, and it had been left with some parts half-finished and others wholly finished. Syracuse came this close to disaster.

The readers know from hindsight that the Athenians failed in their siege of Syracuse, but Thucydides' comment alerts them to the possibility that things might have worked out very differently. Not only the prominent ἔτυχε right at the beginning of the sentence, but also the preceding account emphasizes how close another outcome was (7.2.1):

... Gongylus, one of the Corinthian commanders, started last with a single ship yet was first to reach Syracuse, slightly before Gylippus, and when he found them getting ready to hold an assembly about putting an end to the war, he stopped and encouraged them by saying that there were other ships still approaching together with Gylippus son of Cleandridas, a commander sent by the Lacedaemonians.

As Stahl notes: 'one thing is clear: *without Gongylos' unscheduled early arrival, Gylippus himself, on his own arrival, might well have found the city in Athenian hands.*'[167] Scholars have noted the similarity of the passage to epic 'Beinahe'–episodes.[168] The 'sideshadowing' of another 'Beinahe'–episode is reinforced by a further epic device, a counterfactual. When the Peloponnesians do not succeed in their siege of Plataea, they try to set the city on fire (2.77.4–6):[169]

---

[166] On the correspondence with 3.49.4, where Thucydides uses the same phrase for the rescue of the Mytilineans, cf. Connor 1984: 187; Hornblower 1994: 158; Stahl 2003: 216. Rood 1998a: 260 also discusses the slightly different case of 8.33.3. On the prominence of the passage, see Kern 1989: 80–2; Gribble 2006: 450–1. Connor 1984: 187 argues that Thucydides' comment provides the readers with a privileged foreknowledge: while the readers are informed that Syracuse will not be taken, the situation remains tense at the level of the action for some time. However, Rood 1998a: 173 n. 58 shows that this interpretation relies on a misleading translation: 'By such a margin did Syracuse escape from danger' (in the Greek, 'escape' is not mentioned).

[167] Stahl 2003: 214. [168] Rood 1998a: 173; Rengakos 2006b: 294–5.

[169] On counterfactuals in Thucydides, see Flory 1988, who compares them with Homeric counterfactuals. He also notes that there are far fewer counterfactuals in Herodotus (47–8). See also Dover 1988b.

And a blaze resulted of such dimensions as no one had ever seen up to that time, of those intentionally lit; for in the mountains wood rubbed together by the wind has sometimes given rise to fire and flames by itself. But this was big and nearly destroyed the Plataeans after they had escaped the other dangers. A large area of the city inside was unapproachable, and *if a wind had come up to spread the fire, as their enemies hoped, they would not have escaped* (πνεῦμά τε εἰ ἐπεγένετο αὐτῇ ἐπίφορον, ὅπερ καὶ ἤλπιζον οἱ ἐναντίοι, οὐκ ἂν διέφυγον). But it is said that what happened now was this, that heavy rain came with thunder and put out the blaze, and so the danger was averted.

The *irrealis* in the counterfactual signals to the readers that the alternative version did not take place. And yet, in sketching alternative scenarios, counterfactuals serve as another 'sideshadowing' device besides the focus on expectations and 'Beinahe'–episodes.[170] Thucydides' efforts to restore the openness of time mark an important distinction from his predecessor Herodotus as well as other commemorative genres such as epic and tragic poetry. Whereas they keep their recipients safely ahead of the characters through *prolepseis*, Thucydides' readers may know the history of the Peloponnesian War, but the narrative does not capitalize on hindsight – on the contrary, it tries to recreate the presentness of the past when it still was a present. It is worth noting that the efforts of 'sideshadowing' also distinguish Thucydides from most modern historians. As Niall Ferguson in his call for a 'virtual history' and the use of counterfactuals by historians shows, historians of various stripes, ranging from idealism to Marxist materialism, are inclined to downplay contingency.[171] This tendency is owed to the retrospective perspective from which history is written, but it does not do justice to the perspective of the historical agents.

While Thucydides restricts the temporal perspective of the readers to the position of the characters, it is important to note that, in addition to their knowledge of the past, the narrative privileges readers over the characters in two regards. First, in the 'Sicilian archaeology' Thucydides provides his readers with superior knowledge about the past. Another example of this is Thucydides' digression on the end of tyranny in Athens, which alerts the readers to the shaky foundations of democratic decision-making (6.54–9).[172] Second, and more important, the readers' horizon is not limited to one perspective – Thucydides employs various focalizers. For instance, the Athenians do not know what the Sicilians are doing nor do the Sicilians have secure information about the situation in Athens, but readers have

---

[170] For a similar argument, albeit without using the concept of 'sideshadowing', see Hunt 2006: 400.
[171] Ferguson 1997.   [172] Cf. pp. 214–20 and 271–3.

access to both camps. The different perspectives shed light on one another and further correspond with the narrative. Thus, while the mimetic dimension of Thucydides' narrative is reinforced by the avoidance of authorial *prolepseis*, the readers still enjoy a privileged vantage-point that embraces insights into the past and various foci.

(c) Chance
The Sicilian Expedition illustrates well Thucydides' focus on his characters' expectations and affords an impressive example of the gap between expectations and experiences, but my selective reading may foster too narrow a view, namely that the *History* is mostly concerned with failures that are due to miscalculation. And of course, Thucydides' narrative implies the criticism that, owing to corrupt orators, a democracy such as Athens is liable to foster expectations that will be disappointed.[173] At the same time, however, Thucydides also emphasizes that human plans can encounter forces that are beyond control.[174] For example, Athenagoras' argument reveals the intricacies of planning as far as the intentions and actions of other men are involved. His reflections about whether or not it is reasonable for Athens to invade Sicily may be sound, but nonetheless his conclusions prove wrong: human action simply does not obey reason all the time.

It is not necessarily the plans and actions of other men that make the outcome of one's own plans unpredictable. Let me give a minor example from the siege of Syracuse that abounds in sudden and unexpected reversals.[175] The Syracusans try to prevent a complete circumvallation of their city by erecting palisades. In their attempt to reach the Great Harbour from the south, the Athenians manage to take a palisade that the Syracusans have erected in the marsh of Lysimeleia (6.101.3). In an ensuing battle, the Athenians first get the better of their opponents, but suddenly the fleeing Syracusans stop, rout the Athenians and kill Lamachus (6.101.4–6). This reversal allows the Syracusans to proceed to the wall at Epipolae where they destroy the outer circuit and would have easily taken the Athenian fort had it not been for Nicias (6.102.2–3):

But Nicias happened to have been left there (ἔτυχε ... ὑπολελειμμένος) because of illness. He ordered the servants to set fire to all the equipment and timber which had been deposited in front of the wall, since he realized that with no men they

---

[173] Cf. Yunis 1996: 103–9; Ober 1998: 113–21. Connor 1984: 168 is inclined to read the Sicilian disaster as deserved punishment for what the Athenians did to Melos. On this link, see also Kohl 1977: 172–3.
[174] This is forcefully argued by Stahl 2003.
[175] The reversals are emphasized by Rood 1998a: 159–201; Stahl 2003: 189–222.

would not be able to survive in any other way. And it turned out accordingly, for the Syracusans did not continue their advance because of the fire, but withdrew.

The full destruction of the wall and the capture of the Athenian camp after the surprising reversal in the battle are only prevented by the fact that Nicias felt too ill to join combat that day. The role of chance is given emphasis by the prominent position of ἔτυχε at the very beginning of the sentence.[176]

Many similar episodes could be adduced in which chance plays a major role. Even in scenes where no chance is involved, it can be invoked by Thucydides, for instance when he closes the account of the final battle in the harbour of Syracuse (7.71.7):

The shock of this moment was unprecedented. What they had suffered was very similar to what they had dealt out themselves at Pylus; for when the ships of the Lacedaemonians were destroyed, their men who had crossed over to the island were also lost, and this time it was beyond hope for the Athenians to be saved on land unless something unaccountable happened.

The defeat is devastating, the fate of the Athenian soldiers is sealed and nothing will actually save them, but at this pivotal point in the narrative Thucydides nonetheless uses one of his rare authorial interventions to note that even in this situation something unexpected could happen. The closure is undermined by the emphasis on chance. The mention of chance possibly gains additional weight from the reference to the Pylus episode where chance looms large, as F. M. Cornford points out:

The fleet, bound as it was for Sicily, with instructions to call on the way at Corcyra, where it was urgently needed, would never have put in at Pylus, if a storm had not '*by chance*' driven it to shelter ... It was owing to the accidental continuance of bad weather that from sheer want of something to do '*an impulse seized*' the soldiers to fortify the place ... They had time to finish it because the Lacedaemonians at home were *just then* celebrating a festival ... Just when reinforcements and a supply of arms are urgently needed by the extemporized garrison, a couple of piratical craft come bearing down the wind from the north. They turn out, oddly enough, to be Messenians with forty hoplites aboard and – how very fortunate! – a supply of spare arms.[177]

Chance emerges not only as a prominent force in the narrative, Thucydides also has his characters reflect upon it. For example in the Sicilian Expedition, Nicias ponders on both planning and chance: '... and since I know that we are

---

[176] Cf. *ibid.*: 210.
[177] Cornford 1907: 88–9. For different emphasis, see Rood 1998a: 24–57; Stahl 2003: 138–53. Gomme, Andrewes and Dover 1945–81, III: 488–9, on the other hand, downplay the prominence of chance.

greatly in need of good planning and still more of good fortune – a problem because we are human – I wish to expose myself as little as possible to chance when I sail, but to depart protected as far as reasonably possible by careful preparation'. (6.23.3). However, the Athenians are neither guided by circumspect planning nor is their defeat averted by chance.

One may conclude that Thucydides highlights both failures due to miscalculation and chance as interfering with human expectations. Thucydides does not invoke the gods, but the prominence of failure and chance aligns his narrative with both non-historiographic genres of memory and Herodotus' *Histories*. As I have argued in the first part of this study, contingency of chance also looms large in elegy, epinician, tragedy and oratory to which, in the preceding chapter, I added the *Histories* as another text that foregrounds human fragility. Much as Thucydides is at pains to stress the novelty und uniqueness of his approach, he shares, just as Herodotus, common ground with the genres that he criticizes.

More specifically, like Herodotus, Thucydides uses narrative time and perspective to throw into relief the tension between expectation and experience, but he proceeds in a novel way and thereby creates a different reading experience. While there are artful analeptic juxtapositions of experiences with expectations, very few authorial *prolepseis* guide the readers through the Sicilian Expedition. Therefore, if we leave aside the fundamental difference between the 'as-if' of reading and 'real' experiences, we can say that the reading experience mirrors the experiences at the level of the action with regard to the future.[178] Although the readers have the advantage of hindsight, the temporal restrictions and devices of 'sideshadowing' reinforce the impression of the openness of the action. However, at the same time the multiplicity of perspectives and authorial digressions on the past privilege the readers over the characters. On the one hand, Thucydides' narrative allows the readers to experience contingency of chance to which the characters are exposed in the frame of the 'as-if'. On the other, the privileged stance provides them with a deepened insight into the tension between expectations and experiences. One question remains: does Thucydides' narrative overcome the force of contingency of chance?

8.3.2. Contingency and narrative patterns

While both Herodotus and Thucydides emphasize the fickleness of human life in their narratives, their inclination to attribute contingency of chance to

[178] Cf. Connor 1984: 249.

higher powers is different. It is a widely held belief among scholars of Greek historiography that Thucydides' sobriety and rationality opposes Herodotus' theological worldview. In Chapter 7, section 7.3.1, I have conceded that Herodotus entertains metaphysical interpretations, but I found it necessary to add that he does not present a coherent philosophy of history. Different and mutually exclusive models, notably divine retribution, the envy of the gods and the cycle of good and bad fate, are invoked to explain human suffering in the *Histories*. What about Thucydides? Cornford's attempt to find divine agencies such as Fortune, Hope, Delusion and Eros in the *History* met with much disapproval,[179] and although Jordan made a case that we have to credit Thucydides with a stronger interest in religion than is usually assumed,[180] there are no such explicit references to gods as in Herodotus.[181]

Herodotus does not offer a theory that solves contingency of chance, but his narrative restricts its force through *prolepseis* and patterns which constitute regularity through the exemplary mode of memory and make the reading a safe experience. As we have just seen, Thucydides tends to avoid *prolepseis*. However, scholars have argued that patterns play an important role in his narrative. I shall now turn to these patterns and discuss whether they cancel out contingency of chance. In an ambitious study that has received less attention than it deserves, Virginia Hunter argues that a net of patterns structures Thucydides' account of the Peloponnesian War and that he also has some of his characters learn either from their own experiences or from paradigms.[182]

The overarching pattern, according to Hunter, is that the Athenians' disaster in Sicily parallels the first Spartan invasion of Attica.[183] This pattern is reinforced by several significant repetitions. For example, Lamachus' prediction of how the Sicilians would react to a quick and unexpected attack parallels the Athenians' experiences during the first invasion.[184] Gylippus' reflections about the demoralization of the Athenians, on the

---

[179] Cornford 1907.
[180] Cf. Jordan 1986 (on the role of religion in the Sicilian Expedition, see 144–6), and, more recently, Furley 2006. See, however, Rubel 2000: 129–34, who advocates the traditional view that Thucydides deliberately avoids religion. On Thucydides and religion, see also Oost 1975; Marinatos 1981; Dover 1988a; Hornblower 1992.
[181] Cf. Lloyd-Jones 1971: 137, who notes that in Thucydides the gods are 'conspicuous by their absence'.
[182] Hunter 1973.
[183] See in particular Hunter 1973: 130–1; 145–8. Similarly, Rawlings 1981 argues that Thucydides juxtaposes his two ten-year wars. According to his interpretation, Books 1 and 6, 2 and 7, 3 and 8 mirror one another. However, he argues not so much for an underlying pattern as for a dense net of similarities and differences.
[184] Hunter 1973: 100–1.

other hand, correspond to the experiences of the Spartans on Sphacteria.[185] More prominently, Nicias parallels Archidamus.[186] Like the Spartan king, Nicias warns against the expedition, but becomes its leader. The failure to heed the well-founded warnings leads to defeat in both cases. This observation prompts Hunter to claim that 'Thucydides evidently studied Herodotus with great care and, while eliminating the religious overtones of the morality cycle, captured the essence of Xerxes' downfall.'[187]

Some parallels are striking, but crucial differences as well as the lack of explicit remarks raise doubts as to whether it is justified to speak of a 'pattern' that repeats itself and hence will help Thucydides' readers in assessing the future.[188] As we have seen, the comment in which Thucydides explicitly juxtaposes the final battle in Syracuse with the situation on Sphacteria emphasizes the role of chance and thereby undermines the notion of a pattern.[189]

Hunter's further thesis that characters are shown to learn from their experiences or paradigms is also liable to overinterpretation. To stay with the examples mentioned, the claim that Lamachus' 'main concern is that he not repeat Archidamos' error, i.e. let opportunities pass and so miss the *kairos*,'[190] mixes up implicit correspondences in Thucydides' narrative with the character's motivation. Lamachus may be in a situation similar to that of Archidamus, but Thucydides does not indicate that his strategy relies on learning from Archidamus' mistake. The same applies to Gylippus: 'It is easy to see the source of Gylippus' psychology. He has learned enough from past experiences (*erga*) to see similarities in the present (*logoi*) and to predict the future (*erga*).'[191] However, there is nothing in the text that justifies the assumption that Gylippus is influenced by the exemplum of the past.

---

[185] *Ibid.*: 118–20. [186] *Ibid.*: 127–9. [187] *Ibid.*: 164.
[188] One rather striking parallel that Hunter does not elaborate on is the inversion of land and sea battles in both the Pylus–episode and the Sicilian Expedition. Cf. Macleod 1983a: 142–3; Flory 1993: 119–20.
[189] On the juxtaposition of the Pylus– and the Sicily–episodes, see besides the literature in the above note also Finley 1967: 145–9; Jordan 2000: 77.
[190] Hunter 1973: 101.
[191] *Ibid.*: 120. Another case in point is the Syracusans' change of their naval strategy (7.36) that seems to correspond to the sea battle of the Corinthians with the Athenians (7.34.3–8). Hunter 1973: 91 admits: 'Thucydides does not indicate how many similarities the Syracusans saw in the two situations, for example, whether they thought the hostile, crescent-shaped shore significant. In fact, he does not even state that the Syracusans knew anything about the indecisive battle at Naupaktos.' Later, however, she claims (172): 'But men also learn from the example of others (*paradeigma*). Chapter 5 showed how the Syracusans did just this: following the Corinthian example they made significant innovations in their naval tactics.' This is not only speculative, but even goes against the text which states that the Syracusans learned from their own previous battle against the Athenians (7.36.2).

According to Hunter, Thucydides not only establishes patterns within his narrative, but also invokes patterns through two intertextual foils, the Trojan and the Persian Wars. While Hunter only touches upon these intertexts, they have received more attention in recent scholarship.[192] In what follows, I will examine whether the epic (a) and Herodotean foils (b) in the *History* set up patterns that compensate for contingency of chance.

(a) The Trojan War as foil for the Sicilian Expedition
As is well known, Homer is an important influence on Thucydides. Particularly the account of the Sicilian Expedition seems to evoke the Trojan War time and again.[193] While many specific allusions are debatable, it is difficult to deny striking similarities and the epic colouring of some passages.[194] Building on observations made by Hunter, Lisa Kallet elaborates on the parallels between the two events which are both called στόλος ('expedition').[195] She shows to what extent the reconstruction of the Trojan War in 1.9–11 relies on the model of the Sicilian Expedition. Particularly the comments on the size of the Achaean army and the explanation of the length of the war seem to take their cue from the Sicilian Expedition: oddly, Thucydides asserts that the Achaean army was rather small. This, Kallet points out, corresponds with the implicit criticism of the Athenian fleet as too small. Moreover, Thucydides argues that the siege of Troy took so long because the Achaeans were forced to support themselves with food. Similarly, the Athenian army in Sicily suffered from insufficient funding. Another interesting parallel is the motivation of the allies. Thucydides points out that it was not the obligation incurred through oaths, but the power of Mycenae and its fleet that prompted the Achaeans to gather around Agamemnon. This explanation is reminiscent of the analysis of why the allies fight in the Sicilian Expedition, recalling the prominent role that fear has in the development of the Athenian naval empire.[196] Thus,

---

[192] Hunter 1973: 164–5. On the *History* and Homer, see Strasburger 1972; Bowie 1993; Frangoulidis 1993; Mackie 1996; Allison 1997b; Zadoroinyi 1998; Rood 1999; Kallet 2001: 97–115. For a collection of epic echoes, see Smith 1900. On the *History* and Herodotus, see Cornford 1907: 202–20; Rood 1999; Kallet 2001: 97–115; Rogkotis 2006. Rengakos 2006b discusses Thucydides' narratological debts to Homer and Herodotus.
[193] Cf. Hornblower 1994: 67. [194] Rood 1998b critically assesses the arguments for specific allusions.
[195] Hunter 1973: 165; 1982: 40–1; Kallet 2001: 97–112. The Athenian armada is called a στόλος in 6.31.3; 6, the Achaean forces against Troy in 1.9.2; 10.1.
[196] Hunter 1982: 197–8. Kallet 2001: 113 points out that Thucydides mentions considerations of power and profit that induced the Athenian allies to join the Sicilian Expedition (7.57.1). Further similarities between the Trojan War and the Sicilian Expedition include early victories that are not followed up and the role of fortification, cf. Kallet 2001: 99.

essential aspects in which Thucydides deviates from the Homeric account are obviously modelled on the Sicilian Expedition.

By using the Sicilian Expedition as a template for the Trojan War, Thucydides transforms the earlier war into a foil for the later. The juxtaposition is reinforced by comparisons of the Athenians' enterprise with earlier expeditions.[197] In 6.31.6, Thucydides remarks that 'the expedition became no less famous for the miraculousness of its daring and for the splendour of its sight than for the superiority of the army over those against whom they went, and because it was the greatest voyage from home ever undertaken, with the greatest hope for what would happen compared with the actual circumstances'. In 6.33.5, he has Hermocrates argue: 'Few great expeditions, undertaken either by Greeks or barbarians, which have ventured far from their own land, have succeeded.' And in closing the account of the Sicilian Expedition, Thucydides points out: 'And this Hellenic event turned out to be the greatest connected with this war and, as it seems to me, of Hellenic events which we know from hearsay, the most splendid for those who won and the most wretched for the defeated.'[198] (7.87.5). The Trojan War is not explicitly mentioned in these comparisons, but, being the most prominent war in Greek history, it probably would have been the first to come to the minds of Thucydides' readers.

Furthermore, there are several motifs that evoke the Trojan War as a foil. For example, in both the *Iliad* and the *History*, the desperate situation of the besieging army is expressed by comparisons with a conquered city.[199] More interestingly, not only the story, but also the discourse suggests a juxtaposition of the Sicilian Expedition with the Trojan War as presented in the *Iliad*. In 7.57–8, Thucydides elaborates his claim that 'the greatest number of nationalities came together at this one city' (7.56.4) by listing the forces on both sides. The form of the catalogue that Thucydides chooses is of epic origin. The Homeric ring may be enhanced by the position of the catalogue in the narrative. It precedes the final battle just as the 'Catalogue of Ships' is placed before the battle and therefore has a similar function of retarding the action.[200] Thus, in relying on an epic form of presentation Thucydides reinforces the thematic juxtaposition of Troy with Sicily.

Given all these points, the question arises whether the Trojan War serves as a pattern that underlies the narrative of the Sicilian Expedition and thereby denies contingency of chance. The force of chance which is powerfully

---

[197] On the general tendency of comparing different wars with one another in antiquity, see Rood 1999: 143.
[198] On this last comparison, see pp. 261–2.
[199] Thuc. 7.11.4; 75.5. Cf. Zadorojnyi 1998: 300. For the topos in the *Iliad*, see Morrison 1994. For later parallels in ancient historians, see Rood 1998b: 2 n. 37.
[200] Cf. Schadewaldt 1929: 10–11.

displayed in the narrative would be limited by the regularity of a pattern that was repeated in the past and will recur in the future. However, although some points in Thucydides' reconstruction of the Trojan War are modelled on the Sicilian Expedition, the general relation between the wars is more complex than a simple pattern and it is therefore more appropriate to say that the Trojan War sheds light on the Sicilian Expedition. Three points may suffice to highlight the complexity of the correspondences that Thucydides constructs between the siege of Troy and the expedition to Sicily: first, the Trojan War was the benchmark against which all later wars had to be measured and the comparisons quoted above underscore the size of the Peloponnesian War – according to Thucydides, it was 'a major one and notable beyond all previous wars' (1.1). Thus, the comparison with the Trojan War serves to highlight the dimension of the war which Thucydides is covering.

Second, the foil of an expedition that succeeded throws into relief the failure of the Athenian invasion. While the Achaeans captured Troy, the Athenians suffer total defeat at the hands of the Sicilians, some of whom trace their lineage back to Trojan refugees (6.2.3).[201] I suggest that the Trojan War as a negative foil for the Athenian defeat is reinforced by the Athenians' claim to heroic grandness. Not only is there much pomp in the departure of the fleet, but in arguing for the expedition and defending his own position in the polis, Alcibiades points out (6.16.5):

I know that such men, indeed those men who stood out by brilliance of any kind, were envied during their lifetimes, especially by their peers, then by all the others with whom they came in contact, but that they left behind claims of kinship among later men, even without validity, and, in their fatherland, pride in men who had been no aliens or failures but had been theirs and performed great deeds.

Plutarch cites in his *vita* the otherwise unknown verse 'not the son of Achilles, but Achilles himself' (*Alc.* 23.6) to emphasize Alcibiades' changeability and versatility.[202] The quotation expresses primarily the authenticity of Alcibiades' different modes of conduct – his performances seem to be 'the real thing', not fake – but the comparison with Achilles also illustrates nicely the heroic claim that is implicit in the quoted passage.[203] Thucydides has

---

[201] However, the Athenian ally Egesta is named as one of the cities that were founded by Trojans (6.2.3).
[202] Cf. Bloedow 1990: 1. The same verse seems to be cited in slightly different form in Plut. *Mor.* 51 c (TrGF adesp. 363).
[203] In modern scholarship, cf. Greenwood 2006: 39. Rood 1998b: 2 considers the possibility that Alcibiades' advice that the Athenians at Samos do not attack Athens (8.86.4–5) is modelled on Achilles' restraining of the Achaeans 'when they are eager to return home' (Arg. 1.61 *PEG*), an episode that Proclus mentions in his summary of the *Cypria*. This would reinforce my interpretation, but, as Rood admits, the evidence is scanty.

Alcibiades refer to 'people who claimed descent from Odysseus'[204] and, more importantly, compare his own situation, particularly the envy and mistrust that he is exposed to, to the fate of the heroes at the hands of their contemporaries. He makes the implicit comparison explicit in the following sentence: 'When I with these aspirations am personally assailed for them …' (6.16.6). His argument sways the Athenians who vote to go to Sicily. However, the Sicilian Expedition ends in disaster and the foil of the Trojan War underscores the failure to complete the heroic ambitions that Alcibiades advances.

Third, the Homeric intertext also throws into relief the enormous suffering of the Athenian army. The *Iliad* vividly describes the cruelties of war and gives ample space to the suffering of the heroes.[205] June Allison notes a particularly high density of epic echoes in chapters 7.74 and 75, in which Thucydides reports the utter defeat in the harbour of Syracuse.[206] Potential references to the *Odyssey* further underline the misery of the Athenian soldiers,[207] particularly at the beginning of the 'Sicilian archaeology', where Thucydides mentions the Cyclopes and Laestrygonians as the first inhabitants of Sicily (6.2.1). S. A. Frangoulidis argues: 'The effect then of the referral to these mythic places, at the start of the Sicilian narrative, is to offer an advanced indication of the savage forces that guard Sicily when the Athenians are about to launch their expedition against the land that is otherwise related to the "birth" of Odysseus' troubles during his homecoming.'[208] Significantly, at the end of his account Thucydides mentions that 'few out of many returned home (ἀπενόστησαν)' (7.87.6). I am not convinced that this is a reference to two specific Iliadic passages, as Allison suggests, but the unique use of the Homeric word ἀπονοστεῖν in the *History* is quite likely to evoke the painful *nostoi* of the Achaean heroes from Troy.[209] Possibly, the Iliadic and the Odyssean intertexts interact with one

---

[204] Gomme, Andrewes and Dover 1945–81: ad loc.
[205] Cf. Marg 1976; Griffin 1980; Grethlein 2006a. [206] Allison 1997b: 502.
[207] See Frangoulidis 1993; Mackie 1996, who argues that the Sicilian Expedition is shaped as an inverted *Odyssey*. Rood 1998b: 5 is rather sceptical: 'The allusions to the world of Odysseus, I would argue, should not encourage us to draw detailed comparisons between Thucydides' narrative and the *Odyssey*. Instead, they define Sicily as a distant land with a mythical aura – an aura that explains the "longing for faraway sights" felt by the young men at Athens when they voted to invade Sicily.' I agree with Rood that there seem to be few specific allusions to the *Odyssey*, but I find it hard to deny that the general background of the *Odyssey*, particularly the topic of *nostos*, underscores the notion of suffering.
[208] Frangoulidis 1993: 99. Cf. Connor 1984: 162 n. 9.
[209] Allison 1997b: 512–14. For a critique of her argument, see Rood 1998b: 4.1. On the Homeric echo and the evocation of epic *nostoi*-tales, see Hornblower 1987: 116. Hornblower 2004: 350–1 suggests that Thucydides evokes not only the epic *nostos*, but also the *nostos* of athletes.

another and reinforce the failure and misery of the Athenians: an expedition that is modelled on Agamemnon's siege of Troy turns into something that is more miserable than Odysseus' toilsome *nostos* without gaining glory.

In summary, the complexity of the intertextual relations between the *History* and the Homeric epics makes it difficult to argue that the Trojan War constitutes a pattern that is simply repeated in the Peloponnesian War and that will be repeated again and thereby allows readers to overcome contingency of chance. The epics rather provide a foil that sheds light on the Sicilian Expedition through parallels, contrasts and quantitative differences. The 'plu-past', the past embedded in the past of the narrative, does not prefigure the past, but it helps to better assess it. In juxtaposing the Peloponnesian with the Trojan Wars, Thucydides draws on the exemplary mode of memory, but his use of it is very complex and does not establish clear-cut regularities.

(b) The Persian Wars as foil for the Sicilian Expedition
Besides the Trojan War, the Persian Wars are evoked as a backdrop against which the Sicilian Expedition is to be viewed.[210] Some passages recall both Homer and Herodotus. For instance, the catalogue of the forces at Syracuse may evoke the catalogue of the Greek and the Persian armies in Hdt. 7.61–99 as well as the 'Catalogue of Ships'. It is also plausible to refer the comparisons of the Sicilian Expedition with other wars not only to the siege of Troy, but also to the Persian invasion into Greece. Thucydides' concluding evaluation is a particularly interesting case in point (7.87.5–6):

And this Hellenic event (ἔργον τοῦτο [Ἑλληνικόν][211]) turned out to be the greatest connected with this war and, as it seems to me (δοκεῖν δ' ἔμοιγε), of Hellenic events which we know from hearsay (ὧν ἀκοῇ ... ἴσμεν), the most splendid for the victors and the most wretched for the defeated. For they were entirely defeated in every respect and suffered no little misery at any point, so to speak, in total destruction (καὶ οὐδὲν ὀλίγον ἐς οὐδὲν κακοπαθήσαντες πανωλεθρίᾳ δὴ τὸ λεγόμενον), army, ships, nothing that was not lost, and few out of many returned home (ἀπενόστησαν).

---

[210] Perhaps the foils of the Trojan and Persian Wars reinforce one another. Both events were frequently juxtaposed in different genres and media in the fifth century BCE. The victory over the Persians was claimed to equal the heroic performance against the Trojans. In Thucydides' *History*, however, the Athenians are projected against the background of the Achaean heroes and the Persians. This twofold juxtaposition clashes with the common comparison of the Greeks' stand against the Persians with the siege of Troy and thereby underscores the failure of the Athenians to gain the same glory as the Greek heroes at Troy. While their ancestors had performed a deed worthy of heroic honours, the Athenians have now taken over the role of the failing aggressor.

[211] I do not think that Ἑλληνικόν is a gloss, as Jones, following Krüger, believes.

Although the *comparanda* for the Sicilian Expedition are not specified, the diction evokes Herodotus as well as Homer and thereby invites the readers to juxtapose Thucydides' subject with the Trojan and Persian Wars.[212] To start with, the assertion that the Sicilian Expedition was the greatest event in all Greek wars may recall Hdt. 7.20.1, where Xerxes' invasion is said to surpass all other notable military expeditions.[213] Moreover, as Rood has persuasively argued, ἔργον in the meaning of 'achievement', δοκεῖν δ' ἔμοιγε and ὧν ἀκοῇ ... ἴσμεν have a Herodotean ring.[214] At the same time, ἀπονοστεῖν is epic and the κακός-compositum κακοπαθεῖν, although not attested in Homer, sounds epic.[215] Thucydides also gives the comparison an epic ring by shifting the focus from the greatness of the expedition that Herodotus estimates to the Homeric topic of suffering.[216] If πανωλεθρία alludes to Hdt. 2.120.5, where Herodotus assesses the Trojan War, the link to both Homer and Herodotus is even encapsulated in a single word.[217] Thus, through his diction Thucydides pits the Sicilian Expedition against the Trojan and Persian Wars. In a subtle interplay of form and content, Thucydides gives the Herodotean evaluation of the size of the Persian invasion a Homeric spin, applies it to the Peloponnesian War and ranks it, although only a Hellenic affair, above both the war at Troy and the victory over the Persians.

Besides the comparisons of the Sicilian Expedition with other wars, Cornford noted numerous parallels between Thucydides' account and Xerxes' expedition as reported by Herodotus.[218] For example, the debate at Athens recalls the consultation of Xerxes with his council.[219] Particularly Nicias' warnings are reminiscent of Artabanus' arguments against the invasion.[220] Alcibiades' misapprehension of Sicily and its dangers, on the other hand, mirrors the faulty image of Greece on which Mardonius relies. Both Herodotus and Thucydides emphasize the pompous preparations in

---

[212] I do not think that Thucydides limits his comparison to wars in which Greeks fought versus Greeks. 'Hellenic event' can also signify a war that Greeks fought against barbarians.
[213] On the superlative see Price 2001: 360–1 and Greenwood 2006: 87, who argue for an ironic correspondence with the 'archaeology'.
[214] Rood 1998b: section 4.2.
[215] On ἀπονοστεῖν, see Connor 1984: 162 n. 9; Hornblower 1987: 116; Frangoulidis 1993: 101; Allison 1997b: 512–14, who also comments on κακοπαθεῖν.
[216] This does not mean that Herodotus never reflects on the evils of war, see e.g Hdt. 6.98.2.
[217] See p. 264.
[218] Cf. Cornford 1907: 202–20. For further details, see Rood 1999, particularly 153–4; Rogkotis 2006. While these scholars focus on the similarities between the Sicilian Expedition and Xerxes' invasion, Kallet 2001: 87–97 tries to show that in essential aspects the Sicilian Expedition is modelled on the Ionian Revolt in Herodotus.
[219] See also von Fritz 1967: 727.
[220] On the similarities between Nicias and Artabanus, see Marinatos 1980; Rood 1998a: 166–7.

which the individual boatsmen compete with one another (Thuc. 6.31.3–4; Hdt. 7.19.2), and whereas the emphasis on visual elements and the integration of internal spectators may be owed to a common striving for *enargeia*, the regatta of the Athenian ships to Aegina constitutes a striking parallel to the sea battle of Xerxes' fleet at Abydus (Thuc. 6.32.2; Hdt. 7.44). Furthermore, the libations poured from gold and silver *krateres* by the sailors echo the libations from a golden *phiale* that Xerxes makes (Thuc. 6.32.1; Hdt. 7.54).

It is difficult to pin down verbal allusions to Herodotus – the rare ἅμιλλα for the contests may be one[221] – but the great number of parallels in significant places has prompted Tim Rood to claim that 'the force of the Herodotean parallels drawn by Thucydides is to suggest that the Athenian invasion of Sicily is in some ways a re-run of the Persian invasion of Greece.'[222] This reading allows Rood to argue for a complementary relation between Herodotus and Thucydides.[223] While in the *Histories* time and again the Persian Wars adumbrate the later intra-Hellenic conflicts, Thucydides uses the Persian Wars as a foil for the Peloponnesian War. In one aspect, this argument can be pushed even further. Both authors evoke the Trojan War as an additional foil. In Chapter 7, section 7.2, I argued that in the Syracusan embassy scene and the narrative of the Plataea battle the epic past, the time of the Persian Wars and later intra-Hellenic conflicts shed light on each other. Now we see that Thucydides uses the Trojan as well as the Persian Wars as foils for his account of the Peloponnesian War and can therefore note that both writers set up a panopticon in which three different wars are refracted.

In evoking the Trojan and Persian Wars as foil to the recent past, Thucydides employs the exemplary mode of memory that is so prominent in the poetic and rhetorical genres of memory. In all of these genres as well as in Herodotus, the construction of regularity serves as a powerful counter-strategy against contingency of chance. We have seen that the juxtaposition of the Sicilian Expedition with the Trojan War is too complex to establish regularity. How strong, we have to ask now, is the regularity created by the foil of the Persian Wars? Does it constitute a pattern that is repeated in the Peloponnesian War and is likely to recur?

---

[221] Cf. Rood 1999: 153; Kallet 2001: 86.
[222] Rood 1999: 159. Further parallels could be mentioned. For example, Connor 1984: 173 n. 38 suggests that the messengers sent out by Hermocrates to prevent the Athenians from leaving at night (7.73) are strongly reminiscent of Themistocles' stratagem that lured the Persians into the battle at Salamis (8.75–6).
[223] Rood 1999: 165–6.

Some scholars believe that Thucydides not only projects the Sicilian Expedition against the backdrop of the Persian Wars, but also suggests a Herodotean interpretation of Athens' downfall.[224] Thucydides presents, they argue, the failure of the Sicilian Expedition as due to divine retribution. In this case, the foil of the Persian Wars, together with the Herodotean intertext, would establish a pattern and create regularity. This interpretation mainly relies on a passage the Homeric and Herodotean intertexts of which I have already mentioned (7.87.5–6):

And this Hellenic event turned out to be the greatest connected with this war and, as it seems to me, of the Hellenic events which we know from hearsay, the most splendid for the victors and the most wretched for the defeated. For they were entirely defeated in every respect and suffered no little misery at any point, so to speak, in total destruction (πανωλεθρία δὴ τὸ λεγόμενον), army, ships, nothing that was not lost, and few out of many returned home. This was what happened concerning Sicily.

The only other occurrence of πανωλεθρία in extant classical literature is the passage in which Herodotus concludes his discussion of the epic and other versions of the Helen–story (2.120.5):[225]

But they did not have Helen to give back and the Greeks did not believe that they spoke the truth. To declare my own opinion, this was because the *daimonion* arranged things so that, in their complete annihilation (πανωλεθρίῃ ἀπολόμενοι), they make this clear to mankind that for severe crimes the punishment at the gods' hands is severe (ὡς τῶν μεγάλων ἀδικημάτων μεγάλαι εἰσὶ καὶ αἱ τιμωρίαι παρὰ τῶν θεῶν). That is my view, at any rate.

Since τὸ λεγόμενον can refer not only to a common proverb, some scholars, including Nanno Marinatos Kopff and Hunter Rawlings, have argued that Thucydides alludes to this passage and thereby suggests a Herodotean frame of interpretation, i.e. that the Athenian disaster is to be interpreted as divine punishment. However, the allusion to the passage in Herodotus is not wholly beyond doubt and the interpretative suggestion is far from conclusive. Given the scarcity of the remains of classical literature, arguments based on the singularity of words are always tentative. Moreover,

---

[224] Strasburger 1958: 39 n. 3; Marinatos-Kopff/Rawlings 1978; more tentatively Connor 1984: 208–9 with 208 n. 57. Fisher 1992: 406–7 and Rood 1998b: 4.2 emphasize the aspect of destruction that is more prominent than the idea of divine justice; Kallet 2001: 114–15 argues against the suggestion of a Herodotean interpretation of the Sicilian Expedition 'which would jar if not subvert not only the entire narrative of the expedition, but also the *History* as a whole' (115). I believe that Kallet is right and will try to show that the intertext even invites a critical view of Herodotus.
[225] Cf. pp. 156–8.

the adjective πανώλεθρος is frequently used in tragedy, and this makes it rather tempting to see τὸ λεγόμενον as marking a conventional phrase. On the other hand, the strong Herodotean ring of the whole passage supports a reference to Herodotus.[226] If we therefore side with the majority of scholars and accept the allusion, one could assume that it only conveys the idea of 'total destruction'. At the same time, the prominence of the passage in Herodotus makes it at least arguable that the whole of Herodotus' concluding remark on the Trojan War is evoked. I believe that in this case though, the allusion does not suggest Herodotus' reflection on divine justice as a template for the interpretation of the Peloponnesian War, but rather questions it and points out Thucydides' superiority over Herodotus.[227]

Ironically, my argument hinges on the one other passage that Marinatos-Kopff and Rawlings adduce to buttress their interpretation, Nicias' speech in 7.77. After the devastating defeat in the harbour of Syracuse, Nicias addresses the remaining troops and encourages them not to give up hope. The obvious Herodotean tone of the speech,[228] it is argued, affords evidence for an interpretation of the Peloponnesian War along Herodotean lines. However, in general and in particular with an author as complex as Thucydides, character speech ought not to be read as a direct expression of the author's opinion. What we need instead is a close reading of the speech within its context.

First, it is noteworthy that Nicias employs different topoi and explanatory models that may not directly contradict one another, but do not make for a coherent whole either. At the beginning, Nicias points out that others have suffered worse: 'there have been men who were saved from even more terrible situations than this' (7.77.1). While remaining with the same argumentative pattern, he shifts the focus from the situation to the suffering subject and remarks that he himself who is 'second to no one in good fortune' (7.77.2) shares the same misery as his men. Both arguments gain their consolatory force from implicit conclusions that are drawn *a maiore ad minus*. Then Nicias switches to a moral argument: 'And yet I have spent my life in many devout actions toward the gods and many just and irreproachable ones toward men. Accordingly, my hope for the future is strong, despite all, and in the light of what we deserve our disasters certainly do not terrify me' (7.77.2–3). The following sentence elaborates on the argument that bad

---

[226] Cf. Connor 1984: 208 n. 57; Kallet 2001: 114–15. For a more detailed weighing of the arguments, see Rood 1998b: 4.1. Against the intertextual link, see Gomme, Andrewes and Dover 1945–81: ad loc.
[227] For an extended version of this interpretation, see Grethlein 2008a.
[228] Cf. Westlake 1968: 203; Jordan 1986: 146.

deeds will be punished, while good deeds will be rewarded, but also introduces the idea that there are limits to good fortune: 'For enough has gone well for the enemies, and if, with our expedition, we caused the envy of one of the gods, we have already been punished sufficiently.' (7.77.3).

There are some stretches and tensions in Nicias' argument:[229] he adduces his personal moral integrity, but makes the argument that good deeds will be rewarded for the whole army. The moralistic scheme also clashes to some extent with the emphasis on his moral integrity – if he is such a good person, why is he exposed to such extreme suffering? Furthermore, the moralistic scheme does not really square with the idea of divine envy, which is based on the notion that human good fortune is limited. While the first focuses on moral behavior, the latter depends on the degree of bliss. I do not want to over-emphasize these tensions, but it is worth stressing that the incoherence does not make Nicias' view an attractive interpretative framework for readers. Instead, Nicias' argument is clearly conditioned by the speech context, the desire to console and to encourage his troops.[230]

Thucydides does not provide his readers with an explicit comment on this speech, but, only a few paragraphs above (7.69.2), he has closed his indirect account of Nicias' previous speech with the remark that Nicias was

saying other things as well which men in such a situation would mention if they are not guarding against appearing to speak in platitudes (ἀρχαιολογεῖν), very similar things for all situations, references to women and children and ancestral gods, but in their current consternation they believe them to be helpful (ὠφέλιμα νομίζοντες) and cry them out.

The negative connotation of ἀρχαιολογεῖν[231] as well as the tension between the universal use of such arguments in all kinds of situations and the belief that they will help in this particular situation cast a critical light on Nicias' argument. The criticism is made even sharper by the word ὠφέλιμος that evokes Thucydides' own claim to provide a useful account and thereby establishes a contrast between Nicias' mistaken belief and the *History*.[232]

The explicit critique of Nicias in 7.69.2 prepares the implicitly critical presentation of his speech in 7.77, as the polemic against ἀρχαιολογεῖν applies well to 'ideas about the relation between god and man, which resemble those of Pindar and Herodotus'.[233] What is more, Nicias'

---

[229] Cf. Gomme, Andrewes and Dover 1945–81: ad 7.77.1: 'His logic is not impeccable ...' Westlake 1968: 203 argues that Nicias' argument is 'old-fashioned'.
[230] Cf. Macleod 1983a: 144–5.   [231] See Grethlein 2008a: 135–6.
[232] Cf. Lateiner 1985: 205.   [233] Westlake 1968: 203.

reflections on divine justice are evaluated by the further course of the action. Instead of the salvation that he promises, the suffering gets worse and worse, the Athenians are first exposed to the Syracusans' attacks and those who survive end up in quarries, where they miserably perish. Taken together, the inconsistencies of Nicias' speech and its interaction with the narrative do not invite the reader to apply this frame of interpretation to the Sicilian Expedition. On the contrary, the way in which the Herodotean model of divine justice is integrated into the narrative demonstrates that it fails to explain reality. In his deconstruction, Thucydides indicates that such models are desperate, but inappropriate, attempts to cope with suffering. I therefore suggest that, if there is an allusion to Herodotus in Thuc. 7.87.6, it drives home the point not only that the event described by Thucydides surpasses Herodotus' topic, but also that Herodotus' take on history is inappropriate.

This interpretation can be backed up by a fresh look at Thucydides' final praise for Nicias: 'So for such reasons or very similar ones he died, certainly the least deserving of all Hellenes, at least in my time, to arrive at such a degree of misfortune because of his total devotion to virtue.' (7.86.5). Scholars have focused on the question of the extent to which this assessment of Nicias ties in with the role that he has in the narrative.[234] At the same time, it is worth noting that Thucydides' praise picks up a central idea in Nicias' speech in 7.77, merit and its relevance.[235] Seen from this angle, Thucydides not only expresses his appreciation of Nicias, but also comments on the worldview that Nicias outlined in that speech: virtue did not save him from a most horrible end, and so there seems to be no divine justice.

Thus, the very passage on which scholars have relied to argue that Thucydides casts the Sicilian Expedition in a Herodotean mould rather deconstructs the notion of divine retribution that Herodotus puts forward in his assessment of the Trojan War. Even if we leave aside this critical jibe at Herodotus, the similarities between the Sicilian Expedition and Herodotus' Persian Wars do not suffice to establish a pattern that rules out contingency of chance. Besides differences in the course of events – for instance, whereas the Syracusans decide to prevent the Athenian army from fleeing, the Persians can return after their defeat – decisive factors are different. Herodotus elaborates on the differences between Greeks and Persians, which in part contribute to the successful defence. The Syracusans' victory over the Athenians, on the other hand, is due to their similarity.[236] Furthermore, at the core of Thucydides' analysis, we find the detrimental role of democratic decision-making that is specific to the Athenian disaster.

[234] Cf. Rood 1998a: 183–4.   [235] Cf. Lateiner 1985: 209.   [236] Cf. Rood 1998a: 162.

Instead of providing a clear-cut pattern, Herodotus' Persian Wars rather shed light on some aspects of the Peloponnesian War. Most prominently, the Herodotean foil emphasizes the inversion in Athens' history. While the Athenians helped to save Greece from the Persians, they have now become a threat to Greek freedom. What the Sicilians now expect in case of a victory is exactly what the Athenians did less than a century ago: 'Immediately, the other Hellenes would partly be liberated, partly be freed from fear (for the remaining power of the Athenians would be incapable of shouldering the war that would subsequently be brought against them), and they themselves, credited with responsibility for this, would be greatly admired both by the rest of mankind and by men thereafter.' (7.56.2).[237] That the foil of the Persian Wars emphasizes the inversion rather than marking a pattern is further indicated by the fact that nothing suggests that the Syracusans will become the new tyrants of Greece. In Herodotus' narrative, on the other hand, a net of *prolepseis* foreshadow Athens' succession to Persia in the cycle of empires.[238]

Thucydides shares with Herodotus and recollections of the past in poetry and oratory not only the emphasis on contingency of chance, but also the use of the exemplary mode of memory. As his predecessor, he deviates from poetic and rhetorical memory in that he uses the exemplary mode of memory not for purposes of glorification or to buttress claims, but to shed critical light on the recent past. Thucydides' juxtapositions of different times are even subtler and more complex than those of Herodotus, so complex indeed that the regularity created is too slight to offer a significant counterweight against contingency of chance. Unlike in Herodotus, there are no patterns which create stability.

8.3.3. *The usefulness of the* History

Thucydides rarely provides *prolepseis* that contrast expectations with experiences; instead his readers are more or less fully exposed to the contingency of chance unfolding in the plot. Nor does he draw on the Trojan and

---

[237] As Rood 1998a: 161–2 points out, this echoes Pericles' claim that Athens is worthy of admiration now and in the future (2.41.4; cf. 2.39.4). Thucydides also has Hermocrates say in indirect speech that the Athenians' 'skill at sea was neither inherent nor permanent, but despite being more the landsmen than the Syracusans they had become seafarers because they were forced to by the Medes, and those who matched daring against daring men, such as the Athenians, appeared most troublesome to them. And now they themselves, just as the Athenians terrorized their neighbours, sometimes with no advantage in strength but attacking with boldness, would have the same effect on their opponents.' (7.21.3).
[238] Cf. p. 172 n. 79.

Persian Wars as patterns that establish regularity. Nonetheless, Thucydides' claim to usefulness implies that his work somehow helps his readers to cope with contingency of chance (1.22.4):

> And the results, by avoiding patriotic storytelling, will perhaps seem the less charming for listening. Yet if those who will wish to look at the plain truth about both past events and those that at some future time, in accordance with human nature, will recur again in similar or comparable ways judge them useful, this will suffice. It is composed rather as a possession for all time than a competition piece to be heard for the moment.

Thucydides promises not only a better understanding of the past, but also insights that are useful for assessing the future.[239] And yet, given the absence of patterns combined with the prominence of failure and chance, the question arises: to what extent can Thucydides' narrative help the readers better understand the future? Does the *History* convey anything beyond the insight that the only 'constancy and predictability of human nature' is to be *'found in the inconstancy of its behavior'*, as Hans-Peter Stahl claims?[240] I would like to discuss three aspects of the *History's* usefulness, the content (a), the method (b) and the reading experience (c).

(a) Content
History may not repeat itself, but underlying 'human nature' makes events similar or comparable.[241] In other passages too, Thucydides refers to 'human nature'. His comment on the Corcyrean *stasis* is particularly illuminating:[242] 'And many hardships afflicted the cities during the civil wars, hardships which happen and will always happen as long as men have the same nature (φύσις ἀνθρώπων), sometimes more and sometimes less strong, varying in their forms as each change of fortune occurs.' (3.82.2). As in 1.22.4, Thucydides remarks that 'human nature' makes past, present and future comparable, while at the same time pointing out that there are no simple repetitions. That Thucydides is not only interested in specific events, but also in what they reveal about man at a general level comes to the

---

[239] Cf. pp. 210–11 with references to scholarship.
[240] Stahl 2003: 98. For the tension between chance and intelligence in Thucydides, see besides Edmunds 1975 also de Romilly 1956b: 175–6; Parry 1989b: 176; Farrar 1988: 157; Marincola 2001: 87–8.
[241] On τὸ ἀνθρώπινον in Thucydides, see the literature given by Moles 2001: 203 n. 24. See also Crane 1998: 295–303 and Sahlins 2004: 117–24 on Thucydides' essentialism.
[242] See also the narratorial voice in 2.50.1; the Athenians in 1.76.2–3; Cleon in 3.39.5 and the Spartans in 4.19.4. On Thucydides' interest in the general, see de Romilly 1956b: 51; Moles 1993: 108–9; 2001: 203.

fore in his tendency to use abstracts.[243] This interest in constants of human life marks a crucial distinction from the ideal of objectivity fostered by Historicism.[244] While Thucydides' emphasis on accuracy is reminiscent of the Historicist endeavour to figure out *'wie es wirklich gewesen'* and induced scholars in the nineteenth century CE to see in him a kindred spirit, his interest in the transhistorical strikes a rather different tone and shows that the *History* is based on an essentialist view of human life.[245]

This is illustrated by Thucydides' assessment of the Trojan War. As we have seen, the reconstruction of the Trojan War in 1.9–11 relies on the template of the Sicilian Expedition.[246] Thucydides takes for granted that the relevance of financial support and the mechanisms of power politics have stayed the same over time, an assumption that a Historicist reading would challenge. It is this transhistorical level of life on which part of the *History's* claim to usefulness rests. Thucydides' account may not establish patterns, but, at a more abstract level, the revelations about human nature allow the reader to better assess the future.

The content of the *History* can be useful in a more specific way. In section 8.2, I suggested that some speeches have meta-historical significance. Their references to the past are not fixed in writing, but nonetheless mirror the historian's act of memory and can therefore be read as implicit self-reflection. Some other references to the 'plu-past', the past embedded in the past of the narrative, which is not limited to speeches, demonstrate the usefulness of solid historical knowledge and illustrate the complex ways in which the past can elucidate the present beyond the notion of anthropological constants.[247] For instance, Thucydides notes very pointedly at the beginning of the Sicilian Expedition that the Athenians went to Sicily without knowing the island's history and present circumstances (6.1.1). With the knowledge that he himself presents in the 'Sicilian archaeology' the Athenians would have acted differently. Thus, the 'Sicilian archaeology' proves the relevance of historical knowledge *via negationis*.

There are other cases in which the invocation of a 'plu-past' provides positive meta-history. The foils of the Trojan and Persian Wars, for example, may mirror the uses that Thucydides envisages for his *History*. They do

---

[243] Cf. Kallet 2006: 345.
[244] For an interesting discussion of Thucydides against the background of Historicism, see Moles 2001.
[245] See the critical judgement by Sahlins 2004: 118: '... a history based on such foundations is decidedly anticultural – and in the same measure antihistorical'.
[246] See pp. 257–8.
[247] For similar arguments, albeit without the term 'meta-history', see Rawlings 1981: 254–63; Kallet 2001: 118–20; 2006: 359.

not provide a pattern that is simply repeated, but they illuminate many aspects of the Peloponnesian War. Similarly, Thucydides' account of the Peloponnesian War may help later generations improve their understanding of their own present and even facilitate a realistic assessment of the future. The critical reader may object that the allusions to Homer and Herodotus are merely learned games with predecessors. However, the reconstruction of the Trojan War on the basis of the Peloponnesian War shows that Thucydides envisages a deeper comparison. In the same way in which the 'plu-past' is cast in the template of the past, the past can help to make conjectures about the future. Thus, these intertextual relationships are not merely literary exercises, but establish a meta-historical dimension in the *History*.

I have touched upon two passages that are particularly interesting for such a meta-historical reading. In section 8.1.2, I examined Thucydides' deconstruction of the tyrannicide, which under his critical scrutiny is not much more than the culmination of a love affair. There are at least two significant links between the digression on the tyrannicide and its context, the witch-hunt after the mutilation of the Herms and the desecration of the Mysteries in 415 BCE. I have already pointed out that the Athenians' sloppy treatment of the past contrasts with their over-anxiety in the present. While the Athenians do not bother to acquire solid knowledge about the past, but simply believe a distorted tradition, they are over-sensitive toward present conspiracies. The Athenians' approaches to the past and the present not only contrast with each other, they are also causally linked. It is the all too negative image of tyranny that makes the Athenians extremely sensitive to anybody in an outstanding position.[248] Thus, their exaggerated suspicions in the present situation are the result of unquestioned assumptions about the past. As Hans-Peter Stahl puts it:

> It is precisely this *false myth* which becomes *in its turn* – a hundred years after the fact! – *a concrete political factor*, in that it excites the people's fear of tyranny to such a degree that *again* the domestic peace of the city is destroyed and the very order of Athenian society is threatened ... Thucydides shows historical *misconception as a direct cause* of action which has jumped the rails of rational control.[249]

What is more, the deficient knowledge of the past leads to exactly the kind of tyranny that the Athenians want to avoid. The imprisonment and persecution of citizens who are suspected to have been involved in

---

[248] Cf. Taylor ²1991: 82–3.   [249] Stahl 2003: 8. See also Kallet 2006.

conspiracies evoke Hippias' reign after the murder of his brother.[250] The parallel is underscored by the adjective 'harsh' ('χαλεπός'). At the beginning of his discussion of the tyrannicide, Thucydides says: 'Since the people understood through hearsay that the tyranny of Peisistratus and his sons had become harsh (χαλεπήν) in its last stage, and furthermore that it had been overthrown not by themselves and Harmodius but by the Lacedaemonians, they were in constant fear and held everything in suspicion.' (6.53.3). When Thucydides returns to the narrative about the year 415 BCE, he writes: 'Taking all this to heart and recalling what they knew about it from hearsay, the people of Athens were at this time harsh (χαλεπός) and suspicious of those who stood accused over the Mysteries, and they had the impression that all had been done for an oligarchic and tyrannical conspiracy.' (6.60.1). The repetition of 'harsh' ('χαλεπός') marks the fact that in their fear of tyranny, the Athenian people have themselves established a tyranny and thereby indicates the detrimental consequences that a deficient knowledge of the past can have.

The phrase 'oligarchic and tyrannical conspiracies' bolsters a further analogy.[251] Some scholars argue that the murder of Hipparchus and the expulsion of Hippias serve as a mirror for the persecution of Alcibiades.[252] In both cases, outstanding leaders are assaulted by the lower classes.[253] While it can be doubted that the description of Aristogeiton as 'citizen of the middle class' ('μέσος πολίτης') has a negative ring[254] and makes him a counterpart of the lower class citizens and non-citizens that accuse Alcibiades, it is difficult to deny that the fate of Hippias in some ways prefigures Alcibiades' career. Not only does the positive evaluation of Hippias' regime before the assassination of his brother parallel the important role that Thucydides ascribes to Alcibiades,[255] but it is also striking that Thucydides looks beyond the tyrannicide and reports that Hippias finally

---

[250] Cf. Pearson 1949; Momigliano 1971: 32; Connor 1977: 108; 1984: 179–80; Rood 1999: 180–1.
[251] See also Thuc. 6.15.4. Cf. Rawlings 1981: 110.
[252] See particularly Rawlings 1981: 101–12. See already Schadewaldt 1929: 84–94 and also Connor 1984: 178–9; Farrar 1988: 148; Thomas 1989: 243. Scholars have also argued for other parallels, not all of them convincing. Hunter 1973–4: 124, for example, sees a parallel between Harmodius' and Aristogeiton's conspiracy and Demosthenes' operation at Pylus. On the other hand, Stahl 2003: 6 argues against the parallels between 514 BCE and 415 BCE (see also Ridley 1981: 27; Tsakmakis 1995: 212–13). However, I do not think that Stahl's and Rawling's readings are mutually exclusive. They rather reinforce one another.
[253] Cf. Rawlings 1981: 101–2; 109–10.
[254] Cf. Tsakmakis 1995: 192. On Thucydides' presentation of Aristogeiton as a 'middling' man, see Wohl 2002: 7–8.
[255] In 6.15, Thucydides remarks that the persecution of Alcibiades ruined Athens, cf. Taylor ²1991: 84.

joined Darius and fought against Athens at Marathon. This establishes a strong parallel to Alcibiades who would join Athens' present opponent, Sparta.[256]

Thus, on the one hand, the digression on the tyrannicide serves to point out the detrimental consequences of the Athenians' misunderstanding of the past for their present politics. On the other hand, the digression establishes a foil that illuminates the present and the future, with the career of Hippias foreshadowing the fate of Alcibiades. Thucydides uses the very 'plu-past' that the Athenians fail to heed to enrich his account of the past so that the same story both demonstrates the detrimental consequences of historical ignorance and shows how to use the past.

The Plataean Debate offers a similar case.[257] As I have argued, the juxtaposition of the speeches by the Plataeans and Thebans reveals the bending and colouring to which the past is exposed in such diplomatic speeches. Yet, while the arguments may prove futile at the level of the action, the Persian Wars as evoked by them help the reader better assess the Peloponnesian War. Most strikingly, the glorious unified fight against Persia underscores the misery of the intra-Hellenic struggle: 'The battleground for Hellenic freedom had become an Hellenic butchering ground.'[258] The destruction of a *lieu de mémoire* as prominent as Plataea forcefully marks the abandonment of the pan-Hellenic unity that had saved the Greeks from the Persian conquest.

Moreover, the Thebans accuse the Plataeans of *attikismos* and thereby cause the readers to ponder whether Athens has taken over the role of Persia. Not only characters, but also the narratorial voice levels at the Athenians the reproach that they 'enslave' other Greek poleis.[259] Seen from this perspective, Thucydides' *History* spells out Athens' role as heiress to the Persian Empire, which is adumbrated at the end of Herodotus' *Histories*.[260]

At the same time, the inversion of Athens' role in Greece invites the readers to reflect on the speed of changes and the underlying forces. The juxtaposition of Persian and Peloponnesian Wars may prompt readers to ask questions about why power corrupts and what the role of fear in politics is. Thus, the references to the Persian Wars, albeit without success at the

---

[256] Cf. Momigliano 1971: 32; Connor 1984: 180; Vickers 1995: 199; Rood 1998a: 181.
[257] Cf. Chapter 8, section 8.2.2.
[258] Price 2001: 110. Cf. Orwin 1994: 70. The Plataeans sharply juxtapose past and present in 3.57.2; 3; 59.2. On the Persian Wars as a contrast to the Peloponnesian War in Thucydides, see also Rood 1999: 149–52.
[259] Cf. the Corinthians in 1.68.1; 68.3; 121.5; 122.2; 124.3; narratorial voice in 1.98.4. On this reproach, see Price 2001: 127–89.
[260] Cf. Cornford 1907: 201.

level of the action, evoke the Persian Wars as a contrast, as a model and as a starting point for the Peloponnesian War. Thucydides not only demonstrates the deficiencies and the final failure of using the past in oratory, he also subtly uses the past evoked by the characters to give his own account more depth. This way of using the 'plu-past' in the digression on the tyrannicide and the Plataean Debate to shed light on the past of his account illustrates the ways in which, in addition to anthropological constants, his narrative may prove useful for his readers. Thucydides' application of the exemplary mode of memory is very cautious and subtle – the *History* provides its readers not so much with patterns as with a manifold, complex foil that allows for a better understanding of any other time.

(b) Method

This does not exhaust the *History's* usefulness. Not only its content, but also its method is instructive. Lisa Kallet suggests that the *History* offers its readers an insight into Thucydides' workshop.[261] Yet, while in her strongest example, the digression on the tyrants, Thucydides shows how he has gained his superior knowledge,[262] otherwise he is rather at pains to conceal the procedures of his inquiry.[263] I would therefore prefer to argue that the *History* teaches not so much how to do history, but that instead Thucydides demonstrates the importance of his method in areas outside historiographical research. Striking echoes and similarities between Thucydides' methodological reflections and his narrative indicate that the *History's* standards of accuracy are also relevant in politics.[264]

In my discussion of the digression on the tyrannicide, I noted that the Athenians' investigations are reminiscent of the Thucydidean method. The Athenians' desire to 'examine the affair closely and find out' ('βασανίσαι[265] τὸ πρᾶγμα καὶ εὑρεῖν') and not 'to let anyone accused, however worthy he seemed, escape without trial (ἀνέλεγκτον διαφυγεῖν) on account of the informers' vileness' (6.53.2) echoes Thucydides' critcism of accounts that are ἀνεξέλεγκτα (1.21.1) and the preceding reflection in 1.20.1: 'Such, then, I found (ηὗρον) to be ancient history, although it was difficult to trust every piece of evidence. For men accept one another's accounts of past events, even if they are about their own countries, with a uniform lack of examination (ἀβασανίστως).'

---

[261] Cf. Kallet 2006.   [262] Cf. *ibid.*: 340–4.   [263] Cf. Morrison 2004: 96.
[264] Ober 1998: 94–104 makes a similar argument for the Mytilinean Debate.
[265] On the legal connotation of βασανίζειν see Hornblower 1987: 107; Tsakmakis 1998: 252 n. 47.

In section 8.1.2, I argued that the striking echoes draw attention to crucial differences between the Athenians and Thucydides. From the angle that I am taking here, the similarity of the activities in writing history and in doing politics is remarkable. Both writer and politician investigate and try to find the truth. The same similarity between historiography and politics is borne out in other passages. To give an example from the Sicilian Expedition, the Egestans promised to support the Athenians financially if they intervened on their behalf: 'The Athenians called an assembly and heard from the Egestans and their own envoys much that was attractive and untrue (ἐπαγωγὰ καὶ οὐκ ἀληθῆ), in particular, as for the money, that a great amount was available in the temples and the treasury. They then voted to send sixty ships to Sicily ...' (6.8.2).

Very pointedly, Thucydides fully unmasks the Egestans' plunder only later when the Athenians discover how their envoys had been tricked into believing that the Egestans had great sources of wealth at their hands (6.46).[266] The repeated references and the piecemeal disclosure give the deceit a prominent place in the narrative. In the quoted passage, 'attractive and untrue' ('ἐπαγωγὰ καὶ οὐκ ἀληθῆ') echo Thucydides' interest in truth and his critique of the *logographoi* whose accounts are 'more attractive for listening than with regard to truthfulness' ('ξυνέθεσαν ἐπὶ τὸ προσαγωγότερον τῇ ἀκροάσει ἢ ἀληθέστερον', 1.21.1). Had the Athenians applied the same critical accuracy to the news from Segesta that Thucydides follows in his reconstruction of the past, they might have been spared a big disaster.

Another even stronger echo of 1.21.1 can be found in the Melian Dialogue, where the Athenians start out with the following remark (5.85):

Since the speeches are not open to the public, clearly in order to avoid that, through a continuous presentation, the people would be taken in, for once hearing from us things that are appealing and hard to refute (ἐπαγωγὰ καὶ ἀνέλεγκτα) (for we understand that this is the aim of bringing us before a small group), make it even safer as you sit here: do not decide on every aspect in one speech but by responding immediately to what seems to be said unfavourably.

The parallel between προσαγωγόν and ἐπαγωγόν is reinforced by ἀνέλεγκτον, which echoes Thucydides' rejection of poetic and rhetorical accounts that are ἀνεξέλεγκτα (1.21.1). No matter how we evaluate the Athenians' point, it shows that the very criteria that define Thucydides' account are also relevant in the realm of politics.

The letter in which Nicias describes the misery of the army in Sicily to the Athenian assembly illustrates further similarities (7.8.2):

[266] Cf. Mader 1993; Kallet 2001: 27–31; 69–79.

Because he was afraid that the messengers would not report the facts, be it because of incompetence in speaking, or because they have a defective memory (μνήμης ἐλλιπεῖς γιγνόμενοι), or because they speak to please the crowd (πρὸς χάριν τι λέγοντες), he wrote a letter in the belief that this would be the best way for the Athenians to learn his own opinion, not obscured by the messenger, and to deliberate about the facts.

As Emily Greenwood notes, the juxtaposition of words and deeds recall Thuc. 1.22 and μνήμης ἐλλιπεῖς is reminiscent of the problems with memory that Thucydides is facing in reporting speeches.[267] More significantly, 'speaking to please the crowd' recalls the 'reports which for the most part have forfeited credibility over time by winning victories as patriotic fiction (μυθῶδες)' (1.21.1).[268] Also the letter itself evokes Thucydides' agenda (7.14.4):

I could send you a different and more pleasant (ἡδίω) message than this but certainly not a more useful one (χρησιμώτερά γε), if you need accurate knowledge (σαφῶς εἰδότας) of the situation here for your deliberation. While at the same time I know your nature – that you wish to hear what is most pleasant (ἥδιστα) but make accusations later, if the results are not consistent with it – I considered it safer to reveal the truth (τὸ ἀληθές).

Nicias strives to convey 'accurate knowledge' that is useful. Likewise, Thucydides hopes that his account will be useful to those 'who wish to look at the plain truth' (1.22.4). Both character and author contrast their truthful writings with oral presentations that are merely pleasant to hear.[269] The echoes reveal that the critical accuracy with which Thucydides reconstructs the past also matters in the assessment of the present in politics. Perhaps, this interpretation can be further supported by John Moles' reading of 1.22.4. Moles notes that ὅσοι δὲ βουλήσονται evokes the ὁ βουλόμενος formula in Athenian inscriptions and thereby invokes the authority, permanence and the 'open-access' quality of inscriptions.[270] From the angle that I am taking here, a further connotation seems possible. In applying a formula of decrees to the reception of his own work, Thucydides may also hint at its political relevance.

---

[267] Greenwood 2006: 78.   [268] Cf. Flory's analysis of μυθῶδες (1990).
[269] However, the distinctions are not that sharp and the parallel between letter and *History* is not free of ambiguity. Greenwood 2006: 78 rightly points out that Thucydides presents the letter as it is being read out in the assembly and that the messengers report additional words from Nicias (7.10). See also Morrison 2004: 102–3. Further aspects deserve attention, for example the correspondences between Nicias' letter with his speech against the Sicilian Expedition, cf. Greenwood 2006: 79–80. Zadorojnyi 1998 also argues that the letter includes a marked Homeric echo through which Nicias stylizes himself as Agamemnon.
[270] Moles 1999: 2 and 6.

(c) Reading experience

There is yet a further aspect in which the *History* can claim to be useful. As we have seen, Thucydides avoids *prolepseis* and his reticence with authorial interventions, the numerous vignettes and devices of 'sideshadowing' give the readers the feeling of witnessing events directly. Thus, the very act of reading challenges the reader to assess the current situation and to speculate about the future. In this way, reading the *History* becomes an exercise in an essential task of everyday as well as political life. James Morrison suggested that 'in putting the reader in a position analogous to that of historian and statesman, in forcing the reader to make connections and juxtapose arguments, the *History* lives as an interactive text.'[271] This reading of the *History* ties in nicely with my narratological approach that emphasizes the structural analogy between the experience of reading and the experiences at the level of the action. As I argue elsewhere, reading duplicates the temporal structure of real life experiences in the frame of the fictional 'as-if'.[272]

However, one point needs clarification. The reader's labours not only parallel, as Morrison claims, Thucydides' labours, but in some respects they are inverse. Chapter 1.22.1–3 is among the most discussed passages in Greek literature and this is not the place to enter into any of the numerous controversies.[273] What is important for my argument is that Thucydides not only juxtaposes speeches with deeds, but that he also clearly distinguishes between the ways of reconstructing them. While he can claim that his account of the deeds is based on what he or his informants have witnessed, the speeches are given in accordance with 'what was especially required in the situation' ('τῶν αἰεὶ παρόντων τὰ δέοντα', 1.22.1).[274] Thus, the speeches are made to fit the requirements of the context. Thucydides reconstructs the speeches on the basis of the deeds that he knows. This is not only an assertion, but seems actually to be the way in which Thucydides composed some speeches, as Virginia Hunter's

---

[271] Morrison 1999 (quotation from p. 126). In a related paper (2000), Morrison reads the Melian episode as a test case where the readers can apply the insights they have gained in reading Books 1 to 4. See also Connor 1984, who argues that the *History* requires a 'participatory' style of reading; Arnold 1992, who focuses on the reception of the speeches; and, more recently, Yunis 2003: 198–204; Kallet 2006: 336.

[272] Cf. Grethlein 2006a: 192–203.

[273] I follow the detailed and lucid discussion of the 'Redensatz' by Egermann 1972, which unfortunately has been widely ignored in Anglo-American scholarship. See also Erbse 1989: 131–4. For further literature, see Orwin 1994: 207–12; Greenwood 2006: 63–7.

[274] On τὰ δέοντα, see the reflections of Moles 2001: 207–9. Moles 1993: 105 makes the fascinating if not wholly convincing suggestion that τὰ αἰεὶ παρόντα means 'the always present things'. This would establish an interesting ring with 'a possession for all time' ('κτῆμά τε ἐς αἰεί', 1.22.4).

exemplary discussion of 7.34–41 suggests.[275] The readers' situation is inverse. The speeches of the characters form the basis on which the readers, parallel to the characters, are challenged to make guesses about what is going to happen. The different temporal directions, retrospective for the historians, prospective for characters and readers, lead to an inverse relation of speeches and deeds.

Despite this inversion, the activities of the historian on the one hand and the characters and the readers on the other are similar.[276] This is borne out by Thucydides' evaluation of Themistocles (1.138.3):

Through his native intelligence and without preparing or supplementing it by study, he was with the briefest deliberation the most effective in decisions about immediate situations and the best at conjecturing what would happen farthest into the future; whatever he was engaged in he was capable of explaining, over matters in which he had no experience he was not incapacitated from judging adequately. In particular he foresaw what better or worse possibilities were still concealed in the future. To sum up, this man, by natural ability, with rapid deliberation, was certainly supreme in his immediate grasp of what was necessary (αὐτοσχεδιάζειν τὰ δέοντα).

Themistocles' foresight is paralleled by Pericles who considers himself 'a man inferior to no one in judging what is necessary (γνῶναί τε τὰ δέοντα) and in explaining it' (2.60.5). Both statesmen excel in figuring out and communicating their insights in speeches; Thucydides, on the other hand, bases the reconstruction of his speeches on τὰ δέοντα given by the deeds.[277] The use of τὰ δέοντα for assessing the past and the future indicates that, despite the inverse relation to speeches and deeds, the historian, the characters and the readers draw on the same method of reasoning and conjecturing.[278]

To sum up, Thucydides does not cancel out contingency of chance, but nonetheless his *History* can claim to be useful against it at different levels. The readers are provided with insights into constants of human life such as fear and the dynamics of power and also receive a foil against which the present can be assessed. Moreover, Thucydides indicates that his standards of accuracy are relevant for both reconstructing the past and assessing the

---

[275] Hunter 1973: 85–94.
[276] Staley 2002 points out striking similarities between the reconstruction of the past by historians and the assessment of the future in the form of scenarios.
[277] On the parallels established by τὰ δέοντα, see also Moles 2001: 207–8. Moles 2001: 215 points out further parallels between 1.22 and 1.138.3.
[278] The parallels between Thucydides and Pericles have been widely noticed. See e.g. Edmunds 1975: 212–14; Darbo-Peschanski 1987: 138–40; Farrar 1988: 187–9; Rood 1998a: 292; Crane 1998: 38–61.

present and future. Finally, the very reading of the *History* constitutes an exercise in the art of conjecturing and reasoning that forms an important aspect of life in general and politics in particular. Owing to the open form of the narrative and yet in the safe frame of the 'as-if', the readers are challenged to consider what is going to happen next on the basis of the characters' perspectives.

8.4. CONCLUSION

Modern scholarship makes Thucydides look as if he is suffering from a multiple personality disorder. Many historians tend to see in him an old colleague, or at least a kindred spirit. They trust his account, rely on it for their own reconstructions of Greek history and also find in his methodological rigour the foundation of their own works. If we leave the History department and go next door to Political Science, we encounter a very different Thucydides, one who mercilessly analyzes the mechanisms of power politics. His disregard for ethical issues makes him a hard-boiled realist. Yet another Thucydides is read in the Greek original and can be found in Classics departments. This Thucydides is a rather sly narrator who has taken extensive classes on prose composition with Homer and Herodotus. Thanks to Simon Hornblower and others, the rather dry narrative, which put generations of students to sleep, has turned out to be an artful and elaborate construction.

While 'Thucydides *historicus*' and 'Thucydides *politicus*' stand at the beginning of venerable traditions and while 'Thucydides *narrans*' is viewed against the backdrop of his predecessors, I have tried to assess Thucydides afresh by locating him in the contemporaneous field of memory. On the one hand, the need to assert the new genre of historiography comes to the fore in Thucydides' efforts to set his approach off against other accounts of the past. In methodological reflections that are far more pronounced than what we find in Herodotus, Thucydides polemicizes against poets as well as orators. The medium of writing, the focus on the recent past and the independence of any particular polis that already distinguish Herodotus from the non-historiographic genres of memory are aggressively pointed out as marking the *History*'s superiority. The meta-historical significance of embedded speeches that I have argued for in Herodotus is reinforced by pointed echoes of Thucydides' own methodological reflections.

On the other hand, the idea of history that underlies the *History* shares much common ground with non-historiographic memory. Contingency of chance figures prominently in the account of the Peloponnesian War.

Whereas Herodotus uses a dense net of anachronies reminiscent of the epics to emphasize the rule of chance at the level of the action and simultaneously overcome it for his readers, Thucydides by and large avoids *prolepseis* and, through various devices of 'sideshadowing', makes his readers experience the plot from the perspective of the characters, privileged only through *analepseis* and the insight into various perspectives. Nor is the insecurity of human life overcome through recurring patterns.

Contingency of chance not only appears more forceful in Thucydides than in Herodotus, but it is not distanced any more. In Herodotus, contingency of chance that the epic and tragedy banish into 'heroic vagueness' serves as a template for the recent past, albeit mostly the past of the barbarian 'other'. Thucydides, on the other hand, elucidates the fragility of human life in the even more recent past of Greece itself. The tragedy of Athens to which Herodotus carefully alludes is Thucydides' major theme. Whilst Thucydides may not distance contingency of chance nor overcome it through *prolepseis* and patterns, nonetheless his claim to usefulness implies that he at least equips his readers to cope with it: his account provides precious insights into the *conditio humana*, illustrates methodological rigour that is crucial also in politics and offers an exercise in how to assess the future.

The exemplary use of the past that Thucydides propagates both aligns his work with, and sets it off from, other media of memory. Like poets and orators, Thucydides directly juxtaposes past and present; however, as in Herodotus, the juxtaposition does not help to glorify the present or legitimize claims, but rather sheds critical light on the present. This pragmatic dimension of the *History* is a far cry from the ideal of objectivity that positivist historians pursue.

CHAPTER 9

Epilogue: Historical fevers, ancient and modern

The cover of Stanley Lombardo's translation of the *Iliad* shows soldiers in full gear leaving a boat and heading towards a clouded beach where machine guns and a tank await them (Figure 1).[1] The landing of the allies in Normandy at the end of World War II as cover illustration nicely visualizes the achievements of the translation which Richard Martin, on the other side of the cover, hails with the following words: 'The narrator's voice sounds contemporary without losing authority or resonance, while his heroes from an archaic time speak a racy, hard-bitten idiom completely recognizable to our own Iron Age.' At first glance, the implicit juxtaposition of the Trojan War with World War II may remind us of the use of the Trojan War as a foil for current or recent wars that we have encountered time and again in the course of this study: Mimnermus stylizes a Smyrnean hero as Diomedes *redivivus*, Simonides juxtaposes the Greeks who fought at Plataea with Achilles, in the *Persae* the battle of Salamis is cast in an epic register and Herodotus and Thucydides evoke the siege of Troy to shed light on the Persian and the Peloponnesian Wars.

And yet there is a crucial difference. The ancient juxtapositions of the Trojan War with more recent wars are straightforward and ignore the differences that separate the times. Mimnermus portrays the Smyrnean soldier as a heroic *promachos* and even Thucydides, who argues that the Peloponnesian War superseded all earlier wars in its size, builds his reconstruction of the Trojan War on straight conclusions drawn from the Peloponnesian War, assuming that the dynamics of power and the logic of military expeditions have not changed. The effect of the cover of Lombardo's translation, on the other hand, relies on the awareness of the temporal gap between World War II and the siege of Troy. The prospective readers are struck by the discrepancy between their notion of heroic combat and the '*Stahlgewitter*' of twentieth-century warfare

[1] Lombardo 1997.

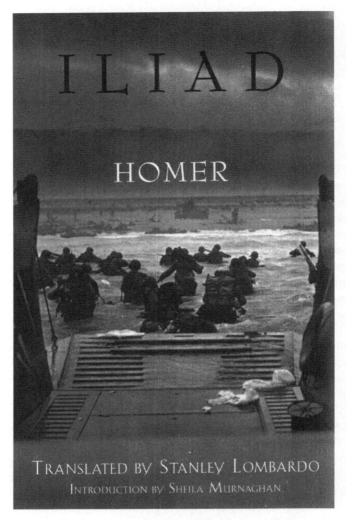

Figure 1. Cover of Stanley Lombardo's *Iliad* translation. *Homer: Iliad*, translated by Stanley Lombardo. © 1997 by Hackett Publishing Company, Inc. Reprinted by permission of Hackett Publishing Company, Inc. All rights reserved.

that the photograph conveys. The illustration arouses attention through an alienation effect and suggests that the translation under the cover removes the dust from the *Iliad* and, more than classicistic translations, renders the alien world of ancient epic accessible and meaningful to a modern audience.

Historical fevers, ancient and modern

The deliberate clash between heroic and twentieth-century warfare illustrates Reinhart Koselleck's thesis that around 1800 CE the topos 'historia magistra vitae', so popular in Antiquity and the Middle Ages, lost much of its appeal.[2] The increasing awareness of the uniqueness of historical events and epochs undermined the utility of the direct juxtaposition of different times that is at the core of exempla. Koselleck's thesis may be a bit schematic. The exemplary mode of memory has not completely vanished and while professional historians are sceptical of comparisons of different events that neglect the specific temporal and cultural circumstances, it is still tempting to derive conclusions about the present from parallels in the past.[3] On the other hand, this study has shown that the use of exempla in the fifth century BCE is quite complex. Both Herodotus and Thucydides challenge the legitimizing use of exempla and in Herodotus a general changeability further undermines the exemplary mode of memory.[4] Nonetheless, whereas in classical Greece the exemplary view of the past looms large in a wide range of commemorative genres, including the first historians who replace the goals of glorification and legitimization with a rather critical thrust, the modern emphasis on the uniqueness of epochs has made it harder to juxtapose directly past with present events.

In ancient Greece, the past is far less of a foreign country than it is in the modern world.[5] The heroic past may be larger than life, but the differences from the present are quantitative rather than qualitative and the very recent past can be cast in a heroic register. The modern shift in the perception of the past can be further illustrated by artistic representations. In his introduction to *Futures Past*, Koselleck describes Albrecht Altdorfer's painting '*Die Perserschlacht*' (Figure 2) and the reaction of Friedrich Schlegel to it.[6] The portrayal of the battle at Issos (333 BCE) shows much love for details; on the flags we even find the numbers of the troops as given by Curtius Rufus. Nonetheless, as Schlegel notes three hundred years later, the Persians look more or less like the Turks

---

[2] Koselleck 1985: 21–38. See also Lübbe 1977: 269–74; Lowenthal 1985: 364–5.
[3] For example, in his study of memory in modern Calymnus (Greece), Sutton 1998: 119–48 emphasizes the prominence of analogies. An interesting case mentioned by Crane 1998 reveals that the exemplary mode of memory can still be found in modern academia: at the beginning of World War I, a reading of Thucydides' Melian Dialogue was staged at the University of Toronto, with the Athenians as Germans, the British as Spartans and the Belgians as Melians.
[4] I elaborate on the intricacies of exempla in Herodotus and Thucydides in Grethlein (forthcoming a).
[5] 'The past is a foreign country' stems from the beginning of Hartley's *The Go-Between* (1953) and is used as a title by Lowenthal 1985.
[6] Koselleck 1985: 3–5.

284   *Epilogue*

Figure 2. Albrecht Altdorfer, *Battle of Issos*. Bayerische Staatsgemäldesammlungen – Alte Pinakothek.

who besieged Vienna in the very year when the painting was made, 1529 CE. While Altdorfer did not distinguish between warfare in Antiquity and the sixteenth century, but simply presented the ancient battle in a contemporary mould, Schlegel is aware of the gap between the times and their specific features. The anachronism in Altdorfer's painting is as glaring for us as it was for Schlegel.[7]

A similar difference can be noticed between representations of the past in ancient Greece and the Modern Age. Scholars have noted that presentations of myths in the fifth century BCE mirrored the more recent past.[8] The paintings of the Centauromachy, the Amazonomachy and Theseus' encounter with Minos on the Athenian Theseion offered a dense net of analogies with the Persian Wars. For example, the parallel between fighting the Amazons and the Persians, both exponents of transgression and hubris, is reinforced by an Amazon named Dolope, who not only evokes Cimon's defeat of the Dolopian pirates, but also recalls the medism of the Dolopes in 480 BCE.[9] Many further cases could be adduced in which, parallel to the literary texts discussed in this study, artistic presentations of myths served as mirrors for the recent past. More instructive for my argument though is the observation that Greek artists cast archaic and recent events in the same register.[10] Therefore, if no names are ascribed, it is often hard to decide whether the events represented are mythical or contemporary, as modern scholarly debates show. For instance, most archaeologists assume that the friezes on the Athena–Nike temple on the Acropolis depict recent battles of Greeks versus Persians and Athenians against Greeks.[11] Some scholars, however, advocate the view that scenes from the Trojan War are represented.[12] Or, to give an example from vase-painting, a scene on a cup of the Bryguspainter in Oxford has been interpreted as the theft of the Palladium by Odysseus and Diomedes as well as the Greek raid on the Persian camp at Plataea (Figure 3).[13] While medieval artists cast the past in a

---

[7] On the notion of anachronism, see Grethlein 2009a. See also Tonkin 1992: 10 on the presentation of the past in a contemporary register in the Middle Ages.

[8] See, for example, Castriota 1992, who examines the Cimonian monuments, the Cnidian Lesche, the Stoa Poikile and the Parthenon. The interpretation of the analogies is debated though; while for instance Francis 1990 argues for allusions to specific events, other scholars including Hölscher 1998 are more careful and see the analogies at a more abstract level, referring to dichotomies such as hubris–civilisation.

[9] Cf. Castriota 1992: 44. For the analogies between the paintings of the Theseion and the Persian Wars, see also Woodford 1974; Francis 1990: 49–50.

[10] Cf. Boardman 2002: 157–82. See also Lissarrague 1984; Giuliani 2003: 283–4, who argues that the dichotomy 'myth – everyday life', so dear to traditional scholarship, fails to do justice to many vase paintings; *ibid.* (forthcoming). On the representation of historical events in general, see Hölscher 1973.

[11] Cf. Hölscher 1973: 91–8; Stewart 1985.

[12] Cf. Felten 1984: 123–4 and Knell 1990: 148. On the difficulties of identifying the scenes of temple friezes, see Robertson 1975: 349; Burn 1989: 62; 69.

[13] Beazley ²1963: 399: Oxford, Ashm. Mus. 1911.615 from Cervetri augmented by frg. New York, Metr. Mus. of Art 1973, 175.2. Both interpretations are suggested by Herford 1914. While Beazley ²1963: 31 is

Figure 3. Detail of Brygos Cup (AN1911.615). Ashmolean Museum, University of Oxford.

contemporary mould, ancient artists rather mythicize the recent past or at least present recent and archaic events in the same register. Neither, however, heeds the individuality of epochs that is at the core of modern historical thinking.

The thesis that in ancient Greece the past was less of a foreign country than in the modern western civilization is supported by yet another observation. As Ortwin Dally points out in a forthcoming study, there are no signs of architectural restoration programmes before the Hellenistic Age.[14] This is not due to a lack of interest in the past – as we have seen the Greeks were very much under the spell of their past – but the idea of restoration presupposes the notion that the past is different from the present in specific ways and therefore worth preserving. By the same token, in classical Greece special items were collected in temples, but

---

inclined to favour the mythical interpretation, other scholars have suggested that yet another contemporary scene is depicted, the rise of the spirits of two warriors of Marathon that are going to protect Greece against the Persians, cf. Barrett and Vickers 1978: 17–18; Kron 1997: 65–6.

[14] See the chapter 'Vorstufen der "Denkmalpflege"' in Dally (forthcoming). On restoration in ancient Greece, see also Buchert 2000.

there are no museums in our sense.[15] The discrepancy between past and present that leads to restoration programmes and 'musealization' in the Modern Age was felt less strongly and did not therefore impede the direct juxtaposition of the past with the present.

Christian Meier notes that, just like Koselleck's *Sattelzeit*, the fifth century BCE was a time of change and saw the coinage of many new terms to signify the innovations. Nevertheless the notions of development and change had little prominence in ancient Greece: 'It is true that other processes were observed – more broadly based processes such as the growth of knowledge, skills, and material resources, or the increase in the size and power of the poleis – but these observations seem to have been largely peripheral, and there is no term to designate the processes as such.'[16] Meier's thesis ties in nicely with my argument, as a stronger awareness of change would have led to an emphasis on the uniqueness of epochs and would thereby have challenged the exemplary mode of memory. However, my explanation deviates from his. According to Meier, it was the 'politicization' that impeded the 'temporalization': 'Politicization was the central tendency of change in the ancient world, and this precluded temporalization ... It follows that in the ancient world men were conscious above all of action and human ability rather than of change, and this is reflected in the whole of their culture.'[17] I do not see how exactly the emphasis on action should have prevented the Greeks from paying more attention to temporal processes, in particular since, as Meier himself acknowledges, 'politicization' and 'temporalization' are linked with one another in the *Sattelzeit*. I prefer to think that the relative insignificance of change and development is due to the same reason as the importance of exempla, namely the strong perception of contingency of chance, which marks a crucial difference between ancient and modern ideas of history.

As I have tried to demonstrate, there is not a monolithic idea of history in classical Greece, but, depending on the socio-cultural context and

---

[15] See, for example, the list of votives in the Lindian temple chronicle, cf. Higbie 2003: 163–86. On the preservation of old goods in temples, see Pritchett 1979: 240–8; Boardman 2002: 8 (cf. 27). For further reflections, see Grethlein 2008b: 45–6. While museums are emblematic of memory in the modern western world, they can also be found in other cultures; for African museums that predate the colonization, see Mbunwe-Samba 1989: 116.

[16] Meier 1990: 181. See also Higbie 2003: 206–7: 'Greeks seem to have believed in a much greater continuity between their past and present than we understand there to have been. Unless there was evidence or a reason to suggest otherwise, they understood that their lives were much as their ancestors had been, which enabled them to imagine current customs, such as religious practices, retrojected into the past.'

[17] Meier 1990: 185–6.

narrative forms, the past is remembered in various ways – Clio not only likes cosmetics, she also has many faces. Nonetheless, all the commemorative genres analyzed in this study gravitate around the tension between the strongly felt contingency of chance and the construction of continuities and regularities. The perilous force of chance makes it hard to construct linear developments. Where humans are subject to *tyche* or the will of the gods, who are unpredictable and, unlike the god of the Judeo-Christian tradition, do not pursue a plan in history, there is little ground for developments.[18] Continual ruptures challenge not only long-term processes, but also actions and identities. Traditions and exempla answer the destabilizing force of chance, the former through the creation of continuities, the latter through the construction of regularities.

On the other hand, around 1800 CE the notion of development becomes more and more prominent, first in the idea of progress, then in organic models of development.[19] As Koselleck shows, the horizon of expectations supersedes the space of experiences and while the future is viewed as an open space, the past appears as a process that leads to the present.[20] This shift is attested by the new singular terms history/ *Geschichte/histoire/storia*, which denote not only the representation of the past but also the past as a single process with a dynamic of its own.[21] Besides depriving chance of its power, the notion of development also challenges traditions and exempla, as its trajectory goes against linear continuity and regularities.

Needless to say, the idea of development was not invented around 1800 CE. There are '*Kulturentstehungslehren*' in the fifth century BCE[22] and, although Thucydides emphasizes the transhistorical 'human nature' ('τὸ ἀνθρώπινον'), he notes crucial changes over time in his 'archaeology'. By the same token, the exemplary and traditional modes of memory

---

[18] The relevance of the Judeo-Christian view of history for the modern notion of history is emphasized in Löwith's classical study (1949). More recently, see Hardtwig 1991 on the religious aspects of Historicism.

[19] The rise of the modern notion of history, particularly the relation between late Enlightenment historiography and Historicism, is the subject of a fierce debate. For a brief survey with further literature, see Grethlein 2006a: 100–1. Of course, modern historical thinking is not limited to the notion of development, but is rather multi-faceted. Focusing on the construction of the dichotomy 'antiquity–modernity' in the eighteenth and nineteenth centuries CE, Vlassopoulos (forthcoming) distinguishes between alterity, proximity, polarity and immanency as models of linking the past to the present. Nonetheless, it is safe to claim that the idea of development that agrees with Vlassopoulos' category of alterity is a particularly distinct and prominent feature of historical thinking in the Modern Age.

[20] Koselleck 1985: 3–69. [21] Koselleck 1975: 647–58.

[22] See, for example, Edelstein 1967; Müller 1968; Dodds 1973; Dihle 1988; Meier 1990: 186–221; Utzinger 2003: 97–229.

are still in use in our world. And yet, the templates of exempla and traditions were far more prominent in classical Greece, whereas the idea of development did not dominate memory before 1800 CE. The catastrophes of the twentieth century CE have shaken belief in progress, the end of history has been announced and academic historiography, after an extended flirtation with sociology, has come under the sway of anthropology, but nonetheless the concept of development is still our master narrative for the past.[23] Significantly, in ancient Greek, on the other hand, there is no equivalent for our word 'history' in the singular, which was only created when the diversity of *res gestae* was seen as a development with its own dynamic.

The difference can be traced back to different perceptions of contingency. It is widely assumed that contingency gained relevance only in the modern world, whereas in antiquity it was marginal, if known at all.[24] This belief rests not only on a very narrow selection of ancient texts, mostly Aristotle, but also relies on a mistaken concept of contingency. As I pointed out in the introduction, contingency as '*quod est nec impossibile nec necessarium*' has two sides, freedom and chance. If we follow this definition of contingency and also take into account the literary genres discussed in this study, then it becomes obvious that contingency was not nonexistent in Antiquity, but that it was perceived differently than in the Modern Age.[25] The Greeks foregrounded the destabilizing force of contingency of chance. On the other hand, in the wake of the Modern Age, where the future opens as a realm of opportunities, contingency is primarily experienced as the freedom of action. While the focus on chance needs to be counterbalanced by continuity and regularity, the freedom of action makes history appear as a development and hence challenges traditions and exempla.

Let me return to the starting point of this study: not only our age, but also classical Greece was obsessed with the past. However, the reflections of this epilogue feed the suspicion that the grip of the past was different. The Greeks' obsession with their past and the modern historical fever rely on different ways of coping with the temporality of human life. What about the grip of the present on the past that has come to the fore as a

---

[23] Oexle 1996 argues convincingly that our historical thinking still shares the major assumptions of Historicism. See also Steenblock 1991. Even approaches that question the idea of development as forcefully as Foucault's work have some common ground with Historicism, cf. Fulda 2000.

[24] See, for example, von Graevenitz and Marquard 1998b: XII; Wetz 1998: 82. For a fuller argument against this view, see Grethlein 2006a: 102–4.

[25] Makropoulos 1997 shows that the perception of contingency is a socio-cultural construction.

significant feature of memory in non-historiographic genres as well as in the works by Herodotus and Thucydides? Positivist historians may see here a crucial difference from their own works, which aim at an objective representation of the past. And indeed, modern scholarly studies generally abstain from using the past to legitimize present claims and do not even claim to provide lessons from the past. That being said, the present inscribes itself into each reconstruction of the past, even, or particularly, those which lay claim to objectivity. To use a spatial metaphor, the view of a mountain depends on the vantage-point of the spectator.[26] This study has not only taken its cue from the contemporary historical fever, but the very assumption that different cultures have different ideas of history is indebted to a Historicist notion of history. It would have made little sense to the Greeks and, alas, it will be no 'possession for all time', and yet, I hope that the view has made the effort worthwhile.

---

[26] The relevance of the vantage point from which the past is reconstructed is already emphasized by Chladenius 1742: 189. For a classical reflection on this, see Collingwood 1965: 53–5; for the metaphor of the mountain, see e.g. Carr 1961: 30–1; Demandt 1978: 220–2; Shrimpton 1997: 6.

Appendix: Lengthy historical narratives in Tyrtaeus and Mimnermus?

Ewen Bowie's influential articles have established the thesis that there were elegies with lengthy historical narratives.[1] In this note, I review the evidence for his two main cases, Tyrtaeus' *Eunomia* and Mimnermus' *Smyrneis*. Many scholars believe that in the *Eunomia* Tyrtaeus evoked the past, especially the first Messenian War, as a foil to the present.[2] The *Eunomia*, it is assumed, contained a lengthy part dealing with the earlier subjection of the Messenians that was meant to encourage the Spartans in the current conflict, which is generally identified as the second Messenian War.[3] This assumption is, I believe, based on a misreading of fr. 2 W^2 and on the questionable assignment of further fragments to the *Eunomia*.[4]

Besides the famous account of procedures in the assembly which Plut. *Lyc.* 6 and Diodorus 7.12.6 give in slightly different form (fr. 4 W^2),[5] only *P. Oxy.* 2824, partly overlapping with a quotation in Strabo 8.4.10 p. 362, can be safely attributed to the *Eunomia* poem (fr. 2 W^2).[6] The assignment of fr. 5, 6 and 7 W^2, on the other hand, relies solely on the assumption that the *Eunomia* dealt with the capture of Messene. Let us take a closer look at fr. 2 W^2 to see if this assumption is justified:

---

[1] Bowie 1986; 2001.
[2] See Bowra 1938a: 44–5; Dover 1964: 193; Walter 1993: 166–9; Meier 1998: 243–72.
[3] However, the attestations of the Messenian Wars are late and Luraghi 2002: 239 with n. 33 challenges their historicity. For a more traditional view on the Messenian Wars, see Parker 1991; 1993; Cartledge 2002²: 109–11. For a reading of Tyrtaeus' poems against the background of the Messenian Wars, see Tarditi 1983.
[4] See the reconstruction by Walter 1993: 166–9 and Meier 1998: 270–1, who assume that fr. 2, 4, 5, 6 and 7 W^2 all belong to the *Eunomia*. Bowie 1986: 30 is inclined to attribute fr. 5–7 W^2 to the *Eunomia*; in 2001: 46–7, however, he is more careful about fr. 5 W^2 at least.
[5] The *communis opinio* takes fr. 4 W^2 as a reference to the Great Rhetra. Recently, this has been contested by van Wees 1999 who argues that the *Eunomia* antedates the Great Rhetra. For my argument, this question can be left aside. For further literature, see the list given by van Wees 1999: 1 n. 1.
[6] The attribution of fr. 4 W^2 to the *Eunomia* has been questioned by Meyer 1892: 229 n. 1 and von Blumenthal 1948: 1947. Indeed, neither Plutarch nor Diodorus states that their quotes come from the *Eunomia*, but, given the topic of their quotes, the constitution of Sparta, the *communis opinio* rightly assigns the fragment to the *Eunomia*, see e.g. Steinmetz 1969: 63; Podlecki 1984: 103.

```
         ]...υι.[
    ]..ε θεοπρο[π
         ]..φ..ενακ[
    ]. μαντειασαν[
         ]τειδεταθή.[
    ]πάντ' εἶδεν.[
         ἄ]νδρας ἀνιστ[αμεν
    ]ι[.]ηγαλα[
         ]..[...]θεοῖσί φί[λ
    ]ω πειθώμεθα κ[
         ]αν ἐγγύτεροι γέν[εος·
    αὐτὸς γὰρ Κρονίωνˏ καλλιστεφάνου ˏπόσις ῞Ηρης
    Ζεὺς Ἡρακλείδαιςˏ ἄστυ δέδωκε τόˏδε,
    οἷσιν ἅμα προλιπˏόντες Ἐρινεὸν ˏἠνεμόεντα
    εὐρεῖαν Πέλοπˏοιˏ ˏνῆσον ἀφικόˏμˏεθα
         ]γλαυκώπ[ι]δος[
```

Verses 12–15 are the first reference to the Dorian migration, be it historical or not: 'For the son of Cronus himself and husband of fair-crowned Hera,/ Zeus, has given this town to the descendants of Heracles,/ with whom we left windy Erineus/ and came to the wide island of Pelops.' It has been argued that the town mentioned in line 12 is Messene, and that Tyrtaeus makes it a gift from Zeus to back up Spartan claims.[7] However, no matter whether we follow the reading of the papyrus or Strabo's text,[8] 'this town' is very unlikely to refer to Messene. According to fr. 5 W², Messene was taken by Theopompus only two generations earlier;[9] the town in fr. 2 W², on the other hand, was given to the Heraclidae when they first invaded the Peloponnese. 'This town' therefore seems to refer to Sparta.

Moreover, the verses are not so much about the foundation of Sparta in general, but Tyrtaeus remarks more specifically that Sparta was given to the Heraclidae who are carefully distinguished from the 'we' signifying the Spartan people. Thus, Zeus' gift is invoked not to establish a claim to Sparta, but to underscore the authority of the royal families, which traced their lines back to the sons of Heracles. This ties in well with a tentative restoration of the preceding verses: In line 9, θεοῖσι φί[λ reminds us of the characterization of Theopompus as θεοῖσι φίλος in fr. 5 W² 1; in 10, the

---

[7] Cf. Steinmetz 1969: 61–2; Meier 1998: 257.
[8] For fr. 2 W² 13 Strabo has: Ζεὺς Ἡρακλείδαις τήνδε δέδωκε πόλιν. *P. Oxy.* 2824 reads:]ἄστυ δέδωκε το [. While Gentili and Prato (1979/²2002) follow Strabo's text, West favours the papyrus.
[9] However, Schwartz 1899: 429 suggests that 'fathers of our fathers' refers to ancestors in general. See also Luraghi 2003: 110–11. Even if this is right, Theopompus is later than the Heraclidae.

Lengthy narratives in Tyrtaeus and Mimnermus? 293

papyrus reads πειθώμεθα,[10] in the following line we can decipher ἐγγύτεροι γέν[εος. The most plausible reconstruction is that an exhortation to follow the kings is explained by their closeness to the gods, which is then illustrated by the fact that Zeus gave them the city of Sparta.[11]

This reading of fr. 2 W² goes well with fr. 4 W² in which the right of the kings to lead the assembly is emphasized. A further link between the two fragments is established by the mention of oracles in fr. 2 W² (θεοπρο[π, 2; μαντειασαν[, 4) that may well hark back to or anticipate the oracle in fr. 4 W².[12] Thus, the two fragments that can be safely attributed to the *Eunomia* deal with constitutional issues, particularly the position of the kings, which is reinforced by a reference to the foundation of Sparta. It cannot of course be ruled out that the poem also dealt with the Messenians, but there is nothing to suggest this.[13] Therefore the attribution of fr. 5, 6 and 7 W² to the *Eunomia*, which is based merely on the assumption that the poem dealt with the Messenian War, is untenable.[14]

The quotation of fr. 5 W² may even indicate that it belongs to a different poem. Immediately before Strabo introduces fr. 2 W² 12–15 with the words 'in the elegy which they entitle *Eunomia*', he evidently refers to fr. 5 W² in which Tyrtaeus mentions the battles of his fathers' fathers: 'Tyrtaeus says in his poems that the first conquest of them took place at the time of the fathers' fathers.' It would be odd if Strabo, giving two quotes from the same poem in one passage, first referred to ποιήματα in general and then, for the second quote, named the poem. We cannot press the case too hard, as we do

---

[10] However, a cautionary note may be called for here: In the *editio princeps*, Turner cannot decipher the fourth letter and justifies his choice of πειθώμεθα instead of πειρώμεθα with lines 11–12.

[11] The quotation in Strabo 8.4.10 p. 363 was interpreted along these lines by Jacoby 1918: 285 and Andrews 1938: 96–7 already before *P. Oxy.* 2824 was published by Turner 1971. Now, this interpretation can be bolstered by the preceding lines. See also Bowra 1938a: 44–5; Tarditi 1983: 10–11. In 1986: 30–1, Bowie deems it possible that πειθώμεθα belongs to a speech; in 2001: 46–7, however, he is sceptical.

[12] Cf. van Wees 1999: 6.

[13] The only vague hint that the war against the Messenians may have featured somewhere in the *Eunomia* could be seen in Arist. *Pol.* 7, 1306b37–1307a2, where he adduces Tyrtaeus' *Eunomia* as evidence that *staseis* easily arise in wars and adds: 'For some, pressed hard by the war, deemed it worthy to redistribute the land' ('θλιβόμενοι γάρ τινες διὰ τὸν πόλεμον ἠξίουν ἀνάδαστον ποιεῖν τὴν χώραν', 1307a1–2). Yet, it is unclear whether this comment is based on a reading of Tyrtaeus or whether Aristotle merely links the *Eunomia* to the tradition on Tyrtaeus. Even if we assume that it is a reliable reference to Tyrtaeus (and I strongly doubt it), this would not suffice to prove that the *Eunomia* contained a description of the Messenian War. Cf. van Wees 1999: 2: 'All we can safely say is that *Eunomia* must have contained at least one allusion to demands for the redistribution of land.'

[14] Luraghi 2003: 111–12 even doubts that fr. 6 and 7 W² describe the fate of the Messenians. However, given the introductory statement of Pausanias, his scepticism seems unnecessary. See van Wees 2003: 35 n. 6. In 2002: 235, Luraghi notes that the state which is described in fr. 6 and 7 W², should not be mistaken for helotry. Different interpretations are given by von Blumenthal 1948: 1950; Meier 1998: 267; Luginbill 2002: 410.

not know the sources that Strabo used for his quotations, but, granted that he had access to the poems in their full length, it is very unlikely that fr. 5 W² came from the *Eunomia*. Our material, it can be concluded, does not support the suggestion that the *Eunomia* was a poem of a length that would have rendered a performance at a symposium problematic.

What about Mimnermus' *Smyrneis* – does it give a long account of Smyrna's history *ab ovo*? Let us see what the fragments allow us to say about it. Explaining the use of ἐνδέχεσθαι in a passage from Antimachus, the commentator quotes a distich from the *Smyrneis*: 'So the men around the king charged, after he had given the word of command, making a fence with their hollow shields' ('ὡς οἵ πὰρ βασιλῆος, ἐπε[ί ῥ'] ἐ[ν]εδέξατο μῦθον,/ ἤ[ϊξ]αν κοίληι[ς ἀ]σπίσι φραξάμενοι', fr. 13a W²).

It is highly likely that the following statement in Pausanias refers to the same poem: 'Mimnermus, who composed elegiac verses on the battle of the Smyrneans with Gyges and the Lydians, says in the proem that the more ancient Muses are daughters of Uranus and that the other, younger Muses are children of Zeus.' (9.29.4 =fr. 13 W²). If we read fr. 13a W² against the backdrop of fr. 13 W², we can conclude that the distich describes a scene in the Smyrneans' fight against the Lydians and that the king is to be identified with Gyges. While these two fragments can be safely ascribed to the *Smyrneis*, the assignment of fr. 9 W², which gives an account of Smyrna's foundation,[15] and fr. 14 W², the praise of a brave Smyrnean, rests on speculations about the content of the poem.[16]

Nonetheless, Bowie argues that the *Smyrneis* comprised a whole book in the Hellenistic editions and presented an account of Smyrna's history from its foundation.[17] Bowie's reconstruction rests on the following assumptions: first, he believes that the opposition of αἱ κατὰ λεπτὸν [ῥήσιες][18] to ἡ μεγάλη γυνή in the prologue of Callimachus' *Aitia* refers to two works of

---

[15] See Klinger 1930: 79–80; de Marco 1939–40: 338–9, who suggests that the fragment either came at the beginning of the poem, which he deems more likely, or belonged to a reply given to the king's speech concluded by fr. 13a W² (341–2); Bowie 2001: 48. At first glance, it looks as if fr. 9 W² might go together with fr. 10 W² (Strabo 14.1.3 p. 633): 'The Pylian Andraemon (founds) Colophon, as Mimnermus too says in the *Nanno*' ('Κολοφῶνα δὲ Ἀνδραίμων Πύλιος (κτίζει), ὥς φησι καὶ Μίμνερμος ἐν τῇ Ναννοῖ'). However, in fr. 9 W², Andraemon is not mentioned and the foundation of Colophon is merely touched upon. Cf. Jacoby 1918: 286–7.

[16] While Szadeczky-Kardoss 1968: 945–6 and Steffen 1973: 64 attribute fr. 14 W² to the *Smyrneis*, Jacoby 1918: 293–6 and Allen 1993: 9 argue that it stems from another elegy. Vetta 1983: XXIII is, in my opinion, right to leave the question open. See also Gentili and Prato 1979/²2002 who list it under *incertae sedis*.

[17] Bowie 1986: 28–9.

[18] The text of *Aitia* 11–12 is corrupt and Rostagni's supplement ῥήσιες, on which Bowie's reading depends, is not undisputed. See e.g. Asper 1997: 156 and, for a survey of various conjectures and interpretations, Allen 1993: 146–56.

Mimnermus, one being a collection of short poems, called *Nanno*, the other the long *Smyrneis*. Second, he suggests that these two works are to be identified with the two books of Mimnermus mentioned by Porphyrion on Hor. *epist.* 2.2.21.[19] Third, he claims that the name 'tall lady' bears Callimachean wit by not only pointing out the length of the poem, but by also alluding to the Amazon from whom the city received its name. He therefore deems it likely that the *Smyrneis* also dealt with the foundation of Smyrna by the Amazon and is inclined to attribute fr. 9 W² to the poem.

The brilliance of Bowie's argument makes it easy to forget how frail our basis for any conclusions about length and content of the *Smyrneis* actually is. It is far from sure that Callimachus' 'tall lady' refers to a work by Mimnermus at all, let alone to the *Smyrneis*.[20] Many other suggestions have been made.[21] Even if Bowie's interpretation of the *Aitia*–prologue is right, his conclusion that the *Smyrneis* comprised one of the two books mentioned by Porphyrion rests on speculation and the allusion to the Amazon Smyrna would have worked well without an account of the foundation, not to mention the fact that the Amazon is not referred to in fr. 9 W².

Bowie's reconstruction also raises a new problem. Like other scholars before him, Bowie ascribes fr. 9 W² to the *Smyrneis*. However, Strabo, to whom we owe the fragment, attributes the passage to the *Nanno*. This obviously contradicts Bowie's basic thesis that *Nanno* and *Smyrneis* are two separate books. Supposing that fr. 9 W² belonged to the *Smyrneis*, it is more likely that the *Smyrneis* was part of a collection of poems called *Nanno* than that, as Bowie must suggest, *Nanno* and *Smyrneis* contained partly the same material or Strabo misattributed the verses.[22] This challenges Bowie's argument for a book-length elegy. Moreover, fr. 9 W² looks like a rather brief and perfunctory account of the foundation of Smyrna and, if it was not part of a speech,[23] it does not lend itself as evidence for an extensive foundation myth in the *Smyrneis*.[24]

If on the other hand fr. 9 W² was not part of the *Smyrneis*, then the slender evidence for a full-blown account of Smyrna's history shrinks even

---

[19] Both points were made by Colonna 1952 and have been accepted by West 1974: 74; Gentili/Prato 1979/²2002 on T 10; Töchterle 1980; Pretagostini 1984: 132; Allen 1993: 146–56. However, they have been effectively questioned by Müller 1988: 203–5.
[20] Even West 1974: 74 who favours Colonna's idea concedes: '... ἡ μεγάλη γυνή, which it is possible to take as a reference to the *Smyrneis* ..., though that is only one of several possible explanations of the enigmatic words.'
[21] See the bibliography in Lehnus 2000: 45–7.   [22] Cf. Müller 1988: 203–6.
[23] Against this possibility, see Jacoby 1918: 270.
[24] Despite its shortness, fr. 9 W² is a very important early testimony for the Ionian migration. See for an interpretation in this context Dihle 1962: 258–63.

further and Bowie's argument rests merely on the speculative interpretation of Callimachus' *Aitia*–prologue.[25] No matter how we turn it, the case for a long chronological narrative of Smyrna's history is weak. All that we know is that the *Smyrneis* contained an account of a battle against Gyges. Of course, it cannot be ruled out that other events were referred to, but perhaps the conflict with Gyges was the main theme of the poem, or perhaps this and other past successes were part of an exhortation to act with the same bravery in the present.[26] Both possibilities would remove the *Smyrneis* from the list of historical elegies understood as lengthy chronological accounts, and, in the latter case, the *Smyrneis* would support Sider's thesis that the presentation of the past in elegy tends to be intertwined with other themes, in this case perhaps an exhortation.[27]

In addition to Tyrtaeus' *Eunomia* and Mimnermus' *Smyrneis*, Bowie further adduces the testimonies for Semonides' *archaiologia Samion* and Xenophanes' *ktisis*–poem to argue for historical elegies too long to be performed at symposia. However, we know virtually nothing about these poems, and Bowie himself concedes that the *archaiologia Samion* may have been a forgery[28] and the 'foundation of Colophon and the colonization of Elea in Italy' is said to be in ἔπη.[29] While this does not necessarily mean that it was in hexameters, it surely does not make it an elegy either.

---

[25] The fact that the *Smyrneis* had a proem invoking the Muses does not prove much about its length. As Bowie 1986: 29 n. 85 himself admits, Solon fr. 13 W² opens with an invocation to the Muses, while only having 76 lines. I am intrigued by the idea that the reference to two Muses mirrors the treatment of the ancient and recent past (Jacoby 1918: 296–8; Rutherford 2001: 42 n. 41), but again this is no evidence that the *Smyrneis* contained a chronological account. Bowie 2001: 62 adds that the pair of Muses could reflect other distinctions as well, e.g. the distinction between pan-Hellenic myth and the *ktiseis* of poleis. There is an interesting parallel in Timotheus, *Persae* fr. 791, 211–12: 'because I disregard the older Muse/ with my young songs' ('ὅτι παλαιοτέραν νέοις/ ὕμνοις Μοῦσαν ἀτιμῶ'). Hordern 2002: ad 203 refers the dichotomy old–young not to the content, but the style of the *nomos*. See also Timotheus, *Persae* fr. 296, where the old Muse is bidden farewell and the relation of old and new is compared to Zeus – Cronus.

[26] Cf. Jacoby 1918: 267; Klinger 1930: 79–80; de Marco 1939–40: 338–9; Cook 1958–9: 27; Dihle 1962: 275, who thinks that the war with Alyattes must be seen as the background of the whole *Smyrneis*; Boedeker and Sider 2001b: 5 n. 6. On the other hand, Steffen 1973: 62 and 72 objects to the idea that the present situation was referred to in the *Smyrneis*.

[27] However, Sider 2006: 334 does not question Bowie's reconstruction of the *Smyrneis*.

[28] Bowie 1986: 31 n. 98. According to Jacoby FGrH 3b: 456, it cannot be ruled out that in the sixth century BCE a *ktisis* of Samos was composed, but he argues that the title is late and that, if such a poem existed, it may have been as short as Tyrtaeus' *Eunomia* or Solon's *Salamis*. On the *archaiologia Samion*, see also Pellizer 1983: 26–7.

[29] Morever, Jacoby FGrH 3b: 296 suspects that the testimony about Xenophanes' *ktisis* of Colophon and Elea has been made up by Lobon of Argos. Cf. Untersteiner 1971: CCL–CCLIV.

Bibliography

Accame, S. (1951) *Ricerche intorno alla guerra corinzia.* Naples.
Aélion, R. (1983–4) 'Silences et personages silencieux chez les Tragiques' *Euphrosyne* 12: 31–52.
Albini, U. (1964) *Andocide. De Pace.* Florence.
   (1967) 'Lettura dei *Persiani* di Eschilo' *PP* 22: 252–63.
Alcock, S. E. (2002) *Archaeologies of the Greek Past. Landscape, Monuments, and Memories.* Cambridge.
Alexanderson, B. (1967) 'Darius in the *Persians*' *Eranos* 65: 1–11.
Allen, A. (1981) 'Mimnermus and Athena' *Maia* 33: 207–8.
   (1993) *The Fragments of Mimnermus. Text and Commentary.* Stuttgart.
Allison, J. W. (1983) 'Pericles' policy and the plague' *Historia* 32: 14–23.
   (1997a) *Word and Concept in Thucydides.* Atlanta.
   (1997b) 'Homeric allusions at the close of Thucydides' Sicilian narrative' *AJPh* 118: 499–516.
   (2001) '*Axiosis*, the new *Arete*. A Periclean metaphor for friendship' *CQ* 51: 53–64.
Aloni, A. (2001) 'The Proem of Simonides' *Plataea Elegy* and the circumstances of its performance', in *The New Simonides. Contexts of Praise and Desire*, eds. D. Boedeker and D. Sider. Oxford: 86–105.
Aly, W. (1969) *Volksmärchen, Sage und Novelle bei Herodot und seinen Zeitgenossen. Eine Untersuchung über die volkstümlichen Elemente der altgriechischen Prosaerzählung* (2nd edn.). Göttingen.
Ameis, K. F. and C. Hentze (eds.) (1896/1894) *Homers Ilias für den Schulgebrauch erklärt. I–II* (3rd and 5th edn.). Leipzig.
Andersen, Ø. (1978) *Die Diomedesgestalt in der Ilias.* Oslo.
Andrews, A. (1938) 'Eunomia' *CQ* 32: 89–102
Arnold, P. E. (1992) 'The persuasive style of debates in direct speech in Thucydides' *Hermes* 120: 44–57.
Arnott, G. (1973) 'Euripides and the unexpected' *G & R* 20: 49–64.
Asheri, D. (1993) 'Erodoto e Bacide. Considerazioni sulla feda di Erodoto negli oracoli (Hdt. VIII 77)', in *La Profezia nel Mondo Antico*, ed. M. Sordi. Milan: 63–76.
Asper, M. (1997) *Onomata allotria. Zur Genese, Struktur und Funktion poetologischer Metaphern bei Kallimachos.* Stuttgart.

Assmann, J. (1992) *Das kulturelle Gedächtnis. Schrift, Erinnerung und politische Identität in frühen Hochkulturen*. Munich.
  (2000) 'Gedächtnis I.' *RGG*⁴ 3: 523–5
Austin, N. (1994) *Helen of Troy and Her Shameless Phantom*. Ithaca, NY.
Avery, H. C. (1964) 'Dramatic devices in Aeschylus' Persians' *AJPh* 85: 173–84.
Avezzù, G. (1985) *Apologia per l'uccisione di Eratostene; Epitafio*. Padua.
Backès, J.-L. (1984) *Le Mythe d'Hélène*. Clermont-Ferrand.
Bacon, H. H. (1961) *Barbarians in Greek Tragedy*. New Haven, CT.
Bakhtin, M. M. (1981) *The Dialogic Imagination. Four Essays*. Austin, TX.
Bakker, E. (1997) 'Verbal aspect and mimetic description in Thucydides', in *Grammar as Interpretation. Greek Literature in its Linguistic Contexts*, ed. E. Bakker. Leiden: 7–54.
Barrett, A. A. and M. Vickers (1978) 'The Oxford Brygos cup reconsidered' *JHS* 98: 17–24.
Barrett, J. (1995) 'Narrative and the messenger in Aeschylus' Persians' *AJPh* 116: 539–57.
  (2002) *Staged Narrative. Poetics and the Messenger in Greek Tragedy*. Berkeley, CA.
Bauer, G. (1963) *'Geschichtlichkeit'. Wege und Irrwege eines Begriffs*. Berlin.
Baumgartner, H.-M. (1997) *Kontinuität und Geschichte. Zur Kritik und Metakritik der historischen Vernunft* (2nd edn.). Frankfurt.
Beale, W. (1978) 'Rhetorical performative discourse. A new theory of Epideictic' *Philosophy and Rhetoric* 11: 221–46.
Bearzot, C. (1997) '*P. Oxy.* 3965: Considerazioni sulla data e sull' ispirazione dell' elegia di Simonide per la battaglia di Platea', in *Akten des 21. Internationalen Papyrologenkongresses*. Berlin: 71–9.
Beazley, J. D. (1963) *Attic Red-Figure Vase-Painters* (2nd edn.). Oxford.
Belloni, L. (1982) 'L'ombra di Dario nei *Persiani* di Eschilo. La regalità degli Achemenidi e il pubblico di Atene' *Orpheus* 3: 185–99.
  (1988) *Eschilo. I Persiani*. Milan.
Bichler, R. (1985) 'Die "Reichsträume" bei Herodot' *Chiron* 15: 125–47.
  (2000) *Herodots Welt. Der Aufbau der Historie am Bild der fremden Länder und Völker, ihrer Zivilisation und ihrer Geschichte*. Berlin.
Bischoff, H. (1932) *Der Warner bei Herodot*. Diss. Marburg.
Blass, F. (1887) *Die Attische Beredsamkeit. I. Von Gorgias bis zu Lysias* (2nd edn.). Leipzig.
Bloedow, E. F. (1990) '"Not the son of Achilles, but Achilles himself": Alcibiades' entry on the political stage at Athens II' *Historia* 39: 1–19.
  (1993) 'Hermocrates' strategy against the Athenians in 415 B.C.' *AHB* 7: 115–24.
  (1996) 'The speeches of Hermocrates and Athenagoras at Syracuse in 415 BC' *Historia* 45: 141–58.
Blumenberg, H. (1979) *Arbeit am Mythos*. Frankfurt.
von Blumenthal, A. (1948) 'Tyrtaios' *RE* VII A 2: 1941–56.
Boardman, J. (2002) *The Archaeology of Nostalgia. How the Greeks Re-created their Mythical Past*. London.

Bodnar, J. (1992) *Remaking America. Public Memory, Commemoration, and Patriotism in the Twentieth Century*. Princeton, NJ.
Boedeker, D. (1988) 'Protesilaos and the end of Herodotus' *Histories*' *ClAnt* 7: 30–48.
  (1993) 'Hero cult and politics in Herodotus. The bones of Orestes', in *Cultural Poetics in Archaic Greece. Cult, Performance, Politics*, eds. C. Dougherty and L. Kurke. Cambridge: 64–177.
  (1995) 'Simonides on Plataea: narrative elegy, mythodic history' *ZPE* 107: 217–29.
  (1998) 'Presenting the past in fifth-century Athens', in *Democracy, Empire, and the Arts in Fifth-Century Athens*, eds. D. Boedeker and K. Raaflaub. Cambridge, MA: 185–202.
  (2000) 'Herodotus' genre(s)', in Depew and Obbink (2000a): 97–114.
  (2001a) 'Heroic historiography. Simonides and Herodotus on Plataea', in Boedeker and Sider (2001a): 120–34.
  (2001b) 'Paths to heroization at Plataea', in Boedeker and Sider (2001a): 148–63.
  (2002) 'Epic heritage and mythical patterns in Herodotus', in *Brill's Companion to Herodotus*, eds. E. Bakker, I. de Jong and H. van Wees. Leiden: 97–116.
Boedeker, D. and D. Sider (eds.) (2001a) *The New Simonides. Contexts of Praise and Desire*. Oxford.
  (2001b) 'Introduction', in Boedeker and Sider (2001a): 3–6.
Bollack, J. (1963) 'L'or des rois. Le mythe de la *Deuxième Olympique*' *RPh* 89: 234–54.
Bosworth, A. B. (2000) 'The historical context of Thucydides' funeral oration' *JHS* 120: 1–16.
Bowie, A. (1993) 'Homer, Herodotus, and the beginnings of Thucydides' *History*', in *Tria Lustra. Essays and Notes Presented to John Pinsent (Liverpool Classical Papers 3)*, ed. H. D. Jocelyn. Liverpool: 141–7.
Bowie, E. (1986) 'Early Greek elegy, symposium and public festival' *JHS* 106: 13–35.
  (1990) '*Miles ludens?* The problem of martial exhortation in early Greek elegy', in Murray (1990a): 221–9.
  (2001) 'Ancestors of historiography in early Greek elegiac and iambic poetry?', in *The Historian's Craft in the Age of Herodotus*, ed. N. Luraghi. Oxford: 45–66.
Bowra, C. M. (1938a) *Early Greek Elegists*. Cambridge, MA.
  (1938b) 'Xenophanes, Fragment 1' *CPh* 33: 353–67.
Bradley, R. (2002) *The Past in Prehistoric Societies*. London.
Bradley, R. and H. Williams (eds.) (1998) *The Past in the Past. The Re-use of Ancient Monuments*. London.
Bremmer, J. N. (1990) 'Adolescents, symposion, and pederasty', in Murray (1990a): 135–48.
Broadhead, H. D. (1960) *The Persae of Aeschylus*. Cambridge.
Bruce, I. (1966) 'Athenian embassies in the early fourth century B.C.' *Historia* 15: 272–81.
Brunnsaker, S. (1971) *The Tyrant-Slayers of Kritios and Nesiotes: A Critical Study of the Sources and Restorations* (2nd edn.). Stockholm.

Brunt, P. A. (1953) 'The Hellenic league against Persia' *Historia* 2: 135–63.
Bubner, R. (1984) *Geschichtsprozesse und Handlungsnormen. Untersuchungen zur praktischen Philosophie*. Frankfurt.
Buchert, U. (2000) *Denkmalpflege im antiken Griechenland. Maßnahmen zur Bewahrung historischer Bausubstanz*. Frankfurt.
Buck, R. (1988) 'The Sicilian expedition' *AHB* 2: 73–9.
Buffière, F. (1956) *Les mythes d'Homère et la pensée grecque*. Paris.
Burckhardt, A. (1924) *Spuren der athenischen Volksrede in der alten Komödie*. Diss. Basel.
Burian, P. (1997) 'Myth into muthos: the shaping of tragic plot', in *The Cambridge Companion to Greek Tragedy*, ed. P. Easterling. Cambridge: 178–208.
Burkert, W. (1974) 'Die Absurdität der Gewalt und das Ende der Tragödie. Euripides' *Orestes*' *A&A* 20: 97–109.
  (1985) 'Das Ende des Kroisos. Vorstufen einer herodoteischen Geschichtserzählung', in *Catalepton. Festschrift für Bernhard Wyss zum 80. Geburtstag*, ed. C. Schäublin. Basel: 4–15.
Burn, L. (1989) 'The art of the state in late fifth-century Athens', in *Images of Authority. Papers Presented to Joyce Reynolds. (Proceedings of the Cambridge Philological Society, Suppl. 16)*. eds. M. M. Mackenzie and C. Roueché. Cambridge: 62–81.
Burnett, A. P. (1989) 'Performing Pindar's Odes' *CPh* 84: 283–93.
  (2005) *Pindar's Songs for Young Athletes of Aigina*. Oxford.
Burzacchini, G. (1995) 'Note al nuovo Simonide' *Eikasmos* 6: 21–38.
Butler, A. F. (1905) *Herodotus VII*. New York, NY.
Bux, E. (1960) 'Art. Logographen' *RE* XIII.1: 1021–7.
Cagnazzi, S. (1986) 'L'archaiologein di Nicia (Tucidide VII,69,2)' *Athenaeum* 64: 492–7.
Cagnetta, M. (1984) 'Platea, ultimo atto' *QS* 19: 203–12.
Calame, C. (2000) 'Temps du récit et temps du rituel dans la poétique grecque. Bacchylide entre mythe, histoire et culte', in Darbo-Peschanski (2000): 395–412.
Carey, C. (1989) 'The performance of the victory ode' *AJPh* 110: 545–65.
  (1991) 'The victory ode in performance: The case for the chorus' *CPh* 86: 192–200.
  (1995) 'Pindar and the victory ode', in *The Passionate Intellect. Essays on the Transformation of Classical Traditions. Presented to Prof. I. G. Kidd*, ed. L. Ayres. New Brunswick, NJ: 85–103.
  (2007a) 'Pindar, place, and performance', in *Pindar's Poetry, Patrons, and Festivals. From Archaic Greece to the Roman Empire*, eds. S. Hornblower and C. Morgan. Oxford: 199–210.
  (2007b) 'Epideictic oratory', in *A Companion to Greek Rhetoric*, ed. I. Worthington. Malden, MA: 236–52.
Carne-Ross, D. (1976) 'Weaving with points of gold: Pindar's *Sixth Olympian*' *Arion* N.S. 3: 5–44.
Carr, H. C. (1961) *What Is History?* New York, NY.

Carrara, P. (1977) *Eretteo*. Florence.
Carter, M. F. (1991) 'The ritual functions of epideictic rhetoric. The case of Socrates' funeral oration' *Rhetorica* 9: 209–32.
Cartledge, P. (1993) *The Greeks. A Portrait of Self and Others*. Oxford.
　(2002) *Sparta and Lakonia. A Regional History 1300 to 362 BC* (2nd edn.). London.
Castellani, V. (1986) 'Clio vs. Melpomene; or, why so little historical drama from classical Athens?' *Themes in Drama* 8: 1–16.
Castriota, D. (1992) *Myth, Ethos, and Actuality. Official Art in Fifth-Century B.C. Athens*. Madison.
Chaniotis, A. (1988) *Historie und Historiker in den griechischen Inschriften. Epigraphische Beiträge zur griechischen Historiographie*. Stuttgart.
Chatelet, F. (1962) *La naissance de l'histoire. La formation de la pensée historique en Grèce*. Paris.
Chiasson, C. C. (1983) 'An ominous word in Herodotus' *Hermes* 111: 115–18.
　(1986) 'The Herodotean Solon' *GRBS* 27: 249–62.
　(2003) 'Herodotus' use of Attic tragedy in the *Lydian logos*' *ClAnt* 22: 5–36.
　(2005) 'Myth, ritual, and authorial control in Herodotus' story of Cleobis and Biton (*Hist.* 1.31)' *AJPh* 126: 41–64.
Chladenius, J. M. (1742) *Einleitung zur richtigen Auslegung vernünftiger Reden und Schriften*. Leipzig (reprint Düsseldorf 1969).
Christ, M. R. (1994) 'Herodotean kings and historical inquiry' *ClAnt* 13: 167–202.
Clader, L. L. (1976) *Helen. The Evolution from Divine to Heroic in Greek Epic Tradition*. Leiden.
Clairmont, C. W. (1983) *Patrios Nomos. Public Burial in Athens during the Fifth and Fourth Centuries B.C. The Archaeological, Epigraphic-Literary and Historical Evidence*. Oxford.
Clarke, M. (2008) *Making Time for the Past. Local History and the Polis*. Oxford.
Classen, J. and J. Steup (1862–1922) *Thukydides. I–VIII*. Berlin.
Clay, J. S. (1999) 'Pindar's Sympotic Epinicia' *QUCC* 62: 25–34.
Cobet, J. (1971) *Herodots Exkurse und die Frage der Einheit seines Werkes*. Wiesbaden.
Cogan, M. (1981) *The Human Thing. The Speeches and Principles of Thucydides' History*. Chicago, IL.
Cole, T. (1991) *The Origins of Rhetoric in Ancient Greece*. Baltimore, MD.
Collingwood, R. G. (1946) *The Idea of History*. Oxford.
　(1965) *Essays in the Philosophy of History*. Austin, TX.
Colonna, A. (1952) 'Mimnermo e Callimaco' *Athenaeum* 30: 191–5.
Confino, A. (1997) 'Collective Memory and Cultural History. Problems of Method' *The American Historical Review* 102: 1386–403.
Connerton, P. (1989) *How Societies Remembers*. Cambridge.
Connor, W. R. (1977) 'Tyrannis polis', in *Ancient and Modern. Essays in Honor of Gerard F. Else*, eds. J. H. D'Arms and J. W. Eadie. Ann Arbor, MI: 95–109.
　(1984) *Thucydides*. Princeton, NJ.
　(1985) 'Narrative discourse in Thucydides', in *The Greek Historians. Literature and History. Papers Presented to A. E. Raubitschek*, ed. M. H. Jameson. Stanford, CA: 1–17.

(1990) 'City Dionysia and Athenian democracy', in *Aspects of Athenian Democracy*, ed. W. R. Connor. Copenhagen: 7–32.
Conte, G. B. (1994) *Genres and Readers. Lucretius, Love Elegy, Pliny's Encyclopedia*. Baltimore, MD.
Cook, J. M. (1958–9) 'Old Smyrna, 1948–1951' *ABSA* 53/54: 1–34.
Corcella, A. (1984) *Erodoto e l'analogia*. Palermo.
Cornford, F. M. (1907) *Thucydides Mythistoricus*. London.
Court, B. (1994) *Die dramatische Technik des Aischylos*. Stuttgart.
Crahay, R. (1956) *La littérature oraculaire chez Hérodote*. Paris.
Crane, G. (1996) *The Blinded Eye. Thucydides and the New Written Word*. London.
 (1998) *Thucydides and the Ancient Simplicity. The Limits of Political Realism*. Berkeley, CA.
Creuzer, G. F. (1845) *Die historische Kunst der Griechen in ihrer Entstehung und Fortbildung* (2nd edn.). Leipzig.
Croally, N. T. (1994) *Euripidean Polemic. The Trojan Women and the Function of Tragedy*. Cambridge.
Crotty, K. (1982) *Song and Action. The Victory Odes of Pindar*. Baltimore, MD.
Csapo, E. and M. Miller (1998) 'Democracy, empire, and art: Towards a politics of time and narrative', in *Democracy, Empire, and the Arts in Fifth-Century Athens*, eds. D. Boedeker and K. Raaflaub. Cambridge, MA: 87–126.
Currie, B. (2004) 'Reperformance scenarios for Pindar's odes', in *Oral Performance and Its Context*, ed. C. J. Mackie. Leiden: 49–69.
 (2005) *Pindar and the Cult of Heroes*. Oxford.
Curtius, E. (1886) 'Ueber zwei Kunstausdrücke der griechischen Literaturgeschichte', in *Kleine Schriften. II. Ausgewählte Abhandlungen wissenschaftlichen Inhalts*, ed. E. Windisch. Leipzig: 239–54.
Dalfen, J. (1974) *Polis und Poiesis. Die Auseinandersetzung mit der Dichtung bei Platon und seinen Zeitgenossen*. Munich.
Dally, O. (forthcoming) 'Rückblick und Gegenwart. Vergleichende Untersuchungen zur Visualisierung von Vergangenheitsvorstellungen in der Antike' *Ergänzungsheft. Jahrbuch des Deutschen Archäologischen Instituts*.
Darbo-Peschanski, C. (1987) 'Thucydide: historien, juge' *Metis* 11: 109–40.
 (ed.) (2000) *Constructions du temps dans le monde grec ancien*. Paris.
Davidson, J. (1991) 'The gaze in Polybius' *Histories*' *JRS* 81: 10–24.
Dawe, R. D. (1963) 'Inconsistency of plot and character in Aeschylus' *PCPhS* 189: 21–62.
 (1982) *Sophocles. Oedipus Rex*. Cambridge.
Debnar, P. E. (1996) 'The unpersuasive Thebans (Thucydides 3.61–67)' *Phoenix* 50: 95–110.
 (2001) *Speaking the Same Language. Speech and Audience in Thucydides' Spartan Debates*. Ann Arbor, MI.
Deffner, A. (1933) *Die Rede bei Herodot und ihre Weiterbildung bei Thukydides*. Diss Munich.

Deichgräber, K. (1952) 'Das griechische Geschichtsbild in seiner Entwicklung zur wissenschaftlichen Historiographie', in *Der listsinnende Trug des Gottes. Vier Themen des griechischen Denkens*. Göttingen: 7–56.
Demand, N. (1975) 'Pindar's *Olympian 2*, Theron's faith, and Empedocles' *Katharmoi*' *GRBS* 16: 347–57.
Demandt, A. (1978) *Metaphern für Geschichte. Sprachbilder und Gleichnisse im historisch-politischen Denken*. Munich.
Dentzer, J.-M. (1982) *Le Motif du Banquet Couché dans le Proche-Orient et le Monde Grec du VIIème au IVème Siecle avant J.-C*. Rome.
Depew, M. and D. Obbink (eds.) (2000a) *Matrices of Genre. Authors, Canons, and Society*. Cambridge, MA.
 (2000b) 'Introduction', in Depew and Obbink (2000a): 1–14.
Deubner, L. (1932) *Attische Feste*. Berlin.
Deufert, M. (2004) 'Situationsbezogenheit und Improvisation in der frühgriechischen Lyrik: Der Festsaal in der Symposionselegie des Xenophanes', in *Text und Handeln. Zum kommunikativen Ort von Minnegesang und antiker Lyrik*, ed. A. Hausmann. Heidelberg: 23–45.
Dewald, C. (2005) *Thucydides' War Narrative. A Structural Study*. Berkeley, CA.
Dickson, K. M. (1995) *Nestor. Poetic Memory in Greek Epic*. New York, NY.
Dihle, A. (1962) 'Zur Datierung des Mimnermos' *Hermes* 90: 257–75.
 (1988) 'Fortschritt und Goldene Zeit', in *Kultur und Gedächtnis*, eds. J. Assmann and T. Hölscher. Frankfurt: 150–69.
Dillery, J. (1995) *Xenophon and the History of his Times*. London.
Dodds, E. R. (1973) *The Ancient Concept of Progress and other Essays on Greek Literature and Belief*. Oxford.
Dougherty, C. (1993) 'It's murder to found a colony', in *Cultural Poetics in Archaic Greece. Cult, Performance, Politics*, eds. C. Dougherty and L. Kurke. Cambridge: 178–98.
 (1994) 'Archaic Greek foundation poetry: Questions of genre and occasion' *JHS* 114: 35–46.
Dover, K. J. (1964) 'The poetry of Archilochos' in *Archiloque (Entretiens Hardt 10)*. Geneva: 181–212.
 (1968) *Lysias and the Corpus Lysiacum*. Berkeley, CA.
 (1988a) 'Thucydides on oracles', in *The Greeks and Their Legacy. Collected Papers*, ed. K. J. Daves. Oxford: 65–73.
 (1988b) 'Thucydides' historical judgement: Athens and Sicily', in *The Greeks and their Legacy. Collected Papers*, ed. K. J. Daves. Oxford: 74–82.
Duff, D. (ed.) (2000) *Modern Genre Theory*. Harlow.
Dunn, F. (2007) *Present Shock in Late Fifth-Century Greece*. Ann Arbor, MI.
Easterling, P. (1989) 'City settings in Greek poetry' *PCA* 86: 5–17.
 (1997) 'Constructing the heroic', in *Greek Tragedy and the Historian*, ed. C. Pelling. Oxford: 21–37.
Ebert, J. (1972) *Griechische Epigramme auf Sieger an gymnischen und hippischen Agonen*. Berlin.
Edelstein, L. (1967) *The Idea of Progress in Classical Antiquity*. Baltimore, MD.

Edmunds, L. (1975) *Chance and Intelligence in Thucydides*. Cambridge, MA.
  (1993) 'Thucydides in the act of writing', in *Tradizione e Innovazione nella cultura Greca da Omero all' età Ellenistica. Scritti in onore di Bruno Gentili II.*, ed. R. Pretagostini. Rome: 831–52.
Edwards, M. (1999) *Ancestral Geographies of the Neolithic. Landscapes, Monuments, and Memory*. London.
Edwards, M. J. (1995) *Greek Orators IV. Andocides*. Warminster.
Egermann, F. E. (1972) 'Thukydides über die Art seiner Reden und über seine Darstellung der Kriegsgeschehnisse' *Historia* 21: 575–602.
Erbse, H. (1979) 'Über Herodots Kroisoslogos', *Ausgewählte Schriften zur Klassischen Philologie*. Berlin: 180–202.
  (1987) 'Zwei Fragen zur Geschichtsbetrachtung des Thukydides', in *Agora. Zu Ehren von Rudolph Berlinger (Perspektiven der Philosophie. Neues Jahrbuch 13)*. Amsterdam: 331–46.
  (1989) *Thukydides-Interpretationen*. Berlin.
  (1992) *Studien zum Verständnis Herodots*. Berlin.
  (1999) 'Über Pindars Umgang mit dem Mythos' *Hermes* 127: 13–32.
Ermatinger, E. (1897) *Die attische Autochthonensage bis auf Euripides*. Berlin.
Erskine, A. (2001) *Troy between Greece and Rome. Local Tradition and Imperial Power*. Oxford.
Farrar, C. (1988) *The Origins of Democratic Thinking. The Invention of Politics in Classical Athens*. Cambridge.
Feeney, D. (2007) *Caesar's Calendar. Ancient Time and the Beginnings of History*. Berkeley, CA.
Fehling, D. (1989) *Herodotus and his Sources. Citation, Invention and Narrative Art*. Leeds.
Felten, F. (1984) *Griechische tektonische Friese archaischer und klassischer Zeit*. Waldsassen.
Ferguson, N. (1997) 'Introduction. Virtual history. Towards a 'chaotic' theory of the past', in *Virtual History: Alternatives and Counterfactuals*, ed. N. Ferguson. London: 1–90.
Finley, J. H. (1967) *Three Essays on Thucydides*. Cambridge, MA.
Fisher, N. R. E. (1992) *Hybris. A Study in the Values of Honour and Shame in Ancient Greece*. Warminster.
Fitzgerald, W. C. (1983) 'Pindar's *Second Olympian*' *Helios* 10: 49–70.
Flashar, H. (1969) *Der Epitaphios des Perikles. Seine Funktion im Geschichtswerk des Thukydides*. Heidelberg.
Flory, S. (1978) 'Laughter, tears and wisdom in Herodotus' *AJPh* 99: 145–53.
  (1980) 'Who reads Herodotus' *Histories*?' *AJPh* 101: 12–28.
  (1987) *The Archaic Smile of Herodotus*. Detroit, MI.
  (1988) 'Thucydides' hypotheses about the Peloponnesian War' *TAPhA* 118: 43–56.
  (1990) 'The meaning of τὸ μυθῶδες (1.22.4) and the usefulness of Thucydides' History' *CJ* 85: 193–208.

(1993) 'The death of Thucydides and the motif of "land and sea"', in *Nomodeiktes. Greek Studies in Honor of Martin Ostwald*, eds. R. M. Rosen and J. Farrell. Ann Arbor, MI: 113–23.
Flower, H. I. (1991) 'Herodotus and Delphic traditions about Croesus', in *Georgica. Greek Studies in Honour of George Cawkwell*, eds. M. A. Flower and M. Toher. London: 57–77.
Flower, M. A. and J. Marincola (2002) *Herodotus. Histories Book IX.* Cambridge.
Föllinger, S. (2003) *Genosdependenzen. Studien zur Arbeit am Mythos bei Aischylos.* Göttingen.
Ford, A. (2002) *The Origins of Criticism. Literary Culture and Poetic Theory in Classical Greece.* Princeton, NJ.
Forde, S. (1989) *The Ambition to Rule. Alcibiades and the Politics of Imperialism.* Ithaca, NY.
Fornara, C. W. (1971a) 'Evidence for the date of Herodotus' publication' *JHS* 91: 25–34.
(1971b) *Herodotus. An Interpretative Essay.* Oxford.
(1983) *The Nature of History in Ancient Greece and Rome.* Berkeley, CA.
(1990) 'Human history and the constraint of fate in Herodotus', in *Conflict, Antithesis, and the Ancient Historian*, ed. J. W. Allison. Columbus, OH: 25–45.
Fowler, R. L. (1987) *The Nature of Early Greek Lyric. Three Preliminary Studies.* Toronto.
(1996) 'Herodotus and his contemporaries' *JHS* 116: 62–87.
(2006) 'Herodotus and his prose predecessors', in *The Cambridge Companion to Herodotus*, eds. C. Dewald and J. Marincola. Cambridge: 29–45.
Fox, M. and N. Livingstone (2007) 'Rhetoric and historiography', in *A Companion to Greek Rhetoric*, ed. I. Worthington. Malden, MA: 542–61.
Foxhall, L. and H.-J. Gehrke (eds.) (forthcoming) *Intentionale Geschichte – Spinning Time.* Stuttgart.
Francis, E. D. (1990) *Image and Idea in Fifth-Century Greece. Art and Literature after the Persian Wars.* London.
François, E. and H. Schulze (eds.) (2001) *Deutsche Erinnerungsorte. I–III.* Munich.
Frangoulidis, S. A. (1993) 'A pattern from Homer's *Odyssey* in the Sicilian narrative of Thucydides' *QUCC* 44: 95–102.
Fränkel, H. (1962) *Dichtung und Philosophie des frühen Griechentums* (2nd edn.). Munich.
(1977) *Die homerischen Gleichnisse* (2nd edn.). Göttingen.
Friedman, R. (2006) 'Location and dislocation in Herodotus', in *The Cambridge Companion to Herodotus*, eds. C. Dewald and J. Marincola. Cambridge: 165–77.
Friedrich, W. H. (1973) 'Der Tod des Tyrannen. Die poetische Gerechtigkeit der alten Geschichtsschreiber – und Herodot' *A&A* 18: 97–129.
Frisch, P. (1968) *Die Träume bei Herodot.* Meisenheim.
von Fritz, K. (1967) *Die Griechische Geschichtsschreibung. I–II.* Berlin.
Fulda, D. (2000) 'Historiographie-Geschichte! oder die Chancen der Komplexität. Foucault, Nietzsche und der aktuelle Geschichtsdiskurs', in *Zukunft der*

Geschichte. Historisches Denken an der Schwelle zum 21. Jh, ed. S. Jordan. Berlin: 105–22.
Fuqua, C. (1981) 'Tyrtaeus and the cult of heroes' *GRBS* 22: 215–26.
Furley, W. D. (1996) *Andokides and the Herms. A Study of Crisis in Fifth-Century Athenian Religion*. London.
  (2006) 'Thucydides and religion', in *Brill's Companion to Thucydides*, eds. A. Rengakos and A. Tsakmakis. Leiden: 415–38.
Gadamer, H.-G. (1986) *Wahrheit und Methode. Grundzüge einer philosophischen Hermeneutik* (5th edn.). Tübingen.
Gagarin, M. (1976) *Aeschylean Drama*. Berkeley, CA.
Gaiser, K. (1975) *Das Staatsmodell des Thukydides. Zur Rede des Perikles für die Gefallenen*. Heidelberg.
Garner, R. (1990) *From Homer to Tragedy. The Art of Allusion in Greek Poetry*. London.
Garrity, T. F. (1998) 'Thucydides 1.22.1: Content and form in the speeches' *AJPh* 119: 361–84.
Gathercole, P. and D. Lowenthal (eds.) (1990) *The Politics of the Past*. London.
Gehrke, H.-J. (1985) *Stasis. Untersuchungen zu den inneren Kriegen in den griechischen Staaten des 5. und 4. Jahrhunderts v. Chr.* Munich.
  (1994) 'Mythos, Geschichte, Politik – antik und modern' *Saeculum* 45: 239–64.
  (2001) 'Myth, history and collective identity. Uses of the past in ancient Greece and beyond', in *The Historian's Craft in the Age of Herodotus*, ed. N. Luraghi. Oxford: 286–313.
Gelzer, T. (1985) 'Μοῦσα αὐθιγενής. Bemerkungen zu einem Typ Pindarischer und Bacchylideischer Epinikien' *MH* 42: 95–120.
Gentili, B. (1965) 'Mimnermo' *Maia* 17: 379–85.
  (1968) 'Epigramma ed elegia', in *L'épigramme Grecque (Entretiens Hardt 14)*: 37–81.
  (1988) *Poetry and Its Public in Ancient Greece. From Homer to the Fifth Century*. Baltimore, MD.
Gentili, B. and G. Cerri (1983) *Storia e biografia nel pensiero antico*. Rome.
Gentili, B. and C. Prato (eds.) (1979/²2002) *Poetae elegiaci. Testimonia et fragmenta. I-II*. Leipzig.
Georges, P. (1994) *Barbarian Asia and the Greek Experience. From the Archaic Period to the Age of Xenophon*. Baltimore, MD.
Gerber, D. E. (1997) 'Elegy', in *A Companion to the Greek Lyric Poets*, ed. D. E. Gerber. Leiden: 89–132.
  (1999) *Greek Elegiac Poetry. From the Seventh to the Fifth Centuries BC*. Cambridge, MA.
Gianotti, G. F. (1971) 'Sull' *Olimpica seconda* di Pindaro' *RFIC* 99: 26–52.
Gildersleeve, B. L. (1885) *Pindar. The Olympian and Pythian Odes*. London.
Giuliani, L. (2003) *Bild und Mythos. Geschichte der Bilderzählung in der griechischen Kunst*. Munich.
  (forthcoming) 'Gibt es eine Ikonographie der Vergangenheit?', in Foxhall and Gehrke (forthcoming).

Goetz, H.-W. (1999) *Geschichtsschreibung und Geschichtsbewußtsein im hohen Mittelalter*. Berlin.
Goldhill, S. (1984) *Language, Sexuality, Narrative. The Oresteia*. Cambridge.
  (1986) *Reading Greek Tragedy*. Cambridge.
  (1988) 'Battle narrative and politics in Aeschylus' *Persae*' *JHS* 108: 189–93.
  (1990) 'The Great Dionysia and civic ideology', in *Nothing to Do with Dionysos? Athenian Drama in Its Social Context*, eds. J. J. Winkler and F. Zeitlin. Princeton, NJ: 97–129.
  (1991) *The Poet's Voice. Essays on Poetics and Greek Literature*. Cambridge.
  (2000) 'Civic ideology and the problem of difference: the politics of Aeschylean tragedy, once again' *JHS* 120: 34–56.
Gomme, A. W. (1954) *The Greek Attitude to Poetry and History*. Berkeley, CA.
Gomme, A. W., A. Andrewes and K. J. Dover (1941–81) *A Historical Commentary on Thucydides. I–V*. Oxford.
Gommel, J. (1966) *Rhetorisches Argumentieren bei Thukydides*. Hildesheim.
Goodenough, W. H. (1980) *Description and Comparison in Cultural Anthropology*. Cambridge.
Goodwin, W. W. (1866) 'Note on Thucydides, 1.22.' *Proceedings of the American Academy of the Arts and Sciences* 6: 329–30.
Gossmann, E. (1908) *Quaestiones ad Graecorum Orationum Funebrium Formam Pertinentes*. Diss. Jena.
Gotteland, S. (2001) *Mythe et rhétorique. Les exemples mythiques dans le discours politique de l'Athènes classique*. Paris.
Gould, J. (1985) 'On making sense of Greek religion', in *Greek Religion and Society*, eds. P. E. Easterling and J. V. Muir. Cambridge: 1–33.
  (1989) *Herodotus*. London.
von Graevenitz, G. and O. Marquard (eds.) (1998a) *Kontingenz*. Munich.
  (1998b) 'Vorwort', in von Graevenitz and Marquard (1998a): XI–XVI.
Green, P. (1970) *Armada from Athens*. New York, NY.
Greenwood, E. (2006) *Thucydides and the Shaping of History*. London.
Grethlein, J. (2003a) *Asyl und Athen. Die Konstruktion kollektiver Identität in der griechischen Tragödie*. Stuttgart.
  (2003b) 'Die poetologische Bedeutung des aristotelischen Mitleidbegriffs. Überlegungen zu Nähe und Distanz in der griechischen Tragödie' *Poetica* 35: 41–67.
  (2004) '*Logográphos* und Thuc. 1.21.1' *Prometheus* 30: 209–16.
  (2005) 'Gefahren des λόγος. Thukydides' '*Historien*' und die Grabrede des Perikles' *Klio* 87: 41–71.
  (2006a) *Das Geschichtsbild der Ilias. Eine Untersuchung aus phänomenologischer und narratologischer Perspektive*. Göttingen.
  (2006b) 'Individuelle Identität und Conditio Humana. Die Bedeutung und Funktion von γενεή im Blättergleichnis in *Il.* 6, 146–9' *Philologus* 150: 3–13.
  (2006c) 'The manifold uses of the epic past. The embassy scene in Hdt. 7.153–163' *AJPh* 127: 485–509.
  (2006d) 'How old is Nestor?' *Eikasmos* 17: 11–16.

(2007a) 'Diomedes Redivivus. A new reading of Mimnermus fr 14 W²' *Mnemosyne* 60: 102–11.
(2007b) 'The hermeneutics and poetics of memory in Aeschylus' *Persae*' *Arethusa* 40: 363–96.
(2007c) 'Variationen des "nächsten Fremden". Die *Perser* des Aischylos im 20. Jahrhundert' *Antike und Abendland* 53: 1–20.
(2008a) 'Eine herodoteische Deutung der Sizilischen Expedition (Thuc. 7.87.5f.)?' *Hermes* 136: 129–42.
(2008b) 'Memory and material objects in the *Iliad* and the *Odyssey*' *JHS* 128: 27–51.
(2009a) 'From imperishable glory to history. The *Iliad* and the Trojan War', in *Epic and History*, ed. K. Raaflaub. London.
(2009b) 'How not to do history. Xerxes in Herodotus' *Histories*' *AJPh* 130: 195–218.
(forthcoming a) '*Historia magistra vitae* in Herodotus and Thucydides?', in *Ancient History and Western Historical Thought. The Construction of Classical Time(s)*, ed. A. Lianeri. Cambridge.
(forthcoming b) 'Beyond intentional history. A phenomenological model of the idea of history', in Foxhall and Gehrke (forthcoming).
Gribble, D. (1998) 'Narrator interventions in Thucydides' *JHS* 118: 41–67.
  (1999) *Alcibiades and Athens. A Study in Literary Presentation*. Oxford.
  (2006) 'Individuals in Thucydides', in *Brill's Companion to Thucydides*, eds. A. Rengakos and A. Tsakmakis. Leiden: 439–68.
Griffin, J. (1980) *Homer on Life and Death*. Oxford.
Griffith, M. (1975) 'Man and the leaves: A study of Mimnermos fr 2' *CSCA* 8: 73–88.
  (1998) 'The king and the eye. The rule of the father in Greek tragedy' *PCPhS* 44: 20–84.
Griffith, R. D. (1991) 'Oedipus's bloodthirsty sons: Love and strife in Pindar's Second Olympian Ode' *ClAnt* 10: 46–58.
Griffiths, A. H. (1976) 'What Syagros said. Herodotus 7, 159.' *LCM* 1: 23–4.
van Groningen, B. A. (1945) *Herodotus' Historiën met inleiding en commentaar*. Leiden.
  (1953) *In the Grip of the Past. Essay on an Aspect of Greek Thought*. Leiden.
Grossmann, G. (1950) *Politische Schlagwörter aus der Zeit des Peloponnesischen Krieges*. Zürich.
Gumpert, M. (2001) *Grafting Helen. The Abduction of the Classical Past*. Madison, WI.
Halbwachs, M. (1980) *The Collective Memory*. New York, NY.
Hall, E. (1989) *Inventing the Barbarian. Greek Self-Definition through Tragedy*. Oxford.
  (1996) *Aeschylus. Persians*. Warminster.
Halliwell, S. (1998) *Aristotle's Poetics* (2nd edn). Chicago.
Hammond, N. G. L. (1952) 'The arrangement of the thought in the proem and in other parts of Thucydides I' *CQ* N.S. 2: 127–41.
Hampe, R. (1952) 'Zur Eschatologie in Pindar's *zweiter Olympischer Ode*', in *Hermeneia. Festschrift O. Regenbogen*. Heidelberg: 46–65.

Hansen, M. H. (1984) 'Two notes on Demosthenes' symbouleutic speeches' *C&M* 35: 57–70.
Hardtwig, W. (1991) 'Geschichtsreligion – Wissenschaft als Arbeit – Objektivität. Der Historismus in neuer Sicht' *HZ* 252: 1–32.
Harris, E. M. (1998) 'Review of M. J. Edwards, Greek Orators IV. Andocides' *CR* 48: 18–20.
  (2000) 'The authenticity of Andokides' *De Pace*. A subversive essay', in *Polis & Politics. Studies in Ancient Greek History*, eds. P. Flensted-Jensen, T. Heine Nielsen and L. Rubinstein. Copenhagen: 479–505.
Harrison, T. (2000a) *The Emptiness of Asia. Aeschylus' Persians and the History of the Fifth Century*. London.
  (2000b) *Divinity and History. The Religion of Herodotus*. Oxford.
Hartley, L. P. (1953) *The Go-Between*. London.
Havelock, E. (1964) *Preface to Plato*. Oxford.
Heath, M. (1988) 'Receiving the komos. The context and performance of epinician' *AJPh* 109: 180–95.
Heath, M. and M. Lefkowitz (1991) 'Epinician performance' *CPh* 86: 173–91.
Heck, K. and B. Jahn (eds.) (2000) *Genealogie als Denkform im Mittelalter und Früher Neuzeit*. Tübingen.
Heidegger, M. (1986) *Sein und Zeit* (16th edn.). Tübingen.
Hellmann, F. (1934) *Herodots Kroisos-Logos*. Berlin.
Hellwig, A. (1973) *Untersuchungen zur Theorie der Rhetorik bei Platon und Aristoteles*. Göttingen.
Heni, R. (1977) *Die Gespräche bei Herodot*. Heilbronn.
Henige, D. P. (1974) *The Chronology of Oral Tradition. Quest For a Chimera*. Oxford.
Herford, M. A. B. (1914) 'A cup by Brygos at Oxford' *JHS* 34: 106–13.
Herrman, J. (2004) *The Athenian Funeral Orations*. Newburyport.
Herrmann, H.-V. (1980) 'Pelops in Olympia', in *Stèlè. Tomos eis mnèmèn N. Kontoleontos*. Athens: 59–74.
Herzfeld, M. (1986) *Ours Once More. Folklore, Ideology, and the Making of Modern Greece*. New York, NY.
Herzfeld, M. (1991) *A Place in History. Social and Monumental Time in a Cretan Town*. Princeton, NJ.
Heuß, A. (1973) 'Motive von Herodots lydischem Logos' *Hermes* 101: 385–419.
Higbie, C. (2003) *The Lindian Chronicle and the Greek Creation of their Past*. Oxford.
Hobsbawm, E. and T. Ranger (eds.) (1983) *The Invention of Tradition*. Cambridge.
Hogan, J. C. (1972) 'Thucydides 3.52–68 and Euripides' *Hecuba*' *Phoenix* 26: 241–57.
Hohti, P. (1976a) *The Interrelation of Speech and Action in the Histories of Herodotus*. Helsinki.
  (1976b) 'Die Schuldfrage der Perserkriege in Herodots Geschichtswerk' *Arctos* 10: 37–48.
Hölscher, L. (1999) *Die Entdeckung der Zukunft*. Frankfurt.

Hölscher, T. (1973) *Griechische Historienbilder des 5. und 4. Jahrhunderts v. Chr.* Würzburg.
  (1998) 'Images and political identity: The case of Athens', in *Democracy, Empire, and the Arts in Fifth-Century Athens*, eds. D. Boedeker and K. Raaflaub. Cambridge, MA: 153–83.
Holtorf, C. (2005) 'Geschichtskultur in ur- und frühgeschichtlichen Kulturen Europas', in *Der Ursprung der Geschichte. Archaische Kulturen, das Alte Ägypten und das Frühe Griechenland*, eds. J. Assmann and K. E. Müller. Stuttgart: 87–111.
Holtsmark, E. B. (1970) 'Ring composition and the *Persae* of Aeschylus' *SO* 45: 5–23.
Hordern, J. H. (2002) *The Fragments of Timotheus of Miletus*. Oxford.
Hornblower, S. (1987) *Thucydides*. Baltimore, MD.
  (1991–6) *A Commentary on Thucydides. I–II*. Oxford.
  (1992) 'The religious dimension to the Peloponnesian War, or, what Thucydides does not tell us' *HSPh* 94: 169–97.
  (1994) 'Introduction', in *Greek Historiography*, ed. S. Hornblower. Oxford: 1–72.
  (2001) 'Epic and epiphanies. Herodotus and the "New Simonides"', in Boedeker and Sider (2001a): 135–47.
  (2004) *Thucydides and Pindar. Historical Narrative and the World of Epinikian Poetry*. Oxford.
Hornblower, S. and C. Morgan (2007) 'Introduction', in *Pindar's Poetry, Patrons, and Festivals. From Archaic Greece to the Roman Empire*, eds. S. Hornblower and C. Morgan. Oxford: 1–43.
How, W. W. and J. Wells (1912) *A Commentary on Herodotus. I–II*. Oxford.
Hubbard, T. K. (2001) '"New Simonides" or old Semonides? Second thoughts on *POxy* 3965 fr 26', in Boedeker and Sider (2001): 226–31.
  (2004) 'The dissemination of Epinician lyric: pan-hellenism, reperformance, written texts', in *Oral Performance and Its Context*, ed. C. J. Mackie. Leiden: 71–93.
Huber, L. (1965) 'Herodots Homerverständnis', in *Synusia. Festgabe für Wolfgang Schadewaldt*, eds. H. Flashar and K. Gaiser. Pfullingen: 29–52.
Hude, C. (1912) *Lysias*. Oxford.
Hude, K. (1927) *Herodoti Historiae. I–II* (3rd edn.). Oxford.
Hudson-Williams, H. L. L. (1948) 'Thucydides, Isocrates, and the rhetorical method of composition' *CQ* 42: 76–81.
Hunt, P. (2006) 'Warfare', in *Brill's Companion to Thucydides*, eds. A. Rengakos and A. Tsakmakis. Leiden: 385–413.
Hunter, V. (1973) *Thucydides, the Artful Reporter*. Toronto.
  (1973–4) 'Athens Tyrannis. A new approach to Thucydides' *CJ* 69: 120–6.
  (1982) *Past and Process in Herodotus and Thucydides*. Princeton, NJ.
Hurst, A. (1981) 'Observations sur la *deuxième Olympique* de Pindare' *ZAnt* 31: 121–33.
  (1983) 'Temps du récit chez Pindare (*Pyth.* 4) et Bacchylide (11)' *MH* 40: 154–68.
  (1985) 'Aspects du temps chez Pindare', in *Pindare (Entretiens Hardt 31)*, ed. A. Hurst. Geneva 1985: 155–97.

Husserl, E. (1928) *Vorlesungen zur Phänomenologie des inneren Zeitbewusstseins.* Halle.
Huxley, G. L. (1975) *Pindar's Vision of the Past.* Belfast.
  (1959) 'Mimnermus and Pylos' *GRBS* 2: 101–7.
  (1963) 'Two notes on Herodotus' *GRBS* 4: 5–8.
  (1969) *Greek Epic Poetry from Eumelos to Panyassis.* London.
  (1989) *Herodotus and the Epics.* Athens.
Huyssen, A. (1995) *Twilight Memories. Marking Time in a Culture of Amnesia.* London.
Immerwahr, H. R. (1954) 'Historical action in Herodotus' *TAPhA* 85: 16–45.
  (1956) 'Aspects of historical causation in Herodotus' *TAPhA* 87: 241–80.
  (1960) '*Ergon*. History as monument in Herodotus and Thucydides' *AJPh* 81: 261–90.
  (1966) *Form and Thought in Herodotus.* Cleveland, OH.
Irwin, E. (2005) *Solon and Early Greek Poetry. The Politics of Exhortation.* Cambridge.
Irwin, E. and E. Greenwood (2007) 'Introduction. Reading Herodotus, reading Book 7', in *Reading Herodotus. A Study of the Logoi in Book 5 of Herodotus' Histories*, eds. E. Irwin and E. Greenwood. Cambridge: 1–40.
Jacoby, F. (1913) 'Herodotos' *RE Supplement-Band II*: 205–520.
  (1918) 'Studien zu den älteren griechischen Elegikern I. Zu Tyrtaios II. Zu Mimnermos' *Hermes* 53: 1–44, 262–307.
  (1944) 'Patrios nomos. State burial in Athens and the public cemetery in the Kerameikos' *JHS* 64: 37–66.
  (1949) *Atthis. The Local Chronicles of Ancient Athens.* Oxford.
Jaeger, W. (1932) 'Tyrtaios über die wahre ἀρετή', in *Sitzungsberichte der Preuß. Akad. d. Wissenschaften.* Berlin: 537–68.
Jeismann, M. (ed.) (1999) *Mahnmal Mitte. Eine Kontroverse.* Cologne.
Jones, C. P. (1999) *Kinship Diplomacy in the Ancient World.* Cambridge, MA.
de Jong, I. (1999) 'Aspects narratologiques des *Histoires* d'Hérodote' *LALIES* 19: 217–75.
  (2001) 'The anachronical structure of Herodotus' *Histories*', in *Texts, Ideas, and the Classics. Scholarship and Theory in Classical Literature*, ed. S. Harrison. Oxford: 93–116.
Jordan, B. (1986) 'Religion in Thucydides' *TAPhA* 116: 119–47.
  (2000) 'The Sicilian Expedition was a potemkin fleet' *CQ* 50: 63–79.
Jost, K. (1936) *Das Beispiel und Vorbild der Vorfahren bei den attischen Rednern und Geschichtsschreibern bis Demosthenes.* Paderborn.
Jung, M. (2006) *Marathon und Plataiai. Zwei Perserschlachten als lieux de mémoire im antiken Griechenland.* Göttingen.
Kagan, D. (1981) *The Peace of Nicias and the Sicilian Expedition.* Ithaca, NY.
Kakridis, J. (1975) 'Licht und Finsternis in dem Botenbericht der *Perser* des Aischylos' *Grazer Beiträge* 4: 145–54.
Kallet, L. (2001) *Money and the Corrosion of Power in Thucydides. The Sicilian Expedition and Its Aftermath.* Berkeley, CA.

(2006) 'Thucydides' workshop of history and utility outside the text', in *Brill's Companion to Thucydides*, eds. A. Rengakos and A. Tsakmakis. Leiden: 335–68.
Kannicht, R. (1969) *Euripides. Helena. I. Einleitung und Text*. Heidelberg.
Kapp, E. (1930) 'Review of W. Schadewaldt, Die Geschichtsschreibung des Thukydides. Ein Versuch' *Gnomon* 6: 76–100.
Kartes, B. (2000) *Der Epitaphios des Lysias*. Saarbrücken.
Kennedy, G. A. (1963) *The Art of Persuasion in Greece*. Princeton, NJ.
(1994) *A New History of Classical Rhetoric*. Princeton, NJ.
Kern, P. B. (1989) 'The turning point in the Sicilian Expedition' *CB* 65: 77–82.
Kierdorf, W. (1966) *Erlebnis und Darstellung der Perserkriege*. Göttingen.
Kinzl, K. (1978) 'Demokratia. Studie zur Frühgeschichte des Begriffes' *Gymnasium* 85: 117–27, 312–26.
Kirchberg, J. (1965) *Die Funktion der Orakel im Werke Herodots*. Göttingen.
Kirchhoff, A. (1878) *Über die Entstehungszeit des herodotischen Geschichtswerkes* (2nd edn.). Berlin.
Kirchner, H. (1954) 'Über das Verhältnis des schriftlosen frühgeschichtlichen Menschen zu seiner Geschichte' *Sociologus* 4: 9–22.
Kirk, G. S. (1985) *The Iliad: A Commentary. I: Books 1–4*. Cambridge.
(1990) *The Iliad: A Commentary. II: Books 5–8*. Cambridge.
Kirkwood, G. M. (1958) *A Study of Sophoclean Drama*. Ithaca, NY.
Kitto, H. D. F. (1961) *Greek Tragedy* (3rd edn.). London.
(1966) *Poiesis. Structure and Thought*. Berkeley, CA.
Klinger, W. (1930) 'Un fragment de l'élégie guerrière de Mimnerme. Son importance et l'époque où elle fut composée' *Bulletin International de l'Académie Polonaise de Sciences et des Lettres:* 78–83.
Knell, H. (1990) *Mythos und Polis. Bildprogramme griechischer Bauskulptur*. Darmstadt.
Kock, B. (1925) 'Leokorion' *RE* 12/2: 2000–1.
Kohl, W. (1977) *Die Redetrias vor der sizilischen Expedition (Thukydides 6,9–23)*. Meisenheim am Glan.
Köhnken, A. (1971) *Die Funktion des Mythos bei Pindar. Interpretationen zu sechs Pindargedichten*. Berlin.
(1983) 'Mythical chronology and thematic coherence in Pindar's Third Olympian Ode' *HSPh* 87: 49–63.
Konstan, D. (1983) 'The stories in Herodotus' Histories. Book I' *Helios* N.S. 10: 1–22.
(1987) 'Persians, Greeks and empire', in *Herodotus and the Invention of History*, ed. D. Boedeker (Arethusa 20): 59–73.
Koselleck, R. (1975) 'Geschichte, Historie. V. Die Herausbildung des modernen Geschichtsbegriffs' *GG* II: 647–91.
(1985) *Futures Past. On the Semantics of Historical Time*. Cambridge, MA.
Koster, S. (1970) *Antike Epostheorien*. Wiesbaden.
Kowerski, L. (2005) *Simonides on the Persian Wars. A Study of the Elegiac Verses of the 'New Simonides'*. New York, NY.

Krischer, T. (1977) 'Die enkomiastische Topik im Epitaphios des Perikles' *Mnemosyne* 30: 122–34.
Kron, U. (1999) 'Patriotic heroes', in *Ancient Greek Hero Cult*, ed. R. Hägg. Stockholm: 61–83.
Krummen, E. (1990) *Pyrsos Hymnon. Festliche Gegenwart und mythisch-rituelle Tradition als Voraussetzung einer Pindarinterpretation (Isthmie 4, Pythie 5, Olympie 1 und 3)*. Berlin.
Kühner, R. and B. Gerth (1898) *Ausführliche Grammatik der griechischen Sprache II. Satzlehre. I–II* (3rd edn.). Hannover.
Kuhnt-Saptodewo, S. (2006) *Getanzte Geschichte. Tanz, Religion und Geschichte auf Java*. Vienna.
Kullmann, W. (1956) 'Zur Διὸς βουλή des Iliasproömiums' *Philologus* 100: 132–3.
Kurke, L. (1991) *The Traffic in Praise. Pindar and the Poetics of Social Economy*. Ithaca, NY.
  (1999) *Coins, Bodies, Games, and Gold. The Politics of Meaning in Archaic Greece*. Princeton, NJ.
  (2000) 'Charting the poles of history. Herodotos and Thoukydides', in *Literature in the Greek and Roman Worlds*, ed. O. Taplin. Oxford: 133–55.
Lachenaud, G. (1978) *Mythologies, religion et philosophie de l'histoire dans Hérodote*. Lille.
Lamb, W. R. M. (1976) *Lysias*. Cambridge, MA.
Lamberton, R. and J. J. Keaney (eds.) (1992) *Homer's Ancient Readers. The Hermeneutics of Greek Epic's Earliest Exegetes*. Princeton, NJ.
Lambin, G. (1988) '"Ἔλεγος et ἐλεγεῖον' *RPh* 62: 69–77.
Lanata, G. (1963) *Poetica pre-platonica. Testimonianze e frammenti*. Florence.
Landmann, G. P. (1974) 'Das Lob Athens in der Grabrede des Perikles. Thukydides II 34–41' *MH* 31: 65–95.
Lang, M. (1954–5) 'The murder of Hipparchus' *Historia* 3: 395–407.
  (1984) *Herodotean Narrative and Discourse*. Cambridge, MA.
Lasserre, F. (1976) 'L'historiographie grecque à l'époque archaïque' *QS* 4: 113–42.
Lateiner, D. (1977) 'No laughing matter: A literary tactic in Herodotus' *TAPhA* 107: 173–82.
  (1985) 'Nicias' inadequate encouragement (Thucydides 7.69.2)' *CPh* 80: 201–13.
  (1989) *The Historical Method of Herodotus*. Toronto.
Lattimore, R. (1939) 'The wise adviser in Herodotus' *CPh* 34(1): 24–35.
  (1943) 'Aeschylus on the defeated of Xerxes', in *Classical Studies in Honor of W. A. Oldfather*. Urbana: 82–93.
  (1951) *The Iliad of Homer*. Chicago.
Lattimore, S. (1999) *Thucydides. The Peloponnesian War*. Indianapolis, IN.
Layton, R. (ed.) (1994) *Who Needs the Past? Indigenous Values and Archaeology*. London.
van Leeuwen, J. (1964) *Pindarus' Tweede Olympische Ode. I–II*. Leiden.
Lefèvre, E. (1987) 'Die Unfähigkeit, sich zu erkennen. Unzeitgemäße Betrachtungen zu Sophokles' *Oidipus Tyrannos*' *WJA* 13: 37–58.
  (2001) *Die Unfähigkeit, sich zu erkennen. Sophokles' Tragödien*. Leiden.

Lefkowitz, M. (1981) *The Lives of the Greek Poets*. London.
  (1988) 'Who sang Pindar's victory odes?' *AJPh* 109: 1–11.
  (1995) 'The first person in Pindar reconsidered – again' *BICS* N.S. 2: 139–50.
Legendre, P. (1985) *L'inestimable objet de la transmission. Essai sur le principe généalogique en Occident*. Paris.
Legrand, P.-E. (1937) 'Hérodote croyait-il aux oracles?', in *Mélanges A.-M. Desrousseaux*. Paris: 275–84.
Lehnus, L. (2000) *Nuova bibliografia callimachea (1498–1998)*. Alessandria.
Lendle, O. (1990) 'Κτῆμα εἰς αἰεί. Thukydides und Herodot' *RhM* 133: 231–42.
Lendon, J. E. (forthcoming) 'Historians without history: Against Roman historiography', in *Cambridge Companion to Roman Historians*, ed. A. Feldherr. New York.
Lenz, L. (1986) 'Zu Dramaturgie und Tragik in den *Persern*' *Gymnasium* 93: 141–63.
Lesky, A. (1947) *Thalatta. Der Weg der Griechen zum Meer*. Vienna.
Lévy, E. (1976) *Athènes devant la défaite de 404. Histoire d'une crise idéologique*. Paris.
Liebsch, B. (1996) *Geschichte im Zeichen des Abschieds*. Munich.
Linforth, I. M. (1928) 'Named and unnamed gods in Herodotus' *Univ. Calif. Publ. Class. Phil.* 9/7: 201–43.
Lipsius, J. H. (1886) *Quaestiones logographicae*. Leipzig.
Lissarrague, F. (1984) 'Autour du guerrier', in *La cité des images. Religion et société en Grèce antique*, eds. C. Bérard and J. P. Vernant. Paris: 35–48.
Lloyd, A. B. (1988) *Herodotus, Book II. Commentary. I–II*. Leiden.
Lloyd-Jones, H. (1968) 'The Cologne Fragment of Alcaeus' *GBRS* 9: 125–39.
  (1971) *The Justice of Zeus*. Berkeley, CA.
  (1985) 'Pindar and after-life', in *Pindare (Entretiens Hardt 31)*, ed. A. Hurst. Geneva: 245–79.
  (1994) 'Notes on the New Simonides' *ZPE* 101: 1–3.
Lobel, E. (1954) '2327: Early Elegiacs' *The Oxyrhynchus Papyri* 22: 67–76.
Lombardo, S. (1997) *Homer's Iliad*. Indianapolis, IN.
Long, T. (1987) *Repetition and Variation in the Short Stories of Herodotus*. Frankfurt.
Loraux, N. (1973) '"Marathon" ou l'histoire idéologique. A propos des paragraphes 20 a 26 de l'oraison funèbre en l'honneur des soldats qui allèrent au secours des Corinthiens (attribuée a Lysias)' *REA* 75: 13–42.
  (1975) 'HBH et ANDREIA. Deux versions de la mort du combattant athénien' *Ancient Society* 6: 1–31.
  (1980) 'Thucydide n'est pas un collègue' *QS* 12: 55–81.
  (1986a) *The Invention of Athens. The Funeral Oration in the Classical City*. Cambridge.
  (1986b) 'Thucydide a écrit la Guerre du Péloponnèse' *Metis* 1: 139–61.
Lowenthal, D. (1985) *The Past is a Foreign Country*. Cambridge.
  (1996) *Possessed by the Past. The Heritage Crusade and the Spoils of History*. New York, NY.
Löwith, K. (1949) *Meaning in History. The Theological Implications of the Philosophy of History*. Chicago, IL.

Lübbe, H. (1977) *Geschichtsbegriff und Geschichtsinteresse. Analytik und Pragmatik der Historie.* Basel.
Luce, T. J. (1991) 'Tacitus on "history's highest function". *Praecipuum munus annalium (Ann.* 3.65)' *ANRW II* 33.4: 2904–27.
Luginbill, R. D. (2002) 'Tyrtaeus 12 West: Come join the Spartan army' *CQ* 52: 405–14.
Luppe, W. (1993) 'Zum neuesten Simonides. *P. Oxy.* 3965 fr. 1 / 2327 fr. 6' *ZPE* 99: 1–9.
 (1994) 'Die Korinther in der Schlacht von Plataiai bei Simonides nach Plutarch (Simon. fr. 15 und 16 W²; *P. Oxy.* 3965 fr. 5)' *APF* 40: 21–4.
Luraghi, N. (1994) *Tirannidi arcaiche in Sicilia e magna Grecia. Da Panezio di Leontini alla caduta dei Dinomenidi.* Florence.
 (2002) 'Helotic slavery reconsidered', in *Sparta. Beyond the Mirage*, eds. A. Powell and S. Hodkinson. London: 227–48.
 (2003) 'The imaginary conquest of the Helots', in *Helots and their Masters in Laconia and Messenia. Histories, Ideologies, Structures*, eds. N. Luraghi and S. E. Alcock. Cambridge, MA: 109–41.
 (2008) *The Ancient Messenians. Construction of Ethnicity and Memory.* Cambridge.
Lurje, M. (2004) *Die Suche nach der Schuld. Sophokles' Oedipus Rex, Aristoteles' Poetik und das Tragödienverständnis der Neuzeit.* Munich.
Maass, E. (1887) 'Untersuchungen zur Geschichte der griechischen Prosa' *Hermes* 22: 566–95.
Macan, R. W. (1908) *Herodotus. The Histories. The Seventh, Eighth, and Ninth Books. I–II.* London.
Mackie, C. J. (1996) 'Homer and Thucydides. Corcyra and Sicily' *CQ* N.S. 46: 103–13.
Mackie, H. (2003) *Graceful Errors. Pindar and the Performance of Praise.* Ann Arbor, MI.
Macleod, C. W. (1983a) 'Thucydides and tragedy', in *Collected Essays.* Oxford: 140–58.
 (1983b) 'Thucydides' Plataean debate', in *Collected Essays.* Oxford: 103–22.
Mader, G. (1993) 'Rogue's comedy at Segesta (Thucydides 6.46). Alcibiades exposed?' *Hermes* 121: 181–95.
Magnien, V. (1922) 'Emploi des démonstratifs chez Homère' *BSL* 23: 156–83.
Makropoulos, M. (1997) *Modernität und Kontingenz.* Munich.
 (1998) 'Modernität als Kontingenzkultur. Konturen eines Konzepts', in *Kontingenz*, eds. G. von Graevenitz and O. Marquard. Munich: 55–79.
de Marco, V. (1939–40) 'Studii intorno a Mimnermo' *RIL* 73: 311–50.
Marg, W. (1965) '"Selbstsicherheit" bei Herodot', in *Herodot. Eine Auswahl aus der neueren Forschung*, ed. W. Marg (2nd edn.). Darmstadt: 290–301.
 (1976) 'Kampf und Tod in der Ilias' *WJb* 2: 7–19.
 (1991) *Herodot. Historien. I–II.* Munich.
Marinatos, N. (1980) 'Nicias as a wise advisor and tragic warner in Thucydides' *Philologus* 124: 305–10.
 (1981) *Thucydides and Religion.* Königstein.

Marinatos-Kopff, N. and H. Rawlings (1978) '*Panolethria* and divine punishment' *PP* 182: 331–7.
Marincola, J. (1997) *Authority and Tradition in Ancient Historiography*. Cambridge.
　(2001) *Greek Historians*. Oxford.
　(2006) 'Herodotus and the poetry of the past', in *The Cambridge Companion to Herodotus*, eds. C. Dewald and J. Marincola. Cambridge: 13–28.
　(2007) 'Speeches in classical historiography', in *A Companion to Greek and Roman Historiography. I*, ed. J. Marincola. London: 118–32.
Marquard, O. (1986) 'Apologie des Zufälligen. Philosophische Überlegungen zum Menschen', in *Apologie des Zufälligen. Philosophische Studien*. Stuttgart: 117–39.
Marsa Positano, L. (1946) 'Nugae' *PP* 1: 359–72.
Martin, R. (1989) *The Language of Heroes. Speech and Performance in the Iliad*. Ithaca, NY.
Masaracchia, A. (1977) *Erodoto, Libro VIII delle Storie: La Battaglia di Salamina*. Verona.
Maurizio, L. (1997) 'Delphic oracles as oral performances. Authenticity and historical evidence' *ClAnt* 16: 308–34.
Mazzarino, S. (1966) *Il pensiero storico classico I*. Bari.
Mbunwe-Samba, P. (1989) 'Oral tradition and the African past', in *Who Needs the Past? Indigenous Values and Archaeology*, ed. R. Layton. London: 105–18.
McCall, M. F. (1986) 'Aeschylus in the *Persae*. A bold strategy succeeds', in *Greek Tragedy and Its Legacy*, eds. M. Cropp, E. Fantham and S. E. Scully. Calgary: 43–9.
McKay, K. J. (1975) 'Mimnermos Fr. 13, 9ff Diehl (Fr. 14 West)' *Hermes* 103: 373.
Meier, C. (1988) *Die politische Kunst der griechischen Tragödie*. Munich.
　(1990) *The Greek Discovery of Politics*. Cambridge, MA.
Meier, M. (1998) *Aristokraten und Damoden. Untersuchungen zur inneren Entwicklung Spartas im 7. Jahrhundert v. Chr. und zur politischen Funktion der Dichtung des Tyrtaios*. Stuttgart.
Meiggs, R. (1972) *The Athenian Empire*. Oxford.
Meiggs, R. and M. D. Lewis (1969) *A Selection of Greek Historical Inscriptions to the End of the Fifth Century B.C.* Oxford.
Meineke, A. (1857) *Ioannis Stobaei Florilegium. I–IV*. Leipzig.
Melchinger, S. (1979) *Die Welt als Tragödie. I*. Munich.
Merkelbach, R. (1967) 'Ein Alkaios-Papyrus' *ZPE* 1: 81–95.
Meyer, Eduard (1892) *Forschungen zur Alten Geschichte I*. Halle.
　(1899) *Forschungen zur Alten Geschichte. II*. Halle.
Meyer, Elizabeth (2008) 'Thucydides on Harmodius and Aristogeiton, tyranny, and history' *CQ* 58: 13–34.
Michelini, A. (1982) *Tradition and Dramatic Form in the Persians of Aeschylus*. Leiden.
Mikalson, J. D. (1983) *Athenian Popular Religion*. Chapel Hill, NC.
　(2003) *Herodotus and Religion in the Persian Wars*. Chapel Hill, NC.
Miller, M. (1963) 'The Herodotean Croesus' *Klio* 41: 89–92.
Mills, S. (1997) *Theseus, Tragedy and the Athenian Empire*. Oxford.

Missiou, A. (1992) *The Subversive Oratory of Andokides. Politics, Ideology and Decision-Making in Democratic Athens.* Cambridge.
Mitsis, P. (1988) 'Xerxes' entrance. Irony, myth, and history in the *Persians*', in *Language and the Tragic Hero. Essays in Honor of G. M. Kirkwood*, ed. P. Pucci. Atlanta, GA: 103–19.
Moles, J. (1993) 'Truth and untruth in Herodotus and Thucydides', in *Lies and Fiction in the Ancient World*, eds. C. Gill and T. P. Wiseman. Exeter: 88–121.
  (1996) 'Herodotus warns the Athenians' *Papers of the Leeds International Latin Seminar* 9: 259–84.
  (1999) "Ἀνάθημα καὶ Κτῆμα: The inscriptional inheritance of ancient historiography' *Histos* (www.dur.ac.uk//Classics//histos//1999//moles.html).
  (2001) 'A false dilemma: Thucydides' *History* and historicism', in *Texts, Ideas, and the Classics. Scholarship, Theory, and Classical Literature*, ed. S. J. Harrison. Oxford: 195–219.
  (2002) 'Herodotus and Athens', in *Brill's Companion to Herodotus*, eds. E. Bakker, I. de Jong and H. van Wees. Leiden: 33–52.
Molyneux, J. H. (1992) *Simonides. A Historical Study.* Wauconda, IL.
Momigliano, A. (1936) 'Per la storia della pubblicistica sulla κοινὴ εἰρήνη nel IV sec. a. C' *ASNP* II 5: 97–123.
  (1971) 'L'excursus di Tucidide in VI, 54–59', in *Studi di storiografia antica in memoria di Leonardo Ferrero.* Torino: 31–5.
Moraux, P. (1954) 'Thucydide et la rhétorique' *LEC* 22: 3–23.
Morgan, K. A. (1993) 'Pindar the professional and the rhetoric of the komos' *CPh* 88: 1–15.
Morrison, J. V. (1994) 'Thematic inversion in the *Iliad*. The Greeks under siege' *GRBS* 35: 209–27.
  (1999) 'Preface to Thucydides: Rereading the Corcyrean conflict (1.24–55)' *ClAnt* 18: 94–131.
  (2000) 'Historical lessons in the Melian episode' *TAPhA* 130: 119–48.
  (2004) 'Memory, time, and writing: Oral and literary aspects of Thucydides' *History*', in *Oral Performance and its Context*, ed. C. J. Mackie. Leiden: 95–116.
  (2006) 'Interaction of speech and narrative in Thucydides', in *Brill's Companion to Thucydides*, eds. A. Rengakos and A. Tsakmakis. Leiden: 251–77.
Morson, G. S. (1994) *Narrative and Freedom. The Shadows of Time.* New Haven, CT.
Morstein-Marx, R. (2004) *Mass Oratory and Political Power in the Late Roman Republic.* Cambridge.
Most, G. W. (1985) *The Measures of Praise. Structure and Function in Pindar's Second Pythian and Seventh Nemean Odes.* Göttingen.
  (1986) 'Pindar, *O.* 2.83–90' *CQ* N.S. 36: 304–16.
Moyer, I. S. (2002) 'Herodotus and an Egyptian mirage: The genealogies of the Theban priests' *JHS* 122: 70–90.
Mülke, M. (2000) 'Phrynichos und Athen: Der Beschluß über die *Miletu Halosis* (Herodot 6, 21, 2)', in *Skenika. Beiträge zum antiken Theater und seiner*

Rezeption. Festschrift zum 65. Geburtstag von H.-D. Blume, eds. S. Gödde and T. Heinze. Darmstadt: 233–46.
Müller, C. W. (1988) 'Die antike Buchausgabe des Mimnermos' *RhM* 131: 197–211.
Müller, R. (1968) 'Antike Theorien über Ursprung und Entwicklung der Kultur' *Das Altertum* 14: 67–79.
Munn, M. (2000) *The School of History. Athens in the Age of Socrates*. Berkeley, CA.
Munson, R. V. (2001) *Telling Wonders: Ethnographic and Political Discourse in the Work of Herodotus*. Ann Arbor, MI.
Murray, O. (1982) 'Symposion and Männerbund', in *Concilium Eirene 16/1*, eds. P. Oliva and A. Frolíková. Prague: 47–52.
  (1983a) 'The Greek symposion in history', in *Tria Corda. Scritti in onore di Arnaldo Momigliano*, ed. E. Gabba. Como: 257–72.
  (1983b) 'The symposium as social organisation', in *The Greek Renaissance of the Eighth Century B.C. Tradition and Innovation*, ed. R. Hägg. Stockholm: 195–9.
  (ed.) (1990a) *Sympotica. A Symposium on the Symposion*. Oxford.
  (1990b) 'Sympotic history', in Murray (1990a): 3–13.
Nagy, G. (1986) 'Ancient Greek epic and praise poetry: Some typological considerations', in *Oral Tradition in Literature. Interpretation in Context*, ed. J. Foley. Columbia, MD: 89–102.
  (1990) *Pindar's Homer. The Lyric Possession of an Epic Past*. Baltimore, MD.
Nenci, G. (1998) *Erodoto, Le Storie. Libro VI: La battaglia di Maratona*. Verona.
Nesselrath, H.-G. (1996) 'Herodot und der griechische Mythos' *Poetica* 28: 275–96.
Neumann, U. (1995) *Gegenwart und mythische Vergangenheit bei Euripides*. Stuttgart.
Nicolai, R. (1995) 'κτῆμα ἐς αἰεί. Aspetti della fortuna di Tucidide nel mondo antico' *RIFC* 123: 5–26.
Nicolai, W. (1986) *Versuch über Herodots Geschichtsphilosophie*. Heidelberg.
  (1998) 'Aischylos' Perser', in *Aspekte des Geschichtsdramas. Von Aischylos bis Volker Braun*, ed. W. Düsing. Tübingen: 12–30.
Nietzsche, F. (1954) *Werke in drei Bänden. I–III*. Munich.
Nilsson, M. P. (1951) *Cults, Myths, Oracles, and Politics in Ancient Greece*. Lund.
Nisetich, F. J. (1980) *Pindar's Victory Songs*. Baltimore, MD.
  (1988) 'Immortality in Acragas: Poetry and religion in Pindar's Second Olympian Ode' *CPh* 83: 1–19.
  (1989) *Pindar and Homer*. Baltimore, MD.
Nora, P. (1984–92) *Les lieux de mémoire. I–III.3*. Paris.
Norden, E. (1983) *Die antike Kunstprosa vom VI. Jh. v. Chr. bis in die Zeit der Renaissance* (9th edn.). Stuttgart.
Norlin, G. (1966) *Isocrates. I*. Cambridge, MA.
Nouhaud, M. (1982) *L'utilisation de l'histoire par les orateurs attiques*. Paris.
Obbink, D. (2001) 'The genre of Plataea. Generic unity in the New Simonides', in Boedeker and Sider (2001a): 65–85.
  (2006) 'A new Archilochus poem' *ZPE* 156: 1–9.
Ober, J. (1989) *Mass and Elite in Democratic Athens: Rhetoric, Ideology and the Power of the People*. Princeton, NJ.

(1998) *Political Dissent in Democratic Athens. Intellectual Critics of Popular Rule.* Princeton, NJ.
Ober, J. and B. Strauss (1990) 'Drama, political rhetoric, and the discourse of Athenian democracy', in *Nothing to Do With Dionysos? Athenian Drama in Its Social Context*, eds. J. J. Winkler and F. Zeitlin. Princeton, NJ: 237–70.
Oexle, O. G. (1996) 'Meineckes Historismus. Über Kontext und Folgen einer Definition', in *Historismus in den Kulturwissenschaften. Geschichtskonzepte, historische Einschätzungen, Grundlagenprobleme*, eds. O. G. Oexle and J. Rüsen. Cologne: 139–99.
Oost, S. I. (1975) 'Thucydides and the irrational: Sundry passages' *CPh* 70: 186–96.
Orwin, C. (1994) *The Humanity of Thucydides*. Princeton, NJ.
Paduano, G. (1978) *Sui Persiani di Eschilo. Problemi di focalizzazione drammatica*. Rome.
Page, D. L. (1936) 'The elegiacs in Euripides' *Andromache*. Greek poetry and life', in *Essays Presented to Gilbert Murray*. Oxford: 206–30.
  (1951) 'Rev. E. Diehl, Anthologia Lyrica Graeca' *CR* N.S. 1: 11–14.
  (1962) *Poetae Melici Graeci*. Oxford (=*PMG*).
  (1963) 'Archilochus and the oral tradition' *Archiloque (Entretiens Hardt 10)* Geneva: 119–63.
  (1974) *Supplementum Lyricis Graecis*. Oxford (=*SLG*).
Pallantza, E. (2005) *Der Troische Krieg in der nachhomerischen Literatur bis zum 5. Jh. v. Chr.* Stuttgart.
Parke, H. W. (1977) *Festivals of the Athenians*. London.
Parker, R. (1983) *Miasma. Pollution and Purification in Early Greek Religion.* Oxford.
  (1997) 'Gods cruel and kind: Tragic and civic theology', in *Greek Tragedy and the Historian*, ed. C. Pelling. Oxford: 143–60.
Parker, V. (1991) 'The dates of the Messenian Wars' *Chiron* 21: 25–47.
  (1993) 'Some dates in early Spartan history' *Klio* 75: 45–60.
Parry, A. (1972) 'Thucydides' historical perspective' *YClS* 22: 47–61.
  (1989a) 'Classical philology and literary criticism', in *The Language of Achilles and Other Papers*, ed. A. Parry. Oxford: 141–7.
  (1989b) 'The language of Thucydides' description of the plague', in *The Language of Achilles and Other Papers*, ed. A. Parry. Oxford: 156–76.
Parsons, P. (1992) '3965: Simonides, Elegies' *The Oxyrhynchus Papyri* 59: 4–50.
  (2001) 'These fragments we have shored against our ruin', in Boedeker and Sider (2001a): 55–64.
Pasquali, G. (1923) 'Mimnermo' *SIFC* N.S. 3: 293–303.
Patterson, C. (2006) 'Citizen cemeteries in classical Athens?' *CQ* 56: 48–56.
Pavese, C. O. (1995) 'Elegia di Simonide agli Spartiati per Platea' *ZPE* 107: 1–26.
Pearson, L. (1941) 'Historical allusions in the Attic orators' *CPh* 36: 209–29.
  (1949) 'Note on a digression in Thucydides (VI, 54–59)' *AJPh* 70: 186–9.
Pelling, C. (1991) 'Thucyides' Archidamus and Herodotus' Artabanus', in *Georgica. Greek Studies in Honour of George Cawkwell*, eds. M. Flower and M. Toher. London: 120–42.

(1997a) 'Aeschylus' *Persae* and history', in *Greek Tragedy and the Historian*, ed. C. Pelling. Oxford: 1–19.
(1997b) 'East is East and West is West – or are they? National stereotypes in Herodotus' *Histos* 1.
(2006a) 'Speech and narrative in the *Histories*', in *The Cambridge Companion to Herodotus*, eds. C. Dewald and J. Marincola. Cambridge: 103–21.
(2006b) 'Homer and Herodotus', in *Epic Interactions. Perspectives on Homer, Virgil, and the Epic Tradition. Presented to Jasper Griffin by Former Pupils*, ed. M. J. Clarke. Oxford: 75–104.
(2007) 'Aristagoras (5.49–55, 97)', in *Reading Herodotus. A Study of the Logoi in Book 5 of Herodotus' Histories*, eds. E. Irwin and E. Greenwood. Cambridge: 179–201.
Pellitzer, E. (1983) 'Sulla cronologia, la vita e l'opere di Semonides Amorgino' *QUCC* N.S. 14: 17–28.
(1990) 'Outlines of a morphology of sympotic entertainment', in Murray (1990a): 177–84.
Perlman, S. (1961) 'The historical example, its use and importance as political propaganda in the attic orators' *Scripta Hierosolymitana* 7: 150–66.
Péron, J. (1974) *Les images maritimes de Pindare*. Paris.
Pickard-Cambridge, A. (1968) *The Dramatic Festivals of Athens* (2nd edn., revised by. J. Gould and D. M. Lewis). Oxford.
Plant, I. M. (1999) 'The influence of forensic oratory on Thucydides' principles of method' *CQ* N.S. 1: 62–73.
Podlecki, A. J. (1984) *The Early Greek Poets and Their Times*. Vancouver.
(1993) 'Κἀτ' ἀρχῆς γὰρ φιλαίτιος λεώς: The concept of leadership in Aeschylus', in *Tragedy, Comedy and the Polis*, ed. A. H. Sommerstein. Bari: 55–79.
Pohlenz, M. (1948) 'Zu den attischen Reden auf die Gefallenen' *SO* 26: 46–74.
Poltera, O. (1997) *Le langage de Simonide: Étude sur la tradition poétique et son renouvellement*. Bern.
Porciani, L. (2001) *Prime forme della storiografia greca. Prospettiva locale e generale nella narrazione storica*. Stuttgart.
Powell, J. E. (1938) *A Lexicon to Herodotus*. Cambridge.
Pownall, F. S. (1995) 'Presbeis Autokratores: Andokides' *De Pace*' *Phoenix* 49: 140–9.
Prato, C. (1968) *Tirteo*. Rome.
Preiß, A. (ed.) (1990) *Das Museum. Die Entwicklung in den 80er Jahren*. Munich.
Pretagostini, R. (1984) *Ricerche sulla Poesia Alexandrina*. Rome.
Price, J. J. (2001) *Thucydides and Internal War*. Cambridge.
Primavesi, O. (2000) 'Nestors Erzählungen. Die Variationen eines rhetorischen Überzeugungsmittels in der *Ilias*', in *Rede und Redner. Bewertung und Darstellung in den antiken Kulturen*, eds. C. Neumeister and W. Raeck. Möhnesee: 45–64.
Prince, G. (2003) *A Dictionary of Narratology* (2nd edn.). Lincoln, NE.
Prinz, K. (1997) *Epitaphios Logos. Struktur, Funktion und Bedeutung der Bestattungsreden im Athen des 5. und 4. Jahrhunderts*. Frankfurt.

Pritchett, W. K. (1979) *The Greek State at War, III: Religion.* Berkeley, CA.
  (1985) *The Greek State at War, IV.* Berkeley, CA.
Pucci, P. (1992) *Oedipus and the Fabrication of the Father. 'Oedipus Tyrannus' in Modern Criticism and Philosophy.* Baltimore, MD.
Raaflaub, K. (1987) 'Herodotus, political thought, and the meaning of history', in *Herodotus and the Invention of History*, ed. D. Boedeker (Arethusa 20): 221–48.
  (2002a) 'Herodot und Thukydides: Persischer Imperialismus im Lichte der athenischen Sizilienpolitik', in *Widerstand – Anpassung – Integration. Die griechische Staatenwelt und Rom*, eds. N. Ehrhardt and L.-M. Günther. Stuttgart: 11–40.
  (2002b) 'Philosophy, science, politics: Herodotus and the intellectual trends of his time', in *Brill's Companion to Herodotus*, eds. E. Bakker, I. de Jong and H. van Wees. Leiden: 149–86.
  (forthcoming) 'Ulterior motives in ancient historiography. What exactly and why?', in Foxhall and Gehrke (forthcoming).
Race, W. H. (1979) 'The End of *Olympian* 2. Pindar and the *Vulgus*' *CSCA* 12: 251–67.
  (1997) *Pindar, I–II.* Cambridge, MA.
Raubitschek, A. E. (1941a) 'Two notes on Isocrates' *TAPhA* 72: 356–64.
  (1941b) 'The heroes of Phyle' *Hesperia* 10: 284–95.
Rawlings, H. R. (1981) *The Structure of Thucydides' History.* Princeton, NJ.
Rebuffat, R. (1966) 'Hélène en Égypte et le romain égaré (Hérodote, II, 115, et Polybe, III, 22–24)' *REA* 68: 245–63.
Redfield, J. (1985) 'Herodotus the tourist' *CPh* 80: 97–118.
Regenbogen, O. (1930) 'Herodot und sein Werk. Ein Versuch' *Die Antike* 6: 202–48.
  (1961) 'Die Geschichte von Solon und Krösus. Eine Studie zur Geistesgeschichte des 5. und 6. Jhs', in *Kleine Schriften*, ed. F. Dirlmeier. Munich: 101–24.
Rehm, R. (2002) *The Play of Space. Spatial Transformation in Greek Tragedy.* Princeton, NJ.
Reinhardt, K. (1916) *Parmenides und die Geschichte der griechischen Philosophie.* Bonn.
Reitzenstein, R. (1893) *Epigramm und Skolion. Ein Beitrag zur Geschichte der alexandrinischen Dichtung.* Giessen.
Rengakos, A. (1984) *Form und Wandel des Machtdenkens der Athener bei Thukydides.* Stuttgart.
  (2004) 'Strategien der Geschichtsdarstellung bei Herodot und Thukydides – oder Vom Ursprung der Historiographie aus dem Geist des Epos', in *Geschichtsdarstellung. Medien – Methoden – Strategien*, eds. V. Borsò and C. Kann. Cologne: 73–99.
  (2006a) 'Homer and the historians: The influence of epic narrative technique on Herodotus and Thucydides', in *La Poésie Épique Grecque. Métamorphoses d'un Genre Littéraire (Entretiens Hardt 52).* Geneva: 183–209.
  (2006b) 'Thucydides' narrative: The epic and Herodotean heritage', in *Brill's Companion to Thucydides*, eds. A. Rengakos and A. Tsakmakis. Leiden: 279–300.

Renthe-Fink, L. von (1964) *Geschichtlichkeit. Ihr terminologischer und begrifflicher Ursprung bei Hegel, Haym, Dilthey und Yorck*. Göttingen.
Rhodes, P. J. (1994) 'In defence of the Greek historians' *G&R* 41: 156–71.
Richardson, N. J. (1986) 'Pindar and later literary criticism in antiquity' *Papers of the Liverpool Latin Seminar* 5: 383–401.
  (1993) *The Iliad: A Commentary*. VI: Books 21–4. Cambridge.
Ricoeur, P. (1990) *Time and Narrative. I–III*. Chicago, IL.
  (2004) *Memory, History, Forgetting*. Chicago, IL.
Ridley, R. T. (1981) 'Exegesis and audience in Thucydides' *Hermes* 109: 25–46.
Robertson, M. (1975) *A History of Greek Art. I–II*. Cambridge.
Rogkotis, Z. (2006) 'Thucydides and Herodotus. Aspects of their intertextual relationship', in *Brill's Companion to Thucydides*, eds. A. Rengakos and A. Tsakmakis. Leiden: 57–86.
Roisman, H. M. (2007) 'Right rhetoric in Homer', in *A Companion to Greek Rhetoric*, ed. I. Worthington. Malden, MA: 429–46.
de Romilly, J. (1956a) 'L'utilité de l'histoire selon Thucydide', in *Histoire et Historiens dans l'antiquité. Entretiens sur l'antiquité classique tome IV*. Geneva: 41–81.
  (1956b) *Histoire et Raison chez Thucydide*. Paris.
  (1963) *Thucydides and Athenian Imperialism*. Oxford.
  (1966) 'La condamnation du plaisir dans l'oeuvre de Thucydide' *WS* 79: 142–8.
  (1971) 'La vengeance comme explication historique dans l'oeuvre d'Hérodote' *REG* 84: 314–37.
  (1985) *La crainte et l'angoisse dans le théâtre d'Eschyle*. Paris.
Rood, T. (1998a) *Thucydides. Narrative and Explanation*. Oxford.
  (1998b) 'Thucydides and his predecessors' *Histos* 2.
  (1999) 'Thucydides' Persian Wars', in *The Limits of Historiography. Genre and Narrative in Ancient Historical Texts*, ed. C. S. Kraus. Leiden: 141–68.
  (2006) 'Objectivity and authority: Thucydides' historical method', in *Brill's Companion to Thucydides*, eds. A. Rengakos and A. Tsakmakis. Leiden: 225–49.
Rosaldo, R. (1980) *Ilongot Headhunting 1883–1974. A Study in Society and History*. Stanford, CA.
Rose, P. W. (1982) 'Towards a dialectical hermeneutics of Pindar's *Pythian* X' *Helios* 9: 47–73.
  (1992) *Sons of the Gods, Children of Earth. Ideology and Literary Form in Ancient Greece*. Ithaca, NY.
Rosén, H. B. (1987–97) *Herodoti Historiae. I–II*. Leipzig.
Rosenbloom, D. (1993) 'Shouting "fire" in a crowded theater. Phrynichos' *Capture of Miletos* and the politics of fear in early Attic tragedy' *Philologus* 137: 159–96.
  (1995) 'Myth, history, and hegemony in Aeschylus', in *History, Tragedy, Theory*, ed. B. Goff. Austin, TX: 91–130.
Rosenmeyer, T. G. (1968) 'Elegiac and elegos' *CSCA* 1: 217–31.
  (1985) 'Ancient literary genres. A mirage?' *Yearbook of Comparative and General Literature* 34: 74–84.

Rosivach, J. V. (1987) 'Autochthony and the Athenians' *CQ* 37: 294–306.
Rösler, W. (1980) *Dichter und Gruppe. Eine Untersuchung zu den Bedingungen und zur historischen Funktion früher griechischer Lyrik am Beispiel Alkaios.* Munich.
  (1990) '*Mnemosyne* in the *Symposion*', in Murray (1990a): 230–7.
  (1991) 'Die 'Selbsthistorisierung' des Autors. Zur Stellung Herodots zwischen Mündlichkeit und Schriftlichkeit' *Philologus* 135: 215–20.
  (2002) 'The *Histories* and writing', in *Brill's Companion to Herodotus*, eds. E. Bakker, I. de Jong and H. van Wees. Leiden: 79–94.
Rossi, F. (1967–8) 'La "stratega" di Tirteo' *AIV* 126: 343–75.
Rossi, L. E. (1971) 'I generi letterari e le loro leggi scritte e non scritte nelle letterature classiche' *BICS* 18: 69–94.
  (1983) 'Il simposio greco arcaico e classico come spectacolo a se stesso' *Spectacoli conviviali dall' antichità classica alle corti italiene dell' 400. Viterbo*: 41–50.
Rowe, G. O. (1966) 'The portrait of Aeschines in the *Oration on the Crown*' *TAPhA* 97: 397–406.
Rubel, A. (2000) *Stadt in Angst. Religion und Politik in Athen während des Peloponnesischen Krieges.* Darmstadt.
Ruck, C. A. P. (1972) 'Marginalia Pindarica' *Hermes* 100: 143–69.
Rüsen, J. (1982) 'Die vier Typen des historischen Erzählens', in *Formen der Geschichtsschreibung*, ed. R. Koselleck. Munich: 514–605.
  (1983) *Historische Vernunft. Grundzüge einer Historik I: Die Grundlagen einer Geschichtswissenschaft.* Göttingen.
  (1986) *Rekonstruktion der Vergangenheit. Grundzüge einer Historik II: Die Prinzipien der historischen Forschung.* Göttingen.
  (1989) *Lebendige Geschichte. Grundzüge einer Historik III: Formen und Funktionen des historischen Wissens.* Göttingen.
Rutherford, I. (2001) 'The New Simonides. Toward a commentary', in Boedeker and Sider (2001a): 33–54.
Rutherford, R. (1982) 'Tragic form and feeling in the *Iliad*' *JHS* 102: 145–60.
Sahlins, M. D. (1985) *Islands of History.* Chicago, IL.
  (2004) *Apologies to Thucydides. Understanding History as Culture and Vice Versa.* Chicago, IL.
Saïd, S. (1981) 'Darius et Xerxès dans les *Perses* d'Eschyle' *Ktema* 6: 17–38.
  (1988) 'Tragédie et renversement. L'example des *Perses*' *Metis* 3: 321–41.
  (1989) 'L'espace d'Euripide' *Dioniso* 59: 107–36.
  (2002) 'Herodotus and tragedy', in *Brill's Companion to Herodotus*, eds. E. J. Bakker, I. De Jong and H. V. Wees. Leiden: 117–47.
Salapata, G. (2002) 'Myth into cult: Alexandra/Kassandra in Lakonia', in *Oikistes. Studies in Constitutions, Colonies, and Military Power in the Ancient World. Offered in Honor of A. J. Graham*, eds. V. B. Gorman and E. W. Robinson. Leiden: 131–59.
Sanz Morales, M. (2000) 'La cronología de Mimnermo' *Eikasmos* 11: 29–52.
Sauge, A. (1992) *De l'épopée à l'histoire. Fondement de la notion de l'historié.* Frankfurt.
Scardino, C. (2007) *Gestaltung und Funktion der Reden bei Herodot und Thukydides.* Berlin.

Schachter, A. (1998) 'Simonides' elegy on Plataia: The occasion of its performance' *ZPE* 123: 25–30.
Schadewaldt, W. (1929) *Die Geschichtsschreibung des Thukydides. Ein Versuch.* Berlin.
  (1974a) 'Die *Perser* (Daten)', in *Wege zu Aischylos II*, ed. H. Hommel. Darmstadt: 3–6.
  (1974b) 'Ursprung und frühe Entwicklung der attischen Tragödie', in *Wege zu Aischylos I*, ed. H. Hommel. Darmstadt: 104–47.
Schapp, W. (1976) *In Geschichten verstrickt. Zum Sein von Mensch und Ding* (2nd edn.). Wiesbaden.
Schiappa, E. (1999) *The Beginnings of Rhetorical Theory in Classical Greece.* New Haven, CT.
Schmid, P. B. (1947) *Studien zu griechischen Ktisissagen.* Freiburg.
Schmitt, A. (1988) 'Menschliches Fehlen und tragisches Scheitern. Zur Handlungsmotivation im Sophokleischen "König Ödipus"' *RhM* 131: 8–30.
Schmitt Pantel, P. (1992) *La cité au banquet. Histoire des repas publics dans les cités grecques.* Rome.
Schmitz-Kahlmann, G. (1939) *Das Beispiel der Geschichte im politischen Denken des Isokrates.* Leipzig.
Schneeweiß, G. (1975) 'Kroisos und Solon', in *Apophoreta (Festschrift U. Hölscher)*, ed. A. Patzer. Bonn: 161–87.
Schneider, C. (1974) *Information und Absicht bei Thukydides. Untersuchung zur Motivation des Handelns.* Göttingen.
Schneider, H. (1912) *Untersuchungen über die Staatsbegräbnisse und den Aufbau der öffentlichen Leichenreden bei den Athenern in der klassischen Zeit.* Berlin.
Schnyder, B. (1995) *Angst in Szene gesetzt. Zur Darstellung der Emotionen auf der Bühne des Aischylos.* Tübingen.
Schott, R. (1968) 'Das Geschichtsbewußtsein schriftloser Völker' *ABG* 12: 166–205.
Schroeder, O. (1914) *De laudibus Athenarum a poetis tragicis et ab oratoribus epidicticis excultis.* Göttingen.
von der Schulenburg, S. (ed.) (1923) *Briefwechsel zwischen Wilhelm Dilthey und dem Grafen Paul Yorck von Wartenburg, 1877–1897.* Halle.
Schulz, E. (1933) *Die Reden im Herodot.* Diss. Greifswald.
Schwartz, E. (1899) 'Tyrtaeos' *Hermes* 34: 428–68.
  (1929) *Das Geschichtswerk des Thukydides* (2nd edn.). Bonn.
Schwinge, E.-R. (1996) 'Zu Thukydides' historischer Erzählung' *Poetica* 28: 297–326.
  (1997) 'Tyrtaios über seine Dichtung (Fr. 9 G.-P.= 12 W)' *Hermes* 125: 387–95.
  (2008) *Komplexität und Transparenz. Thukydides: Eine Leseanleitung.* Heidelberg.
Schwyzer, E. and A. Debrunner (1950) *Griechische Grammatik, II. Syntax und syntaktische Stilistik.* Munich.
Scullion, S. (2006) 'Herodotus and Greek religion', in *The Cambridge Companion to Herodotus*, eds. C. Dewald and J. Marincola. Cambridge: 192–208.
Seager, R. (1967) 'Thrasybulus, Conon and Athenian imperialism, 396–386 B.C.' *JHS* 87: 95–115.
Sedgewick, G. G. (1948) *Of Irony, Especially in Drama.* Toronto.

Segal, C. (1974) 'Time and the hero: The myth of Pindar's *Nemean* 1' *RhM* 117: 29–39.
    (1986) *Pindar's Mythmaking: The Fourth Pythian Ode*. Princeton, NJ.
van Seters, J. (1983) *In Search of History: Historiography in the Ancient World and the Origins of Biblical History*. New Haven, CT.
Shanske, D. (2007) *Thucydides and the Philosophical Origins of History*. Cambridge.
Shapiro, S. O. (1994) 'Learning through suffering: Human wisdom in Herodotus' *CJ* 89: 349–55.
Shaw, P.-J. (2001) 'Lords of Hellas, old men of the sea. The occasion of Simonides' Elegy on Plataea', in Boedeker and Sider (2001a): 164–81.
Shimron, B. (1989) *Politics and Belief in Herodotus*. Stuttgart.
Shrimpton, G. S. (1997) *History and Memory in Ancient Greece*. Montreal.
Sicking, C. M. J. (1995) 'The general purport of Pericles' funeral oration and last speech' *Hermes* 123: 404–25.
Sider, D. (2001) '"As is the generation of leaves" in Homer, Simonides, Horace and Stobaeus', in Boedeker and Sider (2001a): 272–88.
    (2006) 'The New Simonides and the question of historical elegy' *AJPh* 127: 327–46.
Sideras, A. (1971) *Aeschylus Homericus*. Göttingen.
Siewert, P. (1985) 'Zur Wahrheitssuche bei Thukydides und vor attischen Gerichtshöfen des 5. Jh. v. Chr.', in *Römische Geschichte, Altertumskunde und Epigraphik. Festschrift für Artur Betz*, eds. E. Weber and G. Dobesch. Vienna: 565–74.
Simon, E. (1983) *Festivals of Attica*. Madison, WI.
Simpson, M. (1969) 'The chariot and the bow as metaphors for poetry in Pindar's odes' *TAPhA* 100: 437–73.
Slater, W. J. (1984) '*Nemean One*. The victor's return in poetry and politics', in *Greek Poetry and Philosophy. Studies in Honour of Leonard Woodbury*, ed. D. E. Gerber. Chicago, IL: 241–64.
    (ed.) (1991) *Dining in a Classical Context*. Ann Arbor, MI.
Slings, S. R. (2000) *Symposium: Speech and Ideology. Two Hermeneutical Issues in Early Greek Lyric, with Special Reference to Mimnermus*. Amsterdam.
Smarczyk, B. (2006) 'Thucydides and epigraphy', in *Brill's Companion to Thucydides*, eds. A. Rengakos and A. Tsakmakis. Leiden: 495–522.
Smith, C. F. (1900) 'Traces of epic usage in Thucydides' *TAPhA* 31: 69–81.
Smith, C. F. and A. G. Laird (1908) *Herodotus. Books VII and VIII*. New York, NY.
Snell, B. (1928) *Aischylos und das Handeln im Drama*. Leipzig.
    (1952) 'Homer und die Entstehung des geschichtlichen Bewußsteins' in *Varia Variorum Festgabe für Karl Reinhardt*. Münster: 2–12.
Solmsen, F. (1982a) 'Achilles on the islands of the blessed. Pindar vs. Homer and Hesiod' *AJPh* 103: 19–24.
    (1982b) 'Two crucial decisions in Herodotus', in *Kleine Schriften III*. Hildesheim: 78–109.
Solmsen, L. (1943) 'Speeches in Herodotus' account of the Ionian Revolt' *AJPh* 64: 194–207.

(1944) 'Speeches in Herodotus' account of the Battle of Plataea' *CPh* 39: 241–53.
Sommerstein, A. (1989) *Aeschylus. Eumenides.* Cambridge.
Sourvinou-Inwood, C. (1989) 'Assumptions and the creation of meaning: Reading Sophocles' *Antigone*' *JHS* 109: 134–48.
    (2003) *Tragedy and Athenian Religion.* Lanham, MD.
Stadter, P. A. (1973) *The Speeches in Thucydides.* Chapel Hill, NC.
    (1992) 'Herodotus and the Athenian arche' *ASNP* III 22: 781–809.
Stahl, H.-P. (1968) 'Herodots Gyges-Tragödie' *Hermes* 96: 385–400.
    (1975) 'Learning through suffering? Croesus' conversations in the *History* of Herodotus' *YCS* 24: 1–36.
    (2003) *Thucydides: Man's Place in History.* Swansea.
Staley, D. J. (2002) 'A history of the future' *H&T* 41: 72–89.
Stanford, W. B. (1942) *Aeschylus in His Style.* Dublin.
Starr, C. G. (1968) *The Awakening of the Greek Historical Spirit.* New York, NY.
de Ste. Croix, G. E. M. (1972) *The Origins of the Peloponnesian War.* London.
Steenblock, V. (1991) *Transformationen des Historismus.* Munich.
Steffen, V. (1973) 'De Mimnermi *Smyrneide*', in *Scripta Minora Selecta I.* Wroclaw: 60–75.
Stehle, E. (2001) 'A bard of the iron age and his auxiliary muse', in Boedeker and Sider (2001a): 106–19.
Stein, H. (1969) *Herodotos* (8th edn.). Dublin.
Steiner, D. T. (1986) *The Crown of Song in Pindar.* London.
    (2001) *Images in Mind. Statues in Archaic and Classical Greek Literature and Thought.* Princeton, NJ.
Steinger, G. (1957) *Epische Elemente im Redenstil des Herodot.* Diss. Kiel.
Stein-Hölkeskamp, E. (1989) *Adelskultur und Polisgesellschaft. Studien zum griechischen Adel in archaischer und klassischer Zeit.* Stuttgart.
Steinmetz, P. (1969) 'Das Erwachen des geschichtlichen Bewußtseins in der Polis', in *Politeia und Res Publica. Beiträge zum Verständnis von Politik, Recht und Staat in der Antike,* ed. P. Steinmetz. Wiesbaden: 52–78.
Stella, L. A. (1947) 'Studi Simonidei. I Per la cronologia di Simonide' *RFIC* 24: 1–24.
Stewart, A. F. (1985) 'History, myth, and allegory in the program of the temple of Athena Nike, Athens' *Studies in the History of Art* 16: 53–73.
Stierle, K. (1979) 'Erfahrung und narrative Form. Bemerkungen zu ihrem Zusammenhang in Fiktion und Historiographie', in *Theorie und Erzählung in der Geschichte,* eds. J. Kocka and T. Nipperdey. Munich: 85–118.
Strasburger, H. (1958) 'Thukydides und die politische Selbstdarstellung der Athener' *Hermes* 86: 17–40.
    (1972) *Homer und die Geschichtsschreibung.* Heidelberg.
    (1975) *Die Wesensbestimmung der Geschichte durch die antike Geschichtsschreibung* (3rd edn.). Wiesbaden.
    (1982) 'Herodot und das perikleische Athen', in *Studien zur Alten Geschichte II.,* eds. W. Schmitthenner and R. Zoepfel. Hildesheim: 592–626.
Strauss, B. S. (1987) *Athens after the Peloponnesian War. Class, Faction and Policy 403–386 BC.* Ithaca, NY.

Stupperich, R. (1977) *Staatsbegräbnis und Privatgrabmal im klassischen Athen*. Diss. Münster.
Sutton, D. E. (1998) *Memories Cast in Stone. The Relevance of the Past in Everyday Life*. Oxford.
Szádeczky-Kardoss, S. (1968) 'Mimnermos' *RE Supplementum* XI: 935–51.
Talamo, C. (1973) 'Per la storia di Colofone in età arcaica' *PP* 28: 343–75.
Taplin, O. (1972) 'Aeschylean silences and silences in Aeschylus' *HSCPh* 76: 57–98.
  (1977) *The Stagecraft of Aeschylus. The Dramatic Use of Exits and Entrances in Greek Tragedy*. Oxford.
  (1990) 'Agamemnon's role in the *Iliad*', in *Characterization and Individuality in Greek Literature*, ed. C. Pelling. Oxford: 60–82.
Tarditi, G. (1983) 'Tirteo: Momenti di una campagna di guerra' *Aevum* 57: 3–13.
Tarkow, T. A. (1983) 'Tyrtaeus 9 D. The role of poetry in the new Sparta' *AC* 52: 48–69.
Taylor, M. W. (1991) *The Tyrant Slayers. The Heroic Image in Fifth Century B.C. Athenian Art and Politics* (2nd edn.). Salem, MA.
Thalheim, T. (1901) *Lysias*. Leipzig.
Thalmann, W. G. (1980) 'Xerxes' rags. Some problems in Aeschylus' *Persians*' *AJPh* 101: 260–82.
Theunissen, M. (2000) *Pindar. Menschenlos und Wende der Zeit*. Munich.
Thomas, R. (1989) *Oral Tradition and Written Record in Classical Athens*. Cambridge.
  (1992) *Literacy and Orality in Ancient Greece*. Cambridge.
  (2000) *Herodotus in Context. Ethnography, Science and the Art of Persuasion*. Cambridge.
  (2006) 'The intellectual milieu of Herodotus', in *The Cambridge Companion to Herodotus*, eds. C. Dewald and J. Marincola. Cambridge: 60–75.
  (2007) 'Fame, memorial, and choral poetry: The origins of Epinikian poetry – an historical study', in *Pindar's Poetry, Patrons, and Festivals. From Archaic Greece to the Roman Empire*, eds. S. Hornblower and C. Morgan. Oxford: 141–66.
Thompson, W. E. (1967) 'Andocides and Hellanicus' *TAPhA* 98: 483–90.
Thummer, E. (1957) *Die Religiosität Pindars*. Innsbruck.
Töchterle, K. (1980) 'Die μεγάλη γυνή des Mimnermos bei Kallimachos' *RhM* 123: 225–34.
Todd, S. C. (1993) 'Review of A. Missiou, The subversive oratory of Andokides' *CR* 43: 20–2.
Tompkins, D. P. (1972) 'Stylistic characterization in Thucydides' Nicias and Alcibiades' *YCS* 22: 181–214.
Tonkin, E. (1992) *Narrating Our Pasts. The Social Construction of Oral History*. Cambridge.
Treves, P. (1941) 'Herodotus, Gelon, and Pericles' *CPh* 36: 321–45.
Tritle, L. (2006) 'Warfare in Herodotus', in *The Cambridge Companion to Herodotus*, eds. C. Dewald and J. Marincola. Cambridge: 209–23.
Troeltsch, E. (1913) 'Die Bedeutung des Begriffs der Kontingenz', in *Gesammelte Schriften II*. Tübingen: 769–78.

Tsagarakis, O. (1977) *Self-expression in Early Greek Lyric Elegiac and Iambic Poetry*. Wiesbaden.
Tsakmakis, A. (1995) *Thukydides über die Vergangenheit*. Tübingen.
  (1998) 'Von der Rhetorik zur Geschichtschreibung: Das 'Methodenkapitel' des Thukydides (1,22,1–3)' *RhM* 141: 239–55.
Turner, E. G. (1971) '2824. Tyrtaeus, *Eunomia*' *The Oxyrhynchus Papyri* 38: 1–3.
Untersteiner, M. (1971) *Senofane. Testimonianze e frammenti. Introduzione, traduzione e commento*. Florence.
Usher, S. (2007) 'Symbouleutic oratory', in *A Companion to Greek Rhetoric*, ed. I. Worthington. Malden: 220–35.
Utzinger, C. (2003) *Periphrades Aner. Untersuchungen zum ersten Stasimon der Sophokleischen Antigone und zu den antiken Kulturentstehungstheorien*. Göttingen.
Vandiver, E. (1991) *Heroes in Herodotus. The Interaction of Myth and History*. Frankfurt.
Vansina, J. (1985) *Oral Tradition as History*. Madison, WI.
van der Veen, J. E. (1996) *The Significant and the Insignificant. Five Studies in Herodotus' View of History*. Amsterdam.
Vellacott, P. (1977) 'Has good prevailed? A further study of the *Oresteia*' *HSCPh* 81: 113–22.
Veneri, A. (1976) 'Ancora su Mimnermo, fr. 13,9 ss. Diehl (14 West)' *QUCC* 22: 23.
Verdenius, W. J. (1989) 'Pindar, *O*.2.83–6' *Mnemosyne* 42: 79–82.
Verdin, H. (1977) 'Les remarques critiques d'Hérodote et de Thucydide sur la poésie en tant que source historique', in *Historiographia antiqua. Commentationes Lovanienses in honorem W. Peremans septuagenarii editae*. Leuven: 53–76.
Verity, A. (2007) *Pindar. The Complete Odes*. Oxford.
Vernant, J.-P. (1988) 'Tensions and ambiguities in Greek tragedy', in *Myth and Tragedy in Ancient Greece*, eds. J.-P. Vernant and P. Vidal-Naquet. New York, NY: 29–48.
Vetta, M. (1983) 'Introduzione. Poesia simposiale nella Grecia arcaica e classica', in *Poesia e simposio nella Grecia antica. Guida storica e critica*, ed. M. Vetta. Rome.
  (1992) 'Il simposio: La monodia e il giambo' *Lo spazio letterario della Grecia antica. I: La produzione e la circolazione del testo. Tomo 1, La polis* Rome: 177–218.
Vickers, M. J. (1995) 'Thucydides 6.53.3–59: Not a "digression"' *DHA* 21: 193–200.
Vidal-Naquet, P. (1988a) 'Aeschylus, the past and the present', in *Myth and Tragedy in Ancient Greece*, eds. J.-P. Vernant and P. Vidal-Naquet. New York, NY: 249–72.
  (1988b) 'Oedipus between two cities. An essay on *Oedipus at Colonus*', in *Myth and Tragedy in Ancient Greece*, eds. J.-P. Vernant and P. Vidal-Naquet. New York, NY: 329–59.
Vivante, P. (1972) 'On time in Pindar' *Arethusa* 5: 107–31.

Vlassopoulos, K. (forthcoming) 'Constructing antiquity and modernity in the eighteenth century. Alterity, proximity, polarity, immanency', in Foxhall and Gehrke (forthcoming).
Walbank, F. W. (1957) *A Historical Commentary on Polybius. I.* Oxford.
  (1960) 'History and tragedy' *Historia* 9: 216–34.
Walker, A. (1993) '*Enargeia* and the spectator in Greek historiography' *TAPhA* 123: 353–77.
Walker, H. J. (1995) *Theseus and Athens*. New York, NY.
Walsh, G. B. (1984) *The Varieties of Enchantment. Early Greek Views of the Nature and Function of Poetry*. Chapel Hill, NC.
Walter, U. (1993) *An der Polis teilhaben. Bürgerstaat und Zugehörigkeit im Archaischen Griechenland*. Stuttgart.
Walz, J. (1936) *Der Lysianische Epitaphios (Philologus, Supplementband 29, Heft 4)*. Leipzig.
Waterfield, R. (1998) *Herodotus. The Histories*. Oxford.
Waters, K. H. (1966) 'The purpose of dramatisation in Herodotus' *Historia* 15: 157–71.
  (1971) *Herodotos on Tyrants and Despots. A Study in Objectivity*. Wiesbaden.
  (1985) *Herodotos the Historian. His Problems, Methods and Originality*. London.
Weber, L. (1922) 'Perikles samische Leichenrede' *Hermes* 57: 375–95.
von Weber, O. (1955) *Die Beziehungen zwischen Homer und den älteren griechischen Lyrikern*. Bonn.
van Wees, H. (1999) 'Tyrtaeus' *Eunomia*. Nothing to do with the *Great Rhetra*', in *Sparta. New Perspectives*, eds. S. Hodkinson and A. Powell. London: 1–41.
  (2002) 'Herodotus and the past', in *Brill's Companion to Herodotus*, eds. E. J. Bakker, I. de Jong and H. van Wees. Leiden: 321–49.
  (2003) 'Conquerors and serfs. Wars of conquest and forced labour in archaic Greece', in *Helots and their Masters in Laconia and Messenia. Histories, Ideologies, Structures*, eds. N. Luraghi and S. E. Alcock. Cambridge, MA: 33–80.
West, M. L. (1974) *Studies in Greek Elegy and Iambus*. Berlin.
  (1992) *Iambi et Elegi Graeci. I–II* (2nd edn.). Oxford. (=W²)
  (1993) 'Simonides Redivivus' *ZPE* 98: 1–14.
  (1995) 'The date of the *Iliad*' *MH* 52: 203–19.
  (2006) 'Archilochus and Telephos' *ZPE* 156: 11–17.
West, W. C. (1970) 'Saviors of Greece' *GRBS* 11: 271–82.
Westlake, H. D. (1968) *Individuals in Thucydides*. Cambridge.
  (1969) *Essays on the Greek Historians and Greek History*. Manchester.
  (1977) 'Athens and Amorges' *Phoenix* 31: 319–29.
Wetz, F. J. (1998) 'Kontingenz der Welt – ein Anachronismus? ', in *Kontingenz*, eds. G. von Graevenitz and O. Marquard. Munich: 81–106.
White, H. (1973) *Metahistory. The Historical Imagination in Nineteenth-Century Europe*. Baltimore, MD.
  (2005) 'Metahistory', in *The Routledge Encyclopedia of Narrative Theory*, ed. D. Herman. London: 302.

von Wilamowitz-Moellendorff, U. (1877) 'Die Thukydideslegende' *Hermes* 12: 326–67.
  (1913) *Sappho und Simonides*. Berlin.
Wilke, B. (1996) 'De mortuis nihil nisi bene. Elaborierte Mündlichkeit in den attischen Grabreden', in *Vergangenheit und Lebenswelt. Soziale Kommunikation, Traditionsbildung und historisches Bewußtsein*, eds. H.-J. Gehrke and A. Möller. Tübingen: 235–55.
Willcock, M. M. (1995) *Pindar. Victory Odes. Olympians 2, 7, 11; Nemean 4; Isthmians 3, 4 and 7*. Cambridge.
Wilson, P. (1996) 'Tragic rhetoric: The use of tragedy and the tragic in the fourth century', in *Tragedy and the Tragic*, ed. M. S. Silk. Oxford: 310–31.
Winnington-Ingram, R. P. (1983) *Studies in Aeschylus*. Cambridge.
Wiseman, T. P. (1979) *Clio's Cosmetics. Three Studies in Greco-Roman Literature*. Leicester.
Wohl, V. (2002) *Love Among the Ruins. The Erotics of Democracy in Classical Athens*. Princeton, NJ.
Woodbury, L. (1966) 'Equinox at Acragas. Pindar, *Ol*. 2.61–62' *TAPhA* 97: 597–616.
Woodford, S. (1974) 'More light on old walls. The Theseus of the Centauromachy in the Theseion' *JHS* 94: 158–65.
Woodman, A. J. (1988) *Rhetoric in Classical Historiography. Four Studies*. London.
Wormell, D. E. (1963) 'Croesus and the Delphic oracle's omniscience' *Hermathena* 97: 20–2.
Worthington, I. (1991) 'Greek oratory, revision of speeches and the problem of historical reliability' *C&M* 42: 55–74.
  (1994) 'History and oratorical exploitation', in *Persuasion. Greek Rhetoric in Action*, ed. I. Worthington. London: 109–29.
Xydas, C. C. (1982) 'Loci lyrici emendandi' *Parousia* 1: 322–8.
Yatromanolakis, D. (2001) 'To sing or to mourn? A reappraisal of Simonides 22 W²', in Boedeker and Sider (2001): 208–25.
Yerushalmi, Y. (1996) *Zakhor: Jewish History and Jewish Memory*. Seattle, WA.
Yorck von Wartenburg, P. (1956) *Bewußtseinsstellung und Geschichte. Ein Fragment aus dem philosophischen Nachlaß*. Tübingen.
Young, D. C. (1983) 'Pindar *Pythians* 2 and 3. Inscriptional ποτέ and the "poetic epistle"' *HSCPh* 87: 31–48.
  (1984) *The Olympic Myth of Greek Amateur Athletics*. Chicago, IL.
Yunis, H. (1996) *Taming Democracy. Models of Political Rhetoric in Classical Athens*. Ithaca, NY.
  (2003) 'Writing for reading. Thucydides, Plato, and the emergence of the critical reader', in *Written Texts and the Rise of Literate Culture in Ancient Greece*, ed. H. Yunis. Cambridge: 189–212.
Zacharias, W. (1990) *Zeitphänomen Musealisierung. Das Verschwinden der Gegenwart und die Konstruktion der Erinnerung*. Essen.
Zadorojnyi, A. V. (1998) 'Thucydides' Nicias and Homer's Agamemnon' *CQ* 48: 298–303.

Zeitlin, F. I. (1990) 'Thebes: theater of self and society in Athenian drama', in *Nothing to Do with Dionysos? Athenian Drama in Its Social Context*, eds. J. J. Winkler and F. I. Zeitlin. Princeton, NJ: 130–67.

Zerubavel, E. (2003) *Time Maps. Collective Memory and the Social Shape of the Past.* Chicago, IL.

Ziolkowski, J. E. (1981) *Thucydides and the Tradition of Funeral Speeches at Athens.* New York, NY.

Index locorum

Aeschin.
  3.190 78
Aesch.
  Pers. 13, 74–104, 133, 144,
    195, 281
    10 79
    14–64 79
    21–32 77
    33–58 77
    80 88
    87–92 79
    93–100 80, 89
    102–7 79–80
    114–25 80
    117–19 97
    126–31 76
    140–3 80
    161–7 80
    181–210 80
    185–6 89
    213 91
    215–25 80
    225 80
    244 85
    248 86
    261 76–7
    285–9 86–7
    289 97
    290–5 87
    295 87
    361–2 81, 84
    369–73 81
    454–5 84
    473–5 85
    529–31 92–3
    579–80 97
    598–605 89
    645–6 95
    694–702 87
    701–2 87
    709–11 95
    725 84
    730 97
    739–43 90
    742 84
    744–6 80
    753–8 82, 84
    759–62 82
    759–86 81
    760 82
    774–5 81
    780–6 82
    781 82
    782 82
    782–3 82
    786 82
    803–4 81
    818–28 90–1
    849–51 93
    852–906 95
    1019 93
  Supp.
    604 100
    605 100
    607 100
    610 100
    621 100
Alc.
  fr. 298 V 72
  fr. 348 V 72
Andoc.
  de pace 14, 107, 125, 126–44,
    172, 186, 204
    1–12 130
    2 129
    3 132
    6 131
    7 134
    8 134, 138
    10–12 130
    13–16 130
    13–27 130

Index locorum

  15–16 133
  17–23 130
  18–19 137
  21–2 137
  24–7 130
  28–32 130
  29 129, 131–2
  31 134
  32 129
  33 137
  33–4 130
  33–41 130
  35–6 130
  37 137
  38 138
  40 138
  41 138
Antiph.
 Poiesis
  fr. 189
   KA 1–5 101
Archil.
 fr. 13 W² 5–9 59
Arist.
 Rh.
  1365a31–3 168
  1411a2–4 168

Bacchyl.
 3 78
 3.58–66 44

CEG
 393.4 42
Cologne Papyrus
 nr. 2021 72

Dem.
 13.
  21 140
 18.
  194 141
 22.
  14 143
  15 143
 60.
  107
  1 123
  9 124
  10–11 124
  12 123
  28 179
Diod. Sic.
 7.12.6 291

Eur.
 Or.
  696–703 100
  884–949 100
  1072 100
  1079 100
 Supp.
  160 100
  231–3 100
  728–30 100
 TrGF
  1113a (=1040N²) 134

Gorg.
 DK 82 B 5–6 107

Hdt.
 1 171
 1.1–5 150
 1.5–6 171
 1.5.3 150
 1.5.4 176, 189, 191
 1.13 197
 1.13.2 197
 1.26–94 187–96
 1.30 188
 1.31 188
 1.32.1 194–5
 1.32.1–9 189
 1.34–45 189
 1.34.1 197
 1.34.2 189
 1.43.3 199
 1.45.2 199
 1.53.3 197
 1.54.1 197
 1.56.2–68 198
 1.59 179
 1.66.2 198
 1.69–70 198
 1.70.3 198
 1.71–85 189
 1.71.1 198
 1.71.2–4 198
 1.85 199
 1.86 199
 1.86.5 199
 1.90.3–4 199–200
 1.91.1–5 200
 1.91.6 200
 1.207 191
 1.207.1 191
 1.207.2 190
 2 206

Hdt. (cont.)
  2.23 155–6
  2.112 152
  2.112–20 151–8
  2.113–15 152
  2.116 152
  2.116.1 155
  2.116.2 154–5
  2.117 152
  2.118–19 153
  2.120 153
  2.120.5 156–7, 262, 264
  3.33 194
  3.36.3 192
  3.40.2 195
  3.125.2 195
  4.110–17 178
  4.205 193
  5.92 ζ2 155
  6.98.2 170
  7 127
  7.9–10 127
  7.19.2 262–3
  7.20.1 262
  7.43 171
  7.44 263
  7.46.4 195
  7.54 263
  7.61–99 261
  7.133–7 193
  7.133.2 193
  7.153–63 158, 160–73
  7.158 160
  7.159 160–1
  7.160 160
  7.161 160
  7.161.2–3 167
  7.161.3 160–1, 167
  7.162 160–1, 168
  8.3.1–2 167, 184
  9.16.4 204
  9.25.2–3 174
  9.26–7 158, 160, 173–86
  9.26.2 175
  9.26.2–7 174
  9.26.7 175
  9.27 175
  9.27.5 175
  9.33.2 181
  9.37 182
  9.46–49.1 179
  9.48.1–2 180
  9.53.2 180
  9.58.2–4 180
  9.64.1 180
  9.64.2 182
  9.65.2 194
  9.73 182
  9.73.3 183
  9.83 91
  9.85 184
  9.116 171
Hom.
  Il.
    1 36, 164
    1.125 162
    2 77, 126–7
    2.486 67
    2.553–4 167
    3.202 126
    3.351–4 158
    4.399–400 66
    5.62–3 134–5
    5.85–94 65
    5.93 66
    5.93–6 65–6
    5.96 66
    5.800–24 67
    6.145–9 190
    6.289–91 152
    7 163, 164
    7.67–91 162
    7.96–102 162
    7.109–19 162–3
    7.124–8 163
    7.125 161–2
    7.132–3 163
    7.133–56 163
    7.157 163
    7.157–8 163
    9 164, 166
    9.411–16 33, 36, 124
    9.443 105
    9.524–99 105
    9.527 105
    11.603–4 135
    11.765–90 163
    14.84–7 157
    16.31–2 158
    18.61 76
Hyp.
  6 107
  6.32 125
  6.35 124
  6.42 124
Isoc.
  4.8 77
  4.82 105

4.9 139
6.42 142–3

Lycurg.
  62 139
  106 139
Lys.
  2.
    14, 105–26, 128, 133–5
    1 115, 119
    2 119, 224
    3 114, 117–19
    3–16 110
    4 110
    4–6 109
    6 114, 117, 120
    7–10 109
    11 110
    11–16 110
    17 110, 114
    17–19 110–11
    18–19 110
    20 111, 114
    21–6 112
    22 120
    23 114, 117–18
    26 114–15
    27 112, 120
    27–43 112
    32 114
    34 112
    38 112
    44–7 112
    48 112
    49–53 112
    51 116
    54 115
    54–7 112
    55 112, 133–4
    56–7 112
    58 112
    60 114–15
    61 114, 116
    61–5 113
    64 115
    67 113
    67–70 113
    69 113–14, 116
    70 113
    75 108
    79 117
    81 117
  25.
    21–3 140
    25–7 140

  30.
    18 140
  34.
    127

Mimn.
  fr. 2 W^2 62
    1–2 59
    11–16 59
  fr. 9 W^2 57, 294–5
    2 58
    4 58
    6 58
  fr. 13a W^2 52, 55, 294
  fr. 13 W^2 55, 294
  fr. 14 W^2 58–9, 64–8,
    124, 294
    2 67
    3 66
    4 66
    5 66

Paus.
  9.29.4 294
  10.7.6 69
Pind.
  Ol.
    1.55–64 43
    2 19–46
    2.1–7 23
    2.2 37–8
    2.4 28
    2.6 25, 42
    2.7 25, 28
    2.8 25, 30, 38
    2.8–9 42
    2.8–10 30–1
    2.8–11 24
    2.9–10 28
    2.10 25, 27
    2.11 25
    2.12 31
    2.12–15 25, 27, 29, 31–2, 37
    2.14 27
    2.15 38
    2.15–17 23, 38
    2.15–22 23
    2.16 34
    2.16–17 34
    2.17 31, 34
    2.17–18 25–6
    2.18 34
    2.18–20 34
    2.18–22 23
    2.19 26, 34

Pind. (cont.)
    2.19–20 26
    2.20 26
    2.22–3 38
    2.22–30 23
    2.23 26, 31
    2.24–31 26
    2.30–1 23
    2.30–4 23
    2.32–3 30
    2.32–4 23
    2.35–6 27
    2.35–7 26
    2.37 26
    2.38 27
    2.38–9 39
    2.38–40 26
    2.38–45 23
    2.40 26
    2.41–2 26
    2.42 40
    2.43–5 27
    2.45 27, 28
    2.46 28, 39
    2.46–7 27
    2.46–9 23
    2.48–9 31
    2.49–51 40
    2.51–4 34
    2.51–6 23
    2.55–6 28
    2.56–7 30
    2.57–81 23
    2.57–83 29
    2.61–2 30
    2.61–7 29
    2.62–3 31
    2.62–7 30
    2.63–5 30
    2.67 29
    2.68–83 29
    2.72–4 31
    2.76 31
    2.77 31
    2.79–80 36
    2.79–83 36
    2.83–5 36
    2.83–9 23
    2.83–91 35
    2.89–91 36
    2.89–100 23
    2.91–5 42
    2.92 34
    2.95–100 34
    2.96 34
    2.97 34
    2.98 34
    2.98–100 37
    2.99 34
    2.100 34
    3.6–9 32
    7.20–33 45
    7.34–53 45
    7.54–71 45
    9.23–5 41
    12.3 43
    12.5–8 43
    13.91 43
Pyth.
    1.61–5 45
    2.21–41 43
    3.114–15 45
    4 45
    8.95–6 43
    10.12–13 44
    12.28–32 43
Isthm.
    1.14–17 44
    4.67–9 (49–51) 44
    4.71–2 (53–4) 44
    7.43–8 43
    8.1 45
Nem.
    6.15–16 44
    6.28a–30 45
    7.12–13 45
    10.37–8 44
    10.45–6 44–5
    11.37–44 46
Pl.
  Menex.
    235a6–10 226
    235c4–5 116
    236e3–7 125
    237a7 123
    246a5–6 123
    249b8–c4 125
  Symp.
    221c 164
Plut.
  De Herodoti malignitate
    872C–E 53
  Mor. [De mus.]
    1134a 69
  Vit. Alc.
    23.6 259
  Lyc.
    6 291
PMG
    893–6 71

Porph.
  On Hor. *epist.*
    2.2.21 295
P. Oxy. 47
  2303
    fr. 1a 72
  2327 48
    fr. 5 (= 1–4 fr. 11 W²) 50–1
    fr. 6 50–1, 60
  2824 291
  3965 48, 60
    fr. 26 60
  4708 71

Simon.
  fr. 11 W² 47–73
    1–4 50
    10–14 51
    13 55
    15–18 51, 54
    16 63
    18 55
    19–20 51
    20–8 51, 54–5
    21 63
    24–6 53
    25–6 53
    29–37 53
    34 53
    37–8 53
    41 53
  fr. 15 W² 53
  fr. 16 W² 53
  fr. 19 W² 60–2
  fr. 20 W² 60–2
    1–4 60
    5–12 60
    12 60
    14 60
Stesich.
  Palinode
    fr. 192–3 *PMG* 153
Stesimbr.
  FGrH 107 F 9 *apud* Plut. *Per.* 8 124
Soph.
  OT
    397 101
    397–8 102
Str.
  8.4.10 p. 362 291

Thuc.
  1 218
  1.1 259
  1.1–19 206

1.1.1 223
1.4 218
1.9–11 257, 270
1.10 213
1.20–1.1 206–7
1.20–2 15, 151–2, 205–14, 221, 225
1.20.1 219, 274
1.20.2 214, 216, 219
1.20.3 210, 219, 222
1.21.1 68, 207–8, 210, 219–24, 236, 274–6
1.21.2 206–7, 209
1.22 207, 276
1.22.1 277
1.22.1–3 277
1.22.2 218
1.22.3 226, 238
1.22.4 71, 208, 210–13, 222–4, 236–7, 269, 276
1.23.1–3 207
1.23.5–6 238
1.24 211
1.26.3 234–5
1.73.2 142
1.73.4–74 234–5
1.101–3 235
1.105.2–3 235
1.108.4–5 235
1.112.1 132
1.138.3 278
2.2–6 229
2.27 235
2.27.2 235
2.34 221
2.34.1–7 121
2.35–46 220–8
2.35.1 225
2.35.2 225
2.35.3 226
2.36.2 223
2.36.3 223
2.36.4 223
2.37.1 217
2.37.2 217
2.37.3 217
2.38 217
2.40.4 217
2.40.5 227
2.41.2 222, 228
2.41.3 228
2.41.4 68, 124, 222, 224, 228
2.42.1 224
2.42.2 223, 228
2.43.2 223
2.44.4 224
2.45.1 224
2.46.1 223

Thuc. (cont.)
2.60.5 278
2.63.2 244–5
2.65.3–4 227–8
2.65.8 226–7
2.65.9 217
2.77.4–6 250–1
3.38.4 224
3.42.6 209
3.43.2 209
3.52–68 127, 220–1,
    228–39
3.52.2 230
3.53–9 230
3.53–67 185
3.53.4 235–6, 238
3.54.3 233
3.54.3–4 231
3.54.5 235
3.55.1 234
3.56.2 230
3.56.4–5 231
3.57.2 231
3.57.2–3 231
3.57.3 232
3.58.3 230–1
3.58.4 232
3.58.5 231
3.59.2 231
3.61–7 230
3.61.1 236
3.61.2–62.2 233
3.62.5 235
3.65.2 231
3.66.1 236
3.66.2 231
3.67.6 236
3.68.4 237
3.82.2 269
5.26.5 236
5.45.1 209
5.85 209, 275
5.89 237
6 214, 241
6.1.1 270
6.2.1 260
6.2.3 259
6.6.1 241
6.8.2 209,
    244, 275
6.9–14 243
6.12.1 244
6.13.1 244
6.15.4 245
6.16–18 243

6.16.2 42
6.16.5 259
6.16.6 260
6.18.3 244
6.20–3 243
6.20.4 243
6.22 244
6.23.3 253–4
6.24.3 241
6.26.2 244
6.30.2 248
6.30.2–31.1 241
6.31.3–4 247, 262–3
6.31.6 248, 258
6.32.1 263
6.32.2 263
6.33–4 246
6.33.1 247
6.33.4 247
6.33.5 246, 258
6.35.2 246
6.36–40 246
6.36.4 246
6.37.1–2 246
6.41.2–4 246
6.42.1 243
6.46 275
6.48 243
6.52.2 243
6.53.2 219, 274
6.53.3 272
6.54–9 206, 214–20, 251
6.54–60 206
6.54.1 214–15
6.54.1–4 215
6.54.3 215, 217
6.54.4 215
6.54.5 217
6.54.5–7 215
6.54.6 217
6.55 215
6.55.1 218
6.56–9 15
6.56.1 215
6.56.2–3 215
6.57 215
6.57.3 216
6.58 215
6.59.1–3 215
6.59.4 215
6.60.1 272
6.60.5 219
6.61.1–2 219
6.101.3 252
6.101.4–6 252

6.102.2–3 252–3
7 241
7.2.1 250
7.2.4 250
7.8.2 275–6
7.14.4 276
7.34–41 277–8
7.56.2 268
7.56.4 258
7.57–8 258
7.69.2 266
7.70.3 247
7.71.7 253
7.74 260
7.75 260
7.75.3 248
7.75.4 248
7.75.5 248
7.75.6–7 248
7.75.7 244
7.77 265–7
7.77.1 265
7.77.2 265
7.77.2–3 265
7.77.3 265–6
7.86.5 267
7.87.5 258
7.87.5–6 261, 264
7.87.6 260, 267
Tyrt.
  fr. 2 W^2 291–4
    2 293
    4 293
    9 292
    10 292–3
    11 293
    12 292
    12–15 292–3
  fr. 4 W^2 52, 69, 72, 291, 293
  fr. 5 W^2 52, 56–8, 291–4
    1 57, 292
    1–8 56
    2 57
  fr. 6 W^2 291, 293
  fr. 7 W^2 291, 293

Xenoph.
  fr. 1 W^2
    17–18 70
    19–24 70
    23 211–12
Xen.
  Hell.
    6.3.6. 143

Index of Greek words

ἀγών 209, 236
ἀγώνισμα 208–9, 224, 236
ἀλαθής 34
ἀλήθεια 212, 219, 225–6
ἁμαρτία 83
ἀναποδίζειν 155
ἀνέλεγκτος 219, 274–5
ἀποίητος 38
ἀπονοστεῖν 260, 261–2
ἀποφαίνεσθαι 157
ἀρχαιολογεῖν 266
ἀρχή 138–9
βασανίζειν 219, 274
τὰ δέοντα 212, 277–8
διδασκαλία 224
εἰρήνη 139
ἐξαλείφειν 231
ἐπαγωγός/προσαγωγός 209, 275
ἐραστής 215, 217–18
ἑταιρεία 100
εὔθυνος 91
εὐκλεής 36
ζήτησις 219

καταφανές 157
κίβδηλος 198
κλονεῖν φάλαγγας 66
κοσμεῖν 223–4, 236
κτῆμα ἐς αἰεί 213, 236
τὸ λεγόμενον 264–5
λιταί 36
μαρτύριον 222, 236
μυθῶδες 207–8, 276
πανωλεθρία/ πανωλεθρίη 157, 262, 264
πανώλεθρος 265
παραποιεῖν 154–5
ἐς τὸ παραχρῆμα 209, 222, 236
πίστις 219, 222
ποιεῖν 38, 158
τὸ σαφές 212, 222
σημεῖον 212, 222
τεκμήριον 222, 236
τέρπειν/ἀτερπέστερος 222, 224
τυγχάνειν 250, 252–3
ὑμνεῖν 223–4
χαλεπός 272

General Index

Abydus 263
Académie française 2
Acamas 99
accuracy, historical 3, 132–3, 210
Achaeans 163, 257, 259–60
Achilles 30, 33, 36, 50–1, 54, 63, 105–6, 124, 135, 158, 163–6, 172, 259, 281
Acragas 25, 30–1, 41–2
Acropolis 285
Adrastus 27–8, 99, 109–10, 114, 199
Aegina/Aeginetan(s) 112, 130–2, 185, 235, 263
Aegospotamoi 112
Aeschines 78
Aeschylus
 Eum. 99, 103
 Sept. 98
 Supp. 99
Aeschylus, *Pers.*
 borderline between Greeks and Persians blurred 88–92
 catalogues 77
 compared with *Halosis Miletou* 87–8, 98
 contingency of chance 79–85
 continuity/traditional mode of memory 81–2, 97
 epic colouring 75–7
 evoking pity and fear in Athenian audience 86–92
 expectations and experiences of characters 79–81
 gnomai 89–91
 hymn to victory 88
 messenger as epic bard 76–7
 reception of play in Athens 86–95
 regularity/exemplary mode of memory 81–2, 93–5
 spatial distance 75
 warning against Athenian imperialism? 91–2
Aetna 45
afterlife 25–6, 29–33, 36
Agamemnon 66, 157, 160, 162, 164–6, 172, 257, 261

agon 64, 68, 69, 124, 151, 182, 209, 224, 228, 234
Ajax 72
Alcaeus 72–3, 142
Alcibiades 42, 164, 217, 219, 243–5, 247, 259–60, 262, 272–3
Alcimidas 44
Alcmaeonids 215–16
Alcock, S. 3
Alexander (Macedonian king) 179
Alexander (Paris) 152–4, 157
Allison, J. 260
Altdorfer, A., *Die Perserschlacht* 283–5
Alyattes 197
Amasis 195
Amazon(s) 109–11, 114, 120–1, 143, 175, 177–8, 285, 295
Amazonomachy 78, 110, 285
Amompharetus 180
Amorges 130–2
anachronism 285
anathema, Greek at Delphi 185, 231
Anatolia 188
Andocides, *de pace*
 Athenian defeats 133–4
 casting Athenian past in tragic frame 134
 continuity/traditional mode of memory 131, 135
 empire 137–9
 and epic 134–5
 family tradition 131–2
 historical blunder 132–3
 oligarchic leaning 136–9
 publication 128–9
 reflection on exempla 129
 regularity/exemplary mode of memory 129–32, 135
 use of past for critical purpose 135
Antimachus 294
Aphidnae 183
Aphrodite 152, 156
Apollo 36, 44, 78, 80, 185, 199–200

Arcadia 198
'archaeology of the past' 2, 3
Archidamus 229, 256
Archilochus 48, 59, 71
Ardys 197
Areithoos 163
Argos/Argives 99–100, 110–11, 130, 175, 177
Arimnestus 182
aristocrats 41–2, 73, 100, 131, 142, 216
Aristogeiton 71, 214–18, 272
Aristotle 8, 13–14, 86–8, 92, 98, 102, 106, 168–9, 289
  concept of *hamartia* 102
  Rh. 106, 168
  theory of reception 86–7
art, representation of past in 281–90
Artabanus 127, 195, 201, 262
Artaphrenes 81
Artayctes 171
Artemisium 51, 112, 231
Asia 70, 81, 97, 188
Aspasia 123
Athena 45, 66–7
Athena–Nike temple 285
Athenagoras 246–7, 252
Athens/Athenian(s) 2, 13–4, 53, 60, 68, 75, 78, 84–6, 88–92, 94, 96–104, 107–45, 160–3, 167–8, 170–89, 193–4, 196, 198, 202, 204, 208, 214–21, 227–30, 233–5, 238, 240–64, 267–8, 270–6, 280, 285
Atossa 74, 80, 82, 84–95, 101
Attica 182–3, 255
attikismos 233, 273
Atys 189, 199
autochthony 110–11, 167
auxesis 67, 207, 213
awareness, historical 11

Bacchylides 19, 44, 78
Bakhtin, M. 4, 249
Barca 193
Barrett, J. 76–7
'Beinahe'-episodes 250–1
Bellerophontes 43, 190
Bergk, Th. 51
Berlin 1
Biton 188
Boedeker, D. 161–2, 208
Boeotia/Boeotian(s) 130, 174, 219, 229, 231, 233
Bosporus 85
Boston Historical Society 1
Bowie, E. 2–3, 52, 68–9, 291, 294–6
Brygus 285–6
Bubner, R. 7
Bundy, E. L. 23

Cadmus 23, 30–1, 39
Caledon 106
Callias 143
Callimachus 294–6
  Aitia – prologue 294–6
Callinus 71
Cambyses 191–2, 194, 201
Candaules 197
Carthaginians 160
Cassandra 72
Castor 44
catharsis 87–8, 98
Centauromachy 285
Ceryces 143
chance 7–15, 287–9
Chios 60
Chronus 23, 31, 38
Cimon 132–3, 285
Cleades 185
Cleobis 188
Clio 288
Coes 201
Collingwood, R. G. 11
Colophon 58
'competition piece' 208–9, 213, 224, 236
Connor, W. R. 247
'content of the form' 5, 19, 33
contingency 6, 289
  of action 7, 8, 28, 289
  of chance 7–15, 25–9, 59–62, 103–4, 254–5, 287–9
  of chance vs. moral fault 83–5, 102–104
  continuity 9–11, 25, 27–8, 39, 59–62, 103–4, 113–16, 288–9
Corcyra/Corcyrean(s) 234–5, 269
Corinth/Corinthian(s) 53, 112–3, 115–6, 130
Cornford, F. M. 253, 255, 262
counterfactuals 250–1
Crane, G. 213
Creuzer, G. F. 208
Croally, N. T. 98, 101
Croesus 44, 78, 150, 171, 187–201
Cronus 29, 31
Crotty, K. 42
Curetes 106
Curtius Rufus 283
Cyclopes 260
Cypria 152, 157
Cyrus 189–92, 200–1

daimonion 153, 157, 193, 264
Dally, O. 286
Danae 88
Danaids 99–100
Danaus 100

dance, as commemorative medium 2
Darius 74, 80–5, 90–1, 93–5, 97–8, 101, 112, 201, 215, 273
Decelea/Decelean(s) 143, 182–3
Decelean War 143
Decelus 182–3
deixis 114
Delian League 97
deliberative oratory
  distorting history for the sake of argument 132–3
  history of 126–7
  preference for recent past 142–4
  regularity/exemplary mode of memory 139
Delphi 185, 197, 231–2
Demaratus 201
Demeter 194
democracy 100, 110–11, 113, 126, 130, 136, 142, 215–19, 228, 246, 252
  and oratory 126–7, 252
Demophon 99
Demosthenes 107, 123–4, 132, 141, 143
development 9–11, 15, 25, 287–9
Diagoras 45
Dilthey, W. 6
Diomedes 64–7, 70, 124, 128, 281, 285
Dionysia, Great 13, 96–7, 103–4, 109, 122
Dionysius 208
Dipaea 182
Dolope (Amazon) 285
Dolopes/Dolopian 285
Dorian dress 80, 88
Dorian migration 292
Dostoevsky, L. 249

Echemus 174–5, 177, 179
Egestan(s) 130, 241, 243–4, 275
Egypt/Egyptian(s) 152–7, 193, 195
Eion epigrams 78, 171–2
ekklesia 247
Elea/Elean(s) 182
elegy
  contingency of chance 59–62
  continuity/traditional mode of memory 57–8, 62
  direct speech 55
  and epic 55–6, 62–8
  focus on polis 52–3, 63, 71–2
  'historical'/'narrative' 13, 47, 59–62, 291–6
  mythic narratives 63
  performance 68–72
  regularity/exemplary mode of memory 54–8, 62
  'sympotic' 13, 47, 59–62
Eleusinian Mysteries 143
enargeia 242, 248, 263

Enlightenment, Age of 15
envy, divine 83–5, 89, 103, 194–5, 255, 266
epic poetry, *see also* Homer
  contingency of chance 62, 190
  on recent past 63
  performance 70
  speeches 105–6, 126
Epicrates 136
Epidamnus 234
Epilycus 130
epinicean poetry
  and epic 33, 35–7
  and prophecy 37
  as speech–act 40
  contingency of chance 43, 46
  continuity/traditional mode of memory 43–6
  integrating victor into community 42–3
  performance 40–1
  regularity/exemplary mode of memory 43–6
Epipolae 252
epitaphios logos
  avoidance of naming individuals 133
  and epic 117, 124–5
  and tragedy 122, 125
  as speech–act 124–5
  contingency of chance 108–9, 116–17
  continuity/traditional mode of memory 123–5
  evidence for 107
  overcoming individual loss at the level of the polis 109
  praeteritio of Athenian past 122–3
  regularity/exemplary mode of memory 125
  ritualized setting 121–2
  structure 107
Ereuthalion 163
ergon, see logos–ergon
Ergoteles 42
eros 217–18
Erythrae 174
Eteocles 26, 40
Euboea 130, 132
Euripides 99–101
  Heracl. 99
  HF 99
  Med. 99
  Or. 100
  Phoen. 98
  Supp. 98–101
Europa 150
Europe 1, 171
Eurystheus 99, 109–10
exempla, *see* memory, exemplary mode
expectations
  horizon of 7, 288
  expectations and experiences 7, 79–81

experiences
    space of 7, 288
expression, polarized 86

Ferguson, N. 251
Fitzgerald, W. C. 28
Flashar, H. 221
'floating gap' 111–12
Flory, S. 212–13
Flower, M. A. 183
Four Hundred 140
Frangoulidis, S. A. 260
Freiburger Narrenzunft 1
'Future past' 170, 172

Gadamer, H.-G. 8, 33, 81
garlands 31–2
Gelon 160–1, 164–9
genealogy 11, 62–3, 82, 88
generations, comparison of 66, 116, 119, 123, 163, 224
genres, literary 4
    competition of 64, 67–8, 123–4, 151–2, 156
    narrative form 5
    performance 5
    socio-political setting 5
Geraneia 116
Gianotti, G. F. 24
Glaucus 190
glory, imperishable 33, 117, 213
gnomai
    in epinicean poetry 19, 43
    in tragedy 89–92
Gobryas 201
gods, difficult to name 85
Goldhill, S. 96
Gomme, A. W. 232
Gorgias, *epitaphios logos* 107
Green, P. 249
Greenwood, E. 276
van Groningen, B. A. 2, 19
Gyges 52, 55, 58, 197, 294, 296
Gylippus 250, 255–6

Hall, E. 88
hamartia 102
Harmodius 71, 214–18
Hecataeus 153
Hector 153, 162–3, 166
Hegel, G. W. F. 8, 33, 81
hegemony, Athenian 112–13, 115, 167, 170, 172, 177, 181–2, 186
Hegesistratus 182
Heidegger, M. 6
Helen 14, 126, 150–3, 156–7, 179, 182–3, 186–7, 193, 206, 264

Heliadae 45
Hellanicus 214
Hellespont 112, 195
Helots 235
Heracles 25, 28, 32, 44, 99, 110, 174, 177, 292
Heraclidae 110–11, 114, 122, 174–5, 177, 292
Heraeum 180
'heritage crusade' 1
Hermocrates 246–7, 258
Herms, mutilation of 214, 219, 271
Herodotus 3–4, 12, 14–15, 68, 88, 91, 103, 127, 135, 149–206, 208–9, 211, 213, 216, 220, 228–9, 234, 239–41, 247, 251, 254–7, 261–8, 271, 273, 279–80, 281, 283, 290
    combining *analepsis* with *prolepsis* 182–3
    contingency of chance 190, 195–6, 203–4
    contingency of chance emphasized by narrative form 196–200
    contrast between characters and readers 196–202
    critique of Homer 152–8
    Croesus-*logos* 187–202
    'cycle/wheel of human affairs' 190–2
    divine envy 194–5
    divine retribution 192–4
    and *epitaphioi logoi* 177–9
    Greeks–barbarians 204
    Helen-*logos* 14, 151–8, 187, 193, 206
    Homeric echoes 161–7
    juxtaposition of Persian with Trojan Wars 171–3
    method 155–6
    oracles 198
    oral presentations and publication of work 151, 173, 187, 209
    pan-Hellenic stance 150–1, 187, 203, 208
    patterns 172, 190, 201–2, 203
    references to recent and current struggles of Athens against other Greeks 170, 172, 181–6, 202, 204
    regularity/exemplary mode of memory 171–3, 176, 181–7, 202–4
    Sauromatian *logos* 178
    similarity with Homer 157–8, 190, 201, 203
    speech duel at Plataea 173–86
    speeches 158–87
    Syracusan embassy scene 14, 158, 160–74, 176, 181, 183–7, 220, 263
    and tragedy 201
    wise adviser 191
Hieron 44, 45, 78, 196
Higbie, C. 3
Hipparchus 214–17, 272
Hippias 214–16, 272–3
Hippocleas 44

General Index

'*historia magistra vitae*' 283
Historicism, Age of 15, 270, 290
historicity (defining historical nature of humans) 6, 8
historie 156, 203
historiography, Greek 3
  continuity with other commemorative genres 150
  local: different from Herodotus and Thucydides 151 n. 5
  not determined by performative context 15
  not yet established as genre in fifth century BCE 149, 151, 205, 209, 221
  pragmatic dimension of 159
  preference for recent past 150
  meta-historical significance of speeches 149
  speeches, *see* Herodotus *and* Thucydides
  tension between tradition and innovation 149–50
  use of past for critical purposes 135
historiography, modern
  downplaying contingency 251
  focus on developments 289
history
  as singular term 8, 288
  distinct from memory 10–11
  idea of, phenomenological model of 5–11
  'intentional' 6
  no equivalent term in Greek 289
  'virtual' 251
Homer 14, 33, 36–7, 55, 60, 62–8, 76, 83, 94, 105–6, 108, 120, 126, 145, 149, 151–6, 158, 160–1, 167, 170, 187, 190, 201, 203, 206–9, 213, 222, 224, 257–62, 264, 271, 279
  Aristeia of Diomedes 70
  'Catalogue of Ships' 77, 167, 258, 261
  Doloneia 70
  Il. 5, 14–15, 63, 66–7, 71, 77, 105, 134–5, 152–8, 161–2, 164, 166, 187, 190, 203, 258, 260, 281–2
  Od. 260
Hornblower, S. 33, 279
Hunter, V. 255–7, 277–8
Hurst, A. 24, 45
Hyllus 174, 177
Hyperides 107, 123–5

identity, constructed by memory 11, 41, 72, 121, 144, 178
Ilium 171
Iliupersis 78
Immerwahr, H. R. 172, 223
immortality,
  through praise 14, 33–7, 62–3, 109, 117–21, 145
  'transient' 33, 45
Ino 23, 26, 29, 31, 38–9

Io 150
Iolaus 44
Ionian revolt 88
Ionian science 14, 213
irony, tragic 101–2
Irwin, E. 65, 71
Island of the Blessed 29–33, 36, 116
Isocrates 77, 105, 139, 142–3
  Paneg. 105
Issos 283
Isthmus 174, 219
Ithaca 56
Ithome, Mt. 132, 182, 235
Ixion 43

Jacoby, F. 66, 208, 216
de Jong, I. 201
Jordan, B. 247, 255

Kallet, L. 257, 274
Kerameikos 122, 127, 221
'kinship diplomacy' 143–4, 234
Kirchhoff, A. 168
kleos 33, 36, 54, 63
Koselleck, R. 7–8, 283, 287–8
Kowerski, L. 47, 51–2, 62
Kurke, L. 42–3

Labdacids 39–40
Lacedaemonians 165, 198
Laestrygonians 260
Laius 101
Lamachus 243, 252, 255–6
Lampsacus 215
Lefèvre, E. 102
Leocoreion 216
Leonidas 54
Leontinoi 243
Leos 216–17
Libya 153
lieu(x) de mémoire 2, 6, 235, 273
Lindian chronicle 3
liturgies 136
Lloyd-Jones, H. 43
logographos 127, 151, 207–9, 219, 275
logos–ergon 63, 105, 118–20, 175, 225–6, 228
Lombardo, S. 281
Loraux, N. 2, 107, 121, 129, 211
Lowenthal, D. 1
Lurje, M. 102
Lycaon 67
Lydia/Lydian(s) 78, 188, 192, 197–8, 294
Lysias, *epitaphios logos* 14, 105–29, 133–5, 140, 144, 196, 224
  as speech-act 117–21

Lysias, *epitaphios logos* (*cont.*)
  contingency of chance 116–17
  continuity 109–17
  defeat as expression of Athens' greatness 112–13
  pedagogical function 118–21
  regularity 115–17
  temporal vagueness 113–15
Lysimeleia 252

Macedonia/Macedonian(s) 179
Macleod, C. W. 230
Marathon 78, 85, 112, 115, 122, 175, 177, 179, 185, 215, 273
Mardonius 127, 174, 179–80, 182, 262
Mardus 81–2
Marinatos-Kopff, N. 264–5
Marincola, J. 183
Martin, R. 281
Massagetae 191
Medea 99, 150
medismos 233
Medus 81
Megabazus 201
Meier, C. 287
Meineke, A. 64
Melampus 182
Meleager 105–6
Melissus 44
memory
  accidental mode of 9
  aristocratic traditions 139
  as distinct from history 10–11
  'collective' 2
  'cultural' 2, 6, 235
  democratic 133
  developmental mode of 9, 25
  exemplary mode of 9, 25, 44, 55–7, 78–9, 94, 127–33, 232–5, 261, 268, 283–90
  exemplary mode, *a maiore ad minus* 57, 95, 127
  exemplary mode referring to one's own tradition 140
  exemplary and traditional modes of 57–9, 66, 115–16, 131, 140, 232–3
  polyphony of 129, 135, 141–2, 287–8
  'social' 2
  socio-political relevance 142, 145
  traditional mode of 9, 25, 44–5, 57–8, 131, 232–5, 288–9
Memphitis 152
Menelaus 100, 152–3, 156, 158, 162–3
Menestheus 78, 163, 167
Mermniads 197, 201
Messene/Messenian(s) 52, 56–7, 182, 291–3
Messenian Wars 291

meta-history/meta-historical 107, 149, 159, 166, 173, 203, 220–1, 228, 235, 239, 240, 270–1, 279
metaphor
  of bow for poetry 35–6
  of erasure for annihilation of city 231–2
  of *eros* for citizens' adherence to democracy 218
  of leaves for humans 59–60, 62, 190
  of plant for humans 27, 39, 169
  of spring for soldiers 168–70
Metroon, Council Hall 78
Middle Ages 283
Miletus 88
Miltiades 132
Mimnermus 13, 48, 52, 57–9, 67–8, 71, 73, 78, 94, 114, 124, 127–8, 151, 281, 295
  Nanno 295
  Smyrneis 58, 69, 291, 294–6
Minos 285
mise-en-abyme 94–5, 98, 101, 220, 235
Missiou, A. 136–7
Modern Age 7, 8, 10, 285, 287, 289
Moira 80
Moles, J. 211, 276
monomachia 175, 179–80
Morrison, J. 277
mors immatura 33, 36, 124, 169
Morson, G. S. 249
Most, G. 19
Munson, R. V. 178
Munychia 78
'musealization', museum 1, 286–7
Muses 51, 54–5, 67, 76, 156, 294
  invocation of 54–5, 63, 296 n. 25
Mycenae 257
Myronides 133
Mysteries scandal 214, 219, 271–2
myth
  in elegy 63, 71
  in epinicean poetry 19, 43
  flexibility 99, 101, 133
  and history 110, 143, 144

National Mall 1
Nestor 135, 163–6, 169
'New Simonides' 2, 13, 47–73, 78, 117, 172, 207–8
  containing reflection on human fragility? 60–2
  content 50–2
  pan-Hellenic stance 53
  performance 69–70
  regularity/exemplary mode of memory 54–5
Nicias 243–6, 252–3, 256, 262, 265–7, 275–6
Nicomachus 140
Nietzsche, F. 1
Nora, P. 2, 10

General Index

Normandy 281
North America 1
nostos 43, 89, 91, 260–1

Obbink, D. 52, 62
Ober, J. 131
Odysseus 56, 89, 126, 157, 163–4, 213, 261, 285
Oedipus 23, 26–9, 33–4, 39, 81, 99, 101–2
Oenoe 78
oligarchs in Athens 136–7
Olympia 32
Olympian games 25, 28, 32
oral, *see* societies, oral *and* traditions, oral
oratory
  attempt to avoid impression of elitism 131, 139–40
  continuity/traditional mode of memory 140
  and democracy 126–7, 252
  distortion of past for the sake of argument 132–3
  focussing on recent events 142–4, 212
  judicial, deliberative, epideictic 106
  rise of 105–6
  and tragedy 141
  tragic view of Athenian history 141–2
Orestes 99–100, 103
Oroites 195
orphism 29
Oxford 285

Palladium 285
Panathenaea 69, 215
Paris 36
Parker, R. 141
Parsons, P. 53
past
  as 'foreign country' 283, 286
  and polis 71–2, 104, 144, 150, 208, 228
  preference for mythic past 150
  preference for recent past 142–4, 175, 212
  recent past in heroic register 44, 55–7, 64–8, 75–9, 94, 105 n. 3, 144, 281, 285–6
  as terrain for socio-political struggles 139, 145
patrios politeia 140
Patroclus, 135, 158
patronymic 28
patterns, narrative 15, 28, 40, 172, 188, 200–2, 203, 241, 254–70, 274, 280
Pausanias (author) 52, 69, 294
Pausanias (Spartan general) 53–4, 185
Peisistratids 96, 179, 215–18
Peisistratus 272
Pelasgus 99–100
Peleus 30, 105, 163–5
Pelling, C. 101
Peloponnese/Peloponnesian(s) 53, 113, 174, 250, 292

Peloponnesian War 109, 133–4, 143, 182–4, 205–7, 209, 213, 221, 229, 241, 251, 255, 259, 261–3, 265, 268, 270–1, 273–4, 279, 281
Pentecontaetia 137, 139, 235, 238
Pericles 15, 68, 107, 121–8, 164, 168–70, 183, 206, 217, 221–9, 240, 244–5, 278
  Samian funeral speech 107, 124
Perseus 88
Persia/Persian(s) 14, 51, 55, 63, 74–7, 79–86, 88–98, 102–3, 110–12, 120–1, 164, 171–2, 174–5, 178–80, 182, 184–5, 188–9, 191, 193–5, 197, 199, 204, 229, 231–3, 261–3, 267–8, 273–4, 283, 285
Persian Wars 13, 15, 48, 51, 54, 74, 77–8, 105, 110–17, 122, 143, 167, 170–2, 178, 182, 185–6, 203–4, 230–5, 257, 261–4, 267, 271, 273–4, 281, 285
  as foil for Sicilian Expedition 261–8, 270–1, 273–4
  epicized 77–8
Phereclus 134
Pheretime 193
Philip 141
philolaconism in Athens 136–7
Phoenix 105–6
Phrynichus 88
  Halosis Miletou 13, 74, 86–8, 98
  Phoenissae 74
Phthie 163, 165
phylai 216
Pierides 63
Pindar, *Ol.* 2
  anachronies 38–9
  contingency of chance 26–8
  continuity/traditional mode of memory 25, 27–8, 39
  and epic 35–7
  eschatology 29–33
  narrative form 37–40
  Ol. 3 as commentary on *Ol.* 2 32
  Pindar's role for transcendence of time 34–40
  regularity/exemplary mode of memory 28, 39–40
  structure 23–4
Piraeus 113, 247–8
Pisa 25
Pittacus 72
pity and fear 87–92
Plataea/Plataean(s) 14, 47, 51–3, 55, 62, 112, 127–8, 158, 160, 170, 173–4, 176, 178–9, 181–9, 220, 228–38, 240, 250, 263, 273, 281, 285
Plato 116, 123
  Menex. 107, 125, 226
  Symp. 164
'plu-past' 94, 172, 239, 261, 270–1, 273–4

Plutarch 53, 248, 253
  Vit. Alc. 259
polis
  and athletic victor in elegy 42–3
  continuity of 59–60
  prominence in elegy 52–4, 71–2
Polybius 159
Polycrates 195
Polyneices 26, 27, 40
pote, inscriptional 78–9
praeteritio 122–3, 223
praise 23, 34–7, 67, 223–4
Priam 153
Price, J. 231
Priscian 51
Protesilaus 171
Proteus 152–3, 157
Psyttaleia 81
public festivals 13, 41, 69–70, 73, 96, 103
Pylades 100
Pylus 253
Pythia 197–8, 200

Rawlings, H. 264–5
regularity 9–11, 25, 28, 39–40, 55, 104, 115–16, 128, 263, 268, 288
Rengakos, A. 201
restoration, architectural 286–7
Rhea 31
rhetoric, *see epitaphios logos*, deliberative oratory, oratory
Rhodes 45
ritual, creating regularity and continuity 13–14, 96–7, 122, 123, 125
Rood, T. 262–3
Rowe, G. O. 141
Rutherford, I. 62

Sadyattes 197
Sahlins, M. 2
Salamis 13, 74–5, 77–8, 86, 88, 94, 98–9, 112, 133, 174, 185, 194, 281
Samian War 124, 168
Sandanis 198, 201
Sardis 198–9
Sattelzeit 287
Schapp, W. 6
Schlegel, F. 283–5
Schmitt, A. 102
Scythia/Scythian(s) 178
Segesta 275
Semele 23, 26, 29, 31, 38, 39
Semonides, *archaiologia Samion* 52, 296
Shoah Memorial in Berlin 1

Sicilian Expedition 241–3, 250, 252–4, 257–64, 267, 270, 275
Sicily/Sicilian(s) 30–1, 161, 165, 242–7, 251–2, 255, 257–60, 262–3, 268, 270, 275
Sider, D. 47, 52, 60–2, 73, 296
Sideras, A. 76
'sideshadowing' 242, 248–52, 254, 277, 280
Sidonia 152
Sigeum 215
Simonides 47–73, 108, 117, 120, 128, 145, 151, 281
Smyrna/Smyrnean(s) 52, 57–8, 64, 66–7, 78, 124, 127, 281, 294–5
Snell, B. 83
societies, oral 1, 111
Socrates 116, 123, 164, 226
Solon 188–9, 194, 197, 199–201
Sophanes 182–3
Sophocles 101
  Ant. 98
  OC 98–9
  OT 98, 101–2
Sourvinou-Inwood, C. 99
Sparta/Spartan(s) 41, 51–4, 57, 78, 113, 128–33, 136–7, 140, 142–3, 152, 160, 165–9, 173–5, 179–85, 193–4, 198, 215, 219, 229–32, 235–9, 255–6, 273, 291–3
speech-act 14, 37, 40, 108, 120, 125, 165
Sphacteria 255–6
Sphinx 102
Stahl, H.-P. 216, 250, 269, 271
Stesichorus, *Palinode* 153
Stoa Poikile 78, 171–2
Stobaeus 60
stasis 181, 231, 243, 269
Strabo 58, 292–5
Suda 48, 51
Susa 74
Syagrus 160–70
symposium 13, 41–2, 68–72, 73, 96, 126, 144, 145, 151, 187, 294
  and aristocratic identity 41, 71–2
  and partisan interests 72
Syracuse/Syracusan(s) 130, 160, 164, 166, 169, 242–3, 246–8, 250, 252–3, 256, 260–1, 265, 267–8

Talthybius 193–4
Tanagra 182
Tantalus 43
Tarentum 246
Tegea/Tegean(s) 160, 173–84, 229, 234, 240
Teisamenes 181–2
Telephus 71
Tellus 188
temporality 6

General Index

Theaeus 44
theatrokratia 224
Thebes/Theban(s) 98–9, 101, 110, 127, 204, 228–38, 240, 273
Themistocles 133, 278
Theopompus 57, 292
Thermodon River 178
Thermopylae 112
Theron 13, 19, 23–45, 63, 81, 92
Thersander 23, 27–8, 32–3, 39–40, 81
Thersites 126
Theseion 285
Theseus 99, 179, 182–3, 285
Thessaly 174
Thetis 33, 36
thinking, historical 11
Thirty, regime of 113, 115–16, 130, 140
Thomas, R. 3, 4, 139, 216
Thrasybulus 78
Thucydides 3–4, 12, 14–15, 42, 68, 71, 107, 121–2, 124, 127, 132, 135, 142, 149–52, 185, 202–4, 205–80, 281, 283, 288, 290
  accuracy 210–11, 218–20, 222–5, 226, 274–6
  and Homer 247, 257–62, 271
  and modern historians 211, 270, 280
  and tragedy 247
  and writing 211, 238, 279
  'archaeology' 206–7, 213, 240, 288
  avoiding *prolepseis* 241–2, 244, 247, 251–2
  critical of Athenian democracy 216–20, 227–8, 271–3
  claim to usefulness 210–11, 213–14, 237–9, 268–79
  compared with Herodotus 205, 206, 241–2, 254, 255, 263, 268, 280
  contingency of chance 252–4, 267, 278, 280
  continuity/traditional mode of memory 232–5, 240
  Corcyrean Pathology 231
  distancing himself from Herodotus 261–8
  enargeia 248–252
  essentialist idea of history 270
  gods 255
  Herodotean echoes 261–8, 271
  human nature 210–11, 269–70
  influenced by Ionian science 213
  influenced by rhetoric 212–13, 236
  interest in human psychology 241
  Melian Dialogue 234, 237, 275
  method 206–14, 218–20, 274–6
  '*Methodenkapitel*' 207
  Mytilinean Debate 231
  on *logographoi* 208–9, 212–14, 224–5
  on poets 207–8, 213–4, 222
  on tyrannicide 214–20, 270–3
  on tyranny of Peisistratids 215–18
  patterns 254–68
  Periclean funeral speech 15, 107, 121, 168–9, 206, 217, 220–9, 240
  Persian Wars as foil for Sicilian Expedition 261–8, 270–1, 273–4
  Plataean Debate 15, 185, 206, 220–1, 228–40, 273–4
  political relevance of work 227, 274–6
  Pylus episode 253
  reading experience 277–9
  regularity/exemplary mode of memory 232–5, 240, 261, 267–8, 274
  'Sicilian archaeology' 242, 245, 251, 260, 270
  Sicilian Expedition 240–68
  'sideshadowing' 249–52, 254, 277
  similarities between Athens and Syracuse 246–7
  speeches 220–40, 242–7, 265–6, 277–8
  Syracuse similar to Athens 246, 247
  Trojan War as foil for Sicilian Expedition 257–61, 270–1
  use of inscriptions 218
time
  narrated and narrative 5, 38, 92, 196
  'new' ('*Neuzeit*') 8
  'vulgar' 6
Tlepolemus 45
Tolstoy, F. 249
traditions, *see* memory, traditional mode
  invented 6, 11
  oral 2, 3, 111, 139, 156, 216
tragedy
  asylum 99
  and Athens 99–103
  contingency of chance 97, 102–4
  continuity/traditional mode of memory 97, 103
  distancing of controversial issues 100–1
  historical 74
  issue of responsibility 102–3
  the 'other' 96–8
  pluriform and polyphonous 83
  regularity/exemplary mode of memory 97, 103
  ritual context 96–7, 103
Trojan War 15, 77–8, 152–4, 157–8, 160, 163, 167, 171–2, 213, 257–63, 265, 267, 271
  as foil for Persian Wars 15, 54–5, 77–8, 94, 171–3, 281
  as foil for Sicilian Expedition 257–61, 270–1
  historicity not doubted 153
Troy/Trojan(s) 51, 54–6, 76–7, 94, 124, 128, 152–3, 156–7, 165–6, 175, 193, 257–62, 281
Turks 283–4
tyche 5 n. 29, 43, 288

Tydeus 66
Tyndaridae 182–3
Tyrtaeus 13, 48, 52, 57, 59, 71, 73, 78, 94, 114, 291–3
   Eunomia 52, 69, 72, 291, 293–4, 296

'vagueness, heroic' 75, 79, 93–5, 98, 108, 125, 144, 171, 280
van Wees, H. 169
Ventura Surf Chapter 2
'*verbis facta exaequare*' 105, 122, 226
Vienna 284

warner, 'tragic' 244
Washington DC 1
'we', time-transcending 57–8, 114
West, M. L. 48, 50–1, 53, 55, 68–9
Woodbury, L. 29

Woodman, T. 159, 212–13
World War II, compared with Trojan War 281–3

Xenocrates 40
Xenophanes 48, 70–1, 142, 153
   ktisis–poem 52, 296
   symposium-elegy 211–12
Xenophon, *Hell.* 143
Xerxes 74, 79–85, 88–97, 102–3, 112, 127, 160, 165–6, 171, 194–5, 201, 262–3

Yorck von Wartenburg, P. 6
Yunis, H. 245

Zacynthus 182
Zeitlin, F. 98
Zeus 25, 31, 36–7, 88, 292–3
'zooming-devices' 99–100

Printed in Great Britain
by Amazon.co.uk, Ltd.,
Marston Gate.